THE INK OF MELANCHOLY

THE INK OF MELANCHOLY

Faulkner's Novels from *The Sound
and the Fury* to *Light in August*

ANDRÉ BLEIKASTEN

INDIANA UNIVERSITY PRESS

For Aimée

This book is a publication of

Indiana University Press
Office of Scholarly Publishing
Herman B Wells Library 350
1320 East 10th Street
Bloomington, Indiana 47405 USA

iupress.indiana.edu

First paperback edition 2017

The paper used in this publication meets the minimum
requirements of American National Standard for Information Sciences—
Permanence of Paper for Printed Library Materials, ANSI 239.48-1984.

Manufactured in the United States of America

The Library of Congress has cataloged the original edition as follows:

Bleikasten, Andre.
The ink of melancholy: Faulkner's novels from The sound
and the fury to Light in August / Andre Bleikasten
Includes bibliographical references. p. cm.
ISBN 0-253-31200-0 (alk. paper)
1. Faulkner, William, 1897–1962—Criticism and interpretation.
2. Melancholy in literature. I. Title
PS3511.A86Z6298   1990
813'.52—c20   89-45357
CIP

ISBN 978-0-253-02299-8 (paperback)
ISBN 978-0-253-02343-8 (ebook)

1 2 3 4 5   21 20 19 18 17 16

CONTENTS

PREFACE

Take the sum total of the texts produced over the course of a writer's career and assembled under the authority of his name—what we usually designate, rightly or wrongly, as a "life's work," an *oeuvre*. How describe its weave and its thread? How trace its trajectory? From what vantage points, at what distance, under what assumptions, according to what rules and procedures?

An *oeuvre:* sheets of printed paper bound together, a set of volumes aligned on a library shelf—an occupied space, a body of writing, a solid monument. You can see it, you can touch it, you can even read it. But once you have started reading, another much more elusive space opens up, a space neither in this world nor out of it, and you enter a silent, ghostly city of words, seemingly completed yet never at rest, inviting endless decipherings, and always promising, asymptotically, the final closure in which all would be (be)held together.

Before acquiring the fixed contours of provisional immortality, however, the monument will have been hammered out more or less haphazardly, by fits and starts, ruptures and resumptions, over a span of time. It will have taken time to make it, and time, in due course, will take it back and leave us with the fading splendor of its ruins.

Writing has its own beat, not to be confused with the pulse of the writer's life. Any great work of fiction, though, carries inscribed in it the paradox of a life betrayed and recaptured, of a life that has chosen to write itself rather than to live itself, and hence can be read (allegorically and etymologically) as *bio-graphy* or even *auto-bio-graphy*. For, whatever its announced purpose and intended referent, is not writing, at least writing with any claim to originality, also—with all the ambiguities of the reflexive, all the deceptions of doubling—writing oneself?

Not that any "true" self has ever been delivered and preserved by words. Language is a public space belonging to no one, writers play losing games with names, and the monuments of literature always turn out to be cenotaphs: they outlast their builders, and so does the name engraved on the tombstone, but the grave itself is empty.

What lies buried in a writer's work is at best a singular absence. Writing begins where living recedes. So, why not acknowledge once and for all what Faulkner called the "immitigable chasm between all life and all print," stick to print, and leave life alone?

Formalist readings (especially New Critical readings) did their best to obliterate biographical and sociohistorical contexts and to hypostatize literature as such. Presumed to be autonomous and autotelic verbal artifacts, literary texts were to become the sole objects of critical concern. Yet "the death of the author," periodically reannounced since Mallarmé, has not laid his ghost to rest. Few critics today will attempt to explain a writer's work in biographical terms, but the author's prestige as creator has remained intact, and whenever we discuss texts as parts of a "work," the only justification we can find for examining them together is what we take to be their common origin, the fact that they were written and signed by the same individual. It is possible, of course, to circumvent the empirical traces of that individual by just preserving his name as a convenient trademark. Neverthelesss, author and *oeuvre* are two reciprocally defining and enabling notions. You cannot discard one without discarding the other.

Or are they nothing more than twin fantasies? "The word 'oeuvre,'" Roland Barthes once remarked, "is already imaginary," and so is the word *author*: in common parlance, at least, the former suggests coherence of form and meaning, the latter a verifiable point of origin and source of authority. That both terms are heavily fraught with ideology certainly needs no further demonstration. And yet, once *work* and *author* have been divested of their traditional aura, we are left, to put it in the vaguest manner, with something we know to have been written by someone under given circumstances of time and place—a set of données whose interrelatedness has to be taken into consideration and, if possible, articulated and accounted for.

The question of the relation of man to writer and of life to work cannot be dismissed out of hand as irrelevant to critical inquiry. To content oneself with setting the "higher" order of art against the messiness of life is just to perpetuate a romantic-modernist piety. For, to begin with, a man's life is never sheer confusion. Reality may look chaotic, but no sooner are we born than we are caught in the nets of language, and language orders and processes most of what we call our "experience." Art, on the other hand, is not all balance and beauty and never was. We have all been trained to admire literary texts as smooth silken surfaces; a less idealizing look will show that they are all made of bits and pieces, and that their language bristles with paradoxes, ambiguities, and contradictions which no amount of exegetical expertise will ever resolve.

Life and writing are both dynamic fields of colliding forces, halfway between order and contingency. So would the wager not be, rather, to relate the text of the *oeuvre* to its pre-text, to that which is written *avant la lettre?* To find out whether and how they can be read together?

Written fictions are fabricated with words, paper, and ink, and they necessarily arise within language, from myriads of other fictions, but even though they never directly "express" or "reflect" life, it seems safe to assume that, in some way, the accidents of life have left their mark on them. Which does not mean that the principles of their production are themselves of the order of the living. Considered from the outside, the curve of a "life's work" may seem parallel to the continuous unfolding of a "lifeline," and so has often been likened to an organic process, a series of programmed transformations from birth through maturity to death. Since the advent of Romanticism, organicist assumptions have become so common and so "natural" in literary criticism that their validity has seldom been seriously questioned. Their sole basis, though, is a cluster of metaphors within a rhetoric that dares not state its name. Works of art are thus identified with works of nature and, by an imperceptible slippage from the descriptive to the normative, "organic" unity or wholeness has eventually imposed itself as one of the major criteria of aesthetic assessment.

The prolonged success of these metaphors is hardly surprising. The very nature of the relationship which the critic entertains with his object seems to encourage him to adopt an organicist approach: he generally has to deal with completed books and established canons, so that the temptation is always strong to read and admire a writer's work as a necessary miracle. In construing it as the accomplishment of some preestablished design, we satisfy our need for totality, coherence, and order, and yield to our desire for unified form and full meaning: if everything is already virtually present in the "seed," the beginning cannot be separated from the end. Everything, then, acquires instant teleological justification, and each phase in the writer's production comes to define itself as a rigorously necessary moment in relation to the overall design and sovereign purpose of the work.

Such tidy orderings and patternings require of course the performance of a few illusionistic tricks, not unlike those resorted to by the slicker novelists. For the sake of the cause—and for the effect—one devises clean critical fictions from which all trace of disorder and randomness has been carefully erased. In trying to rationalize and totalize, one forgets that for those who surrender to its fascination and accept its risks, writing is also an excessive and disruptive gesture, the fresh violence of a rebeginning, and that a true text is also, and perhaps above all, the newness which, unpredictably, in defiance of all intentions, calculations, and expectations, *falls* on the page.

Today, we are no longer so certain that works of art grow like trees or are erected like cathedrals. The necessity of their coming into existence is no longer taken for granted. And yet they strike us as organized totalities, and we cannot conceive such structures without postulating an organizing principle, a motive force, a telos. "I know perfectly well I'll never know," say the sophisticated critics of today, "but just the same. . . ." How can they renounce the right to knowledge, abandon the claim to their share of truth? If they no longer pursue the "true meaning" of literary works, the urge to explain is as strong as ever, and beyond it the ambition to bring into the light of day the hidden law of a writer's work, whether the latter be perceived panoptically, in what is presumed to be its completed totality, or step by step, according to the internal historicity of its deployment. Whatever our theoretical premises, we cannot do without the tacit belief that every literary text conceals somewhere in its folds the secret of its production.

Admittedly, over the past decades critics have become much more self-conscious about the validity of their aims and procedures. There is probably still a lingering expectation that certainties ought to be attainable, and the hope of turning literary criticism into an autonomous and rigorous scientific discipline is slow to die. But criticism too has now entered "the era of suspicion." There is no reason, however, to be overly distressed by this state of affairs. It might serve as a gauge for a lighter, more mobile and more alert reading, which, instead of imprisoning a text in our or its reasons, would allow us to become aware of its unreason, of its hazards and its errors, of all that calls attention to the extra-vagance of its play.

With William Faulkner, this play is dauntingly complex. Faulkner was a writer of fierce independence and vaulting ambition who thought of himself as an "author" in the fullest sense. Literature was to him what it had been to the greatest writers from Romanticism to Symbolism and what it was for nearly all Modernists: an extremely jealous goddess demanding total devotion and deserving heroic sacrifices, including that of the writer's life. Much like Flaubert and Conrad, James and Joyce, Proust and Kafka, he was in quest of a language that would be more than language, and, like them, he strove in his own way, with his own resources and ruses, for the wholeness and perfection of the "well-wrought urn," sometimes even subscribing to the extreme idealistic assumption, most eloquently stated by Mallarmé, that, if the world exists at all, it is destined to end up in or as a book, the Book: "it takes only one book to do it. It's not the sum of a lot of scribbling, it's one perfect book, you see. It's one single urn or shape that you want. . . ."

How Faulkner saw and dreamed himself as a writer and how he thought about writing is interesting to know but tells us little about what he accomplished—the less so as most of his public statements about art and literature reflect the dominant aesthetic discourse of his day. As with Proust and Joyce, there is far more daring and innovation in his novelistic practice than in his half-hearted attempts at articulating his poetics. It is important to remember, however, that for him as for them the urge to write sprang from a passionate desire for self-affirmation and self-realization. Boldly asserting his authority, insisting on his demiurgic powers with almost Balzacian self-confidence, Faulkner was determined to create a "cosmos of his own," existing for and by itself, of which he would be "sole owner and proprietor." Of the great literary undertakings of the first half of the twentieth century, none, assuredly, was carried out with more unyielding resolve and greater resourcefulness. Among the creators of modern fiction, Faulkner was indeed one of the most stubborn, most cunning, and most vigilant, and if one must deny him, as one would any writer, the unqualified, unconditional liberty of godlike creation, his achievement as a novelist testifies to *mastery* of the highest order gained at the price of long and patient work. The nature and limits of that mastery may be questioned, but we cannot fail to recognize the dazzling evidence of its practice.

But Faulkner was modern too in his constant readiness to dare. Throughout his career he took risks, and he knew how to fail. Like all true writing ventures, his enterprise was also a series of raids into unmapped territory, or—to resume the play metaphor—a series of solitaires, gambles now won, now lost, strange

new games the very rules of which were unknown to the player before they
started.

"To understand fictional creation," wrote André Malraux, "is to understand
that a novelist also carries out what he has *not* conceived. The creative act
which will give birth to the novel shines ahead of the conceivable, at its margin,
like a pilot fish." For Faulkner, writing fiction was indeed this mysterious
venture beyond the conceivable toward the unconceived. At the beginning he
was only a wistful Narcissus lost in a library, and from the borrowed glimmer
of the early poems to the rich *moiré* patterns of his first great novels he had a
long road to travel. Only when he started what was to become *The Sound and
the Fury* did the "pilot fish" make its appearance. At once it drew him along
to the high seas.

By then Faulkner had become not just a competent novelist but one of the
major literary voices of his generation. *The Sound and the Fury* marked the
beginning of a period of strenuous work and stunning inventiveness. Published in 1929, a few months after *Sartoris*, Faulkner's last apprentice novel, it
was followed by *As I Lay Dying* in 1930, *Sanctuary* in 1931, *Light in August* in
1932. Four of Faulkner's finest novels thus succeeded one another within four
years, and each of them was a new departure. More masterpieces were to
come, at slightly longer intervals, from *Absalom, Absalom!* (1936) through *The
Wild Palms* (1939) and *The Hamlet* (1940) to *Go Down, Moses* (1942). The period
from the late twenties to the early forties was in Faulkner's career one of
unique and nearly unbroken fertility, and the creative outburst on which it
opens—from *The Sound and the Fury* to *Light in August*—touches indeed on the
miraculous.

It is the four children of this miracle that I have attempted to read, separately
and together, careful both to discern for each what constitutes its singularity,
its difference, and to find out how they take meaning from their relations to
each other.

To respond as fully as possible to the pull and provocation of Faulkner's
texts, I have tried to read them first of all with that "evenly suspended" or
"poised" attention which Freud recommended to analysts—keeping theoretical presumptions and interpretive hypotheses at bay as long as possible. But
the best one can hope for is that issues are not foreclosed prematurely. It is
never a question of canceling, even provisionally, all critical distance and
settling into a cozy and innocent "tête-à-texte," as if Faulkner's novels had
never been read before. No one ever reads entirely by himself; no one ever
simply reads "what is there." The questions which a text poses are, first and
foremost, those we ask of it, and they are seldom *ours:* more often than not
they are unknowingly prompted by the *Zeitgeist.*

My involvement with Faulkner's work started in the sixties, when literary
studies in France were at last awakening from the dogmatic slumber of
Lansonian positivism and debate about literary theory and critical methods
began to occupy an unprecedented place in French intellectual life. The
nouvelle critique started with thematic approaches in the wake of Gaston

Bachelard and phenomenology; then came the structuralist wave, the emergence of linguistics as a model for the "human sciences" (as they are called in my country), the Lacanian "return to Freud," the Althusserian "return to Marx," new developments in poetics and narrative theory, and finally what now goes by the loose designation of poststructuralism. Like many Frenchmen of my generation, I did my best to absorb all these trends as they came along (that is, before they hardened into new orthodoxies or softened into recipes for critical fast food, and well before they were recycled for academic mass consumption in America). But what counted more than fads and fashions was the excitement of my encounters with individual authors: Maurice Blanchot, Jean-Pierre Richard, Jean Starobinski, Roland Barthes. . . .

They taught me how to read and how not to read. I would like to think, however, that my own reading of Faulkner belongs to no system, to no school except, on occasion, the *école buissonnière*. Nor do I pretend to provide a totalizing interpretation. My business is not with meaning as such but with the production of meanings and also with suspensions of and resistances to meaning. So, rather than process Faulkner's fiction through some prefabricated grid, I have attempted—without fetishizing them—to concentrate on the texts themselves: to pay close attention to the motivations and circumstances of their composition (whenever the available information permitted), to do justice to the rich array of their themes, structures, and textures, to trace their various protocols and the endless interplay of their tropes and codes, to scrutinize their points of emphasis and repetition as well as their rifts and gaps. And whenever and wherever it seemed worthwhile, I have also attended to their implications in biographical, sociocultural, and historical terms.

There is no substitute for close reading. Not that reading closely is necessarily reading well, nor that a happy blend of acquired skills and native grace frees one from method. Yet a method, after all, is nothing but a "going after," a road taken to get to some place, and there is clearly no "royal way" to reach the heart of a highly complex work such as Faulkner's (supposing that it has a heart and that one can reach it). While every judiciously conducted approach undoubtedly allows us to discover and understand one of its many facets, none is likely to restore it for us with all the vigor and diversity of its *relief*.

Ideally, literary criticism would be stereoscopic, and perhaps what it most needs today is something like the "thick description" which Clifford Geertz recommends to his fellow anthropologists. I have therefore multiplied the "takes," proceeding by successive essays according to the occasion and its needs, seeking for each novel the critical tools and idioms most likely to illuminate its functioning and to reveal its stakes. My purpose is not to put Faulkner's novels on the rack so as to make them confess their secrets. It is not so much a question of *exposing* them to the light of contemporary scientific discourse as of *developing* (as one would a photographic negative) an entire body of insights and wisdom already stored away in their folds. Faulkner's work always outraces what might be said about it, and whatever we may say has already been said, in its own manner, obliquely, through a language of feints and enigmas or silences, by the texts themselves—*en passant*. And what retains us there is precisely the impossibility of dwelling there. Faulkner's texts are not deposits of fixed and final meaning for us to decipher; they are discharges of mental energy, fields of turbulence, records of battles won and lost, and we never find them again in the same state as we left them. It is in vain that we select our finest arrow; at the moment of shooting, the target is already somewhere else.

STRASBOURG, OCTOBER 1988

ACKNOWLEDGMENTS

This book was originally my *thèse de doctorat d'Etat* and appeared in its original French version in 1981 as *Parcours de Faulkner*. Earlier versions of parts one and two were published separately in English translations by Indiana University Press, the former, entitled *Faulkner's As I Lay Dying*, in 1973, the latter, entitled *The Most Splendid Failure*, in 1976. Partial translations of the chapters on *Sanctuary* and *Light in August* have been published in various periodicals and collections. Most of the chapters have been extensively revised and expanded for the present publication.

Over the years I have accumulated debts to many people and institutions. I wish to renew my thanks to the Fulbright and Smith-Mundt Foundations and to the American Council of Learned Societies for financing my first research visits to the United States in 1967 and 1969-70, to James B. Meriwether for inviting me to the University of South Carolina as visiting research professor in 1976, to the Rockefeller Foundation for allowing me to spend a month at the Bellagio Study and Conference Center in 1985, and to William Carroll and John T. Matthews for inviting me to teach Faulkner at Boston University in 1987. My thanks are also due to the Alderman Library of the University of Virginia and the William Faulkner Foundation, for granting me access to the Faulkner materials in their possession. I should also like to express my gratitude to my friends and fellow Faulknerians Michel Gresset, Lothar Hönnighausen, Arthur F. Kinney, Ilse Dusoir Lind, Michael Millgate, Giliane Morell, François Pitavy, and James B. Watson for their continued interest in my work, and especially to Millicent Bell, John T. Matthews, Noel Polk, Stephen M. Ross, and Philip Weinstein for giving my manuscript very careful reading and making many valuable suggestions. Finally, I wish to thank Roger Little, Jean Paira, and Joe Breines, who have assisted me very generously with the translations.

EDITIONS CITED AND ABBREVIATIONS

With regard to *The Sound and the Fury, As I Lay Dying, Sanctuary,* and *Light in August,* the first editions are listed below, but the page references are to the corrected texts of the 1987 Vintage editions. With regard to the other works, references are to the first edition unless otherwise specified.

AA   *Absalom, Absalom!,* New York: Random House, 1936.

AILD   *As I Lay Dying,* New York: Jonathan Cape and Harrison Smith, 1930; Vintage, 1987.

CS   *Collected Stories,* New York: Random House, 1950.

ELM   *Elmer,* James B. Meriwether and Dianne L. Cox, editors, *Mississippi Quarterly,* 36 (Summer 1983), 337-460.

EPP   *Early Prose and Poetry,* edited with an introduction by Carvel Collins, Boston: Little, Brown, 1962.

ESPL   *Essays, Speeches & Public Letters,* edited by James B. Meriwether, New York: Random House, 1966.

FA   *Father Abraham,* edited by James B. Meriwether, New York: Random House, 1984.

FAB   *A Fable,* New York: Random House, 1954.

FD   *Flags in the Dust,* edited by Douglas Day, New York: Random House, 1973; Vintage edition, 1974. Vintage edition cited.

FU   *Faulkner in the University,* Frederick L. Gwynn and Joseph L. Blotner, editors, Charlottesville: University Press of Virginia, 1959.

GB   *A Green Bough,* New York: Harrison Smith and Robert Haas, 1933; *The Marble Faun and A Green Bough,* New York: Random House, 1965.

GDM   *Go Down, Moses,* New York: Random House, 1942.

H   *The Hamlet,* New York: Random House, 1940.

ID   *Intruder in the Dust,* New York: Random House, 1948.

LA   *Light in August,* New York: Harrison Smith and Robert Haas, 1932; Vintage, 1987.

LG   *Lion in the Garden: Interviews with William Faulkner 1926-1962,* James B. Meriwether and Michael Millgate, editors, New York: Random House, 1968.

M   *The Mansion,* New York: Random House, 1959.

MAR   *The Marionettes* (MS facsimile), edited with an introduction and

<table>
<tr><td></td><td>textual apparatus by Noel Polk, Charlottesville: University Press of Virginia, 1977.</td></tr>
<tr><td>MAY</td><td>Mayday (MS facsimile), South Bend, Indiana: University of Notre Dame Press, 1977; typeset edition, introduction by Carvel Collins, Notre Dame and London: University of Notre Dame Press, 1980. Typeset edition cited.</td></tr>
<tr><td>MF</td><td>The Marble Faun, Boston: Four Seas, 1924; The Marble Faun and A Green Bough, New York: Random House, 1965.</td></tr>
<tr><td>MOS</td><td>Mosquitoes, New York: Boni and Liveright, 1927.</td></tr>
<tr><td>NOS</td><td>New Orleans Sketches, edited with an introduction by Carvel Collins, New York: Random House, 1968.</td></tr>
<tr><td>P</td><td>Pylon, New York: Harrison Smith and Robert Haas, 1935.</td></tr>
<tr><td>R</td><td>The Reivers, New York: Random House, 1962.</td></tr>
<tr><td>RN</td><td>Requiem for a Nun, New York: Random House, 1951.</td></tr>
<tr><td>SAN</td><td>Sanctuary, New York: Jonathan Cape and Harrison Smith, 1931; Modern Library, 1932; Vintage, 1987.</td></tr>
<tr><td>SAR</td><td>Sartoris, New York: Harcourt, Brace, 1929.</td></tr>
<tr><td>SF</td><td>The Sound and the Fury, New York: Jonathan Cape and Harrison Smith, 1929; Vintage 1987.</td></tr>
<tr><td>SL</td><td>Selected Letters of William Faulkner, edited by Joseph Blotner, New York: Random House, 1977.</td></tr>
<tr><td>SO</td><td>Sanctuary: The Original Text, edited by Noel Polk, New York: Random House, 1981.</td></tr>
<tr><td>SP</td><td>Soldiers' Pay, New York: Boni and Liveright, 1926.</td></tr>
<tr><td>T</td><td>The Town, New York: Random House, 1957.</td></tr>
<tr><td>T13</td><td>These Thirteen, New York: Jonathan Cape and Harrison Smith, 1931.</td></tr>
<tr><td>U</td><td>The Unvanquished, New York: Random House, 1938.</td></tr>
<tr><td>US</td><td>Uncollected Stories, edited by Joseph Blotner, New York: Random House, 1979.</td></tr>
<tr><td>VS</td><td>Vision in Spring, with an introduction by Judith L. Sensibar, Austin: University of Texas Press, 1984.</td></tr>
<tr><td>WP</td><td>The Wild Palms, New York: Random House, 1939.</td></tr>
</table>

INTRODUCTION

MASKS AND MIRRORS

L'origine de l'oeuvre, ce n'est pas la première
influence, c'est la première posture.

Roland Barthes

Tous les romans ne sont que des pistes
brouillées.

Louis Aragon

Et in Arcadia ego

How does one become "Faulkner"? How could a young minor poet of the
twenties, writing Decadent verse in his native Mississippi, grow into one of
the major novelists of our century? A naive question, prompted by our desire
to understand beginnings in terms of endings, but we cannot help wondering,
even if the question is to be left unanswered.

Faulkner was no precocious genius. There was no instantaneous flowering,
as for Büchner or Rimbaud; nor did Faulkner resemble Flaubert, who from his
boyhood revered literature like a goddess. If Faulkner's logophilia started
fairly early, his vocation to writing was slow in declaring itself, and his literary
beginnings were not particularly impressive. They belong not so much to the
history of Faulkner's creation as to the limbo of its prehistory, a time of latency,
turbulence, and languor, when writing was just one possibility among others.

Everything began with postures and impostures. In August 1919, when, at
twenty-two, Faulkner published his first poem, "L'Apres-Midi d'un Faune,"[1]
and added a *u* to his patronym, he no doubt was already claiming his right to
be different, but the signer was not yet a writer: he was *playing* the Poet, just
as in the years following his return from the Royal Air Force training camp in
Toronto, after "they had stopped the war on him,"[2] he acted and watched
himself acting—in "real" life?—the romantic parts of Bohemian, Dandy, and
Wounded Warrior,[3] or as he was to play the Gentleman Farmer in his later
years.

The curtain rises on the ambiguous, shadowy theater of Narcissus. On
reflections, delusions, deceptions. On masks, mirrors, mimicry. On roles tried

out and discarded like costumes for a ball. At this uncertain stage of Faulkner's life the genuine and the contrived, the real and the imaginary, the person and its personae were so entangled as to be virtually indistinguishable. To call the personae false identities would be misleading, for there was no "true" identity to project or to conceal, and it was precisely through the interplay of impersonations that Faulkner's self was seeking to work out its difference, and perhaps also to prolong the adolescent excitement of playing with potentialities and deferring the moment of settling into the routines of socially acceptable adulthood.

According to Ovid, Narcissus became Narcissus—a figure of legend, a figure to be read—at the fatal instant when he mistook his own image in the watery mirror for another person. For Faulkner, becoming "Faulkner" started likewise with the troubling sameness-in-otherness of mirror images, the uncanny fascination of *doubles*. Except that he was not so purely self-involved as to do without a stage and an audience. To discover the actor, the poseur, we need only look at the photographs taken by his mother after his discharge from the RAF: they show us a sad-eyed, slim young man, almost Chaplinesque with his tiny moustache and his cane, posing before the camera in various military accoutrements with the self-conscious casualness of the shy.[4] To pose, as the dictionary will tell us, is "to represent oneself in a given character or as other than what one is."[5] But has anybody ever found his identity without first faking it, and are not all self-representations fabrications and frauds? And what was young Billy, the demobilized cadet, the Count No 'Count, outside the poses he struck and the roles he played?

The war had ended before the would-be hero could sail for France, much less engage the enemy and get properly shot.[6] After his missed exit into Valhalla new stages had to be set up and new parts provided. Hence the various roles. And at this point Faulkner the performer was one with Faulkner the writer. Playing roles and writing poems answered the same contradictory wishes: the desire to reveal and the desire to conceal; the impulse to establish contact and the equally pressing need to maintain a safe distance; the urge to find *one* self, to "cut a figure" in the world, to be singled out for recognition, to exist at last under the gaze of others, and the stubborn refusal to become what he was expected to be in a tradition-bound small southern town.

Putting oneself into words surely takes more time and talent than putting oneself into a uniform, and written words always end up wrapping themselves around the writer's absence. Yet in one sense all of Faulkner's fictions can be read as luxuriant outgrowths of the half-narcissistic, half-exhibitionistic theatricality of his early postures: they are all acts of disclosure and concealment, confession and deception, affirmation and withdrawal, and monuments to a self ever to be.

Selves are fictions anyhow—more or less random and more or less ingenious combinations of images and identifications. Selves are texts, motley tissues woven from reminiscences and borrowings: the patterns may be new and original, the material never is. This may sound by now like a post-Freudian cliché, but the suspicion that our little egos are all second-hand has been there all along. And Faulkner too must have had his doubts, for like all truly creative people, he probably was too self-divided or, to put it less negatively, too many-selved ever to achieve a firm and fixed sense of his own identity. Keats, his patron saint, went so far as to assert that the poet "has no self,"[7] and one could indeed argue that lack of "proper" selfhood is the price to be paid for what Keats, in another well-known letter, called "negative capability," the ability to dwell in "uncertainties, mysteries, doubts, without any irritable reaching after fact and reason."[8] For a writer, and particularly for a dramatist or a novelist, a fictionmaker, it is undeniably an advantage not to be too sure where he stands and who he is, and so to be able to extend his self into other selves, to weave its text into a rich tapestry for others to contemplate and for others to acknowledge as his own.

His own, yet never owned, never possessed. Identity, for a writer, is found and lost, inscribed and erased in the palimpsest of his writing, and it has never been *his* to begin with. "A book," as Proust noted, "is a product of a different self from the self we display in our habits, in our social life, in our vices."[9] And Faulkner said pretty much the same thing when he called a book the writer's "dark twin."[10] A secret, untamed, more authentic self? Perhaps, or at least a graph or glyph of his deepest desire, but also a more public self, for no sooner has he trusted it to language and bound it in a book than it is taken away from him and appropriated by his readers, assuming existence only insofar and as long as the pattern that informs his every sentence is recognized by them as his signature, the unique unmistakable inscription of a proper name.

Faulkner did not become "Faulkner" overnight. It took time. In the poems and poetic sequences of his youth and early manhood, from "The Lilacs" (1920) to *Helen: A Courtship* (1926),[11] the weaving of the tapestry had hardly begun, and what would gradually grow into an intricate and highly original design was at best a fumbling outline. As Phil Stone, Faulkner's friend and early mentor, put it in his preface to *The Marble Faun*, the pastoral cycle published in 1924: "These are primarily the poems of youth. . . . They also have the defects of youth—youth's impatience, unsophistication and immaturity."[12]

Until recent years, Faulkner's poetry had received little serious consideration, and most of the rare studies devoted to the subject were understandably concerned with the question of sources.[13] The discernible influences are indeed many, and remarkably heterogeneous: they range from Elizabethan lyric and pastoral verse through the Romantics and the Victorians to early Modernists such as Yeats, Conrad Aiken, and T. S. Eliot. To these must be added the French Decadents and Symbolists adopted by the Aesthetic movement of the nineties: Mallarmé (from whom Faulkner borrowed the title of his first published poem) and Verlaine (four adaptations of whose poems he published in the *Mississippian*, the newspaper of the University of Mississippi, in 1920).[14] Like most literary beginnings, Faulkner's offer a dense and clearly visible network of intertextuality, but beneath the thick quilt of quotations (often on the verge of plagiarism) there is not much of a text. Indeed, amid all these voices, past and present, his own is a bare whisper. When Eliot published *Prufrock and Other Observations*, his first volume of poems, in 1917, he had already discarded the literary conventions of the late Victorians and achieved a manner distinctively his own; the nineteen lyrics of *The Marble Faun*, on the other hand, conform to a pallid poetic code already obsolete at the time of their composition. Had Faulkner persevered as a poet, he might have evolved eventually a personal style (in some of the poems he was later to publish in *A Green Bough* there are hints of what it would have been like), but *The Marble Faun* reads too much like the self-conscious exercises of a belated epigone of *fin-de-siècle* writers to appeal to the modern reader, and we probably would not pause to consider them had they not become—to borrow a nice phrase from Mary McCarthy—the sacred droppings of a holy bird.

At best the slender neo-Romantic poems collected in this volume have the wistful charm of elegant mood pieces; at worst they are absurdly high-flown; for the most part their precious diction, contorted syntax, stereotyped imagery, and cloying musicality strike one as remorselessly "poetic." They are without doubt apprentice work. But the apprentice is an avid and fast learner, and for all its weaknesses *The Marble Faun* cannot be dismissed as mere scale-practicing or as the effusions of a callow dilettante. It not only evinces a keen awareness of literary traditions; like *Vision in Spring*[15] and Faulkner's other poem sequences, it also bears witness to meticulous craftsmanship and—most important with regard to future developments—to his incipient concern for form and structure. *The Marble Faun* is indeed already a "highly complex literary exercise," one which "would scarcely have been attempted by an unlettered, accidental poet."[16]

Yet it is perhaps primarily as poeticized self-projection that *The Marble Faun* solicits our attention. If as a work of literature it has little of substance to offer, it has indeed a great deal to tell about Faulkner as a young man and beginning writer. In a twice mythic Antiquity, reimagined by the Romantics and the Symbolists, Faulkner found one of his first masks, a mask already referred to in the book's oxymoronic title: immobile at the center of the poetic scene, the marble faun is clearly the most pregnant figure of this "cold pastoral." As an inherited literary figure, he represents here potentially what the faun has represented to the Western imagination since the advent of Christianity: a sensuous pagan dream of freedom and innocence under the aegis of Pan the Goat-God; a nostalgic reminder of the elemental, freshly flowing energies of a lost Arcadia—a place and time in which man, half animal, half god, was still allowed to roam the earth and to gratify his wildest desires, unburdened by sin and sorrow.[17] Faulkner's faun, however, has little in common with his fairly ribald *Belle Epoque* homologue in Mallarmé's eclogue. Turned into stone, caught in the coldness of mute marble, he can only listen to the tender music of Pan's flute; he cannot answer its call. Desire, with him, has darkened into mourning and melancholy, and not even in his dreams has he known the full blaze of noon. The impenitent ravisher of nymphs has become a sighing and shivering voyeur with a wintry heart; Dionysiac ardor has given way to morose delectation:

> Why am I sad? I?
> Why am I not content? The sky
>   Warms me and yet I cannot break
> My marble bonds. That quick keen snake
> Is free to come and go, while I
> Am prisoner to dream and sigh
> For things I know, yet cannot know,
> 'Twixt sky above and earth below.
> The spreading earth calls to my feet
> Of orchards bright with fruits to eat,
> Of hills and streams on either hand;
> Of sleep at night on moon-blanched sand:
> The whole earth breathes and calls to me
> Who marble-bound must ever be.[18]

Another famishing Tantalus, doomed to passive awareness and barren knowledge, wistfully watching the promising spectacle of life from which he is forever exiled, the marble faun emblematizes the contradictions and dilemmas of a young dreamer still entangled in the frustrations of adolescence and of a would-be writer still uncertain of his true vocation. Uneasily poised between the extravagant aspirations of his youth and the as yet remote accomplishments of his adulthood, both tempted by the austere perfections of art and attracted by the proffered riches of the real world, Faulkner, at this point, was obviously too self-involved to achieve a working relationship with either.

The Marble Faun is of course also an invitation to teleological fallacy. Reading it with the benefit of hindsight, we cannot help decoding it as a seminal text foreshadowing works to come. Its elaborate formal organization prefigures the far bolder and even more intricate patterns of Faulkner's fiction; its thematic orchestration points ahead to a number of later motifs. Its nature imagery and seasonal framework, for example, were to be reused in the complex symbolic structures of the novels, and the pastoral mode was likewise to reemerge in wholly different guises: *As I Lay Dying* has been termed "a pastoral elegy";[19] *Light in August* might be defined as a pastoral tragedy, and the pastoral element is even more prominent in the Snopes trilogy.

Moreover, the faun's predicament embodies polarities and antinomies to be found again in all of Faulkner's later texts: stasis versus motion, confinement versus freedom, consciousness versus experience, dream versus reality, self versus world. And in his tortured impotence he may also be seen as the first adumbration of Faulkner's generic "sick hero."[20] For some of his divided male characters the ultimate dilemma will be life or death, yet their existential malaise usually begins with an acutely felt inner contradiction, the disturbing sense of being dead-in-life. Their predicament, like the faun's, is less an alternative than an aporia: "to be *and* not to be."

Lastly, insofar as he is a statue, a likeness carved in and preserved by stone, Faulkner's faun might also be viewed as an early illustration of what was to become the writer's major paradigm of the work of art: like a figure on an urn or a frieze, the marble faun evokes the Keatsian paradox of arrested motion so often referred to in Faulkner's fiction.

Still, for us, retrospectively, his major import is that of a poetic self-portrait: he is Faulkner's first persona (from *per-sonar:* to sound through), the elegiac double of a young writer in all but solipsistic isolation, whose creative powers are still waiting for release and for whom literature is as yet not so much an imperious vocation as a consoling fiction, a drowsy dreamland for solitary souls. The portrait, however, no more refers back to a prior identity than did the various poses which Faulkner then foisted upon his friends and neighbors. The resemblance is here nothing more than a redoubled semblance. It is the portrait, rather, which retroactively generates its model, the theatrical double which conjures up the mirage of an original backstage self. For what does the mask both mask and unmask if not a lack, a gap, an uncomfortable condition of vacancy? And it is only a short step from the marble mask to the lunar Pierrot of *Vision in Spring*[21] and *The Marionettes*, the Symbolist one-act play that Faulkner wrote in a fine calligraphic hand, illustrated with pen and ink drawings, and bound himself during the autumn of 1920.[22]

Mon ami Pierrot

Preceding by a few years the final draft of *The Marble Faun*, this dream play is likewise *fin-de-siècle* with a vengeance, and even more heavily dated because of all the moods, motifs, and mannerisms it borrows from the Symbolists. Here is its décor:

> The sky is a thin transparent blue, a very light blue merging into white stars in regular order, and a full moon. At the back center is a marble colonnade, small in distance, against a regular black band of trees; on either side of it is the slim graceful silhouette of a single poplar tree. Both wings are closed by sections of wall covered with roses, motionless on the left with a peacock silhouetted against the moon. In the middle foreground is a pool and a fountain.[23]

Stars and trees "in regular order," slim poplars in perfect symmetry, black-and-white contrasts, a marble colonnade, a pool, and a fountain: it would be difficult to imagine a more radically stylized setting. Again, as in *The Marble Faun*, we have been transported into the exquisite arrangements of the formal garden—*à la française*, half classical, half rococo, with a rigorously geometrical pattern; nature denatured, displaced, and denied. Ellison, the owner of the

Domain of Arnheim, might have designed it; Beardsley might have drawn it: not forgetting the moon, the roses, and the peacock.

And here, in his ample white costume, with his drooping sleeves and his wan face, is Pierrot, the evanescent hero of the play, first drawn by Faulkner in a style precisely Beardsleyan, then described (the description becoming the caption of the drawing):

> Pierrot is seated at right front in a fragile black chair beside a delicate table. His left arm is curved across the table top, his right arm hangs beside him, and his head rests upon his curved arm, face toward front. He appears to be in a drunken sleep, there is a bottle and an overturned wine glass upon the table, a mandolin and a woman's slipper lie at his feet. He does not change his position during the play. He is dressed in white and black. Flung across the chair back is a scarf of black and gold Chinese brocade.[24]

Where does Faulkner's besotted Pierrot come from? From Verlaine's Watteauesque *Fêtes Galantes*? From Jules Laforgue's bittersweet *fumisteries* (via Aiken and Eliot)? From Ernest Dowson or, again, from Beardsley, Dowson's illustrator, who, late in his short life, used the Pierrot mask for the artist's self-portrait as a dying clown? When Faulkner wrote his play, Pierrot had been for several decades the tragicomic emblem of the alienated artist, and his vogue in French, then European art and literature was such that it would be pointless to trace him back to a unique model.[25] It hardly matters from whom he was borrowed. But it is noteworthy that in projecting himself into a *commedia dell'arte* character adopted by high culture, the young Faulkner played once again a role from the slightly shopworn repertoire of the Decadents.

The role, however, has been slightly altered. Faulkner's Pierrot is neither Pedrolino, the lumpish lover of the Italian theatrical tradition, nor even the Hamletized tragic or neurotic clown depicted by Gautier, Verlaine, and Laforgue, but a furtive seducer, a kind of lunar Don Juan, resembling his predecessors only in his misogyny and his phantomlike ways. Besides, the *dramatis personae* include two Pierrots: the drunken and sleeping Pierrot, onstage throughout, described in the second paragraph, and the rakish "Shade of Pierrot," who is the play's protagonist. Faulkner's new double, then, is himself double, a figure divided between stasis and motion, silence and speech—just like the marble faun. And the theater is again a mental theater: as Noel Polk points out, "the action of the play takes place in Pierrot's head, either as a dream of himself as the would-be lover, like Mallarmé's and Faulkner's fauns, or as a guilt-ridden dream of remorse over what he has done to Marietta."[26]

As for Marietta, a Columbine without Columbine's saucinesss, it is easy to see how much she owes to Mallarmé's Hérodiade and to Wilde's bejeweled Salomé.[27] Building again upon a well-established literary tradition, Faulkner appropriates a figure already abundantly mythologized: the Belle Dame sans Merci, the *femme fatale*, seducer and destroyer of men, whose demonic powers fascinated poets, novelists, dramatists, painters, and composers from the late nineteenth century to the early decades of ours. Of this dark myth of womanhood the Marietta of Faulkner's play offers only a pale, diminished reflection. Yet she is the first in a line of narcissistic virgins, most of whom will appear in his early novels. It is remarkable too that while Pierrot is rather perfunctorily treated and disappears in the middle of the play (his portrayal in the illustrations is much more inventive), Marietta emerges as its focal figure and is in fact Faulkner's first dramatized female character. Like the nymphs of the poems, she is first of all a prey of male lust, but, like the marble faun, she attempts to understand and voice her own desires, and hence may be seen as another, this time feminine persona of the writer, a portrait of Narcissus as Echo. Narcissism is once again a central issue. Formal garden, fountain, peacocks, jewels, candles, roses, and the ubiquitous cold moon, all these standard symbols of artificial splendor are suggestive of Marietta's morbid self-love and barren beauty. Enraptured by her own body, she admires herself in the reflections of the pool, and she eventually dies in her desolate autumnal garden, not for having been seduced and abandoned but because in her extreme narcissism she could trade her beauty only against death. Or is it more than death? After her return, Marietta, studying her reflection, discovers that she has not changed, that she is as beautiful as ever. But her beauty is now beyond life and sex, having become a hostage to both death and art. One of the attendant figures compares her to "an ivory tower" and "a little statue of ivory and silver," her hair turns into gold, her breasts become jewels, her hands "two links of silver chain" or "little pieces of smoothe silver."[28] Metaphors repeat themselves and multiply with such luxuriance around Marietta that they eventually smother her. Her literal death is by water, her textual death by rhetoric. By the end of the play, the deserted maiden has been fetishized into a hard, glittering icon.[29]

Distaste for organic matter and lavish use of mineral imagery had been one of the hallmarks of French poetry from Gautier and Baudelaire to the Parnassians, and jewels, ivory, and silver are also conspicuous motifs in Wilde's *Salomé*. There is indeed little in *The Marionettes* that has not been pinched from the iconic and rhetorical code of the Decadent and Symbolist traditions. But the route that takes Marietta from the anguished awakening of desire through sexual initiation to a premature death will be retraced with much more insight and subtlety in Faulkner's fiction. From this outdated staging of a fatal seduction, fantasies and obsessions begin to take on a shape that we cannot fail to identify in retrospect as typically Faulknerian. The final vignette of the play encapsulates them with almost allegoric simplicity: it shows Pierrot from behind, staring at his reflection in a mandorla-shaped mirror, between two funeral—some would say "phallic"—candlesticks, with dead Marietta lying on a couch at his feet.[30] Narcissus, Eros, and Thanatos: this is indeed the mythic and phantasmal constellation within which Faulkner's fiction will unfold itself, at least up to *The Sound and the Fury*.

Both masks and mirrors, Faulkner's early texts poeticize the unresolved tensions and unfulfilled wishes of prolonged adolescence. But the narcissism reflected in them is seldom merely the amorous capture of a subject by his own image. Far from losing themselves in the ecstatic contemplation of themselves, the male characters with whom the young Faulkner identified resent their self-confinement and are in fact all fervid "nympholepts." Pierrot dreams of himself as an irresistible lover; the more prudish faun is disconsolate because he is "marble-bound." All of Faulkner's juvenilia speak the language of desire. However narcissistic, the scene of representation is presided over by Eros, with alluring nymphs and naiads gliding across moonlit gardens or leafy groves, fleetingly offered to the lusting eye, yet never to be possessed. Let us note, too, that the addressees of the neatly hand-lettered, hand-illustrated, and hand-bound *art nouveau* booklets which Faulkner produced between 1921 and 1926 were nearly all women: *Vision in Spring,* an early sequence of love poems, was written for Estelle Oldham Franklin, his boyhood sweetheart and future wife; one copy of *The Marionettes* was dedicated to her daughter; *Mayday* and *Helen: A Courtship* were gifts for Helen Baird, another woman he loved; *The Marble Faun,* his first published book, was dedicated to his mother, the first object of his affections. These booklets were not only texts *about* desire and love; they were their messengers and would probably not have been manufactured with such excruciating care had they not been intended as signed offerings, graceful propitiatory gestures in a coy game of seduction. As Dawson Fairchild observes in *Mosquitoes:* "I believe that every word a writing man writes is put down with the ultimate intention of impressing some woman that probably don't care anything at all for literature."[31]

(Self-)Criticism

Writing, for Faulkner, was at first little more than the literary encoding of a series of private moves: a way of playing hide-and-seek with his theatrical selves, a way of parading and a way of wooing. A young man with a penchant for belles lettres, he used literature as a vehicle for thinly disguised self-expression and self-dramatization, and the static scenarios of the pastoral poem or the dream play perfectly suited his needs. What Yeats wrote of late-nineteenth-century poets fairly applies to him: "At once the fault and the beauty of the nature-description of most modern poets is that for them the stars, and streams, and the leaves, and the animals, are only masks behind which go on the sad soliloquies of nineteenth century egotism."[32]

As early as 1925, however, when describing the "pilgrimage" that had taken him from Swinburne's flamboyant romanticism to Shakespeare, Keats, and Housman, Faulkner willingly admitted that his love of poetry had begun as a youthful pose:

I was not interested in verse for verse's sake then. I read and employed verse, firstly for the purpose of furthering various philanderings in which I was engaged, secondly, to complete a youthful gesture I was then making, of being "different" in a small town. Later, my concupiscence waning, I turned inevitably to verse, finding therein an emotional counterpart far more satisfactory. . . .[33]

It is significant too that the pieces of literary criticism which Faulkner published between 1920 and 1925 read so often like oblique comments and speculations on his own poetic endeavors. In the writers whom he reviewed, he perceived echoes of his own moods and perplexities and seldom failed to detect those blind spots and shortcomings which he probably knew to be also his. Thus, in his review of William Alexander Percy's *In April Once*, he compared the author to "a little boy closing his eyes against the dark of modernity which threatens the bright simplicity and the colorful romantic pageantry of the middle ages with which his eyes are full."[34] And in noting that Percy "—like alas! how many of us—suffered the misfortune of having been born out of his time,"[35] he no doubt spoke for himself too.

Faulkner's early critical pieces reveal as much about the preoccupations of their author as about the writers—poets, playwrights, novelists—they are supposed to discuss. One recurrent concern in them is the relationship between art and the artist or, more precisely, the psychological if not psychosexual roots of literary creation. "Writing people," he remarks in one of his reviews, "are all so pathetically torn between a desire to make a figure in the world and a morbid interest in their personal egos."[36] However brief his own experience of writing, it had already taught him that narcissism is both the mainspring of artistic creation and its most insidious poison. Hence his reservations about Joseph Hergesheimer, a fashionable author of the twenties, whose *Linda Condon* he reviewed in his final *Mississippian* piece. Faulkner charged him with "a deliberate pandering to the emotions"[37] and argued that, however brilliant, his book was too self-complacent to be considered a novel:

> It is more like a Byzantine frieze: a few unforgettable figures in silent arrested motion, forever beyond the reach of time and troubling the heart like music. His people are never actuated from within; they do not create life about them; they are like puppets assuming graceful but meaningless postures in answer to the author's compulsions, and holding these attitudes until he arranges their limbs again in other gestures as graceful and meaningless.[38]

Faulkner's arguments could easily be turned around on the author of *The Marionettes*. Self-criticism by proxy, once again: this charming little world of postures and gestures is that of the lunar Pierrot and the marble faun. Yet Faulkner would not abandon the puppet imagery nor give up his penchant for still scenes. But at this point he was already fully aware that he had to find ways to go beyond the mannered aestheticism of his apprentice work. His condemnation of Hergesheimer's static art prefigures in reverse what he was later to state as the true artist's primary ambition: "to arrest motion, which is life, by artificial means and hold it fixed so that a hundred years later, when a stranger looks at it, it moves again, since it is life."[39]

Noteworthy too in these short critical essays is Faulkner's call for a truly national literature capable of taking advantage of the as yet unexplored riches of American experience and of "the lustiest language of modern times."[40] This kind of preoccupation was by no means new: for several generations American writers had been expressing the same hopes and doing their best to fulfill them. Surprisingly, in 1922 Faulkner still deplores that his country "has no drama or literature worth the name."[41] But far from finding "America aesthetically impossible,"[42] he firmly believes in the future of an authentically American literature and asserts the need for most writers to have strong cultural roots: "art is preeminently provincial: i.e., it comes directly from a certain age and a certain locality."[43] Not that he was ever tempted by regionalism; even at this tentative stage his literary ambitions by far exceeded those of a local colorist. But the crucial discovery he then began to make was that literature, like anthropology, is a matter of "local knowledge" and that his experience of the South would provide him with all he needed to build a world of his own: "a man with real ability finds sufficient what he has to hand."[44]

Textual twins: "The Hill" and "Nympholepsy"

The discovery of the literary potential of his homeland probably hastened Faulkner's conversion to narrative prose. Had this conversion not occurred, his particular talents would probably have withered in the rarefied air of post-Romantic lyricism. At best he might have become a good minor poet after having been a mediocre one, but certainly not the great writer we know and admire today. This does not mean that the poetic impulse had to be given up, far from it; but to become truly fecund it had to be absorbed and energized by the urge to tell the tale of the tribe, which, for Faulkner, turned out to be a much more vital need than the fastidious distillation of private emotion.

The passage from poetry to prose was no sudden turnabout, however. Even though the young Faulkner thought of himself primarily as a poet, his passion for poetry had never precluded experiments in other genres and modes. He had been writing stories and prose sketches since his boyhood; he continued to do so during the early twenties and, as we have seen, tried his hand at drama and criticism. And perhaps one should recall his real talent for drawing, which, according to Carvel Collins, made him briefly envision parallel careers in the graphic arts and writing.[45] Poetry, to him, was clearly literature in its purest and noblest form, but at no time was it his unique medium.

"Landing in Luck," Faulkner's first published short story, appeared in the *Mississippian* on November 26, 1919.[46] Narrating the disastrous first solo flight and miraculous landing of Cadet Thompson, it is undeniably an autobiographical fiction, inspired by Faulkner's recent experience in a

Canadian training camp. Its manner prefigures the opening scene of *Soldiers' Pay*, but there is not much to praise in it: its anecdote is thin, its humor tame, its style flat. Faulkner's start as a storyteller was remarkably unremarkable. No one, after reading the story, could have predicted his career as a novelist.

More than two years after this inauspicious beginning, on March 10, 1922, the same journal published "The Hill."[47] As Henri Thomas, its French translator, notes, this short sketch is "an attempt at poetic prose rather than a fiction—a poem in prose quite in accordance with the Baudelairian canon."[48] It is also a piece of apprenticeship replete with Swinburnian reminiscences, but more than any of Faulkner's early writings it looks ahead to his fiction. Pastoral conventions begin to recede, and the formal stage settings give way to a rural landscape whose contours are for the first time distinctly those of Faulkner country. However sketchy, the description of the hamlet in the valley, contemplated from the crest of a hill by a "tieless casual," provides the first panorama of what was to become the novelist's mythical Jefferson. Furthermore, the hill-and-valley pattern foreshadows in many ways Faulkner's later use of space symbolism: high and low, verticality and horizontality, ascent and descent are revealingly contrasted, and while the valley and its somnolent hamlet evoke "the joys and sorrows, hopes and despairs"[49] of an earthbound humanity, the hilltop, a high place between sky and earth, suggests—as it often will in Faulkner's novels—the remote possibility of a freer mode of being, high above the muddy flow of time and life. That the experience recorded in the sketch occurs at sunset is equally noticeable. Twilight, as Michel Gresset has pointed out, is to Faulkner, as to many writers of the Anglo-Saxon Symbolist tradition, "the moment of all possible revelations," and in "The Hill" it functions indeed as "the medium or agent of what happens to the tieless casual."[50]

But what, exactly, happens to him? Nothing much. The text refers to "the terrific groping of his mind,"[51] but his mental exertions are of no avail: "for a moment he had almost grasped something alien to him, but it eluded him; and being unaware that there was anything which had tried to break down the barriers of his mind and communicate with him, he was unaware that he had been eluded."[52] Twilight holds out the promise of revelation; the stage seems set for a Joycean epiphany, yet no illumination occurs, and the mind's struggle to break its bonds does not even rise to consciousness. No insight is achieved in the process apart from the sudden realization by the protagonist of "the devastating unimportance of his destiny."[53]

"The Hill" is the evocation of a failed epiphany. Like the petrified faun or the bemused Pierrot and like many of Faulkner's later characters, its hero or rather anti-hero is fated to contemplation without vision. Like the faun, too, he might be taken for a double of that other would-be seer: the artist himself, in his endless striving to see and say the world truthfully. "The Hill" could thus be read as an ironic parable on the inescapable failure of all art and on the mirage of which it is both the product and the production. As Jorge Luis

Borges has suggested in *Labyrinths*, "This imminence of a revelation which does not occur is, perhaps, the aesthetic phenomenon."[54]

For Faulkner himself, however, the composition of this prose sketch was probably the occasion of a major discovery. "Something" that had so far eluded him was at last coming into focus. After a series of various experiments none of which had been conclusive, a kind of precipitation occurred, and "The Hill" was the precipitate. However hesitantly, the lineaments of a unique fictional design were beginning to emerge, according to a pattern which was to assert itself with increasing vigor. And as this configuration was taking shape, writing, for Faulkner, ceased to serve exclusively his need for masked confession. The "tieless casual" can be seen as another of the writer's doubles, but the self he impersonates is neither the lyrical self of *The Marble Faun* and *The Marionettes* nor the anecdotal self of "Landing in Luck." In his utter isolation he may remind us of the faun, but unlike the latter he is a man in motion: the statue has left its pedestal; the cold marble has become living flesh. Moreover, this new character owes certainly as much to Faulkner's social experience as to his familiarity with literature, and in social terms, within the class context of the South, he stands for Faulkner's *other*. No pastoral shepherd but a "casual," a farm laborer, toiling with his hands for bare subsistence, he comes from the lowest stratum of southern society and is the first of the rural "poor whites" portrayed in Faulkner's fiction. Nameless (like most characters in Faulkner's New Orleans sketches and like the later Tall Convict in *The Wild Palms*), voiceless, and "featureless," he is man at his most opaque and inarticulate, and therefore far removed from the self-centered, self-conscious, and loquacious figures of the earlier texts. Identification is still at work, but rather than a static game of mirrors, it is now a reaching out, a move out of self, a quest for otherness. In the series of doubles that mark out Faulkner's early writings the *alter* for the first time appears to take precedence over the *ego*.

"The Hill" thus points to a significant shift from other as self to self as other. A small breach has been opened in the stronghold of narcissism; a displacement, a decentering, has occurred that allows Faulkner to start in turn on his way and to begin the fertile wandering of his writing venture. And it is in the course of this wandering that he will find his true territory.

"The Hill" is indeed "a double threshold: to Faulkner's world and to Faulkner's universe, the physical setting of the Yoknapatawpha novels and the inner theater of the literary creation."[55] True, it is only a rudimentary sketch, with little more than discreet hints of future developments. That the seeds were there, however, is amply confirmed by "Nympholepsy," an expanded version of "The Hill" presumably written three years later, and published only in 1973.[56]

"Nympholepsy" is the "dark twin" of "The Hill." Again a lone farmhand climbs a hill at sunset, contemplates the prospect from its top, and then descends into the valley; yet there is more of a story here than in the earlier sketch. Dramatic tension is generated by the fleeting apparition of a female figure, first glimpsed far off as "a golden light among dark pines,"[57] then frantically pursued through field and wood by the tale's protagonist. Faulkner here resumes the motif of the amorous chase that he had used in some of his poems (notably in "L'Apres-Midi d'un Faune"), and reverts to the mythological scene (briefly recalled at the close of "The Hill") of the pastoral: while the pursued maiden turns into a tantalizing nymph, the "tieless casual" is cast in the role of the lusting faun. Without ceasing to be out of reach, the "something" that he failed to grasp here materializes in the desirable flesh of a woman. The still confrontation of self and world has become a bewildering close encounter with the other sex.

It would seem, then, that the object of the quest has undergone a decisive transformation: instead of the austere, almost abstract drama of inaccessible knowledge, "Nympholepsy" stages the nightmare of impeded sexual possession.

In following the call of desire, the farmhand has stumbled unawares into forbidden space, watched over by a remote deity both indifferent and tyrannical:

> And above all brooded some god to whose compulsions he must answer long after the more comfortable beliefs had become out-worn as a garment used everyday. And this god neither recognized him nor ignored him: this god seemed to be unconscious of his entity, save as a trespasser where he had no business being.[58]

This enigmatic god might well be Pan the Sinister.[59] The man, at any rate, is panic-stricken and seized by the terror of "abrupt and dreadful annihilation."[60] Soon he finds himself running, and as he crosses a stream on a footlog, he slips off balance and falls:

> Then the water took him. But here was something more than water. The water ran darkly between his body and his overalls and shirt, he felt his hair lap backward wetly. But here beneath his hand a startled thigh slid like a snake, among dark bubbles he felt a swift leg; and, sinking, the point of a breast scraped his back. Amid a slow commotion of disturbed water he saw death like a woman shining and drowned and waiting, saw a flashing body tortured by water; and his lungs spewing water gulped wet air.[61]

The coveted body turns out to be the lure of death. Woman is death, death is woman. Water is their common metaphor, a trope of desire and death that runs through all of Faulkner's fiction. Engulfment, drowning, death by water is in Faulkner erotic death par excellence, as is attested by his early poems, *The Marionettes*, and *Mayday* as well as by Quentin's suicide in *The Sound and the Fury* and the pervasive flood imagery of *The Wild Palms*.[62] But it is in "Nympholepsy" that it is given its first spectacular staging.

The scene is the same as in "The Hill," and yet it is *another scene*, suffused with heady sensuality and drenched in anguish, with something of that ominous "mystical" atmosphere in which the Symbolists found their *frissons*.

With its conspicuously Swinburnian title and lush imagery, "Nympholepsy" is no less dated than the earlier sketch, perhaps even more dated, and of the two versions of the text, "The Hill" is assuredly the more economical, the better controlled. But it is precisely through its voluble abandon that "Nympholepsy" seduces and intrigues the reader, as if it were to tell us what "The Hill" left untold. In reading it, we keep circling around a primal enigma, but for us too the moment of disclosure is forever deferred. The place of origins will not yield its secrets. What we are offered in its stead is the shadow theater of its re-presentation, a retelling of the timeless tales of men and gods recorded by myth, and perhaps a reminder of the legendary scene reported in Ovid's *Metamorphoses*: Diana surprised while she is bathing among her nymphs by the young hunter Actaeon and cruelly punishing the inadvertent intruder for his sacrilegious gaze. "Nunc tibi me posito visam velamine narres / Si poteris narrare, licet."[63] "Tell it, if you can!" the naked goddess says. Faulkner-Actaeon is about to take up the challenge.

The learning of prose

"Nympholepsy" was probably written within the first month or two of Faulkner's second visit to New Orleans in the spring of 1925. He was then moving into a new phase of his literary apprenticeship, a phase predominantly marked by his close and fecund association with Sherwood Anderson, whose example, advice, and encouragement were decisive in his turning from poetry to prose. During his stay in New Orleans Faulkner was still writing poems, and he was to write more in the following years; 1925, however, was the year when prose fiction superseded poetry as his major medium.

It certainly also was a turning point in his intellectual development. In the course of the six months spent in New Orleans, by then the undisputed cultural capital of the South, Faulkner became immersed in the cosmopolitan and bohemian atmosphere of the Vieux Carré. Keeping company with journalists, writers, and painters, and listening to their cafe conversations, he discovered the major cultural trends of the midtwenties and grew aware of such influential figures as Freud, Frazer, Bergson, and Joyce. Not that up to then he had been a benighted provincial nor that he suddenly became a city intellectual, but consorting regularly with people who shared his passion for art and literature must have made him more confident in his own vocation, and the intellectual stimulation he found in New Orleans certainly had a positive impact on his development as a writer. There can be no doubt that the influences he then absorbed—probably through osmosis rather than systematic study—were instrumental in shaping his later work.

Faulkner's literary output during this period offers conclusive evidence of his broadening interests. In 1925 he published two groups of prose pieces: eleven short sketches in a New Orleans literary magazine, the *Double Dealer* (January–February), and a series of sixteen stories and sketches in the Sunday feature section of the *Times-Picayune* newspaper (February–September).[64] In these vignettes Faulkner explored new material and experimented with new styles, modes, and techniques. Admittedly, their language oscillates uncomfortably between high rhetoric and rural dialect, and Faulkner's narrative performance is still often amateurish. The *Double Dealer* pieces are all static mood paintings, close to lyrics in their attempt to crystallize emotions and feelings in timeless patterns, and there is little effective dramatization in the more fully developed *Times-Picayune* stories. Yet here are Faulkner's first attempts at character creation and storytelling, and for all their connections with his earlier writings they demonstrate an unmistakable move in the direction of realism. Anderson's pervasive influence is felt in the choice of familiar, down-to-earth subjects, most often borrowed from the street life of New Orleans. The characters presented in the sketches are cops, cobblers, sailors, longshoremen, tramps, bootleggers, gangsters, whores—common people, most of whom are rootless or belong to the outer fringes of society. With their bright memories of childhood and youth, their withered expectations, and their frustrated longings for love, freedom, or beauty, they often remind one of Anderson's "grotesques" in *Winesburg, Ohio*. At times they are also reminiscent of Stephen Crane, and the legacy of naturalism appears throughout in the use of melodramatic incident, the predilection for outsiders, misfits, and losers, and the general emphasis on low life. Yet Faulkner's stylizing approach to his material clearly departs from the standard techniques of naturalism, having much more in common with the "impressionistic" method then associated with Conrad and Joyce. Under their joint influence, he already sets out to make use of the various possibilities of narrative perspective and narrative voice: whether they are exotic prose poems such as "Wealthy Jew" or vernacular soliloquies such as "Frankie and Johnny," all the vignettes of the *Double Dealer* series are in the first person, focusing on the speaker's inner world, and some of the longer stories, such as "Home" and "Out of Nazareth," offer stretches of interior monologue anticipating *The Sound and the Fury* and *As I Lay Dying*.

Faulkner taught himself prose as he had taught himself poetry: through sedulous and shameless imitation of his predecessors. Yet reading his New Orleans sketches with the benefit of hindsight, we can hardly help a sense of *déjà-vu*. In "Out of Nazareth," for instance, which may be the fictionalized account of a real incident, David, 'the handsome young man met by the narrator and Spratling, foreshadows at once Faulkner's artist figures (he is a poet-tramp like his namesake in "Carcassonne" and owns a copy of *A Shropshire Lad*, as the young Faulkner did), his Christ figures (as the title and several of his attributes suggest), and his earth mothers (notably Lena Grove, the pregnant girl of *Light in August*, whom he resembles in his "calm belief" in Nature). In "The Kingdom of God," the bellowing idiot with cornflower blue eyes, clutching in his hand a broken narcissus flower, clearly prefigures Benjy Compson, the dim-witted brother in *The Sound and the Fury*. Ek, the all too imaginative "raconteur" in "The Liar"—one of the last and best stories published in the *Times-Picayune* and one of the first with a Yoknapatawphalike backcountry setting—anticipates V. K. Ratliff, the superb vernacular narrator of *The Hamlet*. Further hints of later developments could be traced in almost any of the sketches, but perhaps even more striking than all these anticipations is the extreme facility displayed, the amazing promptness and dexterity with which Faulkner picked up the tricks of his trade and assimilated the lessons of his many masters. Not that the sketches possess much intrinsic merit: Faulkner's attempts at reconciling the sonorous rhythms and far-flung imagery of late Romantic poetry with realistic narrative are interesting in terms of his career but at this point their fusion is seldom successfully achieved. Moreover, most of the *Times-Picayune* stories betray hasty writing, and in some of them (as in a number of short stories Faulkner later turned out for national magazines), there is even a touch of the slickly commercial, reminding one that they were also written for money. In literary terms, the New Orleans sketches represent no clear advance over "The Hill," and Anderson's warning to the budding virtuoso was quite to the point: "You've got too much talent. You can do it too easy, in too many different ways. If you're not careful, you'll never write anything."[65]

A trial run: *Soldiers' Pay*

The New Orleans sketches were only a part of Faulkner's output in 1925, for between January 4, the date of his arrival in New Orleans, and July 7, the date of his departure for a five-month tour of Europe, he published not only most of the sketches but also three poems,[66] three essays,[67] and a review,[68] not to mention the manuscripts found after his death.[69] Lastly, during the first months of 1925 Faulkner was busy writing his first novel, *Soldiers' Pay*. Written at the urging of Sherwood Anderson, completed in May 1925, and published in February 1926, this book marks the beginning of Faulkner's career as a novelist. Not surprisingly, it is about World War I and its aftermath, about the war Faulkner had been deprived of and which fascinated him all the more as he had not fought in it. That his motivations in choosing this subject were deeply personal is beyond doubt; during his role-playing period in the twenties the limping war veteran was one of his favorite parts. As can be seen from *Flags in the Dust, A Fable,* and the war stories, the "Great Crusade" of 1914-18 was to haunt his imagination throughout his career. Faulkner's nonexperience of the war may indeed be said to have proved as traumatic to him as actual participation in it had to other Americans of his generation. The wound was there, even though, unlike Hemingway's, it was an imaginary one, and it would keep festering for many years.

Still, Faulkner's deep-felt involvement with the war was not enough to produce a great novel. In the twenties, talented young writers on both sides of the Atlantic were voicing the disillusionment of the postwar generation. In America, Dos Passos drew on his war experience to write *Three Soldiers* (1921);

so did Cummings in *The Enormous Room* (1922). And in 1926, the very year when *Soldiers' Pay* appeared, Hemingway published *The Sun Also Rises*, perhaps the finest novelistic distillation of the bitter postwar mood. It was also a first novel, but while Hemingway found at once his frugal music, Faulkner was still seeking his voice.

In its own way, however, *Soldiers' Pay* is likewise a typical "lost generation" novel, voicing the sense of futility and frustration that then afflicted those whom the war had suddenly made aware of the irretrievable loss of American innocence. But its very typicality dates the novel. By 1926 "postwar disillusionment" had become something of a pose, and such figures as the sad young man, the discharged soldier, and the Fitzgeraldian flapper were already literary stereotypes. Nothing gets sooner out of fashion than fashion. Faulkner's first novel is too much of a fashionable book, a harlequin costume designed and manufactured by all the literary couturiers of the day. There are suggestions of James Branch Cabell's urbane eroticism and Joseph Hergesheimer's languid elegancies, of Aldous Huxley's clever juggling with ideas and T. S. Eliot's "Waste Land" mood. Even Beardsley, the dominant model of Faulkner's early drawings, has left his mark, and throughout one also senses his persistent fidelity to the obsolete mannerisms of the Decadents and the indiscreet if not incongruous proximity of his recent poetic past.[70]

Faulkner's shortcomings in *Soldiers' Pay* are those one would expect in a first novel: extreme self-consciousness, too many echoes and reminiscences, too many directions taken at once. The attempt to graft poetry onto prose is hardly more convincing here than it was in the New Orleans sketches. Yet to this attempt the book owes its distinctive quality as an experiment in fiction. In abandoning poetry for prose, Faulkner did not settle for a lesser medium—or if he did it was with the hope that its possibilities could be enlarged in such ways as to make it an art form of equal dignity. And to Faulkner as to Flaubert, James, Conrad, and Joyce, such an ambition could be achieved only if prose fiction was as tightly controlled and as rigorously disciplined as poetic discourse. In his first novel the experiment no doubt miscarried; yet, as Michael Millgate judiciously notes, "what gives *Soldiers' Pay* its special character is its origin as a novel about the war and its aftermath written by a young writer self-consciously pursuing the abstract formalism of late romantic prose."[71] Indeed, the most remarkable feature of the book is perhaps that from the outset of his novelistic career Faulkner made so clean a break with the conventions of realistic fiction.

What unity the novel possesses it owes to pattern rather than plotting. The narrative does not follow orderly chronological progression; nor is there a stable dramatic focus: characters flit in and out, brief scenes and vignettes follow one another in kaleidoscopic succession. The time sequence is repeatedly broken up, unrelated actions are linked through montagelike juxtaposition, and discrepant moods are telescoped for ironic effect—contrapuntal techniques reminiscent of Joyce (see, for instance, section 7 in chapter VII, which is clearly indebted to the "Circe" chapter in *Ulysses*) and foreshadowing the fugal structures of Faulkner's later fiction. Furthermore, to harmonize his disparate materials Faulkner resorts to structural devices he had used in *The Marble Faun* and would use again with greater sophistication in his mature work: emphasis on the progress of the seasons; incorporation of literary allusions and mythical references, reliance on reverberant repetition of imagery and symbol, elaborate modulation of theme and motif. What is lost in narrative coherence and continuity is in some measure regained through compositional tightness.

The overall effect of *Soldiers' Pay* is therefore one of deliberate disjointedness as well as intricate patterning. Not that it really works: the novel's structure suffers from overelaboration, its stylistic texture from overwriting. While Faulkner manages to be aggressively modernistic, he fails to be truly modern. It should be urged, however, that in writing his first novel he was already fully aware of the potentialities of his medium and determined to exploit them to their limit.

Soldiers' Pay also deserves close attention as a nexus between Faulkner's early poetry and prose and the novels to come. Insofar as the book has a dramatic focus it is centered upon the mute motionless figure of Donald Mahon, a maimed, disfigured, hemiplegic, aphasic, and nearly blind soldier back from the war, and the novel's action may be said to develop as a kind of last vigil around his long dying, as the action of *As I Lay Dying* will develop around Addie Bundren's. A general pattern is thus established, to be reused in a number of later works: some fading figure—a shadowy presence or a haunting absence rather than a fully realized character—becomes the static center which sets everything in motion and around which all the other characters revolve in concentric circles, each of them responding in his own way to the focal figure. In this respect, Donald Mahon, Caddy Compson, Addie Bundren, Laverne Shumann, Thomas Sutpen, and Flem Snopes occupy similar positions and fulfill similar functions, however much they may differ as characters. At the same time Donald is also related to a significant series of male figures. In Faulkner's earlier work he is prefigured by the marble faun, severed like him from life's motion, and has his direct prototype in the terribly injured airman evoked in "The Lilacs," a poem written in 1920 and later published in *A Green Bough*.[72] On the other hand, he is himself a crude prefiguration of later heroes such as Bayard Sartoris and in some measure even anticipates Quentin Compson, the death-haunted young man of *The Sound and the Fury*.

Moreover, through Donald's drama Faulkner begins to sound one of his major themes: time. Donald is only the empty shell of a man, a living corpse with neither past nor present, imprisoned in a timeless limbo from which there is no return to life and no escape into death. Deliverance is denied him as long as he has not recovered his memory, that is, consciousness of his identity. Only when the elusive past is eventually recaptured as he remembers his encounter with the enemy plane does death become a possibility again. Then at last, the past having been reunited for a fleeting moment to the present, Donald again has a future, even though, ironically, it is a future of nothingness. Time and memory, consciousness and identity: Faulkner's readers will recognize here the nucleus of later thematic developments. And in a sense the desperate gropings of Donald's memory in the darkness of his last agony may be read as the inverted programmatic emblem of Faulkner's own quest: for the writer as for his first fictional hero, the struggle for selfhood passes perforce through anamnesis, the difficult exhumation of a buried past. Of this past Donald must retrieve at least a shred before he can die his own death; Faulkner's task will be likewise a work of recollection and reappropriation. He too will have to remember—not in order to die but to be (re)born into writing, which is both life and death.

A figure of death among the living, Donald also serves as a grim reminder of war amid the preposterous bustle of a small southern town. In this dual function he is set over against Januarius Jones, the fat and fatuous satyr whose grotesque erotomania is counterpointed against the dying soldier's silent suffering. While the one represents the war veterans and their harrowing experience of violence and death, the other is made to embody the futility of the postwar civil world. The contrast between these polar figures is further emphasized by the opposition of Donald's heroic romanticism and Januarius's vulgar hedonism; it is given additional significance by the two characters' suggested relatedness, for Januarius, the priapic clown, turns out to be a travesty of what Donald was before the war: an ardent young lover, with "the serenity of a wild thing, the passionate serene alertness of a faun."[73] Their implicit antagonism, then, is also that of a before and an after, of an idealized past and a debased present. Donald's love affair with Emmy was an idyll of grave and tender sensuality; all that Januarius is capable of is ludicrous lust.

Soldiers' Pay is as much a novel about sex and love as about war and death, and in associating the funeral wake with a farcical erotic ballet, it comes to resemble a *danse macabre*. Sex and death, "the front door and the back door of the world,"[74] are throughout intimately linked, and it is of course no accident that Donald's burial coincides with Emily's final surrender to the lecherous Jones. Contrived coincidences such as these no doubt show how heavy-handed Faulkner was then apt to be in his use of life's little ironies. A subtler treatment of the two themes would certainly have required more maturity. Faulkner's feelings about death are still largely indebted to the romantic reveries of adolescence, and for all its display of smartness and cynicism his handling of the sex comedy is likewise immature. But death and sex are acknowledged from the first as the controlling powers of man's fate, and in his first novel Faulkner already describes a whole range of responses to both—responses varying widely according to whether the characters in-volved are soldiers or civilians, young or old people, men or women. The sexual or sentimental subplots develop around three feminine figures, two of whom are unmistakable adumbrations of later heroines. One is Cecily Saunders, Donald's former fiancée: spoiled, shallow, selfish, eager to please yet unable to love, she is portrayed as "the symbol of a delicate bodyless lust"[75] and satirized as "a papier-mâché Virgin."[76] While recalling the Marietta of

Marionettes and the naiads of Faulkner's early poems, Cecily inaugurates the series of "epicene" flappers of his early novels, and her acid grace and sexy sexlessness are traits to be found again in Temple Drake, the equally frail but even more disquieting heroine of *Sanctuary*. At the other extreme is Emily, the constant nymph: simple, submissive, tender-hearted, inarticulate, described throughout the novel in terms of animal imagery, the first of Faulkner's earth mothers. The third figure, Margaret Powers, is a neurotic war widow, another Lady Brett Ashley, who, instead of collecting lovers, seeks to assuage her sense of guilt through a sacrificial gesture. Yet, although she becomes Donald's mothering nurse, Faulkner describes her as a Beardsleyan avatar of the femme fatale. Much like Januarius Jones, she is in fact an excrescence of his juvenile infatuation with the Decadents, with no recognizable posterity in his mature fiction.

A great deal of Faulkner's characterization in *Soldiers' Pay* is derivative and inconsistent. In creating his characters he relies too much on currently popular types or falls back on outdated literary models. The symbolic significance they are invested with is all too often contradicted by the functions they are asked to assume within the realistic context of the narrative, and their motivations are sometimes highly implausible.[77] For all its weaknesses, however, Faulkner's characterization is never divorced from structure, and one cannot fail to be struck by the elaborate care with which the novel's characters are grouped, balanced, and contrasted. Revealing, too, as far as female characters are concerned, is the crystallization in Faulkner's first novel of the two complementary mythic images of woman which, however qualified and differentiated, were to underlie all his fiction: Eve, the archetypal mother, and Lilith, the perennial temptress.

Less obvious, but surely as pertinent to an inquiry into Faulkner's growth as a writer, are the ways in which the characters and situations presented in *Soldiers' Pay* relate to his personal experience and fantasies. He must have written the book with an awareness that most of his early expectations had come to nothing. His youthful love affair with Estelle Oldham had been thwarted by her marriage to another man.[78] His heroic dreams, as we have seen, had been likewise betrayed by reality. His prospects as a writer were as yet largely problematic. It therefore seems safe to assume that the sense of frustration and failure conveyed by the novel had roots in the author's recent past. The harshness of Faulkner's portrayal of Cecily Saunders certainly owes something to the bitterness he felt toward Estelle after her betrayal, and her own later testimony bears out one's suspicion that he had taken her as a model.[79] The autobiographical relevance of the novel's male characters is even easier to trace. A number of physical and biographical details connect Donald to the young Faulkner, and through this wounded war pilot a favorite impersonation of Faulkner's finds its way into fiction for the first time. Donald's funeral becomes in a sense the symbolic burial of Faulkner's dream of military glory and heroic death. And while Donald stands as the pathetic embodiment of the *dream*, other characters turn out to be ironic or even comic sketches of the *dreamer*, especially Julian Lowe, the callow cadet and hero-worshiper to whom Donald, the fallen Icarus, comes to represent all the glamor of gallant romance, and Gilligan, the demobilized private who, like Faulkner, never got across to the Western front. What unites the novel's male characters is their common experience of frustration. Hampered heroes, mocked lovers, all of them. For even as they are defeated in their heroic aspirations they are thwarted in their erotic yearnings: Donald is forsaken by Cecily; George Farr, the fickle girl's eventual husband, is tormented by morbid jealousy; Gilligan's love for Margaret Powers is a hopeless affair; and even Januarius Jones's frantic woman-chasing is destined to end more often than not in grotesque fiascos.

Whether shown in pathetic or comic light, whether portrayed with sober sympathy or satiric detachment, Faulkner's frustrated male characters are all in some measure self-extensions into the feelings and gestures of possible surrogates. In *The Marble Faun* Faulkner used only one persona; in *The Marionettes* there were already two Pierrots; here in *Soldiers' Pay* the writer's self is split into a plurality of fragmentary doubles. And not only does none of them represent him whole. Each one redoubles a double; that is, each is made to relay a self-*image* and not at all to stand for a *real* single self. In *Soldiers' Pay* written fiction starts its devious game with the fictions of life, and irony and humor are already at play, creating distance and preventing fiction from turning into mere imaginary wish fulfillment. True, the movement toward full dramatization has barely begun; the author's presence beneath his various masks is still heavily felt. Yet even though *Soldiers' Pay* still evinces a fair amount of narcissistic self-involvement, it also marks the beginning of a necessary process of exorcism.

A divertissement: *Mosquitoes*

Faulkner's next novel, *Mosquitoes* (1927), is generally considered to be his weakest, and the author dismissed it himself as mere apprentice work: "This one, if I could write it over, I probably wouldn't write it at all. I'm not ashamed of it, because that was the chips, the badly sawn planks that the carpenter produces while he's learning to be a first-rate carpenter, but it's not a—not an important book in my list."[80] *Mosquitoes*, though, is by no means a sloppy novel. Like *Soldiers' Pay* and the earlier poem sequences, it is a firmly structured and intricately patterned piece of work. There is a Prologue and an Epilogue; its four central chapters and many internal subsections are arranged within a meticulous chronological scheme. Once again Faulkner experiments with montage effects and uses various narrative devices, from multiple perspective to internal focalization and stream of consciousness.[81] True, his formal and technical innovations belong already to the tradition of the new. As in *Soldiers' Pay*, many influences may be traced, and by and large they are the same as those of the earlier novel. Particularly conspicuous are the numerous verbal echoes from the early Eliot.[82] Among novelists Faulkner's greatest debt is probably to the chatty Aldous Huxley of *Crome Yellow, Antic Hay*, and *Those Barren Leaves*. The circumstances—a miscellaneous group of people thrown onto their own resources—are of a kind that the English novelist would have liked; the characters—artists, writers, dilettantes, their patrons and hangers-on—are of the intellectual type that he favored; and as an isolating device to justify unbroken conversation among them, Faulkner's yacht functions much like Huxley's country houses. *Mosquitoes* was a venture into the then fashionable "novel of ideas," and one might argue that it was a faux pas, a misguided foray into a genre alien to Faulkner's own gifts, that in trying to equal the witty sophistication and flippant cynicism of his British model he could only go astray. Yet when reread today, Huxley's novels seem hardly less dated than Faulkner's attempt to compete with him. The point is perhaps simply that conversation novels seldom age well.

After the sketches, *Mosquitoes* is the first literary trace of Faulkner's New Orleans experience. Its characters are borrowed from the artistic bohemia of the Vieux Carré in the midtwenties, and a number of them can be identified as in a *roman à clef*.[83] But most of those who recognized themselves in the portraits (among them Sherwood Anderson, the model for the novelist Dawson Fairchild, and William Spratling, the sculptor on whom he partly patterned Mark Gordon) had some reason to complain of the cruelty of the portraitist. Indeed, *Mosquitoes* often resembles a private settling of accounts. Faulkner's sojourn in New Orleans had certainly been a very useful experience, and from Anderson he had received all the assistance and encouragement he could expect. Yet, although he was too honest ever to deny his debt, his was in some measure the ingratitude one so often encounters in writers toward their erstwhile patrons and benefactors. It had not taken him long to detect the limitations of Anderson's literary talent, and, as with Hemingway, the naughty impulse soon followed to poke fun at the elderly novelist through pastiche of his style[84] and eventually to caricature the man himself. *Mosquitoes* may thus be viewed as a gesture of irreverence toward a literary father figure. More generally, with regard to Faulkner's development, it appears as an act of repudiation: by ridiculing the shallow intellectuality of the New Orleans world he rejected his own past and asserted his independence as a writer.

Like *Soldiers' Pay*, *Mosquitoes* is largely satire, and one of Faulkner's favorite targets is again sex, or rather what it had come to be in the post-Victorian, pseudo-"liberated" society of the twenties: endemic pruriency, an obsession feeding on impotence and sterility, what D. H. Lawrence was later to call "sex in the head." Sexuality, as depicted in the novel, is either thwarted or perverted, and even sexual identity becomes problematic. Gender roles are confused or inverted: except for Gordon, men are effeminate, women are masculinized, and girls will be boys. Echoing the *fin-de-siècle* motif of androgyny, Faulkner describes an enervated bisexual world.[85] His characters include a lesbian poetess and an undersexed poet, and even those who stick to heterosexual standards are at the very least crippled by neurotic repression. The more grotesque characters are to be found among the older people: Mrs. Maurier, the wealthy widow and silly patroness of the arts; Dorothy Jameson, the male-chasing painter; and above all the Prufrockian Mr. Talliaferro. As in *Soldiers' Pay*, the old are contrasted with the young.[86] In their own inarticulate and heedless way, however, the young are just as egotistical as their elders, and the couples they form in the novel suggest rather equivocal brother-sister relationships. And whether old or young, everybody seems to succumb to the same inertia. "This is kind of funny, aint it?" Jenny says. "They are not going anywhere, and they don't do anything."[87] Indeed, apart from talking and drinking and flirting, nothing happens aboard the *Nausikaa*. Only Patricia, Mrs. Maurier's lively niece, tries to break out of this stifling little world. Yet the closest she comes to sexual adventure is with the placidly sexy, Eulalike Jenny, and her escapade with the steward David ends in disaster. Again as in *Soldiers' Pay*, the ballet of desire is little more than the empty flutter of marionettes.

Yet if sexuality looms as large in *Mosquitoes* as it does in Faulkner's first novel, the thematic configuration within which it appears is fairly different. The emphasis is not on sexual perversion alone; it is also on the utter barrenness of verbal intercourse: "Talk, talk, talk: the utter and heart-breaking stupidity of words. It seemed endless, as though it might go on forever. Ideas, thoughts, became mere sounds to be bandied about until they were dead."[88] Conversation, as defined by the novel's narrator, is at best an absurd parlor game, a mere travesty of articulate and meaningful communication. Anticipating Addie's diatribe in *As I Lay Dying*, Fairchild denounces the "sterility" of language: "You begin to substitute words for things and deeds, like the withered cuckold husband that took the Decameron to bed with him every night, and pretty soon the thing or the deed becomes just a kind of shadow of a certain sound you make by shaping your mouth a certain way."[89]

This seemingly irreducible antagonism between the actuality of experience and the unreality of words is dramatized in the novel by the division of the characters into doers and talkers. Those who evince true vitality and are capable of meaningful action are people of few words, like the close-lipped Gordon, perhaps the only authentic artist in the group. Mr. Talliaferro, on the other hand, is both an insufferable chatterbox and a pathetically inept lover who sells ladies' lingerie but knows next to nothing about their bodies. For him and his like, words become paltry surrogates for the experience they are either unable or unwilling to accept and make their own. Garrulity thus functions as an index of futility and failure, while taciturnity signals unimpaired powers to live and create.

The notion, both stated in the novel and exemplified by its characters, that words and deeds are at variance was of course not new; it was in fact a commonplace at a time when there was a widespread revulsion from rhetorical abstractions and pseudo-intellectual verbiage among writers. Moreover, Faulkner's invectives against verbosity are given an ironic twist by his self-conscious indulgence in the very sins the novel is supposed to denounce, and one may wonder to what extent the irony was intended. Still, the emergence of the language theme calls for attention, since the problematic relationship of language to outer and inner reality—its claim to referentiality and expressiveness—informs much of Faulkner's later fiction and embodies itself in many of his later heroes and anti-heroes. Talliaferro, coming after Januarius Jones, the hardly less ludicrous would-be Don Juan of *Soldiers' Pay*, is one in a long series of intemperate talkers that include Horace Benbow, the voluble lawyer of *Flags in the Dust* and *Sanctuary*, and the ghostlike Reporter of *Pylon*. As to the tall, masculine Mark Gordon, he belongs unquestionably to the sturdy race of Faulkner's quiet and silent men.

The complex relations between life and language were to become one of Faulkner's abiding concerns. They are not merely a recurring theme in his novels; his whole work may be read as an ever-renewed attempt to bridge the gap between words and things and to restore language to the throbbing energies of life. Significantly, in *Mosquitoes*, Fairchild, the writer, while denouncing the futility of talk, expresses the belief that "words brought into a happy conjunction produce something that lives, just as soil and climate and an acorn in proper conjunction will produce a tree."[90] For Faulkner the contradiction between language and life, if never finally resolved, could be coped with through the creation of another idiom: the idiom of art. What art is and should be, how it relates to the world and to the artist's self—these are precisely the questions raised in this early novel, as if, before embarking on his great venture, he had felt the need to clarify his position and outline a poetic of his own.

Mosquitoes has been called Faulkner's "Portrait of the Artist."[91] As far as literary merit is concerned, the comparison with Joyce's first major achievement is hardly to Faulkner's advantage; yet the two novels do resemble each other in that both are early attempts at defining a workable *ars poetica* as well as tentative statements of their authors' ambitions. Further, there is evidence that *A Portrait of the Artist as a Young Man* was in Faulkner's mind when he wrote his second novel. Stephen Dedalus and Mark Gordon, the two dominating artist figures, are alike in their arrogant aloofness, and both are associated with the hawk. There are also unmistakable analogies between Joyce's and Faulkner's definitions of aesthetic experience: Joyce's "enchantment of the heart" is echoed by Faulkner's "Passion Week of the heart,"[92] and Joyce's "silent stasis" by Faulkner's "frozen time."[93] Another common trait is the assimilation of art to life. For Stephen the moment of inspiration is that privileged instant when "in the virgin womb of the imagination the word was made flesh,"[94] and his proclaimed ambition is "to recreate life out of life."[95] In *Mosquitoes* Fairchild likens artistic creation to procreation, and Julius Wiseman, the "Semitic Man," reflects that "Dante invented Beatrice, creating himself a maid that life had not had time to create."[96] Yet in both novels art is also envisioned as a negation of life, since life thus recreated is forever preserved from mortality. While Stephen dreams of creating "a living thing, new and soaring and beautiful, impalpable, imperishable,"[97] Gordon's marble torso of a girl is described as "passionate and simple and eternal in the equivocal derisive darkness of the world."[98]

To turn from Joyce's *Portrait* to Faulkner's *Mosquitoes*, however, is to perceive significant differences in formulation and emphasis. If both are indebted in their theorizings to the tradition of romantic idealism and borrow part of their aesthetic lexicon from Christianity, Faulkner's reflections, unlike Joyce's, owe nothing to Scholastic philosophy and Thomist theology and are far more sketchy and much less peremptory than the highly ambitious speculations attributed to Stephen. Furthermore, in *Mosquitoes* Faulkner's views on art and literature are not fully represented by any character but emerge dialogically from the novel's conversations and action. Gordon, Fairchild, and Julius are no doubt its most articulate theorizers, but each has his own assumptions. Their assumptions change, however, and by the time we reach the *Walpurgisnacht* of the Epilogue, they have become largely consonant in their common repudiation of art as an end in itself.[99]

While Stephen's theory of art—not to be mistaken for that of Joyce himself when he wrote the *Portrait*—is still pretty close to pure aestheticism (as can be seen from its contemptuous dismissal of kinesis), Faulkner, at this point in his career, is beginning to move from the shallow idealism of his literary beginnings to what might be termed, for lack of a better phrase, the tragicomic realism of his major works. True, Fairchild still celebrates "the splendid and timeless beauty" achieved by artistic genius, but art is now also defined as a "passion," and what is stressed is not so much its "ecstasy" as its "agony." Sorrow and suffering are seen to be at the dark core of both art and life: "Only an idiot has no grief," Gordon says at the close of the novel, "only a fool would forget it. What else is there in the world sharp enough to stick to your guts?"[100] The shift away from aestheticism is not only illustrated by the converging changes undergone by Gordon, Fairchild, and Julius in the final section but also tellingly emblematized by two artifacts: the marble torso and the clay mask. Gordon's first masterpiece is "the virginal breastless torso of a girl, headless, armless, legless, in marble temporarily caught and hushed yet passionate still for escape."[101] Like the Keatsian urn, the statue fuses passion and art, motion and stasis; yet its beauty is "marble-bound," and its perfect form has been obtained through a process of subtraction and abstraction—that is, through a deliberate denial or, at least, diminishment of life—and, more specifically, through a willful cancellation of sex, the transformation through mutilation of a female body into a fascinating fetish.[102] Gordon's Baudelairian *rêve de pierre* is an androgynous dream; at this point even he has not yet broken free from the sterile bisexual or asexual world to which most of the other characters belong. His later achievement—the mask of Mrs. Maurier—is something very different:

> It was clay, yet damp, and from out its dull dead grayness Mrs. Maurier looked at them. Her chins, harshly, and her flaccid jaw muscles with savage

verisimilitude. Her eyes were caverns thumbed with two motions into the dead familiar astonishment of her face; and yet, behind them, somewhere within those empty sockets, behind all her familar surprise, there was something else—something that exposed her face for the mask it was, and still more, a mask unaware.[103]

The very choice of material and model points to the new direction taken by Gordon's art. The gray earthiness of clay is given precedence over the cold purity and hard splendor of marble, and instead of a beautiful young girl the sculptor has chosen this time to portray a silly old woman. While the virginal torso embodied a solitary dream of sexless beauty and timeless youth, the mask reveals the humble truth of a human face; the former sprang from the romantic impulse to sever art from life, the latter from the wish to relate it back to life. Not that Gordon reverts to a tamely academic imitation of "nature"; in its harsh expressionistic stylization and grim concentration on essentials, the hollow-eyed mask of Mrs. Maurier rather suggests a figure by Giacometti or a portrait by Rouault: it is life surprised, seized upon, and stripped to its tragic core (or perhaps rather to its essential inessentiality: the mask behind the mask), the startling revelation of a heretofore unsuspected world of "love and life and death and sex and sorrow."[104] The implied aesthetic here is a far cry from Gordon's earlier stance, and it has little in common with the theory expounded by Stephen in the *Portrait*. If one insists on analogies with Joyce, its spirit comes in fact much closer to the definition he gave of "the classical temper" in *Stephen Hero*, the first draft of the *Portrait*:

The classical temper . . . ever mindful of limitations, chooses rather to bend upon those present things and to work upon them and fashion them that the quick intelligence may go beyond them to their meaning which is still unuttered.[105]

Joyce defined the classical temper in opposition to the romantic one, "an insecure, unsatisfied, impatient temper which sees no fit abode here for its ideals and chooses therefore to behold them under insensible figures."[106] His trajectory was from the poses of late Romanticism to his own highly idiosyncratic and utterly unconventional kind of "classicism." But only in *Ulysses* did he achieve the firm grasp of concrete particulars, the mature impersonal detachment, and the dramatic power which allegiance to the classical temper required. As to Faulkner, he may be said to have followed a broadly similar route, and his aesthetic purposes were likewise conceptualized before they began to be put to full use and redefined in the creative process. In both cases theory ran ahead of practice. Gordon's portrait of Mrs. Maurier is assumed to penetrate beyond appearances to the hard kernel of truth; as a character in the novel, however, she remains a cardboard figure of grinning silliness.

At the outset of their literary careers Joyce and Faulkner alike were anxious to reach a fuller understanding of the relation between life and art. What strikes one in both is that the quest for a workable aesthetic went along with a search for identity. What probably mattered both to Joyce and to Faulkner was less the discovery of a consistent poetic than finding out about themselves as writers. Their ruling concern was one of self-definition in terms of life and art, not articulation of a theoretical creed of universal validity. Yet in this respect it is again interesting to see how widely they differed. Fitting squarely into the tradition of the *Künstlerroman*, Joyce's *Portrait* focuses on the single figure of Stephen Dedalus and is largely patterned on Joyce's own experience. Even though the portraitist's intentions have long been an object of ardent controversy among Joyce critics, there can be no doubt that the portrait of Stephen is a self-portrait. Whatever the distance assumed between the author and his hero and no matter how much irony may be involved in the distancing, it is indeed the "portrait of the artist as a young man." With Faulkner the autobiographical impulse is more elusive, more decentered, more dissemi- nated. Had he completed "Elmer," the story of a young American painter he started to write before *Mosquitoes*, during his first visit to Europe,[107] his second novel might have been a comic portrait of the artist. But the point is precisely that he did not finish "Elmer." Even in his first two novels it is fairly obvious that Faulkner does not belong with the confessional school of the Wolfes, Fitzgeralds, and Hemingways, those barely masked autobiographers who never ceased to embroider on their own life stories.

Admittedly, as we have seen, he also started by telling about himself, but the more he told, the more he lost himself in his fictions. In *Mosquitoes* as in *Soldiers' Pay*, instead of focusing on a single double, the writer's self explodes into a whole constellation of partial selves. In the first novel the stage was crowded with soldier figures; in the second one finds a similar proliferation of artist and pseudo-artist figures. Both series are related in various ways to Faulkner's own fantasies (his role-playing during the postwar years providing the link beween fantasy and fiction). *Soldiers' Pay* portrays the writer as a returned soldier; *Mosquitoes* depicts him as both artist *and* aesthete. For while Gordon, the true artist, may be said to represent the writer's ideal self and potential future, the dilettantes surrounding him embody the distortion or betrayal of that ideal and are so many versions of Faulkner the "failed poet."

Noteworthy too in this connection are the furtive appearance made in the novel by the author under his own name as "a little kind of black man," introducing himself to one of the young women as a "liar by profession,"[108] and the fact that Faulkner has his characters comment disparagingly on three poems he would later publish in *A Green Bough*.[109] The dominant note of *Mosquitoes* is wry and impish self-mockery, and what it points to is Faulkner's increasing impatience with the posturings of his early aestheticism. Like *Soldiers' Pay*, his second novel is still largely a fiction of the self, but it is also a purging of the ego, a salubrious exercise in distancing and ironizing, and a sincere attempt at clarification. Its literary merits are no doubt slight compared with those of his major achievements, yet it is never tedious, and whenever Faulkner's native genius for humor comes to the fore (as in the superb tall tale about the sheep farm in the swamp, where flock and farmer undergo a farcical metamorphosis into fish), it is truly entertaining. For all its anachronistic mannerisms and blatant borrowings, Faulkner's language comes out unabashed, with an alertness all its own. The book's mischievous charm and infectious exuberance have lost little of their appeal. Lillian Hellman, in reviewing the novel, found it "full of the fine kind of swift and lusty writing that comes from a healthy, fresh pen."[110] Conrad Aiken called it "a distinctly unusual and amusing book" but added regretfully that "it is good enough to make one wish it were better."[111] In Faulkner's development, *Mosquitoes* is indeed little more than a divertissement of intermittent brilliancy; it probably also was a necessary detour through alien territory—the last detour before he began at last to touch his true ground.

Coming home: *Sartoris/Flags in the Dust*

Faulkner finished *Flags in the Dust*, his third novel, on September 29, 1927, four days after his thirtieth birthday and only one year after the completion of *Mosquitoes*. After several rejections, it was eventually published in 1929 in a shortened version as *Sartoris*.[112] Faulkner told Jean Stein in his 1955 interview what this novel meant to him:

> With *Soldiers' Pay* I found out writing was fun. But I found out after that not only each book had to have a design but the whole output or sum of an artist's work had to have a design. With *Soldiers' Pay* and *Mosquitoes* I wrote for the sake of writing because it was fun. Beginning with *Sartoris* I discovered that my own little postage stamp of soil was worth writing about and that I would never live long enough to exhaust it, and by sublimating the actual into apocryphal I would have complete liberty to use whatever talent I might have to its absolute top. It opened up a gold mine of other peoples, so I created a cosmos of my own.[113]

While working alternately on *Flags in the Dust* and "Father Abraham," his first attempt at a Snopes novel,[114] Faulkner thus came to realize how right Sherwood Anderson had been in advising him to write about "that little patch up there in Mississippi where [he] started from."[115] Now he was at last taking possession of his true territory—a territory which his imagination would expand and transmute into a teeming world of words.

As Conrad noted, "In truth every novelist must begin by creating for himself a world, great or little, in which he can honestly believe."[116] This is precisely what Faulkner did in the first of his Yoknapatawpha novels. Not only is the setting for the first time Jefferson, Mississippi, but many of the characters that are to return in his later fiction—the Sartorises, the Snopeses, Horace and Narcissa Benbow, Dr. Peabody, the MacCallums, and a host of minor figures—here make their first appearance, and one gets the impression that many more are waiting in the wings. In the course of the creative process Faulkner's approach to his material was to change time and again, but in *Flags in the Dust* the données of his "world" were already fully assembled. Faulkner considered this panoramic novel the very "germ of [his] apocrypha";[117] to us, his readers, it appears in retrospect as a fascinating source book, an almost inexhaustible reservoir of potentialities.

Reading it, one can hardly fail to be struck at once by the almost Balzacian scope of these *scènes de la vie de province*. Never before had Faulkner paid such scrupulous attention to the social and regional context; never before had he attempted to evoke a particular place at a particular time in such painstaking detail. As Douglas Day points out, "Faulkner clearly wished to make of his novel an anatomy of the entire Yoknapatawpha social structure, excluding only the Indian."[118] In the shortened version published in 1929, the emphasis falls on the Sartoris clan, yet even there the social spectrum is still fairly wide, ranging from town to country, from white to black, from the old patrician families and the rising middle class to the yeomen and the sharecroppers. All these classes and categories are carefully differentiated through their respective codes of behavior, and actions, characters, and setting are for the first time closely interrelated. In *Soldiers' Pay* the choice of a southern locale had little bearing on the novel's pattern and meaning; in *Flags in the Dust* the spirit of the place became a presence pervasively felt. At every page one senses the subtle pressures of a stratified and hierarchized social order and the inescapable power of shared values and common traditions. *Flags in the Dust*, one of Faulkner's most markedly southern novels, is the portrait of a traditional rural society as firmly rooted in space and time as Hardy's Wessex or Joyce's Dublin.

In writing it Faulkner drew more than ever on his own experience. But whereas in the two previous novels his starting point had been a fairly recent and narrowly personal past, he now came to use broader segments and deeper strata of his memory, reaching back to early recollections and reaching out concentrically toward his family, his town, and his county and toward the South, past and present, real and mythic, to which they all belonged. As Faulkner himself stated in a letter to Malcolm Cowley, his prestigious great-grandfather, Colonel William Clark Falkner, "was prototype of John Sartoris,"[119] the towering ancestral figure invoked on the novel's threshold. Many other characters in the book were likewise modeled on members of his own family and on Oxford citizens he knew or had heard about.[120] What prompted Faulkner to recreate the familiar world of his childhood and youth was, at least at the outset, the desire to make up beforehand for an impending loss and to conquer time through the ruses of art: "All that I really desired," he wrote in commenting upon the composition of *Flags in the Dust*,

> was a touchstone simply; a simple word or gesture, but having been these 2 years previously under the curse of words, having known twice before the agony of ink, nothing served but that I try by main strength to recreate between the covers of a book the world as I was already preparing to lose and regret, feeling, with the morbidity of the young, that I was not only on the verge of decrepitude, but that growing old was to be an experience peculiar to myself

alone out of all the teeming world, and desiring, if not the capture of that world and the feeling of it as you'd preserve a kernel or a leaf to indicate the lost forest, at least to keep the evocative skeleton of the dessicated [sic] leaf.[121]

As so often with Faulkner, the writing impulse sprang from a private sense of lack and loss. Yet more was involved than nostalgia for a passing world and the desire to rescue it from oblivion. With *Flags in the Dust* Faulkner began to realize—as some of his heroes would after him—that his own individual existence, the fate of his family, and the destiny of the South were so inextricably interwoven that, as man and writer, he had to come to grips with all of it. From then on, writing, for him, was to be less and less a matter of romantic self-concern. His novels would still be autobiography in a sense, yet to the extent only that all great literary fictions are: not mirrors of the self nor even self-probings so much as sympathetic immersions into the opaqueness of other selves and imaginative forays into the familiar strangeness of the world.

Writing, to Faulkner, would be henceforth an active, restless interrogation of the world. *Flags in the Dust* puts us on the threshold of this interrogation, even as it puts us on the threshold of Faulkner's *oeuvre*. The threads with which it will be woven are now all in the writer's hand, and yet his third novel prolongs the autobiographical fabulations of the two previous books, and two at least of its major characters—Bayard Sartoris and Horace Benbow—are still related in many ways to his private personae.

Through Bayard, his problematic hero, Faulkner reverted to the war theme, which he had begun to deal with in *Soldiers' Pay*. Like Donald Mahon, Bayard is a fighter pilot home from the war; Donald's physical wounds are paralleled by Bayard's psychic injuries, and both are found in a condition that isolates them from their family and community. In both cases, too, a woman—Margaret Powers for Donald, Narcissa Benbow for Bayard—comes to represent a transitory and illusory promise of recovery and reinsertion in life. Equally noteworthy is the motif of the double linked to both characters. In *Soldiers' Pay* the dying Donald is set off against the dead Donald of the past; in *Flags in the Dust* the "dying" Bayard is likewise contrasted with Johnny, his dead twin brother; and in both novels the dead figures—the faunlike Donald, the wild but lovable Johnny—suggest a lost ideal of warm, carefree vitality. At this point, however, the similarities end. Whereas Donald was but a rudimentary totem of the dying hero, Bayard is an almost fully realized character; while the former was a passive sufferer, the latter, caught up in "the dark and stubborn struggling of his heart,"[122] is shown to be both agent and victim of his sad fate. Donald has already gone through the ordeal of heroism but must recapture the past to be able to die; with Bayard, the decisive test has not yet occurred, and in assiduously courting death he does his utmost at once to live up to the Sartoris past and to escape from its burden. The most obvious cause of Bayard's suicidal course is beyond doubt his shattering experience of the war; he is one of those airplane pilots of World War I of whom Faulkner said that "in a way they were dead, they had exhausted themselves psychically."[123] Yet his compulsive death wish is given further significance in terms of family relationships, notably with reference to Johnny. Bayard's intense emotional involvement with his twin brother is marked throughout by narcissistic ambivalence: while blaming himself for Johnny's death, he "kills" him anew in burning his mementos; while loving him as his alter ego, his mirror image, he envies him for embodying all too well the heroic perfection of his ideal self. For to achieve heroic status it takes more than courage or even temerity: a lightness of being, an inborn elegance of gesture, an aristocratic contempt for death, virtues which Johnny had in abundance and which Bayard lacks. Johnny's jump from the flaming plane, as remembered and retold (in three different versions) by his brother, its horrified and rapt witness, was an act of triumphant self-affirmation; Bayard's violent but trivial end, while testing an experimental airplane that no one else would fly, completes a process of sullen self-destruction begun long before.

Bayard is the first of Faulkner's melancholy mourners. His are the split feelings of the bereaved, but unbearably intensified by his very closeness to the lost brother. Divided between the urge to rejoin him in death and the desire to survive, beset at once by grief and guilt, resentment and shame, he resorts to dangerous actions—riding a wild stallion, racing and wrecking cars, and eventually flying an unsafe plane—as a release from inner tension. And as later for Quentin Compson or David Levine, self-inflicted death will be the only way out, since only through death—a death reenacting and countering Johnny's—can he hope to achieve identification with his idealized brother and expunge his guilt.

Horace Benbow's self-destructiveness is less flamboyant, yet he too is a young war veteran (he has been overseas in the YMCA service organization), readjusting with difficulty to the routines of civilian life, the gray everydayness of the everyday. Bayard and Horace were clearly meant to be seen as antithetical and complementary figures; their coupling is particularly evident in *Flags in the Dust*, where Horace figures much more prominently than in *Sartoris*. Significantly, they meet only once in the novel (in the Thanksgiving scene) and never interact in any way. Indeed, as characters they could hardly be further apart: Bayard is one of Faulkner's arrogant, harshly masculine heroes; Horace, a lover of Venetian glassware and the poetry of Keats, appears throughout as a futile aesthete. Their opposition exemplifies polarities already adumbrated in Faulkner's earlier fiction and to recur in varying patterns in the later work: furious action versus passive suffering; aggressive masculinity versus effeminacy; inarticulate brooding versus febrile intellectuality. For all their differences, though, Bayard and Horace are "lost generation" figures alike in their aimless self-absorption and self-estrangement, and the former's morbid fascination with his dead twin brother originates in the same kind of regressive drive as the latter's platonically incestuous love for his sister.

It is also clear, as Cleanth Brooks has pointed out,[124] that as characters both are unmistakably romantics. Presented alternately as a fallen angel and a cold demon, Bayard is in many ways a twentieth-century descendant of the archetypal Romantic hero, and his literary lineage can be traced back to Milton's Satan, to the Gothic villain, and above all to the Byronic rebel.[125] Horace, on the other hand, embodies the carefully cultivated disenchantment and ironic self-awareness of late Romanticism and Decadence, and his effeteness, his "air of fine and delicate futility,"[126] relate him back to Faulkner's Prufrock and Pierrot figures. Yet more to the point perhaps than the two characters' all too obvious literary ancestry is their significance with regard to their creator. In their complementarity they may be said to represent the dual trend of Faulkner's youthful romanticism—a romanticism from which he was not yet totally cured and which his characters are intended not so much to express as to exorcise. Less schematically than Donald Mahon, Bayard stands for the failure of Faulkner's *heroic* dream: the desire to transcend finiteness and achieve glory through the apotheosis of a violent, self-willed death: "If . . . you could only crash upward, burst; anything but earth."[127] And the same yearning is equally apparent in Horace, the disillusioned dilettante, under the guise of the *aesthetic* temptation. Where Bayard seeks to enter the timeless world of heroic romance, Horace, the dreamer, voyages "in lonely regions . . . beyond the moon"[128] and tries to find refuge in the stilled perfection of art. One is the portrait of the young man as a would-be hero; the other, like the protagonist of "Elmer" and the pseudo-artists of *Mosquitoes*, the ironic portrait of the young man as a poet *manqué*.[129]

The contrasting but parallel destinies of Bayard and Horace dramatize a conflict central to nearly all of Faulkner's fiction: the conflict between what might be called the *vertical* impulse, that is, the idealistic—heroic or aesthetic—urge to rise above the contingencies of time and flesh toward the transcendence of absolute freedom, and the humble, never to be silenced demands of life. The two characters' inability to meet these demands can perhaps best be seen in their failure to come to terms with sexuality. Bayard has been a poor husband to his first wife and is not saved by his marriage to Narcissa, and he obviously prefers the company of men and horses to that of women. Horace, it is true, feels deeply attracted to the other sex, but his immaturity and misogyny (women, to him, are either virgins or whores) are shown both in his equivocal attachment to his sister and in his degrading love for Belle Mitchell, a vulgar and voluptuous divorcée. Bayard denies love because he is in love with his death; Horace debases it because he is in love with his sister. In Quentin Compson, heir to both, these two loves will be one.

Bayard and Horace belong with Faulkner's many paired figures. And not only are they doubles to each other; their doubling is ironically underscored by the emergence of another, outrageously grotesque double of both: Byron Snopes (himself doubled by his hired amanuensis, young Virgil Beard), the first of the Snopeses to make an appearance on Faulkner's stage and one of his first and most disturbing comic villains. Byron, a bookkeeper at the Sartoris bank, is introduced as a "hillman of indeterminate age, a silent man who performed his duties with tedious slow care."[130] A Caliban among would-be Ariels, Byron is poles apart from Horace and Bayard, and yet, as Judith

Wittenberg observes, he represents "a parodically extreme version of their plights in both his attitudes and his behavior."[131] As in *Soldiers' Pay*, frustration is here again the common fate of all young males. But there is more than that. Between Byron, the half-crazed redneck, and Horace, the neurotic gentleman, parallels intriguingly multiply as the novel progresses. Like Horace, Byron is attracted to Narcissa; his obscene anonymous letters to her incongruously replicate the florid epistles of her brother. In Byron's raw fantasies and ungrammatical language Horace's "unravish'd bride" becomes an available whore. Both are frustrated lovers if not figures of impotence; both eventually turn from Narcissa, the forbidden object of desire, to another, more accessible woman, only to be frustrated again. On the other hand, in his utter isolation, his desperate brooding, and his barely controlled fury Byron also reveals affinities with Bayard (even their names echo each other); interestingly, Narcissa responds to the physical presence of her husband as well as to the lustful absence of her secret suitor with something like fearful fascination. Byron's sordid story provides the novel with a kind of parodic subplot, a grimacing replica in low life of what goes on in the upper spheres.[132] As in *Sanctuary*, with which *Flags in the Dust* has so much in common, we find here razor-sharp divisions between classes (as well as between races); yet, while the social distance is shown to be unbridgeable, it is also shown to be artificial, and in both novels Faulkner measures the lower against the higher so as to bring the higher down. Like Popeye, Horace's demonic double in the later novel, Byron ironically points to the squalid underside of Horace's romantic reveries. The decadent scions of the Jefferson bourgeoisie look even shabbier once we have watched the antics of their aping inferiors.

Flags in the Dust is Faulkner's third series of variations on the tragicomedy of sex and love: love rejected (Bayard-Narcissa), love as bondage (Horace-Belle), incestuous love (Horace-Narcissa), and sheer voyeuristic lust (Byron-Narcissa). And again the *chassé-croisé* of amorous pursuits is counterpointed against a dance of death. Bayard's suicidal race is as central to this novel as Donald's mute last agony was to *Soldiers' Pay*. Yet the double theme of sex and death here is given richer resonance through Faulkner's purposeful use of the southern background. The modern rootlessness and restlessness of Bayard and Horace are set off against the relative order and stability of a settled rural community in which traditional standards still prevail. What is more, the present drama is brought into significant perspective by being related to the familial and communal past. Like *Soldiers' Pay* and *Mosquitoes*, *Flags in the Dust* has a cyclic structure, and its action unfolds within the cosmic time symbolized by the return of the seasons (the narrative proceeding from the early spring of 1919 to the spring and early summer of 1920). It also develops, however, out of the shadowy depths of a remote but ever-recurring past. *Flags in the Dust* is "peopled with ghosts of glamorous and old disastrous things,"[133] and for the first time in Faulkner's fiction the living are shown to be the helpless hostages of the dead.

Time comes to be felt as an active, shaping force whose "definite presence"[134] is already intimated in the first pages of the novel through the ritual, almost necromantic incantation of the formidable phantom of Colonel John Sartoris, the long-dead founder of the family line. Owing to the repeated recalls of past figures and events (mainly through the reminiscences of old Bayard, old Will Falls, and Miss Jenny Du Pre, the three survivors of time past and major exponents of the Sartoris myth), story time is extended and made to span four generations of Sartorises, all of which are also represented in the novel's present, with the conspicuous exception of the parental one (young Bayard's parents), which Faulkner will focus on in his next two books. The area of speculation and investigation is thus expanded beyond the narrow confines of the contemporary scene, allowing the narrator to manipulate different time levels and to order them in various perspectives. Past and present are woven into a dizzying design of recalls and repetitions, so that young Bayard, the novel's twentieth-century protagonist, invites comparison not only with his dead twin brother but also with the patriarchal figure of the Colonel and with his namesake, the daredevil Carolina Bayard of Miss Jenny's memory who was killed in the Civil War. Analogies are so many that the past almost appears as a rehearsal of the present and the present a reenactment of the past. The Sartorises turn into replicas of one another (the confusion being perversely encouraged by the play on homonymies: there are two "Cunnels," three Bayards, and three Johns); their destinies become so many variations on the same heroic theme, their brutal exits so many exemplifications of the Sartoris way of death.

Yet, rather than a pious recelebration of the heroic legend of the South, *Flags in the Dust* is in fact Faulkner's first inquiry into its genesis, the still hesitant beginning of the archaeology of southern myth and southern history that will be pursued much more effectively and much more radically in *Absalom, Absalom!* and *Go Down, Moses*, his other two genealogical novels. What calls for attention here is not so much the Sartoris tale as the telling and retelling through which it came into being, the subtle alchemy of memory, imagination, and discourse by means of which facts have been gradually enriched, embellished, and woven into the finer fabric of fiction. The process of myth-making is clearly seen at work in Miss Jenny's account of the Carolina Bayard's raid during the Civil War. What had been "a hare-brained prank of two heedless and reckless boys wild with their own youth" becomes through the rhetoric of her narration "a gallant and finely tragical focal point to which the history of the race had been raised from out of the old miasmic swamps of spiritual sloth by two angels valiantly fallen and strayed."[135] What haunts the Sartorises, then, is not at all a "real" past but a gaudy legend of their own fabrication—a verbal and imaginary construct, a "family romance" abstracted from reality, not unlike the artifacts shaped by the novelist himself. Like fiction-writing, myth-making is above all a way of ordering experience, of plotting it into a narrative and lending it beauty, value, and significance.

But myths can also kill, and in *Flags in the Dust* the impact of the family myth on the male twentieth-century Sartorises is indeed shown to be disastrous. The last glimpse we get of the prestigious Colonel Sartoris is his statue towering above the Jefferson graveyard, his head "lifted a little in that gesture of haughty arrogance which repeated itself generation after generation with a fateful fidelity."[136] There could be no more apposite emblem of his posthumous role in the novel. While alive he had vainly pursued his "dream"; now that "the dreamer has purged himself of the grossness of pride with that of flesh," the dream has "shaped itself fine and clear."[137] To his offspring he has bequeathed a game and a name, but the game is "outmoded and played with pawns shaped too late and to an old dead pattern," and the name has "death in the sound of it."[138] No longer a symbol of cultural order, no longer a tutelary spirit presiding over the community of the living, the Ancestor has become a bloodthirsty idol. "Sartoris" has turned into a categorical imperative, the password of a hereditary obligation to die a vainglorious death. The stubborn persistence of the same "dream" and the recurrence of the same spectacular "gestures" from generation to generation are, however, no safeguard against disorder and decline. Whether identification with the dead forefather succeeds or fails, it must end in self-destructive violence; but as the repetition scheme unfolds in time it turns out to be an entropic process, and the present is at best a paltry copy of the past. While the Civil War is remembered by everybody as a glamorous saga, World War I is seen as senseless confusion. Admittedly, Johnny was still able to meet the demands of the ancient code of honor with proper panache, but young Bayard missed his wartime rendezvous with death, and all the shameful survivor can hope to achieve is a prompt retreat from infamy.

There may be justification for heroism if the hero is bound to a social order and pays allegiance to a common ethic and a common cause; there is none in a community that has no use for it. The heroism of the Sartorises was heroics to begin with, a series of theatrical gestures prompted by an exhibitionistic yearning for a "heaven in which they could spend eternity dying deaths of needless and magnificent violence while spectators doomed to immortality looked eternally on."[139] Selfless dedication has never been their forte; though its performance postulates an admiring audience, all the Sartoris dream pursues is the transfiguration of a private "apotheosis." Gambling with life and death, however, cannot be imposed like a duty. Hence the tyranny of the family myth has reduced the acting out of their heroic fantasies to an obsolete pantomime, enclosing all male Sartorises within the compulsive patterns of murderous repetition.

There is much in Flags in the Dust to support such a reading, yet we can never know for sure whether we are intended to regard the Sartorises as the blind victims of their own schemes or as the helpless pawns of a cruel cosmic Player. In the last analysis, Flags in the Dust is an ambiguous novel—or, more precisely, an equivocal one. It is not ambiguous as The Sound and the Fury and Absalom, Absalom! are; its uncertainties proceed from a muddled purpose rather than from a deliberate strategy. Faulkner's attitude toward the Sartoris myth, as reflected in his often sonorous rhetoric and in his handling of the narrative point of view, is ambivalent in ways reminiscent of Miss Jenny's split perspective in the novel: even though he is able to see the myth in the light of irony, he cannot as yet free himself completely from its dark spell, divided as he himself is at this point between sentimental allegiance to a glamorized southern past and the impulse to call into question its "heritage of humorless and fustian vainglory."[140]

Flags in the Dust stands midway between the dreamy romanticism of his adolescence and the complex critical awareness he was to reach in his mature fiction. In all respects a transitional work, it may be said to represent the end of his apprenticeship. It cannot be counted among his great achievements. There is just too much of everything: too many detailed descriptions (landscapes, houses, barns, gardens, interiors), too many wordy dialogues, too much obtrusive authorial comment. Faulkner is trying to cram too many novels into one; he does not know yet what to leave out in order to let the reader in. *Flags in the Dust* is like a storehouse or a treasure chest, in which materials are accumulated for the works to come. Everything is there ready to hand but not yet fully mastered, not yet fully owned.

Lacking the fine sense of economy and the powerful concentration of effect of the major works, *Flags in the Dust* did not turn out to be "THE Book," as Faulkner had hoped.[141] It was nonetheless an impressive advance over his previous work and a decisive step in his development as a novelist. If he had not yet found his voice, he had discovered and started to map out his world. Through its shaping and reshaping, truths would be invented and enacted in the very process of writing: truths become fictions, fictions become truths—or, to borrow a phrase from *Absalom, Absalom!*, that "might-have-been which is more true than truth."[142]

One

The Struggle with the Angel

I

THE QUEST FOR EURYDICE

Regarder Eurydice, sans souci du chant, dans l'impatience et l'imprudence du désir qui oublie la loi, c'est cela même, *l'inspiration*.

Maurice Blanchot

A pregnant emptiness. Object-loss, world-loss, is the precondition for all creation. Creation is in or out of the voice; *ex nihilo*.

Norman O. Brown

"The most splendid failure"

With *The Sound and the Fury* something happened to Faulkner that had never happened before and would never happen again. For us, his readers, this novel is the first of his major works, a quantum leap in achievement; for the writer, however, it was much more than a book: a sudden release of creative energies, a turning point in his career, a unique experience in his life. On what the experience meant to him we are fortunate to have his own retrospective comment in the two versions of the introduction he wrote during the summer of 1933 for a new edition of the novel that was to be published by Random House.[1] Of his many statements on *The Sound and the Fury*, none provides fuller insight into the book's genesis, and, what is more, none gives us as sharp a sense of the emotional climate in which it was conceived and written.

> I wrote this book and learned to read. I had learned a little about writing from Soldiers' Pay—how much to approach language, words: not with seriousness so much, as an essayist does, but with a kind of alert respect, as you approach dynamite; even with joy, as you approach women: perhaps with the same secretly unscrupulous intentions. But when I finished The Sound and The Fury I discovered that there is actually something to which the shabby term Art not only can, but must be applied. I discovered then that I had gone through all that I had ever read, from Henry James through Henty to newspaper murders, without making any distinction or digesting any of it, as a moth or a goat might.

After The Sound and The Fury and without heeding to open another book and
in a series of delayed repercussions like summer thunder, I discovered the
Flauberts and Dostoievskys and Conrads whose books I had read ten years ago.
With The Sound and The Fury I learned to read and quit reading, since I have
read nothing since.[2]

It is with these startling reflections that Faulkner's introduction begins. If *The
Sound and the Fury* was a revelation, it was first of all the revelation of
Literature, through the sudden (re)discovery of all the major novelists with
whom Faulkner had just joined company. True, he had read them before, but
if we are to believe his testimony, his first reading had been nothing but
consumption without "digestion." His second reading, on the contrary, was
a process of assimilation carried to its furthest limits, that is, to the point where
reading becomes writing. What Faulkner implicitly acknowledges here is that
the relationship between reading and writing is one of reversibility: reading
is always a virtual writing, and writing always a way of reading. In working
on his fourth novel, he rediscovers the texts of his predecessors in the production of his own and becomes aware of how they interact in the chemistry of
his own writing. Not that his novel simply derives from others: the process at
work is one of radical transformation, a way of displacing and, eventually,
replacing its models. *The Sound and the Fury*, then, may be considered a
rereading of Flaubert, Dostoevsky, and Conrad—a reading at once attentive
and forgetful, fascinated and treacherous, and, by virtue of its very infidelity,
creative. The gesture of appropriation is also a gesture of dismissal. From now
on, Faulkner can dispense with reading others. It will be enough for him to be
his own reader.

The Sound and the Fury marks Faulkner's decisive encounter with Literature,
his final entry into its infinite text, a space in which novels are endlessly born
out of novels. With *Flags in the Dust* he had discovered that his experience as
a southerner could be used for literary purposes; with *The Sound and the Fury*
he came to realize that, far from being the mere expression or reflection of prior
experience, writing could be in itself an experience in the fullest sense.

What Faulkner then experienced was the pure *adventure* of writing, free of
any preestablished design. "When I began it," he notes, "I had no plan at all.
I wasn't even writing a book."[3] And he felt free too from any external pressure
or constraint; he did not even care about getting published. The commercial
failure of his previous books became an encouragement to disregard the
demands of the publishers as well as the expectations of his potential public.
The Sound and the Fury would be a strictly private affair: "One day I seemed to
shut a door between me and all publishers' addresses and book lists. I said to
myself, Now I can write."[4]

Having cleared the ground, Faulkner discovered in himself the heretofore
unsuspected power to write freely—not just for superficial "fun" but for his
deepest pleasure: "Now," the text goes on, "I can make myself a vase like that
which the old Roman kept at his bedside and wore the rim slowly away with
kissing it."[5] *The Sound and the Fury* thus became the occasion for a doubly

significant experience: through the reversal from "reading" into writing, Faulkner was at last able to appropriate his literary legacy and to transmute it into a creation irreducibly his own; yet this breakthrough to mastery was not simply a matter of artistic maturation, and it would not have been possible, perhaps, without the onrush of emotion he experienced during the composition of the novel. What made the writing of *The Sound and the Fury* such an extraordinary experience was probably more than anything else its being quickened by the dark energies of desire.

The work of art has been defined in psychoanalytic terms as a *transnarcissistic* object, meant to establish a connection between the narcissism of its producer and that of its consumer.[6] But with *The Sound and the Fury* the creative impulse, at least in its earlier phase, seems to have been rather *intranarcissistic*. The object to be shaped was to serve no other purpose than self-gratification. Giver and receiver were to be identical. As to the object itself, its narcissistic nature and function are emphasized through the image of the Tyrrhenian vase kept by the old Roman at his bedside and whose rim is slowly worn away by his kisses. Another reminder of the urn of Keats's ode, the vase is of course a paradigm of the beautiful and potentially timeless artifacts produced by art. But the point here is that the aesthetic is made one with the erotic.[7] The kissed vase is clearly a libidinal object, a fetish, standing *instead* of something else, the mark and mask of an absence. It functions as a surrogate or supplement—an assumption fully confirmed by the last sentence of Faulkner's text: "So I, who had never had a sister and was fated to lose my daughter in infancy, set out to make myself a beautiful and tragic little girl."[8]

Through the detour of a fiction, Faulkner thus attempted to make up for a lack. And the impatience and impetus of his desire were such that he felt irresistibly carried away, propelled beyond himself by what he was to call an "ecstasy":

> that other quality which The Sound and The Fury had given me . . . : that emotion definite and physical and yet nebulous to describe: that ecstasy, that eager and joyous faith and anticipation of surprise which the yet unmarred sheet beneath my hand held inviolate and unfailing, waiting for release.[9]

According to Faulkner's account of his creative experience, none of his novels sprang up more miraculously. *The Sound and the Fury*, it would seem, was an unexpected grace, a gift of the gods, and this mediumlike sense of being written through, of calling something into being he did not know he contained, was never to return. When he wrote his next book, *Sanctuary*, "there was something missing; something which The Sound and The Fury gave me and Sanctuary did not."[10] When he began *As I Lay Dying*, he knew "that it would be also missing in this case because this would be a deliberate book."[11] And with *Light in August* it had become clear to him that this "something" would elude him forever and that "whatever novels [he would] write in the future would be written without reluctance, but also without anticipation or joy."[12]

This quasi-trancelike condition was radically different from "the cold satis-faction"[13] he would derive from his later works; nor can it be compared to the lighthearted ludic approach asssociated with his earlier novels. Are we to assume, therefore, that this experience was unmitigated creative euphoria, sweet surrender to afflatus, and that *The Sound and the Fury* was written under the spell of an irrepressible and infallible inspiration? In his introduction of 1933 Faulkner emphasizes that "this is the only one of the seven novels [he] wrote without any accompanying feeling of drive or effort, or any following feeling of exhaustion or relief or distaste."[14] This assertion is flatly con-tradicted, however, by some of his later statements on the novel. Thus, in one of the class conferences he held at the University of Virginia in 1957, he declared: "It was the one that I anguished the most over, that I worked the hardest at, that even when I knew I couldn't bring it off, I still worked at it."[15] To wonder when Faulkner told the truth is not the right question to ask, for the whole truth lies precisely in the contradiction: *The Sound and the Fury* was the child of care as well as of inspiration, of agony as well as of ecstasy.

Something of the same seeming contradiction may be detected in Faulkner's evaluation of the novel. In October 1928, after typing its final version, he proudly told his friend and literary agent Ben Wasson: "Read this, Bud. It's a real sonofabitch."[16] Yet whenever he was questioned about *The Sound and the Fury*, he referred to it in terms of "failure."[17] True, he considered it "the most gallant, the most magnificent failure,"[18] but a failure it was all the same. There had been others before; with this book, however, Faulkner met failure in a deeper, more inescapable sense—failure as the very destiny of all artistic endeavor. What then became evident to him was the sobering truth that, as Samuel Beckett put it, "to be an artist is to fail, as no other dare fail," and that "failure is his world and the shrink from it desertion."[19] Had Faulkner remained a writer of talent only, he would never have reached that awareness. Less paradoxically than it might seem, it was when the powers of language appeared to be within his grasp as never before that he came to recognize the *necessity* of failure.

Faulkner's description of the novel's genesis reads like a record of abortive attempts:

> That began as a short story, it was a story without plot, of some children being sent away from the house during the grandmother's funeral. They were too young to be told what was going on and they saw things only incidentally to the childish games they were playing, which was the lugubrious matter of removing the corpse from the house, etc., and then the idea struck me to see how much more I could have got out of the idea of the blind self-centeredness of innocence typified by children, if one of those children had been truly innocent, that is, an idiot. So the idiot was born and then I became interested in the relationship of the idiot to the world that he was in but would never be able to cope with and just where could he get the tenderness, the help, to shield him in his innocence. I mean "innocence" in the sense that God had stricken him blind at birth, that is, mindless at birth, there was nothing he could ever do about it.

And so the character of his sister began to emerge, then the brother, who, that Jason (who to me represented complete evil. He's the most vicious character in my opinion I ever thought of), then he appeared. Then it needs the protagonist, someone to tell the story, so Quentin appeared. By that time I found out I couldn't possibly tell that in a short story. And so I told the idiot's experience of that day, and that was incomprehensible, even I could not have told what was going on then, so I had to write another chapter. Then I decided to let Quentin tell his version of that same day, or that same occasion, so he told it. Then there had to be the counterpoint, which was the other brother, Jason. By that time it was completely confusing. I knew that it was not anywhere near finished and then I had to write another section from the outside with an outsider, which was the writer, to tell what had happened on that particular day. And that's how that book grew. That is, I wrote that same story four times. None of them were right, but I had anguished so much that I could not throw any of it away and start over, so I printed it in the four sections. That was not a deliberate *tour de force* at all, the book just grew that way. That I was still trying to tell one story which moved me very much and each time I failed, but I had put so much anguish into it that I couldn't throw it away, like the mother that had four bad children, that she would have been better off if they had all been eliminated, but she couldn't relinquish any of them. And that's the reason I have the most tenderness for that book, because it failed four times.[20]

Like many great modern novels—*Ulysses* and *The Magic Mountain* come at once to mind—*The Sound and the Fury* began by taking the form of a short story in the mind of its creator.[21] The novel form was almost resorted to as a *pis aller*, and the entire book may thus be seen as the outgrowth of an initial failure: Faulkner's incapacity to complete the narrative within the limits of the short story, which he considered "the most demanding form after poetry."[22] What is more, failure informs the very pattern of the novel, since its four sections represent so many vain attempts at getting the story told. Most readers will of course dismiss this confession of impotence as an excess of modesty. Yet Faulkner's insistence on his failure was no pose. Experience had already taught him that "being a writer is having the worst vocation . . . a lonely frustrating work which is never as good as you want it to be."[23]

The Sound and the Fury had first been the sudden opening up of a boundless field of possibilities, the happy vertigo of a creation still unaware of its limitations, whose movement bore Faulkner along in quick elation, as if he were the entranced beholder of his own inventions. But once the wonder of this privileged first moment was dispelled and the book was no longer the bright mirage of desire but a work in progress, doubt and anxiety took over. And when Faulkner looked back on what he had accomplished, he knew that his work was "still not finished,"[24] that the story he so wanted to tell, the only one really worth the telling, was still to be told.

The Sound and the Fury was Faulkner's first great creative adventure. It assured him at once a major place in what has been, since Hawthorne, Poe, and Melville, the great tradition of failure in American literature. Like his American ancestors and like other modern writers from Flaubert and

Mallarmé through Joyce, Kafka, Musil, and Beckett, it led him to the experience of the impossible. According to Faulkner himself, failure was the common fate of all writers of his generation: "All of us failed to match our dream of perfection."[25] Whether the blame falls on the artist or on his medium, language, everything happens as though writing could only be the gauging of a lack. Creation then ceases to be a triumphant gesture of assertion; it resigns itself to be the record of its errors, trials, and defeats, the chronicle of its successive miscarriages, the inscription of the very impossibility from which it springs.

Hence novels tend to turn into extended metaphors for the hazardous game of their writing. Novelists no longer seek to give life a semblance of order by relying on well-rounded characters and well-made plots. Instead of following a logical sequential pattern, events are subordinated to the process of the fictitious discourse itself as it takes shape or fails to do so—unfolding, infolding, progressing, regressing, turning in on itself in a never-completed quest for form and meaning.[26] What is told then is not only a story but the venture of its telling: the novel tends to become the narrative of an impossible narrative. Commenting upon *The Man without Qualities,* Musil once observed that "what the story of this novel amounts to is that the story which it should tell is not told."[27] Faulkner might have said as much of *The Sound and the Fury.* The fragments of his narrative flout our expectations of continuity, order, and significance, and we have to accept them as such, in all their random brokenness and final provisionality. Faulkner's text is as much the locus as the product of its gestation.

Desire at work

The Sound and the Fury grows out of and refers back to an empty center, which one might paradoxically call eccentric or define—to borrow a phrase from Wallace Stevens—as a "center on the horizon,"[28] insofar as it represents at once the novel's origin and its *télos,* its generating principle and the ever-receding object of its quest. Which is to say again that the novel arises out of the emptiness of desire in much the same way dreams do. Like dreams, it aims at a fictive wish fulfillment, as can be seen clearly from Faulkner's own statements. Indeed, the processes at work in the writing of *The Sound and the Fury* in many ways invite comparison with the metonymic and metaphoric procedures of dream-work. Yet it is perhaps even more enlightening to relate them to what Freud termed *Trauerarbeit,* the "work of mourning" whereby the psyche seeks to detach itself from a lost love-object. Writing, as André Green argues,

> presupposes a wound, a loss, a bereavement, which the written work will transform to the point of producing its own fictitious positivity. No creation goes without effort, without a painful labor over which it carries a pseudo-victory. It

can only be a pseudo-victory because it is short-lived, because it is always contested by the author himself who feels the tireless urge to start again, and hence to negate his previous achievements, or at least to reject the idea that the result, no matter how satisfactory it may have seemed, is his last word. . . . Reading and writing are a ceaseless work of mourning. If there is a pleasure to be found in the text, we always know that this pleasure is a surrogate for a lost gratification, which we are trying to recover through other means.[29]

That literature functions as a substitute is an assumption verified by Faulkner's own testimony: "the beautiful and tragic little girl" whom he set out to create through the power of words was manifestly intended to fill a vacancy. His introduction refers to absence ("I, who had never had a sister") as well as to mourning ("fated to lose my daughter in infancy"), equating in retrospect the imaginary *lack* with an actual *loss*. And interestingly, the seminal image of the novel is focused on the grandmother's death, and Faulkner's initial concern was with the Compson children's reactions to this event:

It struck me that it would be interesting to imagine the thoughts of a group of children who were sent away from the house the day of their grandmother's funeral, their curiosity about the activity in the house, their efforts to find out what was going on, and the notions that would come into their minds.[30]

As I Lay Dying, whose composition is chronologically close to that of *The Sound and the Fury*, similarly revolves around a mother's death, and mourning, the coming to terms with loss (or the failure to do so), figures prominently in much of Faulkner's later fiction. Mourning, then, is not only a possible key to the process of Faulkner's creation but also a motif readily traced in the novels themselves. One would like to know what its emergence at this point means in psychobiographical terms; yet, apart from the hints one can find in Faulkner's comments and above all in his fiction, there is little to gratify our curiosity. *The Sound and the Fury*, Faulkner told Maurice-Edgar Coindreau, his French translator, was written at a time when he "was beset with personal problems."[31] What these "personal problems" actually were must remain a matter of speculation.

It is fairly obvious, however, that the novels written during those years, especially *The Sound and the Fury* and *As I Lay Dying*, are novels *about* lack and loss, in which desire is always intimately bound up with grief and death. And it is clear too that they have sprung *out of* a deep sense of lack and loss—texts spun around a primal gap.

In *The Sound and the Fury* this gap is reduplicated and represented in the pathetic and intriguing figure of Caddy Compson, the lost sister. Even when the novel was still a vague project in the author's mind, "the beautiful and tragic little girl" was already there, and we find her again in the basic image which was to inform the whole book:

perhaps the only thing in literature which would ever move me very much: Caddy climbing the pear tree to look in the window at her grandmother's funeral while Quentin and Jason and Benjy and the negroes looked up at the muddy seat of her drawers.[32]

Out of this emotion-packed image the novel grew. In retrospect, one is tempted to read it as the latter's prefiguration, or at least as a foreshadowing of its dominant themes: an image of innocence confronted with what eludes and threatens it; an image of childhood caught on the brink of forbidden knowledge—evil, sex, death. To Faulkner it must have presented itself as an enigma to be questioned, a secret to be deciphered, and in this respect one should note the emphasis given in the little tableau to the act of seeing and watching: the three brothers looking up at Caddy's muddy drawers; Caddy looking in the window at the funeral preparations. Curiosity about sex and dying prompts their common desire to see. Yet while the boys' curiosity comes close to sexual voyeurism, their reckless sister is fascinated by the mystery of death. Caddy is the only one to climb the tree of knowledge; her brothers stay timidly below and are content with staring at the stain on her drawers. Caddy occupies in fact an intermediary position, suspended as she is between her brothers and the intriguing scene of death—a reminder, perhaps, of the mythic mediating function of woman through whom, for man, passes all knowledge about the origins, all knowledge about the twin enigmas of life and death.

One could carry the investigation further and point out the striking parallels between this scene and the "primal fantasies" postulated by psychoanalysis. The symbolic significance of the scene lies first of all in its insistence on perplexed watching. Hinging upon the question of origins, as all *ur*-fantasies do, it relates a desire to *know* back to the primitive, infantile wish to *see*. As to the ultimate objects of the children's curiosity, they are clearly designated as death and sex, but the point is that in the spatial pattern of the scene the brothers are to Caddy as Caddy is to the window, thus suggesting a virtual equation of sex (the muddy drawers) with death (Damuddy's funeral).[33] Equally noteworthy in this connection is the fact that the boys are peering at a little girl's drawers—that which both conceals and betrays her sexual identity. According to Freud, "probably no male human being is spared the terrifying shock of threatened castration at the sight of the female genitals."[34] True, there is no such shock in Faulkner's evocation of the scene; yet, curiously enough, when Freud accounts for the nature of certain fetishes by "the circumstance that the inquisitive boy used to peer up the woman's legs towards her genitals,"[35] he seems to be describing the very position of the Compson brothers in relation to Caddy. Moreover, even though castration is not referred to explicitly, it is suggested by the intersection of sex and death. Castration—the equivalent of death in the language of the unconscious—provides a further link between the two themes.

The whole scene may thus be read as the emblem of a dual revelation: the simultaneous discovery of sexual difference and of death. The working out of the episode of Damuddy's death in the first section of the novel definitely bears out such a reading. Revelation (etymologically the removal of the *velum*, the veil) becomes there quite literally a denudation, a laying bare: on the day when their grandmother dies, Caddy undresses at the branch—an act to which Quentin responds with violence by slapping her (20-21)—and the scene is strangely echoed by Caddy's later allusions to the "undressing" of the dead mare, Nancy, by the buzzards (38) and to the possibility of an identical fate for Damuddy's corpse (40). Once again, sex and death are brought into resonance through a common motif.

While pointing forward to what is at stake in the novel, the seminal scene also sheds light on the author's deeper motivations, for in a sense these curious children, confronted with the mysteries of sex and death, are the fictive delegates of that supreme voyeur who is none other than the novelist. He too wants to see and know. Just as we, his readers, do.

"The beautiful one"

At the heart of the enigma: Caddy, a turbulent little Eve, rash and defiant, perched on a pear tree,[36] and already significantly associated with the Edenic innocence of trees and with mud, symbol of guilt and sin. It is her story—and that of her daughter Quentin, Caddy's debased copy—that Faulkner wanted to tell in *The Sound and the Fury*: "a tragedy of two lost women."[37] And the privileged place this book held in his affection is inseparable from his abiding tenderness for Caddy: "To me she was the beautiful one, she was my heart's darling. That's what I wrote the book about and I used the tools which seemed to me the proper tools to try to tell, try to draw the picture of Caddy."[38]

It is hardly surprising that Faulkner should have spoken of Caddy with the accents of love.[39] Wasn't she from the outset a creation of desire? Before becoming the "real" sister of Benjy, Quentin, and Jason in the novel, Caddy had been Faulkner's imaginary one, invented to make up for a lack. Yet fiction here does not play the customary game of illusion; it does not work out as a consoling substitute. For Caddy is exposed as a fiction within the fiction, her presence in the novel being rendered in such a way as to make her appear throughout as a pure and poignant figure of *absence*. Caddy, "the beautiful one," is no sooner found than she is lost again. *The Sound and the Fury* does not celebrate the (imaginary) triumph of desire but reduplicates its necessary defeat. This novel is Faulkner's first descent into Hell, and Caddy remains his ever-elusive Eurydice.

That is why Caddy, the novelist's secret muse and the very soul of the novel, cannot be considered the heroine of the book in any traditional sense. A chimera to the author, she never ceases to be a chimera in the novel. To lament that she escapes satisfactory definition is hardly relevant, for she is both more and less than a "character": she is at once the focal and the vanishing point, the bewitching *image* around which everything revolves. From the writer's mind she has slipped into the narrators'; from being Faulkner's private fantasy she becomes the obsessive memory of the Compson brothers, without ever really assuming shape and substance in the space of fiction.

One might even argue that Caddy is little more than a blank counter, an empty signifier, a name in itself devoid of meaning and thus apt to receive any meaning. Her function within the novel's semantic structure could be compared to that of a joker in a game of cards: the word *Caddy* assumes meaning only in relation to the contextual network within which it occurs, and since, from one section to another, it is drawn into different verbal environments, woven into different textures, it is invested with ever-renewed significances. *Caddy* is a sign, with all the arbitrariness of the sign, and Faulkner's keen awareness of the chancy and shifting relationships between word and thing, language and meaning, is attested on the very first page of the novel by his deliberate punning on *caddie* and *Caddy*.[40] The homophony is confusing to Benjy, who mistakes *caddie* for the name of his beloved sister, and also, ironically, to the reader, who at this point realizes that the setting is a golf course but is not yet in a position to understand what *caddie* evokes in Benjy's mind or why it makes him moan with grief. Like most openings in fiction, the golf course scene establishes the rules of the game to be played by the readers. By exploiting from the outset the polysemy of words, Faulkner disorients the reader, frustrates his expectations, and alerts him to the trickeries and duplicities of language, as if to warn him that the world he is about to enter is not *his* world. The words used in Benjy's monologue may be simple, but their familiar surfaces soon turn out to be extremely deceptive. We must learn the alphabet and grammar of his idiolect before we can begin to discover what his fumbling speech is all about.

Words are an inexhaustible source of ambiguities and confusions, so that the communication they permit is always liable to misapprehensions. Words are signs everyone assembles in transitory patterns and fills with private significances that often make sense for him alone. What *caddie* means for the golfers differs from what it means for Benjy; what it means for Benjy differs from what it means for us. Yet in its active emptiness and extreme plasticity, language possesses formidable powers, and the random utterance of two syllables is enough to arouse Benjy's anguish and grief.

Caddy is just a name, or the deceptive echo of a name. On the day when the novel begins—April 7, 1928—the person to whom it refers has been missing from the Compson family for many years. Benjy's moaning points at once to an absence, which the perception of anything however remotely related to his lost sister instantly quickens and thickens in his vacant mind. To Benjy, Caddy is the nearest of absences. His memory has no memories. He cannot remember, nor can he forget. For him it is as though Caddy had only departed a few seconds ago: her trace is forever fresh, and the merest sensation lends her absence agonizing immediacy. In surprisingly similar ways, Caddy also haunts her brother Quentin, holding him in her spell, leaving him no rest and no escape except in death. And even to Jason, for all his declared indifference and contempt, she will be a festering wound.

Yet at the same time—precisely because she is nothing but a haunting memory—Caddy remains to the end an elusive figure, not unlike Proust's "creatures of flight." She is the presence of what is not there, the imperious call of absence, and it is from her tantalizing remoteness that she holds her uncanny power over those she has left.

All the scenes of the past that come to beset memory bring her closer and remove her further away. Of Caddy nothing remains but a series of snapshots, vivid and unreal, in which her fleeting image is forever fixed:

> *Only she was running already when I heard it. In the mirror she was running before I knew what it was. That quick, her train caught up over her arm she ran out of the mirror like a cloud, her veil swirling in long glints her heels brittle and fast clutching her dress onto her shoulder with the other hand, running out of the mirror. . . .*(92)

Barely glimpsed, Caddy the (no longer "unravish'd") bride at once vanishes, and all that a glance could grasp was a silent rush reflected in a mirror. What lingers in the memory is at best the reflection of a reflection.

Or consider this other obsessive image of the lost sister, likewise linked to an event that Quentin cannot forget, the loss of her virginity: Caddy no longer caught running away, but immobilized in the silent suddenness of her appearance: *"One minute she was standing in the door"* (91).[41] Whether Caddy's silhouette is fleetingly reflected in a mirror or emerges unexpectedly in the doorway, there is each time the same disturbing oscillation between absence and presence, the same paradoxical sense of receding proximity or close remoteness.

Caddy is associated time and again with the immaterial and the impalpable: reflections (74, 87, 92, 171), shadows (92, 178), moonlight (92), a cloud (92), a breath (171), "a long veil like shining wind" (45). Caddy's evanescence in space constantly parallels her inaccessibility in time. Not that she is ever etherealized into a conventionally "poetic" creature. But insofar as she must remain the evasive object of desire and memory, she can be approached and apprehended only in oblique ways. Caddy cannot be described; she can only be *circumscribed*, conjured up through the suggestive powers of tropes. A realistic rendering of the character is out of the question. Only the ruses and indirections of poetic discourse can do justice to the burning absence which Caddy "embodies" in the novel.

Literally nowhere, Caddy is metaphorically everywhere. Her presence/absence becomes diffused all over the world, pointing, like so many feminine figures of Faulkner's earlier and later work, to an elemental complicity between Woman and the immemorial Earth. Her swiftness and lightness relate her to the wind; her vital warmth to "the bright, smooth shapes" of fire (65); her muddy drawers and treelike odor[42] to the fecundity and foulness of the land. Yet above all Caddy is the most enticing and most pathetic of Faulkner's nymphs. In the entire novel there is scarcely a scene in which Caddy does not appear in close conjunction with *water*. It is in the creek branch near the Compson house that she wets her dress and drawers on the day of Damuddy's death (19-21); it is in the same branch that Quentin and Caddy wash off the stinking mud of the pig trough after the Natalie incident (158); and it is there again that Quentin finds his sister, sitting in the water, one summer evening, after the family has discovered her affair with Dalton Ames (171). Lastly, in the third section, Jason remembers her standing over her father's grave in a drenching rain (232). Throughout the novel, water is Caddy's element, and like Caddy herself it is drawn into an extremely ambiguous symbolic pattern. In the branch scenes it is primarily the lustral water of purification rituals, and it would be easy to supply further illustrations of its cleansing function: Caddy, at fourteen, washing off the perfume to quiet Benjy (48); Caddy, washing her mouth after kissing Charlie in the swing (55); and, finally, Benjy pulling at his sister's dress, dragging her into the bathroom after the loss of her virginity (78-79). After these ritual ablutions, Caddy "smells like trees" again, except in the last scene where Benjy keeps on crying even after Caddy has bathed herself.

Water, however, is not only a symbol of purity. If it possesses a restorative power, at least in the eyes of the novel's characters, and if Faulkner at times suggests its function in Christian baptism (it rains on the night Benjy's name is changed), there are also many intimations of its erotic quality. Bathing, in particular, seems to prompt a kind of soft, sensuous, almost sensual intimacy between water and flesh, and to prurient eyes the spectacle of this tender complicity may become both a scandal and a temptation. In the insidious caress of water, in the way it reveals the body in its embrace, there is something all but immodest which, even in the early childhood scene at the branch, disturbs and alarms young Quentin. For him, who then begins to act as a guardian of Caddy's "honor," the sight of the drenched dress clinging to his sister's body is no longer an innocent spectacle. And when he slaps her for having undressed, he introduces by this very gesture the first suspicion of evil into a hitherto intact childhood world.

In Quentin's reminiscences and reveries, flesh and sex are repeatedly linked to suggestions of dampness and fluidity, and as the hour of his death draws nearer, it almost seems as if the waters were slowly rising, submerging his mind and memory, bringing him ever closer to the instant of his drowning. Thus, in the long breathless memory sequence in which he relives his poignant encounter with Caddy at the branch and his subsequent meeting with Dalton Ames near the bridge (171-87), water saturates the whole atmosphere with a silent drizzle. Quentin inhales the smell of the rain, breathes in the scent of honeysuckle wafted on the humid warmth of twilight. And out of all this mugginess emerges the body of his nymph-sister—water made flesh:

> I ran down the hill in that vacuum of crickets like a breath travelling across a mirror she was lying in the water her head on the sand spit the water flowing about her hips there was a little more light in the water her skirt half saturated flopped along her flanks to the waters motion in heavy ripples going nowhere renewed themselves of their own movement I stood on the bank I could smell

the honeysuckle on the water gap the air seemed to drizzle with honeysuckle and with the rasping of crickets a substance you could feel on the flesh. (171-72)

Once more woman's body—"her hips," "her flanks"—is associated with running water, and as Quentin watches his sister lying there, he cannot help thinking back to the day long past when she had soiled her dress and drawers: "do you remember the day damuddy died when you sat down in the water in your drawers" (174). Quentin himself is aware of the symbolic relationship between the two scenes; in retrospect the childhood episode acquires a premonitory meaning, Caddy's muddy drawers becoming an emblem of her defilement, of what Quentin considers to be an indelible stain on her honor: her fall from sexual innocence. This irremediable loss is the focal point of Quentin's obsession, an obsession eagerly feeding on every sense impression: the sight of flowing water, the smell of rain and honeysuckle, the chirp of crickets, shadows, warmth, moisture, everything melts into "a substance you could feel on the flesh." Quentin's obsession, as described here, is by no means the abstract mania for which it has been all too often mistaken by critics. Experienced at first in the sultry profusion of immediate sensations, the traumatic shock is relived by Quentin's memory with hallucinatory intensity.

There is no Proustian reunion, though, for Faulkner's hero. Caddy risen out of the past through the sortileges of memory is not Caddy recaptured. Memory only serves to exacerbate a sense of loss. The past is recollected in fever and pain, not in tranquillity, and the camera obscura of memory turns out to be a torture chamber. It is never a shelter; happy memories have no place in it. As far back as it can reach, Quentin's memory encounters a Caddy *already* lost: as if she had resented her brother's jealous vigilance from the outset and were impatient to flee from the prison of innocence in which he would forever keep her, she is always seen rebelling against his demands, always on the point of running away. In this respect, the scene of the muddy drawers—one of the earliest among the childhood incidents recalled in his monologue—is equally prophetic: it marks the beginning of the ineluctable movement that is to separate him from his sister. From this childhood scene to Caddy's wedding, nearly all the fragments of the past that erupt in Quentin's mind are related to Caddy's "betrayal," and each of his painful memories reenacts one moment in the process of her desertion.

Presence in absence, nearness in distance, nothing perhaps better sums up the paradox of Quentin's haunted memory than *odor*. A subtle emanation from things and beings, odor, as Sartre writes, is "a disembodied body, vaporized, remaining entire in itself, yet turned into volatile essence."[43] Like memory, it is a diffuse presence, a felt absence, a tantalizing intimation. Like symbols, it acts by indirection: to the extent that it always has the power to evoke something other than itself, to point an absence, one might consider it a "natural" metaphor. Small wonder, then, that the fragrance of *honeysuckle* is the most pregnant and most poignant symbol in the Quentin section.

Quentin associates Caddy with the odor of honeysuckle, just as Benjy associated her with the smell of trees. But whereas in the first section "she smelled like trees" functions as an index of Caddy's sexual innocence and vanishes as soon as the latter is compromised (see, for example, the perfume incident, 48-49), the meaning of honeysuckle in Quentin's monologue changes as Caddy changes, and its scent is irremediably corrupted when it comes to reek in his nostrils as the smell of her sex and sin. It is noteworthy that "honeysuckle," which occurs about thirty times in section 2, is nowhere as frequent as in the scene immediately following Quentin's discovery of his sister's loss of virginity (171-87): the scent of honeysuckle then becomes the pivot in a shifting complex of sense impressions. After blending into the uncertain grayness of twilight (108), it combines with the humidity of the atmosphere (172), "coming up in damp waves" (177) or drizzling like the rain (177). Through the cross-play of synesthesia, honeysuckle is made to encompass and condense the entire field of sensory experience: something at once smelled, seen, and felt, it suffuses the whole scene. Yet, while metamorphosing and expanding across space, the smell also seems to flow back to Caddy as to its source, and Quentin refers to it as though it were a carnal secretion on the surface of her skin: "the smell of honeysuckle upon her face and throat" (169); "it was on her face and throat like paint" (173). Quentin comes to resent the cloying odor as a rank indiscretion, an almost obscene exuding of the innermost secrets of the flesh. Associated with Caddy's lovemaking in the swing by the cedars and eventually equated with Caddy herself, it stands in his mind for "the bittersweet mystery of sisterly sex"[44] as well as the unbearable scandal of its violation. Quickening his obsession, it becomes the very emblem of his anguish and torment: "after the honeysuckle got all mixed up in it the whole thing came to symbolize night and unrest" (194). In his confrontation with Caddy about Dalton Ames, his sister reminds him that he once liked the smell (176); now he hates it, cursing "that damn honeysuckle" (171). So hateful has it become to him that it even oppresses him physically, making him gasp for breath: "I had to pant to get any air at all out of that thick grey honeysuckle" (173). The sweet "honey" of sisterhood, which Quentin so avidly "suckled" in his childish greed, has thickened into a suffocating substance and now has the bitter taste of loss.

Trees, water, twilight, honeysuckle—all the nature imagery related to Caddy, so far from calling attention to itself as symbolic, seems to grow out of the soil of subjective experience while being at the same time inextricably bound up with the sensible world. It never hardens into the fixed patterns of allegory; its manifold symbolism originates in the dynamic exchanges between a self and its environment. If some of these images run through several sections, they can never be separated from the singular voice in whose discourse they occur: reflecting both transient moods and abiding obsessions, they belong to the shifting landscapes of individual minds.

Yet the focal ambiguity to which all these images invariably refer is that of Caddy herself. For Caddy exists only in the memories of her brothers, and if we come to know what she represents for and means to Benjy, Quentin, and

Jason, we never discover what she actually is. Hence her contradictory faces: in turn sister and mother, virgin and whore, angel and demon, she at once embodies fecundity and foulness, the nostalgia for innocence and the call to corruption, the promise of life and the vertigo of death. She is what woman has always been for men: the figure par excellence of the Other, a blank screen onto which to project their desires and their fears, their love and their hate. And insofar as this Other is a myth and a mirage, a mere fantasy of the self, it is bound to be a perpetual deceit and an endless source of disappointment. Caddy, to borrow a phrase from Paul Claudel, is "the promise that cannot be kept, and her grace consists in nothing else."[45]

Even so, she is more than the sum of these fantasy images. Faulkner's triumph in creating Caddy is that her figure eventually transcends the abstract categories and rigid patterns in which her brothers attempt to imprison her, just as she escapes any facile sentimentalizing or demonizing on the author's part. Not that the reader is enabled to infer a "true" picture of Caddy from the information he is given in the novel. There is little doubt, of course, that she possesses the vitality, the courage, the capacity for love and compassion which her self-centered brothers and parents so sadly lack.[46] It is quite obvious, too, that she is both the tragic victim of her family and the unwitting agent of its doom. But to focus exclusively on Caddy's assumed psychology or to dwell at length on her moral significance is to miss the point. Caddy was elusive to her creator; so she is to her brothers in the novel, and so she must remain to the reader. She cannot be assessed according to the same criteria as the other characters, for she belongs in the last resort to another space, to what might be called the novel's utopia. "The true life is absent," Rimbaud wrote. Caddy is a pathetic emblem of that desired other life, while her fate poignantly confirms its impossibility in a world of alienation and disease.

Henry James thought that "a story-teller who aims at anything more than a fleeting success has no right to tell an ugly story unless he knows its beautiful counterpart."[47] The story of the Compsons is indeed "an ugly story"; Caddy, the daughter and sister of the imagination, the figure projected by "the heart's desire," is "its beautiful counterpart." Let us remember, however, that from the very beginning she was conceived of as a beautiful *and* tragic little girl. Caddy is a dream of beauty wasted and destroyed. Her presence/absence at the center and periphery of the novel signals the unfulfillment of the writer's desire as well as the inescapable incompletion of his work. Caddy's beauty is the beauty of failure.

II

THE AGONY OF DISPOSSESSION

> Quand les enfants commencent à parler, ils
> pleurent moins.
>
> Jean-Jacques Rousseau

Translated from silence

Echoing its Shakespearean title, the first section of *The Sound and the Fury* presents itself as "a tale told by an idiot."[1] Who has not dreamed of writing such a tale? For if it could be done, one would at last tell a true story. "*Idiôtès*, idiotic," as Clément Rosset reminds us in his delectable little treatise on idiocy, "means simple, particular, unique; then, through a semantic extension whose philosophical significance is of great import, a person bereft of intelligence, a being devoid of reason. All things, all persons are thus idiotic inasmuch as they exist only in themselves, that is, are incapable of appearing otherwise than where they are and as they are: incapable, therefore, and in the first place, of being *reflected*, of appearing in the double of the mirror."[2] The real as such is what is "simple, particular, unique." To have an idiot speak, then, would be to convey its essential simplicity, to give dumbness a tongue, to accede to a language without reflection and division. Is this not precisely what Faulkner has attempted in writing the impossible monologue of Benjy?

A lesser novelist would have presented Benjy as an interesting case of mental retardation. To Faulkner he is first of all a being of language, an *idio-lect*. A writer's ruse, to be sure, but a fertile one: from the outset, the reader is jolted into a *text* that refuses to fit into his prior reading experience. Instead of allowing us to settle in the familiar world of fictional make-believe, Faulkner points at once to the specific premises of his own creation, compelling us to find out for ourselves by what rules it is governed. Interestingly, it is in the first section that his writing is at its most experimental, that the most radical departure from the traditional novel occurs. There are modern novelists who begin by lulling the reader into a false sense of security and then make him gradually realize the arbitrariness of their fictions. Faulkner's strategy here is far more abrupt: the shock comes without delay, and nowhere in the novel is the effect of "defamiliarization" sharper than at its beginning. Benjy's monologue is not merely a tour de force; it is also a coup de force, a brutal summons to give up our reading habits.

Not that the novel's opening section confounds comprehension. Most sentences in it are perfectly grammatical, and taken one by one, nearly all of them make sense. Moreover, reported conversation, developing into scenes or at least scene fragments, occupies more than half of Benjy's monologue—a monologue that, strictly speaking, is no monologue at all but rather a *polylogue*, a patchwork of many voices seemingly recorded at random by an unselective mind.[3] Yet Benjy's own idiolect stands out the more startlingly for being interwoven with the speech of others. Throughout the section it serves as a private code meant to suggest the workings of a severely limited mind. Privacy, in this case, does not entail distortion and obfuscation, as it will in Quentin's monologue. What makes Benjy's section so disturbingly odd is rather an excess of simplicity. Its lexical repertoire is restricted to a minimum;[4] its syntax conforms to elementary patterns and evinces an extremely rigid word order.[5] As Irena Kaluza has pointed out, the typical Benjy sentence comes very close to what transformational grammar describes as *kernel sentences*: "simple, declarative, active, with no complex verb or noun phrase."[6] The impression of simplicity is further strengthened by the repetitiveness of the diction and by the systematic flattening out of the relationships between clause units, most of which are either asyndetic or paratactical. At first sight there is indeed nothing to relieve the stark uniformity of Benjy's speech but the recurrence of a few phrasal motifs ("Caddy smelled like trees") and a number of unusual lexical combinations ("my hands saw it").

It is clear, then, that Benjy's code is primarily established through *reduction*. Lexical variation and syntactic modulation are kept within very narrow bounds; language is stripped to its barest essentials, generating a discourse as far removed from the formality of literary tradition as from the looser patterns of living speech. Such discourse is usually referred to as "stream of consciousness." In the present case, "stasis of consciousness" would probably be a more accurate phrase. It is true that we are allowed to travel through Benjy's kaleidoscopic mind, and insofar as the logic of his mental processes is that of chance associations, his speech may be categorized as "interior monologue." Yet its overall effect is one of inflexible rigidity and ceaseless fragmentation rather than free, spontaneous flux. Benjy's words look fragile and frozen, as if they arose out of a wintry silence. They form sentences without ever developing into sequences of sustained reverie, let alone articulate thought. Each sentence hardens into a discrete unit, a brittle concretion of meaning, standing by itself in utter isolation, and as they accumulate, they become a random collection of atoms—all equal, adding together, never adding up.

The movement of Benjy's speech is most often one of slow dispersion, so steady and so even as to acquire at times the hypnotic quality of massive immobility. What is thus achieved is a very singular *monotone*, whereby the plurality of voices echoed in his monologue are muted and homogenized into a distant murmur. Faulkner's technique of linguistic reduction ends by creating an uncanny sense of neutrality (as befits a gelding), as though the section developed in a vacuum and was floating free of speaker, author, and reader alike.

Flatness is mitigated, however, by subtle changes of pitch and tempo. On closer inspection, Benjy's speech even appears to follow a carefully modulated dramatic curve. The section begins at an almost leisurely pace with extended narrative units devoted to relatively minor incidents (4–15: the delivery of Uncle Maury's message to Mrs. Patterson on December 23, 1900; a trip to the cemetery in 1912). After reverting to the present (15–19), it then moves on to a fairly detailed account of the day of Damuddy's death in 1898 (19–44), interrupted with increasing frequency by memories of Caddy's wedding (23–25, 42–43, 43–44, 45–46) and of three other deaths in the family (32–34: Quentin; 34–37, 38–40: Mr. Compson; 37–38: Roskus). There follows a sequence of thematically related episodes centering on the process of Caddy's growing alienation from Benjy: Caddy uses perfume (46–49); Benjy must sleep alone at thirteen (49, 50–51); Caddy with Charlie in the swing (53–55), the latter incident leading up to the parallel present scene with her daughter Quentin (55–58). Benjy's memories then focus more and more sharply on the agony of loss: the episode of his assault on the Burgess girl (59–61) is associated with his desire for Caddy's return as well as with the nightmare of his subsequent castration; the long scene of his renaming (64–82), on the other hand, is above all a poignant reminder of his sister's love and kindness. Moreover, the quick alternation of past and present scenes emphasizes the magnitude of his losses: Quentin's treatment of Benjy is contrasted with Caddy's; the happy memories linked with the name-change scene are set over against the atmosphere of nasty bickering prevailing in the Compson family under Jason's reign. As the past erupts into the present with ever-increasing urgency, Benjy's mind is set spinning. The feverish shuttling back and forth between his memories suggests an emotional crescendo, climaxing in what is to Benjy as much as to Quentin the most unbearable of all memories: Caddy's loss of sexual innocence (78–79).

A wild undercurrent of intensities runs beneath the still surface of Benjy's speech, and its presence can be intermittently felt in the very texture of his language. Whenever moments of extreme tension or confusion are recorded, the blank order of Benjy's syntax breaks down. Words then begin to dash and crash into one another; ellipsis combines with staccato repetition to produce the kind of breathless and pathetic stammering which we find, for example, in Benjy's account of his drunkenness on the day of Caddy's wedding (23–25), or in his recalling of the fateful incident with the schoolgirls (60–61).

Fort / da

The limits of Benjy's language designate the limits of his world. There is no central "I" through whose agency his speech might be meaningfully ordered;

in like manner, there is no sense of identity to make his experience *his*. The severe restrictions imposed on his linguistic abilities reveal the extent of his mental deficiencies. All that is left to Benjy is sensory reflex, emotional response, perception without intellection, and a capacity for the raw intensities of pleasure and pain. He is humanity at its most elemental and most archaic, the zero degree of consciousness. His quasi-tropistic reactions to the conditions he meets are all he *is*.

Benjy's monologue sends us back to the confusions of the presubjective, prelogic, animistic world of infancy. Since there is no distinction between "I" and "non-I," there can be no boundary between inner and outer space and nothing to focalize what Benjy does, perceives, or suffers. Hence the startling *eccentricity* of all his experiences: sensations, perceptions, and emotions are accorded exactly the same status as objects and occurrences in the outer world; everything is *out there*, in scattered fragments, and Benjy is at best the bemused watcher of what is happening to him.

Only once, toward the end of his monologue, does Benjy refer to himself in the reflexive form: "*I got undressed and I looked at myself, and I began to cry*" (84). What he saw in the mirror was of course his mutilated body; the scene is like a "mirror stage" in reverse: for Benjy there is no "jubilant assumption" of the unified body but only the stark evidence of castration.[7] His morselized body is not any more his own than his mind; each part of it seems to act autonomously: his throat makes sounds of its own (46), his hand "[tries] to go back to his mouth" (68), and even the pain of burning is something external to him:

> I put my hand out to where the fire had been.
> "Catch him." Dilsey said. "Catch him back."
> My hand jerked back and I put it in my mouth and Dilsey caught me. I could still hear the clock between my voice. Dilsey reached back and hit Luster on the head. My voice was going loud every time. (67–68)

Benjy's monologue is punctuated with cries of pain, and his reactions to external stimuli are throughout extremely sharp. Yet his pain is nobody's pain; just pain, a blind discharge of impersonal emotion.

The world reflected by the Benjy section possesses a kind of oneness in that it seems to admit of no distinction, no differentiation, no distance. At first reading, at least, it presses down upon us with all the weight of its *in-difference*. It does not take us long, however, to realize that Benjy's is a fractured world. Nothing here suggests the plenitude of experience which the romantic tradition (mistakenly) attributes to primitives and small children. Benjy's relationship with his environment is by no means symbiotic, and since his condition prevents him from ever gaining any hold on it, he is bound to be the plaything of circumstance. Nakedly exposed to whatever blow fate or chance aims at him, Benjy is the quintessential victim.

Not that his life is one of unrelieved misery. What gives it its basic rhythm is rather a perpetual oscillation between serenity and anguish. Benjy's sensibility knows no transition, no in-between, only abrupt switches from contentment to pain, from pain to contentment, invariably signaled by crying or silence:

> I tried to pick up the flowers. Luster picked them up, and they went away. I began to cry. (63)

> "What you howling for now." Luster said. "Look there." The fire was there. I hushed. (66)

> the fire went away. I began to cry. (67)

> "Here." Dilsey said. "Stop crying now." She gave me the slipper, and I hushed. (69)

> "Take that cushion away, like I told you." Mother said. "He must learn to mind."
> The cushion went away.
> "Hush, Benjy." Caddy said. (73)

All these scenes exemplify the same pattern. Jimson weed, fire, the cushion, and Caddy's slipper are things which Benjy likes. When they "go away," he starts crying or howling; when they "come back" (another recurrent phrase in his monologue), he "hushes." Things and persons come and go, materialize out of nowhere, and vanish with magic suddenness: the jimson weed is there or gone, and it is the same with the cushion (73, 82), the bowl (80), or any other object. There is, then, at least one distinction registered by Benjy's mind: the opposition of presence and absence. They are the two categories into which his whole universe is divided, and they make all the *difference*.

Benjy's unfailing responsiveness to the disappearance and return of objects brings to mind the *fort/da* game described by Freud in *Beyond the Pleasure Principle*. One day Freud watched a little boy playing with a wooden reel: "What he did was to hold the reel by the string and very skilfully throw it over the edge of his curtained cot, so that it disappeared into it, at the same time uttering his expressive 'o-o-o-o' [standing for 'fort' = 'gone']. He then pulled the reel out of the cot again by the string and hailed its reappearance with a joyful 'da' ['there']."[8] Freud's interpretation of the game is that by staging the disappearance and return of the reel the little boy symbolized his "great cultural achievement—the instinctual renunciation . . . which he had made in allowing his mother to go away without protesting."[9] This is precisely what Benjy fails to do: he cannot manage loss, he cannot renounce; he can only howl in impotent protest.

The pathos of his destiny lies largely in this total inability to master and symbolize absence, especially the absence of the one person who matters to him: Caddy. His sister "was the whole world to him,"[10] so that with her departure his whole world has dissolved into emptiness. For Benjy all possible forms of presence and absence relate back to, and are metaphors of, the presence and absence of Caddy, and it is of course not fortuitous that all the objects mentioned above are in some way associated with her.

Caddy disparue

Everything in the first section hinges upon the brother-sister relationship, and as much could be said of the second and, to a lesser extent, of the third. For the first time in Faulkner's fiction this relationship becomes both thematic focus and structuring principle. The three brothers form the plural *subject* of narrative discourse; the sister turns out to be its primary *object*. The former are present through their *voices*; the latter is the absent/present figure ceaselessly evoked—or *invoked*—in their monologues. Thematically, the brother-sister relation is just as central: it exemplifies the ambiguous relation of desire to its lost object, while functioning at the same time as a paradigm for most of the tensions and conflicts represented in the novel.[11]

Its primacy is of course as evident in Quentin's as in Benjy's section, yet it is in the opening monologue that its basic significance can be most easily grasped. For in the childlike idiot's mind there are none of the obliquities and evasions, none of the ruses and rationalizations that characterize the (necessarily bad) conscience of the adolescent or the adult. Here again reductive procedures are at work: the first section reduces the novel's thematic concerns to a "kernel sentence," and in a sense the two following sections are merely elaborations of what Benjy at once exposes with absolute candor.

His monologue leads us straightaway into a world ruled over by what Faulkner was later to call "the blind self-centeredness of innocence."[12] Incurably childish, unaware of good and evil,[13] Benjy has no links with his environment but those arising from his immediate needs. If infancy and innocence are interchangeable concepts, he is indeed an innocent. One should not forget, however, that the date of his monologue is that of his thirty-third birthday. If innocence has been preserved in him, it has been at the terrible cost of degeneracy. Trapped in an adult body, his indestructible childhood, so far from being grace, exhibits the grotesque grimace of abjection.

What childhood means for Benjy is first and foremost a condition of utter helplessness, reducing him to total and permanent dependence upon others. And yet his wishes can make no compromise with reality: his are at once the child's extreme demands and the child's impotence to achieve its aims. His predicament could be summed up in a single word: *lack*. And the little he had he lost.

Most scenes in which Benjy is directly implicated are scenes of dispossession. One of his earliest memories is the rainy November day in 1900 when his name was changed from Maury to Benjamin[14] at his mother's request: the name change suggests not only a loss of identity but also Benjy's repudiation by Mrs. Compson. Another reminder of dispossession is the loss of the

Compson pasture, sold by his father to finance Quentin's year at Harvard and to pay for Caddy's wedding. And eventually, after his assault on a schoolgirl, Benjy will even lose his sex.

A degenerate *puer aeternus*, stripped to naked need, devoid of intelligence and memory, deprived of language and robbed even of sex and name, Benjy is the bleak sum of his lacks and losses. His most severe loss, however, was the loss of Caddy. Although he does not suffer from it as Quentin does, he continues waiting for his sister at the gate, hardly knowing what he is waiting for. In Faulkner's own words, Caddy, "that fierce, courageous being . . . was to him a touch and a sound that maybe he heard on any golf links and a smell like trees."[15] All he knows, or rather senses, is that someone or something is missing. Still, the seesaw movement, touched off by the merest sensation, which over and over again tugs Benjy's mind back to the Caddy of his childhood, seems to bespeak an inarticulate obsession with a past forever vanished.

"To that idiot," Faulkner said, "time was not a continuation, it was an instant, there was no yesterday and no tomorrow, it all is this moment, it all is [now] to him. He cannot distinguish between what was last year and what will be tomorrow, he doesn't know whether he dreamed it, or saw it."[16] Yet Benjy's present lacks the fullness of presence. If he existed in the perfect enclosure of a timeless world, it would be hard to understand why the very sound of Caddy's name makes him whimper with grief. "The witless know only loss and absence," the narrator of *A Fable* remarks, "never bereavement."[17] But to sense loss takes at the very least a subliminal awareness of the difference between *was* and *is*. And if Benjy is not granted a minimal sense of the future, how to explain his waiting at the gate after Caddy's departure? True, it is routine waiting, one of Benjy's immutable rituals; it is waiting nonetheless, although, paradoxically, it is waiting for a return of the past, a way of negating time. Benjy has no consciousness of time, but his consciousness is in time. And if to him there is nothing before and nothing after the instant, this "nothing" forms a kind of halo around the present moment, contaminating it with its nothingness. Not unlike Quentin's, Benjy's present is extremely thin ice, cracking at every step, and both brothers experience it as a perpetual falling or sinking in. Rather than living in a perpetual now, Benjy may be said to live in a temporal limbo, a no man's land *between* past and present, a spectral space in which they echo each other in bewildering and agonizing confusion. Or one might liken this "time" to a creviced and pitted terrain, with holes that are so many traps laid by the past.

Benjy is the prisoner of his past and forever exiled from it, forever "waiting at the gate." His whole monologue is like Quentin's a stubborn quest for the long-lost sister, or at any rate for the warmth, security, and order she represented to him.[18] A futile quest: if his memories of Caddy's tender care are as vivid as ever, they give him no lasting comfort; and if he is occasionally allowed to relive past moments of happiness, his speech dwells more readily on all the incidents presaging the final loss of his sister. Many of the remembered scenes record the progress of Caddy's sexual maturation and of her consequent estrangement from him: Benjy recalls the day when Caddy for the first time put on perfume and did not smell anymore like trees (46–49); he recalls the evening when he saw her in the swing with Charlie (53–55); he remembers being thirteen and Dilsey telling him he is too old to sleep with his sister (49–51); he remembers pulling at Caddy's dress to get her into the bathroom after she lost her virginity (78–79), and crying when he saw her in her wedding veil on the day of her marriage (23–25, 42–46). Most of the events recalled in the first section are either anticipations or consequences of Benjy's major loss, like the death of his brother Quentin and his own sexual mutilation. The image of Caddy projected by Benjy's monologue is primarily that of the beloved and loving sister; yet, because of her desertion and all its fateful effects, she can also be seen already as the unwitting instrument of disaster and the main cause of Benjy's present misery.

Captive desire

What the first section makes obvious, too, is the extent to which the brother-sister relationship is patterned on that of child and mother. For Benjy, Caddy is definitely a mother surrogate; it is she who replaced Mrs. Compson, the failing mother, and of all the family she alone appears to have given him genuine love. But for Caddy he would never have escaped from autistic isolation. As Faulkner himself put it: "the only thing that held him into any sort of reality, into the world at all, was the trust that he had for his sister . . . he knew that she loved him and would defend him, and so she was the whole world to him. . . ."[19] Benjy's love for his sister-mother is absolute, but absolute only in its demand: the infantile dependence on which it is based rules out reciprocity. Benjy does not love Caddy so much as Caddy's love, and in his fierce narcissism he would like this love to be given to nobody else. His keen jealousy when Caddy begins to be "unfaithful" to him leaves no doubt about his possessiveness. And his "love" is far from being innocent if by innocence we mean the absence of any sexual component in his relationship with her. Benjy would not be so extraordinarily alert to his sister's sexual development nor so preoccupied with her virginity if sexuality played no part in his own desire. His desire is innocent only inasmuch as, unlike Quentin's, it is free from any sense of inner conflict and guilt.

Further evidence of this is provided by the Burgess girl episode. It is surely no accident that the scene of Benjy's unique attempt at sexual intercourse occurs at the very place where he used to meet Caddy when she, like the Burgess girl, came back from school. Benjy once again confuses past and present, mistaking today's girl with yesterday's Caddy. The implications of this error should not be overlooked; if the Burgess girl functions as a substitute for Caddy, then Benjy's sexual aggression must be viewed as an attempt at incest, and castration as his punishment for violating the primal taboo. In the second section, we shall be told about another incident with a young girl, likewise unconsciously equated with Caddy (Quentin calls her "sister"), and Quentin will be similarly accused of sexual misconduct. The parallelism of the two scenes points to the many connections between the first and the second section, and it is interesting to note that the incest motif already emerges here with its usual correlate, castration.

With Benjy, incestuous desire is no fantasy as it is with Quentin. If left free to act, he would yield to his urges without the slightest sense of guilt. Is he then to be seen as a fictional embodiment of the Freudian id? It has been argued that each of the first three sections of *The Sound and the Fury* may be viewed as a dramatization of one of the agencies of Freud's second "topography," the monologues of Benjy, Quentin, and Jason corresponding respectively to the id, the ego, and the superego.[20] It seems highly improbable that any such psychoanalytic allegorizing was in Faulkner's mind when he wrote the novel, and it would be preposterous to reduce his characters to dressed-up Freudian concepts. Yet if handled with due caution, the parallel proves enlightening, especially with reference to the first section. Benjy's protracted infancy, his lack of selfhood, his utter amorality, and the uninhibited urgency of his sexual impulse in the Burgess girl episode are assuredly features relating him to the reservoir of drive energy Freud designated as the id. Even more interesting perhaps, his monologue recalls the "primary processes" of the unconscious. In contrast to verbalized, logically ordered conscious thinking, psychoanalysis describes these processes as nondiscursive, iconic, and illogical. Although the Benjy section is a verbal construct devised by a conscious mind, the mental functioning it suggests comes pretty close to the processes Freud detected in dream-work and in the formation of neurotic symptoms. As we have already seen, Benjy's speech is indeed Faulkner's paradoxical attempt to write a nondiscursive discourse, to verbalize the nonverbal, and it reads indeed to an amazing extent like a text of the unconscious in its disregard of time and logic, its ignorance of negation and contradiction, and its evident reliance on the dream mechanisms of condensation and displacement.

There is more to it, however, even from a Freudian point of view. The emphasis in the first section falls on infancy, on the unconscious, on the id, yet the superego, the repressive agency, is also there. Not that it plays any role in Benjy's mind, but it is *represented*, externalized in physical space. Like Quentin's, Benjy's desire is already *barred*; what distinguishes them is that in Benjy's case the barrier is plainly visible and tangible. While Quentin's tragedy is played out on a purely internal stage, Benjy's drama is given a symbolic *mise en scène* in the outer world.

The space in which the idiot moves is a space of enclosure, rigorously circumscribed, bristling with defenses—a prefiguration of the state asylum at Jackson behind whose bars he will eventually be confined. His successive black caretakers—Versh, T. P., Luster—keep constant watch over him and control his every move. Confinement is suggested from the first words of Benjy's monologue: "*Through the fence,* between the curling flowers, I could see them hitting" (3, italics added). If he is allowed to look through the fence, he does not have permission to go beyond it. Yet what lies beyond is precisely one of the three things which, according to Faulkner,[21] he loves most: "Benjy's pasture," sold to pay off the family debts. The fence is thus a concrete token of dispossession and exclusion, while the closed-in pasture may be said to symbolize all that Benjy has lost. In the imaginary topography of his world, the pasture, since converted into a golf course, stands for the primeval Garden, access to which is henceforth forbidden; it also reminds one—ironically—of the *hortus conclusus,* the enclosed garden of the Song of Songs. Its symbolic function is the more manifest as it is almost immediately connected with the memory of Benjy's sister: it is from the former pasture that he hears the sound of her name. And it is equally revealing that, a page later, as he tries to crawl through the honeysuckle-choked fence and his clothing snags on a nail, he relives for the first time a moment of his childhood with Caddy, the present scene suddenly dissolving to give way to a cold winter setting many years ago (4–5, first passage in italics). The fence is the limit separating the present from the lost Eden of childhood, and the many references to it throughout the monologue (*fence* occurs five times in the first paragraph alone, and thirteen times in the first three pages) make it an eloquent emblem of Benjy's captivity.

Benjy resents being fenced in and constantly tries to break through barriers. When he is in the house, he wants to go outside; when he is in the yard, he runs down to the gate: "'Couldn't keep him in.' Versh said. 'He kept on until they let him go and he come right straight down here, looking through the gate'" (7). Another key word of the first section, *gate* belongs to the same set of symbols as the fence. But the gate is not only a limit and an obstacle; it can also become an opening and give access to the *other* world. As a promise of escape, it exercises an irresistible attraction over Benjy. Every day he runs down to the gate and stays there like a sentry on duty or, to use one of Jason's animal metaphors, like an imprisoned bear clutching at the bars of its cage (see 292). As long as he is confined to this cage, he never stops whining and whimpering; as soon as he is let out, his crying ceases. Thus on Easter Sunday, before leaving for church with Dilsey, he is wailing "quietly and steadily" (333), and nothing, apparently, can console him. Yet once he has gone through the gate, he hushes, as if suddenly delivered from his unnamable torment: "They passed out of the gate. 'Now den,' [Dilsey] said. Ben ceased" (334). The gate symbolizes Benjy's blind yearning for freedom, but let us not forget that this yearning is one with his desire for Caddy's return. If he continues to wait there for her every day, it is because he hopes (without knowing he hopes) that she will come home again as she used to as a schoolgirl. His ritual waiting is propitiatory magic: "*He think if he down to the gate,*" T. P. explains to Mrs. Compson, "*Miss Caddy come back*" (59). "Nonsense," the latter replies, and nothing indeed could be more nonsensical than Benjy's obstinate denial of time and refusal of loss.

"Trying to say"

Only once does Benjy find the gate unlocked and manage to escape the adults' vigilance:

> It was open when I touched it, and I held to it in the twilight. I wasn't crying, and I tried to stop, watching the girls coming along in the twilight. I wasn't crying.
> "There he is."
> They stopped.
> "He can get out. He won't hurt anybody, anyway. Come on." "I'm scared to. I'm scared. I'm going to cross the street."
> "He can get out."
> I wasn't crying.
> "Dont be a fraid cat. Come on."
> They came on in the twilight. I wasn't crying, and I held to the gate. They came slow.
> "I'm scared."
> "He wont hurt you. I pass here every day. He just runs along the fence."
> They came on. I opened the gate and they stopped, turning. I was trying to say, and I caught her, trying to say, and she screamed and I was trying to say and trying and the bright shapes began to stop and I tried to get out. I tried to get it off of my face, but the bright shapes were going again. They were going up the hill to where it fell away and I tried to cry. But when I breathed in, I couldn't breathe out again to cry, and I tried to keep from falling off the hill and I fell off the hill into the bright, whirling shapes. (60–61)

This is Benjy's retelling of the episode with the schoolgirls and, if we may say so, his personal version of what happened on that fateful day. What did Benjy want of the passing girls? The close repetition of "trying to say" stresses the urgency of his desire: to seize the unexpected opportunity of communication and so break the isolation in which Caddy's departure has left him. This desperate need for communication is expressed here by the wish to speak and be heard, the very wish that all of Benjy's monologue is at pains to fulfill. For is not the entire section a "trying to say"?[22] And is not *The Sound and the Fury*, more than any other of Faulkner's works, the one in which he tried and failed to say what he wanted to? It is perhaps no mere coincidence that when, years later, he spoke of his "failure," he used the very terms he had attributed to Benjy.[23] But while it is interesting to speculate upon the wider implications of the phrase, it is also necessary to attend to its ambiguity within the immediate context of the scene. Apart from a few details ("I caught her," "she screamed"), nothing here suggests a sexual assault. Yet it is as such that Benjy's behavior is construed by the girls and by the adults who are told about the incident.

And Faulkner's comments leave no doubt either as to the sexual character of the attempted "communication."[24] That it should be obscured in the text hardly surprises us: sex and violence are very often treated elliptically in Faulkner's fiction, and more explicitness would have been inconsistent with Benjy's inability to articulate his impulses and emotions. What is more amazing, however, is that an attempt at sexual intercourse should be masked as a wish for verbal communication.

"Trying to say" (mark the intransitive use of the verb) thus refers at once to the writer's creative endeavor and to the character's crude sexual impulse. Beyond Benjy's story, it brings to mind what we know about the psychological circumstances of the novel's birth, confirming our assumption that *The Sound and the Fury* is itself an extended metaphor for a nameless desire. Exploiting the duplicities of language, taking advantage of its gaps, Faulkner's fiction *reveals* itself as a desire for utterance—"trying to say"—and *conceals* at the same time what it is in essence: an utterance of desire, a discourse endlessly spiraling around the focus of its secret fascination—the unspoken, the unspeakable, the mute powers of sex and death.

Childhood and death

In Benjy's monologue sex and death are never far away and are always seen in close conjunction. Thus in Benjy's memory the Burgess girl scene (sexual aggression) and the castration scene (sexual death) are significantly juxtaposed. Furthermore, the anesthesia prior to the surgical procedure depriving Benjy of his manhood is itself suggested through extremely ambiguous imagery. Everywhere else in the section "the smooth, bright shapes" are associated with euphoric sensations: the fast flow of houses and trees during his drives to the cemetery (13), the sight of fire (65, 74), and above all the memory of going to sleep with Caddy (13, 85). Here the luminous shapes also herald sleep, but a sleep that is suffocation ("I couldn't breathe out again"), falling ("I fell off the hill into the bright whirling shapes"), descent into death.[25]

This interweaving of images of life and death is typical of Benjy's section. Throughout, without ever being named, death is a haunting presence. Thus the earliest episode, the water splashing incident at the creek branch which Benjy harks back to more frequently and lengthily than to any other,[26] is overshadowed by Damuddy's death. From the memory of this death Benjy's mind slips imperceptibly to all the other deaths that have occurred in the family: the return of Quentin's body after his suicide at Cambridge (32–34), Mr. Compson's death and funeral (34–37, 38–40), the death of Roskus, Dilsey's husband (37–38). In his chaotic memory, these successive deaths are so entangled as to resemble an obsessive harping on a single occurrence, a ritual homage to Death. To this must be added the macabre image of Nancy, the mare shot by Roskus and "undressed" by the buzzards, whose carcass Benjy glimpsed in a ditch one moonlit night (38, 40). His mind is of course not death-ridden as Quentin's is; death is something that he cannot comprehend, but there is ample evidence that its mystery weighs on him very heavily. Moreover, Benjy senses the imminence and presence of death with an infallible animal instinct. When Mr. Compson dies, he howls at death like Dan, the dog, and even before his father dies, he "smells" his impending end (38–40). Benjy's uncanny divination powers in this field are indeed as keen as his flair for sex.

Lastly, there is Benjy's curious penchant for graveyards. The visit to the family cemetery is one of the first scenes recalled in his monologue (10–13), and it is on another of these funeral trips that the novel ends. The cemetery is invariably the goal of the only outings allowed Benjy; ironically, his contacts with the external world are restricted to the immutable Sunday ritual of the pilgrimage to the family dead. The special significance that the place has for him is further emphasized by the fact that one of his favorite games is playing with what Dilsey and Luster call his "graveyard" (64)—a blue bottle, perched on a little mound, into which he sticks stalks of jimson weed. Benjy's private graveyard may be taken as a derisory symbol of all his losses.[27] The nasty smell of jimson weed has come to replace the clean smell of trees associated with Caddy. Considering that the weed was used by southern Negroes in contraception and abortion and was given obscene names by the hill people of Mississippi because of its phallic form,[28] it is tempting to regard it also as an ironic symbol of lost manhood. Benjy's game is a mourning rite, a primitive commemoration of loss and death. The miniature graveyard and its fetid flowers condense all the ambiguities of his shrunken world—a world as close to its beginnings as to its end, forever arrested in its blind innocence, no sooner born than dead.

The virtues of idiocy

"He was a prologue," said Faulkner of Benjy, "like the gravedigger in the Elizabethan dramas. He serves his purpose and is gone."[29] At first sight none could qualify less for such a role than Benjy, and the choice of an idiot's point of view was obviously something of a gamble. Yet Benjy does serve his purpose, or rather his purposes, with admirable efficiency. "I was trying," the author explained later, "to tell this story as it seemed to me that idiot child saw it."[30] So the first section was to create the illusion of a mind registering what happens or recalling what happened without understanding in the least the multiple connections between the events. The illusion works: reading Benjy's section, we see the world through the eyes of early childhood. To use again a comparison often made by critics, the idiot's mind seems to function like a camera or a tape recorder out of human manipulation and control. Benjy is in a sense the novel's most reliable narrator: insofar as the recorded facts escape manipulation, his monologue achieves an objectivity in sharp contrast to the sections that follow. Yet what ensures his trustworthiness is paradoxically also what compromises his narrative competence. As he is unable to order his memories and perceptions in a temporal perspective, his point of view is actually no *point* of view at all, and his telling of the Compson story is the very negation of narrative.

There is, then, a definite loss in immediate intelligibility. There are substantial gains and subtle rewards, however, for those readers who are willing to play the novel's game and are capable of the imaginative openness and intellectual alertness which the first section and, for that matter, the whole novel demand. It is true that Benjy provides no orderly dramatic exposition, but if one pays close attention to Faulkner's montage and to his identification devices—the changes in typeface to indicate time-shifts,[31] the names of Benjy's successive guardians, the carefully planted verbal clues—a broad outline of the story will emerge, and in fact no section tells us as much about the childhood and adolescence of the Compson children as the first. Supplying information shorn of explanation and evaluation, Benjy's monologue is a proto-narrative held in timeless suspension, waiting for the reader to give it form and meaning: it does not tell a story but creates within us the possibility of telling one—or several.

This does not mean, as was insinuated by Faulkner's early critics, that the first section is nothing but a perverse puzzle. That the burden of narrative organization and interpretation is transferred from narrator to reader does not imply that the latter is confronted with mere confusion, nor that he is free to arrange the material he is given at his will. The seeming chaos of Benjy's section conceals what might be termed a *vertical* order, an order, that is, in which the horizontal linearity of external chronology is replaced by a synchronic patterning of internal relationships. The compressed juxtapositions in the monologue constitute virtual superimpositions through which similarities as well as differences come to light. As can be seen, for instance, from the juxtaposition of the two scenes in the swing, the one with Caddy, the other with her daughter, Quentin (53–55), the past may be turned into an implicit comment upon the present, the present into an ironic reminder of the past. Throughout the section past and present as well as distinct time units within the past are counterpointed to suggest both continuities and contrasts. Scenes or scene fragments separated in time tend to fall into groups and to form chains by reason of their common elements: thus the Caddy scenes, the death scenes, the dispossession scenes. And these chains are integrated in their turn into larger complexes of meaning. So the linking of four death episodes with Caddy's wedding points to the common significance of those events for Benjy in terms of loss and foreshadows the metaphoric equivalence of sex and death underlying the second section. Clearly, then, the arrangement of narrative data, random though it may seem, does possess a logic and a purpose. Its disconcerting effect upon the reader is easy to account for: fiction traditionally relies on syntagmatic (or metonymic) developments; here the ordering is paradigmatic (or metaphoric).[32] In contrast to the literalness of its linguistic texture, the overall structure of Benjy's discourse is therefore essentially *symbolic*, allowing thematic configurations to emerge much more forcibly than would have been possible within the sequential framework of standard narration.

Subordinating narrative exposition to abrupt scenic presentation and substituting thematic implication for discursive comment, the first section grants the reader an intuitive foreknowledge of the issues at stake and engages him in the process of interpretation even before he has been able to piece the story itself together. Benjy appears from the outset as a key figure and even more so in retrospect. He is only a mirror, but a mirror the more trustworthy for being without "reflection." What his monologue tells us is the truth, albeit not the whole truth. It is against Benjy that all the other characters of the novel are measured.[33] Yet he is not only the touchstone and revelator of the Compson family; the supreme irony is that he is also its living emblem. Granted, he cannot be called to account like his brothers, and, as Faulkner himself notes, he is not "rational enough even to be selfish."[34] Yet one can hardly fail to be struck by the many ways in which he anticipates Quentin and even Jason: "the blind self-centeredness of innocence" is the very core of his being; as we shall see, the same phrase applies to Quentin and Jason, the only major difference between them and Benjy being that they refuse to outgrow their "innocence" whereas the idiot is forever doomed to it. Benjy and his brothers are alike in their basic narcissism, their refusal of change, their denial of life's motion—disquieting innocents, all of them.

The first section—the story of the miserable child-man—may thus be said to represent the whole Compson drama in reduced form. It tells us almost all there is to know, but it does so with a deceptive mixture of opaqueness and transparency. To yield its rich harvest of ambiguities and ironies, the prologue must be read again—as an epilogue.

III

THE YOUNG MAN,
DESIRE, AND DEATH

Denk: es erhält sich der Held, selbst der
Untergang war ihm
Nur ein Vorwand, zu sein: seine letzte Geburt.

Rainer Maria Rilke

The discourse of obsession

If Benjy's monologue serves as a prologue to the whole novel, it is with the section immediately following it that it has its closest affinities. Again Caddy is "the center on the horizon," the remote and haunting figure in which death and desire meet and merge. Again everything revolves around the brother-sister relationship: like Benjy's, Quentin's love for Caddy is jealous, exclusive, excessive, but while the idiot's urges barely emerge from primal need, Quentin's are desire in its fullest, or rather emptiest, sense: a desire that nothing can ever truly satisfy, a desire incommensurate with any real object, gliding from substitute to substitute down to the very last—death. In Benjy's childish attachment to his sister there is little more than an indiscriminate hunger for love; Quentin's feelings are rooted in the same archaic soil, but they are refracted through the deceptive prism of an adult or at least adolescent mind and must be traced through a far more devious discourse. His monologue does not so readily reveal the hidden pattern of its disorder.

To switch from the first to the second section is to pass from the simple (the "idiotic") to the complex; it means leaving the limbo of blank innocence to be thrust into a private hell of anguish and guilt. Quentin certainly remains an innocent inasmuch as innocence may be equated with "blind self-centered-ness." But his relationship with Caddy is a much more intricate affair. The idiot's helpless dependency on his sister results from his stunted mental growth. With Quentin the blockage is of a subtler kind, and it is only toward the end of his adolescence that its negative implications come to be fully felt. Benjy's love for Caddy hardly strikes us as abnormal once we know that he is

fated to perpetual childhood; Quentin's, on the other hand, develops into a
morbid passion whose outcome can only be despair and death.

Hence the changes intervening at this point in the novel's thematic development. In the first section the dual reference to desire and death never becomes
articulate; it must be inferred from the symbolic patterning of the idiot's
monologue. In the second section the two poles of Benjy's wordless anxiety
are no longer submerged: desire and death can be easily identified in
Quentin's double narcissistic obsession with *incest* and with *suicide*.

Obsession is not only what his monologue conveys; it implodes in it,
informing and deforming the very texture of its language, and is at once the
principle of its disorder and the key to its twisted logic. Like Benjy's idiocy, it
operates up to a point as a reductor, derationalizing speech by its disruptive
impact on the hierarchical structures of grammar.[1] Linguistically, there are
obvious similarities between the two monologues, and especially when Quentin records "present" actions and perceptions, he often uses strings of minimal
sentences strongly reminiscent of Benjy's speech: "When I finished breakfast
I bought a cigar. The girl said a fifty cent one was the best, so I took one and
lit it and went out to the street. I stood there and took a couple of puffs, then
I held it in my hand and went on toward the corner..."(94). But with Quentin
the breaking-up process is taken a step further: syntactic order is not only
reduced to elemental patterns but repeatedly dismantled. There is not only an
impoverishment in grammatical and logical relationships; the clauses themselves tend to fall apart:

> ... *getting the odour of honeysuckle all mixed She would have told me not to let me sit
> there on the steps hearing her door twilight slamming hearing Benjy still crying Supper
> she would have to come down then getting honeysuckle all mixed up in it.* (148)

> ... *hands can see cooling fingers invisible swan-throat where less than Moses rod the
> glass touch tentative not to drumming lean cool throat drumming cooling the metal the
> glass full overfull cooling the glass the fingers flushing sleep leaving the taste of
> dampened sleep in the long silence of the throat....* (199)

In such passages the collapse of syntax is almost complete. All we are left with
is a perplexing cluster of words, with subjects and predicates all adrift.
Language breaks asunder into random particles, and even the speaking
subject subsides in *"the long silence of the throat."*

For all its rough edges, however, Quentin's is in fact the most subtly
modulated speech in the novel and the one that offers the greatest flexibility
in tone, pace, and style, ranging from clear narrative prose to opaque stream
of consciousness and from Benjy's "reduced" syntax to Faulkner's rhetorical
manner. Quentin is at times a standard first-person narrator (mainly in
recounting the events of his last day but also in reporting certain scenes of his
past); the point is that he proves unable to fulfill his narrative function with
sustained consistency and that whenever painful private memories or fantasies surge forth, he loses control over his words. Again and again Quentin

attempts to tell his story in orderly fashion; again and again his narrative gets caught in the vortex of his obsessions. Many paragraphs in the second section begin quite conventionally as controlled narration, only to end in erratic interior discourse. And this entropic tendency also characterizes the monologue as a whole. The closer one gets to its emotional climax (Quentin's decisive encounter with Caddy at the branch, 171–87), the less Quentin masters his language; the deeper he moves into his monologue, the less he *speaks* and the more he *listens* to the myriad voices of the past. That these effects were all carefully calculated by the author can be easily seen from the changes he made in revising his manuscript. Formally, the manuscript is still fairly traditional in many respects: unpunctuated passages are rare, reported speech is generally presented between quotation marks, speakers are easy to identify, and it almost looks as if some of the unconventional devices used in this section had been gradually discovered during the process of composition, to be systematized once the manuscript was completed. Thus, in the manuscript version of the climactic scene with Caddy, the suppression of punctuation marks occurs later than in the final version (77 in the holograph, beginning with "All right let go"; cf. 185 in the published text), and the removal of capitals occurs even later (78 in the holograph, beginning with "anytime he will believe me"; cf. 187 in the published text). It is clear, then, that in revising the manuscript Faulkner radicalized the experimental character of his writing and thereby emphasized the dreamlike "interior" quality of Quentin's monologue.[2]

What the confusion thus achieved is meant to render is of course Quentin's emotional turmoil, but paradoxically it also testifies to his greater intelligence: his mind works hardly more logically than Benjy's, yet it runs at higher speed and ranges over a far more extended network of associations. There are twice as many time-shifts in the second section (about 200) as in the first (about 100), and the shuttling back and forth between past and present is at times so swift as to convey the impression of a mind running on several tracks at one and the same time.

In contrast to the deliberateness of his external actions, Quentin's mental activity betrays throughout a feverish restlesness. Erratic, elliptical, full of unexpected detours and sudden turnabouts, his thought processes are those of a frantically busy mind. At the same time, however, they also reveal a captive mind, compulsively racing within the closed circle of its memories and fantasies. While Benjy's memory seldom repeats itself, Quentin's is ceaselessly driven back to the same scenes of the past, and the persistent recurrence of identical words (*Caddy, water, shadow, door, honeysuckle,*) and identical phrases and sentences (*Did you ever have a sister?; One minute she was standing there; Father I have committed*) gives his monologue the incantatory rhythm of a litany. From first to last the syntax of fragmentation is counterbalanced by a closely patterned rhetoric of repetition, a rhetoric suggesting, as so often in Faulkner, stasis as well as motion.

The martyrdom of the comedian

These reiterative patterns are an index of the specific quality of Quentin's experience. His present, as we shall see, is a reenactment of his past; his future is his past in waiting. Unlike Benjy, however, Quentin has a history. Yet can he be considered in any strict sense the *subject* of its telling? In point of fact, the unspoken speech attributed to him can hardly be called *his*, for it is not any more than Benjy's the discourse of a single person. Again, many voices, past and present, are heard, and within this polyphonic ensemble Quentin's own enjoys no special privilege.[3] The very fragmentation of his speech, its dream-like incoherence and obsessive redundancy belie the postulate of a stable "I" presiding over its enunciation. Quentin's "monologue" is not a dialogue of self with self; what it records is the process through which the entire fabric of a self is unraveled. Insofar as there is still an ego at play, it is not at all the agent of mediation, integration, and adjustment which American ego psychology supposes it to be. Modern French psychoanalysis might prove more helpful here, for its ego concept is much more relevant to what we find in the second section: an ego that is the locus of alienating identifications rather than the location of identity.

Quentin's drama is that of the "poor player," trying out various parts, none of which he is able to appropriate and sustain. His quest for selfhood amounts to little more than a desperate search for models to imitate.[4] Like the other members of his histrionic family (except Benjy and Caddy), he attempts to dramatize and dignify his existence by projecting himself into ennobling roles, and Mr. Compson as well as Shreve, Spoade, and Herbert Head are quite aware of his role-playing.[5] The characters he would impersonate are those provided by the repertoire of his culture: Jesus, the saint of Christian tradition (St. Francis of Assisi), the medieval knight (Galahad), the romantic hero (Byron), the southern gentleman. That there should be so many literary echoes in his monologue is hardly surprising; the quixotic Quentin lives in a world of words and books, a museum of romance, and his existence is thus doubly fictive: he is a character acting characters, an unsubstantial "I" lost in the maze of its fictions and myths.

Selfhood, then, is at best a theatrical creation. The core of Quentin's being is deceit, division, nonidentity. Nothing in him or around him seems real. His speech drags us into a space corroded by absence, a space inside out and outside in, with neither landmarks nor boundaries, just as it plunges us into a time out of time, collapsing rather than elapsing, in which the self is shattered by the reciprocal exclusion of being and having been (199). Besides, isn't this monologue, like Addie's in *As I Lay Dying*, a posthumous speech? Faulkner, as if to underscore how little reality he bestows upon Quentin, makes him speak after he is dead. As Sartre writes, "all Faulkner's art aims to suggest to us that Quentin's soliloquy and his last walk are already his suicide."[6] The voice we listen to in the second section is a voice out of nowhere—no body's voice.

What is offered instead is the tormented landscape of a mind, an interlacing of tracks and traces, a palimpsest of desire and memory. As we read and reread it, we eventually make out the pattern of a trajectory, tortuous and paradoxical, and beneath that trajectory we cannot but sense a slow blind surge toward death. Where and when did this lethal course begin? There are no simple beginnings, but it is suggested more than once that, had Quentin not been deprived of maternal love, his life might have taken a different course: *"If I could say Mother. Mother"* (108), or again *"if I'd just had a mother so I could say Mother Mother"* (197). And the same poignant sense of abandonment is revealed by Quentin's remembrance of the picture in the story book:

> When I was little there was a picture in one of our books, a dark place into which a single weak ray of light came slanting upon two faces lifted out of the shadows. . . . I'd have to turn back to it until the dungeon was Mother herself she and Father upward into weak light holding hands and us lost somewhere below even them without even a ray of light. (198)

Quentin's projection of the family situation onto this scene of darkness and confinement is eloquent evidence of parental neglect. Both parents failed the Compson children, but in this Rorschach test it is significantly the mother who is equated with the dungeon. The cold, egotistical Mrs. Compson has become a lightless prison-womb to her children, keeping them captive, as securely as she would have by possessive love, through what she denied them. Or, to borrow another of Quentin's metaphors, she poisoned them once and for all: *"Done in Mother's mind though. Finished. Finished. Then we were all poisoned"* (116).

For this poison there is no antidote; from this darkness, there is no escape. None of the Compson children will ever succeed in fleeing from it, whatever their individual responses to the original trauma. Quentin had no mother, but he had a sister. Like Benjy, he turned to her for the love his mother denied. Yet in shifting allegiance from mother to sister he has perhaps also transferred to her his early resentment of the mother's betrayal. Even in the earliest childhood scenes he appears as a moody, introverted boy with a very ambivalent attitude toward his sister, and it is equally remarkable that this ambivalence is matched from the outset by suspiciousness with regard to sex.

Wallowing in sin

The most revealing episode in this respect is the scene in which Quentin and Natalie, a neighbor girl, are "dancing sitting down" in the barn (155–56). When Quentin sees his sister standing in the door watching their little game, he immediately breaks off and hurls abuse at Natalie: *"Get wet I hope you catch pneumonia go on home Cowface"* (156). Then he jumps into the hog wallow:

> *I jumped hard as I could into the hogwallow the mud yellowed up to my waist stinking*

I kept on plunging until I fell down and rolled over in it . . . mud was warmer than the
rain it smelled awful. (156–57)

Telling Caddy that he was "hugging" Natalie, he expects her to be offended,
but his sister does not "give a damn" about what happened. Upset by her
indifference, he then angrily smears mud from his own body onto hers while
she scratches at his face. After which, reconciled at last, the two children go to
the branch and sit down in the water, washing off the malodorous mud.

Everything in this childhood scene in some way anticipates Quentin's
future actions and attitudes. His leap into the hog wallow is the enactment of
an old Puritan metaphor, the symbolic performance of what his first and no
doubt last sexual experiment means to him: yielding to the urges of the flesh
equals wallowing in filth.[7] Mud becomes quite literally the substance of sin:
water (and as such related to the whole complex of water symbolism pervading the novel), but with its transparency gone, its fluidity thickened into sticky
stinking matter—a concrete image of sexual nausea. Just as in *Sanctuary* and
Light in August, sexuality here is linked with the unclean and the viscous, and,
through the implicit reference to pigs, with loathsome animality.[8]

The hog wallow scene dramatizes the revulsion following Quentin's timid
attempt at sexual initiation. The ritual mudbath is both a symbolic reenactment of the previously mimed sexual act and its nullification. In much the
same way as Christmas, after his discovery of woman's "periodical filth,"
shoots a sheep and steeps his hands in "the yet warm blood of the dying
beast,"[9] Quentin, by wallowing in the mud, resorts to homeopathic magic,[10]
curing evil by evil. One might add that his strange ritual on this occasion is
strongly reminiscent of the defense mechanism known in the study of compulsive neuroses as "undoing" (*Ungeschehenmachen*).

The "dirty girls"

At once a confession of guilt, an act of penance, and a cleansing rite, Quentin's
gesture foreshadows the magical actions through which he will attempt time
and again to ward off the threats of the world, not only during his childhood
and adolescence but up to and even *in* his suicide. Magical too is the code by
which he lives and acts: in the last analysis all his perception of good and evil
comes down to that of the pure and the impure. The summum bonum is
equated in his mind with his sister's intact virginity; his nostalgia for lost
innocence is above all the dream of a sexless life. In his monologue Quentin
recalls Versh's story about a self-castrated man (132). But castration—an idea
which has been haunting him and a possibility he must have envisaged for
himself—does not appear to him as a satisfactory alternative. Castration
would simply be a *pis-aller*, for it would not obliterate the memory of having
had a sex: "But that's not it. It's not not having them. It's never to have had
them then I could say O That That's Chinese I dont know Chinese" (132).

Quentin wishes sex were an alien language. If it were all Greek or "Chinese" to him, then he could at last feel safe. For to know about sex is already to share in evil knowledge and to partake of sin.

The ultimate goal of Quentin's angelism turns out to be *aphanasis*, the radical extinction of sexual desire itself, and its correlate is a deep-seated hatred of its most common object, woman. Quentin's is the Puritan (and Miltonic) version of the Fall: Eve was the beginning of evil; it was through her that the innocence of Eden was lost. Although he clings to the southern myth of Sacred Woman-hood and will defend Woman's honor to the last (as is shown by his fight with Gerald Bland a few hours before his suicide), Quentin's faith in her purity has been shattered by his sister's promiscuity. His monologue reverberates with Mr. Compson's cynical remarks on women, and for all his protests and denials he has apparently come to acknowledge the bitter truth that "women are never virgins" (132), that they are by nature impure, that is, impure like Nature herself. One quickly senses that the revered icon of the Immaculate Virgin screens a darker image, not far removed from Jason's definition of women as bitches. Quentin shrinks from so much candor, yet womanhood, in his monologue, is constantly linked to suspect images and sensations—softness, warmth, wetness, darkness—and particularly to dirt.[11] As with other male characters in Faulkner's fiction, we find in Quentin a morbid concern with the physiological evidence of woman's "impurity," menstruation:

> Because women so delicate so mysterious Father said. Delicate equilibrium of periodical filth between two moons balanced. Moons he said full and yellow as harvest moons her hips thighs. Outside outside of them always but. Yellow. Feet soles with walking like. Then know that some man that all those mysterious and imperious concealed. With all that inside of them shapes an outward suavity waiting for a touch to. Liquid putrefaction like drowned things floating like pale rubber flabbily filled getting the odour of honeysuckle all mixed up. (147)

Woman's delicacy and suavity are a decoy; the sanctuary of her body hides an ignoble secret: the filth of sex, at once the periodically renewed promise of fecundity (hinted at by the references to the moon and to harvests and by the symbolism of yellow) and the threat of mortal engulfment. In Quentin's diseased imagination the menstrual flow and "liquid putrefaction" are con-fused in the same obscene streaming.

Templum aedificatum super cloacam: Tertullian's definition of woman perfect-ly sums up Quentin's view.[12] His equating of woman with dirt is confirmed, moreover, by at least three of the female figures evoked in his monologue: Caddy, Natalie, and the little Italian girl Quentin meets at Cambridge on the day of his suicide. Caddy is the girl with the "muddy drawers,"[13] and in Quentin's memory Natalie too is a "dirty girl": twice he recalls Caddy's sarcastic remark when he teased and taunted her about her first kiss: "*I didnt kiss a dirty girl like Natalie anyway*" (153, 154). As to the "present" episode with the Italian girl, it alternates significantly with the account of the Natalie scene, and one of the links between the two scenes is precisely the "dirty girl" motif: Quentin's new "sister" is also "a little dirty child" (143), and his descriptions of her draw attention to "her dirty dress" (146), her "dirty hand" (151), and "her filthy little dress" (152). The dirt is made even more repellent by moisture and warmth: "She extended her fist, it uncurled upon a nickel, moist and dirty, moist dirt ridged into her flesh" (145). And the suggestion of disgust is further strengthened by animal similes with phallic connotations: "Her fingers closed about [the two coppers], damp and hot, like worms" (145); "She had a funny looking thing in her hand, she carried it sort of like it might have been a dead pet rat" (159).[14] All these touches lend the scene of Quentin's encounter with the girl a faintly nauseous atmosphere and emphasize the eerie, almost ominous effect of her silent presence at his side. The girl is an echo of the past and a prefiguration of the future; while taking Quentin back to his childhood as the ironically rediscovered sister, she is also, in her uncanny silence, her dark stare, and her inexplicable stubbornness in following him everywhere, a symbol of Fate, an avatar of "little sister Death," and she is finally another metaphor of soiled innocence, a reminder of the defilement whose unbearable memory is soon to be washed away by the waters of the Charles River.

In Quentin's daily behavior this concern with purity and impurity is reflected by a compulsive need for order and cleanliness. Spots and stains make him uneasy, and nothing annoys him more than other people's slovenliness.[15] Even as a child, he resented the fact that Louis Hatcher's lantern was not spotlessly clean (130). Similarly, during his interview with Herbert Head, his sister's vulgar fiancé, he is anxious lest the lighted cigar which the latter has put on the mantel should cause a blister (125),[16] and after his fist fight with Gerald Bland, his first question is not about possible injury but about the bloodstains on his vest (188). At no moment, however, is his preoccupation with cleanliness and order more conspicuous than during the elaborate preparations for his suicide. After lamentably failing to put order into his life, Quentin very methodically sets about putting order into his death:

> I laid out two suits of underwear, with socks, shirts, collars and ties, and packed my trunk. I put in everything except my new suit and an old one and two pairs of shoes and two hats, and my books. I carried the books into the sitting-room and stacked them on the table, the ones I had brought from home and the ones *Father said it used to be a gentleman was known by his books; nowadays he is known by the ones he has not returned* and locked the trunk and addressed it. The quarter hour sounded. I stopped and listened to it until the chimes ceased.
>
> I bathed and shaved. The water made my finger smart a little, so I painted it again. I put on my new suit and put my watch on and packed the other suit and the accessories and my razor and brushes in my hand bag, and wrapped the trunk key into a sheet of paper and put it in an envelope and addressed it to Father, and wrote the two notes and sealed them. (91–92)

Quentin is determined to leave everything in impeccable order. His death, at least, shall be no mess. As if to reassert *in extremis* the aristocratic code he failed to live by, he wants his exit to be a gentleman's. Hence the fastidious care he takes of his personal hygiene and clothing. Here he is, on the last morning of his life, taking a bath, shaving, donning a new suit. Later, at the close of his monologue, this funeral toilet is resumed and completed: after his altercation with Bland, Quentin returns home, cleans his bloodstained vest with gasoline, washes his face and hands, changes his collar, shirt, and tie (197). Here is the record of his very last gestures:

> The last note sounded. At last it stopped vibrating and the darkness was still again. I entered the sitting room and turned on the light. I put my vest on. The gasoline was faint now, barely noticeable, and in the mirror the stain didnt show. Not like my eye did, anyway. I put on my coat. Shreve's letter crackled through the cloth and I took it out and examined the address, and put it in my side pocket. Then I carried the watch into Shreve's room and put it in his drawer and went to my room and got a fresh handkerchief and went to the door and put my hand on the light switch. Then I remembered I hadnt brushed my teeth, so I had to open the bag again. I found my toothbrush and got some of Shreve's paste and went out and brushed my teeth. I squeezed the brush as dry as I could and put it back in the bag and shut it, and went to the door again. Before I snapped the light out I looked around to see if there was anything else, then I saw that I had forgotten my hat. I'd have to go by the postoffice and I'd be sure to meet some of them, and they'd think I was a Harvard Square student making like he was a senior. I had forgotten to brush it too, but Shreve had a brush, so I didn't have to open the bag any more. (205)

In its tedium of detail Quentin's flat, factual report faithfully reflects the manic meticulosity of this ultimate inspection. Yet behind the mechanical succession of controlled gestures one senses a consciousness no longer fully present to itself or to the world, registering the actions of the body as if from a distance, a consciousness more than ever astray, and it is remarkable that for all the scrupulous attention given to his final preparations, Quentin twice nearly forgets a detail. Is it because he cannot help thinking of his imminent suicide? And does he go through all these futile motions to avert the thought of death? It seems safe to assume that they are a last diversion maneuver, but perhaps all this absent-minded fussiness testifies even more to a radical incapacity to welcome death, an inability to *want* it at the very moment when it appears most desirable.[17]

Besides, it is not at all evident that Quentin desires it, and if we were not informed of his design and alerted by the chilling flatness of his report, his actual intentions might be easily misinterpreted. In the extreme care he lavishes on his body and clothing there is a suggestion of coquetry, a touch of narcissistic self-concern that one would hardly expect from a man on the point of committing suicide. Quentin spruces himself up as if he were going out for a date. The ambiguity is hardly ambiguous: Quentin's suicide is indeed a lover's date.

Detours of desire

In order to retrace the complex process that has led Quentin to choose death, let us return for a moment to the prophetic hog wallow scene. Quentin's game with Natalie was the beginning of his initiation into sex. Now *before* Caddy's return to the barn he enjoys the game and apparently feels no compunction about his pleasure. Only when Caddy comes back and surprises him hugging the girl does the love game make him feel guilty and distraught. Then he begins to panic, for he suddenly realizes (although his realization remains subliminal) that the intrusion of sex into his life threatens to compromise forever his unique relationship to Caddy. To stave off this menace, it becomes indispensable that his sister should acknowledge its seriousness by a firm disavowal of what she has seen. As Caddy does not react in the expected way, he smears her body with mud. Symbolically, he thus drags her down with him into the mire of sin, forcing her to share his assumed guilt and so reestablish- ing—in evil—the intimacy that his game with Natalie had put in jeopardy. After that they can both go to the branch and purify themselves in its water: the illusion of innocence is provisionally restored.

Quentin's puzzling behavior in the course of this ritual defilement and purgation clearly shows that what matters to him is not so much the preser- vation of sexual innocence, whether his own or Caddy's, as the safekeeping at any cost of the absolute mutuality of a dual relationship. Innocence to him is a means rather than an end, and if he is so anxious to preserve it, it is firstly because it is a token of isolation, safety, and peace. Conversely, if he recoils from sexuality, it is primarily because it imperils his exclusive bond to his sister. Even at this early stage Quentin is prepared to go to any lengths to keep her out of the world's clutches; no price seems too high, and he is willing to pay even that of sin provided that the sin committed is a common sin calling for common punishment. In this childhood scene he compels his sister to share his mudbath. When, later, Caddy is "soiled" by the loss of her virginity, he insists no less on restoring their intimacy, but it is his turn then to join the fallen virgin in the filthy waters of sin.

From the sex game in the barn to the ritual cleansing in the branch, the episode is also prophetic and paradigmatic in that it involves a *triangular* relationship and foreshadows later scenes with similar situations, but in which the roles will be ironically reversed. Here the triad consists of Quentin, Natalie, and Caddy, and tension arises as soon as it is formed, that is, from the moment Caddy appears in the doorway of the barn. The little drama which then takes place curiously resembles a banal adultery story: Quentin, Natalie, and Caddy virtually play the parts of husband, mistress, and betrayed wife. Expecting Caddy to be jealous and shower reproaches on her faithless partner, Quentin stands ready to plead guilty. The actors, however, do not play the roles they had been given in his private script. In hoping that his sister would play the outraged partner, he has in fact cast her for his own role, one which was already to some extent his in the first branch scene (the splashing incident), and which he will play with ever more pointed jealousy in his subsequent encounters with Caddy: the quarrel after her first flirtation with a "darn town squirt" (153), the long pathetic colloquy about her affair with Dalton Ames (171–87), and the last meeting in her room on the eve of her wedding (140–43). In all those scenes, just as in the early Natalie scene, there are three persons involved, but sex is no longer a childish game and the actors have been allocated different roles: Caddy has replaced Natalie in the part of the "dirty girl," and her lovers have supplanted Quentin. Reverting to the position of the infant within the oedipal pattern, it is he who now plays the thankless role of the *terzo incommodo*.[18]

Proceeding from concurrent desires with Caddy at stake, this triangular relationship is bound to generate conflict. In point of fact, from the yet harmless squabbles of childhood to the poignant confrontation before Caddy's wedding, all the scenes just referred to are scenes of potential or overt violence, and each time Quentin turns out to be its agent or its cause.

Most often Quentin's aggressiveness is aimed at Caddy herself: he slaps her, at fifteen, for having kissed a boy, just as he did at seven after she had taken off her dress; he smears her with mud after the incident with Natalie, and in the climactic scene about Ames he even takes out his jackknife and points it at Caddy's throat.[19] On the other hand, he shows persistent hostility to his sister's lovers: he tries to hit Dalton Ames when he meets him near the bridge (183–84), and during his interview with Herbert Head he deliberately antagonizes his future brother-in-law (123–26). The same pattern of conflict reemerges almost farcically in the two major episodes of Quentin's last day. The episode with the Italian girl culminates in a grotesque inversion of roles. Arrested for "meditated criminal assault" (160), Quentin is now cast in the role of seducer, while Julio, the girl's older brother, successfully assumes the chivalric part of avenger that Quentin could not play: small wonder that Quentin is convulsed with hysterical laughter on realizing the irony of the situation. As to the second episode, the fight with Gerald Bland, it is likewise based on a tragicomic quid pro quo, since it arises from Quentin's unconscious identification of Bland with Caddy's first lover.

The targets of Quentin's aggressiveness do not change, and what it constantly aims at is either the elimination of the hated rival or the punishment of the beloved sister. To recapture the object of his love, he will try anything from physical intimidation to the subtler stratagems of persuasion. His are in fact all the desperate ruses of the frustrated lover. One of his favorite tactics is vilifying his rivals: "*that blackguard Caddy. . . . A liar and a scoundrel Caddy was dropped from his club for cheating at cards got sent to Coventry caught cheating at midterm exams and expelled*" (141). By exposing Head's disreputable past, Quentin hopes he can induce Caddy not to marry him, and there are similar motives to his caustic comments on Caddy's first boyfriends (153) and on Dalton Ames (105). The point is of course that none is more dishonest here than Quentin himself: what worries him is not so much that Ames and Head are no gentlemen as the threat they pose to his love, and he objects to them as he would to any other man taking Caddy away from him.

Another of Quentin's magic tricks is *denial*. When faced with unpleasant facts, Quentin refuses to acknowledge them or tries at least to twist the evidence so as to minimize their significance. Thus he persuades himself and attempts to persuade Caddy that her "infidelities" were not committed of her own free will but forced upon her. Hence his resentment when, questioned about her first kiss, Caddy admits with blunt candor: "*I didnt let him I made him* [kiss me]" (153). Later, when he learns about her affair with Ames, he wants Caddy to admit that she has been raped, and his greatest fear then is that his sister might love her seducer:

> do you love him
> her hand came out I didnt move it fumbled down my arm and she held my hand
> flat against her chest her heart thudding
> no no
> did he make you then he made you do it let him he was stronger than you and
> he tomorrow Ill kill him I swear I will father neednt know until afterward and
> then you and I nobody need ever know we can take my school money we can
> cancel my matriculation Caddy you hate him dont you dont you (172–73)

It should be clear by now that Quentin's desire is above all a desire for Caddy's desire. What is unbearable to him is not that his sister lost her virginity but that she consented to lose it, that she willingly gave herself to Ames and still wants his embraces. What he desperately denies is that she eludes him as *subject* of desire. Contrary to what many commentators and Faulkner himself have contended,[20] Caddy's virginity is not just an abstract concept, a mere emblem of Quentin's idealistic concern for the Compson honor. In Quentin's psychic economy, virginity and incest are the pivots of rigorously interlocking fantasies. If incest refers back to the *interdiction* of desire, virginity represents the permissibility of the forbidden, *the deferred possibility of the impossible*: Caddy's hymen is the veil concealing from Quentin both her future as woman and the truth about his own sex. If the sister has come to occupy the place of the failing mother, it is important to realize that as long as she is a virgin, she is *not yet* (his) mother, and hence *not yet* forbidden to the son/brother. Her intact virginity is for Quentin that which, ideally, authorizes (postponed, unconsummated) incest, and it is also that which guarantees Caddy's inaccessibility to another's desire and the innocence of his own. As long as this double insurance works, Quentin feels safe and pure, and can love his sister as his undisputed property. Conversely, once Caddy's virginity is lost, everything is lost: the closure of Quentin's private world forever fractured, the trustful and seemingly guiltless mutuality of the dual relationship irremediably destroyed.

Then his *passion* truly begins. Its immediate cause is the intrusion of the hateful third party and the ensuing clash of rival claims on Caddy, yet much more than mere rivalry is involved. The intruder is of course at once abhorred and feared as a potential ravisher, but he also acts as mediator, revealer, and catalyst. While portending the breakup of Quentin's intimacy with Caddy, he is also instrumental in dispelling the illusion of its "purity." To Quentin as much as to his sister, his entrance upon the stage means the end of innocence. For even though he will never confess to it, Quentin recognizes in the rival desire a reflection of his own, and as Caddy's body becomes attractive to others, it ceases to be sexless to him.

Hence the extreme ambivalence of Quentin's attitudes toward his rivals. While hating them as Caddy's seducers, he admires and envies them for the virile potency and daring he lacks. Ames and Head realize by proxy his unavowed and unavowable wish: the sexual possession of his sister. No wonder then that he should be such a poor avenger of her outraged honor. His weakness vis-à-vis Caddy's lovers is of the same order as Hamlet's hesitation to kill the usurper of the royal bed: unconscious identification with the successful competitor prevents his wreaking vengeance for the insult.[21]

Quentin's two contradictory wishes—disposing of the rival while becoming like him and taking over his prerogatives—thus come to merge in the fantasy of complete substitution, that is, the fantasy of consummated incest: *"it was I it was not Dalton Ames"* (90) . . . *"you thought it was them but it was me"* (170–71). Quentin's desire at this point becomes an imitation of his rival's, even as in the oedipal situation the son's desire is patterned on the father's. It is noteworthy too that the two male figures who most excite his animosity and admiration—Dalton Ames and Gerald Bland[22]—are to some extent father images: in their ability to seduce and dominate, their sexual potency, physical strength, and sporting prowess (shooting in Ames's case; shooting, rowing, and boxing in Bland's), they embody alike the ideal of *mastery* which Quentin pretends to despise because it is out of his reach.[23]

The question of the Father

The most amazing thing about this father image is that it never coincides with the image of the real father. Not that the latter's role is marginal. Far from it. It is to his father that Quentin addresses himself at the beginning and end of his monologue, as though he expected of him an answer to his questions, an alleviation of his anguish. If Caddy is the primary object of his discourse, Mr. Compson is to a very large extent its implied *receiver*. The entire monologue, frequently punctuated with "Father said," could almost be defined as an imaginary conversation between Quentin and Mr. Compson, a running debate between father and son. In this function of interlocutor in absentia, the figure of the father occupies indeed a key position, and it is significant that when Faulkner revised the manuscript of *The Sound and the Fury*, he saw fit to give him an even greater role.[24]

Quentin, Caddy, Mr. Compson: another triad comes to light, the one that brings us closest to the young man's complex and tragic fate. On the face of it, it is an oedipal triad, and yet Quentin's relations with his father breathe mutual trust and affection. The father/son conflict, so often evoked in Faulkner's fiction, is apparently missing here. Indeed, Quentin's argument with Mr. Compson suggests not so much a duel as a doleful duet, and he feels so close to his father that he makes him his confidant.[25] In his distress and disarray, he turns to him as the one who *knows* and whose knowledge should help him to find a *raison d'être*. But the father's wisdom is a knowledge of death, not of life. His "philosophy," a garrulous nihilism distilled into cynical aphorisms on the absurdity of the human condition, has undeniably left a deep mark on Quentin's own thinking. Its only effect, however, has been to thrust him more irretrievably into despair.

Through his disillusioned *fin-de-siècle* rhetoric Mr. Compson has attempted to rationalize his personal failure; to him it has been a refuge in much the same way as alcohol or his reading of Horace and Catullus. And the one thing his son inherits from him is precisely his failure—a failure which he had likewise inherited from his own father. For, as Faulkner himself was to point out in an interview, in the Compson family failure is congenital:

> The action as portrayed by Quentin was transmitted to him through his father. There was a basic failure before that. The grandfather had been a failed brigadier twice in the Civil War. It was the—the basic failure inherited through his father, or beyond his father.[26]

These comments put Quentin's story in a genealogical perspective—a perspective barely outlined in the novel itself, but which had already begun to emerge in *Flags in the Dust* and was to be further explored in *Absalom, Absalom!* and *Go Down, Moses*. Admittedly, *The Sound and the Fury* lacks the historical dimension of the latter novels, yet it is clear that Quentin's fate is not simply that of a neurotic young man. Not unlike Isaac McCaslin's in *Go Down, Moses*, his tragedy is a tragedy of inheritance. Beyond his individual failure lies the bankruptcy of at least two Compson generations, and beyond that again the disease and decay of a whole culture.

What Mr. Compson represents to his son is all this past, and through this past he has a hold over him. Mr. Compson is weak, and yet, regardless of what he is or does, he has power—a power originating in his *priority*. And because he comes *after* his father, Quentin is inevitably caught up in a test of fidelity. Through his father, he is heir to the southern tradition, to its aristocratic code of honor and its puritanical ethic. When this pattern of values is passed on, however, it has already lost its authority, the more so in this case as its appointed transmitter is an inveterate skeptic. Quentin clings to it with desperate obstinacy because to him it is the only available recourse against absurdity, and because its very rigidity seems a safeguard of order and integrity. Yet while transmitting the code, his father's voice has taught him its inanity. Quentin's fidelity is an allegiance to values long dead, and in making them *his* he chooses defeat. The southern code has failed; the failure of tradition has become a tradition of failure. In refusing to break with it (as some later Faulkner heroes do), Quentin can only repeat the fatal errors of his fathers.

Why such a sequence of failures? How is one to account for the curse on the Compsons? For what crime is it the punishment? Faulkner gives us a clue in the sequel to the comment quoted above:

> It was a—something had happened somewhere between the first Compson and Quentin. The first Compson was a bold ruthless man who came into Mississippi as a free forester to grasp where and when he could and wanted to, and established what should have been a princely line, and that line decayed.[27]

If Faulkner is to be believed, Quentin's most redoubtable antagonist is none other than this pioneering ancestor, the long-dead founder of the family line; the decisive contest opposes the last of the Compsons to the first, four generations apart, and it is in the "something" that happened between them that we are asked to seek the deeper causes of Quentin's failure. His tragedy is indeed the tragedy of the son, but if we follow the author's suggestions, the overpowering paternal figure with whom Quentin is confronted is not at all his real father: it is embodied in the daunting features of the *Urvater*, the founding father. The quick sketch of him that Faulkner gives us here[28] at once brings to mind other ancestor figures of his fiction: Colonel John Sartoris (briefly referred to at the close of section 2), Carothers McCaslin, the patriarch of *Go Down, Moses*, and Thomas Sutpen, the demonic hero of *Absalom, Absalom!*— men of daring, rapacious and ruthless like Quentin MacLachan Compson, and like him founders of an ill-starred dynasty. In the light of these resemblances, the secret kinship between Quentin and all the other victims of those legendary ghosts can be easily seen, and it becomes more understandable too why Faulkner chose Quentin as principal narrator for *Absalom, Absalom!* Through the history of another southern family, it is that of his own he attempts to decipher, and if he identifies so readily with the young Henry Sutpen, it is not only because of their common obsession with incest but also because both of them are enthralled by the same formidable father figure.

Death has raised these figures to the heights of myth, setting them at an unbridgeable distance and turning them into sovereign ghosts. The ancestor finds in death an extra power over the living; absence makes him godlike. Yet he is a cruel and culpable god: discharging his own guilt by the curse he heaps upon his descendants, he watches jealously over the perpetuation of the "original sin," and so ensures the inexpiable nature of the past.

True, in *The Sound and the Fury* the almost theological implications of this drama are never dwelt upon, and the importance which Faulkner accords retrospectively to the Compson ancestor is by no means evident. The latter plays no visible role in the novel; he is not even mentioned, so that the suspicion grows that Faulkner unwittingly reads his later books into the earlier one. Yet to discount Quentin MacLachan Compson altogether leads one to misunderstand the complex issue of the father-son relationship. For Mr.

Compson's weakness may be said to derive primarily from the fact that he, just like his son, is a powerless hostage to this ancestral shade. In other words, he too has never stopped being an impotent son, and is consequently unfitted to exercise his paternal prerogatives. His failure as parent is symmetrical with Mrs. Compson's: while she refuses to play the part of the love-dispensing mother, he evades the sterner duties of the father.[29] Quentin is thus torn between two equally negative father images: on one hand, the genitor, the living father of the present, weak and kindly, a mere transmitting shaft in the cogs of fate, much too close to his son to be anything other than an elder brother showing him the way to defeat; on the other hand, the mythicized Dead Father, because of whom fatherhood has become an impossibility and sonhood the curse of impotence.

Quentin's drama can therefore have no solution—except in death. The real battle, to paraphrase one of Mr. Compson's remarks, is not even fought. It's no use fighting ghosts. Between the living and the dead the match can never be even. To Quentin, the Ancestor is a mute and massive transcendence, crushing him with all his invisible weight and fating him to helpless paralysis. Nor can Quentin rise up against his real father, for the latter is just as elusive in his weakness as the great-grandfather in his hidden power.

This impasse of the father-son relationship is as fatal to Quentin as his incestuous attachment to Caddy, and the two relationships are in fact closely interdependent. Within the oedipal structure the primal function of the father is to declare the law and guarantee its authority, and inasmuch as it is his task to deflect desire from its first object, the mother, he assumes a crucial role as interdictor. Now it is precisely as lawgiver that Mr. Compson fails his son. Quentin's tragedy is, as we have already seen, originally determined by the absence of the mother—a gap provisionally filled by Caddy and reopened by her desertion, but it can be traced back as well to a rift in the *Name-of-the-Father*, the symbolic function identifying the person of the father with the agency of the law.[30]

The unbridgeable distance between lawgiver and genitor precludes the cultural process of exchange and transmission which would normally lead to the mutual *recognition* of father and son. For Quentin the law functions in a vacuum, ab-solutely, and instead of being accepted as a prerequisite of order and sought after as a protection against the vertigo of forbidden desire, it is suffered as arbitrary violence. The failure is indeed a failure of tradition: the legacy of the dead has become deadly.

To put it another way (yet again in Lacanian terms), the law no longer ensures the transition from the *imaginary* register to the *symbolic* order.[31] Narcissus cannot become Oedipus. To Quentin the mirror hall of narcissism has become a nightmare, yet for want of an intercessor he can find no way out of it.

His incest fantasy testifies to this entrapment, but to interpret it as a resurgence of repressed desire is plainly not enough. For the point about the incest with Caddy is that it is conceived as *confessed* to the father, and what Quentin secretly intends by confessing it to him is to challenge paternal authority, to provoke Mr. Compson into acting at last as the interdicting and punishing father. However desperate, the gamble which Quentin considers is not without hope: the hope that the flagrant transgression of the primal taboo would entail a reaffirmation and restoration of the law, that the very scandal of his sin would set its dialectic into motion again.

In attempting to provoke paternal retaliation, Quentin may be said to seek the symbolic castration which would free him from his bondage to the incestuous wish, and yet there are as many reasons to construe his fantasy as an unconscious ruse to be spared castration. For the fantasy is conjugated in a past tense; incest is referred to as an accomplished fact: "*I have committed incest I said Father it was I . . .*" (90). Quentin's is perhaps actually "the fantasy of having acted out the fantasy,"[32] typical of the compulsive neurotic: "[For him] it is a question of composing his oedipal fantasy *as if it had already been enacted*: the father already killed, the mother already possessed. In return for which castration need no longer be considered; only guilt persists; this is the reason why it can be so intense with him."[33] If we retain this hypothesis in Quentin's case, our first reading of his fantasy has to be reversed, not to be invalidated but rather to allow for a new contradiction: the imaginary confession of incest should then be interpreted as *both* defiance and escape—castration simultaneously sought after and fled from.[34]

Paradoxes and reversals

Overdetermination, multivalence: in the last resort the meaning of Quentin's fantasies proves undecidable. His obsession with incest is not just nostalgia for the lost mother; it is a longing for both reunion *and* separation. Pointing at once to regression and rebellion, it is, much like his other fantasies, a skein of many interweaving threads. And as so often with Quentin, it provides a magic answer to a real dilemma. Halted on the threshold of adulthood, unwilling to encounter reality, terrified by the unpredictable changes the future holds in store for him, Quentin would do anything to turn the clock back and revive the sheltered world of childhood. As he conceives of it, consummated incest would fold his family back on itself and seal it off against the troublesome outsiders. More specifically, as has been suggested before, it would also allow him to reestablish his exclusive relationship with Caddy: "*Then you will have only me then only me then the two of us amid the pointing and the horror beyond the clean flame*" (133). And the same wish for endogamic isolation recurs in his later (imaginary) reply to his father: "*It was to isolate her out of the loud world so that it would have to flee us of necessity and the sound of it would be as though it had never been*" (203). The paradox is twofold, however; it is not simply a question of wresting from sin what innocence failed to preserve but to regain innocence by way of the greatest guilt and of the everlasting punishment that this guilt entails: in Hell Quentin would "guard [Caddy] forever and keep her forevermore *intact* amidst the eternal fires."[35]

Far from being irreducible, it appears then that to Quentin the contradiction between conscience and desire is only provisional, and in some measure it is his very Puritanism that leads him to consider the unforgivable sin of incest. His is a *morale du pire*: the incest once committed, the honor of the Compsons would be rescued through the very excess of disgrace, and evil exorcised by the very enormity of his sin. Quentin's incest fantasy is thus confiscated by his superego, which uses it for its own ends. And, as we shall see, his suicide is likewise a triumph of the id *and* the superego. Springing from the interplay of the same psychic agencies, his incest wish and his death wish are in effect the opposite sides of the same desire.

Quentin's winding path to death reveals the migrations and metamorphoses of this desire under the impact of "melancholy mourning." Freud tells us that in this process the libido, instead of reaching out toward another object, withdraws within the ego, where it serves to establish a narcissistic identification with the lost object. The ambivalence toward the object is preserved, if not strengthened, during that identification, and the intra-psychic conflict is then transformed into a conflict between the ego and the superego: the other is being attacked through the self, the self through the other, and by way of this reversal the murderous impulse may be turned into a suicidal wish.[36] In Quentin's story a similar process can be traced from the initial trauma of loss to the final surrender to death.

Melancholia is closely bound up with narcissism. Small wonder that it preys on the self-sealed Quentin. For he loves Caddy as Chateaubriand's René loves Amélie, as Poe's Roderick loves Madeline, as Melville's Pierre loves Isabel, and as, well before these preromantic and romantic lovers, Narcissus, in Pausanias's version of the myth, loved his twin sister Echo: as his feminine double. The loss of Caddy is therefore a terrible wound to his ego, and it induces at once an intense "work of mourning."[37] An identification occurs with the departed sister, internalizing the conflict and turning aggressiveness into masochism. The shift is already indicated in Quentin's fights with Dalton Ames and Gerald Bland: in front of the former, he ends by fainting "like a girl" (186),[38] and his fight with the latter ends just as lamentably. In looking for trouble with men he knows are stronger than himself, Quentin satisfies his quixotic sense of honor but also tries to gratify his need for humiliation and punishment—a need reinforced by the self-hatred that has come to replace his resentment toward Caddy. In the early childhood scenes Quentin was most often the aggressor; once Caddy is felt to be irrevocably lost, his hostility is turned against himself, and henceforth he is both provoker and provoked, accuser and accused, torturer and victim.

A parallel movement of inversion and introjection converts his murderous impulses into a suicidal drive. Probably no one kills himself who has not begun by wishing the death of another. Quentin is no exception: before his death wish is fulfilled in suicide, it is directed at each of the three points of the triangle. Sometimes it is aimed at the rivals: murder threats against Ames ("Ill kill you," 183),[39] and murderous fantasies about Herbert Head on the eve of his marriage to Caddy ("Quentin has shot Herbert he shot his voice through the floor of Caddy's room," 120–21). Sometimes its object is Caddy herself: "I wish you were dead," (180) says Quentin to his sister when she returns from her date with Ames, or again: "Ill kill you do you hear" (181). Yet in the scene with the knife just before this, the death wish has already begun to turn inward. It matters little whether Quentin actually proposed a "suicide pact" to Caddy or not; the point is that he envisioned it, and as we shall see, his death by drowning is indeed a *double* suicide.

"A wedding or a wake?"

Not that he has ever seriously considered killing his sister. At the crucial moment in this scene, he drops the knife (175), unable to carry through his gesture. His dreams of revenge and murder are only dreams, and whenever it is really a matter of action, Quentin falters—or faints. Just as he shrinks from murder, he recoils from incest, contenting himself with the thought and the word of it, afraid of committing the act. Like the three boys encountered on his last day whom he overhears discussing the money they would get by selling a trout they haven't yet caught, he makes "of unreality a possibility, then a probability, then an incontrovertible fact, as people will when their desires become words" (134). Like the boys', his is a world of wishful thinking and talking, of childish fiats, spells, and incantations, in which you can always say "calf rope" (153). Only Quentin's last fantasy is *deadly* serious, but the sole act of which he proves himself capable is precisely one that frees him forever from any obligation. And it is probably not mere chance that makes him choose the most passive form of death: death by water. His suicide, however well prepared, is less an act of will than an entranced surrender.

Still, if Quentin's death is the last resort of impotence, his suicidal urge—in much the same way as his incest wish—results from multiple and contradictory motivations and aims at resolving their conflict. Death completes the destructive work of his relentless superego.[40] In ending his days, Quentin at last expunges his guilt. Water delivers him from his "shadow," from the curse of being burdened with a body and a sex. Dissolving the foulness of the flesh, it returns his bones to the mineral chastity of sand: "And I will look down and see my murmuring bones and the deep water like wind, like a roof of wind, and after a long time they cannot distinguish even bones upon the lonely and inviolate sand" (90–91). In trying to imagine afterlife, Quentin reverts to the water imagery associated with the ritual cleansings of his childhood and adolescence. What he expects from his suicide is a final purgation, washing him of the sin of existence, effacing the very trace of his having been alive. Only then will guilt be absolved, the debt paid, the law restored.

In Quentin's death reveries, water thus renews its promise of oblivion and peace, and yet it also retains to the last its sexual ambiguity. Water, as we have seen, is in Faulkner a trope of desire and drowning a recurrent metaphor for the lures and perils of sex. In Quentin's destiny the metaphor comes true *to the letter*. However solitary, his end evokes a romantic *Liebestod*, a reunion with the forbidden sister in death; his suicide is incest at last consummated. It is not only the consequence of Caddy's marriage but its symbolic counterpart. "Is it a wedding or a wake?" (93): Shreve's question when he sees Quentin dressed up on the morning of his last day could hardly be more to the point.[41] After Caddy lost her virginity, Quentin for the first time thought of rejoining her in death; his dive into the waters of the Charles River is another attempt to regain possession of the sister-naiad of his lost childhood.

And beyond the sister of his childhood his reveries carry him back to the mother of his birth. The lethal waters soon become maternal waters. The river is lost to sea, a sea imagined as an underworld full of caverns and grottoes (102, 129, 200). Everything is eventually soothed and stilled in the cosmic motherhood of Thalassa. Quentin's death marks the ultimate regression: to the quiescence before birth or, better still, to the stasis before life; to the one and to zero; to the all and to nothingness. Eros and Thanatos are the two powers that tore Quentin's life apart. Through his death their reconciliation is at last accomplished.[42]

IV

OF TIME AND THE UNREAL

> Le temps est le *sens* de la vie (*sens*: comme on
> dit le sens d'un cours d'eau, le sens d'une
> phrase, le sens d'une étoffe, le sens de
> l'odorat).
>
> Paul Claudel

Quentin's time

> When the shadow of the sash appeared on the curtains it was between seven
> and eight oclock and then I was in time again, hearing the watch. (86)

Whereas the first section of *The Sound and the Fury* closes with Benjy slipping
peacefully into the unconsciousness of sleep, Quentin wakes up at the opening
of the second. A painful awakening: being reborn with the day, for him, is to
fall once again into the nightmare of time.

Hardly has he woken when Quentin's consciousness redoubles itself as
consciousness of time, of being trapped in time, and this awareness is all the
more acute as the hint of dawn Quentin sees at his window is the dawn of his
last day. The countdown has begun: from now on each hour, each minute will
bring him closer to the moment of death. From the very first sentence of his
monologue, Quentin's time is a time-for-death or even (insofar as his voice
reaches us from beyond life) a time-in-death.

Yet Quentin does not yield at once to the vertigo of imminence. Resorting
again to magic tricks, he tries at first to outwit time. Could he manage to forget
it, he would be saved: his suicide would then lose its *raison d'être*. Time,
however, will not let itself be forgotten:

> I don't suppose anybody ever deliberately listens to a watch or a clock. You dont
> have to. You can be oblivious to the sound for a long while, then in a second of
> ticking it can create in the mind unbroken the long diminishing parade of time
> you didn't hear. (86)

Quentin's demented time-awareness projects itself onto the external world,
temporalizing space, spatializing time. Everything becomes a virtual signal or

metaphor of time; the whole world is transformed into a gigantic gnomon. The shadow of the sash on the curtains in the room where Quentin wakes is the first of these time symbols. Throughout his last day *shadows*,[1] lengthening or shortening according to the position of the sun, remind him of the ineluctable flight of time, and Quentin watches them, fascinated, as though their slow creeping movement were time itself:

> The shadow hadn't quite cleared the stoop. I stopped inside the door, watching the shadow move. It moved almost perceptibly, creeping back inside the door, driving the shadow back into the door. (92)

But it is his own shadow that most intrigues him. His ambiguous attitude toward it recalls all the symbolism traditionally associated with the *double*. Yet contrary to popular lore, according to which a man's shadow is primarily a representation of the immaterial and immortal soul, Quentin interprets it as an image of the loathed body, and he even gives it an anatomy by referring to its belly (110, 114), its bones (109), and its head (153). To him it is first and foremost a haunting reminder of his mortal bodily self. Its darkness partakes of the darkness of sex, sin, and guilt;[2] it stands for the part of himself he is determined to deny and destroy. Hence his persistent hostility toward his dark twin brother: on many occasions he "walks," "treads," or "tramples" on his shadow (109, 110, 115, 120, 128, 137) or attempts to "trick" it (102, 105, 109, 154), and when he looks down at his shadow on the water, he dreams of holding it under and drowning it (102). While providing further evidence of Quentin's self-division and of his need to punish and be punished, these absurd gestures and childish fantasies also "foreshadow" his suicide: the shadow—a fleeting form without substance—is obviously also a symbol of death.[3]

Time, flesh, death, all of Quentin's obsessions intersect in the shadow motif. Among these obsessions time is perhaps not the deepest, and if it is more often and more openly admitted than the others, it is perhaps just because it is more admissible than the others, and also because in the hours preceding his suicide Quentin has come to identify time as his supreme enemy, the nameless and invisible power that has reduced his dreams to naught and hurls him on to death. Yet the obsession has always been with him and can be traced back to his childhood: already at school Quentin had the habit of counting the seconds and minutes to the bell sounding the end of classes (100). In the narrative of his last day, the obsession is expressed by a profusion of explicit temporal references, especially numerous at the beginning and end of his monologue, and by frequent allusions to anything suggesting time, from natural time indicators such as shadows, the position of the sun in the sky, and the angle of its rays, to man-made instruments of time measurement such as church bells, clocks, and watches.

Nearly all of Quentin's senses are alerted to time. Time is not only something measured by the eye and registered by the mind; its law is inscribed in the organic depths of the flesh, in its rhythms and routines: "Eating the business of eating inside of you space too space and time confused Stomach saying noon brain saying eat oclock" (120). And when time stops being visible, its inescapable progress continues to claim Quentin's attention by the regular repetition of bells chiming and, even more insidiously, by the implacable ticking of his watch. Hence his various attempts to occult or silence time. In the morning, on waking, he begins by turning his watch upside down so as not to see the two hands. A little later, he breaks its crystal and twists off the hands:

> I went to the dresser and took up the watch, with the face still down. I tapped the crystal on the corner of the dresser and caught the fragments of glass in my hand and put them into the ashtray and twisted the hands off and put them in the tray. The watch ticked on. I turned the face up, the blank dial with little wheels clicking and clicking behind it, not knowing any better. (91)

The symbolic significance of Quentin's gesture is obvious enough, and just as manifest is the irony of the scene: what it reveals is not only Quentin's refusal of time but the utter futility of his refusal. For in breaking his watch Quentin hurts no one but himself, and thereafter, throughout the day, the ticking goes on, pursuing him to the very end.

There is as much irony in the ensuing scene: Quentin's visit to the jeweler's shop. He walks past its window at first, feigning not to notice it ("I looked away in time," 94); then, as he sees a clock "high up in the sun" (94), he becomes aware of time again, turns back and enters the shop on the pretext of showing the craftsman his broken watch. But what he really wants to know is whether "any of those watches in the window are right" (95). The negative answer finally given him by the perplexed jeweler[4] is precisely the one he hoped for: if each of the watches tells a different time and none of them is correct, the case of their deception is proven. A last look at the window as he leaves confirms Quentin's conviction of their falseness:

> There were about a dozen watches in the window, a dozen different hours and each with the same assertive and contradictory assurance that mine had, without any hands at all. Contradicting one another. I could hear mine, ticking away inside my pocket, even though nobody could see it, even though it could tell nothing if anyone could. (96)

Immediately afterward Quentin recalls his father's words:

> Father said clocks slay time. He said time is dead as long as it is being clicked off by little wheels; only when the clock stops does time come to life. (97)

These reflections of Mr. Compson's refer to a polarity underlying the entire second section and brought into evidence by Faulkner's very technique: the seemingly irreducible opposition between clock time and the time of consciousness and sensibility—what Sartre called "the time of the heart."[5] The former is a contrivance of man's intelligence, a "symptom of mind-function" (87), a quantitative concept abstracted from reality; the latter constitutes the dense and dynamic medium of our psychic experience. This distinction between spatialized, mechanized, objective time and subjective duration is of course strongly reminiscent of Bergsonism.[6] In Quentin's case, however, there is no ontological benefit in shifting from one to the other, no access to some "truer" dimension of being. Faulkner's rendering of his character's predicament strikes us as "truer" in that it manages to suggest the achronological quality of inner experience, yet for the character himself the immersion in "real" time only means further disarray and dislocation. Time does "come to life" for him, but only to kill him.

Moreover, Mr. Compson's philosophy is not Faulkner's. Rather than a fictional illustration of a preconceived theory of temporality, as Sartre contended, Quentin's monologue is a conjectural representation of a haunted mind, and what it points to is not so much a "metaphysic" as a pathology of time.[7] Isn't neurosis also a failure to come to terms with temporal existence, resulting from a fixation to the past which prevents adjustment to the present and mortgages the future? Quentin's exacerbated chronophobia is above all an index of his immaturity and confusion, as is the utter disconnectedness of his inner time.

Dispersal and sinking

No one has described more judiciously than Sartre this dismantled, exploded time. Only, he forgets to specify that the *present* he analyzes is Quentin's, not Faulkner's:

> One present, emerging from the unknown, drives out another present. It is like a sum that we compute again and again: "And . . . and . . . and then." Like Dos Passos, but with greater subtlety, Faulkner makes his story a matter of addition. Even when the characters are aware of them, the actions, when they emerge in the present, burst into scattered fragments.[8]

One of the most arresting features of this present is indeed the way in which it crumbles away, the jerky movement of its *dispersal*. Bergsonian river metaphors will hardly do here: nothing suggests the continuous flow and felt direction of a *durée*. Quentin's present is a line, but a dotted one. Moments swirl up out of an opaque emptiness and vanish again, following one another without merging into a continuity. On the linguistic level, this disjointedness is reflected, as Sartre again notes (taking the scene of the broken watch as an example), in the splitting up of Quentin's discourse into a multiplicity of short, simple clauses, and the *ands* supposed to connect them rather operate as disconnectors, so that each statement seems to be closed in on itself and large portions of Quentin's narrative produce an uncanny staccato effect.

The other characteristic of Quentin's present is what Sartre aptly calls its *sinking:*[9] no sooner has it surged up than each moment sinks like a stone into the past; no sooner does it recede than it congeals. Hence the self-contradictory sense of time endlessly marking time, of time standing still: "Beneath the sag of the buggy the hooves neatly rapid like the motions of a lady doing embroidery, diminishing without progress like a figure on a treadmill being drawn rapidly offstage" (142). It is true that such paradoxical suggestions of dynamic stasis are quite frequent in Faulkner's novels, but in Quentin's monologue arrested time seems to be the very medium of experience. Constantly oscillating between evanescence and solidification, his present is in fact no present at all. Always a latecomer, his consciousness never adheres to the *now;* it perceives it as a flickering shadow and registers it distractedly. Quentin moves through the present like a sleepwalker; he does not live in it, turned as he is toward the past. To him the present comes to life only when it is dead. And while eating up the present, the past also rules out any projection into the future. Instead of being a possibility, Quentin's death takes on even before it happens the incontrovertible finality of a *fait accompli.*

The enchantments of memory

Present, past, future are apprehended indiscriminately by way of *memory,* and memory bewitches all time into a turbulent stasis. It invades the whole mind and becomes its exclusive function. Much like Benjy, Quentin does not *have* a memory; to a large extent, he *is* his memory. So much so that he tends to forget the pastness of the past, and the hallucinatory reactivation of memory traces sometimes totally obliterates the present moment. Consider, for instance, his ludicrous fight with Gerald Bland: the scene is recounted not by Quentin but by his friend Shreve; Quentin no longer knows why he tried to hit Bland (190); he seems to emerge from the fight as from a confused bad dream, and everything indicates that he is scarcely conscious of what has happened to him. But we learn later that before the incident Bland had boasted about all his girls, and before striking him Quentin had asked: "Did you ever have a sister? did you?" (190). A year earlier Dalton Ames had likewise offended feminine honor, and Quentin had then asked exactly the same question (183). Without being aware of it, Quentin has identified Bland with his sister's first lover, and this identification has sufficed to tip the present into the past. While being beaten up, Quentin relives a scene of his past, and the drubbing he is given by Bland revives once again the humiliating experience of his utter helplessness before his rivals.

Quentin's monologue reads like a palimpsest. Almost every moment of his life opens, backward and/or forward, onto other moments resembling it. The similarity may be due to the return of an earlier situation (as in the fight with Bland and all the triangular scenes) or to the reappearance of an identical background (all the water scenes). It is suggested even more subtly through the recurrence of identical motifs in different spatio-temporal contexts. Thus the equation of the Quentin-Bland scene with the Quentin-Ames scene is surreptitiously prepared by the association bird–water–broken sunlight[10] used in the narrative of Quentin's walk along the river with the little Italian girl:

> There was a bird somewhere in the woods, beyond the broken and infrequent slanting of sunlight. (155)

> The bird whistled again, invisible, a sound meaningless and profound, inflexionless, ceasing as though cut off with the blow of a knife, and again, and that sense of water swift and peaceful above secret places, felt, not seen not heard. (156)

> I looked off into the trees where the afternoon slanted, thinking of afternoon and of the bird and the boys in swimming. (168–69)

The same motif reemerges in the remembered scenes with Ames and Caddy:

> behind him the sun slanted and a bird singing somewhere beyond the sun. (184)

> I heard the bird again and the water. (184, 185)

> her face looked off into the trees where the sun slanted and where the bird. (187)

All these echoes and cross-references induce a disturbing sense of *déjà vu*: we are caught with Quentin in a spellbinding set of specular images in which things and events are perpetually duplicated through the giddy interplay of reflections. For Quentin the present is but a mirror held up to the shadows of the past, a theater of ghosts where nothing is ever first, where nothing ever begins. All Quentin's actions are re-beginnings, compulsive, Sisyphuslike repetitions of an ineffaceable past, and the only possible change he can envision is a gradual degradation in the dreary round of sameness.

The greater the pressure of this memory-ridden time, the emptier Quentin's world. For if the past weighs on the present and shapes it inexorably in its image, it is hardly more real to him. In much the same way as Benjy, he seems to hover "between" the present and the past, that is, in the similarity between the two. Unlike the characters of Joyce and Virginia Woolf, Quentin experiences no epiphany, no "moment of being." Contrary to Proust's world, there is here neither time lost nor time recaptured. The past haunts the present, it never comes to inhabit it. In Proust, memory can be a source of illumination; remembering is far more than a moment of the past relived: "something which, common to both past and present, is much more essential than either of them"[11] crystallizes in the mind, touching off a trans-temporal experience, an ecstasy that allows the self, the "true" self, to rise above the contingency of mere duration and to recognize itself in the plenitude and permanence of its identity. To Quentin there is no such transcendence of time within time; for him, the encounter of present and past, instead of achieving a happy fusion, can only result in agonizing confusion. And in this confusion there is nothing to sustain a stable sense of selfhood. Quentin is so irretrievably lost in it, so racked between past and present that he no longer knows whether he is or has been. *"Non fui. Sum. Fui. Non sum"* (199): coming almost at the close of his monologue, these Latin words epitomize his total failure to reconcile becoming and being, time and identity. Ironically, Quentin then turns at last to the future, the future he had so far chosen to ignore. But the only future he considers is a nonfuture, a simple promise of extinction: "And then I'll not be. The peacefullest words. Peacefullest words" (199).

Since he can neither be himself in time nor escape alive out of time, Quentin seeks refuge in death. But even as he prepares to relinquish the world of the living, he has already begun to die to it or—to be more faithful to the subjective quality of his experience—the world has already begun to die to him. Space has become a place of exile and restless wandering, secretly conquered by *emptiness*:

> The houses all seemed empty. Not a soul in sight. A sort of breathlessness that empty houses have. Yet they couldnt all be empty. (152)

> The road curved on, empty. (152)

> The entrance to the lane was empty. (153)

> The road went on, still and empty, the sun slanting more and more. (155)

Quentin is a lonely traveler in a deserted space whose very atmosphere becomes rarefied: "Even sound seemed to fail in this air, like the air was worn out with carrying sounds so long" (130). In Quentin's disenchanted gaze, the New England décor of his last day shrivels to a "waste land," stirring up by contrast nostalgic recollections of the generous summers of his home country:

> Only our country was not like this country. There was something about just walking through it. A kind of still and violent fecundity that satisfied even bread-hunger like. Flowing around you, not brooding and nursing every niggard stone. Like it were put to makeshift for enough green to go around among the trees and even the blue of distance not that rich chimaera. (129)

In retrospect, the South has come to stand for the lost Eden, the motherland of plenty. New England, on the other hand, reflects Quentin's present state of starvation. Thin colors, thin sounds, thin air, a landscape drained of all vigor—everything bespeaks a world on the verge of exhaustion. Becoming their own replicas, depthless and weightless, things look like "ghosts in broad day" (102). Halfway between life and death, Quentin wanders in a spectral space; even before he left his home country for Harvard, his world had dissolved into a gray limbo of mocking shadows:

> I seemed to be lying neither asleep nor awake looking down a long corridor of gray halflight where all stable things had become shadowy paradoxical all I had done shadows all I had felt suffered taking visible form antic and perverse mocking without relevance inherent themselves with the denial of the significance they should have affirmed thinking I was I was not who was not was not who. (194–95)

As much as through shadow imagery this process of derealization is suggested through the motif of the *mirror*.[12] In Benjy's section, the mirror functions as a beneficent object, associated with Caddy's presence, with the brightness of fire and the safety of an orderly world: "refuge unfailing in which conflict tempered silenced reconciled" (195). In the second section its symbolic meaning is reversed: mirrors are no longer linked with light and fire but with darkness and water, and instead of giving shelter, they become disquieting presences, partaking like shadows of the uncanny nature of the double. In Quentin's memory, the mirror is an emblem of Caddy's departure (87, 92); in his present experience, it stands as a symbol of his wounded narcissism. In the course of his comings and goings on his last day, he looks several times at his reflection: in the morning he stares at his shadow in the river (102); after his fight with Bland, he tries to look at his face in a basin of water (187); later, in the trolley car on the way home, he catches sight of his reflection in a window (193); and before committing suicide he looks at himself in the mirror of his dormitory room for the last time (205).[13] Except in the last instance, all Quentin's mirrors are unstable ones: the quivering surface of water or a windowpane reflecting his face "on the rushing darkness" (197)—liquid mirrors, mirrors silvered with night, reducing everything to a mere flicker of appearances. They only heighten Quentin's sense of unrest and impermanence: in much the same way as his shadow, his mirror image stands for self-division and portends imminent destruction. In his reflection he sees himself as other—unreal, imaginary, dead. "Isn't looking at oneself in a mirror thinking of death?" Paul Valéry asks.[14] The image of his body which Quentin glances at is indeed nothing but the reflection of a reprieved corpse.

Instability, fragmentation, unreality: these are also, in Quentin's quasi-posthumous perception of the world, the essential attributes of *light*. Caught in the ever-renewed interplay of shadows and reflections, light is ceaselessly divided and refracted, scattering through space in myriads of luminous atoms: trees lean over the wall "sprayed with sunlight" (129); the shade of trees is "dappled" (137, 139); "the river [glints] beyond things in sort of swooping glints" (127), and Quentin sees "the last light supine and tranquil upon tideflats, like pieces of broken mirror" (195). Light resembles a swarming of ants: "Sunlight slid patchily across his walking shoulders, glinting along the pole like yellow ants" (140). Or it is held in quivering suspension like a butterfly: "lights began in the pale clear air, trembling a little like butterflies hovering a long way off"

(195). And by a sudden reversal of the simile, "yellow butterflies flickered along the shade like flecks of sun" (140; see also 161).

One is almost tempted to read these suggestive evocations of light and shade as a passing tribute to the beauty of the natural world—Quentin's farewell to the sun before his descent into darkness. The profusion of reflections and refractions, glints and glimmers reminds one at times of the effervescent luminosity of impressionist painting. Yet the multiplying omens of death hardly allow the enchantment to work. The movement of light here is not fluid expansion so much as infinite dispersal, and nothing better defines the space of its reverberation than the image of the *broken* mirror (195). This sense of brokenness combines with Quentin's sharp sensitivity to obliquity or declivity—a spatial cognate, as it were, to the temporal notion of decline: most of Quentin's descriptions include allusions to oblique and downward movements, and obliquity also characterizes the direction of light, often referred to as "slanting" (138, 140, 155). The sun always sheds its light at an angle, and the slant of its beams measures for Quentin the advance and decline of the day, reminding him like the hands of his watch of the irreversible passing of time and the ineluctable approach of death.

The sense of an ending increases as the light of day decreases into *twilight*.[15] As in *As I Lay Dying*, human death is associated with the dying of the day—an association emphasized by Quentin's transferring the waning of light to himself: "As I descended the light dwindled slowly, yet at the same time without altering its quality, as if I and not light were changing, decreasing, though even when the road ran into trees you could have read a newspaper" (193). As though he had already reached the threshold of death, Quentin then feels the burden of time getting lighter: "I could see the twilight again, that quality of light as if time really had stopped for a while, with the sun hanging just under the horizon" (193). The closeness of the end is equally hinted at through the association of twilight and water: "the road going on under the twilight, into twilight and the sense of water peaceful and swift beyond" (193–94). The onset of night and the proximity of water both portend death. But for Quentin they are also reminders of the past, stirring the memory of other scenes connected with grayness and wetness: it was in the same "gray light" (172, 177, 178) that he met his sister at the branch, after finding out about her affair with Ames; it was also in the abetting shadows of twilight that Caddy joined her lovers. Quentin's twin obsessions thus merge one last time, and again he comes to brood on what has become the major symbol of his torment, the odor of honeysuckle:

> When it bloomed in the spring and it rained the smell was everywhere you didnt notice it so much at other times but when it rained the smell began to come into the house at twilight either it would rain more at twilight or there was something in the light itself but it always smelled strongest then until I would lie in bed thinking when will it stop when will it stop. (194)

Shadows and reflections, the flickerings of daylight and the uncertainties of twilight—all these images of instability and impermanence are signs of a world adrift. They symbolize for Quentin the ceaseless movement of becoming, of flux and change, and to him all changes are changes for the worse and all becoming is but a hemorrhage of being.

Reverberating through the final pages of his monologue, *temporary*, "the saddest word of all" (205), points accusingly to the ultimate cause of Quentin's tragedy: time, the universal destroyer, the irresistible agent of defeat and death. His individual experience is thus virtually raised to broader significance; Mr. Compson's rhetoric, at any rate, tends to present the pathetic destiny of the young suicide as an extreme exemplification of our common condition. The father articulates in abstract terms what the son suggests through a chaos of broken images and fragmented memories, namely that man's curse is to be shackled to time: "Father said a man is the sum of his misfortunes. One day you'd think misfortune would get tired, but then time is your misfortune Father said" (119). Time means sundering. It removes us ever further from the presumed plenitude of the origin and brings us ever closer to death. And indefatigably it secretes in us that other form of death, forgetfulness: "Father said That's sad too, people cannot do anything that dreadful they cannot do anything very dreadful at all they cannot even remember tomorrow what seemed dreadful today" (90). It dispossesses us of our memories, dulls and degrades our affections, and wears away even our sorrows:

> it is hard believing to think that a love or a sorrow is a bond purchased without design and which matures willynilly and is recalled without warning to be replaced by whatever issue the gods happen to be floating at the time no you will not do that until you come to believe that even she was not quite worth despair. (204)

Mr. Compson's reflections on time invite us to consider his despair and suicide from a philosophical as well as a psychological perspective. Yet the old drunkard's aphorisms no more express Faulkner's convictions than they provide the key to Quentin's suicide. It is true that Quentin is alarmed at the prospect of losing even his sense of loss, of being robbed of his very despair, and that he clings to it as if its sheer intensity were a protection against nothingness. However, even admitting that his death is *also* a gesture of protest against an absurd world, Quentin dies above all because of his inner weakness, and nothing in his monologue allows us to assume that at the point of death his blind confusion has yielded to tragic lucidity. Quentin *lives* the absurd in the narcissistic vertigo of his obsessions and fantasies; to the end he lacks the detachment which would convert his experience into awareness and so make his suicide a death *against* the absurd. Quentin's is not a philosophical suicide but the predictable end of his long journey into night.

The crux of the matter in the second section is not time; it is Quentin's troubled relationship to time. And as if to belie his failure to live and to invalidate Mr. Compson's a priori rationalizations of it, the monologue itself ironically intimates the possibility of different relationships. One of these is hinted at through the image of the *trout*, whose shadow Quentin watches in the water:

> I could not see the bottom, but I could see a long way into the motion of the water before the eye gave out, and then I saw a shadow hanging like a fat arrow stemming into the current. . . . The arrow increased without motion, then in a quick swirl the trout lipped a fly beneath the surface with that sort of gigantic delicacy of an elephant picking up a peanut. The fading vortex drifted away down stream and then I saw the arrow again, nose into the current, wavering delicately to the motion of the water above which the May flies slanted and poised. . . . The trout hung, delicate and motionless among the wavering shadows. (133–34)

Conjoining stability and suppleness, gravity and grace, the trout stands for a mode of being in which self-possession does not preclude adjustment to a changing environment. The fish achieves balance in the vortex, immobility in motion, eternity in time. Just as Ben, the Bear in *Go Down, Moses*, has always escaped the hunters, the old trout has defied all the fishermen in the area for over twenty-five years (134). Like Ben, the "great ancestor" of the wilderness, it symbolizes endurance, and it is perhaps because it represents to Quentin himself his not yet totally extinguished desire to live on that he asks the three boys to leave "that old fellow" alone (137).[16] It is significant, though, that in his thoughts (the interpolated italicized passage in the description of the trout) this image of life is instantly reversed into a vision of death: the liquid shadow of the fish becomes in his reverie a flickering flame, water turns to fire, the living depths of the river are replaced by the abyss of hell where Quentin imagines himself burning eternally with Caddy (133). Quentin fails to understand the parable of the trout; he can conceive of no immobility other than death.

The obvious parallel to the fish suspended in the water is the bird poised in the air: "in a break in the wall I saw a glint of water and two masts, and a gull motionless in midair, like on an invisible wire between the masts . . ." (101). As the aerial counterpart of the trout, the *gull* is another model of delicate poise and dynamic immobility. Yet its meaning for Quentin is more ambiguous. The gull seems to hover above the flux of time: "I could hear my watch and the train dying away, as though it were running through another month or another summer somewhere, rushing away under the poised gull and all things rushing" (138). But the association of its outspread wings with the hands of a clock turns it into yet another time symbol: "The hands were extended, slightly off the horizontal at a faint angle, like a gull tilting into the wind" (97). Moreover, the gulls are twice described as if they were hanging in space on "invisible wires" (102, 119). Is this to suggest that their freedom is only a deceptive appearance? The image is actually one of *hampered* flight, reflecting Quentin's desperate wish for escape but also its frustration.

"Apotheosis"

In contrast to earth and water, the air comes to represent for Quentin (as for many other Faulkner heroes) the element par excellence of the immaterial, the boundless, the timeless. Earth and water are the emblems of human finiteness; the air stands for the infinite. Hence the positive valuations given in Quentin's dualistic imagination to ascent and flight: to fly is to be free of earth's gravity, to conquer both flesh and time.[17] Nowhere is this striving for transcendence more eloquently expressed than in Quentin's envious and admiring vision of Gerald Bland rowing:

> all things rushing. Except Gerald. He would be sort of grand too, pulling in lonely state across the noon, rowing himself right out of noon, up the long bright air like an apotheosis, mounting into a drowsing infinity where only he and the gull, the one terrifically motionless, the other in a steady and measured pull and recover that partook of inertia itself, the world punily beneath their shadows on the sun. (138)

In contrast to the negative imagery of descent, dispersal, and darkness, we find here the evocation of a solitary and glorious ascent toward the ethereal regions of infinity. The nightmare of time ("all things rushing") and the nausea of matter give way suddenly to a bright dream of escape out of the "puny" world. And it is of course not fortuitous that the fulfillment of this sun dream is granted not to Quentin but to the "royal" son/sun figure of Bland.[18] The heroic transfiguration which the latter embodies in this scene is clearly not for him. Still, as his father suggests in commenting upon his projected suicide, Quentin too is thinking of an "apotheosis":

> you are not thinking of finitude you are contemplating an apotheosis in which a temporary state of mind will become symmetrical above the flesh and aware both of itself and of the flesh it will not quite discard you will not even be dead. (203)

Lacking the energy to match his dream of "apotheosis" in heroic self-immolation, Quentin dies as lamentably as he lived. But he too seeks in death a form of immortalization, and one of the paradoxes of his suicide is that self-destruction becomes a way to self-aggrandizement. For what the suicide is meant to accomplish is the expunction of the abhorred carnal self, and it is in order to get rid forever of his body that Quentin takes care to weight it with two flatirons before diving into the Charles River. Yet in his imaginations of death the destruction of the body is no total annihilation. In the passage already quoted in which he speculates upon his posthumous destiny and evokes his bones at the bottom of the sea, he puts himself in the position of a beholder: "I will look down and see my murmuring bones . . ." (90). Surviving his own death as a disembodied I/eye, Quentin projects himself into afterdeath to be witness to his own dissolution; seeing himself dead, he will not be dead altogether. What he actually expects from his suicide is not at all a state of not-being but rather an *ek-stasis*, that is, literally, a standing outside and beyond his self—without any self-loss.

A divided self, a double death.[19] In his suicide Quentin is once again split into two distinct halves: while the gross corporal self is given over to nothingness without any regrets, the ideal self, having managed to get rid at last of its cumbersome twin brother, is expected to gain full access to the perfect immobility of the timeless. This ultimate scission, though, by no means diminishes the magic virtues and curing powers which Quentin attributes to his suicide. As his father rightly notes, the death he is seeking does not even imply a complete renouncement of the flesh nor a total abrogation of time. Quentin's "apotheosis" is a compromise with eternity: flesh restored to innocence rather than immolated; time arrested rather than abolished; the ego unburdened and exalted rather than destroyed.

This miraculous resolution of all contradictions is of course purely *imaginary*: Quentin's suicide is the ending of an elaborate play performed from first to last in a mock theater, among shadows and reflections, and staged by a Narcissus enthralled by his own image. The passage through the looking glass is eventually achieved by drowning: a reentry into the waters of death/birth, a return of self to self, blotting out all otherness and erasing all difference. But by *whom* is the mirror traversed? An unanswerable question. Quentin tries to make the limits of his ego coincide with the absolute limit of death; he would cross the boundary and pass to the *other* side without ceasing to be himself. It cannot be done. Identity is no more found in death than it was in life. Quentin's rapport with death is impossible; his suicide turns out to be a fool's bargain.

For the protagonist of Tolstoy's story "The Death of Ivan Illyich," the prospect of death means first of all a return to the solitude of the self, but it also reveals to him his existence as irremediably his own: Ivan comes to acknowledge time and to accept death, taking it into himself as the most intimate of possibilities, and is therefore allowed to salvage his banal life from pretense and absurdity before he dies. For Quentin, on the other hand, death is never a possibility but a faked certitude. He keeps playing at hide and seek with himself to the very end, and his game with life and death is throughout a double game. Quentin's encounter with death is in fact nothing more than an ultimate lure, the final mirage before the mirror is shattered. The last of his fictions.

Quentin's story can be read as an ironic version of the familiar journey of the romantic ego: from descent into a private hell to glorious resurrection, from self-loss to self-aggrandizement. Goethe's Werther, Chateaubriand's René, Byron's Manfred, Shelley's Prometheus, and a host of lesser figures at once come to mind. There is of course nothing heroic about Quentin, but his tortured egotism, his alienation from the actual world, and his yearning for the perfection of absolutes are assuredly romantic traits. Like Horace Benbow, Gail Hightower, and Ike McCaslin, he is longing for the stasis and permanence enjoyed by the lovers on Keats's urn. And like his spiritual cousins, he belongs with Faulkner's potential artist or poet figures.[20]

As such he is also, as Faulkner himself came to admit, a self-projection of the author: "Ishmael is the witness in *Moby Dick* as I am Quentin in *The Sound and the Fury.*"[21] Created out of the depths of the novelist's private experience, Quentin is undeniably the most complex portrait of the artist as a young man, and his haunted vision, his anguish and suffering are at the novel's very center. Yet even though Faulkner called him "that bitter prophet and inflexible corruptless judge of what he considered the family's honor and its doom,"[22] Quentin hardly qualifies for the role of "moral agent."[23] Not simply because he is too weak to take significant action, nor because his despair is rooted in neurosis, but because there is nothing behind his moralistic poses and family pieties but plain narcissism. Faulkner himself points out that Quentin is "incapable of love"[24]: there could be no more damning comment. No doubt he is "a sensitive young man," yet seldom has "the sensitive young man" been more thoroughly demystified; no doubt he is a romantic, but in the last resort his romanticism comes down to glorified infantilism. Rip off the noble mask, and you will find Benjy's whining baby face. For all the autobiographical elements that went into the character, Faulkner holds him at a distance and subjects his loveless, life-denying egocentricity to ruthless exposure. What is perhaps most admirable about Quentin's monologue is a unique combination of empathy and critical detachment. For in exposing Quentin's blindness, Faulkner gives the full measure of his own insight and of the extraordinary self-knowledge he must have achieved by the time he wrote *The Sound and the Fury.*

Quentin's suicide in the novel stands for the sacrificial immolation of the writer's alter ego on the scene of writing, and both deaths are responses to death, symbolic acts intended to repair loss and to restore the lost object. Yet whereas Quentin's grief turns to the dry agony of despair and ends in suicide, Faulkner's is converted into the inspired melancholy of art. Quentin had to die of his fictions to allow another fiction to be born.

V

THE POISON OF RESENTMENT

> The petit-bourgeois is the man who has
> preferred himself to all else.
>
> Maxim Gorki

"What I say"

Once a bitch always a bitch, what I say. I says you're lucky if her playing out of school is all that worries you. I says she ought to be down there in that kitchen right now, instead of up there in her room, gobbing paint on her face and waiting for six niggers that cant even stand up out of a chair unless they've got a pan full of bread and meat to balance them, to fix breakfast for her. . . . (206)

In its sarcastic bluntness the opening paragraph of Jason's monologue signals straightaway the distance separating the third section from the previous two. Nothing here is like Benjy's incoherent babble or Quentin's tortuous reveries and reminiscences. Another voice is heard now, harsh, petulant, sardonic; a hysterically self-assertive *speaking* voice. From the interior monologue, with the unpredictable meanderings of its private logic, we switch to the plainer and louder language of the dramatic soliloquy; despite intermittent use of associative patterns, Jason's section owes much more to the vernacular tradition of oral narrative than to the Joycean "stream-of-consciousness."[1] At times it is as though one overheard the unpremeditated talk of someone thinking aloud; more often it is as if one read the verbatim transcript of an impromptu oral account. Unlike Benjy's "trying to say" and Quentin's self-absorbed musings, Jason's discourse at once emphasizes the narrator's awareness of himself in the very act of speaking (through the countless interpolated *inquits:* "I say(s)," "like I say," "what I say") and suggests time and again the silent complicity of a listening *you*, often explicitly referred to in the text, who at any time could become an interlocutor.[2] For all its self-consuming fury, or rather because of it, the rhetoric of Jason's monologue points to an eagerness to communicate, a desire to win over his implied audience which has no parallels in Quentin's or Benjy's section.

What is more, with Jason the novel reverts to its traditional narrative function. A story gets told, and Jason assumes the role of storyteller with almost histrionic glee. As a consequence, there are no longer any serious barriers to our understanding: events usually follow one another in chronological sequence, and even when Jason flashes back to earlier moments, we are hardly likely to get lost.[3] Though he is by no means a reliable narrator, the narrative thus gains clarity and coherence, many gaps in the reader's information are filled in, and the fragments of the Compson story collected in the previous sections begin at last to fall into an intelligible pattern.

Similarly, traditional models reassert themselves in the characterization of the narrator-protagonist. Jason is one of Faulkner's most superb creations, and he is surely a far more complex character than has been generally acknowledged. Yet he acts above all as the comic villain of the piece, and in this role he turns out to be an original combination of several standard types supplied by tradition. With the third section, *The Sound and the Fury* moves into the vicinity of folk comedy—a vein Faulkner was to explore more fully in *As I Lay Dying*, the Snopes trilogy, and *The Reivers*. In his racy colloquial language as well as in his antisocial attitudes, Jason reminds one of the vernacular figures created by the humorists of the Old Southwest. His lineage can be traced back to Simon Suggs and Sut Lovingood,[4] characters whose pungent wit and brutal candor are close to his and who are his peers in cruelty and meanness. Moreover, insofar as his mental and emotional life is reduced to a small set of stock responses, Jason also presents affinities with "humor" in the sense defined by Ben Jonson and most richly illustrated in fiction by Dickens. And lastly one may see him as a distant country cousin of the great railers and misanthropes of Western literature—Homer's Thersites in the *Iliad*, Shakespeare's Timon and the many malcontents of Elizabethan drama, Molière's Alceste, the Gulliver of the last voyage, the spiteful hero of Dostoevski's *Notes from Underground*.[5] To compare Jason to these imposing figures is to do him perhaps too much honor, yet like them he is in his own petty provincial way an implacable man-hater, and in like fashion, too, he takes the role of the satirist,[6] venting his rancor in floods of invective and sarcasm and exposing human folly with merciless eloquence.

Jason equally resembles these famous railers in being both agent and target of the satirical thrust. His whole monologue may be read as a brilliant variation on the classical theme of the satirist satirized.[7] Faulkner's irony here kills two birds with one stone: it works at Jason's expense, since his speech clearly shows him to be a rogue and a fool, but at the same time it operates through his agency at the expense of the other Compsons, reducing the drama of their downfall to the ludicrous proportions of a madhouse chronicle:

> I haven't got much pride, I cant afford it with a kitchen full of niggers to feed and robbing the state asylum of its star freshman. Blood, I says, governors and generals. It's a damn good thing we never had any kings and presidents; we'd all be down there at Jackson chasing butterflies. (265)

Jason has throughout a sharp eye for the incongruous and the grotesque, and as satirist he is all the more redoubtable because Faulkner—the satirist behind the scenes—lends him his own talents for the role. Described without nuance, stripped of everything that might earn them understanding or pity, the protagonists of the family drama now become the typecast actors of a burlesque Southern melodrama halfway between Caldwell and Tennessee Williams: alcoholics for a father and an uncle, a whining hypochondriac for a mother, a shameless trollop for a niece, and a drooling idiot for a brother, such are the *dramatis personae* in section 3. Small wonder that the tale of their mishaps, including Jason's own, turns to Gothic farce.

All these alterations induce a different relationship between reader and narrator. In Quentin's monologue our first response is identification, and it is only on second thought that we come to view the character critically; with Jason, on the contrary, the possibility of identification is undercut by the novelist's irony. The distance between Jason and all those he derides is paralleled by the distance of revulsion separating Jason from the author. To Faulkner, Jason represented, in his own words, "complete evil," and in the same interview he added: "He's the most vicious character in my opinion I ever thought of."[8] Jason, however, is a very disturbing villain, and as John Longley notes, "he is disturbing because we all know he lurks in us."[9] Our response to him is therefore bound to be ambivalent: to the extent that he is held up to ridicule and contempt, identification with him is deflected toward a sense of comic exhilaration arising from the conviction of our moral superiority; we side with Faulkner against Jason or, as Wayne C. Booth puts it, "we take delight in communion, and even in deep collusion, with the author behind Jason's back."[10] Yet Jason cannot be laughed off like a harmless clown, for his speech possesses at times an almost demonic power of persuasion and his mordant wit is hard to resist. This is not to say that we laugh with him (Jason himself is incapable of true laughter), but in reenacting his monologue we cannot help sneering and snickering with him, and insofar as he voices and acts out our own aggressive emotions, he becomes a magnified mirror image of our own rancorous selves.[11]

In this connection it may be tempting to speculate upon the relationship between Jason and his creator. Apparently, the character stands for everything Faulkner abhorred. Yet identification and distancing were at play here just as they were in the second section. To interpret Quentin in merely biographical terms is to yield to romantic fallacy. But it would be quite as wrong to believe that Jason is a grotesque figure projected in cool satirical detachment. That he was removed from Faulkner by the whole range of the novelist's irony is obvious enough. Yet his presence in the book is without any doubt as immediately and as vividly felt as Quentin's; perhaps it is even more compelling in the raw power of its voluble fury. Could it be so compelling, so hallucinatingly "real," if Jason were not somehow related to the deeper springs of Faulkner's creation?

When asked about *The Sound and the Fury* in 1953, Mrs. Maud Falkner, the novelist's mother, made the following comment: "Now, Jason in *The Sound and the Fury*—he talks just like my husband did. My husband had a hardware store uptown at one time. His way of talking was just like Jason's, same words and same style. All those 'you know's.' He also had an old 'nigrah,' named Jobus, just like the character Job in the story. He was always after Jobus for not working hard enough, just like in the story."[12] If we are to believe this testimony, the sources for Jason are not far to seek, and the possibility that he has been partly modeled on Murry C. Falkner and that his voice is quite literally the voice of the father is indeed an intriguing one. One could of course press the point and read the third section as an oedipal settling of accounts. Yet if it was a literary parricide, it was also an act of identification, and in the father the son probably recognized another of his potential selves.

Just as there was a Stavrogin or a Smerdyakov in Dostoevsky, there must have been a Jason in Faulkner. But my concern here is not to find the counterparts of his characters in real life nor even to determine how the characters are related to the ambiguities and complexities of the novelist's psyche, but rather to apprehend them from within the work itself, to see how they relate to one another, and how they function within the thematic structure.

"Blood is blood"

Thematically there is no major break between section 3 and the preceding sections. But the treatment of themes is set in a very different key and it almost looks as if they had been turned inside out. Thus in Jason's monologue, the brother-sister relationship, though hardly less central than in Benjy's or Quentin's, changes its sign from plus to minus: what Jason feels for Caddy is hatred, a hatred as intense and uncontrollable as Benjy's love or Quentin's love-hate. To him as to them she is a rankling memory; for him as for them she has been the instrument of disaster. Not that he misses his sister as his brothers do, but the loss he has suffered is directly related to her: Herbert Head, Caddy's fiancé, had promised him a job in a bank—a promise broken because of her misconduct. The child she had to leave him as a hostage has therefore become "the symbol of the lost job itself" (355), and it is on his niece that he will take out his hatred. What sets Jason apart is essentially his response to loss: Benjy howls in blind protest; Quentin commits suicide; Jason, on the contrary, nurses his rancor and is determined to take revenge.

But blood will tell. "Because like I say blood is blood and you cant get around it" (280): when Jason invokes the family heritage to account for his niece's promiscuity, he is unaware of how much his statement also applies to him. In his monologue he poses as the only sane and sensible man in a world of fools and lunatics and prides himself on his worldly wisdom and his capacity to cope with reality. He believes and would have us believe that he has nothing in common with the other Compsons. This belief, however, is given the lie by his behavior and is just one of his many delusions about himself. In a sense, it is true, Jason is indeed an outsider and has been one since his early childhood. His mother considers him a true Bascomb (208, 225, 230) and seemingly cherishes him as her only child. Not unlike Jewel, Addie Bundren's favorite son in *As I Lay Dying*, Jason has been deeply marked by his mother's preferential treatment, but as Caroline Compson is incapable of loving anyone except herself, he has been little more than a pawn in the destructive game she has been playing with the family. All she has accomplished is to mold Jason in her likeness, and by not allowing him to think of himself as a Compson, she has been quite successful, too, in alienating him from his father, his brothers, and his sister. Of her four children he is undeniably the one most like her in his mean-spirited egoism, his imperturbable smugness, and his petit-bourgeois concern for propriety. On closer examination, however, it becomes clear that he has inherited as much from his father as from his mother. Like Quentin and probably more than Quentin, Jason, in his childhood, had expected his father to behave like a father and was deeply disappointed.[13] Mr. Compson's cynical philosophy has nonetheless left its mark upon his mind as it has upon his brother's: in spite of his bitter contempt for his father, Jason has adopted his principles and erected them into a rigid rule of conduct. His inflexible logic is Mr. Compson's skepticism hardened into dogma, and by pushing it to preposterous lengths, he unwittingly exposes its contradictions and provides the final proof, *per absurdum*, of its impracticality.[14]

Even more surprising, Jason turns out to be in many ways Quentin's homologue. On the face of it, the two characters are of course poles apart, and it seems safe to assume that Jason was originally conceived to serve as a foil to his brother. Beside Quentin, Jason is no doubt a buoyant extrovert. Whereas Quentin, in his adolescent romanticism, flees from "the loud, harsh world," Jason, even though he never feels at home in it, is bustling about with pugnacious energy and is desperately scrambling for success. Most critics have noted the contrast between Quentin's quixotic idealism and Jason's hard-nosed pragmatism. What has been less often noted is that the former's idealism and the latter's pragmatism are equally spurious, and that behind these deceptive facades one finds the same self-centeredness and the same capacity for self-delusion, or, to use again Faulkner's more ambiguous term, the same irreducible "innocence." Jason is in fact merely the negative of his brother—a tougher Quentin who, instead of becoming a suicide, has turned sour.

They do not fly together, but birds of a feather they surely are. Throughout, their actions and attitudes reveal startlingly similar patterns. With both there is a persistent refusal of the Other, an unfailingly hostile response to anything or anyone likely to threaten the closure of their narcissistic world. Only—and it is here that the differences show—while Quentin's aggressiveness turns finally against his ego and ends in self-destruction, Jason's strikes out in petty malice.

Jason misses no opportunity to inflict pain, and as Cleanth Brooks has pointed out, in its resourceful meanness his cruelty goes well beyond that of a Popeye or a Flem Snopes.[15] Its roots are in childhood, as can be seen from the early episode recorded in the first section in which he cuts up the paper dolls which Caddy had made for Benjy (74).[16] Similarly Jason takes a perverse pleasure later in subtly frustrating Caddy's desire to see her daughter (234–35), or in tormenting poor Luster when he burns the two circus tickets before his eyes (293–94). In his own way Jason, just like Benjy and Quentin, remains true to his childhood,[17] and Dilsey is well aware of the childish perversity hidden beneath his adult meanness when she scolds him at the end of the circus ticket scene: "A big growed man like you" (295).

The objects of resentment

Within the family circle Jason can indulge his tyrannical bent and his sadistic whims in full safety. Outside, in his social and professional relations, prudence would normally commend a measure of vigilance and restraint. Yet Jason's animosity is so irrepressible that it breaks out at the slightest provocation and impels him to antagonize whoever comes his way. In all the conversations recalled in his monologue, his own words are nothing but gall and vinegar: he ceaselessly taunts Earl, his former business partner (in fact, his employer since Jason withdrew his money from the business to buy a car), and treats his customers with haughty condescension; he tells off the telegrapher for not keeping him right up to date with the stock reports, quarrels with the sheriff who refuses to help him catch his runaway niece, and provokes an old man into assaulting him in Mottson. Projecting his own malevolence and dishonesty onto others, Jason senses treachery and thievery everywhere, suspects everyone, and regards the whole world as his personal enemy.[18] And on Easter Sunday, during the frantic chase after his niece and the carnival man with the red tie, his morbid suspicion develops into a positively delirious sense of persecution.

If Quentin's divided self is close to schizophrenia, Jason's conspiracy and persecution fantasies belong with the symptoms of paranoia.[19] And the world, as seen by him, is likewise the mirror image of his own neurotic self; it bristles with hostility, and he would have us believe that he only fights back so as to survive in an unfriendly environment. It soon appears, however, that his aggressive behavior is determined beforehand by the contradictory demands of his paranoid disposition. By using every opportunity to antagonize his family and acquaintances, Jason, while finding release for his pent-up rage, also provokes retaliation. The expected counterattacks are indeed an integral part of his singular game, and they serve in fact several purposes: while providing him with a posteriori justifications for his own viciousness, they supply new food for self-pity by confirming him in the role of victim, and gratify as well an obscure need for punishment, as can be seen from the way he courts disaster. In the final pursuit, he even seems to derive a masochistic pleasure from his humiliations: when the sheriff refuses to help him catch his niece, "he [repeats] his story, harshly recapitulant, seeming to get an actual pleasure out of his outrage and impotence" (351).

Jason's bellicose behavior, then, is not just sadism. The persecutor wants to be persecuted; he has been programmed to be in turn assailant and sufferer. Jason may seem much simpler than Quentin (an impression ironically reinforced by his own image of himself in the monologue), but his antagonistic relationship to others proceeds likewise from complex unconscious motivations and points likewise to the devious workings of a sense of frustration and guilt. In both cases, allowances have to be made for the intricate play of displacements, repressions, and reversals. The difference between Quentin and Jason lies not so much in the psychological components of their personalities as in the dynamics of their working out. The basic features are almost identical, but differently combined and differently stressed.

This identity-in-difference can also be traced through the subtle shift from private obsessions to collective fantasies. Unlike Quentin's estrangement from society (not to speak of Benjy's autistic isolation), Jason's relation to it is an odd mixture of rebellion and conformity. His paranoid resentment is surely boundless, and for his ever-ebullient malice any available target will do. It is noteworthy, however, that his animosity flows so many times into the fixed channels of common prejudice.

In its lighter moments Jason's wit is leveled at such harmless stereotypes of folk humor as misers, small-towners, old maids, parsons (223, 285, 287), and, more significantly, intellectuals, "these college professors without a whole pair of socks to their name, telling you how to make a million in ten years . . ." (288). Anti-intellectualism generally goes along with xenophobia, and Jason is no exception to the rule:

> But I'll be damned if it hasn't come to a pretty pass when any dam foreigner that cant make a living in the country where God put him, can come to this one and take money right out of an American's pockets. (221)

A champion of Americanism, hostile to foreigners, Jason also feels quite naturally anti-Yankee as a southerner: "maybe your dam company's in a conspiracy with those dam eastern sharks" (250). Not surprisingly either, his national and regional prejudices are coupled with ethnic prejudice, as evidenced by his strong anti-Jewish feeling—a feeling he expresses with the hypocritical qualifications and reservations that have always been characteristic of the more "respectable" forms of anti-Semitism:

> "I give every man his due, regardless of religion or anything else. I have nothing against jews as an individual," I says. "It's just the race. You'll admit that they produce nothing. They follow the pioneers into a new country and sell them clothes." (219)

And it goes without saying that Jason holds nothing but scorn for blacks:

What this country needs is white labour. Let these dam trifling niggers starve for a couple of years, then they'd see what a soft thing they have. (219)

Like I say the only place for them is in the field, where they'd have to work from sunup to sundown. They cant stand prosperity or an easy job. Let one stay around white people for a while and he's not worth killing. They get so they can outguess you about work before your very eyes, like Roskus the only mistake he ever made was he got careless one day and died. Shirking and stealing and giving you a little more lip and a little more lip until some day you have to lay them out with a scantling or something. (289)

The black, the Jew, the foreigner, the intellectual: so many avatars of the despised and detested Other. In accordance with the standard procedures of bigotry and racism, Jason congeals them into rigid categories and reduces their being to a small set of unalterable predicates: Jews are mercantile and parasitic, Negroes lazy and thievish, etc. Once petrified by prejudice, they become safe objects for hatred and contempt and allow Jason to rejoin the "elite of the ordinary."[20]

Cosi fan tutte

The spectrum of his preconceptions and phobias would of course not be complete without misogyny. Jason is as much a sexist as he is a racist, and, just as on Jews and blacks, he has on women his stock of rancid clichés to degrade their humanity. One index of this dehumanizing process is his use of animal imagery: Jews are likened to sharks (250), blacks to monkeys (292), and women to bitches (206, 305). Another is the way in which Jason objectifies behavior and classifies actions. Whatever a woman may do, she can do nothing that will not fit neatly into his ready-made deterministic patterns: "Just like a woman," he declares when Caddy's check reaches him six days late (218). Yet his assumed knowledge and foreknowledge of feminine behavior do not immunize him against its perils. The trouble with women is that only their unpredictability is predictable; they are so illogical in their arguments, so fickle in their moods and motivations, that anything can be expected any time: "I dont know why it is I cant seem to learn that a woman'll do anything" (280). That is why woman becomes for Jason the supreme enemy: she is to him the most perverse embodiment of irrationality and therefore a permanent challenge to his schemes and calculations, an ever-present threat impossible to avert. And ironically the development of the action in the novel seems to prove Jason right in his fears: he is twice flouted by a woman, the first time by Caddy, whose promiscuity prevents him from getting the promised job, the second time by her daughter Quentin who, by running away with the money stolen from her, again reduces his hopes and projects to nothing.

Jason's misogyny differs from Quentin's in that it does not imply a total repudiation of sexuality. Yet, arising from the same deep-seated suspicion, it leads him likewise to arrest woman in an arbitrary concept. Turning Quentin's half-hearted gyneolatry inside out, Jason spells out what "the champion of dames" had suspected all along but refused to acknowledge, namely, that all women are "bitches." For Quentin this is an unbearable truth which he does his utmost to conceal under the noble trappings of courtly idealism. Jason, on the other hand, seemingly adjusts to it by choosing "a good honest whore" (269) for a mistress. This is not to say, of course, that he is less deluded about women than his brother: the whore is simply the reverse of the virgin—another projection of male fantasy, another reduction of womanhood to faceless archetype.

By debasing woman to the function of a marketable commodity, Jason thinks he can keep his distance from her, the more so as he is careful to establish his liaison with Lorraine on a contractlike commercial basis. Yet his crass "philosophy" about women, so readily translated into action with his docile mistress, no longer serves as a safe strategy where Caddy and her daughter are concerned. Here affective involvement takes the upper hand, as becomes pretty obvious in Jason's dealings with his niece. While money, the abstract, impersonal substitute for all that is desirable, has apparently come to be the sole object of his "positive" emotional investments, Quentin II is a permanent reminder of past frustrations and hence the favorite target of his rage and hatred. Both passions, it should be remembered, are closely related to his sister. Caddy plays the role of money-provider: potentially, insofar as her marriage was to assure Jason a respectable position at her husband's bank; actually, since for fifteen years he has been stealing from her two hundred dollars a month. In other words, it is from Caddy, the departed sister, that Jason expects the gratification of his dearest wishes, and in this respect he reminds one again of Quentin: in Jason, one might argue, Quentin's ambivalence toward Caddy, instead of being internalized, has been dissociated and displaced. This hypothesis is the more plausible as displacement manifestly underlies Jason's relationship to Quentin II, and as the latter nearly comes to occupy in his monologue the central place which her mother held in the previous sections.

Jason's relationship to his seventeen-year-old niece parallels Quentin's relationship to his sister in such a way as to become its parodical reenactment. Indeed, Jason, who performs as the girl's surrogate father, is as compulsively preoccupied with her promiscuity as Quentin was with Caddy's. The reasons given are no doubt different, yet between Quentin's sense of honor and Jason's concern for respectability there is only a difference of degree. Furthermore, Jason is so sincerely outraged by his niece's escapades that a hypocritical care for decorum will hardly do for an explanation. Here again Jason's attitudes are extremely inconsistent, and once more his actual behavior gives the lie to the thoughts and feelings he professes. At one moment he pretends to be indifferent to Quentin's fate: "Like I say, let her lay out all day and all night with everything in town that wears pants, what do I care" (278). But immediately after his indignation explodes:

> These dam little slick haired squirts, thinking they are raising so much hell, I'll show them something about hell I says, and you too. I'll make him think that dam red tie is the latch string to hell, if he thinks he can run the woods with my niece. (278)

Jason rails at "those dam squirts" (216) just as Quentin did, and both use the same colloquial phrase of abuse (see section 2, 153: "It's for letting it be some damn town squirt I slapped you"). His fury here is strongly reminiscent of his brother's resentment of Caddy's early dates. Similarly, in the scene where he confronts his niece (210–17), his brutality parallels—even in particular gestures such as grabbing her arm—Quentin's aggressiveness toward Caddy in many of the scenes described in the second section. The parallel is further emphasized by the girl's defiant attitude, and when she threatens to rip her dress off in front of Jason, one is irresistibly reminded of the scene at the branch on the day of Damuddy's death, when young Caddy took hers off as a challenge to Quentin. In both scenes the gesture of undressing is felt as a provocation, and its effrontery maddens Jason just as it outraged Quentin's prudery. Their being both scandalized by the sight of naked female flesh is a clear index of their puritanical recoil from sex. To Jason as to Quentin, sex is associated with the darkness of sin, and in his monologue woods—the bewitched area that haunted Hawthorne's Puritan sinners—become once again the secret abode of shameful lust: "Are you hiding out in the woods with one of those dam slick-headed jellybeans? Is that where you go?" (211). Significantly too, sexual obsession and ethnic prejudice overlap in the image of the promiscuous Negro girl: "I'm not going to have any member of my family going on like a nigger wench" (217). And it is precisely the same puritan and racist imagery that expresses Quentin's anxiety over his sister's lost honor: "*Why must you do like nigger women do in the pasture the ditches the dark woods hot hidden furious in the dark woods*" (105).

   The ambiguity of such attitudes and such language need hardly be stressed again. While professing to be shocked by his niece's outrageous make-up and slovenly deshabilles, Jason feels secretly titillated and barely manages to conceal his lecherous thoughts:

> if a woman had come out doors even on Gayoso or Beale street when I was a young fellow with no more than that to cover her legs and behind, she'd been thrown in jail. I'll be damned if they dont dress like they were trying to make every man they passed on the street want to reach out and clap his hand on it. (267)

There is an unmistakable touch of prurience and voyeurism about Jason's constant spying on his niece (again reminiscent of Quentin's attitudes toward Caddy), and what impels him to chase her around the countryside through ditches and poison oak is not only the desire to get his money back but also the hope to catch her in the act. The sheer intensity of Jason's animosity toward Quentin points to the depth of his emotional involvement, and it is probably not going too far, as one critic suggested, to relate it to a "deeply repressed incestuous attraction."[21]

The recurrence of similar situations, attitudes, and gestures, as well as the many verbal echoes of section 2 in section 3, provide conclusive evidence of the very close affinities between Quentin and Jason. Yet they also emphasize the contrast between past and present. Instead of the pathetic confrontations recalled in Quentin's monologue, we find here scenes of harsh vulgarity which show how deep the Compsons have sunk under Jason's rule. In the third section everything takes on a more sordid color. Perhaps too a truer color, revealing Quentin as well as Jason in a clearer light. For after all, Quentin's influence upon his sister was no less damaging than Jason's on his niece. More insidiously, his perverted love proved as injurious as outspoken hatred. "If I'm bad," says Caddy's daughter to Jason, "it's because I had to be. You made me. I wish I was dead. I wish we were all dead" (300). Before her, Caddy voiced the same resigned despair, the same awareness of being "bad" (181), and instead of invoking destiny, she could well have accused Quentin of corrupting her. The victims, one of a jealous brother, the other of a vindictive, pseudo-paternal uncle, Caddy and her daughter both recognize themselves as damned in the maleficent mirrors held up to them by their pitiless judges. Quentin and Jason are doubtless not alone in working their wretched fates, but as prosecutors and persecutors they are undeniably instrumental in turning them into "lost women." In the last resort the novel pits the two brothers back to back: Jason is Quentin the censor become torturer; Quentin is Jason with the alibi of high-minded idealism. The third section, in this respect, is not simply a grating repetition of the second; it is also an exposure of Quentin's fevered romanticizing.

"Just let me have twenty-four hours"

Because of their extreme self-absorption and self-delusion, Quentin and Jason alike are destructive to themselves and to others. For the same reasons, they also fail to come to terms with reality, and nothing illustrates this better than their common failure to conquer time. Jason, it is true, does not break his watch; he is not haunted by scenes of his childhood as Quentin was and shows nothing but sneering contempt for tradition. Yet he is trapped in the past as his brothers are, and although memory plays no prominent part in his life, the "outrage" he suffered when Caddy deprived him of the promised job is still an open wound. In his monologue, flashbacks are far less numerous than in Quentin's, but in the one major shift to the past, his thoughts return significantly to his sister (232–37). What sets him apart is that instead of brooding endlessly on Caddy, he takes active steps to make good the affront. Where

Quentin was haunted by an irretrievable past, Jason is obsessed with a lost future which he is at pains to restore. The future he runs after is above all the time of revenge, the ultimate day of triumph when he will at last settle his account with the past. Tomorrow becomes for him the antidote to yesterday.

For him, then, it is not so much a question, apparently, of escaping from time as of catching up with it. From the continual shuttling between store, telegraph office, and home recounted in the third section to the mad pursuit described in the last, Jason's life is nothing but a long and exhausting race against the clock. A ludicrous race as well: Jason's compulsive bustle reminds one of the incongruous frenzy of actors in the early silent movies; like them, Jason is transformed into a grotesquely gesticulating puppet by the jerky acceleration of movement. Always on the alert, always in a hurry, wildly dashing from place to place without ever getting anywhere on time, Jason spends all his energy in sheer waste. Unforeseen and uncontrollable incidents occur at every turn and develop into a series of exasperating contretemps: Jason arrives at the telegraph office an hour after the cotton market has closed; he has run out of blank checks when he needs them to deceive his mother once more; he "just misses" catching his niece and her carnival lover, and so on. Jason never has time enough to master time. The more he works himself up for action, the farther behind he gets: the tantalizing distance between the empty present and the bright, avenging future will never be bridged.

Jason is like a trotting donkey, with a carrot forever dangling beyond his reach. While Quentin dreams of a vertical eternity *above* time, Jason's eternity is an ever-receding mirage lying *ahead,* on the horizontal line of duration. Paradoxically, like all naive believers in "progress," it is in time that he flees time. "Just let me have twenty-four hours" (305), he pleads at the end of his monologue. Those twenty-four hours measure the gap that separates him from the realization of his covetous dream—a dream not far removed, after all, from Quentin's: to retain, to possess, to lay in a treasure-store and to shelter it from the law of loss and change. For Quentin the "treasure" to be hoarded was Caddy's virginity; in Jason the same hunger for self-extension, the same need for exclusive possession manifests itself more prosaically and more economically in the pursuit of money through embezzlement and financial speculation and finds its most eloquent metaphor in the strongbox where he keeps the stolen dollars. But Jason loses his savings just as Quentin lost his sister. All his calculations, ruses, and precautions cannot save him from disaster.

The fool

In the Appendix to *The Sound and the Fury* Faulkner tells us that Jason is "the first sane Compson since before Culloden" and defines him as "logical rational contained."[22] It should be clear by now that Faulkner's statements about him are to be taken *cum grano salis.* In point of fact, the way in which Jason reacts to people and events is every bit as emotional as that of Quentin or, for that matter, Benjy, and his futile attempts to force experience into a rigid order of his own only confirm the likeness. True, his meanly legalistic approach to all practical questions and his propensity to reduce all relationships to business arrangements show us that cold rationality is what he is striving for. But even more than by the unpredictability of events his need for order is flouted by the rashness of his own impulses. Not only does his reason betray him time and again in his dealings with his family; even in business matters it abandons him whenever an important decision is to be made. His performance as a businessman is indeed a poor one, and for all his cupidity and cynicism, he fails miserably in his enterprises. As old Job points out to him, the very excess of his suspiciousness turns against him:

> "You's too smart fer me. Aint a man in dis town kin keep up wid you fer smartness. You fools a man whut so smart he cant even keep up wid hisself," he says, getting in the wagon and unwrapping the reins.
> "Who's that?" I says.
> "Dat's Mr Jason Compson," he says. (288–89)

Jason ends up trapped by his own machinations, and his actions all bear out Job's shrewd remark. Consider his cotton speculations (219–22, 249–50, 260–61, 281–82) or his sporting bets (290–91): they establish beyond any doubt that so far from being reached through cool reasoning his decisions are invariably dictated by whim or vanity or the most puerile spirit of contradiction. Too suspicious to believe in luck, too impulsive to adhere to logic, Jason is doomed to lose out at every turn.

As reflected in his monologue, Jason's thinking is in itself a paltry parody of rational thought. "Once a bitch always a bitch": the opening sentence of his speech exemplifies from the outset the kind of sophistry that warps his reasoning throughout; it is the first of the many unwarranted generalizations that allow his prejudices to posture as plain truths. Most of Jason's ideas and opinions belong in the same category of false induction: they are little more than the rough and ready rationalizations of his rancor and his fears. His ratiocinative mania (another trait of his paranoid personality) demands that every fragment of experience be coerced into procrustean mental patterns and that nothing be left unexplained. But for Jason it is not so much a matter of explaining as of explaining *away*, of reducing complexity to simplicity, of converting otherness into sameness. What he looks for is the magical surrogate of a logical system—a system proving the world to be a vast and sinister conspiracy and thus buttressing his sense of outraged martyrdom.

Jason, however, is not a very imaginative paranoiac, and his mind is far too shallow and conventional to devise a system of its own. What he thinks is neither what *he* thinks nor what he *thinks*. His ideas are all secondhand, and, as we have seen, they all come from the threadbare ideology of his cultural environment. The very texture of his speech testifies to his mental barrenness: its diction is repetitious; its syntax multiplies subordinate clauses but never

masters them, and its whole language tends to freeze into formulas.²³ Jason's
grammar, hardly better than his logic, provides evidence not only of his lack
of education but also of the abysmal vulgarity of his mind. True, his blustering
rhetoric has an acrid flavor of its own, yet at its core his language is dead and
deadening: it immobilizes everything and everyone in a hideous grimace,
creating the arrested image of a world in which a woman will always act "just
like a woman" and black people will be forever "niggers." Behind the accumulation of pseudo-logic and tauto-logic, one senses an atrophied intelligence, frantically feeding on the meager diet of its stale truisms and
sophisms. A nauseous compound of clamorous clichés, a dreary dictionary of
idées reçues: Jason's monologue has nothing else to offer.

Such concepts as rationalism, realism, and pragmatism refer to what Jason
would be, not to what he actually is. His tough-minded stance is just a
self-protective pose, a fragile barrier erected against the world and against his
own folly, and bound to break down in times of stress. The final chase of Miss
Quentin is a case in point. Jason's irrationality, hitherto contained, erupts in a
most spectacular way: in the course of his pursuit, he drops all his pretensions
to sense and sanity, throws prudence to the winds, and rushes headlong
toward disaster. The madness of the Compsons, so often the butt of his jibes,
has not spared him, as even Jason himself comes to realize in his very rare
moments of lucidity:

> Me, without any hat, in the middle of the afternoon, having to chase up and
> down back alleys because of my mother's good name . . . there I was, without
> any hat, looking like I was crazy too. Like a man would naturally think, one of
> them is crazy and another one drowned himself and the other was turned out
> into the street by her husband, what's the reason the rest of them are not crazy
> too. (268)

Jason is "crazy too," and his madness reaches its furious climax on Easter
Sunday, after the disappearance of his niece. Wild fantasizing then comes to
obliterate his precarious sense of reality in ways again reminiscent of Quentin.
Nothing is left of Jason's cocksure aggressive stance, and he now plays the
victim and wallows in self-pity. Yet at the same time, like a true Compson, he
projects himself into heroic characters to sustain and strengthen his vacillating
self-image. Quentin thought of himself as the last medieval knight and likened
his imminent death to the sacrificial death of Christ; similarly assuming that
his petty private affairs are of universal moment, Jason casts himself in the
romantic part of heaven-storming rebel. In his delirious megalomania his
burlesque misadventures are given operatic scale and raised to tragic significance; his opponents are no longer a little slut and a vulgar showman but
"the opposed forces of his destiny" (356), while Jason himself is suddenly
transmogrified into a provincial Prometheus or a seedy Satan:

> From time to time he passed churches, unpainted frame buildings with sheet
> iron steeples, surrounded by tethered teams and shabby motorcars, and it

seemed to him that each of them was a picketpost where the rear guards of Circumstance peeped fleetingly back at him. "And damn You, too," he said, "See if You can stop me," thinking of himself, his file of soldiers with the manacled sheriff in the rear, dragging Omnipotence down from his throne, if necessary; of the embattled legions of both hell and heaven through which he tore his way and put his hands at last on his fleeing niece. (354)

The return to reality is triggered by the harrowing experience of physical humiliation in the scene of Jason's tangle with the old man at Mottson—a scene which, as Duncan Aswell has judiciously pointed out, "might have come straight out of Quentin's day"[24] and closely parallels the latter's fight with Gerald Bland. Quentin tries to hit Bland to avenge a woman's honor; Jason acts no less absurdly in provoking an old man he has never seen before and who has nothing whatsoever to do with his troubles. In both scenes there is a tragicomic misunderstanding, the person attacked being each time a surrogate for the real antagonist out of reach. If Jason considers himself less quixotic than his brother, his blind anger leads him eventually to the selfsame tilting at windmills. His fight, like Quentin's, is shadowboxing in a shadow world, the more ludicrous as he falls and hits his head on a rail before the furious old man has had a chance to get near him with his rusty hatchet. Several other details of the scene further underscore the irony of repetition: references to blood (359–60), inviting comparison with Quentin's bleeding nose, and the question asked by the witness of the incident who believes it was a suicide attempt (360) and asks Jason if the girl he is looking for isn't his sister (361).

The clinching irony, however, comes at the end of the episode, when Jason finds himself a victim so wretched that his plight recalls not only Quentin's impotence but also the utter helplessness of his idiot brother Benjy. His energy drained and his bravado gone, Jason is now like a puppet with its strings broken, and we see him crushed by the bitter humiliation of total defeat:

> He sat there for some time. He heard a clock strike the half hour, then people began to pass, in Sunday and Easter clothes. Some looked at him as they passed, at the man sitting quietly behind the wheel of a small car, with his invisible life ravelled out about him like a wornout sock. . . . (362)

Through Jason's lamentable failure Faulkner makes a kind of poetic justice triumph. Situations and roles are reversed according to the standard patterns of farce and comedy: Jason's story is that of the robber robbed, the persecutor persecuted, the victimizer turned victim. As in the puppet theater, one would be tempted to applaud the downfall of the villain had not the novelist changed his attitude in the meantime. In the final scene of the chase, when Jason, alone and abandoned, slumped behind the steering wheel of his little car, is patiently waiting for one of the despised blacks to drive him home, he is no longer a laughable figure. Not that he suddenly enlists our sympathy. But the contempt heaped upon him throughout the novel gives way now to that respect mingled with pity that Faulkner had grace enough to grant each of his creatures at the hour of extreme solitude or impending death, be they as vile as Popeye, Flem Snopes, or Jason.

The petit bourgeois

From blustering, bullying self-affirmation Jason is thus brought down to abject impotence. By the end of the novel he has been exposed to the core of his being, with no corner of his tortuous mind left unsearched. He now stands before us as a living embodiment of evil, yet his villainy is not to be explained away by the facile assumptions—whether metaphysical, psychological, or sociological—that he was born bad and predestined to play the villain. Neither wholly guilty nor totally innocent, Jason is, like all of Faulkner's defeated characters, the victim of circumstance as well as the agent of his own ruin. Furthermore, insofar as the evil he comes to stand for is rooted in corruption, not only of his family but of society at large, it clearly transcends the narrow limits of his shabby individuality.

The social dimension of the character is indeed crucial for a proper understanding of the third section and for a correct assessment of its significance within the novel. The general movement of *The Sound and the Fury* has often been defined as one of progressive opening, and several critics have pointed to a gradual shift from private to public concerns.[25] There can be no question that Jason's monologue offers a broader perspective than the two previous ones, although his point of view is as narrowly subjective as that of his brothers (indeed more so than Benjy's). It calls the reader's attention beyond the Compson household, and by doing so it allows him to set the family drama in a social context and to relate it to all the pressures and influences of a specific cultural environment.

Yet even more meaningful perhaps than the unfolding of the social scene in section 3 is the way in which society conditions and shapes Jason's very language and thought. None of the first three monologues is more deeply socialized, and none, as we have seen, is more thickly encrusted with ideological deposits. Jason is the only one of the Compson brothers to speak the colloquial idiom of his region and the only one to seek a social identity. Both Benjy and Quentin are outsiders: the former is separated from the world by mental deficiency, the latter estranged from it through his neurotic obsessions. Jason's case is different, since he is at least trying to find his niche in society: "I've got a position in this town" (217), he tells his niece, and throughout the novel we can see him making desperate efforts to put up a front, to keep the family name—what is left of it—intact in the eyes of public opinion. The irony is of course that he fails to do so. Jason does not enjoy the esteem of his fellow citizens, and the Jefferson community only tolerates him because of the respectable position once held by his family. So he too comes close to being an outsider, and he is at any rate too marginal, too much of an eccentric to be considered truly representative of his milieu.

Still, a southerner he is, and although we should make allowance for the exaggerations and distortions of satire, there is no doubt that his portrait is to some extent a radioscopy of the southern mind. But to what South does Jason belong, the old or the new? Is he a Sartoris or a Snopes? It has been argued that in contrast to Quentin, the last defender of the aristocratic code, Jason stands for the crass materialism of the rising Snopeses.[26] That he has much in common with Snopesism, as it is portrayed in Faulkner's trilogy, no reader would of course think of denying. Jason abandons, or thinks he abandons, all allegiance to the values of the traditional South, and cynically congratulates himself on his lack of moral scruples (263); his greed, dishonesty, and meanness rival anything Flem Snopes can offer. It is hardly surprising, then, that in a society in which Snopesism has become the common standard of behavior, Jason should be the only Compson to survive. But this is precisely what differentiates him from Flem: he just manages to survive; he does not make his fortune. According to Faulkner, Jason was the only member of his family able to stand up to the Snopeses on their own ground.[27] In point of fact, however, he is no match for Flem, and in *The Mansion* the latter has no more difficulty outwitting him than the other citizens of Jefferson.[28] Jason lacks the patient craftiness and cold single-mindedness which pave the way to Flem's success. He is doubtless a very vocal exponent of the new mercantile non-ethic, but his bumbling ineptness in practical matters is a very poor illustration of Snopesism in action.[29] The reason is perhaps that his greed is of another order. The Snopeses are rapacious like beasts of prey; they are driven by the vulgar appetites and coarse ambitions of the rootless upstart, and their rise to money and power is as irresistible as a natural catastrophe. Jason, on the other hand, the last survivor of a degenerate bourgeois family, is caught in the paralyzing contradictions of his heritage; for him, life started with the searing experience of loss, and, do what he will, his blind hunger will never be quenched.

Jason should not be confused then with the rising class of the Snopeses any more than he should be identified entirely with the class of his origins. Jason himself seems to feel uncertain as to where he belongs and shifts grounds according to mood and circumstance. Now he sides with the poor hill farmers (219), now he curses them (223) or denounces their improvidence (286); now he rails at his family's social pretensions, now he acts as the self-appointed defender of the Compson name. It is true that Jason sees himself as a Bascomb, a member of the mercantile and uneducated lower middle-class family of his mother, rather than as an aristocratic Compson, yet in his status anxieties the haunting memory of the Compson past cannot be discounted. Jason feels déclassé, and his sense of social degradation gives his resentment its sharp edge of bitterness. Jason is Faulkner's portrait of the addled petit bourgeois, and through him he has lent an eloquent voice to all the malcontents of the new South of the twenties: decayed aristocrats, grubbing small businessmen, hard-pressed dirt-farming rednecks, all those whom the hazards of the economic system had condemned to grovel in mediocrity and to boil with chronic frustration. Jason speaks for this mass of disgruntled southern whites, and his discourse distills their grievances and complaints with sour precision.

Like most failures and misfits, Jason considers himself the victim of an unfair destiny which has robbed him of his due and pushed him out of his rightful place in society. It is quite remarkable that on the rare occasions when he switches from "I" to "we," it is to voice a sullen sense of solidarity with his anonymous companions of misfortune: "I dont see how a city no bigger than New York can hold enough people to take the money away from *us country suckers*" (270; my italics). But this furtive awareness of a victimization shared with others never leads Jason to a recognition of human interdependence. In characteristic American (and southern) fashion, the feeling of helplessness in the face of inscrutable social and economic powers is overcompensated by a hysterical emphasis on the virtues of individual achievement: "Besides, like I say I guess I dont need any man's help to get along I can stand on my own feet like I always have" (237). Jason's cocky assertions of autonomy sound like ironic echoes of the legendary spirit of independence of the pioneers and frontiersmen from whom Jason is descended, and one might almost take them for a wry take-off on Emersonian "self-reliance." What Jason's brand of individualism is worth we already know: it is nothing but the mask and alibi of his conformity.

Suspiciousness, intolerance, and prejudice round off the portrait, and it goes without saying that these features also belong to the typical petit bourgeois. Xenophobia, anti-Semitism, racism, anti-intellectualism, misogyny: it is in these forms of aggressiveness, sanctioned and encouraged with varying degrees of hypocrisy by society at large, that the petit bourgeois' resentment is eventually channeled and fixed. The political implications of this particular set of stereotyped attitudes and stock responses are obvious enough: Jason and his like are among those strata of American society from which the radical right has always recruited its most ardent supporters. Admittedly, Jason is not a conservative in the classical sense of the word; he has no nostalgia for a bygone world, and he could not care less about tradition. But he comes close to being what Richard Hofstadter termed "the pseudo-conservative"[30]: intent on keeping a good appearance in public, clinging self-righteously to the respectable image of himself in the roles of hard-working businessman, dutiful son, and meritorious breadwinner of the Compson household, Jason conforms to conservative standards as far as his official selves are concerned. And he does not do so out of mere hypocrisy: there is evidence in his monologue that he deludes himself into taking his roles very seriously. Yet this brittle surface of conventionality is cracked over and over again by the barely controlled violence of his anarchic impulses. His is the split attitude of the pseudo-conservative: blind, unthinking adherence to conformity belied by deep-seated dissatisfaction with the established order and sporadically betrayed by displaced gestures of revolt.

Anger, fear, restlessness, paranoid suspicion, status anxiety, ethnic prejudice—all the features listed by Hofstadter as characteristic of the pseudo-conservative syndrome are paralleled in Jason's monologue. Faulkner certainly had no sociological intentions when he wrote *The Sound and the Fury*, but the unfailing sureness of touch with which he portrayed Jason proves beyond any doubt that even at this still early stage of his career he was fully aware of the dialectical interrelatedness of individual and society. To a higher degree perhaps than any of his contemporaries, Faulkner possessed the historical and sociological imagination that succeeds in capturing the spirit of a time and a place. True, the embittered petit-bourgeois mentality dramatized through Jason is not restricted to a single time and a single place. Yet if Jason is not just typical of the South of the early twentieth century, it is precisely because he is so distinctly southern to begin with.

"There are too many Jasons in the South who can be successful, just as there are too many Quentins who are too sensitive to face reality."[31] Faulkner's own comment confirms, if confirmation is needed, the representative character he attributed to these two figures, and it also points to their complementary functions within the novel. Most critics have interpreted this complementarity in historical terms: in Quentin's collapse they see the breakdown of the southern aristocracy; in Jason they see a kind of white-collar redneck and a prophet of Snopesism; and each of them is thus made to stand for one phase in the process of decadence. The contrast, however, should not be emphasized too heavily, for, as we have seen, Quentin and Jason are more deeply brothers than has been generally acknowledged, and the resemblances between them are so disturbingly close that their monologues may be read as different versions of the same script or different performances of the same play. What the play is about is loss: economic loss, loss of power and prestige for what was not so long ago a family belonging to the ruling class, but also, in individual terms, loss of love through loss of self, loss of self through loss of love. Benjy, the dispossessed idiot on the threshold of the novel, embodies this condition of loss at its rawest and most elemental. In Quentin and Jason it assumes the far more elaborate forms of self-estrangement, and through their monologues Faulkner demonstrates with stunning insight how alienation works within the recesses of a mind. Both brothers fail to acknowledge the necessity of loss, and in denying it, they condemn themselves to further failures, further losses, and turn their very lives into absurd antics. Lacking the strength and courage to undertake the perilous journey from innocence to experience and from self to other, neither passes the test of reality, and both remain moral morons. Theirs are essentially stories of failed initiations, stories of fatal self-delusion—catastrophes of innocence and tragicomedies of mistaken identities.

One might argue that alienation is rather psychosexual with Quentin and rather psychosocial with Jason. But this would be yet another oversimplification, for private fantasies and public fables are shown to be complementary aspects of the same fiction-making in both sections, and Quentin's fantasizing must be considered along with Jason's paranoid obsessions as symptoms of the same family disease. Only the fates of the two brothers are really separate:

one pays for alienation with his life; the other manages to survive. But Jason loses his soul in the process, and his survival is at best a tawdry travesty of Faulknerian "endurance."

VI

AN EASTER WITHOUT
RESURRECTION ?

Nous sommes nés pour porter le temps, non
pour nous y soustraire.

Jean-Paul de Dadelsen

The fourth trial

Having, on his own admission, failed to tell his story through the three
Compson brothers, Faulkner resolved "to write another section from the
outside with an outsider, which was the writer, to tell what had happened on
that particular day."[1] But this new extraterritorial voice is neither that of an
omniscient narrator nor that of a detached observer.[2] The narrative approach
here is one found in many of Faulkner's novels: free and flexible, keenly
attentive to what is happening, while engaging at the same time in the process
of interpretation. But if what is reported is not left totally unexplained, there
is no full elucidation either. Meanings are suggested but never asserted.
Faulkner's method is throughout conjectural, and its tentativeness is
evidenced by the recurrence of comparative-conditional clauses (introduced
by *as if* or *as though*) and words or phrases denoting uncertainty (*seemed,
appeared, it might have been*). In this, section 4 differs notably from the preceding
ones: in the first section, we were given raw facts and raw emotions without
discernible meaning; in the second and even in the third, meanings were so
rigidly self-centered constructs as to distort facts altogether; only the last
section avoids the extremes of blank factualness and blind fantasizing. The
monologue from which it differs least is perhaps Quentin's, insofar as the
latter is also quest for meaning, albeit a doomed one; on the other hand, it is
the very antithesis of Jason's: the paranoid Jason has ready explanations for
everything, and, as we have seen, his explanations all narrow down to
murderous prejudice. He is a model of interpretative terrorism, a telling
exemplification of massive ignorance and irrational bias parading as truth,
and serves therefore as a foil to the outside narrator of the fourth section.
Reporting what he sees and hears, and trying to find plausible explanations

without twisting the evidence, this narrator seems more trustworthy than any of the Compsons, but Faulkner carefully refrains from establishing him as a source of undisputable authority. His position is in fact very close to the reader's: sharing in the reader's perplexities rather than answering his questions, he enjoys no other privileges than those of his intellectual and imaginative alertness.

A gray dawn

Distance is the reader's major gain. No longer constrained to adopt the narrowly limited viewpoint of an idiot or the distorted vision of a neurotic, we can at last stand back and take in the whole scene. And yet the opening of the fourth section hardly mitigates the oppressive atmosphere of the previous ones. For being broader, the vision seems just as bleak as before:

> The day dawned bleak and chill, a moving wall of gray light out of the northeast which, instead of dissolving into moisture, seemed to disintegrate into minute and venomous particles, like dust that, when Dilsey opened the door of the cabin and emerged, needled laterally into her flesh, precipitating not so much a moisture as a substance partaking of the quality of thin, not quite congealed oil. (306)

Suggesting the close of day rather than its beginning, the grim grayness of this limbo landscape reminds one of the twilight associated with the Quentin section. Nothing here points to the promise of a world born afresh. Space is enclosed and constricted by "a moving wall of gray light"; humidity, hanging ominously in the air, threatens to crumble into an infinity of "minute and venomous particles, like dust," or assumes the repulsive quality of "congealed oil." Disquieting and desolate, and seemingly fraught with evil intent, the landscape here described would indeed not have been out of place in the second section. And not only does it lack the breadth and depth of living space; with no principle of order and cohesion to sustain it, it looks as though its disintegration were close at hand. It might almost stand as an emblem for the novel, materializing the mental and moral falling asunder of the Compsons, and its metaphorical significance is all the more plausible as the same suggestions of noncohesion occur in the portrait one finds a few pages later:

> Luster entered, followed by a big man who appeared to have been shaped of some substance whose particles would not or did not cohere to one another or to the frame which supported it. His skin was dead looking and hairless; dropsical too, he moved with a shambling gait like a trained bear. His hair was pale and fine. It had been brushed smoothly down upon his brow like that of children in daguerrotypes. His eyes were clear, of the pale sweet blue of cornflowers, his thick mouth hung open, drooling a little. (317)

Here comes Benjy, the idiot, and no reader will fail to recognize him in this lumpish, slobbering giant. His lack of motor coordination recalls his mental debility, his hairless skin and fat body indicate his castrated condition, and his cornflower-blue eyes are reminders of the childish innocence buried within this ungainly mass of adult flesh.

In much the same way the almost caricatural sketches of Jason and Mrs. Compson seem to be just what one would have expected. The physical resemblance between mother and son comes so to speak as a natural extension of their moral affinities:

> When she called for the first time Jason laid his knife and fork down and he and his mother appeared to wait across the table from one another, in identical attitudes; the one cold and shrewd, with close-thatched brown hair curled into two stubborn hooks, one on either side of his forehead like a bartender in caricature, and hazel eyes with black-ringed irises like marbles, the other cold and querulous, with perfectly white hair and eyes pouched and baffled and so dark as to appear to be all pupil or all iris. (323)

The characters so portrayed make for a new sense of reality. Emerging from the claustrophobic ambience of the three brothers' monologues into the common space of the visible, it is as if after *listening* to the voices in the dark, we were suddenly allowed to *see* their owners in broad daylight and to relate each voice to a face and body, and the spectacle is the more startling as what we see strikes us as oddly familiar: the shock which the reader experiences in discovering Benjy or Jason is a shock of recognition.

Of the many changes taking place in the fourth section, this shift from *within* to *without* is the most readily perceptible. But what we have learned through living in the minds of the three brothers comes at once to inform our new mode of perception and to condition our reading. Building on all that precedes it, the reading of the last section is necessarily the "richest," and everything in the text becomes instantly pregnant with significance. All readings of fiction may be said to move from the literal to the symbolic, for as a narrative develops, it is bound to produce meanings which cross-refer and interrelate and combine into complex semantic clusters. In *The Sound and the Fury*, however, this process is deliberately emphasized through Faulkner's fictional strategy: in the first section he maintains the narrative at the most literal level by having the story told by an idiot; in the last, he achieves a maximum of symbolic reverberation by multiplying "objective correlatives" of the distress, disorder, and decay which he had so far been intent on revealing from within.

Easter Sunday begins ironically with a gray dawn, and this gloomy grayness continues almost unabated to the end. When Dilsey appears at her cabin door, she looks at the sky "with an expression at once fatalistic and of a child's astonished disappointment" (307). As a further sinister omen, the air is soon filled with the shrill cries of jaybirds, which southern folklore associates with hell:

> A pair of jaybirds came up from nowhere, whirled up on the blast like gaudy

scraps of cloth or paper and lodged in the mulberries, where they swung in raucous tilt and recover, screaming into the wind that ripped their harsh cries onward and away like scraps of paper or of cloth in turn. Then three more joined them and they swung and tilted in the wrung branches for a time, screaming. (307)[3]

When Dilsey and her family start off for church, the rain has stopped, but the sun is "random and tentative" (335), and when it does manage to shine through, it is so weak that it looks like "a pale scrap of cloth" (332). The countryside around them is desolate as far the eye can see:

A street turned off at right angles, descending, and became a dirt road. On either hand the land dropped more sharply: a broad flat dotted with small cabins whose weathered roofs were on a level with the crown of the road. They were set in small grassless plots littered with broken things, bricks, planks, crockery, things of a once utilitarian value. What growth there was consisted of rank weeds and the trees were mulberries and locusts and sycamores—trees that partook also of the foul desiccation which surrounded the houses; trees whose very burgeoning seemed to be the sad and stubborn remnant of September, as if even spring had passed them by. . . . (336)

It is indeed a dismal landscape, a "waste land" forgotten by spring, and its barrenness, brokenness, and shabbiness are curiously reminiscent of the squalid suburb of New England where Quentin walked with the little Italian girl on the day of his suicide. And just as in Quentin's monologue, the suspicion arises that this world has been drained of its substance, that it is no more than a mirage poised on the edge of the abyss or a flimsy, deceptive décor masking nothingness:

The road rose again, to a scene like a painted backdrop. Notched into a cut of red clay crowned with oaks the road appeared to stop short off, like a cut ribbon. Beside it a weathered church lifted its crazy steeple like a painted church, and the whole scene was as flat and without perspective as a painted cardboard set upon the ultimate edge of the flat earth. . . . (337)

In the center of this unreal scenery stands the Compsons' house. As in other Faulkner novels, its fate is closely bound up with that of the family. The splitting up of the land and the gradual shrinking of the estate betoken economic and social decline, and point as well to the breakup of the family group itself, whose sole male survivor is a bachelor without progeny. As to the dilapidation of "the square, paintless house with its rotting portico" (344), it is yet another sign of the destructive work of time, and so even more specifically is the endless ticking of the clock, "the dry pulse of the decaying house itself" (329). Like Sutpen's mansion in *Absalom, Absalom!*, the Compsons' house, once the stately seat of the genos and the emblem of dynastic pride, has become a monument to decay and death. The destinies of the house and its inmates are neatly summed up in the Appendix, where Faulkner refers to "the rotting family in the rotting house."[4]

All these suggestions of disorder and decay should warn us against a hasty "positive" reading of the final section. The traditional symbols of rebirth are ironically reversed: dawn and spring are described in terms of desolation, and the irony is the more pointed as the action takes place on an Easter Sunday. At first glance, then, the tonality of the section is largely consonant with that of the preceding ones, especially with that of Quentin's monologue. The narrator's eye is certainly less distraught than Quentin's; it is the more remarkable that we are confronted again with the same imagery of destruction and exhaustion.

Counterpoint

Are we to infer that Quentin's vision of despair possesses more general validity than we originally assumed? The conclusion seems warranted by the general "atmosphere" of the fourth section. There is one notable exception, however: the Easter service episode, whose function and significance we have not yet examined. On the other hand, the reader's spontaneous response to imagery and atmosphere is certainly no reliable starting point for a full critical assessment. Yet, if one turns to structure, one apparently reaches very similar conclusions. Thus one critic contends that "a structural analysis of the closing chapter of *The Sound and the Fury* does, in fact, reveal nihilism as the meaning of the whole."[5] Section 4 consists of four distinct narrative units. It begins with a prologue, going from dawn to about 9:30 A.M. and focusing successively on Dilsey (306–20), Jason (320–29), Benjy and Luster (329–32). The three scenes of the prologue foreshadow in order the three more extended narrative sequences on which the novel ends. The first of these sequences (from 9:30 A.M. to 1:30 P.M.) deals with Dilsey's departure for church, the Easter service, and her return home (332–48); the second sequence (chronologically parallel to the first) links up with section 3 and relates Jason's pursuit of Miss Quentin and the carnival man (348–63); the third and last sequence is centered upon Benjy's and Luster's trip to the cemetery, and ends with the incident near the monument to the Confederate Soldier (363–71). However brief, this outline of the section's narrative structure allows one to dispel one or two misconceptions: it establishes irrefutably that Dilsey is not the focal figure throughout and that the narrative of the Easter service does not occupy the whole section. With a writer so deeply concerned with the architectonics of fiction, meaning cannot be dissociated from form, and in a novel like *The Sound and the Fury* the internal patterning of each section is surely as significant as the ordering of the four sections within the book.

Thus the counterpointing of the Easter service and of Jason's futile pursuit of his niece is obviously deliberate. As elsewhere, the montage of parallel actions allows Faulkner to weave a network of identities and differences. Their simultaneity, indicated at the outset by the morning bells tolling at Dilsey's departure (332) as well as at Jason's (348), is repeatedly recalled by references back and forth from one sequence to the other.[6] Through this temporal parallelism the contrasts are made the more conspicuous: the black people walk to the church in almost ritual procession, "with slow sabbath delibera-tion" (337), while Jason is driving to the carnival (a profane travesty of a religious festival) with increasingly frantic haste. The first sequence is marked by a sense of peaceful social communication (illustrated by the exchange of greetings between Dilsey and her friends, 336), and, at church, by religious communion (340); the second emphasizes Jason's extreme isolation: alone in pursuit, alone in defeat. Similarly, Dilsey's humble piety, shared by the black community, is set over against Jason's sacrilegious pride as he defies divine power itself in his Satanic rage (354). Lastly, while the celebration of the Resurrection of Christ brings the promise of eternal life to the faithful, Jason's "passion" ends appropriately in a grotesque parody of death ("So this is how it'll end, and he believed he was about to die," 359).

The Easter service follows a slowly ascending curve culminating in Reverend Shegog's visionary sermon; Jason's tribulations, on the other hand, evoke a furious and farcical dive to disaster. The antithesis is worked out in the smallest details, and from a Christian point of view it is indeed tempting to read it as the opposition between Satan's wretched fall and the glorious Resurrection of Christ. Yet at this point it is important to remember that the Jason sequence comes *after* the paschal episode. True, in the last section Jason no longer appears as formidable as before, and the failure of his chase gives us for once the satisfaction of seeing the forces of evil beating a retreat. Everything suggests, however, that the rout is only temporary and that Jason has lost nothing of his power to harm. And the very order of the episodes tips the balance in Jason's favor: the chase sequence reestablishes Jason in the leading role, even though it ends in his punishment, and so throws us back into the sordid, hate-filled atmosphere of the third section.

Returns

This regressive movement is pursued to the novel's close. From Jason the focus shifts to Benjy; coming full circle, the final pages carry us back to the beginning. Here again, as in the opening section, is Benjy with his guardian Luster. Once more, moaning and whimpering, he squats before his private "graveyard," the small mound of earth with its empty blue bottle and its withered stalk of jimson weed (364); once more, clinging to the fence, he watches the move-ments of the golfers (365). Even Caddy's ghost reappears, summoned by Luster's perverse whispering of her name to Benjy (365), and the latter imme-diately starts bellowing, only to be assuaged by Caddy's satin slipper, "yellow now, and cracked, and soiled" (366).

As for the very last scene, Benjy and Luster's trip by horse and surrey to the town cemetery, it was likewise anticipated in the first section. Yet this time the funeral excursion does not follow its customary route. We first get a glimpse of Benjy almost restored to tranquillity, "his eyes serene and ineffable" (369), clutching his broken narcissus stalk.[7] Yet when, after reaching the Confederate statue in the town square, Luster turns the horse to the left instead of the accustomed right, Benjy once again begins to roar in agony. But then Jason looms up, back from Mottson and seemingly resurrected in all his avenging fury, to reestablish the order violated by Luster's swerve:

> With a backhanded blow he hurled Luster aside and caught the reins and sawed Queenie about and doubled the reins back and slashed her across the hips. He cut her again and again, into a plunging gallop, while Benjy's hoarse agony roared about them, and swung her about to the right of the monument. Then he struck Luster over the head with his fist. (371)

Finding at last an opportunity to vent his anger and frustration, Jason brutalizes the old mare and lashes out at Luster. He even strikes Benjy, whose flower stalk is broken again. Yet order is indeed reestablished, and in the last sentence of the novel, Benjy's world seems to have recovered its balance:

> The broken flower drooped over Ben's fist and his eyes were empty and blue and serene again as cornice and façade flowed smoothly once more from left to right; post and tree, window and doorway, and signboard, each in its ordered place. (371)

Order is restored, but it is as empty as Benjy's idiotic stare or the petrified gaze of the Confederate Soldier (370). It brings to mind the endings of all the earlier sections: the smooth flow of things recalls the "smooth, bright shapes" signaling Benjy's falling asleep, and in its utter meaninglessness the close of the novel also recalls the ultimate absurdity of Quentin's fussy funeral toilette in section 2 and the demented dream closing Jason's monologue in section 3. And what makes the scene so memorable is not so much the final glimpse of peace regained as the ironic effect of contrast resulting from its juxtaposition with Jason's outburst of violence. The title of the book is given here a further illustration, the most startling perhaps in its harsh stridence, and also the most literally accurate: with Benjy's wild howling—"just sound"—and Jason's unleashed rage, there is indeed nothing left of the Compson world but "sound and fury."

In terms of plot, this ending is no ending at all. The final scene with Jason and Benjy puts an arbitrary stop to the action; it does not bring the expected dénouement. No dramatic resolution, whether tragic or comic, is provided; the tensions built up in the course of the narration are left undiminished, and the novel's complexities and ambiguities are as baffling as ever. Thematically, however, the scene is a powerful and poignant echo of the violence and disorder we have been witnessing all along, a condensed representation of all that has been presented before.[8]

The cry and the rhetoric

As in so much of modern fiction, the knots are not untied, the threads not unraveled. Our bafflement at the novel's close is not unlike Benjy's sense of outrage and disorder. All we can do is to return to the beginning and attempt another reading of the book—with little hope ever to find out its supposed secret. Yet the impossibility—for author and reader alike—of reaching a safe conclusion does not imply the absence of all closure. *The Sound and the Fury* is open-ended as far as plot is concerned, and it is inconclusive in its meaning. But this does not prevent it from achieving an aesthetic integrity of its own.

Formal closure should not be confused with semantic closure, and in the present case the former even seems to have been achieved in some measure at the cost of the latter. In traditional fiction endings are pointers to a fixed rationale, outside the text, in the light of which its contradictions are eventually resolved; in *The Sound and the Fury* the ending refers us back to the text itself, that is, to a tissue, a web of words, in which meanings are held in abeyance.

It is therefore wrong to assume that the closure of the final episode with Benjy "shapes the ultimate meaning of the novel"[9] and that this meaning is an authorial corroboration of Mr. Compson's nihilistic pronouncements in the second section. If structure *is* meaning, meaning does not arise from structure alone. The examination of the last section must therefore be taken further: it is not enough to isolate the broad units of the narrative and to see how their ordering inflects significance; it is indispensable as well to scrutinize the finer mesh of the section's texture.

The shift in style is certainly one of the most arresting features of section 4. Free of the restrictions of the interior monologue, Faulkner now seems to speak in his own person, and a richer, denser, more ceremonious style comes to unfold. Previously held in check or fraught with ironic intent, Faulkner's rhetoric now bursts into full flower. Not that it dominates the whole section, but it infuses the prose of the narrative with new energies, and projects a very different light upon the various actors of the drama. Consider, for example, the portrait of Dilsey in the two opening pages:

> The gown fell gauntly from her shoulders, across her fallen breasts, then tightened upon her paunch and fell again, ballooning a little above the nether garments which she would remove layer by layer as the spring accomplished and the warm days, in colour regal and moribund. She had been a big woman once but now her skeleton rose, draped loosely in unpadded skin that tightened again upon a paunch almost dropsical, as though muscle and tissue had been courage or fortitude which the days or the years had consumed until only the indomitable skeleton was left rising like a ruin or a landmark above the somnolent and impervious guts, and above that the collapsed face that gave the impression of the bones themselves being outside the flesh, lifted into the driving day with an expression at once fatalistic and of a child's astonished disappointment, until she turned and entered the house again and closed the door. (306–307)

The portrait cruelly emphasizes Dilsey's deformity and decrepitude, and multiplies the signs of impending death: with her fallen breasts and her dropsical paunch, the old black woman—a mere skeleton wrapped in a skin-bag—appears here as a grim *memento mori*. Yet, solemnized by the abstract magnificence of the epithets (most of which are ponderous polysyllabic Latinisms) and expanded by the suggestive power of the similes, the description goes well beyond the demands of realism, and far from degrading Dilsey to a macabre scarecrow, it raises her to tragic dignity. Dressed in "regal" color—a "dress of purple silk" and a "maroon velvet cape" (306)[10]—she is lent from the outset an aura of majesty which belies the wretchedness of her ravaged, age-worn body. The servant, the descendant of slaves is turned into a sovereign figure. A queen of no visible kingdom, a queen dispossessed and "moribund" but whose "indomitable" skeleton rises in the gray light of an inauspicious dawn as a challenge to death—a paradoxical symbol of that which transcends mortal flesh and triumphs over time, of that which "endures."[11] And similarly ennobled and embellished by the baroque "coruscations" of Faulkner's eloquence, Dilsey's tears become the essence of universal grief: "Two tears slid down her fallen cheeks, in and out of the myriad coruscations of immolation and abnegation and time" (341).

Benjy likewise appears in a different light. The figure of the idiot had gradually faded from the scene; now he comes right to the forefront again, not only in the closing scene but also at the beginning of the section and in the episode in the Negro church. What is perhaps most remarkable about Benjy in the final section is that his presence there is predominantly vocal: apart from the startling visual description we are given at his first appearance, he is more often heard than seen. His cries and whining—made haunting through the repetition of "crying," "wailing," "whimpering," "slobbering," "bellowing"—supply what might be called the basic soundtrack of the section. Never articulated as speech, scarcely human, Benjy's cries are the abject and pathetic expression of his nameless and unnameable suffering:

> Then Ben wailed again, hopeless and prolonged. It was nothing. Just sound. It might have been all time and injustice and sorrow become vocal for an instant by a conjunction of planets. (333)

> But he bellowed slowly, abjectly, without tears; the grave hopeless sound of all voiceless misery under the sun. (366)

> There was more than astonishment in it, it was horror; shock; agony eyeless, tongueless; just sound. . . . (370)

These passages are reminders of Benjy's intense and inarticulate suffering, but in a sense they also suggest the writer's paradoxical gamble in the very act of creation. Indicative of a double deprivation—the absence of happiness and the absence of speech—Benjy's helpless cries convey lack by lack, and in the text this state of extreme dispossession is forcibly emphasized by the recurrence of privative suffixes. Benjy's cries fail to say what he failed to preserve; they are the burning language of absence and the blind eloquence of the absurd. They are nothing: "just sound." This nothing, though, encompasses "all time and injustice and sorrow," "all voiceless misery under the sun." But is this conjunction of nothing and everything not to be found too in what seems to be at the very antipodes of the cry, that is, literature? And is not the voicing of the voiceless, the naming of the nameless also the deepest desire of the writer? Language at its most ambitious refers dialectically back to the inarticulateness of the cry: it is its negation in that it relies on the signifying powers of the word, while being also its completion insofar as it manages to recapture the immediate pathos of the cry. Not that all literature nurses this ambition, but *The Sound and the Fury* is surely a case in point, and may be considered Faulkner's most daring attempt to come as close as possible to that which is both revealed and silenced in the "eyeless" and "tongueless" agony of the cry. It was of course an impossible wager: to keep it was to lose it. For in the pregnant silence of the printed page the cry is no longer a cry; Benjy's whimperings and bellowings, by being named, are absorbed into the mute eloquence of written discourse and appropriated by literature, which turns them into symbols of its own impotence, of its own vanity.

The cry and the rhetoric. From one the novel moves to the other, and the very ordonnance of the book may be said to reflect this movement of reappropriation. The first section is in its extreme confusion the closest approximation to the "voiceless misery" of the cry; the last, where literature reasserts its claims and the writer reestablishes his authority, is seemingly the furthest from it. Yet Faulkner's rhetoric in the final section attempts to preserve something of the primal urgency of the cry, and in a way reverts to it, making it "vocal for an instant" by a conjunction of words. Moreover, this rhetoric obviously gains strength and persuasiveness from coming after Benjy's "sound," Quentin's *cri du coeur*, and Jason's "fury." Far from describing arabesques in the void, it traces them on soil already prepared. When Dilsey and Benjy reappear in the fourth section, they have already gathered so much weight and substance that their metamorphosis into archetypes of endurance and suffering does not strike us as arbitrary allegorizing.

A simple heart

From the particulars of limited individual experience the last section moves toward the universality of the mythic. Without ceasing to be a slobbering idiot, Benjy comes to stand for crucified innocence in the context of the Easter service at the Negro church; the man-child becomes an analogon of Christ. But the character in which the fusion of realism and symbolism is most successfully achieved is without any doubt Dilsey. Even though her function has often been misunderstood or overemphasized, there can be no question that she is the most memorable character in the last section. Technically, the point of view is not hers, and in dramatic terms her role is a limited one. Yet critics should not be blamed too roundly for attributing the last section to her; even Faulkner called it "the Dilsey section."[12] The one truly admirable character in the novel, she had a special place in the writer's affections: "Dilsey is one of my favorite characters, because she is brave, courageous, generous, gentle, honest. She is much more brave and honest and generous than me."[13] She is no less admirable as a literary creation. Her portrait is so sharply individualized and her figure so warm and earthy that the charge of excessive idealization is hardly relevant. As Cleanth Brooks has rightly noted, Dilsey is "no noble savage and no *schöne Seele*."[14] Nor should she be reduced to a racial stereotype. True, she seems to fit rather nicely in the tradition of the black mammy, and her literary lineage is readily traced back to Thomas Nelson Page.[15] However, the point is that her virtues, as they are presented in the novel, owe nothing to race.[16]

That she was meant to counterbalance the Compsons is obvious enough. Her words and actions offer throughout an eloquent contrast to the behavior of her masters. In her role of faithful—though not submissive—servant, Dilsey represents the sole force for order and stability in the Compson household.[17] Not only does she see with tireless diligence and devotion to the family's material needs; she also tries, albeit with little success, to stave off the day of its disintegration. Taking on the responsibilities traditionally assumed by the mother, she comes to replace the lamentable Mrs. Compson as keeper of the house. In the later sections, she appears as Benjy's last resort,[18] and she also defends Caddy and her daughter against Jason, the usurper of paternal authority.

In the face of the whining or heinous egoism of the Compsons, Dilsey embodies the generosity of total selflessness; in contrast to Quentin's tortured idealism and Jason's sordid pragmatism, she also represents the active wisdom of simple hearts. Without fostering the slightest illusion about her exploiters, expecting no gratitude for her devotion, Dilsey accepts the world as it is, while striving as best she can to make it somewhat more habitable. Unlike the Compsons, she does not abdicate before reality nor does she refuse time, which she alone is capable of gauging and interpreting correctly:

> On the wall above a cupboard, invisible save at night, by lamp light and even then evincing an enigmatic profundity because it had but one hand, a cabinet clock ticked, then with a preliminary sound as if it cleared its throat, struck five times.
> "Eight oclock," Dilsey said. . . . (316–17)

In his rage against time, Quentin tore off the hands of his watch. The Compsons' old kitchen clock has but one hand left and its chime is out of order. Yet Dilsey does not take offense at its "lying" and automatically corrects its errors. To her, time is no matter of obsession. Not that she adjusts to it out of mere habit. Her time is not simply a "natural" phenomenon, any more than her moral qualities are "natural" virtues. Faulkner describes her as a Christian, and no analysis of the character can afford to discount the deep religious convictions attributed to her. Hers is a seemingly naive piety, a simple faith unencumbered by theological subtleties, but it gives her the courage to be and persevere which her masters lack, and provides her existence with a definite meaning and purpose. Dilsey envisions everything in the light of the threefold mystery of the Incarnation, Passion, and Resurrection of Christ. In Benjy she sees "de Lawd's chile" (367), one of the poor in spirit promised the Kingdom of God, and for her all human suffering is justified and redeemed in the divine sacrifice commemorated during Holy Week.

Dilsey's attitude toward time proceeds quite logically from the tenets of her Christian faith. Whereas for Quentin, the incurable idealist, time is the hell of immanence, it is transfused with eternity for Dilsey. Not "a tale full of sound and fury signifying nothing," but the history of God's people. The Christ of her belief has not been "worn away by the minute clicking of little wheels" (87); his crucifixion was not a victory by time but a victory over time. Guaranteed in the past by the death and resurrection of the Son of God and in the future by the promise of His return, bounded by the Passion and the Second Coming, time regains a meaning and a direction, and each man's existence becomes again the free and responsible adventure of an individual destiny. Dilsey's Christ-centered faith allows her to adhere fully to all of time's dimensions: her answer to the past is fidelity; the present she endures with patience and humility, and armed with the theological virtue of hope, she is also able to face the future without alarm. While for Quentin there is an unbridgeable gap between the temporal and the timeless, Dilsey's eternity, instead of being an immobile splendor *above* the flux of time, is already present and at work *in* time, embodied in it just as the word was made flesh. Time, then, is no longer felt as endless and senseless repetition; nor is it experienced as an inexorable process of decay. It does have a pattern, since history has been informed from its beginnings by God's design. And it can be redeemed and vanquished, but, as T. S. Eliot puts it in the *Four Quartets,* "Only through time time is conquered."[19] Which is to say that the hour of its final defeat will be the hour of its fulfillment and reabsorption into eternity.

Firmly rooted in the eschatological doctrine of Christianity, Dilsey's concept of time is theo-logical and teleo-logical, not chrono-logical. The assumptions on which it rests remain of course implicit, but it is in this orthodoxly Christian perspective that we are asked to interpret Dilsey's comment after Reverend Shegog's sermon: "I've seed de first en de last. . . . I seed de beginnin, en now I sees de endin" (344; see also 348). Given the context of Easter in which they occur, her words obviously refer to the beginning and end of time, to the Alpha and Omega of Christ. But it goes without saying that they apply as well to the downfall of the Compsons which Dilsey has been witnessing all along. The implication is certainly not that after all the Compsons may be saved, but what the oblique connection between the Passion Week and the family tragedy suggests is that for Dilsey the drama of the Compsons is above all one of redemption denied.

Black Easter

Yet what the Compson story means to Dilsey is not necessarily what it means to us, nor what it was meant to mean. At this point the impossibility of any final interpretation becomes obvious again. For how are we to take the many references to Christianity included in the novel? And how do they relate to this story of decline and death? One may argue that Faulkner's use of them is ironical, that they point—derisively or nostalgically—to a vanishing myth and expose its total irrelevance as far as the Compsons are concerned. Or one may interpret them in terms of paradox, the more legitimately so, it seems, as paradox has been a major mode of Judeo-Christian thought and is indeed central to Christian faith itself. According to whether irony or paradox is taken to be the clue to Faulkner's intentions, diametrically opposed interpretations of the novel will suggest themselves to the reader. But the question is one of effects rather than intentions, and it is extremely difficult to settle, since paradox and irony alike work by way of inversion.

Inversion is one of Faulkner's favorite techniques. In *The Sound and the Fury* its procedures can be traced in many places, but nowhere perhaps are they as consistently and as intriguingly used as in the episode of the Easter service.[20] With regard to the rest of the novel (and more directly to the juxtaposed Jason sequence), the episode fulfills a contrasting function homologous to that of Dilsey in relation to the other characters. And the contrast is so sharp and so unexpected that the reader is jolted into a radically different mood. It is as if a spring of pure water suddenly welled up in an arid desert, or as if the dismal clamor of the accursed family were momentarily suspended to let us listen to a gospel song. But the episode is no less surprising in the detail of its composition and the movement of its development, both of which owe a good deal of their impact to Faulkner's handling of inversion. The sequence opens rather inauspiciously with the description of the desolate setting of Dilsey's walk to the church (335–36): nothing yet heralds the upsurge of Easter joy. A sense of expectancy is soon created, however, by the gathered congregation impatiently awaiting "dat big preacher" (335) from St. Louis. But when he at last arrives, he turns out to be a shabby, monkey-faced gnome:

> when they saw the man who had preceded their minister enter the pulpit still ahead of him an indescribable sound went up, a sigh, a sound of astonishment and disappointment.
>
> The visitor was undersized, in a shabby alpaca coat. He had a wizened black face like a small, aged monkey. And all the while that the choir sang again and while the six children rose and sang in thin, frightened, tuneless whispers, they watched the insignificant looking man sitting dwarfed and countrified by the minister's imposing bulk, with something like consternation. (338–39)

The frustration, though, is turned into starry-eyed wonderment when the preacher begins his sermon:

> His voice was level and cold. It sounded too big to have come from him and
> they listened at first through curiosity, as they would have to a monkey talking.
> They began to watch him as they would a man on a tight rope. They even forgot
> his insignificant appearance in the virtuosity with which he ran and poised and
> swooped upon the cold inflectionless wire of his voice, so that at last, when with
> a sort of swooping glide he came to rest again beside the reading desk with one
> arm resting upon it at shoulder height and his monkey body as reft of all motion
> as a mummy or an emptied vessel, the congregation sighed as if it waked from
> a collective dream and moved a little in its seats. (339)

Belying the shabbiness and grotesqueness of his physical appearance,
Reverend Shegog displays the mesmerizing talents of a brilliant orator. But
there is more to come: a second, even more stunning metamorphosis occurs
when the cold virtuosity of the "white" sermon suddenly bursts into the
incantatory vehemence of "black" eloquence:

> Then a voice said, "Brethren."
> The preacher had not moved. His arm lay yet across the desk, and he still held
> that pose while the voice died in sonorous echoes between the walls. It was as
> different as day and dark from his former tone, with a sad, timbrous quality like
> an alto horn, sinking into their hearts and speaking there again when it had
> ceased in fading and cumulate echoes. (340)

This is the moment of the decisive reversal: the preacher is no longer master
of his rhetoric, nor is he anymore master of his voice. Instead of being the
flexible instrument of his eloquence, the voice, "a voice"—having seemingly
acquired a will of its own—now seizes his body and uses it as its tool. The
tightrope artist has vanished; Shegog has become the docile servant of the
Word:

> He was like a worn small rock whelmed by the successive waves of his voice.
> With his body he seemed to feed the voice that, succubus like, had fleshed its
> teeth in him. And the congregation seemed to watch with its own eyes while
> the voice consumed him, until he was nothing and they were nothing and there
> was not even a voice but instead their hearts were speaking to one another in
> chanting measures beyond the need for words. . . . (340)

The consuming voice not only reduces the preacher to a mere medium of the
Easter message; it reaches out toward the congregation and, delving into the
innermost recesses of souls, unites them in a wordless chant of communion.
The orderly discourse of cold reason, significantly associated with the facile
tricks of "a white man" (339), has given way to the spontaneous language of
the heart, a language moving paradoxically toward its own extinction as it
resolves itself into "chanting measures beyond the need for words." All that
"white" rhetoric could achieve was "a collective dream" (339); what is accomplished now is a truly collective experience, a welding of many into one.
For the first time in the novel, separation and fragmentation are at least

temporarily transcended; consciousness, instead of narrowing down to private fantasy and obsession, is expanded through the ritual reenactment of myth. In this unique instant of grace and ecstasy, all human misery is miraculously transfigured, all infirmities are forgotten, and the preacher's puny silhouette rises before the faithful like a living replica of the crucified God: "his monkey face lifted and his whole attitude that of a serene, tortured crucifix that transcended its shabbiness and insignificance and made it of no moment" (340–41).

The sermon

The reader is now prepared to *listen* to the sermon itself, to its sounds and rhythms, as the congregation listens. Again there will be surprises, ruptures, reversals, but the dominant mood is at present one of trust and exaltation, any remaining doubts being swept away by the intimate certainty of redemption: "I got de ricklickshun en de blood of de Lamb" (341). Yet the sermon begins on a plaintive note, faintly recalling Quentin's obsessions with time and death: "Dey passed away in Egypt, de swinging chariots; de generations passed away. Wus a rich man: whar he now, O breddren? Wus a po man: whar he now, O sistuhn?" (341). There follows a breathless evocation of the persecuted childhood of Christ: "Breddren! Look at dem little chillen setting dar. Jesus wus like dat once. He mammy suffered de glory en de pangs. Sometime maybe she helt him at de nightfall, whilst de angels singin him to sleep; maybe she look out de do en see de Roman po-lice passin" (342). Jesus here becomes the paradigm for martyred innocence, and the relevance of this paradigm to present circumstances is poignantly emphasized by the implicit reference to Benjy, the innocent idiot, sitting amid the black community, "rapt in his sweet blue gaze" (343).

The legendary and the actual, the past and the present are thus not only contrasted, but significantly linked. Myth infuses reality: projected into an immemorial past, Benjy and Dilsey are transformed into archetypal figures through their identification with Christ and the Madonna. Conversely, the remote events of the Passion are brought back to life again and quiver with pathetic immediacy in the compelling vision of the preacher:

> "I sees hit, breddren! I sees hit! Sees de blastin, blindin sight! I sees Calvary, wid de sacred trees, sees de thief en de murderer en de least of dese; I hears de boasting en de braggin: Ef you be Jesus, lif up yo tree en walk! I hears de wailing of women en de evenin lamentations; I hear de weepin en de cryin en de turnt-away face of God: dey done kilt Jesus; dey done kilt my Son!" (342–43)

With the death of Christ, the sermon reaches its nadir. The preacher now witnesses the seemingly absolute triumph of Evil, and his vision becomes one of utter chaos and destruction: "I sees de whelmin flood roll between; I sees de darkness en de death everlastin upon de generations" (343). Yet this note of despair (again reminiscent of the Quentin section) is not sustained, and immediately after everything is reversed by the miracle of the Resurrection. Shadows disperse, death is forever conquered in the glory of the Second Coming:

> "I sees de resurrection en de light; sees de meek Jesus sayin Dey kilt Me dat ye shall live again; I died dat dem whut sees en believes shall never die. Breddren, O breddren! I sees de doom crack en hears de golden horns shoutin down de glory, en de arisen dead whut got de blood en de ricklickshun of de Lamb!" (343)

Although Reverend Shegog's Easter sermon only occupies a few pages in the novel, it looms very large. And while it is true that it would carry even greater weight if Faulkner had chosen to place it at the novel's close, its impact is greater than a purely structural analysis of the fourth section would lead one to expect. Literary meanings and effects are differential, to be sure, but to assess them correctly is not enough to see how they are "placed" within the text; it is also important to measure the amplitude of the differences. For the singularity here is not only one of subject and theme, nor does it merely arise from a tonal switch. A radical reversal occurs, operating on all possible levels and altering the very fiber of the novel's texture. As the narrator's own preliminary comments suggest, another *voice* takes over, which is not that of any speaker in the novel, nor that of the narrator/author—a voice enigmatically self-generated and mysteriously compelling, *the subjectless voice of myth*.

Another language is heard, unprecedented in the novel, signaled at once by the cultural-ethnic shift from "white" to "black," the emotional shift from rational coldness to spiritual fervor, and lastly by the stylistic shift from the mechanical cadences of shallow rhetoric to the entrancing rhythms of inspired speech. Not that this new language dispenses with formal devices: Shegog's sermon, so far from being an uncontrolled outpouring of emotion, is very firmly patterned and makes extensive use of rhetorical emphasis (questions and exclamations) as well as of such classical procedures as parallelism and incremental repetition (most conspicuous in the abundance of anaphoric constructions). The sermon is the ritual retelling of a mythic story fully known by all the members of the congregation: its narrative contents form a fixed sequence, and the mode of its transmission conforms likewise to a stable code. What needs to be stressed, too, is that the specific tradition to which this speech belongs is the folk tradition—well-established, particularly, in African-American culture—of the *oral* sermon.[21] Ritualized as it is, the preacher's eloquence is the eloquence of the spoken word, and Shegog's sermon reads indeed like the transcript of an oral performance. The effect is partly achieved through the faithful phonetic rendering of the black dialect. Yet Faulkner's greatest success is that he has also managed to capture the musical quality of the sermon: the "sad, timbrous quality like an alto horn, sinking into their hearts and speaking there again when it had ceased in fading and cumulate echoes" (340). More than anything else it is this musicality (i.e., that which, in his speech, belongs to another, nonverbal language) that ensures true communication between the speaker and the listeners, and among the audience itself. Myth and music cooperate in this Easter celebration to free all participants from "the need for words" as well as from the tyranny of time. Is it not precisely in their relation to time that music and myth are alike? As Claude Lévi-Strauss has noted, "it is as if music and mythology needed time only to deny it. Both, indeed, are instruments for the obliteration of time."[22]

What matters here is not so much the message conveyed as the collective ceremony of its utterance and its sharing, a ceremony allowing at once personal identity to be transcended and cultural identity to be confirmed. In contrast to the painful and derisory remembrances of the Compsons, the *commemoration* of the mythic event by the black community appears to be a victory over solitude.

The mythic word

Shegog's Easter sermon may be called a triumph of Faulkner's verbal virtuosity. It is noteworthy, however, that this *tour de force* was achieved through a gesture of humility. For the novelist refrained from improving on the tradition of the oral sermon as he found it. There is no literary embellishment, and there is hardly a personal touch one might attribute to the author. Shegog's sermon has been compared with records of sermons actually delivered: the difference between the latter and Faulkner's creation is barely noticeable.[23] Which is to say that, strictly speaking, it is no creation at all, but only evidence of Faulkner's extraordinary mimetic abilities. The writer here lays no claim to artistic originality, and his self-effacement is carried to such lengths that his own voice is no longer heard. Instead we are *truly* listening to the anonymous voice of an unwritten tradition, grown out of ancient roots and periodically revivified by the rites of popular piety—a voice, that is, whose authority owes nothing to the talents of an author. From *auctor* the writer has become *scriptor*, a modest scrivener scrupulously transcribing a prior text.

This is what makes the sermon a unique moment in the novel: it marks the intrusion of the spoken into the written, of the nonliterary into the literary, of the mythic into the fictional, and by the same token it also signals the writer's willing renunciation of his authorial pride and of his prerogatives as a fiction-maker (or, to put it in Heideggerian terms, his capacity to *be spoken* rather than to speak). It becomes tempting, then, to see the preacher-figure as a double of the novelist himself: do not both surrender their identity as speakers/writers to become the vehicles of an impersonal mythic voice?

Given the importance accorded to the biblical text and to the living word in the Christian—and especially in the Puritan—tradition, it is of course hardly surprising that a writer with Faulkner's background should have been fascinated with the voice of myth. In the register of the imaginary, myth is in the novel's last section what fantasy is to the prior ones. Much like fantasy, myth is a creation of human desire negating time and death. However, as long as myth remains an object of collective belief periodically reactivated by ritual, it also fulfills a gathering function and testifies to the permanence of a shared culture. Hence the novel invokes as a last resort traditional mythic values and ritual practices, and finds them in a community in which their sacred aura has been, to all appearances, fully preserved.

Religion is *religio*, what binds man to man, man to God. The novel's last section is clearly haunted by nostalgia for religion as a binding power, but also as a way of seeing if not of knowing. The voice that takes hold of the preacher induces a vision, and this moment of vision, fully shared by the congregation, is in fact the only experience of spiritual enlightenment recorded in the whole book. Illumination or illusion? In Faulkner's text, at any rate, this capacity for vision is set against the chronic blindness of the Compsons.[24] Both Dilsey and Shegog *see*, and their vision is apparently one that goes beyond the confines of time and flesh; it brings order and significance to their lives and gives them the strength to endure pain and loss. To Dilsey, in particular, the preacher's words bring the encompassing revelation of eternity, the mystical and prophetic vision of "the beginning and the ending."

Is this to say that they embody Faulkner's novelistic "vision," and that the Easter service at the Negro church provides the key to the novel's interpretation? For those who read *The Sound and the Fury* from theological premises, there is no doubt about the answer. Comparing the sermon in Faulkner's novel to the legend of the Grand Inquisitor in *The Brothers Karamazov* or to Father Mapple's sermon in *Moby-Dick*, they do not hesitate to invest it with the same central hermeneutic function: "it tells us the meaning of the various signs and symbols as on a geographical map; it tells us how to read the drama, how to interpret the characters of the plot that has been unfolding before us."[25] From there to calling *The Sound and the Fury* a Christian novel is a short step. It is one step too many, however, for although there is much to suggest such an interpretation, there is little, in the last resort, to validate it. Faulkner's work is misread as soon as it is *arrested*, and critics go astray whenever they seek to reduce its intricate web of ambiguities to a single pattern of meaning. *The Sound and the Fury* stubbornly resists any attempt to dissolve its opaqueness into the reassuring clarity of an ideological statement.

That Faulkner's fiction is heavily indebted to the Christian tradition is beyond question, and the writer himself, in his interviews, freely acknowledged the debt.[26] But it is essential to relate it to the specific context of the novelist's creation: to Faulkner, Christianity was first of all an inexhaustible fund of cultural references, a treasure of images and symbols or, to borrow one of his own favorite words, an extremely useful collection of "tools." This, of course, does not settle the question of his relationship to Christianity. There is surely more than a mere craftsman's debt: myth is both the bad conscience and the utopia of Western fiction, and for Faulkner as for many other modern novelists, the Christian myth remains an ever-present paradigm, an ordering scheme, a pattern of intelligibility toward which his fiction never ceases to move as toward a lost horizon of truth, or rather *through* which it is moving to produce its own myths. Faulkner's quest and questioning remain to a very large extent caught up in Christian modes of thought and expression, as can be even more plainly seen in later works such as *Go Down, Moses, Requiem for a Nun,* and *A Fable.* Yet Faulkner's life-long involvement with Christianity entailed no personal commitment to Christian faith, and none of his public pronouncements substantiates the claim that he considered himself a Christian writer. Besides, even if Faulkner had been an avowed believer, the relationship of his work to Christianity would still be problematical, for insofar as it is literature, it displaces the myths on which it feeds. Aspiring to turn fictions into myths, it is fated to turn myths into fictions.

The success of failure

"A work of literature," says Roland Barthes, "or at least of the kind that is normally considered by the critics (and this itself may be a possible definition of 'good' literature) is neither ever quite meaningless (mysterious or 'inspired') nor ever quite clear; it is, so to speak, *suspended* meaning; it offers itself to the reader as a declared system of significances, but as a signified object it eludes his grasp. This kind of *dis-appointment* or *deception* . . . inherent in the meaning explains how it is that a work of literature has such power to ask questions of the world . . . without, however, supplying any answer."[27] Faulkner's fiction fully bears out Barthes's assumptions. The wealth of Christian allusions we find in *The Sound and the Fury* adds immeasurably to its semantic pregnancy, but in the last analysis Christian values are neither affirmed nor denied. Episodes such as the Easter service and figures such as Dilsey are impressive evidence of Faulkner's deep understanding of Christianity, and they seem to hint at possibilities of experience which the ego-bound Compsons have irremediably lost. Yet, as Cleanth Brooks rightly notes, "Faulkner makes no claim for Dilsey's version of Christianity one way or the other. His presentation of it is moving and credible, but moving and credible only as an aspect of Dilsey's own mental and emotional life."[28] The reader's "disappointment" in this respect is all the greater as Faulkner's novel often *seems* to imply the existence of seizable significances: his ironies do suggest a radically negative vision, and his paradoxes bring us very close indeed to the spirit of Christianity. However, the point about Faulkner's ironies and paradoxes is that they are irreducibly *his.* Etymologically, irony implies dissembling, or feigned ignorance, and paradox refers likewise to a hidden truth. If these classical definitions are retained, Faulkner's inversions are neither ironies nor paradoxes: they are not disguised affirmations but statements of uncertainty and modes of questioning.

So the final leap is never made, nor should it be attempted by the reader. Shall we then agree with those critics to whom *The Sound and the Fury* is simply an ingenious montage of contrasting perspectives, a brilliant exercise in ambiguity? To pose the question in these terms is again to miss the point. Those who think that the novel should have a determinable sense and deplore its inconclusiveness are just as mistaken as those who assume that it has one and therefore refuse to acknowledge its indeterminacies. Both approaches fail to acknowledge the specificity of literary discourse and disregard the very impetus of Faulkner's writing. For far from being inert antinomies, its contradictions generate a field of dynamic tension and are in fact what sets his books in motion. The tension is not solved, nor can it be, but this irresolution is to be imputed neither to an incapacity to make up one's mind nor to a masochistic pursuit of failure. No more than to a Christian or a nihilistic statement should *The Sound and the Fury* be reduced to a neutral balancing of contrary views.

To Faulkner the choice was not between affirmation and denial, sense or nonsense, so much as between writing and silence. As soon as words get written, meanings are produced, that is, are both brought forth and exhibited, and the elaborately deceptive uses of language characteristic of literary discourse, far from canceling significance, open up its infinite possibilities. It is true that in their different ways modern and postmodern novelists such as Beckett, Blanchot, and Robbe-Grillet (not to mention the posterity of Rimbaud among poets) have done their utmost to rarefy meaning, to bring literature as close as possible to the condition of silence, and in one sense to do so is every writer's hope. Faulkner, however, was in no way a minimalist. His literary ancestors are to be sought among the more robust of the great nineteenth-century masters, and if we relate him to his contemporaries or quasi-contemporaries, he is clearly closer to the omnivorous Joyce than to the almost anorexic Beckett. His drive was toward more and more, not less and less. And like Joyce, Faulkner pursued his quest in the teeth of absurdity. "Prendre sens dans l'insensé"[29]—to make sense of and in the senseless, to take up one's quarters where absurdity is at its thickest, is how Paul Eluard defined the function of modern literature. The definition also applies to Faulkner's design, and nowhere perhaps is this design more in evidence than in the final section of *The Sound and the Fury*. While the novel's tensions are there raised to an almost unbearable pitch, the shrill irony of its ending leaves them forever unresolved.

Yet simultaneously a countermovement develops, away from absurdity toward some tentative ordering. Faulkner's rhetoric here is both at its most ambitious and at its most humble: at its most ambitious when it gathers its energies to reassert the powers of language and the authority of the writer; at its most humble when it effaces itself behind the sacred eloquence of an Easter sermon and yields to the anonymous authority of the myth. It is most significant, too, that in this section Faulkner's inversions so often take on the colors of paradox. Given their cultural context, these paradoxes seem to call for a Christian interpretation, but one may wonder whether they do not all refer back to the central paradox of the writer's own endeavor. For the writing process also tends to operate a radical inversion of signs; it too draws strength from its weakness and glories in its want. As we have seen, Shegog, the frail vessel of the sovereign Word, may be taken for an analogon of the novelist himself, reaching the point of inspired dispossession where his individuality gives way to the "voice." And the mystical vision granted to the preacher may likewise be said to metaphorize the unmediated vision sought after by the writer. What these analogies seem to point to is the mirage of an ultimate reversal: that which would restore the absolute presence of language to itself and convert its emptiness into plenitude, its fragmentation into wholeness— fiction raised to mythos, speech raised to logos.

It is of course an impossible dream: the quest is never completed, the reversal forever postponed. There is no denouement, no final unknotting. The last section does not provide the hoped-for perspective from which the dissonant earlier sections could be seen as parts of a coherent and under- standable whole. It only introduces us to another, less solipsistic "world," juxtaposed to the worlds of Benjy, Quentin, and Jason but incapable of holding them together. Yet even though the gap between language and meaning is always there, as readers we insist—cannot but insist, as we do with all works of art we wish to understand and make our own—that what falls apart only seems to do so and actually falls together. The illusion cannot be dispelled that the writing process has managed to create an order of its own, assigning each word and sentence to "its ordered place." And it is not just an illusion; there is indeed an order, or rather an ordering, generated out of the very vacuum of language and the very emptiness of desire. The text of *The Sound and the Fury* does hold together, and achieves admirable integrity as an aesthetic design. And while the furious and helpless voices of the Compson brothers exhaust themselves in utter solitude, the patterned incompleteness of *The Sound and the Fury* waits for readers and requires their active participation. Not that they can succeed where the author failed. But if their reading of the novel is not mindless consumption (which it can hardly be), they, too, will take part in the unending process of its production. Reading and rereading the book, they will write it again.

Two

Requiem for a Mother

VII

A "TOUR DE FORCE"

I try all things; I achieve what I can.

Ishmael in *Moby-Dick*

A spectacle of voices

After completing the manuscript of *The Sound and the Fury* in October or November 1928, Faulkner wrote the first version of *Sanctuary*. Not until a year later—on October 25, 1929—did he begin *As I Lay Dying*. Following each other in publication, *The Sound and the Fury* and *As I Lay Dying* did not immediately follow each other in composition, and yet their thematic, technical, and formal affinities are so numerous that they seem to have been written in the same stride.[1]

In *As I Lay Dying*, Faulkner focuses for the second time in his novelistic career on divisions and conflicts within a single family, but the starting point of *The Sound and the Fury*, the "mental image" at its origin—a group of children faced with their grandmother's death—here nearly becomes the focal point, since most of the narrative revolves around a dying, then dead woman, and her long deferred funeral. And as the dead woman happens to be the children's *mother*, the impact of death is much deeper and the pathos of mourning much more compelling.

A death in the family, a family gathered in grief around a parent's remains: *As I Lay Dying*, as we shall see, is yet another story of bereavement, another tale of loss and sorrow. But the mortuary scene unfolds here on a fairly different, seemingly simpler, and at any rate far more rustic stage. Exeunt the princes; enter the peasants. Moving to the lower reaches of southern society, which he had already started to explore in "Father Abraham" and in some of his early sketches and short stories, Faulkner provisionally abandons the declining dynasties of Jefferson to portray a family of poor—tenant or share-cropping?—farmers from the hills of northern Mississippi. In contrast to the Compsons and the Sartorises, the Bundrens count neither governors nor generals among their ancestors; for them there is no genealogical imperative, no familial heritage to come to terms with, and if they are not without pride and honor, they have barely a past beyond the memories of their own lives. The parents are here the alpha of the family alphabet: *A* like Anse, *A* like Addie. In the beginning was the Father and the Mother.

That *As I Lay Dying* deals with a "nuclear" family of poor country people, however, does not imply a radical shift in outlook. The minds of the Bundrens are no less haunted and no less twisted than those of Faulkner's decadent patricians. Neurosis, after all, is not a privilege of the educated; nor do all farmers possess healthy minds in healthy bodies: Faulkner was much too astute to be taken in by old pastoral clichés. To argue, then, that in his third family chronicle Faulkner turns from the pathos of bourgeois melodrama to the laughter of folk comedy would be a gross oversimplification. It is true that the Bundrens stick together as long as their survival as a family is at stake. But their fiercely clannish solidarity in the face of outside danger is no victory over individual anguish; it serves only to mask the conflicts smoldering within the family. As Calvin Bedient notes, the Bundren family is "a terrible and frustrating unit of interlocking solitudes, atomic in structure like a molecule."[2] Family relationships in Faulkner are seldom idyllic, and this novel, setting against each other husband and wife, mother and son, father and daughter, brother and brother, and brother and sister, presents almost the whole range of possible tensions.

Let us note, though, that the composition of the Bundren family reproduces a pattern already used in *The Sound and the Fury* : again there are several sons and *one* daughter. Faulkner himself saw in this similarity the only link between the two books: "If there is any relationship it's probably simply because both of them happened to have a sister in a roaring gang of menfolks."[3] The novels resemble each other much more than Faulkner was willing to admit, and the unmistakable "family likeness" between them is the more arresting as they also share similarities in narrative design and technique. Apart from the last section of *The Sound and the Fury*, both novels consist entirely of unframed, unlocated, and seemingly uncoordinated "interior monologues," and are indeed the only ones in the Faulknerian corpus to rely so heavily on "stream of consciousness." While both are experimental works of stunning originality, *The Sound and the Fury* and *As I Lay Dying* are beyond doubt Faulkner's most ostensibly Joycean texts, and in this respect too they are "sister novels."

In view of these resemblances, the contrasts become the more significant. As we have seen, writing *The Sound and the Fury* was for Faulkner a unique experience, followed by no second miracle. When he wrote *Sanctuary*, "there was something missing; something which The Sound and the Fury gave me and Sanctuary did not."[4] And with the following novel came a similar disappointment:

> When I began *As I Lay Dying* I had discovered what it was and knew that it would be also missing in this case because this would be a deliberate book. I set out deliberately to write a tour-de-force. Before I ever put pen to paper and set down the first word, I knew what the last word would be and almost where the

last period would fall. Before I began I said, I am going to write a book by which, at a pinch, I can stand or fall if I never touch ink again. So when I finished it the cold satisfaction was there, as I had expected, but as I had also expected that other quality which The Sound and the Fury had given me was absent.[5]

A deliberate tour de force: it was nearly always in these terms that Faulkner referred to *As I Lay Dying* in his interviews.[6] Of course, his retrospective comments on the genesis of his novels must be read with caution, for the truths they convey are seldom literal ones. But as much by the speed with which it was written as by the virtuosity of its technique *As I Lay Dying* is indeed a dazzling accomplishment. It has all the appeal of a brilliant impromptu, the beauty of a perfectly executed trapeze exercise. Of all Faulkner's novels, it is perhaps the most agile, the most adroit, the one in which the writer's new-won mastery of his craft and the versatility of his gifts reveal themselves in the most spectacular ways.

This does not mean, however, that it was merely a bravura performance. If Faulkner, at this point, was already an accomplished writer, he was by no means an established author. *The Sound and the Fury*, while a *succès d'estime*, left Faulkner still lacking public recognition, and with *As I Lay Dying* he once again staked his all.[7] What had changed, though, as he later described it, was his relationship to the blank sheet: the "ecstasy" and agony he had experienced when writing *The Sound and the Fury* gave way to an attitude less emotionally charged. No longer attempting the impossible, he approached fiction with greater detachment and probably wrote with greater ease.

Of course, when he claimed in his notorious introduction to the Modern Library issue of *Sanctuary*, three years later, that he wrote his fifth novel "in six weeks, without changing a word,"[8] Faulkner was not quite telling the truth. Although the holograph version was indeed completed in less than seven weeks (the first page of the manuscript bears the date "25 October 1929," and the last page "11 December 1929"), it took him another month to type it, and there is ample evidence of revision in both manuscript and typescript. Yet in point of fact the revisions are all minor, and everything suggests that when Faulkner began to write the novel he was already in full possession of all his materials and knew what shape he would give his book. If the manuscript betrays some hesitation on secondary points, such as the characters' names, the use of italics and tenses, and the order of sections, it seems safe to assume that the overall pattern of the novel was already fixed, and there is little trace of doubt over the method of narrative management or the handling of viewpoints.[9] For all its newness, the fictional technique of *As I Lay Dying* is not the result of long and patient efforts and experiments; it appears to have imposed itself of its own accord, to have arisen from the vision—what Faulkner calls his "dream"—as part and parcel of it:

Sometimes technique charges in and takes command of the dream before the writer himself can get his hands on it. That is *tour de force* and the finished work is simply a matter of fitting bricks together, since the writer knows probably

every single word right to the end before he puts the first one down. This
happened with *As I Lay Dying*.[10]

This technique is paradoxically both more mutedly "modernistic" and more
subtly eccentric than that of *The Sound and the Fury*. It is more traditional
insofar as the novel fully recovers its narrative vocation. The story itself is
fairly simple, and its telling generally follows the sequential order of events,
with just enough retelling to make the narrative stutter a little. Unlike many
of Faulkner's other novels, *As I Lay Dying* hardly tampers with the chronology
of events; narrative digressions are rare. With one major exception—Addie's
achronological monologue—and several minor ones—Cora's and Whitfield's
reminiscences, Darl's childhood memories, snatches of past conversations
between Anse and Addie, the recollection of Dewey Dell's dream, and the
extended flashback on Jewel's acquisition of a horse (113–22)—the unity of
action is respected from start to finish, and the whole tale is perfectly circumscribed in space and time.

Space here is measured by the forty miles separating country from city, the
Bundrens' house in the hills from the town of Jefferson, the end of their trek;
the time is the ten days they need to prepare, undertake, and complete their
expedition, from Addie's last hours to the day after her burial. *As I Lay Dying*
is first of all the account of a *journey* in its most ordinary, most physical sense:
people in motion, their progress in space and time, along roads and across a
river; but it does not take us long to realize that this journey is also a journey
through life to death, through death to life, and that there are as many journeys
as there are travelers. As the narrative unfolds, the Bundrens' progress thus
becomes gradually emblematic of other, less readily traceable trajectories and
transferences, of other displacements and other discoveries, including the
reader's own adventure through Faulkner's words.

The journey is at once the main object of the narrative and the novel's
primary metaphor. The loose episodic plot it provides, however, is simple
enough, and if we leave aside all ironies and complexities and reduce the story
to its most abstract pattern, to what A. J. Greimas would call its "actantial
model,"[11] we can easily see that it is informed by an archetypal scheme, whose
basic functions are apportioned as neatly as in a folk tale or a myth. At the
outset stands the Bundrens' obligation to go and bury Addie at the Jefferson
cemetery. Their journey is the fulfillment of a promise, the carrying out of a
last will. Addie, the dead one, is at the same time *sender* (Greimas's *destinateur*,
the initiator of the action), *receiver* (its posthumous beneficiary), and *object* (the
corpse to be conveyed to the cemetery). With nature (the flood, the fire) as
opponent and the community (Tull, Samson, etc.) as *helper*, the family, as
authorized collective agent, is the *subject-hero*, who successfully undertakes its
perilous mission and is eventually rewarded (new teeth and a new wife for
Anse, a gramophone for Cash, etc.).

The tale is simple; not so the mode of its telling. As in *The Sound and the Fury*,
the story is "told" by a succession of voices, and here again one is reminded

of the earlier novel. Vardaman's and Dewey Dell's confused utterances some-times recall Benjy's stammerings, Darl's much more "literary" sections are close to Quentin's monologue, and the plain vernacular of most speakers echoes Jason's demotic speech. Yet if the convention of "immediate speech" rests on the possibility of transcribing the flux of mental processes and assumes the presence of a half-articulate or even inarticulate inner voice talking to itself, only a few of the novel's sections—Vardaman's, Dewey Dell's, Jewel's, and intermittently Darl's—are "interior monologues." Faulkner no doubt often uses the devices of "stream-of-consciousness" fiction; yet, despite occasional violations of syntax and logic and a few stretches of run-on prose, most of the Bundren monologues clearly serve a narrative purpose, as do even more plainly the speeches by the peripheral characters who form the novel's Greek chorus. The non-Bundren sections are sometimes written in evocative present tense, but all of them are essentially retrospective first-person narra-tives, offering the improvised quality, the changes in tone and tempo, and the many redundancies and hesitancies of a talking voice. And while with Vernon and Cora Tull, the Bundrens' closest neighbors, and with Doctor Peabody, the most intellectual voice among the external commentators, there are still oc-casional hints of inwardness, the monologues ascribed to uninvolved out-siders, such as Samson, Armstid, and Moseley and MacGowan, the two druggists, cannot be called "interior" in any sense, for they sound like frag-ments of a story told orally, lacking only a listening ear. Which is to say that in *As I Lay Dying* the characters' voices tend from the outset to arise from and to reverberate in a public space and hence to imply a social context. As in *Light in August* and other later novels, we can hear behind most individual utteran-ces a corporate community voice—the anonymous and ubiquitous voice of the tribe, with its commonplaces and common pieties as well as its homely, often fairly cynical wisdom. .

At the same time, however, another, extradiegetic voice, which should not be automatically assigned to the novelist himself, blends again and again with the characters' voices and sometimes even eclipses them. The three sharply individualized monologues of *The Sound and the Fury* conformed from first to last to a code of psychological verisimilitude: Benjy's speech, for instance, is a set of stable conventions, and it sticks to them all along, hardly ever exceeding the presumed limits of his idiolect. As much can be said of Quentin or Jason, and it is only in the novel's final section that the novelist-narrator resumes his traditional privileges. In *As I Lay Dying*, on the other hand, the novelist is both nowhere and everywhere. Apparently effacing himself behind his characters, he gives them the floor and lets them tell the tale in their own words. At first glance, or rather at first hearing, *As I Lay Dying* appears indeed to be the most dramatic or most mimetic of Faulkner's novels, for it would seem that there is nothing here but *reported* or *quoted* discourse, unmediated and uncom-mented upon, as it supposedly was thought and felt, if not uttered, by each of the characters.

"Narrative of words" or "narrative of events"?[12] Both and neither. *As I Lay*

Dying can be read either as a "narrative of events" shared by a set of alternating homodiegetic narrators, with no central narrative consciousness to "authorize" the text,[13] or as a "narrative of words" if we assume a higher agency whose function is to record and arrange the characters' soliloquies into a coherent pattern. Yet if such an agency is posited, it becomes obvious that recording and arranging are not its only prerogatives and that mimetic illusion is by no means its major concern. True, when they talk to one another, Faulkner's farmers all speak the same rural idiom, and they often also use it when talking to themselves. But it is not just a matter of faithfully rendering their vernacular or even of exploiting its stylistic resources and modulating it from one section to another according to the speaker's mood and personality. In fact, the verisimilitude of reported speech is repeatedly punctured by various kinds of inconsistencies and implausibilities. For instance, when Anse's talk is quoted by town characters such as Peabody or MacGowan, it is much more heavily dialectal than when reported by his kin or his neighbors: as Stephen M. Ross points out, "*As I Lay Dying* seems to imitate not how a character sounds but how one character sounds to another."[14] This, of course, could be easily interpreted as verisimilitude pushed to extremes and thus be covered under the rubric of advanced realism. But there are much more serious breaches of plausibility: the fact, for instance, that some of Faulkner's characters, notably the Bundrens, speak in their own voice and their rural idiom when they talk to others in the story-world, and through another('s) voice and language when their discourse is supposed to convey their inner-most thoughts. Paradoxically, the deeper we enter the characters' minds and the closer we get to the core of their being, the less their voices sound like their own and the more they sound like Faulkner's. Indeed, on the earthy parch-ment of the Mississippi dialect the novelist continually traces—almost like an imperious signature: Faulkner was here—the arabesques of his own rhetoric, most easily recognizable in the lyrical outbursts, metaphysical reveries, and oracular apothegms of Darl (whose sophisticated diction, elaborate syntax, and startling metaphors are virtually indistinguishable from the writer's own) and in the terse, impassioned eloquence of Addie's single speech in section 40. At any moment a speaker's voice can be augmented so as to render more eloquently the depths and intricacies of his psyche, and even in those charac-ters whose linguistic capacities seem severely restricted—in Vardaman,[15] for example, or Dewey Dell, or Anse—language sometimes takes flight, and from the most halting prose suddenly springs, by virtue of an unexpected metaphor, a poetic vision which transfigures it.

An early reviewer of *Far from the Madding Crowd* complained that Thomas Hardy lent his laborers "expressions which we simply cannot believe possible from the illiterate clods whom he describes."[16] There have been similar complaints about Faulkner's stylistic implausibilities. He too has been berated for making low-bred characters think and talk beyond their means, in a highly rhetorical idiom which is clearly incompatible with what we know about their level of consciousness or their level of education. "His voice is bigger than him," Tull notes about the preacher Whitfield. "It's like they are not the same. It's like he is one, and his voice is one, swimming on two horses side by side across the ford and coming into the house . . ." (81). What holds true for Whitfield holds true in varying degrees for other characters in the novel. Vardaman's voice, for example, is in many places likewise much "bigger than him," so that we must distinguish Vardaman the speaker-narrator from the confused little Bundren in the novel's fictional world. And Darl, the novel's most articulate and powerful voice, is neither Darl, son and brother, nor "the one that folks says is queer, lazy" (22). Vardaman and Darl are in fact both doubly individualized, as acting characters (seen and judged by all the others) *and* as narrative voices (supposedly speaking themselves or their selves), and these two individualizations supposedly refer to the same person. But they never come to validate each other in a "natural" way, even though as readers we cannot help thinking of voice and agent together.

The question of how and where speaking, doing, and selfhood connect must remain a riddle (as it does to Addie in her monologue), and what complicates matters, and apparently makes Faulkner even "worse" than Hardy, is that he is not even consistently inconsistent: at least as far as the Bundrens are concerned, he makes no attempt to produce and maintain for any length the illusion of a single voice and a stylistically homogeneous text. Not only is *As I Lay Dying* a mosaic of monologues, but nearly all the monologues are themselves patchwork pieces. Hence the locus of enunciation becomes extremely problematic.[17] Who is speaking, and to whom? Is there ever anything like a "speaking subject" in control of and answerable for his or her discourse in a definable discursive situation? These questions are already raised in *The Sound and the Fury*, wherein each of the four sections, labeled only by a date, leaves it to the reader to find out who is actually speaking. In *As I Lay Dying*, each of the sections is headed by a proper name, so that the speaker can be identified immediately. And yet our perplexity is here perhaps even greater, for the naming is no reliable identification, and the idiosyncrasy of voices and visions is in fact called into question much more radically than in the prior novel.

Let us note, however, that in Faulkner's later books, beginning with *Light in August*, we shall often find multiple voices and multiple visions mediated by a narrative instance and subsumed by a rhetorical voice integrating them in a broader, more resonant perspective. One might argue, then, that in its still discreet use of an overvoice—or perhaps, more accurately, of a *diagonal voice*—Faulkner's fifth novel anticipates the more elaborate narrative arrangements and more sonorous polyphonic orchestrations to come. Yet, even though *As I Lay Dying* inscribes itself in the continuity of Faulkner's development as a novelist, it remains in many ways a unique and uniquely unsettling performance. Not that it is aggressively antirealistic, but, as it turns out, we can take almost nothing in this novel for granted. Over and over again, it swerves away from customary practice and does so at every level, from typography to narrative management, from punctuation to characterization.

None of Faulkner's other novels offers as many departures from novelistic usage and as many shifts into the unusual and the implausible; none is as often visited by that modern muse whom Jean Cocteau called the "angel of the bizarre."

By traditional standards Faulkner's handling of point of view, for example, is hardly more acceptable than his use of voice. To begin with, the reliability of the narrators is undermined a number of times by irreducible contradictions between their respective accounts of events. To give just one example: one conversation near the Bundrens' house before Darl and Jewel's departure for their lumber loading errand is first reported by Darl, then by Tull. In Darl's version, it is Darl himself who says twice "It means three dollars" (15, 18); in Tull's, the same statement is attributed to Anse (25), and according to Cora, reporting her husband's words, "Darl almost begged them on his knees not to force him to leave [Addie] in her condition" (19). Since we know Anse to be a miser, the monetary motive is more likely to be his. But if Darl's report cannot be trusted on this occasion, how can we be sure that he is not also lying elsewhere?

Furthermore, the narrative perspectives possess as little unity as the voices. As early as in the opening monologue, Darl's point of view is at least double: to describe Jewel, he at once adopts the vantage point of someone "watching [them] from the cottonhouse," and he can see his brother "looking straight ahead," even though he is "fifteen feet behind [him]" (3). Even more unsettling: in his second section, while talking with his father near the back porch, Darl describes what Jewel is doing with his horse in the pasture behind the barn (9–12). These are the first signs of Darl's preternatural clairvoyance, of which there is further, even more disturbing evidence in his circumstantial account of Addie's death (43–48) and his vivid description of Cash working on the coffin during the rainstorm (67–72)—two scenes he reports while he and Jewel are many miles away, hauling a wagonload of lumber—or again in his verbatim anticipation of Dewey Dell's second monologue (*"You could do so much for me if you just would"* 47). Darl's point of view could be anyone's, and so we must credit him with either second sight or a miraculously precise imagination. And the novel's central prosopopeia, Addie's posthumous monologue, when she has been dead for five days, also blatantly challenges verisimilitude.

Lastly, the distinctness of narrative voices and viewpoints is almost systematically blurred by repetition. It is true that iteration occurs in all writing, and moreover it has been from the outset one of the hallmarks of the "colloquial style," an American tradition *As I Lay Dying* unmistakably belongs to.[18] Like Mark Twain, Faulkner makes abundant use of the innate redundancy of vernacular speech in his dialogues. But there is as much repetition in the characters' "thinking." Repetition in fact patterns the novel's entire text, regardless of the stylistic register and the identity of the speaker, operating on all levels—aural, visual, lexical, syntactic, narrative, thematic—and ranging from mere onomatopeias ("Chuck. Chuck. Chuck," 4; "whish. whish. whish,"

76) and words ("The dead air shapes the dead earth in the dead darkness, further away than seeing shapes the dead earth," 58) to phrases ("I believe in God, God. God, I believe in God," 108) and whole sentences. One of Dewey Dell's monologues includes six slightly modified repetitions of the opening statement, "He could do so much for me . . ." (53–58). In Darl's third section, Anse "rubs his hands on his knees" six times within four pages (15–18). And he "keeps on rubbing his knees" at the beginning of the first speech by Tull (25). Sounds and words thus echo one another within sentences; phrases and sentences ricochet within paragraphs and from one paragraph to another, or even from one section to another.

Repetition serves various purposes, from rhythmic effect to rhetorical emphasis and thematic amplification. Furthermore, reiterated phrases, such as Jewel's "goddamn," Cash's "It wont balance," Vardaman's incantatory formulae, and all Anse's sanctimonious clichés, clearly function as devices of characterization. All in all, however, repetition unifies and equalizes rather than individualizes, and in *As I Lay Dying* one of its major effects is to underscore the stock of words and imagery and the syntactic molds which the different narrators and especially the Bundrens share.[19] The degree of repetition in their speeches is indeed extraordinarily high, as if to suggest that in their obsessive repetitiveness they are all alike. It is not the case, as one critic argues, that "verbal repetition supersedes point of view."[20] Individual perspectives are blurred, not canceled. Whatever the stylistic resemblances between them, the reader is unlikely to confuse Vardaman's or Dewey Dell's monologues with Darl's. The point is that in their language as in their thoughts and behavior the Bundrens are both alike and not alike, that they are in every respect intimate strangers or, to put it with more candor, that they constitute a family. Yet once again there is more at issue than psychology. For what must be noted too is that repetition is so densely patterned and so shamelessly foregrounded that it calls attention to itself as formal design and hence also to language per se and in particular to one of its supposedly noble uses: that manic rearrangement of words endlessly the same and endlessly different which we call literature.

In *As I Lay Dying* the mimetic illusion is thus carried to extreme lengths and depths, while being at the same time undercut by manifold transgressions of any possible form of realism. In addition to all these oddities and paradoxes there is the novel's extreme fragmentation. Whereas in *The Sound and the Fury* the monologues are arranged in large, compact blocks, they are split up here into brief sequences; instead of four sections, this much shorter novel offers fifty-nine, shared among fifteen discrete narrators. The longest is seven pages, the average two to four pages, and the shortest ("My mother is a fish," 74) a mere five words. Increased by the swift, almost kaleidoscopic rotation of the sections, this disjointedness is not without effect on our reading experience: each new soliloquy catches the reader off balance, and even though he has a plot to help him out, he is obliged to engage in continual readjustments if he wants to follow the narrative through all its twists and turns. Under such circumstances, the customary pleasures of novel reading are seriously jeopardized: we flit from one point of view to another without ever settling on any, so that imaginary identification with any of the characters becomes highly improbable. *The Sound and the Fury* plunged us by turns into the "stream of consciousness" of Benjy, Quentin, and Jason, and the immersions lasted long enough to allow us to adopt—or to forget—a character's point of view. Here the immersions are so brief that the "stream" does not carry us along. The novel's montage creates an almost Brechtian distance between the characters and ourselves. We watch them and listen to them, but we never cease to be part of the audience. *As I Lay Dying* offers us a *spectacle of voices*.

A collection of holes

Since Roland Barthes, it has become fairly common to use textile imagery in discussing literary texts. For *As I Lay Dying*, however, rather than the web, I would suggest the *net*, which a jocular lexicographer once called a collection of holes tied together with string. *As I Lay Dying* is indeed a kind of net—an open, meshed fabric, a collection of holes tied together with words.

Holes or gaps abound in the novel, literally and figuratively,[21] from the black hole in Darl's bucket, a "round orifice in nothingness" (9), to the holes drilled by Vardaman into Addie's coffin and into her face (66). But let us also note that the entire thrust of the journey is toward the hole in the earth where her corpse will be eventually buried, a hole surprisingly occulted by another hole, a gap in the narrative discourse this time, since the long awaited scene of Addie's interment is not recounted by anyone but just alluded to by Cash, for whom it is predictibly a mere matter of shovels and digging (see 220, 239). As in all Faulkner's novels, much of what has happened and does happen is not fully revealed and is therefore left for the reader's speculation. Despite the many insights we are offered into the characters' most secret thoughts and feelings, their motives often remain tantalizingly unclear (Why did Addie marry Anse?), and we are not even told how much they know about each other (Does Anse know about Addie's adultery? Does Darl know who is Jewel's father?).[22]

Even the visual surface of the novel's typographic design is somehow netlike. None of Faulkner's books offers more textual ruptures and leaves more blanks; none calls attention to itself more insistently as an object for the eye. Black print contends with "white space," and a page such as 74, on which we read nothing but "Vardaman" and, below, the baffling assertion "My mother is a fish," hardly looks like a page from a novel. Even more intriguingly, within the printed text itself distances between words begin inexplicably to widen, as they do as early as the end of Darl's first section—"Chuck Chuck.   Chuck" (4)—or again in Vardaman's last:

I hear the cow a long time, clopping   on the street. Then she comes into the

square. She goes across the square, her head down   clopping   She lows.
There was nothing in the square before she lowed, but it wasn't empty. Now it
is empty after she lowed. She goes on,   clopping   . She lows. (233–34)

These gaps in the text are of course not gratuitous; they have an expressive
function, and in the passages above they can be easily "read" as visualizations
of silence or emptiness. And in Addie's monologue, there can be no doubt
about the sexual significance of the blank designating the "shape of [her] body
where [she] used to be a virgin" (159). Such blanks depend on the words
surrounding them for whatever meaning they may have, but at the same time
they call into question the significance of their verbal context by pushing into
visibility the materiality of the letter itself. A similar defamiliarization is
produced by the drawing of a coffin right in the middle of a sentence in one
of Tull's sections (77): again the smooth, continuous flow of words on the page
is broken; the trace of the speaking voice which the script is assumed to render
is inexplicably interrupted, and the reader becomes uncomfortably aware of
the arbitrariness or conventionality of all sign systems, whether verbal, visual,
or other.

To write is to blacken whiteness, to fill in gaps, to dress wounds. All texts
aspire to the compactness of living bodies. But here the body is dismembered,
the text bursts asunder, the discourse falters and gapes, as if to remind us of
the lure and lability of all writing and to let us glimpse, in the interstices
between words, where nothing can be seen, what words can neither say nor
give up saying—to make us see what they fail to make us hear: the silence of
death, unheard music of all desire.

As I Lay Dying is a tour de force, no doubt, but the writer's force and cunning,
the resources of his mastery, are used here both to weave a text and to tear it
to pieces, to build a fiction and to ruin its pretensions. To seduce and to disturb.
A book which makes of the syncope its cornerstone; a book of ruptures and
interruptions, of breakdowns and silences, but also of joints and links, the
means of producing rhythm and music. A strange, eccentric, uncanny book—
"a little on the esoteric side," as Faulkner once noted in one of his letters[23]—
disconcerting from whatever angle it is approached. Small wonder, then, that
since its first publication it has puzzled all critics, and that, to put an end to
their embarrassment, most of them have hastened to domesticate its strangeness.

More than any other Faulkner novel, *As I Lay Dying* raises the question of
its generic status, as if for once the label "novel" were not quite appropriate.
This is of course a legitimate concern or at least seems to be, given its many
heterodox features. Yet instead of trying to address the issue in its full
complexity, all too often critics have simply attempted to naturalize the book
at the lowest cost, by fitting it into prenovelistic genres such as drama and
epic.

That it partakes of both (as probably all novels do) is obvious enough. Its
affinities with the epic can hardly be denied: the terrible ordeals the Bundrens

undergo in the course of their journey and their valiant struggle against the unbridled elements inevitably bring to mind the heroic exploits of myth and legend. As early as 1934 the French writer and critic Valery Larbaud called attention to the epic quality of the novel and compared Addie to a Homeric queen, "King Anse" to a rustic Ulysses, and Cash to the lame Hephaestus.[24] The very idea which according to Faulkner gave rise to the novel appears in its sheer simplicity to be an epic idea: "I took this family and subjected them to the two greatest catastrophes which man can suffer—flood and fire, that's all."[25] Faulkner's treatment of the idea, however, is anything but epic. Tull notes that the Bundrens "would risk the fire and the earth and the water and all just to eat a sack of bananas" (126); he may be mistaken, but the nobility of their motives is not above suspicion, and heroism is certainly not the novel's central theme. There is nothing here of epic distance, nothing even remotely reminiscent of the wholeness and timelessness of the epic world.

More serious and more judicious, at first sight, are the attempts to relate *As I Lay Dying* to drama. Its fifty-nine juxtaposed monologues, all headed by the speaker's name, give it the look of a play, and the extensive dialogue embedded in the monologues makes it often read like drama. Furthermore, eddies of "stream of consciousness" notwithstanding, the narrative follows a firmly traced course of action and climaxes in a series of highly charged and amply dramatized scenes, including Addie's dying, the river crossing, and the barn fire, so that the novel almost seems to invite theatrical performance. It is hardly surprising, then, that as early as 1935 Jean-Louis Barrault, who regarded Faulkner's text as "drama in its primitive state," should have used it for an experiment in antirealistic theater.[26] But should one go further and catalogue it as either tragedy or comedy?

None would disagree that *As I Lay Dying* lacks the fevered tension and claustrophobic ambiance (at least in its first two sections) of *The Sound and the Fury*. The swirling multiplicity of perspectives precludes identification and promotes detachment, and it may be argued that the novel follows the standard comic pattern from disorder to restoration: it begins with Addie's death and develops through a series of discomfitures, but apart from Darl, the Bundrens all valiantly muddle through and manage to survive. Furthermore, there is humor in abundance and in many hues, from the earthiest to the eeriest, from the most benign folk humor to the blackest *humour noir*, and in all sorts of ways—the raciness of its vernacular, the grotesqueness of its characters (especially Anse, the novel's comic hero), the tall-tale extravagance of many episodes—it could almost be taken for a country farce.[27] But the farce is too grim and too grisly for the book to be considered essentially comic, and the features relating it to tragedy are surely as significant: as we have seen, the story of the Bundrens, like that of the Compsons or the Sutpens, is about a family adrift, with all its tensions and conflicts. It begins with the account of a last agony and ends with scenes of hatred, violence, and madness. And because of their tortured self-awareness and utter isolation, Addie and Darl, the two most memorable characters in the novel, both come very close to being tragic figures.

Epic, tragedy, comedy? This is obviously not the right question to ask. To force the novel into one of the canonical genres is to ignore the fact that it courts them all without marrying any. The distinctive quality of *As I Lay Dying*, and one of the main sources of its strangeness, is precisely that it is not an epic or a tragedy or a comedy but a gamble on being all three at once—a comedy and the reverse of comedy, a tragedy and the derision of tragedy, an epic and the parody of epic.

In no other novel did Faulkner cultivate the jarring note and the incongruous touch with so little restraint and so much relish. Never did he juxtapose or mix literary genres, stylistic registers, and tones of voice to such an extent or at such speed: *As I Lay Dying* constantly wavers between pathos and laughter, horror and farce. The shifting and blending of intensities and the resultant ambivalence of effect are so disorienting that no catharsis is likely ever to work. Deprived of their usual frames and references, readers cannot help being disconcerted. When, at the novel's close, Darl bursts out laughing at the monkeylike spectacle of his banana-munching family, it is hard to tell on which side lies sanity and on which side madness. And in the final scene—which rings like a mocking echo of the recognition scenes one finds in the sentimental novels of the eighteenth century—when Anse, "kind of hangdog and proud too" (242), introduces the new duckshaped and popeyed Mrs. Bundren to his perplexed children, the whole novel seems to tumble into sheer grotesquerie. As for the journey itself, it may seem quite as preposterous as this farcical ending. The undeviating single-mindedness of the Bundrens in pursuing their mortuary task resembles at times the blind obstinacy of burying beetles, and the success of their undertaking is perhaps less a victory of dedicated will than the triumph of inertia. Are we then to conclude that all the virtues and values traditionally attending the strenuous journey are here reversed for the purpose of travesty? The epic overtones may have been intended to point up the monstrous incongruity of this funereal steeplechase. But the burlesque may be as well a half-ironic celebration of that eminently Faulknerian virtue, endurance.

As I Lay Dying is of all Faulkner's novels the one that has provoked the most widely diverging interpretations. For some critics, regarding it from the reassuringly humanistic perspective of Faulkner's later work, it is "the warmest, the kindliest and most affectionate . . . a triumph of fraternal feeling,"[28] "a comic novel rooted in the earth and countryfolk and lighted by a new faith in humanity,"[29] "an affirmation of life in the face of death."[30] For others, more sensitive to its darker sides, it is "the bitterest of [Faulkner's] early novels,"[31] presenting "human existence as an absurd joke,"[32] and celebrating "the victory of death and sterility and infidelity."[33]

Critics are so sharply divided that one sometimes wonders whether they have all read the same book. And yet, no matter how conflicting their interpretations, nearly all of them seem to agree about the need to coerce *As I Lay Dying* into *one* genre, *one* mode, and to reduce it to *one* unequivocal message, that is, to force it into formal classes and ideological categories to which it obstinately refuses to conform. Why not simply admit that it belongs to the most de-generate of genres: to the *novel?* The German Romantics maintained that the novel was a mixed genre, Baudelaire called it a literary "mongrel," and indeed, since its dubious birth, it has been the unabashed and voracious parasite of all the other genres. *As I Lay Dying* is an opportune reminder that the essence of the novel is its novelness. Like *The Sound and the Fury*, it departs from the realistic paradigm inherited from the nineteenth century and does so even more disturbingly than the earlier book. But its novelness is also a rebeginning. To call it "modernistic" or even to see it merely as a "modern" novel does not lead us very far, for the new and the archaic here jostle each other at every step, and if the heritage of realism is indeed repudiated (Faulkner even subtly distancing himself from its late, sophisticated variants, such as the "psychological" realism which had become fashionable in the twenties), *As I Lay Dying*, far from being a literary foundling, fits very nicely into the much broader and richer and older novelistic tradition, beginning with the serio-comic genres of Antiquity and the Middle Ages, whose roots Bakhtin found in the exuberant folk rituals of the carnival.[34] In the uninhibited diversity of its styles, its generous blending of voices and moods, its emphasis on incongruity, its recourse to irony, humor, and parody as well as in its themes and motifs—the interplay of birth and death, madness and scandal, the "world upside down" topos—*As I Lay Dying* clearly partakes of this tradition of irreverence.

The strength of *As I Lay Dying*, its grim seduction, its ever-fresh provocation reside in its carnivalesque freedom, in the way it thumbs its nose at all classifications, sowing meaning as one sows discord. We had better leave it to its eerie playfulness.

VIII

A DYING LIFE, A LIVING DEATH

> So she is at death's door, eh? Hope they can
> pull her through.
>
> W. C. Fields

Beginning

This elusive text, how to seize it? Where should one begin? Since *As I Lay Dying* refuses to accommodate ready-made categories, why not begin where it begins—with its title?

As is now well known, the title of the novel is a quotation from Homer, even as the previous one was from Shakespeare's *Macbeth*. Faulkner borrowed it from Book XI, the "Book of the Dead," of the *Odyssey*, and when asked about it, he quoted a line from the speech of Agamemnon's shade to Odysseus: "As I lay dying the woman with the dog's eyes would not close my eyelids for me as I descended into Hades."[1] "As I Lay Dying," then, is both the title of a novel by Faulkner and a citation from another text by another writer. Intertextuality is already at work, weaving its threads with those of myth and epic, so that, like most of Faulkner's titles, "As I Lay Dying" appears thick with meaning even before the reading of the text has come to flesh it out and justify its appropriateness.

However, to know the literary origin of the title hardly helps to dispel its uncertainties and ambiguities. The titles of most novels are nouns or nominal syntagms. Along with "Go Down, Moses" and "If I Forget Thee, Jerusalem" (the original title for *The Wild Palms*), the title of Faulkner's fifth novel—one of those titles he had in mind before using them for any specific text, and one which he had already applied to two early versions of "Spotted Horses"[2]—is a clause, and a dangling clause at that, a dependent temporal clause dependent on nothing. Something is already missing; the novel's first hole and first riddle are in the title: what happens/happened "as I lay dying"? A sentence has been begun and we expect the statement to be completed, the question to be answered. The expected complement, the main clause, one might argue, is precisely the text which the title presumably announces. The text would then be the title's other half, or the title the first half of the text. Such questions would not have to be raised if the title were a mere superscription or label, but it is both more and less than that. While naming the book and somehow designating its content (as titles normally do), it calls, as it were, for its assistance: it needs the text as much as the text needs it. Nothing in fact prevents us from reading it as the first monologue, for, like all sections in the novel, it is in the first person, and even more than the latter, it is an utterance severed from its occasion. So we can only wonder about the locus and the circumstances of its enunciation. Who utters or uttered these four improbable words, and where and when? Is this the incipient and interrupted monologue of a still indeterminate, empty "I"? Or is it already Addie speaking from her grave? Her single section in the novel proper would then be the title's deferred replica or unfolded repetition. Yet, if we did not speculate about the title *after* reading the novel, this "I" could be read as well as the authorial "I" of an autobiographic (or, more precisely and pedantically, auto-thanato-graphic) text—a hypothesis prompted by the proximity of the author's name and the title on the book cover (in a position similar to that of the narrators' names in relation to their sections). Or could it be you, *hypocrite lecteur,—mon semblable,—mon frère?* For you cannot read the words "As I Lay Dying" without putting yourself in the place of the dying one; reading it, I read about my own dying.

In addition, there is the irreducible ambiguity of "lay." In standard English it is the past tense of "to lie"; in the dialect spoken by the novel's characters it is often used as its present tense, as when Anse advises Addie "to lay still and rest" (33).[3] Does the title refer to someone thinking of his/her imminent death or to a dead one remembering his/her last moments? The second assumption is of course absurd, but we should not forget that posthumous consciousness is also assumed in Addie's monologue. There is just no way to determine the title's tense: perhaps already a way of suggesting that death is a fracture in time which cannot be conjugated in our grammars.

Furthermore, a relation of concomitance, if not equivalence, is posited from the outset between the last agony of an "I" and the action narrated in the novel. The last agony, as we soon learn, is Addie's, to which the first third of the narrative is devoted. The title, then, does not apply to the book in its entirety if taken literally, and yet it stands for the whole novel, as if to forewarn us that Addie's death both exceeds her actual demise and transcends her person, that the Bundrens all share in her dying, and that the journey is itself from first to last a suspense between life and death. And indeed, what the novel is concerned with is not so much death as the process of dying, not so much death as an isolated fact as its mute presence at the heart of life. *As I Lay Dying* works from the start with the double paradox of a dying life and a living death.

In-between

In *As I Lay Dying* life and death never function as antithetical concepts. They are not opposed as being and nonbeing, but rather are defined—if they are at all definable—in terms of mutual inclusion, as death-in-life or life-in-death, and the ambiguous zone of their encounter and exchange constitutes the very *scene* of the novel, the tumultuous baroque stage on which the story of the Bundrens is played out.

Ambiguity manifests itself first of all in a perpetual oscillation between motion and stasis, in their irreducible complementarity and irresolvable contradiction. *As I Lay Dying* depicts figures moving in space: the Bundrens' wagon trundles obstinately along the road; Jewel wheels on horseback around the funeral cortège; the buzzards hover in circles in the hot summer sky. But space itself also moves: roads and signboards "wheel" up and on (see 95–96). Nature is alive and active: a storm bursts, torrential rain sweeps down, the river overflows, and its raging water carries all before it. Few novels give us so intensely the sensation of a seething world. Some pages in the book are pure kinetic poems. Consider this dazzling evocation of Jewel and his horse:

> When Jewel can almost touch him, the horse stands on his hind legs and slashes down at Jewel. Then Jewel is enclosed by a glittering maze of hooves as by an illusion of wings; among them, beneath the upreared chest, he moves with the flashing limberness of a snake. For an instant before the jerk comes onto his arms he sees his whole body earth-free, horizontal, whipping snake-limber, until he finds the horse's nostrils and touches earth again. (11)

Yet the fascination with immobility is certainly as compelling as that with motion. Or rather, what fascinates is the *passage*, sudden or imperceptible, from one to the other, as the continuation of the above scene shows: "Then they are rigid, motionless, terrific" (11). In Faulkner, however, immobility is scarcely ever absolute or final. Stillness is almost always throbbing with latent motion; it is movement beginning or ending, energy dying or gathering force, a tense interval like the lull before the storm: "They stand in terrific hiatus, the horse trembling and groaning. Then Jewel is on the horse's back. He flows upward in a stooping swirl like a lash of a whip, his body in midair shaped to the horse" (11). Hence the self-contradictory concept of "dynamic immobility," Darl's oxymoron when describing Cash at work on Addie's coffin: "Cash works on, half turned into the feeble light, one thigh and one pole-thin arm braced, his face sloped into the light with a rapt, dynamic immobility, above his tireless elbow" (68). In much the same way Vardaman watches Peabody's horses wheeling without moving, like horses on the revolving platform of a merry-go-round: "I strike at them, striking, they wheeling in a long lunge, the buggy wheeling onto two wheels and motionless like it is nailed to the ground and the horses motionless like they are nailed by the hind feet to the center of a whirling plate" (50).

In-between: between motion and immobility, between reality and illusion, between the actual scene and its perception or representation. These are suspended magic moments in the narrative when characters turn into statues and the scene suddenly becomes a tableau. These are also moments in the text in which representation gestures toward itself as pure make-believe. For as we know, "dynamic immobility" names as well the central paradox of Faulkner's aesthetics, of which Keats's urn is the paradigm. We are not allowed to forget that all of the novel's characters are also figures conceived and shaped by an artist, and it is indeed as such that Darl perceives Gillespie and Jewel during the fire scene: "They are like two figures in a Greek frieze, isolated out of all reality by the red glare" (204). Art *spaces* time, subjects it to its own measures and cadences, embalms it in its own forms, and so negates life's motion, even while preserving it. It is a no to death akin to death, and therein lies precisely the paradox. Making art is—or at any rate has been for thousands of years—committing to memory, and all memory is potentially art in that it is already a re-collecting, re-membering, and re-shaping of experienced reality and a stoppage of time. Memory does not think time, nor even think in time; it stores its traces to turn them into images, representations: space again, a secondary space where time is put away and then allowed to come back in our dreams and reveries. But conversely there is no space that is not secretly traversed by temporality. Motion is time's finger making itself visible. And what is immobility if not an infinite slowness? "We go on with a motion so soporific, so dreamlike as to be uninferant of progress, as though time and not space were decreasing between us and it" (95). Similarly, at the time of the river crossing, when Darl is looking at his family on the other bank, the separating interval seems temporal rather than spatial:

> It is as though the space between us were time: an irrevocable quality. It is as though time, no longer running straight before us in a diminishing line, now runs parallel between us like a looping string, the distance being the doubling accretion of the thread and not the interval between. (132)

Metamorphoses

Through this bewildering time-space dialectic, this vertiginous play of movement and stasis, the novel reveals one of its major paradoxes: "fury in itself quiet with stagnation" (156).

This paradox informs all of Faulkner's fiction, but in *As I Lay Dying* it takes on truly cosmic dimensions. What Darl calls "the myriad original motion" (156) is at work not only across the universe but in the universe, that is, within the elements, the substances, and the beings that it compels to transform themselves, sweeping them along in the flux of constant change. All boundaries are crossed or blurred; no identity or function ever solidifies; forms always verge on dissolution and transformation into different patterns. All is fluid and fleeting. Metamorphosis always prevails. Take, for example, the climactic river scene. Water, the element of metamorphosis *par excellence*, springs to life. Here is Tull's description:

The water was cold. It was thick, like slush ice. Only it kind of lived. One part of you knowed it was just water, the same thing that had been running under this same bridge for a long time, yet when them logs would come spewing up outen it, you were not surprised, like they was a part of water, of the waiting and the threat. (124)

Animism is even more pronounced with Darl, and it runs throughout his account of the river scene. Below the water's turbulent surface, he senses the disturbing presence of some marine monster up from the deep, a slumbering Leviathan turning over in its sleep and threatening to awaken at any moment:

Before us the thick current runs. It talks up to us in a murmur become ceaseless and myriad, the yellow surface dimpled monstrously into fading swirls travelling along the surface for an instant, silent, impermanent and profoundly significant, as though just beneath the surface something huge and alive waked for a moment of lazy alertness out of and into light slumber again. (127)

Immediately after, the foam turns to sweat and the river becomes a galloping horse: "It clucks and murmurs among the spokes and about the mules' knees, yellow, skummed with flotsam and with thick soiled gouts of foam as though it had sweat, lathering, like a driven horse" (127). And once in the water, "It is like hands molding and prodding at the very bones" (144).

Nothing, it seems, is left to define the hierarchy of nature's categories or to distinguish reality from unreality. The inanimate comes to life in strange anthropomorphic ways: the land sweats, planks bleed, saws snore, wheels whisper (see 125, 59, 42, 108). A landscape suggests human anatomy: "The path looks like a crooked limb blown against the bluff" (38). Matter loses its materiality and becomes a spectral presence: a log surges out of the water *"for an instant upright upon that surging and heaving desolation like Christ,"* and "upon the end of it a long gout of foam hangs like the beard of an old man or a goat" (134). The human figure, on the other hand, reproduces the shapes and forces of the universe: for Darl, his sister Dewey Dell is like a miniature cosmos (cf. 150). People come to resemble birds, dogs, horses, steers, or cows, as if on the brink of some Ovidian metamorphosis into a lower form of life, while animals take on human characteristics. After the Bundrens' departure, Samson almost mistakes the buzzard he sees in his barn for "one of them," and watches it go away like "an old baldheaded man" (105). Jewel's horse, during the river crossing, flounders in the water, "moaning and groaning like a natural man" (140). It is particularly in the teeth of disaster and death that the kinship of man and beast is acknowledged; they communicate then in their common terror and, in *As I Lay Dying* as in Picasso's *Guernica*, are seen to adopt identical attitudes and expressions. All the world's anguish is reflected in the mules' terrified eyes: "looking back once, their gaze sweeps across us with in their eyes a wild, sad, profound and despairing quality as though they had already seen in the thick water the shape of the disaster which they could not speak and we could not see" (132–33). And here is how Darl describes the look and the last cry of one of the mules as it drowns: "The head of one mule appears, its eyes wide; it looks back at us for an instant, making a sound almost human. The head vanishes again" (135).

Between men and animals, as between men and things, distinctions tend to dissolve through constant transference of properties. *As I Lay Dying* draws us into the whirlpool of a protean world where no thing is a single thing, locked in its essence, identical to itself, and where all things come to resemble and mirror one another in infinite regress. Moreover, *signs* of analogy turn up everywhere. Not only *are* things and beings always something other than themselves, but they always *mean* something else as well, so that everything appears to be both "impermanent and profoundly significant" (127). Everything cross-refers to everything else through a vast, reverberant network of correspondences. The dead fish hiding in the dust, "like it was ashamed of being dead, like it was in a hurry to get back hid again" (27), foreshadows "that pride, that furious desire to hide that abject nakedness which we bring here with us" (42), which Peabody speaks of with regard to Addie. And the sun, "poised like a bloody egg upon a crest of thunderheads" (35), the evening of the storm, is like the cosmic counterpart to Addie's corpse, a broken egg in its casket.

The animate and the inanimate, the human and the nonhuman are brought into a relationship of reciprocal metaphor, and so are Faulkner's language and Faulkner's "world," one mimicking the other without allowing us to determine which is "one" and which the "other." In the never-ending process of slippage and change, everything is thus eventually reabsorbed in the pervasive metaphoricity of a single language and gathered within the frame of a single vision. A baroque vision? Yes, this shifting, swirling world of movement and metamorphoses, of death and madness, of water and fire, has a striking resemblance to the art and literature of the baroque era. Jean Rousset epitomizes "the funereal dream" of the baroque artist as "death in movement in images of movement."[4] There could hardly be a better definition of *As I Lay Dying*.

Life-in-death

Aesthetically, Faulkner's treatment of life and death may be called baroque, but his characters' behavior is also strongly reminiscent of the "immemorial" (to use one of his favorite epithets) attitudes toward death documented by anthropology. "In archaic minds," writes Edgar Morin, "to which elemental experiences are experiences of metamorphosis, of disappearance and reappearance, of transmutation, all death announces a birth, all birth proceeds from a death, every change is analogous to a death-rebirth—and the cycle of human life is inscribed in the natural cycles of death-rebirth."[5] All of

Faulkner's works revolve in the ever-renewed natural cycles of rise and fall, but in none of his novels are life and death so inextricably entwined as in *As I Lay Dying*. This is not to say that as far as his "philosophy" is concerned, Faulkner was in any way a "primitivist," but rather that in this book Faulkner's imagination of death is surprisingly close to the language of myth.

But let us now return from the scene of death to the dying, to the dead, and to the omnipresent dead woman, Addie Bundren. Have we ever left her? The world's body, in which all boundaries between life and death are blurred, in which they even seem to flow into each other, is clearly also the mother's body.

As it is evoked in the novel, Addie's body is a fallen body, a *cadaver* ("cadere": to fall), but the cadaver already offers us an arresting *image* of the impossible division of life and death. In the cadaver, death is materialized and made visible, revealing itself as the decomposition of the human body into inert matter. It is a fascinating object to the extent that "the cadaver is its own image,"[6] its own double, linked to living flesh by a relationship of perfect resemblance and absolute difference, a familiar object become strange, alien—*unheimlich*; a disquieting object become a figure of absence by the disfiguration of a presence, or, to translate it into Darl's language, the "is" of a "was," the "was" of an "is," confronting us with the incomprehensible; an incongruous object, too, as if from another world, and most unwelcome in this one.

The scandalous cadaver confronts us with the physical evidence of death. Hence nothing is more urgent to the survivors than disposing of this unspeakable "thing," than wiping out all material traces so as to better preserve the pious memory of the "dear departed." But in *As I Lay Dying* everything occurs as if the cadaver could not or would not disappear. The time interval between the cadaver's appearance and its burial is prolonged beyond all tolerable bounds. The Bundrens' problem is not unlike Amédée's in Ionesco's play: how to get rid of it? Only at the end of their journey will they succeed in disposing of their mother's body; meanwhile, they are forced to live daily next to a cumbrous corpse.

All the novel's action revolves around the as yet unburied remains of Addie Bundren. *As I Lay Dying* is first and foremost the story of a family struggling with a corpse, the story of an unburiable cadaver,[7] and most of the journey's ordeals stem from the material difficulties of its transportation. Coming thus to impinge on the banality of everyday concerns, death loses much of its portentousness. For the Bundrens, the cadaver is not so much a source of horror and revulsion as a nuisance. So much time and energy are spent moving the coffin about that they almost come to see it as just a load to be transported; they are too absorbed in their immediate tasks (and also, as the outsiders fail to see, in their private thoughts) to realize how shocking the unduly prolonged presence of a rotting corpse may be to others. They even forget about the smell, which all the while attracts buzzards and drives people away. Except for Darl, and probably Cash, none of the Bundrens appears to be conscious at any time of the outrageous nature of their journey, and this guileless disregard for decorum, this stubborn lack of awareness, this surprising familiarity with death—evident from the beginning, when Cash is constructing the coffin in full view of his dying mother—is of course also what makes their undertaking so baffling to the reader. Behind the Bundrens' blindness, however, we find the feigned blindness of the humorist, pretending not to see the scandal and thus keeping death at a distance. As in the grotesque wake scene in *Sanctuary*, the cadaver, treated here like a mere object to be handled, is desacralized, and Gothic horror defused by farce.

But there is more here than black humor. The cadaver's refusal to disappear points to the Bundrens' unwillingness or incapacity to let Addie go or, to put it the other way, to Addie's own refusal to leave, at least as long as she remains unburied. As she lay dying, her family already spoke of her in the past tense, as one would of a dead person, but once she has died, they continue to talk about her in the present tense, attributing needs, thoughts, and intentions to her, as though she were still alive. It is her lingering presence, felt in varying degrees by all of them, that keeps the family together up to their arrival in Jefferson, and it is to all appearances her indomitable will, her "last will," that makes them carry the task through to the end. In answer to Vernon Tull, who shows surprise at his haste and obstinacy, Anse says: "I give my promise. . . . She is counting on it" (126). All the Bundrens seem to assume that Addie is somehow still among them, as if they entertained the old belief that the dead, for a certain time at least, continue to live a life parallel to ours, and little Vardaman even bores holes in the coffin to allow his mother to breathe. But who does not go wild in times of mourning?

Mothers

Addie is both present and absent, alive and dead—present in her death and alive in her absence. She is at once the cadaver among the living and the mother among her children.

Motherhood, in Faulkner, always takes us back to "the pervading immemorial blind receptive matrix, the hot fluid blind foundation—grave-womb or womb-grave, it's all one,"[8] and many of his mother figures tend to become the Cosmic Mothers of mythology. Over and over again they are equated with fertile nature, the mother-earth, the life of everything that lives and the death of everything that dies, and in *As I Lay Dying* the equation applies as much to Dewey Dell,[9] the pregnant young daughter, as to Addie, the dead old mother:

> The dead air shapes the dead earth in the dead darkness, further away than seeing shapes the dead earth. It lies dead and warm upon me, touching me naked through my clothes . . . I feel like a wet seed wild in the hot blind earth.(58)

The pregnant girl's words arise out of the "dead darkness" of a "dead earth," but a new life will be born in the "dewy dell" from the "wet seed wild in the hot blind earth." The mysterious life forces that send tremors through her womb are no different from the ones that make the crops grow. Like Lena Grove, Eula Varner, and the anonymous pregnant woman in *The Wild Palms*, Dewey Dell is described—and describes herself in her own monologues—as an avatar of *natura naturans*. Woman's body is one with the world's flesh: *mundus muliebris*. In a "metaphysical" conceit worthy of John Donne, Darl compares his sister's leg to "that lever which moves the world; one of that caliper which measures the length and breadth of life" (91). And further on, the same correspondence between gynocosm and macrocosm reemerges in one of the novel's most troubling visions: "Squatting, Dewey Dell's wet dress shapes for the dead eyes of three blind men those mammalian ludicrosities which are the horizons and the valleys of the earth" (150).[10]

In similar fashion Addie is associated and associates herself with the earth. But Addie's earth is the dark domain of the dead rather than the womb of the living. Even the little we learn about her origins is connected with graveyards. "I have people. In Jefferson," she tells Anse during one of their first meetings. "They're in the cemetery." And when Anse asks her about her living kin, she says: " I dont know. I never had any other kind" (157).

The "dead earth," the earth of the dead, is the place Addie comes from and the place to which she returns. When Cash looks at her for the last time, he sees "her peaceful, rigid face fading into the dusk as though darkness were a precursor of the ultimate earth" (46). To Peabody, watching her beneath the quilt, she is "no more than a bundle of rotten sticks" (40); to Darl she looks like a "handful of rotten bones" (44). The text, however, connects her repeatedly with images of death *and* life. Addie's last journey, bearing back her body to Jefferson, the place where she was born, is accomplished under the triple sign of birth, sex, and death, and that which encompasses them: time. Cash has made her coffin "clock-shape," and Addie is laid in it in her wedding dress, "head to foot," like a child in its mother's womb at the moment of delivery (77–78). The coffin is the maternal womb and the nuptial bed as well as a box for the dead. Moreover, the long funeral journey, with all its difficulties and delays, will be almost a reenactment of the drama of Addie's erratic destiny, as if it were as hard for her to find rest in death as in life. As Rabi has noted, her journey recalls "the distant tribulations of folklore, where we see the dead painfully reaching the kingdom of souls after a journey full of terrible events."[11] Everything takes place as if the elements were disputing Addie's corpse: air (the possibility of the body being left to the buzzards), water (the immersion of the coffin in the river), fire (the barely avoided cremation during the barn fire), and the earth in which she is finally buried. Not one of the "four countries of death"[12] is missing. For Addie, the passage from life to death is not just the matter of a moment but a quest strewn with ambushes and perils, like the funeral crossings of myth and legend.

And doesn't Addie have her say after the buzzards have already begun to circle above her dead body? Her proud and passionate voice reaches us from beyond time and space, and her posthumous soliloquy tells us about life, about *her* life, how "terrible" it was and how much it exceeded her desperate endeavors to give it shape and significance. As a young schoolmistress, she whipped her pupils so as to conquer isolation and make "[her] blood and their blood flow as one stream" (158). Addie then burned with the desire to immerse herself in "the terrible blood, the red bitter flood boiling through the land" (161). But only during her first pregnancy, when another body was grafted upon hers and she became two in one, did she experience the longed-for commingling with life: her "aloneness had been violated and then made whole again by the violation" (158). And after the first child was born, when she lay awake in the dark, listening to the sounds of the night, she knew that "the land . . . was now of [her] blood and flesh" (159). Like the nurturing earth, she then became the Universal Mother, and even Anse, her husband, was an infant to be suckled: "I would think that if he were to wake and cry, I would suckle him, too" (158). Likewise, after her affair with Whitfield, she claims sole possession of her offspring and equates herself with the Magna Mater: "My children were of me alone, of the wild blood boiling along the earth, of me and of all that lived; of none and of all" (162). Yet even though *As I Lay Dying* invites "mythic" or "archetypal" readings, and even though it may be tempting to compare Addie and Dewey Dell to Demeter and Persephone[13] or to other fertility goddesses, it is important to realize that this mythic discourse is above all Addie's, and that the rhetoric of triumphant motherhood is primarily hers. Her monologue speaks, with somber and sullen eloquence, of life and death and turns them into issues of cosmic magnitude; but what its eloquence both reveals and conceals is *a* life, a singular woman's trivial and turbulent career.

The novel provides a double perspective on Addie, since we come to know her first through the portraits drawn by her kin and neighbors, then by the self-portrait offered in the mirror of her one monologue. None of these portraits is quite to be trusted, but they all reveal, to use Cora's phrase, a "lonely woman, lonely with her pride" (20). Addie never ceased to be torn between her hunger for life's intensities and her loathing of its constraints, between the urge for intimacy with others and the equally imperious wish to preserve her secrecy. The presence within her of these conflicting aspirations, this double movement of acquiescence and refusal, surrender and withdrawal, is enough to set her apart from Faulkner's mythified (and mystifying) mother figures. Imagination, energy, impatience, and pride: Addie's virtues and flaws are those that Faulkner attributes to his most virile heroes and heroines—to Charlotte Rittenmeyer in *The Wild Palms*, for example, another masculinized woman, another adulteress, whose exacerbated, all-demanding romanticism is strangely like her own. One also thinks of Emma Bovary, whom Baudelaire saw as a "bizarre androgyne," an "almost male" being who gives herself "in a quite masculine way to despicable fellows who are not her equals."[14] Addie gives herself, or rather "takes" in the same manner: "So I took Anse" (156). Traditional gender roles have been once again ironically reversed: while Anse, the husband—referred to by Peabody as "his mother's son" (38)—has the inertia and endurance that Faulkner often associated with feminine figures, Addie, the wife, inherits the extravagant and always injurious dreams of men.

That she is also an omnipresent, domineering mother figure is obvious enough. But what about *her* mother? Whose daughter is Addie? In her entire monologue we do not find a word about her own mother. The father, on the other hand—invoked at the beginning and the end of her monologue just as he is in Quentin's in *The Sound and the Fury*—haunts her memory. She hates him for having "planted" her and remembers him only as a voice. But in Faulkner the father's voice is a voice never to be forgotten, and for Addie as for Quentin or for Joanna Burden in *Light in August*, it conveys a crippling wisdom: "I could just remember how my father used to say that the reason for living was to get ready to stay dead a long time" (155). What we find at the origin of the Bundren story, as of nearly all the family stories that Faulkner tells us, is the daunting figure of a dead Father. Preceding and predetermining the mother-child relationship, the father-daughter relationship is here, in every respect, primordial. Genealogically, Addie defines herself by her exclusive relationship to the (dead) father; her children and their relationships to one another will be likewise determined by their exclusive bond to the (dead) mother.

In the Bundren household, Addie is the matriarch, the sovereign mother; within the patriarchal structure of the southern family, she occupies the father's place, assuming his authority, exerting his power.[15] In "taking" Anse, she already usurped the role of seducer traditionally assigned to the male, and she likewise seizes his prerogatives once married. No sooner has Anse made her pregnant than he ceases to be her husband; no sooner has she become a mother than she stops being his wife. After the birth of her first child, Anse, as we have seen, is to her just another infant to suckle. And after Darl's unwanted birth she declares him promptly "dead" (159, 160). In Addie's private script, then, the father of her children hardly matters. Fantasizing herself as the omnipotent Mother,[16] she behaves as if her children were of virgin birth, having seemingly found in *her own* flesh and *her own* blood what she needed (the supplementing phallus?) to fulfill her desire for wholeness, her delirious dream of being One, the One, fount and origin, father-and-mother, single source and ground of all being.

The megalomaniac exaltation of the "narcissistic pregnancy crisis,"[17] however, does not last. With the second pregnancy come bitterness and revolt. Addie turns against her husband with fierce resentment and refuses her second son the love she gave to Cash. And when Darl is born she conceives of her plan of posthumous revenge: "I asked Anse to promise to take me back to Jefferson when I died" (159). She has not yet given up, however, on her dream of maternal apotheosis. What she missed in marriage she hopes to obtain from adultery; what she could not find in domestic virtue she seeks in sin. But to make her feel alive again, the sin must be the most outrageous possible. So her next move is an attempt at hierogamy: a union, if not with God himself, with a man of God, "the sin the more utter and terrible since he was the instrument ordained by God who created the sin, to sanctify that sin He had created" (161). From her sacrilegious and therefore sacred coupling with Reverend Whitfield Jewel is born—the divine child from whom she expects salvation. Then the wild blood boils away, her eruptive vitality begins to subside, and soon there is nothing left for her but "cleaning up the house," putting her accounts in order, and accepting her father's wisdom in "getting ready to die" (162): Dewey Dell and Vardaman, the last two children to be born, will be "given" to Anse to "negative" the child of sin and to replace the rejected one.

Addie's singular arithmetic is further proof that her children have been little more to her than narcissistic self-extensions or objects of exchange. Whether "jewels" or counters, pawns or pledges, they have been throughout her life and are even after her death private possessions and the instruments of her will. Addie has never let them go, has never allowed them to be on their own; they have never broken out of their preoedipal limbo. Cash, Darl, and Jewel are three young men in the prime of life (Cash and Darl must be in their late twenties, Jewel eighteen or nineteen), and yet none of them is married; Addie is the only woman they care about, and none of them shows great interest in sex.[18] It is true, as one critic recently complained,[19] that most discussions of As I Lay Dying assume that Anse's and Addie's progeny are still all children, but the misunderstanding is quite understandable, for in relation to Addie, alive or dead, they are children indeed.

Little wonder, then, that after her death Addie is still the prime mover, keeping her hold on the family while becoming at the same time the nub of all tensions within it. As the novel's circular structure suggests, she is at once the axle and the wheel, the center and the circumference of the circle, the "center on the horizon," as Caddy was in The Sound and the Fury. In As I Lay Dying the family is indeed the body of the mother, and Addie's children are her membra disjecta. As Addie lies dying, so does the whole family, even though its death will be comically followed by an almost instantaneous resurrection after her burial in Jefferson.

Mourning

When he was young, Dr. Peabody "believed death to be a phenomenon of the body," but experience taught him that it is "merely a function of the mind—and that of the minds of the ones who suffer the bereavement" (39). Because of the physical presence of Addie's corpse and the Bundrens' concern with its preservation all along the journey, As I Lay Dying seldom allows us to forget death as "a phenomenon of the body"; yet what it is most concerned with is obviously what is going on in "the minds of the ones who suffer the bereavement."

As I Lay Dying, then, is a novel about mourning. But mourning here is to be understood in cultural as well as psychological terms. The book not only investigates a series of individual responses to a death event, but it also considers mourning as a collective symbolic action performed in the interest of family and society, and much of its humor and pathos derives from the ironic juxtaposition or interplay of *public* mourning, a set of prescribed gestures, attitudes, and practices expressing deference toward the dead one, and *private* grief, the "work of mourning" which all the Bundren children go through in order to accommodate loss.

Mourning is a matter of survival. Death rituals are meant to carry one through bereavement without too much emotional disturbance, to ensure the continuance of a family beyond the demise of one of its members, and thus to maintain the continuity of human life within a given cultural pattern. The survivors must be prevented from yielding either to the impulse to flee from the death scene or to the contrary impulse to follow the deceased into the grave. For life to resume its customary course, death must be both acknowledged and repudiated through a symbolic act, a kind of second death, a canceling repetition which at once duplicates and negates biological extinction.

In this connection it may be worth recalling that for Hegel the performance of the death rite is precisely the family's appointed task.[20] In providing the dead a decent burial the family fulfills its cultural and ethical, that is, its *antinatural* function. For it is above all a matter of preventing the corpse from returning to nature. "The family," Hegel writes, "keeps away from the dead this dishonouring of him by unconscious cravings and abstract elements, puts its own action in place of theirs, and weds the relative to the bosom of the earth, the elemental individuality that passes not away."[21] The family thus "takes upon itself the act of destruction,"[22] subjects the rawness of nature to the higher order of culture, and transforms senseless destruction into a meaningful ritual.

If the funeral duties fall on the whole family, it is woman who, for Hegel, is specifically in charge of the dead, just as it is woman who, within the family, defends the common interests of the living. According to Hegel "womankind" is the sovereign principle of the family, the very foundation of its law, a law both "familial" and "divine" bound to come up against the "human" law, that is, the law of the community, of the city, which is also the law of men. Womankind is therefore the "inner enemy" of the community or, to use Hegel's celebrated phrase, "the everlasting irony in the life of the community" (*die ewige Ironie des Gemeinwesens*).[23]

In *As I Lay Dying* the Bundrens define themselves collectively through their subjection to Addie, a woman, and through their intense involvement in a death rite, so that in one sense they might be said to represent the Hegelian family with almost archetypal purity. Yet at the same time they are also in many significant ways its negative and travesty. For the Bundrens it is no doubt a question of pulling a corpse away from nature, but with regard to the Hegelian pattern, it is not without irony that the remains to be buried are here those of a woman. Instead of being the vigilant keeper of the cult of the dead,

Addie, wife and mother, is its passive object. Admittedly, she keeps ruling over her kin beyond her death, and it is she who has ordered the journey to Jefferson and so set the Bundrens in motion. Nevertheless, by demanding burial in a remote graveyard and imposing on the bereaved the trials of a perilous journey, she is also responsible for the scandalous delay in the completion of the ritual duties.

Yet the death rite begins properly enough. According to Tull's testimony (81–82), the funeral ceremony, presided over by Reverend Whitfield, has even given rise to one of those rare moments when individual isolation is overcome by mutual recognition and acceptance; much as in the Easter service described in the last section of *The Sound and the Fury*, a sense of communion has been induced by the power of the preacher's voice—a voice "bigger than him" (81), as Reverend Shegog's was—and the singing voices of the women.[24] The following burial journey, however, not only postpones the proper completion of the rite of death but also threatens to make the ritual itself pointless. If Addie is not diligently buried, the increasingly obtrusive physicality of her dead body can no longer be ignored and the corpse will return to nature like an animal carcass. A dangerous gap has thus been opened in the cultural order, and as was rightly feared, the eerie proximity of death releases and exacerbates the "unconscious agencies" which the familial rite was meant to dispel. Addie, the unburiable cadaver, the dead one not yet dead, who seems to mock everybody from her coffin, is indeed "the irony in the life of the community"; but to begin with, she is the irony in the life of her own family—a situation not at all anticipated by the philosopher from Jena!

There are more ironies. Hegel, in his speculations on the family, refers to "the reverent devotion (*Pietät*) of husband and wife towards each other."[25] What we learn about Addie and Anse belies this lofty concept of marital love; moreover, their antagonism persists well beyond Addie's death. The reader may wonder whether the funeral journey is the accomplishment of her revenge scheme, a macabre posthumous joke played on Anse;[26] or whether, through another twist of irony, it is Anse's sly revenge on his wife; or—irony of ironies—whether it is both at the same time. True, Anse's public conduct as widower is irreproachable. He does the best he can to respect his wife's last wish, and it is also true that from the dressing out of the dead body through its transportation to the Jefferson cemetery to its placement in the grave, the Bundrens go dutifully through all the ritual gestures and eventually give Addie the burial she wanted. So the letter of Addie's request is indeed fulfilled. But what first appears to be a virtuous struggle to keep a promise looks much less virtuous once we know about the secret motivations. For as it turns out, apart from Jewel and Darl, the most and the least loved sons, they all have reasons of their own for going to town: a new set of teeth and a new wife for Anse, an abortion for Dewey Dell, a gramophone for Cash, bananas and an electric toy train for Vardaman. The convergence of these personal motives no doubt strengthens the Bundrens' determination to undertake the journey, but their self-interested nature throws suspicion on the act of pure piety they are supposed to be accomplishing.

Darl reads on Anse's face "a monstrous burlesque of all bereavement" (69). We might be tempted to extend the phrase to all the Bundrens and to dismiss all their endeavors as ludicrous pantomime, if their monologues did not allow us to find out about the confusions and agonies occasioned by Addie's death.

Grieving

Private grief usually takes much more time than public mourning. By the end of *As I Lay Dying* we learn that the official death rite has been at long last completed, but we shall never know how long it took the Bundrens to complete their "work of mourning," and we may even wonder whether it has been completed at all. How much time has elapsed between the events and their remembering and retelling? There is no way of knowing, even though, as Eric J. Sundquist points out, "many if not almost all the monologues, whether they are in the present or past tense, need to be understood as occurring, or continuing to occur, *after* the chronological end of the action."[27]

Both public and private mourning, however, are processes of transformation, substitution, and repair whose purpose is to come to terms with the death event and to establish a new, viable relationship between the living and the dead. "Mourning," Freud argues, "has a quite specific psychical task to perform: its function is to detach the survivors' memories and hopes from the dead."[28] Similarly, Daniel Lagache points out that mourning consists "in transferring the biological fact to a human level, that is, in 'killing the dead one'."[29] For the Bundrens, "killing the dead mother" is indeed a pressing imperative. And small wonder that to them it is an all but impossible task, that the dying of Addie in their minds takes so much time: of all our dead ones, the mother will always be the least dead. Hence the painful urgency of the "work of mourning," its many amazing ruses and its extraordinary intensity.

Denial of death, ambivalence toward and identification with the dead one—nothing is missing in Faulkner's remarkably perceptive evocation of the mourning process. But even more stunning perhaps is his mastery in rendering the range of individual responses to Addie's death and the feverish fantasizing to which grief, the deeply traumatic experience of loss, gives rise in each of the Bundrens.

With one notable exception: Anse, the husband, who is clearly the least disturbed by the event. Whether in his peculiar way he loved his wife or not may be debated,[30] but of all the Bundrens he is indisputably the fastest in recouping the loss. Anse rushes through mourning and so reaches at one stroke the final stage of the process in which "the ego . . . is persuaded by the sum of the narcissistic satisfactions it derives from being alive to sever its attachment to the object that has been abolished."[31] We must bear in mind, however, that Addie and Anse have been "dead" to each other for quite a long time. In fact, Addie's actual death is an almost jubilant resurrection for Anse. No sooner has she died than he thinks of getting new teeth: "God's will be done," he says. "Now I can get them teeth" (48); no sooner is she buried than she is replaced by another "Mrs. Bundren." With a set of new teeth and a new wife, Anse's manhood is eventually restored, and such a transformation would have been impossible while his castrating wife was still alive. Anse is probably too opaque to himself to be called insincere, but mourning, with him, is little more than the part of grief-stricken widower, a public role which he seems to relish and plays indeed to perfection.

Not surprisingly, given their emotional dependence on their mother, it is the Bundren children who are the most deeply afflicted, and it is with them that the mourning crisis develops into serious psychic disturbance and, for one at least, leads to madness. For them, Addie is indeed what she longed to be but could not be to herself: the Mother, the Other, an encompassing power not to be resisted. What happens to them is the loss of their mother; what threatens them is to be forever lost in her. Their experience of mourning is a replay of loss or rather of *re-loss* inasmuch as the separation from the mother through death reopens the wound of other, earlier separations, beginning with the severing of birth, the initial expulsion out of the maternal body. But at the same time the last separation is the first, for in one sense they have never left their mother's body, they are all still imprisoned in her womb, unborn. Her destruction, then, necessarily means their own, as is perhaps intimated by the river scene, in which the sons are nearly engulfed at the same time as the coffin containing Addie's corpse.

The "mother to be killed," then, is the archaic mother in the full horror and seduction of her lethal power. Yet each of the Bundren children acts out grief and fantasizes anguish in his or her own way, according to age, sex, and above all the child's position in Addie's scheme, and Faulkner has managed to invent for each of them a unique bundle of affects and fantasies.

For Cash, the oldest of Addie's sons, grief is a dirge, the steady sound of his hammering and sawing, under Addie's window, as he works on her coffin. In his case, the "work of mourning" begins before death has actually occurred, and it is work *tout court* . Laboring over every nail and groove that he puts in the coffin, Cash is above all the "good carpenter," proud of his craft, the reasonable and industrious *homo faber*; and the oblong wooden box which he makes "on the bevel" with his own hands, lifting each board high in the air so that Addie may appreciate its fitness, is a last offering to the mother, a *gift*, like the dung-filled bread pan he once brought her from the barn. Jewel, who relates this childhood episode, is not mistaken:

> It's because he stays out there, right under the window, hammering and sawing on that goddam box. Where she's got to see him. Where every breath she draws is full of his knocking and sawing where she can see him saying See. See what a good one I am making for you. (13)

Although blinded by jealousy, Jewel sees very clearly that Cash's ostentatious bustle under Addie's window is an ultimate serenade. Work is Cash's way of communicating with Addie, his means of getting and holding her attention, and thereby assuring that unspoken understanding that has always existed between them. As Addie later recalls in her monologue: "Cash did not need to say it to me nor I to him . . . " (158). But work at this point is also a strategy of self-protection, the most economical way to divert and displace the imminent pain of loss, to separate himself from the lost object. Wood, the material (*materia, materies*) he works with and of which the coffin is made, becomes the metaphoric and metonymic substitute for the mother (*mater*).[32] It is therefore not surprising that the building of the coffin should become for Cash the object of a manic counterinvestment.[33] If he cannot be the "jewel," he can at the very least be the "jeweler" (70), the maker of the perfect shrine in which the mother's precious body is preserved. In nailing Addie into the coffin, Cash encloses himself with her, burying his desire and pain.

As to Jewel, he is, probably even more than Cash, Addie's true son. Because he is the offspring of her sin and rebellion, he has become her idol, her "jewel," her "cross" and her "salvation" (154). What was denied to Darl and the two last born, Jewel was given in abundance. His mother brooded over him with fierce and tender love—"ma always whipped him and petted him more" (16), Darl recounts with envy—and out of this love Jewel's own grew in return, equally ambivalent, equally possessive, equally savage. It is an incestuous and hence forbidden and frustrated attachment, although there is no father to interfere, and just as jealous as Quentin's to Caddy. Its depth and intensity are perhaps best measured by Jewel's inarticulate hatred for all invaders, especially the other family members. Just as Quentin wanted to isolate his sister "out of the loud world," Jewel, as we learn from his single monologue, would kill father and brother to be alone with his mother and be assured forever of exclusive rights:

> It would be just me and her on a high hill and me rolling the rocks down the hill at their faces, picking them up and throwing them down the hill faces and teeth and all by God until she was quiet and not that goddamn adze going One lick less. One lick less and we could be quiet. (14)

Nevertheless, Jewel is too resilient to fall prey to despair or madness. He is the one who rescues Addie's coffin from water and fire, the hero whose exploits and self-sacrifice assure the success of the collective undertaking. To him the road to Jefferson becomes the road of trials, and by the same token mourning becomes a sort of heroic ordeal, like those undergone by the heroes of fairy tale and myth. Besides, his epic exploits in the course of the journey are preceded by herculean labors, which, performed in the secrecy of night, allow him both to buy himself a horse and to test his heroic potential. But Addie cries when he returns; she knows then that Jewel is no longer entirely hers, that the purchase of the horse was his first gesture of self-emancipation. Contrary to Cash's suspicions, Jewel had not been spending his nights with a woman. There was some truth in the elder brother's sexual suspicions, however: with his horse—which he brutalizes and caresses in turn and curses, according to Darl, with "obscene ferocity" (11)—Jewel plays out all the love and all the hate he feels for his mother. *Mutatis mutandis*, the horse is to Jewel what the coffin is to Cash and what the fish is to Vardaman: an object of transference, a surrogate for the lost maternal body as well as an object of narcissistic identification.[34] As Darl, the clairvoyant one, keeps repeating: "Jewel's mother is a horse" (89).

For Dewey Dell, the Bundrens' only daughter, who is barely out of adolescence, Addie's death is yet another, entirely different experience. More organically than any of her brothers, she senses the closeness of life and death, which is hardly surprising if we remember that the loss of her mother almost coincides with her sexual initiation and with the beginning of her first pregnancy. Dewey Dell's discovery of death is at one with her outrage at the life growing inside her body and slowly transforming it: "I feel my body, my bones and flesh beginning to part and open upon the alone, and the process of coming unalone is terrible" (56). So the daughter goes through the same experiences as her mother: in pregnancy Dewey Dell discovers, as Addie did, her destiny as begetter, and like her mother, she is snatched from "aloneness" only to be thrown back to it.[35] And now her solitude is made all the more irremediable by the death of the only person who could (or so she thinks) have understood and relieved her distress. Her first sexual experience, her pregnancy, her mother's death all come too soon for her. Time, life, death, everything goes too quickly: "I heard that my mother is dead. I wish I had time to let her die. I wish I had time to wish I had. It is because in the wild and outraged earth too soon too soon too soon. It's not that I wouldn't and will not it's that it is too soon too soon too soon" (106). Dewey Dell thinks she has no time for mourning because, as she discovers with dismay, time is already her despotic master: *"That's what they mean by the womb of time: the agony and the despair of spreading bones, the hard girdle in which lie the outraged entrails of events"* (106). There is apparently more urgent business for her than grieving over her mother's death: the labor of bearing and giving life. Yet in her own way Dewey Dell mourns as much as do her four brothers. She too makes desperate attempts to "kill the dead mother," but to do so would be to kill at the same time the mother in her, the mother she is herself becoming. Hence her *idée fixe:* the abortion which, if successfully performed, would be both the real liquidation of the fetus and the symbolic murder of the mother.

Vardaman, the youngest, certainly experiences as much confusion, anguish, and bewilderment as any of the children. Here is how Darl describes him at his dying mother's bedside:

> From behind pa's leg Vardaman peers, his mouth full open and all color draining from his face into his mouth, as though he has by some means fleshed his own teeth in himself, sucking. He begins to move slowly backward from the bed, his eyes round, his pale face fading into the dusk like a piece of paper pasted on a failing wall, and so out of the door. (45)

Vardaman is a small child in the face of death, experiencing the shock of loss in its most primal form. For him the death of his mother is something literally inconceivable, carrying with it the threat of the dissolution of his entire world. Hence, of all the Bundrens, he is both the most energetic in his search for an explanation of it and, with Dewey Dell, the most desperate in denying the mother's death. With Vardaman, grief generates a kind of savage rhetoric, in which metaphor and metonymy are figures not of speech so much as of thought and action. Indeed, in his prelogical mind it is enough for two events to be linked by some analogy or to be contiguous in space or time to become virtually identical. Thus his need to find causes makes him first place the blame on Peabody, who arrived shortly before Addie's death, and, being unable to take revenge on the doctor himself, he beats his horses. Temporal coincidence likewise triggers the association of his mother with the big fish he caught some hours before her death. When the fish was caught, it was whole and Addie was alive. She stopped being when the fish became no-fish. If the fish were still alive, so would his mother be, and since the death of the fish depended on his volition, it must be possible to backtrack, obliterate its occurrence, and then his mother could also be restored to him.

Addie must and does continue to live for Vardaman, either in her coffin or as a fish,[36] because he feels his own life and identity depend on her survival, whatever shape the latter may assume. The process of mourning makes him regress to that anxiety-ridden stage of early childhood analyzed by Melanie Klein in which object relations are not yet completely formed and the differentiation of self from nonself has not yet taken place.[37] Not surprisingly, he responds to Addie's death with oral fantasies of dismembering and reincorporation, acting out mourning in what might be called the *(endo)cannibalistic* mode. Revealing, too, are his destructive impulses before and after her death, and here again one is reminded of Klein's scenarios of infantile violence. He first swears at the fish he has caught (as Jewel, whom he imitates, does at his horse), "cusses it like a grown man, standing a-straddle of it" (27), and instead of gutting it as his father asks, chops it up with an axe and "comes around the house, bloody as a hog to his knees" (34). After Addie's death, however, what bothers him most is the idea that the fish will be "cooked and et" (52). For Vardaman, eating the fish means appropriating not only its flesh but its vital principle. If the fish is Addie, if Addie is the fish, then, as in a cannibalistic feast, eating it is also a reappropriation of his mother, a transubstantiation of her soul and flesh into the soul and flesh of her kin, and a victory of life over death: "And tomorrow it will be cooked and et and she will be him and pa and Cash and Dewey Dell and there wont be anything in the box and so she can breathe" (60). Instead of provoking anxiety, Vardaman's fish fantasy thus becomes one of restorative re-membering. "It can hardly be an accident," writes Michel Gresset, "if [Addie's] dying coincides with the actual preparation of an evening meal, the main dish of which, the fish, is said to be 'full of blood and guts as a hog.'"[38]

In relation to Vardaman's fantasies, *As I Lay Dying* could be read as the account of a eucharistic communion rite or a totemic meal. Reappropriation and reincorporation of the lost object is, at one point in the process, what all mourning attempts. However, insofar as oral fantasies become one with the incestuous urge to regress to the maternal womb, they can only lead to an impasse, so that death, no longer held at bay, becomes indeed a contagious disease. To mourn in its active sense (*faire son deuil*, as the French say: to *do* one's mourning, as one does one's duty or one's room) is to learn how to lose someone so as not to lose oneself. Regression and identification with the dead are probably necessary detours of mourning, but its successful completion requires detachment from the dead, the capacity to remember them as dead (instead of continuing to desire their living presence), and to accept the ineluctability of death itself. With the Bundrens, the failure to complete the funeral rite within normal time limits may be seen as the public counterpart of their difficulty in completing their private mourning. Yet, as we have already noted, three of the four Bundren brothers manage by one means or another to represent their loss through animal totems or surrogate objects. Apart from Jewel's horse, their crudely symbolic substitutions appear to be more or less hasty psychic *bricolages* effected under severe emotional strain: they undoubtedly indicate that the sons are still bound to their mother, but they perhaps also constitute the beginning of the overdue separation from her.

The river scene—the Bundrens' trial by water—serves in this respect as a summation and reenactment of the whole mourning process. Like the rampaging Mississippi in "Old Man," the river rushes along with destructive violence, drowning pigs and mules and threatening to engulf all the Bundrens. But however masculine its fury, the water is also once again a feminine element. Mixed with the earth—the water is muddy, black, or yellow—and therefore doubly feminine, it may be said to represent the primordial matter in which all life is made and unmade. And the fact that Addie's coffin tips over and is almost carried away by the current (Vardaman says that his mother moves about like a fish in water and expects Darl to rescue her), confirms, if confirmation were necessary, its ambiguously maternal character.[39] If the death rite begins with a break from the mother, the immersion of the three older sons during the river crossing marks their return to the mother womb, at once a symbolic death and a baptism, a rebirth.[40] Just as Addie must die a second time in order to be dead, her children must be reborn so as to be able to live on, and their second birth, the symbolic one, is at once a confirmation and a cancellation of the first birth, the real one which has become the imaginary.

Irony, however, secretly hollows out these ritual patterns and makes us wonder about their symbolic import. To what extent are we to take them seriously? *As I Lay Dying* reminds us that writing is not only working through grief but also playing with loss: the *Trauerarbeit* develops into a *Trauerspiel*, a representation of, or a game with mourning. And the suspicion lingers that this might all be mere travesty. Addie's posthumous tribulations are perhaps nothing more than those of a rotting corpse; the funeral rite itself is perhaps but a grotesque mummery; and nothing in the text allows us to affirm that the ordeal in the river is to be read as a successful initiation. And yet it would seem that the journey has not been entirely pointless, that it has taught the Bundrens how to travel, how to traverse flooded rivers and transfer violent emotions, how to displace corpses and replace mothers. In their own bumbling way, they do cope with motion, time, and change—with what Faulkner considered to be the essence of life.[41] Only one fails, only one leaves the river empty-handed: Darl.

IX

TURNS OF MADNESS

Les hommes sont si nécessairement fous que
ce serait être fou par un autre tour de folie
de n'être pas fou.

Blaise Pascal

Disorder

If the story of the Compsons is "a tale told by an idiot, full of sound and fury,"
As I Lay Dying is in many ways a tale of madness told by a madman. As in
Shakespeare's tragedies, madness and chaos are everywhere—in the antics
and agonies of man, but also in the apocalyptic disorder of the world. In the
first sections, it is true, we are still on firm ground, in an ordered space which
the eye can master and size up at its leisure. Yet if Darl's opening monologue
describes the setting with almost geometric precision, the scene soon starts to
crack or to float. Nothing is anchored to its place: "A feather dropped near the
front door will rise and brush along the ceiling, slanting backward, until it
reaches the down-turning current at the back door" (18). Gradually we slip
into an unfamiliar, phantasmagorical dimension where the ordinary laws of
perception no longer obtain. Acoustics are disrupted: in the Bundrens' house
on the hill sounds travel most oddly; voices are heard nearby, disembodied
and sourceless: "As you enter the hall, they sound as though they were
speaking out of the air about your head" (18). Sounds have a strange habit
especially of "ceasing without departing":

> Cash labors about the trestles, moving back and forth, lifting and placing the
> planks with long clattering reverberations in the dead air as though he were
> lifting and dropping them at the bottom of an invisible well, the sounds ceasing
> without departing, as if any movement might dislodge them from the immedi-
> ate air in reverberant repetition. (67)

When the women at the funeral cease their keening songs, Tull remarks, "it's
like [the tunes] hadn't gone away. It's like they had just disappeared into the
air and when we moved we would loose them again out of the air around us,

sad and comforting" (81–82). By some inexplicable power of remanence, sounds linger on in endless "reverberation," remaining as spectral traces even when they are no longer audible. Everything that strikes the senses seems destined to persist beyond its disappearance. Nothing ever altogether vanishes; and nothing, on the other hand, is ever fully present, here and now. Few words recur more often in this novel than *fading*. Sounds and sights hang in perpetual suspension, vacillating between receding presence and nearby absence, as in Darl's singular description of shadows: "Upon the impalpable plane of [the air] their shadows form as upon a wall, as though like sound they had not gone very far away in falling but had merely congealed for a moment, immediate and musing" (67–68). Concrete things dematerialize; shadows acquire substance. A similar phenomenon occurs in the scene where the Bundren brothers carry Addie's coffin to the wagon; when the "box" slips from Darl's hands, it slides "down the air like a sled upon invisible snow, smoothly evacuating atmosphere in which the sense of it is still shaped" (88). And just as sounds, shadows, and objects do, so events leave a wake: after the crossing, when the wagon has finally been hauled out of the river, "it is as though upon the shabby, familiar, inert shape of the wagon there lingered somehow, latent yet immediate, that violence which had slain the mules that drew it not an hour since" (143).

Another significant anomaly, particularly evident in the night scenes, is the frequent reduction of space to two dimensions. For transparent space, in which perspectives are clearly ordered, is substituted an opaque space, with neither depth nor relief, against which objects appear flat. In the scene of Addie's death this flatness is twice suggested: when Vardaman leaves the bedside, we see "his pale face fading into the dusk like a piece of paper pasted on a failing wall" (45), and a page later, the dying woman's face is similarly blurred in the twilight, floating in the darkness, "detached upon it, lightly as the reflection of a dead leaf" (46). This transformation of volumes into surfaces is particularly noticeable with regard to characters, who are sometimes reduced to the insubstantial fragililty of paper-thin silhouettes. But it is also found in descriptions of the setting. Thus, in the other night scene, which shows Cash busy finishing the coffin, one finds the following simile: "Upon the dark ground the chips look like random smears of soft pale paint on a black canvas" (67).

All these depthless landscapes and weightless figures drain the world of its substance and weave a flimsy fabric of eerie appearances with nothing real behind. And everywhere destruction threatens. Nature holds its breath in anticipation of impending disasters. Before Addie's death, the storm gathers on the horizon, light takes on a copper hue, the air smells of sulphur, and the sun is covered with blood. Hallucinating, *unheimlich*, too, is the night scene in which Cash saws the last planks for the coffin by the feeble light of a lantern: the atmosphere is electric; noises, lights, shadows—the whole setting assumes a supernatural aspect, and again there is the reek of sulphur. Hell is not far away.

Another world surges up from within the one we know, fantastic and terrifying, and one cannot tell whether it is given up to demoniacal violence, to the wrath of the old Testament God, or to the cruel whim of that evil demiurge whom Faulkner invokes in his novels. When the rain, awaited and feared for so long, finally starts to fall, it sweeps down with a sudden violence suggestive of the biblical Deluge: the "first harsh, sparse, swift drops" are "big as buckshot, warm as though fired from a gun; they sweep across the lantern in a vicious hissing" (68). Rain here is not a promise of regeneration but a threat of destruction, the first manifestation of the cosmic forces which are going to be unleashed against the Bundrens. The descent into Hell has begun. The wagon is soon to become Charon's ferry; the river crossing, like that of the Styx or Acheron, marks the Bundrens' entry into the nether world. In their accounts of the scene, Darl, the visionary dreamer, and Tull, the man of sense, both give the impression of escaping from a terrible cataclysm. Darl describes the scene in apocalyptic terms:

> that single monotony of desolation leaning with that terrific quality a little from right to left, as though we had reached the place where the motion of the wasted world accelerates just before the final precipice. (132)

Tull speaks as someone who has seen the jaws of Hell open:

> the bridge shaking and swaying under us, going down into the moiling water like it went clean through to the other side of the earth, and the other end coming up outen the water like it wasn't the same bridge a-tall and that them that would walk up outen the water on that side must come from the bottom of the earth. (123)

The fiendish savagery of nature reaches a paroxysm here. For the Bundrens it is the decisive ordeal. Not the last, of course, since after the ordeal by water they have to undergo the ordeal by fire. But Darl's description of the barn fire does not have the same sustained apocalyptic intensity; it is more spectacular than visionary, and attention focuses more on the heroic figure of Jewel than on the scene itself. Water rather than fire seems to be the dominant element in *As I Lay Dying*; water, the prime agent for trans-formation, is also the prime agent of formlessness, the universal dissolver, and hence "the cosmos of death."[1] And through the highly "pregnant" image of the swollen river it is also once again closely associated with femininity and motherhood, and with the fantasies of engulfment which occur so often in the sexual nightmares of Faulkner's males. As in "Old Man," the supreme calamity is imagined here as a liquid debacle, and as in *The Sound and the Fury* and *Sanctuary* dissolution is referred to so often that it becomes one of the novel's leitmotifs. Revealingly, it appears for the first time in section 12, in the wood-loading scene, which coincides with Addie's dying and may therefore be read as its symbolic counterpart:

about the shattered spokes and about Jewel's ankles a runnel of yellow neither water nor
earth swirls, curving with the yellow road neither of earth nor water, down the hill
dissolving into a streaming mass of dark green neither of earth nor sky. (45)

Vardaman takes up the motif in his description of the horse: "It is as though
the dark were resolving him out of his integrity, into an unrelated scattering
of components. . . . I see him dissolve . . . and float upon the dark in fading
solution" (52). The danger of dissolution is also a permanent threat to man, as
can be seen in Darl's description of Cash, after the latter has been rescued from
the flooded river. Although Cash has not been in the river for more than a few
moments, it looks as if the insidious erosion of water had already started to
corrupt his flesh: "His face appears sunken a little, sagging from the bony
ridges of eye sockets, nose, gums, as though the wetting had slacked the
firmness which held the skin full" (142). For Darl the human body is nothing
but an ephemeral "clotting" likely to dissolve at a moment's notice into "the
myriad original motion" (149–50).

The terrestrial equivalent of dissolution is uprooting, another motif in the
novel. Each existence draws its life-force from the earth, and the most eloquent
symbol of elemental life in *As I Lay Dying* is "the wet seed wild in the hot blind
earth" (58). Dying, then, means being torn from the native soil, and Addie's
death certainly suggests such an uprooting: Jewel compares his mother's
hands to unearthed roots (13), and when she dies, her face seems to float in
the dusk, light and detached, like "the reflection of a dead leaf" (46). Significantly, it is in Darl's monologues that references to uprooting are the most
numerous. Almost all of them occur in sections 34 and 37, where Darl relates
the river episode and its consequences:

> Above the ceaseless surface they stand—trees, cane, vines—rootless, severed
> from the earth. (127)

> as if the road too had been soaked free of earth and floated upward . . . . (129)

> [The drowned mules] roll up out of the water in succession, turning completely
> over, their legs stiffly extended as when they had lost contact with the earth.
> (135)

> Jewel and Vernon are in the river again. From here they do not appear to violate
> the surface at all; it is as though it had severed them both at a single blow. . . .
> (149)

That Darl should see images of uprooting and severance everywhere need
not surprise us: they reflect his own rootlessness, his own severance from the
sustaining mother earth. Similarly, the fluid world of metamorphosis mirrors
his nonidentity, and his apocalyptic vision his inner collapse. Darl's
landscapes are inscapes; through the scenes he describes it is his own vertigo

that he tries to fix in words. Darl is the novel's great stage manager. The hallucinated theater of *As I Lay Dying* is invented in his gaze and created through his words.

The queen's fool

As has often been noted, of the novel's fifteen narrators, Darl is by far the most prominent. With nineteen sections out of fifty-nine, he takes on single-handed one-third of the narrative and thus occupies a highly privileged position as narrator. His reliability as such may be disputed, but his point of view is beyond contest the richest and the most flexible, his gaze the sharpest, his language the most spellbinding.

Darl also occupies a unique position within—and outside of—his family. Even more inescapably than Quentin's in *The Sound and the Fury*, his drama is rooted in what Faulkner calls elsewhere "the tragic complexity of motherless childhood."[2] Addie had not wanted her second son; she has never accepted him, never loved him, and he waits in vain by her deathbed for her to recognize him at last, if only by a look, as her son.[3] Darl considers himself motherless: "I cannot love my mother because I have no mother" (84). His statement is both literally and figuratively true, for to him the mother has always been already lost, and so her death is above all an agonizing reminder of the original loss. This relationship to absence, however, is not an absence of relationship. The most cruel irony, perhaps, is that of all the Bundren children Darl is the most deeply riveted, the most rigorously subjected to his mother *because* of the very love which he has been denied. His brothers, as we have seen, all end up somehow displacing their grief and replacing Addie: Jewel with a horse, Vardaman with a fish, Cash with a coffin. But Darl's mother is literally irreplaceable. Neither coffin nor fish nor horse, she is the mother he cannot call mother.[4] Darl will never be able to part from her. How could he relinquish what he could never call his own?

Never having had a mother, Darl is more surely possessed by her than any of his brothers. Darl's eyes, as Dewey Dell describes them, are "full of the land dug out of his skull and the holes filled with distance beyond the land" (23); the "land runs out" of them (106).[5] Now the fertile land is what Addie identifies with in her monologue: Darl *has* no mother, but in many ways he *is* his mother. His gaze is hers—not reembodied, but disembodied, excarnated. His tormented awareness is hers, raised to the second power—but adrift, cut off from its soil, ab-solute. Hence only by way of destruction can he rejoin his mother, and if he sets fire to the barn sheltering her coffin, he does so perhaps not only "to rid the earth of something which should have been under ground days ago"[6] but also to avenge himself on Addie and to take possession of her at last through a second death of which he would be the sole cause.

With the other members of the family, Darl's relations are not all negative. A long-standing tacit complicity unites him to Cash, a complicity fully (though not publicly) acknowledged by the latter after Darl has set fire to the barn: "it looked like one of us would have to do something.... And me being the oldest, and thinking already the very thing that he done" (216–17). With Vardaman, his equally unloved youngest brother, he achieves a measure of mutual understanding through the affinity of madness and childhood, and through a common uncertainty about identity. With Dewey Dell and Jewel, on the other hand, Darl's relations are strained, and their hatred for him erupts with savage violence at the end of the journey. Dewey Dell fiercely resents his having caught her with Lafe and his knowing the secret of her pregnancy. Confused and ambivalent, the relationship between Darl and his sister, then, may be read as a remote reflection of the incestuous love of Quentin for Caddy in *The Sound and the Fury*. Darl, however, is not jealous of his sister's lovers as Quentin is, and her honor hardly matters to him. His jealousy is directed at Jewel, the beloved son, his triumphant rival. It is resentful jealousy that prompts the cruel questions he needles Jewel with, all of which are either about Addie's impending death—"Do you know she is going to die, Jewel?" (35)—or about Jewel's illegitimacy—"Jewel . . . whose son are you?" (195); "Your mother was a horse, but who was your father, Jewel?" (195). It is jealousy and malice, too, that inspire his maneuver—real or fantasized?[7]—to prevent Jewel from being present at his mother's death.

No one reading *As I Lay Dying* can fail to be struck by the enormous importance Jewel is given in Darl's monologues. "Jewel and I . . . "; so starts his first section, and of the eighteen others attributed to him, ten open similarly with a reference to the resented and envied brother (cf. sections 5, 10, 21, 23, 25, 27, 32, 42, 48, 50); apart from the last, there is not a single one that does not begin or end with him. Even when Jewel is not within sight, Darl's clairvoyant eye follows him at a distance, scrutinizing his every action with unflagging, hypnotized attention (cf. the italicized passages in sections 3 and 42). Why this chronic fascination? Jewel is the *other* as *I* see him: erect, smooth, hard, and compact like wood or stone. With "his pale eyes like wood set into a wooden face" and his "rigid gravity" (3), Jewel is—or rather *appears to be*—everything Darl is not and cannot be: the fullness coveted by his emptiness, the strength envied by his weakness, the hard, bright "jewel" which blinds his night. Darl is mesmerized by his younger brother as Sartre's *pour-soi* is by *en-soi*. Jewel *is*, and all the more so since he is unaware: "Jewel knows he is, because he does not know that he does not know whether he is or not" (72). *He* is; therefore *I* am not: such is Darl's *cogito* in reverse. For he is not only uncertain of his identity, he doubts his very existence: "I dont know what I am. I dont know if I am or not" (72).

Bereft of all lineage, unloved and rootless, nobody's son, Darl is the merest fluid gesture of a being. Consciousness is apparently all he has to give him a hold on reality, but what reality is there for him outside the flickering light of the perceiving and thinking mind? As Darl argues in the metaphysical reverie at the close of his sixth section,[8] when consciousness fades away, as he (mistakenly) thinks it does in sleep, the uncertainties of being yield to the certainty of nothingness: "And before you are emptied for sleep, what are you. And when you are emptied for sleep, you are not. And when you are filled with sleep, you never were" (72). Sleep fills the body and empties the mind; sleep "is is-not" (72). It would seem that for Darl all states of being are mental states. *Esse est percipi.* Even the rain and the wind shaping the wagon with its load of lumber "shape it only to Jewel and me, that are not asleep" (72), and once they are asleep, the wagon will no longer be.

At the end of his reverie, however, Darl reverses his extreme idealistic position, as if he were frightened by its implications: "Yet the wagon *is*, because when the wagon is *was*, Addie Bundren will not be" (72). Even though he already knows his mother has died, he is not prepared to face her death and so flatly denies it, not unlike Vardaman seeking in the permanence of ordered family relationships a reassurance against loss and doubt: "Jewel *is*, so Addie Bundren must be. And then I must be, or I could not empty myself for sleep in a strange room. And so if I am not emptied yet, I am *is*" (72). In his metaphysical vertigo, Darl clings to his awareness of being aware and to the presentness of the present moment: "I am *is*" is probably the closest he ever comes to affirming the *hic et nunc* of his own self. The affirmation, however, is at once tempered if not belied by the elegiac postscript with which his reverie ends: "How often have I lain beneath rain on a strange roof, thinking of home" (72). The closing three words not only tersely epitomize Darl's estrangement but point as well to the private origins of his existential anguish. "Thinking of home" means being far from home. Darl cannot help thinking of home, because he has no home and never had one. Homeless, rootless, motherless. With him homesickness or, to say it in Greek, nostalgia, has become an ontological disease.

Powerless to bring itself into stable focus within a recognizable shape, incapable both of gathering itself around a fixed center and of establishing meaningful connections with the outer world, feeling itself under the constant threat of emptiness, Darl's consciousness is everywhere out of place. All rooms are finally "strange rooms" to him; exile is his permanent address. Hence, too, his plural self or, to borrow one of his own phrases, his "perverse ubiquity" (48). His clairvoyance and his telepathic powers may be said to spring from his very weakness; they are side effects of his deficiency in being. Without anything to ballast him or contain it, his mind can range freely in space and identify itself with any other mind it encounters on its way. Because he is nothing himself, he can become anyone, and anyone looking at him looks at his own "naked" double, stripped of his masks by Darl's mirroring gaze. As Tull notes: "It's like he had got into the inside of you, someway. Like somehow you was looking at yourself and your doings outen his eyes" (111).

What makes Darl a tragic figure is that he is painfully aware of his predicament. While Jewel does not know that he *is*; Darl knows that he *is not* and suffers from the acute awareness of his nonexistence. Having no identity to moor him in existence, no solid self to give him weight and balance, Darl wanders in a world itself corroded by unreality and impermanence, a world forever on the brink of chaos and extinction. Almost everywhere in his monologues we can sense his obsession with disintegration and dissolution, with the irresistible onrush of time—an obsession which is to him both terror and temptation: "If you could just ravel out into time. That would be nice. It would be nice if you could just ravel out into time" (193).

Such an obsession is not necessarily a symptom of insanity. According to Faulkner, however, "Darl was mad from the start,"[9] and it is noteworthy that in the novel outsiders such as Cora, Tull, and Samson find him "queer" from the outset (the word occurs five times with reference to him). Most readers will probably remember him as "queer" too, and yet there is little in the early Darl sections to suggest plain insanity, and even in the later ones his *actions* seem rather more reasonable than those of the rest of the family. Even his setting fire to the barn may be justified on rational and even moral grounds, and shortly before the Bundrens reach Jefferson, it is Darl who rescues Jewel from a knife fight. It is true, though, that his monologues point to a precarious mental balance, and one might argue that nearly all the classic symptoms of schizophrenia are soon discernible: withdrawal from reality, loss of vital contact with others, disembodiment and splitting of self, obsession with identity, sense of isolation and deadness, armageddonism (the sense that "the end of the world is nigh" apparent in Darl's account of the river scene).[10] So it comes as no real surprise that with the added ordeals of the journey, Darl succumbs to madness. It hardly matters, though, whether his psychotic syndrome is borne out by nosography. What makes it significant *in the novel* is that his schizoid condition is bound up with his foreclosed sonhood, and it is also worth recalling that Faulkner intended Darl's madness to be perceived simultaneously as a breakdown and a breakthrough. When asked about Darl's clairvoyance, Faulkner responded:

> Who can say how much of the good poetry in the world has come out of madness, and who can say just how much of super-perceptivity the—a mad person might not have? It may not be so, but it's nice to think that there is some compensation for madness. That maybe the madman sees more than the sane man. That the world is more moving to him. That he is more perceptive. He has something of clairvoyance, maybe, a capacity for telepathy.[11]

For Faulkner, then, Darl's madness is not just distress and disorder, not just an illness to be treated by doctors and nurses behind the walls of an asylum. Madness also stands, as it did for the Romantics, for insight and vision, a vision calling into question all received forms of knowledge and challenging the convenient distinctions and categories with which we shield our lives from the strangeness of otherness.

Further, if Darl passes for mad, he certainly does not hold a monopoly on unreason. Can there be a more senseless undertaking than the Bundrens'? To Vardaman, the child, it is the incomprehensible folly of adults.[12] And Armstid's reflection that Vardaman has become "nigh as crazy as the rest of them" (182) strongly suggests that in the eyes of their neighbors the whole

Bundren family has indeed gone mad. Yet their enterprise is also madness in the eyes of Darl, who is supposed to be mad. There must be reason, then, in his madness, a reason that contests the reason of reasonable people. Even stolid Cash comes to wonder about the legitimacy of discriminating between reason and unreason:

> Sometimes I aint so sho who's got ere a right to say when a man is crazy and when he aint. Sometimes I think it aint none of us pure crazy and aint none of us pure sane until the balance of us talks him that-a-way. It's like it aint so much what a fellow does, but it's the way the majority of folks is looking at him when he does it. (215–16)

There is good reason to think that by the end of the journey Darl's mind is truly deranged. But who can tell what "good reason" is? In the last resort, the boundary between sanity and insanity is but the arbitrary division mark of a social order, and mere ways of talking and seeing turn out to be ways of ordering and classifying and institutionalizing violence. Like race and gender, madness only exists as defined by and confined in collective discourse and collective perception, and the programmed fate of the madman is to end up immured within the walls of an asylum.

Darl's laughter

In his last monologue Darl bursts out laughing, and his uncontrolled, hysterical laughter bursts forth as would a truth long hidden and suddenly come to light. "What are you laughing at?" (235), he wonders. Is he laughing, as he first believes, at the pistols of the two men who put him on the train for Jackson? Is it because he has become a public nuisance, a danger for society, an object of police surveillance? So far Darl has been merely considered "queer," and he might have ended his days as the village idiot had he not set fire to a barn. When private property and vital economic interests are at stake, family solidarity becomes a luxury which the Bundrens can no longer afford: "It wasn't nothing else to do," says Cash. "It was either send him to Jackson, or have Gillespie sue us, because he knowed some way that Darl set fire to it" (215).

Ironically, as Darl has become a threat to familial, economic, and social order, his existence must be at last taken into account. Yet it is acknowledged only to be at once discarded. Like the two gentlemen who arrest Joseph K. at the end of The Trial, the two state officials with the shaven necks come to enforce the law. But why are their coats "mismatched" (235)? Are we to regard them as the vindictive delegates of Anse and Addie, Darl's equally "mismatched" parents?[13] The family drama, it would seem, is not yet over. Prepared for by a sexual pun on "riding," the explicit reference to "incest" (the only one in the entire novel) suggests that Darl's arrest and incarceration are the public conclusion of a very private nightmare. And there is more of it in what follows:

> A nickel has a woman on one side and a buffalo on the other; two faces and no back. I dont know what that is. Darl had a little spy-glass he got in France at the war. In it it had a woman and a pig with two backs and no face. I know what that is. "Is that why you are laughing, Darl?" (235)

Originally a "nickel" designated a dwarf or a devil. And there is indeed something "dia-bolic" (rather than "sym-bolic") about this nickel. For the woman and the buffalo are forever disjoined, even though they are the two sides of the same coin. Beauty and the Beast? Woman ideally exempted from the assaults of male animality? The inviolate virgin, the unsoiled mother? Darl does not know "what that is," and neither do we. But he knows what he has seen in the "little spy-glass" he has brought from France: the reverse image of "a woman and a pig with two backs and no face,"[14] that is, the primal scene itself. Is that what he is laughing at? Is he laughing because he has witnessed the obscene spectacle of parental coupling and has discovered the shabby secrets of his family, of all families? Or is he laughing to defend himself against the guilt and anguish induced by the return of the forbidden scene?

"The falling man does not laugh at his own fall," writes Baudelaire, "unless he is a philosopher, a man who has acquired, through habit, the capacity of promptly duplicating himself and of witnessing like a disinterested spectator the phenomena of his ego."[15] Darl is indeed a spectator, though by no means a disinterested one, and in his own untutored way he is also a philosopher, a man thinking about the ultimates of existence. The trouble with him is that he thinks more than is good for him or, as Tull puts it in his cautious sagacity, "he just thinks by himself too much" (64). Madness, in his case, is also an *excess of thinking*. But how can thinking be excessive? How to measure its excess if not by what society holds to be the norm? In Darl's final monologue, when he talks about himself in the first and the third person and addresses himself in the second, most readers diagnose psychotic cleavage, but it could be as well a fit of speculative self-reflexivity. Is this a madman's or a philosopher's laughter? Or could it be both?

In the closing pages of *The Sound and the Fury* Benjy bellows because things are out of order; Darl laughs because they fall back into order: the Bundrens have at last accomplished their funeral mission; Addie is buried and about to be replaced by Anse's new bride; and Darl will soon be in his rightful place among the madmen, inside the asylum walls. "Down there it'll be quiet," Cash tells him reassuringly, "with none of the bothering and such. It'll be better for you, Darl" (221). For Darl, however, resignation is yet to come, and the question remains as urgent as ever. Three times he questions himself on what it is that makes him laugh, and his replies are three salvos of yeses, which, instead of answering his questions, in turn pose a question, since what he says "yes" to is just as cryptic as what he is laughing at. This repeated "yes" is at least as ambiguous as Quentin's vehement denial at the end of *Absalom, Absalom!* and therefore only increases our puzzlement. Perhaps Darl expresses a final attempt to cling to life, perhaps his consent to the living death which awaits him at Jackson. But the "yes" is just as likely to be a bitterly ironic "no," another instance of that defiant "no" that so many of Faulkner's heroes utter in the face of their destiny when they are succumbing to it.

But why should we continue speculating about the motives of Darl's laughter? The point of it is perhaps precisely that it is pointless; what makes it so unsettling is perhaps precisely that it has no object at all. Darl cannot know what he is laughing at because he is laughing at nothing in particular. And hence at everything. At the nothingness of it all. His is pure laughter, boundless, devastating, *tragic* laughter.[16]

To be or not to be one self

From the depths of his own madness, Darl discovers—and makes us discover—the madness of the world. It is a discovery which goes hand in hand with that of death: madness and death represent the two poles of a single anxiety, for in *As I Lay Dying* madness appears, to use Michel Foucault's phrase, as "the already-here of death" (*le déjà-là de la mort*).[17]

Faulkner has been likened to the medieval painters and sculptors of *danses macabres*;[18] his vision and art often bring to mind Brueghel and Bosch. *As I Lay Dying* indeed makes one think of the end of the Middle Ages, of that moment of Western culture when the Ship of Fools came to occupy the place in the collective imagination previously held by the Dance of Death. This shift, as Foucault points out, was not a clean break: "What is in question is still the nothingness of existence, but this nothingness is no longer considered an external, final term, both threat and conclusion; it is experienced from within as the continuous and constant form of existence."[19] In *As I Lay Dying* the two themes are as intimately linked; they crystallize around the two most significant figures in the novel: Addie and Darl. Addie embodies the obsession of death: "I could just remember how my father used to say that the reason for living was to get ready to stay dead a long time" (155). And throughout the novel the concrete presence of the putrid corpse acts as a reminder of nothingness as "an external, final term," as "threat and conclusion." In Darl's lucid madness, on the other hand, nothingness is experienced "from within as the continuous and constant form of existence":

> How do our lives ravel out into the no-wind, no-sound, the weary gestures wearily recapitulant: echoes of old compulsions with no-hand on no-strings: in sunset we fall into furious attitudes, dead gestures of dolls. (191)

It is from the dual perspective of death and madness that *As I Lay Dying* raises the question of identity, but what makes it immediately relevant to the novel is the identity crisis associated for at least three of the Bundrens with the mourning process.

To Anse, Cash, and even Jewel, Addie's death poses no real threat, for they are what they are, solidly, and no matter how much they differ one from another, they are alike in their rigidity and fixity. They are people who give nothing away and allow no one any purchase on them. Language cannot betray them: Jewel is inarticulate; Cash is sparing of his words (at least in the early sections); Anse is content with empty words and gestures, which is only another way of saying nothing. They either act or do not act, but in Anse's voluble laziness, just as in Jewel's headlong violence or Cash's passion for work, one senses the same stubborn inflexibility, the same imperviousness. Jewel retains throughout the novel the same petrified—to be true to Faulkner's images one should say "lignified"—air, and a similar stiffness is discernible in Cash as well: during the storm, he keeps working on the coffin, totally unaffected by the drenching rain, as single-minded and composed as before, the motion of his saw continuing with the regularity of a piston, "as though it and the arm functioned in a tranquil conviction that rain was an illusion of the mind" (68). As for Anse, he is all words and no work (with a strong belief, however, in the deeds . . . of others), and it is his formidable self-centered inertia which acts as his shell. But inside the shell there is probably only emptiness, just as behind Jewel's wooden mask there is perhaps nothing but wild energy and blind pain. Only Cash, despite his robot gestures and his narrow mind, almost ends by convincing us that he has also something like a soul. Apart from this one exception, identity seems to be won and preserved only at the cost of a benumbed and deadened consciousness.

Settling on an identity means settling in it. Darl, Vardaman, and Dewey Dell resemble one another in that for them this settling-in process has not yet occurred or cannot occur. Their selves have neither form nor substance and are apt to fade out entirely. Dewey Dell is haunted by the nightmare of extinction, the living death she went through one night: *"I couldn't think what I was I couldn't think of my name I couldn't even think I am a girl, I couldn't even think I"* (107). "I am not anything," says Vardaman under the shock of Addie's death (52); "I dont know what I am. I dont know if I am or not," says Darl (72). It is in them that what Peabody calls "that abject nakedness which we bring here with us" (42) is the most unprotected. Hence their need to establish boundaries, to define their identity in relationship to other identities, and to assert their separateness, so as to be able to defend themselves against the world. Its simplest expression is mere naming, a recall of who is who, as when Dewey Dell says: "He is Lafe and I am Dewey Dell" (53). With Darl, as we have seen, it takes the form of reasoning: "Jewel *is*, so Addie Bundren must be. And then I must be, or I could not empty myself for sleep in a strange room. And so if I am not emptied yet, I am *is*" (72). As for Vardaman, after fleeing into the dark barn he first imagines Jewel's horse resolved "out of his integrity into an unrelated scattering of components" and then finds it (the horse's as well as his own) restored when he senses within the animal's hide and bones something "detached and secret and familiar, an *is* different from my *is*" (52).

The most vulnerable in his isolation, the most exposed in his nakedness is of course Darl. Nobody and nothing shelters him, and he does not even have the pride which drives the others to hide their nakedness. Even more than Dewey Dell and Vardaman, he is incapable of defining himself within a proper individuality; and like his sister, he is even deprived of his solitude, since, having no boundaries, his consciousness is constantly drawn outside his being. Yet whereas Dewey Dell's self is caught in the body's opacity and jeopardized by the process of becoming "unalone" in pregnancy and childbirth, Darl's is inescapably and irreversibly dissipated in the void.

Consciousness without identity or identity without consciousness is ultimately the alternative that confronts each of the Bundrens. The only choice seems to be between the deadness of identity and the madness of nonidentity. Addie's troubled fate in its manifold ironies aptly illustrates this dilemma: throughout her life she has passionately sought her true self, but only in death can she escape her unappeasable desire for wholeness and acquire identity— identity as a corpse, a lifeless residue, and identity in the minds of others, as a haunting ghost. Similarly, Darl's search finds its paradoxical conclusion in insanity, since it is only when he is acted upon like an object that he becomes real to himself—in the third person, as a stranger, a madman. Whoever tries to reconcile awareness and identity discovers in himself the nothingness of existence and finishes either by giving up—as Addie did in bitter resignation—or by giving way to his vertigo like Darl. To be without identity is to experience death in life. With nothing to focus on or to relate to, consciousness is left dangling in a vacuum; at once caught up in solipsistic self-torment and threatened by dissolution in the impersonal flux of time and life, it achieves neither true separateness nor true relatedness, and so is bound to succumb to despair or madness.

From these dangers Anse has safely escaped. He has been quick to find his selfhood; the very weight of his inertia provides him with the aplomb that was denied to Addie and Darl. For his wife, however, Anse is dead before his death: "And then he died. He did not know he was dead" (160). Just as Jewel does not know that he *is*, Anse will never realize that he is "dead." Both of them are deficient in consciousness and seem to owe their being to the very fact of their unawareness; as Darl would say, they are because they don't know they are. Their *sum* implies no *cogito*; instead of referring to the transcendence of an ego infused with the certainty of its own existence, their identity is somehow exterior to them—an objective identity like that of things, compact and closed.

Not to be conscious of oneself may of course also be equated with nonentity, and identity established at this cost is also a form of death-in-life, not by dissolution this time but by congealing. And it is a form of madness too. In *As I Lay Dying* madness is prowling everywhere; Darl is not its only prey. There is the madness of distracted subjectivity, but the lack of inwardness is also a kind of insanity, probably much more frequent than the other and therefore less willingly acknowledged as such. The novel exemplifies both categories. The first is pathetic with Vardaman and Dewey Dell, tragic with Darl and Addie; the second is rather comic but no less disturbing. Kierkegaard, one of the first to comment on "objective" madness, noted:

> This type of madness is more inhuman than the other. One shrinks from looking into the eyes of a madman of the former type lest one be compelled to plumb there the depths of his delirium, but one dares not look at a madman of the latter type at all, from fear of discovering that he has eyes of glass and hair made from carpet-rags.[20]

It is only a short step from these glass eyes to Anse's cinder eyes. Yet in Faulkner's fiction reification is seldom equivalent to total dehumanization. Anse's appalling callousness, for instance, should not be confused with Cash's stoic imperviousness, although the two characters are alike in their outward grotesqueness. Moreover, with Faulkner, the least aware are often those who endure. Anesthetizing consciousness might then be interpreted as a way of taking up fate's challenge and making oneself immune to its blows, a paradoxical ruse to forestall any danger which, from within or without, threatens to submerge and destroy one's integrity. Playing possum becomes a strategy of survival, feigning death a victory over death. By making himself like an object, inert and insensitive, man acquires a hard crust against which fate comes knocking and bouncing and an immobility which seems to deprive fate of its most redoubtable weapon: time.

Astonishment

It is most significant too that Faulkner retains for all his characters the human privilege of astonishment. It is found in its purest and most concentrated form in Anse, who is not only surprised at what happens but also shows surprise at his very surprise: "He looks around, blinking, in that surprised way, like he had wore hisself down being surprised and was even surprised at that" (28). Yet the other Bundrens evince a similar capacity for amazement and wonder. One finds it in Darl's compulsive questioning, in Dewey Dell's stupor at her pregnancy, in the helpless bewilderment into which Vardaman is thrown by his mother's death, or again in the "expression of furious unbelief" (201) registered on Jewel's face when the fire occurs. This astonishment is beyond reason and unreason; as Cash puts it, "It's like there was a fellow in every man that's done a-past the sanity or the insanity, that watches the sane and the insane doings of that man with the same horror and the same astonishment" (221).

Even among the simplest and the most simple-minded, an inner distance produced by astonishment makes them incredulous and horrified spectators of their own lives. Whether their actions are reasonable or not, Faulkner's characters never stop being surprised at what they do or rather at what they are made to do, at what they endure and suffer. Astonishment is always their first response to "outrage"—one of Faulkner's key words; *As I Lay Dying*, along with *Light in August, Absalom, Absalom!*, and the "Old Man" sections of *The Wild Palms*, is the novel in which it recurs most insistently. The term is used here in two senses—one social, the other moral and metaphysical— which echo each other ironically. Outrage is first a violation of common decency; it is the scandal the Bundrens cause by inflicting the stench of the corpse on their neighbors. "It's a outrage. A outrage," cries Rachel Samson (103), and some seventy pages later Lula Armstid expresses her indignation in identical terms (174). But the real outrage, the genuine scandal lies else- where: it is in everything that baffles, humiliates, and crushes man, in all the violence which accident or fate makes him suffer. Its most visible manifesta- tion in the novel is the series of natural catastrophes which shower down on the Bundrens in the course of their journey, and first of all the rain so often referred to by Darl, Anse, and Tull in the opening sections. This rain is expected by everybody and known to be imminent. Yet when it finally starts to fall, Anse "lifts his face, slack-mouthed, the wet black rim of snuff plastered close along the base of his gums; from behind his slack-faced astonishment he muses as though from beyond time, upon the ultimate outrage" (68). And a bit later in the same scene, Anse looks up at the sky again "with that expression of dumb and brooding outrage and yet of vindication, as though he had expected no less" (69). The astonishment provoked by the outrage, then, is not the shock of the unexpected but stupefaction at the occurrence of the ines- capable. Like the Tall Convict adrift on the raging waters of the Mississippi in "Old Man," Anse "expected no less"; he knows that what happens was due to happen. The event confirms his expectation, and his outraged air suggests at once a canny innocence and an uncanny wisdom, "a wisdom too profound or too inert for even thought" (45).

Anse absorbs the sense of outrage, turning it into placid astonishment and turning astonishment into inertia. The scandal is recognized but immediately accepted as inevitable. The same is not true of the other Bundrens. Contrary to Anse's, their astonishment indicates (as did *étonnement* in seventeenth-cen- tury French tragedy) violent emotion, an upheaval of their whole being. Far from being the furtive blinking of a sleepy mind, a kind of fatalistic complicity with the irremediable, it marks for Addie the beginning of indignation and revolt. Thus, when she realizes that she is pregnant for the second time, she passes straight from disbelief to murderous rage: "At first I would not believe it. Then I believed I would kill Anse" (158). Her astonishment is not dulled into lethargic resignation but directly provokes her proud will to riposte: in order to avenge the outrage to her "aloneness" she makes her husband promise to go and bury her in Jefferson when she is dead.

The funeral journey was conceived as an act of rebellion and a last revenge against fate, and Addie bequeaths her refusal to submit to all her children except Darl. Caught in the same trap as her mother, Dewey Dell similarly rebels against what happens to her and, through her efforts to have an abortion, likewise attempts to escape her destiny. Vardaman too refuses to give in to events and busies himself effacing the outrage inflicted upon him by his mother's death through the exorcisms of his private magic. Jewel's astonishment instantly flares up into fury—the fury in which he finds the energy of his heroism. Darl's, on the contrary, failing to find release in action or be deadened in inertia, endlessly turns in on itself in tortured speculation and is eventually aggravated into madness. Darl perfectly exemplifies the outraged onlooker of whom Cash speaks at the end of the novel; he is indeed only that: a fascinated and impotent stare, overwhelmed by the horror of what it sees.

Astonishment at outrage is the encounter of innocence and evil. Or perhaps even more simply the first collision of mind and reality. For the first and last outrage, to human consciousness, is perhaps the discovery that things are the way they are and happen the way they happen, and that we can do so little about it. As Tull puts it, "it's liable to strike anywhere, like lightning" (63). Sooner or later, the worst will occur anyway; in the end man is always the loser.

Whether struck by stupor or driven to impotent rebellion, Faulkner's characters are above all victims. An obscure curse seems to weigh on them, but they are not guilty. To explain the misfortunes of the Bundrens, one could no doubt look for those responsible and incriminate Addie's destructive pride or Anse's massive egoism. But as Faulkner himself pointed out in an interview,[21] there is no villain in the story other than the absurd convention which makes the family drag the corpse as far as Jefferson and all the evil forces let loose against them during their journey. Evil here seems to be on the world's side. It is of course also within man, but there is little to suggest that it springs from man. In *As I Lay Dying* Faulkner's pessimism—insofar as such a label can be applied to his tragicomic vision—is less moral than metaphysical. Sin, guilt, and retribution are not really at issue, and the historical, social, and racial context of the South, in which all these themes are treated in most of the novelist's other works, is hardly perceptible here. Hence *As I Lay Dying*, even though it is as thoroughly southern in its texture and ambiance as any of Faulkner's novels, may be read as an almost timeless fable. The human beings it presents seem to date from before history, yet they have already been driven from paradise, if they are not already doomed and damned. The effects of the primal curse are indeed strongly felt, but Faulkner does not here, as in his other novels, raise questions about the origins of the malediction. What he shows us instead is the naked scandal of existence, both in its derisory everydayness and through the extremes of madness and death. The decomposing corpse dragged along the road is the *memento mori*, a grim reminder of the radically contingent and irremediably finite nature of man; death is, as Addie early learned from her father, what invalidates all life. As for madness, the other aspect of the scandal, it designates here—like Benjy's idiocy in *The Sound and the Fury*—the intolerable paradox of utter degeneration linked to absolute innocence.

Faulkner, too, it seems, is astonished at the scandal of this "terrible life," and his novel echoes this astonishment very closely. Astonishment might be defined as the zero degree of philosophy; it is at once the expression of our stupidity, our ignorance, or our innocence (we would not be astonished if we knew) and the first sign of a questioning intellect (if we were certain that there is nothing to be known, we would not be astonished either). Yet if all speculative thinking starts from naive wonder, it always ends by disowning its humble origins. In its desire to make sense of nonsense, it is at pains to play down absurdity and to provide neat explanations for what appears revolting to the spontaneous mind. In the systems it erects, evil is never more than a moment or an element in the universal order. Perhaps this is even the main purpose of philosophical systems and religious doctrines: to hush up the scandal, to explain evil away, to make the world acceptable. Nothing like that happens in *As I Lay Dying*: Faulkner does not allow us to move beyond astonishment, refuses to ask questions or to dispel wonder; he is content to record over and over again that initial moment when a human consciousness runs into the intolerable and experiences the shock of outrage. No lesson is drawn, no wisdom offered. *As I Lay Dying*, which in one sense is perhaps the most purely metaphysical of Faulkner's novels, is probably also his least philosophical.

X

THE REAL AND ITS REPRESENTATIONS

Wir wissen sehr früh, denke ich, dass wir mit
unserm Gehirn nicht denken und mit unserer
Sprache nicht sprechen können, denken aber
doch immer mit unserem Gehirn und reden
mit unserer Sprache, das Leben lang.

Thomas Bernhard

Words for things

Through another tour de force, *As I Lay Dying* manages to tell of people's lives
while saying nothing about them. One after another the characters appear out
of no definable place or time and speak as if on an empty stage, telling what
they have to tell; then they vanish as suddenly and as inexplicably as they
arrived. They all tell fragments of their own or others' stories, voice wonder
at their life or outrage at their miseries; but somehow their speeches do not
add up, do not fall into place, do not quite make sense. Even if they end up
telling a complete story, their words seem to arise from and fade into a strange
silence, and once we have read the book it is almost as if we had been watching
a mystifying pantomime.

   As to the novelist himself, he no doubt pulls the strings of his marionettes,
controlling their every gesture and lending them his words. But for once he
seems to have left himself out of the telling, as if to remind us that his own
voice can exist only as writing, as text, that is, as nonvoice, apart from and
perhaps above the "dead sound" of everyday language, in the inked silence
of the printed word. Yet *As I Lay Dying* also reminds us that the writer's
worded silence may somehow accommodate the stubborn silence of reality
itself. For if reality as such, the ultimate reality lurking behind all our symbol
systems, is by definition beyond meaningful articulation, if it has absolutely
nothing to say, the truest language would be one which allowed the world to
come noiselessly in on its own. *As I Lay Dying* is a rare sample of such language:
a text of fiction doubling the opacity of the real with its own enigma.

Yet in its very enigma it also interrogates the relationship—or lack of relationship—between world and language. What link is there between reality as such and our representations and interpretations of it? And how do our feelings and actions relate to what we think and say? These questions are explicitly posed by Addie Bundren, the novel's focal figure, and we know her disillusioned answer:

> I would think how words go straight up in a thin line, quick and harmless, and how terribly doing goes along the earth, clinging to it, so that after a while the two lines are too far apart for the same person to straddle from one to the other. (160)

Verticality and horizontality, air and earth, lightness and weight, all the contrasts point here to an irreducible chasm between word and world, saying and "doing." Addie protests against the unbearable lightness of language. Words, for her, are lifeless abstractions, forms devoid of substance; like children's balloons, they rise and vanish into thin air. While language is commonly assumed to be both referential and expressive, neither of these functions is acknowledged by Addie. Words, she contends, fail to make contact with the world around and within us. And not only do they fall short of their presumed referents; the trouble with them is not just that they do not lead anywhere but that they are perversely misleading: instead of conveying the facts and feelings of life, words serve to cloak their absence and are in fact the tenuous traces of their withdrawal and loss. To Addie words are in the last resort all *negatives*, denying the existence or, to put it the other way around, asserting the nonexistence of what they are supposed to signify. Yet she also knows that in the daily exchanges of speech, the negativity of language is consistently denied for practical purposes of deception and manipulation. Speech prevents true knowledge and blocks authentic communication, but it allows people "to use one another by words like spiders dangling by their mouths from a beam, swinging and twisting and never touching" (158). To talkers such as Anse, Cora, and Whitfield it serves no other purpose than to keep life at a safe distance and to promote either complacent self-delusion or deliberate fooling of others: "fear was invented by someone that had never had the fear; pride, who never had the pride" (157–58), and what Anse calls love is only the lack of love, "just a shape to fill a lack" (158).

Language, according to Addie, divides and degrades its users. For true communication or, even better, for actual communion to take place, we had better abandon language and try other ways of relating to others. This is why, when she was a schoolteacher, Addie gave her students whippings, compelling them to acknowledge her existence through mute violence, through the nonverbal, purely physical idiom of flesh and blood: "Now you are aware of me! Now I am something in your secret and selfish life" (155). Addie wants knowledge to be mutual acknowledgment; she wants her knowledge of others to reach all the way to what they are and their knowledge of her to reach all the way to her own experience, so that knowing will be sharing.

For Addie playing the games of language is a betrayal of one's "duty to the alive, to the terrible blood," and the only language worth heeding is the wordless language buried in language, the only speech worth listening to is the "voiceless speech" of "the dark land" (161). Words must be emptied of their emptiness, so as to let in silence. This is why in her lonely musings, at night, Addie's mind sets out to work its way through names until the names are erased:

> Anse. Why Anse. Why are you Anse. I would think about his name until after a while I could see the word as a shape, a vessel, and I would watch him liquify and flow into it like cold molasses flowing out of the darkness into the vessel, until the jar stood full and motionless: a significant shape profoundly without life like an empty door frame, and then I would find that I had forgotten the name of the jar. (159)

Like Faulkner's, Addie's thinking is intensely visual and always prone to trope. Elsewhere in her monologue she "sees" people as spiders and sin as garments. Here she also substitutes a series of concrete images for the abstract word, replaces "Anse" with a shape, which turns out to be that of a container, a vessel, a jar, but instead of leading to a fuller understanding or making room for deeper intimacy, the whole metaphorical process ends up with an empty frame, void of life if not of meaning, and with the obliteration of her husband's very name. Far from restoring Anse to his concrete, preverbal reality, his unnaming by Addie reduces him to the nonentity she took him to be to begin with.

The powers of language

On her first pregnancy Addie discovered simultaneously that "living was terrible" and "that words are no good; that words dont ever fit even what they are trying to say at" (157). When she was with child for the second time, however, she realized that whatever its inadequacy, language holds formidable powers. Words are traps laid out for our weakness, and Addie's rage comes from having allowed herself to be caught in them: "It was as though [Anse] had tricked me, hidden within a word like within a paper screen and struck me in the back through it" (158). She resented Anse at first, but soon found out that he had been taken in just like herself: "then I realised that I had been tricked by words older than Anse or love, and that the same word had tricked Anse too . . ." (158–59).

Experience—especially experiences directly involving her body: sex, pregnancy, childbirth, and mothering—is what makes Addie aware of the ultimate futility of words, but it also teaches her to acknowledge their insidious power. People think they can appropriate and master language and use it for their own ends, but it is language that uses them and makes game of them, urging them to act in ways they never intended.

No one is outside the prison-house of language. As Julius Kaufman puts it in *Mosquitoes*, the human being is not only the only symbol-making, speaking animal; he belongs to "that species all of whose actions are controlled by words."[1] Man is forever caught up in the webs of significance he himself has spun, and Kaufman even goes so far as to grant language absolute priority and primacy by reversing its presumed relationship to reality: "It's the word that overturns thrones and political parties and instigates vice crusades, not things: the Thing is merely the symbol for the Word."[2] *As I Lay Dying* is a telling exemplification of this priority and could thus be read as an ironic fable on the tyranny of language. Is the entire action of the novel not the direct result of what today linguists would call a speech act, that is, a vow, a promise, Anse's *word* to Addie? Utterances can be acts; no matter how removed it may seem from the felt quality of experience, language is instrumental in shaping it. Like it or not, we are born into the public space of language, just as we are born into flesh, time, and mortality. Language defines and determines our social being and is thus part of the intricate network of constraints which pattern our lives.

If the search for truth in and through language most often leads to the disappointing encounter with an empty form, this empty form conceals an active force whose laws are inescapable. But it is precisely to language's law, the law of the Other, the mediacy of the cultural or symbolic order, that Addie refuses to yield, since, as we have seen, in submitting to the Other, she would have to renounce her narcissistic and incestuous dream of being One. Addie, we should remember, has her own private score to settle, and she would not indict language with so much vehemence had she not started believing in a straightforward equivalence between words and things. Taking words at their face value and envisioning language as a lexicon rather than a syntax, she is at bottom a disillusioned Cratylist: having assumed a purposeful analogy between signifiers and referents, she feels betrayed when she finds out that the relations between them are arbitrary conventions.

Addie's views on language are naively static, and whatever credit we might wish to give them is ruined by the ironies of her monologue. It is one irony that this impassioned eulogy of the raw energies of life is entrusted to a dead woman. It is another irony that language is here at once the target, the arrow, and the bow. Addie's resentment against words is conveyed through words, and her use of them bears witness to their persuasive power. Indeed, in its rich array of figures and tropes, its firmly controlled syntax, and its dense sound patterning, her speech is a superb feast of (Faulknerian) rhetoric. Yet what does rhetoric achieve? It is a third irony that, despite their eloquence, Addie's words too do not "fit even what they are trying to say at."

This final irony is the more sobering as it undercuts the common assumption that a man's or a woman's life can be apprehended as a meaningful pattern and hence becomes narratable only after death. Walter Benjamin claimed that an individual's existence "first assumes transmissible form at the moment of his death," and that "death is the sanction of everything that the storyteller can tell."[3] Now in *As I Lay Dying* the reader is indeed willing to take Addie's monologue for her sincere confession and spiritual testament. Her words reach us from the far side of death, with the authority of death. But her posthumous summing up provides no final illumination. In point of fact it produces more heat than light. After reading it, we no doubt know more about her feelings and motivations than before, but in death as in life, in muteness as in speech, Addie remains a secret, shrouded figure, a figure ultimately reconcealed in what was intended to reveal her. Her last will is an ultimate riddle, for her words neither offer the expected explanation of her destiny nor fully elucidate her relationship to the lives of her husband and children. Or rather, while adding to our understanding of the Bundrens, they render that understanding even more difficult; while shedding light on the family inter-connections, they make them even more opaque.

Addie's monologue thus proves her both right and wrong. She is right in distrusting language, and her own speech demonstrates that whenever we attempt to articulate our deepest thoughts and feelings, our most eloquent utterances are at best pathetic stammerings. Marlow, in *Lord Jim*, might be commenting on Addie's soliloquy when he points out that "the last word is not said,—probably shall never be said. . . . There is never time to say our last word—the last word of our love, of our desire, faith, remorse, submission, revolt"[4] Never: not even in death, if death could speak. But at the same time Addie is wrong in assuming that language can be dispensed with and in suggesting that she at any rate has resisted its lures with some success. Not only are words the vehicle for her postmortem self-justification (how could it be otherwise?), but her indulgence in language is such that we cannot but suspect her of still valuing its expressive resources and still believing in its capacity to render experience significant and even to articulate truth. And from the very account of her life, it is evident too that while apparently shunning words in her search for a silent, ecstatic fusion with elemental forces, Addie has never ceased to make of things and events "the symbol for the Word." Consider for a moment how carefully she stages her adulterous liaison with Whitfield:

> I would think of sin as I would think of the clothes we both wore in the world's face, of the circumspection necessary because he was he and I was I; the sin the more utter and terrible since he was the instrument ordained by God who created the sin, to sanctify that sin He had created. While I waited for him in the woods, waiting for him before he saw me, I would think of him as dressed in sin. I would think of him as thinking of me as dressed also in sin, he the more beautiful since the garment which he had exchanged for sin was sanctified. I would think of the sin as garments which we would remove in order to shape and coerce the terrible blood to the forlorn echo of the dead word high in the air. (161)

It is true that in Addie's recounting of her affair with Whitfield the deceitful outward signs are once more set over against a hidden truth. In identifying the sin of adultery with a secular garment, she opposes it to the presumed sacredness of her sexual bond to a man of God. Sin, she intimates, is to innocence what costumes are to bodies and what words are to things. The clothing/sin is to her the insignia of concealment and fraud, whereas the shedding of clothes allows the emergence of the "naked truth" of life and sex.

Yet truth is a matter of meaning, and Addie wants meaning as much as being. In translating her memories into metaphors, in dressing them up in rhetoric, she betrays her ardent desire to infuse them with a new life and to transfer her past experience to the order of a discourse she might call her own. For all her distrust of words, she is still yearning for *symbols*, that is, motivated sign-relations between language and world. Just as Hester Prynne, in *The Scarlet Letter*, turns the gorgeously embroidered letter into a defiant emblem of her sin, Addie's imagination transmutes her adultery into an emblematic ornament, the more so as she associates it with her lover's priestly vestments. Sin or, rather, the exquisite awareness of sin is what gives her clandestine encounters with Whitfield their thrill, value, and beauty. And let us also note that these encounters only acquire meaning in relation to "the forlorn echo of the dead word high in the air" (just as, later, the Bundrens' journey only acquires meaning in relation to the forlorn echo of her own dead word). People and deeds matter to Addie only to the extent that they can be exalted to the glory of the sign and—even better —invested with the numinous prestige of the broken taboo, and what she expects from her guilty love is sanctification through violation. Sacrilege, to her, is a shortcut to a sacred realm of transcendental presence and meaning which she hopes will save her life from the diminishments of the everyday and single out her destiny as unique. And we might say as much of the other important experiences in her life. Addie does not seek to gain mastery over life, nor does she try very hard to lose herself in its random flux; she wants it to be meaningful, and she wants above all her own life to be meaningful within the universal pattern of things, never suspecting that meanings are the secretions of language and that the only meaning our lives can have is the meaning we *bring* to them. Addie's world, then, is in no way the speechless world of blood and earth which she so rhapsodically invokes but a private fiction of her own making. And if her monologue may be said to echo the novelist's own concerns and to reflect to some extent his own ambivalence toward language, it would be a serious mistake to regard her as his authorized mouthpiece.[5]

From Mallarmé to Rimbaud to Beckett, from Hölderlin to Hofmannsthal to Rilke, from Melville to Stein to Cage, silence has been one of the major obsessions and recurrent temptations of modernity. Whenever literature reaches out beyond the limits of language, it is brought to the threshold of silence. Faulkner, as we have already seen in discussing the Easter celebration in *The Sound and the Fury*, clearly shared the modern yearning for the unsayable. But for a writer, as long as he goes on writing, silence can only be the metaphor of another and better language. Silence, to him, is not a mute absence but the word within the word. Faulkner well knew that "pure" silence can be found only in death and that in the world of the living, silence, as Sartre put it in his work on Flaubert, "is itself a verbal act, a hole dug in language."[6] His own views on language need not be sought elsewhere than in his practice as a writer, and the fact that he chose language as his medium and was true to it to the very last proves that he did not despair of the power of words, under certain conditions, to approach truth.[7] His novels do question language, but they also demonstrate that there is no questioning outside language and that questioning language within language is precisely the writer's business. They therefore also denounce the misuses to which language lends itself and the diseases to which it is vulnerable. Grandiloquence (from which Faulkner himself was not altogether immune) is a case in point. As Clément Rosset has noted, grandiloquence "is fundamentally a sort of accident of language, a slippage, a dragging, whose effect is to render the real with words whose relationship to reality has been visibly lost: a failed language in more or less the same sense in which psychoanalysts, when they refer to a slip or to certain memory lapses, would speak of failed acts—a failed language in the sense that it misses the real."[8]

All language, of course, is in the last analysis a failed or fallen language. Discourses, however, fail more or less lamentably; some are clearly more remote from reality than others. And if none ever fully succeeds in bridging the gap that separates reality from its representations and divides people from people, this gap is not necessarily the abyss of imposture or bombast. Indeed, for Faulkner, language, rather than being only the instrument of our lies and divisions, can become "that meager and fragile thread . . . by which the little surface corners and edges of men's secret and solitary lives may be joined for an instant now and then before sinking back into the darkness where the spirit cried for the first time and was not heard and will cry for the last time and will not be heard then either."[9] Faulkner's whole work is precisely a wager on that possibility, and it has all the anxiety and uncertainty of a wager. It is the novelist's ever-renewed attempt to reconcile silence with speech, experience with form, life with art, his unflagging effort to build the reality of his work on the unreality of words and his never-dying hope to turn fictions into truths.

The wager is won in *As I Lay Dying*, a novel about what happens to minds and bodies, a novel about the necessities and contingencies of our lives in their inscrutable immediacy and their familiar strangeness, that which is least amenable to orderly thought and conceptual articulation. All lives have beginnings and ends, but we cannot think ourselves back or forward beyond language, for we need words to think in the first place. Birth and death, the two extremes, are time-boundaries which elude the time of experience and awareness and so are by definition beyond all possibility of representation. How could words, which are themselves ruled by the law of repetition, express the origin and the end? But—to misquote a famous aphorism—what we cannot speak about we must write about and consign to the page. The writer cannot give up trying to say the unsayable. He will never say it in his own name (he no more knows what he says than anyone else, yet at least he is aware of that), but his text can say it in his stead. Of course, such a text must be of such porous matter, of such loose weave, that reality is free to pass through it. The real never appears where it is most expected; it cannot be found in words but in between, not in the text but in its fringes and fissures.

The carpenter and the madman

In order for language to find its way back to the real, one needs to break its established patterns, to transgress its accepted boundaries, to sweep away the gray dust of accumulated meanings and restore the sign to its uncertainty. Writing, at its fullest, is at once work and madness: such is the lesson, in this novel, of the little parable of the carpenter and the madman. Cash, the "good carpenter," works with wood as a writer does with words and builds his coffin as a writer writes his books: carefully, methodically, attentive to measurement, adjustment, and balance, and with an anxious concern that his work hold together. For the perfection of his work is what holds his self together. In shaping and building objects in the world, he gives form and meaning to his life. His are the humble heroism and sober pride of the skilled worker. His maniacal absorption in the *how* of his work, however, seems to make him oblivious to what he is working toward; the technical means and instruments have become ends in themselves. In his eagerness to make things right, he has almost forgotten what he is making, or why. This is what renders Cash both comic and disquieting from his very first appearances in the novel. Like the grotesque carpenter of *Moby-Dick,* he seems to have alienated himself in his function, and for his know-how he has paid the price of a monstrous blindness. One will also notice that if Cash knows how to make a neat, faultless object, that object is a casket, a death-object, a wooden box destined to receive a rotting cadaver—another "shape to fill a lack" or another lack to fill a shape. What he has shaped and produced is a fine piece of work, not a true work of art. There is surely madness in his compulsive perfectionism, but it is an artisan's madness, not an artist's.

The artist's madness falls to Darl. He is to Cash what unreason is to reason. Or what poetry is to plain prose. Cash traces limits, erects enclosures, builds fences and boxes, arranges a habitable space, and cautiously entrenches himself there. He is on the side of common sense and common prejudice, of discipline and decency, work and property, law and order; he stands for the comfort of received values and the conformity of proper behavior, or, if you will, the narrow worldly wisdom of a well-tempered humanism. He is no doubt capable of sympathy and compassion, and there even is some evidence that by the end of the journey his awareness has expanded. But there are strict limits to his feelings for other people, as there are strict limits to his demands on life: the only extra his modest soul is yearning for is a bit of nice music from the "graphophone." Darl, on the other hand, is always *elsewhere;* as even Cash comes to realize, "This world is not his world; this life his life" (242). He is destined to be forever an onlooker and an outsider, floating in a limbo—a space without boundaries, a time without measure, a world without pattern and purpose, which either has yet to begin, as if it were hesitating on the threshold of its birth, or is already destroyed and extinct. Hence his thought and his gaze have neither roots nor limits, which is indeed insanity in the eyes of common sense.

But were the perspective to be reversed, the *other* madness—the everyday madness of everybody that passes for sanity—would come forth as a hideous or preposterous grimace under the gaze of the one we call mad. Darl is nothing, but he sees all, which is far more than society is willing to tolerate. To see all is to know too much. All the family secrets are known to Darl. His uncanny gaze sees through the postures of honor and pride and penetrates the other family members in the solitude of their desire and of their shame. But it also discloses the world's otherness, the inscrutable primal forces masked by the precarious conventions and arrangements of social life. If Darl is a voyeur, he is also a seer, and inasmuch as his experience of unreason provides flashes of insight into another, darker world, beyond the grasp of reason and the bounds of society, it sustains an essential relationship to truth.

Is Darl then to be read as the figure of the visionary artist? If Cash is a comic representation of the novelist-craftsman, is Darl Faulkner's portrait of the novelist-poet? Yes, except that he is a poet without poems, a novelist without novels, an artist without an *oeuvre*. Darl as narrator no doubt resembles the novelist (in particular the ubiquitous, omniscient novelist of the good old days) in that he is granted privileged access to other minds and is endowed with special gifts for expressing what goes on there. His preternatural clairvoyance could easily be mistaken for an exceptionally vivid and sensitive imagination. Yet Darl's power of language is a twice borrowed power (borrowed from the writer, who does not possess it either), and his madness is without resource or recourse; it is helplessness on its way to destruction. Hence he can be only the novelist's accursed double. To write is no doubt to run the risk of madness, to venture to its very threshold, to wander in its margins, and thus to take on its radical questioning; but as long as one produces a work, one avoids its deadly threat. As Michel Foucault notes: "There is no madness except as the final instant of the work of art—the work endlessly drives madness to its limits; *where there is a work of art, there is no madness*; and yet madness is contemporary with the work of art, since it inaugurates the time of its truth."[10]

As I Lay Dying is a text haunted by death and madness, a text written under their double threat, but at the same time it holds its own against them. Faulkner, unlike his helpless madman, will once again have protected his bid, without gain or loss. Or rather, he will have successfully brought off the tour de force of keeping his losses—by betting on words.

Three

The Blackness of Darkness

XI

"THE MOST HORRIFIC TALE"

Dollars damn me.

Herman Melville

A "cheap idea"?

"This book was written three years ago. To me it is a cheap idea, because it was deliberately conceived to make money."[1] Thus begins the Introduction that Faulkner wrote for the Modern Library issue of *Sanctuary* in 1932, one year after its original publication. Such brazen admission of venality could of course only add to the already scandalous reputation of the novel and confirm the worst suspicions of its (mostly British) detractors. Faulkner's self-deprecatory statements were promptly seized upon to disparage the novel and discredit the novelist, so that for several decades Faulkner scholars busied themselves demonstrating that neither *Sanctuary* nor Faulkner's comments on it offer valid justification for the charge of premeditated sensationalism.

Today *Sanctuary* no longer needs defense, and having learned how to read the notorious Introduction, we have come to realize that a good deal of it is tongue-in-cheek and mischievous provocation. Faulkner first recalls the commercial failure of his earlier books: "I had been writing books for about five years, which got published and not bought" (337). His financial situation worried him the more as in the months following the submission of the original manuscript of *Sanctuary* he had married Estelle Oldham, a divorcée with two children, and run into debt to buy a fine antebellum house. Faulkner was in desperate need of money. How could his economic needs be reconciled with fiction writing?

> I took a little time out, and speculated what a person in Mississippi would believe to be current trends, chose what I thought was the right answer and invented the most horrific tale I could imagine and wrote it in about three weeks and sent it to Smith, who had done *The Sound and the Fury* and who wrote me immediately, "Good God, I can't publish this. We'd be both in jail." (338)

The manuscript having been rejected by Harold Smith, his publisher, Faulkner had to find a job and ended up working at the power plant of the University of Mississippi. It was there, night after night, that he wrote *As I Lay Dying*. Then, a month after the publication of this novel in 1931, apparently without warning, he received the galley proofs of *Sanctuary*:

> Then I saw that it was so terrible that there were but two things to do: tear it up or rewrite it. I thought again, "It might sell; maybe 10,000 of them will buy it." So I tore the galleys down and rewrote the book. It had been already set up once, so I had to pay for the privilege of rewriting it, trying to make out of it something that would not shame *The Sound and the Fury* and *As I Lay Dying* too much and I made a fair job. . . . (339)

So it was only after revising the original version that Faulkner agreed to the publication of *Sanctuary*, and close examination of the available textual evidence (especially collation of the unrevised galleys and the published text) leaves no doubt whatever about the determination and thoroughness with which the revision was carried out.[2] It is on the evidence of the final version that he wanted the novel to be judged, as he told an interviewer in Japan in 1955:

> Remember, the one you read was the second version. At that time I had done the best I could with it. The one that you didn't see was the base and cheap one, which I went to what sacrifice I could in more money than I could afford, rather than to let it pass. The one you saw was one that I did everything possible to make it as honest and as moving and to have as much significance as I could put into it.[3]

Sanctuary, then, is anything but the shoddy potboiler it was once reputed to be. In their eagerness to whitewash Faulkner, however, critics have tended to dismiss his Introduction as a sardonic joke and to deny the possibility that originally the novel may indeed have been conceived to make money. Yet there is good reason to assume that making money was at any rate one incentive for writing *Sanctuary*, and so the pecuniary motive—never denied by Faulkner[4]—should not be prudishly ignored.

The Introduction tells us that after writing *The Sound and the Fury* Faulkner "believed [he] would never be published again" (338). So far he had made no serious effort to conquer a large audience, at least not in his novels. *Soldiers' Pay* and *Mosquitoes*, his first two novels, had been written "for the sake of writing because it was fun."[5] With *Flags in the Dust* came the sudden discovery of the "little postage stamp of native soil" and of its literary potential. And then came the "ecstasy" of *The Sound and the Fury*, Faulkner's true birth into writing. With *Sanctuary* everything changed again. Until then Faulkner had considered writing in essentially personal terms, as an individual's unmediated relationship to language and a free playful production of texts.

Sanctuary, on the other hand, seems to have been designed from the outset as a *product* to be sold.

Not that it had taken Faulkner that much time to discover the laws of the literary market, but he now came to fully realize that it was not enough to be a *writer*, that he had also to achieve full public recognition as an *author*. To live by his pen, he had to sell, and in order to sell, he had to attract customers. Melville had made the same sobering discovery after publishing *Moby-Dick*.

In a market-oriented society books are bound to be commodities, and the novel, an almost exclusively popular genre before it was taken over by the Flauberts and the Jameses, has been a machine-made, mass-produced commodity right from the beginning. No grand bourgeois, Faulkner could not live on his private means as Flaubert had done. In 1916, when he was working as a bookkeeper in his grandfather's bank, he told Estelle that money "was a contemptible thing to work for."[6] But now, having to earn a living and support a family, he could no longer write just to please himself, "for fun," or to pursue his lofty ideal of Literature. If his books were to make a reasonable profit, he had to consider his potential middle-class middlebrow readers and to meet their expectations at least to some degree. When writing *The Sound and the Fury*, he had followed his own star, feeling free to listen to his inner voices and sustained throughout by the exalting illusion of totally uninhibited creation. Now there was a third party: the anonymous average Mississippian whose conventional, fashion-shaped notions of literature had to be taken into account and with whom Faulkner now tried to identify so as to find out what kind of story was most likely to appeal to him.

Thus, while *The Sound and the Fury* had been a strenuously private book, conceived in secrecy and written in solitude, *Sanctuary*, originally intended to achieve popular success, was to be much more of a public novel.

Yet if the most patent reason for this turnabout was the banal desire to make money, there were surely other motivations involved. Faulkner then had serious reasons to doubt the possibility of a successful literary career. In attempting to find a larger audience, he was probably also trying to reassure himself against his doubts, to immunize himself against failure, to prove—to himself as well as to the world—that he too was capable of manufacturing a best-seller. And to expand his readership, he was prepared to take the risk of being misread.

In other words, for Faulkner the recourse to a "cheap idea" was perhaps not only a desperate move to solve his financial problems but also the index of an important change in the economy of his writing, a change prompted by the awareness that the haughty solitude in which he had entrenched himself while writing *The Sound and the Fury* could become an impasse. One might even argue that the provisional *encanaillement* of his genius was indispensable, for it allowed him to escape the lure of an overly self-centered relationship to writing which, had it lasted too long, might have become fatal to the pursuit of his enterprise as a novelist.

The two versions

Close study of the different versions of *Sanctuary* is in this respect quite instructive, fully confirming the hypothesis of a decisive *redistribution*.[7] But let us first dispel some further misconceptions and misunderstandings. After reading the Introduction one might assume that Faulkner set out to bowdlerize the first version to make his tale less "horrific." The revision process, however, was not self-censoring. Not only was there no toning down of the more scabrous episodes taken over from the galleys, but new scenes were introduced which added to the violence and intensified the horror: thus the lynching of Goodwin, only mentioned as a threat in the galleys, is described in vivid detail in chapter XXIX of the final version. Contrary to what might have been expected, the purpose of Faulkner's revisions was not to bring the novel into conformity with current standards of taste and propriety. What really bothered him was not the "shocking" character of the book but its failure to meet his high standards of craftsmanship, its inadequacy as a novel: "You can't print it like this," he told his publisher, "it's just a bad book."[8] The refusal to have the text published in its early version was due not to tardy moral scruples but to aesthetic reasons.

As it stands now, *Sanctuary* is one of Faulkner's most straightforward narratives. The first version was a much more complicated affair. There were many shifts in time-sequence and point of view, yet they were carelessly cobbled together, lacking the internal necessity which they possess in *The Sound and the Fury* and in most of Faulkner's later novels. The narrative started with Horace Benbow's visit to Goodwin in jail, three weeks after the latter's arrest (cf. the beginning of chapter XVI in the published book), then proceeded to explore Horace's past through a long series of flashbacks. As Faulkner came to realize, the first version was marred by the complacent prolixity of its early chapters, the lameness of its resolution, and its overall failure to dramatize events. He therefore undertook to rearrange the narrative sequences more chronologically and to unroll the plot at brisker pace. He also discarded most of the first six chapters devoted to Horace, and what he preserved—Horace's conversations with Narcissa, Miss Jenny, and Ruby about the events at the Old Frenchman place as well as his discovery of Temple Drake's participation in them—was transferred to the middle of the novel (chapters XV to XVII in the published book). Equally worth noting are the changes made at the opening and toward the end. In the original version the novel ended with Popeye's hanging; in the published version Faulkner added a naturalistic account of Popeye's childhood (chapter XXXI, 317–24) and has the novel end on an elegiac note with the autumnal scene staging Temple Drake and her father in the Luxembourg Gardens.[9] And after having long hesitated about the opening scene, Faulkner judiciously chose the superb spring scene, which in the earlier versions appeared only in the second chapter.

The most conspicuous and most significant alteration, however, is the drastic reduction of Horace Benbow's role. His strange destiny in Faulkner's fiction was to be twice sacrificed, for already in *Sartoris* he had lost the dominant position he had been accorded in *Flags in the Dust*. But while his demotion then had been imposed on Faulkner by his editor, this time it was his free decision. In the unrevised galleys, Horace is still the unique focal figure: the first six chapters concentrate on his private problems (especially his troubled, ambiguous relationships with women: mother, sister, wife, stepdaughter), and whatever we are later told of Temple and Popeye is mediated through his consciousness; the reader is seldom allowed to forget that the whole story is Ruby's account of it as remembered by him. In the final version, on the other hand, his mediating presence is less heavily felt, and the story is as much Temple's. Furthermore, the role played by Horace in this novel is his last role in Faulkner's fiction: after *Sanctuary* we shall not meet him again.[10]

What did Horace Benbow stand for? Generically, he belongs to the category of the *intellectual*, a character-type often found in Faulkner's fiction, especially in the early and late novels. His literary ancestry might be traced back to Don Quixote and Hamlet, and his closest models are obviously Prufrock and the Pierrot figure. Sociologically, he typifies the better-educated portions of the southern bourgeoisie—a late, extenuated version of the southern gentleman, a descendant of the "Cavaliers" without their legendary manliness. For if in his multiple guises the Faulknerian intellectual always appears—at least to himself—as a noble soul, a high-minded idealist, a chivalric champion of ladies, a generous protector of the weak and the oppressed, his lofty virtues are inevitably undermined by a flaw of the will, a failure of nerve, a blindness to reality, an incapacity to cope with experience—and, more intriguingly, by a kind of fascinated complicity with the very evil he pretends either to ignore or to fight. With the nameless, cadaverous reporter of *Pylon*, Horace Benbow is one of the most satiric versions of this character-type. A bookish dreamer and garrulous aesthete, he fails in all he undertakes, and if in *Sanctuary* he manages for a while to escape the futility of his life, it does not take him long to get back to it.

Now in social and even psychological terms the intellectual is obviously the kind of character who bears the closest resemblance to the author himself, and the attraction Horace had for Faulkner was indeed so powerful that he very nearly made him the protagonist of two of his novels. Whatever may have been his models in life and literature, Horace clearly belongs with the fictional alter egos through whom Faulkner was both running after and fleeing from his own identity. As we have seen, the production of second selves started with his early attempts at poetry and was pursued in his first novels. *The Sound and the Fury* marked the first great turning point: in Quentin's feverishly solipsistic monologue, self-projection reached at once its greatest intensity and its highest power of exorcism; his monologue, however, is fitted into a polyphonic ensemble, and the social satire of the third section as well as the mythic discourse of the fourth testify to Faulkner's desire to gain distance from a character in a sense too close, too fraternal, and to go beyond the purely personal drama he was associated with.

The downgrading of Horace in the final version of *Sanctuary* seems to be attributable to similar motives. Its first version took Faulkner back not only to *The Sound and the Fury* but also to *Flags in the Dust*, a novel in which the stories of the Benbow and Sartoris families were in the foreground and Horace's various personal problems—his marital worries, his quasi incestuous attachment to his sister Narcissa, and his equivocal attraction to his teenage stepdaughter, Little Belle—were dealt with at tedious length. A good deal of this Benbow material was carried over to the first version of *Sanctuary*. In the published text it has receded to the background, as if in the meantime Faulkner had become tired of the neurotic disturbances of his jaded quadragenarian. It is true that Horace nonetheless remains a hovering presence in most of the book, its defeated "central intelligence"; his fantasies and obsessions are still there, but they are left largely unexplained and are dissociated from his private tragicomedy to be projected onto another screen and acted out on another, larger scene: the theater of cruelty of which Temple and Popeye are the sinister stars.

What has been changed is the manner of representation, the way in which the fantasies operate in the field of fiction. Displaced, rearranged, and partly disjoined from the figure who so far served as their mooring point, they now invade and saturate the whole narrative texture, organize its script, and provide its leading actors. In a sense it might still be said that the whole story of *Sanctuary* is "a dream filled with all the nightmare shapes it had taken [Horace] forty-three years to invent" (233),[11] that it flows out of his sadomasochistic fantasies, even as the disastrous events recounted in *Pylon* actualize the reporter's. In both novels, however, the bad dream is cut loose from the dreamer and comes true in the external world, assaulting him from the outside and suffocating him with the full weight of reality.

Ejected from his "sanctuary," Horace is faced with an unsuspected world of violence and corruption. The confrontation is his reality test, the occasion for his "discovery of evil."[12] It hardly matters that the initiation fails, that for Horace it is finally nothing but a brief excursion into Inferno. What matters is the terrifying spectacle of unfolding evil itself. Its violence and horror far exceed Horace's neurotic imaginings, even though it is also a mirror in which every reader may recognize the magnified reflection of his own abjection.

It is the massive, inexorable, and inscrutable reality of a general, all-infecting evil that Faulkner now brings into daylight, forcing Horace, himself, and the reader to understand, or at least to *see*. For all the ambiguities attached to it, *Sanctuary* signals the final shift from self-interrogation—in all sorts of devious ways which critical distancing and irony did not quite immunize against narcissistic complacency—to a more radical questioning of the world at large.

In the development of Faulkner's fiction *Sanctuary* thus represents a new forward step . Not that it improves upon his earlier works nor even matches their accomplishments. There is progress nonetheless insofar as a new direction has been taken, a new fictional strategy deployed. Faulkner was deeply convinced of the need for an artist to change, and it was out of the question for him to do again what he had done before.

In *Sanctuary* the immediate, contingent incentive to change was no doubt the desire to turn his craft into a profitable business. Hence, to begin with, the choice of a shocking subject, the relative conventionality of the technique, the return to a more linear type of narration, and the adoption of a more traditional and more mass-oriented mode of fiction.

Of all Faulkner's novels, this one, at least in its visible fable, is by far the most unabashedlly *melodramatic*; the "most horrific tale" could only be the most predictable tale. *Sanctuary* tells an old story already told by Richardson, Walpole, M. G. Lewis, and many others: that of the maiden and the monster, the virgin and the villain. Extreme nightmarish situations, criminal passions, violent actions, confinement and thwarted escape, rape and murder—none of the staples of the melodramatic stock-in-trade seem to be missing. Critics have rightly stressed Faulkner's indebtedness to Gothic fiction and to the "hard-boiled" detective novel of the twenties, two popular subgenres closely related to melodrama as far as characterization, plotting, and atmosphere are concerned, and for which the French use the same phrase: *roman noir*.[13]

To recognize the importance of these debts is by no means to imply that *Sanctuary* is an inferior work. Admittedly, if novelists are assumed to stick with the "human" (i.e., the average, the ordinary) and if all worthwhile novels are expected to offer "well-rounded," lifelike characters, with complex feelings and emotions interacting in recognizable social contexts, *Sanctuary* largely fails the test. Yet to read it with such expectations is to misread it by asking it to conform both to the outdated conventions of nineteenth-century realism and the more recent ones of the "psychological novel." This is precisely how it was read by most of its early reviewers and by a number of its later critics, who either deplored its "superficiality" or zealously repsychologized it so as to reclaim it for "serious" fiction.[14] *Sanctuary* is not to be faulted for lacking nuance, delicacy, and depth, and we had better read it on its own terms, in its sustained shrillness, as one of the most exemplary of "American Gothics."[15]

Like all truly innovative novels, however, *Sanctuary* transcends the generic constraints within which it is expected to work. Faulkner pretends to play the game of popular fiction and deftly appropriates its tricks, chills, and thrills; but in appropriating them, he makes them serve his own purposes. *Sanctuary* is unmistakably melodramatic in the calculated excesses of its lurid tale of sex and violence; like Gothic fiction it appeals to the readers' submerged fantasy lives and plays on their most primitive fears and desires. But at the same time it evinces a sense of outrage and derision seldom found in popular fiction. Formulaic melodrama is black-and-white; *Sanctuary* is black, down to its humor. There is no innocent maiden to redeem the corruption of the villain, no virtue to be rewarded in the end; the battle of Good and Evil turns out to be an empty show. In avoiding the pieties and simplicities of moral manichaeism, Faulkner cut melodrama from its traditional ideological assumptions.

Sanctuary displays a concentrated harshness, an astringency probably unique in Faulkner's work. A furious impatience, too, which leads to a hardening and thickening of his novelistic manner and entails multiple reductions. The polyphony of *The Sound and the Fury* and *As I Lay Dying*, gives way to a single narrative voice, and multiple perspective yields to the vision of a single *eye*, exorbited, enlarged by horror or revulsed with disgust. The characters are likewise flattened and stylized by the brutal strokes of a ruthless caricaturist. Time is contracted into a staccato succession of highly charged moments, and space shrinks, as if beset by fear.

Psychoanalysis relates the writing process to dreamwork and assumes fantasy structures to lie beneath all literary texts. In *Sanctuary* Faulkner's method of simplification and compression and his Poelike concentration of effect evoke indeed the *condensation* mechanisms at work in dreams. And if all fictions are reshuffled and reworked fantasies, they appear here to be startlingly close to the textual surface. To call the novel a "Freudian nightmare" (a phrase about as inept as "Freudian symbol" or "Freudian insight") does not tell us anything about how it works as a text, but it is unquestionably to its closeness to dreamwork and fantasy patterns that it owes its dark power, the uncanny charge of raw intensities assailing us as we read Faulkner's "most horrific tale."

All of Faulkner's novels feed on anxieties, and in nearly all of them one senses the helpless fury of outrage and rejection. In *Sanctuary* these feelings are taken to extremes. Anguish here appears in its most elemental form, as *terror*, and refusal is conveyed in *nausea*, its most organic, most immediately physical manifestation.

XII

TERROR AND TRANSGRESSION

Mere anarchy is loosed upon the world,
The blood-dimmed tide is loosed, and
  everywhere
The ceremony of innocence is drowned.

W. B. Yeats, "The Second Coming"

Mondo cane

Of the many remarkable beginnings to be found in Faulkner's fiction none is more arresting than the overture of *Sanctuary*. From the outset the reader is thrust into a haunted, spellbound space. The novel starts rather undramatically with the description of two silent characters in a natural setting, but at once there is a quality of brooding stillness, incipient tension, and indefinite menace, a chilling sense of the "uncanny" that prompts at once a faint shiver of malaise.[1]

"From beyond the screen of bushes which surrounded the spring, Popeye watched the man drinking" (3): Popeye is there right from the start, enigmatic and ominous, "hidden and secret yet nearby" (3), like the "clockwork" bird about to sing its three notes, and he is there as though he had always been there, an ambushed watcher, unseen and unassailable, patiently waiting for his prey. Holding Benbow, the man kneeling at the spring, in his gaze, Popeye already appears in a position of power, Horace—watched, exposed, vulnerable—in a position of weakness. The presentation of the two characters could hardly be more sharply contrasted: whereas Horace is as yet barely individualized (in the first two pages he is simply "the other man"), Popeye, named as soon as he appears, is, as Jean-Jacques Mayoux has noted, "already entirely *present*."[2] His ill-boding presence imposes itself straightaway through the double privilege of name and gaze; the luridly expressionistic portrait that soon follows makes it even more disquieting:

[Benbow] saw, facing him across the spring, a man of under size, his hands in his coat pockets, a cigarette slanted from his chin. His suit was black, with a tight, high-waisted coat. His trousers were rolled once and caked with mud above mud-caked shoes. His face had a queer, bloodless color, as though seen by electric light; against the sunny silence, in his slanted straw hat and his slightly akimbo arms, he had that vicious depthless quality of stamped tin. (3–4)

Originally, Popeye was conceived less as a realistic character than as a pure symbol of evil,[3] and every feature in the portrait is indeed a signature of his malefic essence. Yet even before evil assumes shape and substance in a visible figure, it is that concealed, unseen Other looking at Horace (and looking at us) "from beyond the screen of bushes."

Evil has no beginning; it is that which, inexplicably, is always *already* there, that which has always already begun. Popeye "precedes the novel as a key precedes a musical score. He exists before Horace's perception of him . . . and before the description Horace gives of him. . . . Popeye is not only 'for' Horace, he is there in himself, *an sich.*"[4] The novel arises out of and within his voyeuristic and lethal gaze, and it opens significantly with "from beyond," two words referring to an origin but also to distance, removal, and separation. In the unaccountable distance of the origin, time has already lost its flow and measure. The novel's first sentence describes an optical relation within a scenic space, with no temporal reference given, and the second, instead of starting the narrative by taking us past the first, moves us back to an earlier moment (Horace emerging from the path and kneeling to drink from the spring), a moment prior to that of the incipit. The whole scene thus takes on a suspended and oddly timeless quality, even more strongly emphasized in the original text: "Not only the air, but time, sunlight, silence, all appeared to stand still. The spot, the two figures facing one another decorously, were isolated out of all time."[5]

Popeye's gaze isolates and immobilizes. It is itself "out of all time," even as his pop-eyes are out of flesh—exorbited organs of naked vision. Which is to say that time—or eternity?—is on Popeye's side, that he is from the outset master of the field. His is under all circumstances the advantage of *surprise,* and the novel's opening scene is indeed that of Benbow's "optical rape" by Popeye.[6]

Surprise is followed by suspense. After the shock of the initial encounter comes the endless nightmare of paralyzed waiting. For two hours the two men face each other across the spring which separates their bodies and mingles their reflections—the spring from which one has come to drink and in which the other spits. Motionless, they are watching each other, Popeye holding Benbow at his mercy. Nothing actually happens during their long silent confrontation, but the tension is such that anything might happen at any time. Violence already threatens; the reign of terror has begun.

Terror will strike at random. Tommy, then Temple, caught in Popeye's web, are its first victims. But it should not be forgotten that Popeye, the little gutter Caesar, is himself beset by perpetual fear. No one, here, feels safe; everyone lives in suspicion. As if the worst were bound to happen.

Sanctuary plunges us into an inhospitable world where the presence of the other is invariably resented as an encroachment or felt as a menace of aggression. *Homo homini lupus*: a wolf, or more precisely a dog, as is suggested in the little apologue supplied in the middle of the novel by the grotesque tribulations of Miss Reba's beribboned lapdogs. Now their "bead-like eyes [glare] with choleric ferocity" and "their mouths [gape] pinkly upon needle-like teeth" (153), now they crouch against the wall beneath Temple's bed:

> She thought of them, woolly, shapeless; savage, petulant, spoiled, the flatulent monotony of their sheltered lives snatched up without warning by an incomprehensible moment of terror and fear of bodily annihilation at the very hands which symbolised by ordinary the licensed tranquility of their lives. (163)

There is little difference between these cringing or snarling dogs and mankind as portrayed in *Sanctuary*: the ferocity, the baseness, the bitchery are fundamentally identical.[7] This is *mondo cane*, a dog's world: either the monotony and mediocrity of a kenneled or "sheltered" life, like Narcissa's and that of the Jeffersonian bourgeoisie, or—if ever the cruel and capricious Miss Reba presiding over the destinies of the world expels you from your sanctuaries—"the terror and fear of bodily annihilation." This is precisely what the whole novel is about: the unleashing of terror, the irruption of disorder and violence into a society which thought itself immune to them and will not rest until it has restored order—*its* order. And this is also the point of the test Horace and Temple are put to in the book: suddenly snatched out of the futility of their cozy little lives and catapulted into an alien environment where their codes of conduct no longer obtain, both of them are subjected to the experience of raw evil, an experience which brings no recognition, no gain in self-knowledge to either. Temple, as we see her in the Luxembourg Gardens at the novel's close, seems hardly affected by what she has gone through.[8] As to Horace, his emotional involvement has probably no deeper impact on his life, and eventually he sneaks back to the pink sanctuary of conjugal bondage in a mood of apathetic resignation.

Sanctuary is a stark and powerful dramatization of the workings of evil, and at first reading its frontal assault on our nerves is so brutal as to leave us in a state of shock, benumbed by horror and disgust. The first narrative sequence at the Old Frenchman place in particular seems to function as a machine primarily intended to produce malaise and anguish, to produce them almost physically through the creation of a world of terror and nausea.

The time of nightmare

The prose of *Sanctuary* is as chilling as Kafka's and as glutinous as Céline's, yet its world is unmistakably Faulkner's, and no reader of his fiction can fail to recognize the familiar features of Faulknerian time, its eddies and distortions, its accelerations and decelerations, but intensified and multiplied here by the effects of terror. The panic prompted by impending savagery, the anxiety aroused by foreboding, upset minds and unsettle bodies. Their coordination no longer works. In the grip of terror, it is as though the mind were torn off the body. Here is Temple, just after the car crash: "Still running her bones turned to water and she fell flat on her face, still running" (40). Later, huddled in a corner of Ruby's kitchen, hearing suspect noises beyond the wall, she screams, "feeling her lungs emptying long after all the air was expelled" (54). Or again, after discovering that she is being spied upon by a hidden voyeur: "For an instant she stood and watched herself run out of her body, out of one slipper" (96).

On each of these occasions there is a rupture, a sudden unhinging of consciousness, a breakdown of perception, a loss of coordination and control. Losing all hold on the actual, Temple's mind repeatedly hallucinates intentions into performance and feelings into facts in the vain attempt to keep pace with events, or witnesses in utter amazement the animal reflexes of her body. Whatever she thinks, feels, or does, she is out of phase with the present moment.

Time is out of joint. For Temple, it no longer flows smoothly from one moment to another and is no longer a *now* hinging on a *before* and a *hereafter*. The temporal horizon shrinks, duration contracts and retracts at the approach of the *ineluctable*. Hence a first paradox: time, in *Sanctuary*, appears to be nothing but a blind rush toward disaster, and yet its speed is frozen speed, congealed by the infinitesimal but never bridgeable distance separating it from the actual occurrence of the event. This is indeed the impossible time of nightmares: the vertigo of frenzied acceleration within a "terrific" slowness. Each moment swells into an eternity of terror; time perception tends to shrivel to an agonized sense of *imminence*. For Temple it is little else. No sooner has she arrived at the Old Frenchman place than she lives in the apprehensive expectancy of an unspeakable "something":

> she began to say Something is going to happen to me. She was saying it to the old man with the yellow clots for eyes. "Something is happening to me!" she screamed at him, sitting in his chair in the sunlight, his hands crossed on the top of the stick. "I told you it was!" she screamed, voiding the words like hot silent bubbles into the bright silence about them until he turned his head and the two phlegm-clots above her where she lay tossing and thrashing on the rough, sunny boards. "I told you! I told you all the time!" (107)

Temple's brittle present is nothing but transfixed anticipation, and yet hers is, like that of many Faulkner characters, a futureless future—a past-to-come, memory before the event—as is suggested in the passage above by the rapid tense shift from future ("Something is going to happen to me") to present ("Something is happening to me!"), and from present to past ("I told you it was!").[9]

What Temple dimly knows is that "something" will have happened to her. Hence the paradox of a *future perfect*, twice removed from the actual moment of experience. Dramatized in the double sense of imminence and belatedness, it overshadows both the narrative of the events that lead up to Temple's rape and the account of Red's murder, likewise presented as a *fait accompli* before its actual occurrence. When Temple meets Red for the last time in the roadhouse, she sees him already posthumously, with the eyes of a lubricious widow, both lusting and afflicted:

> She thought that perhaps she had passed out and that it had already happened. She could hear herself saying I hope it has. Then she believed it had and she was overcome by a sense of bereavement and of physical desire. (250)

When the catastrophe at last takes place, the ineluctable turns into the irremediable: time has become destiny. Yet even then there is no encounter with the event, no presence of the present. No sooner has it occurred than it solidifies like cooling lava and becomes a moment forever out of time. Consider how Temple experiences the shooting of Tommy by Popeye:

> To Temple, sitting in the cottonseed-hulls and the corn-cobs, the sound was no louder than the striking of a match: a short, minor sound shutting down upon the scene, the instant, with a profound finality, completely isolating it. . . . (107)

When the curtain rises, the performance is already over. The narrative only retraces the inflexible trajectory that hurls everyone toward disaster. Hence the overpowering sense of fatality which led Malraux to assume that Faulkner invented his characters with the sole purpose of confronting them with the irremediable and of crushing them under their fate.[10]

No one, in Faulkner, is capable of catching up with the "now" of his own experience; no one is capable of recognizing the moment when fate bursts into his life. The event comes upon him, as Sartre put it, "like a thief—comes upon [him] and disappears."[11] Events are never *ad*vents. Far from coinciding with what happens to it, human consciousness is condemned to a perpetual delay. The event is both before and after, menace and memory, imminence and remanence, call and recall. The Faulknerian instant par excellence is perhaps the *fatal instant* whose self-contradictory character has been aptly pointed out by Sartre:

> To say "instant" is to say *fatal instant*. The instant is the reciprocal envelopment of the before by the after; one is still what one is going to cease to be and already what one is going to become. One lives one's death, one dies one's life. One feels oneself to be one's own self and another; the eternal is present in an atom of duration. In the midst of the fullest life, one has a foreboding that one will merely survive, one is afraid of the future.[12]

The instant, then, is never but the black hole in the loop that binds the future to the past, the past to the future, the blind spot of their exchange and their paradoxical reversal. It has no inaugural value; present never wells up as *pure* present. Only later, much later—too late—is the instant apprehended as fatal, that is, acknowledged as a decisive turning point in one's life.

In *Sanctuary* the impossibility of experiencing the present as present finds its most immediate expression in the field of sensory perception, as can be seen from the belated recording by Temple's mind of the fall that interrupted her race. And this impossibility is not only illustrated by scenes *in* the novel. The whole narrative management of *Sanctuary*—even though it may appear more traditionally linear and less overtly subjective than in *The Sound and the Fury* and *As I Lay Dying*—refers us back to the same impossibility and turns out to be governed by the same pattern of *pre*monition and *post*ponement, the same structure of displacement, detour, and delay.

This structure accounts to some degree for the frequency of narrative ellipses. Sooner or later the reader will no doubt find out what has happened, yet when a crucial event occurs, there are fair chances that its telling will be blurred or even skipped over. Like Conrad and James, Faulkner generally prefers to treat climactic moments by indirection or default, announcing them in oblique ways while withholding most of the relevant information and deferring full disclosure as long as possible. This dilatory tactic—sometimes reminiscent of the suspense of detective fiction but obviously obeying other exigencies than that of keeping the reader on the alert—is used for Tommy's murder at the close of chapter XIII and for Red's at the close of chapter XXIV,[13] but its most striking illustration is provided by Faulkner's treatment of Temple's rape. During several chapters hints and presages multiply, and soon we are left in no doubt about what fate has in store for her. Yet by the end of chapter XIII, at the very instant when Popeye is about to commit his crime, narrative discourse fades out. To be more fully informed, the reader must wait for Temple's confession to Horace in chapter XXIII, and even then we learn more about her defensive fantasies before the rape than about the material circumstances of the event itself. These circumstances, especially the nature of the instrument with which the impotent Popeye raped the girl, are revealed only at Goodwin's trial (in chapter XXVIII), when the District Attorney examines Temple and lifts "the stained corn-cob before her eyes" (303).

The instant of the event is conjured away. There is much lingering, however, on its margins, an almost obsessive exploration of its immediate fringes. The *almost* is investigated in its twofold—prospective and retrospective—aspect of *soon* and *no more*. If the instant eludes in its surging immediacy, the rumbling of its approach and the traces of its fading are recorded with excruciating care. Clinging thus to both extremities, the novelist keeps the central enigma intact. And as the two extremities always come to echo each other, the call of the future resounds like a recall from the past, and the obsession with yesterday turns into the presentiment of an ever recurring tomorrow.

The narrative in *Sanctuary* thus derives its singularity from what it leaves out (the preterition of capital scenes) and sets apart (the disjunctions between the perceiving mind and perceived reality, between telling time and events told) as much as from what it conjoins in its paradoxes (the mutual envelopment of past and future, the double vertigo of the ineluctable and the irremediable).

All these features could of course be traced very easily in other Faulkner novels, since they are constants of his narrative strategy and his treatment of time. In *Sanctuary*, however, their implementation meets specific requirements: originally, as we have seen, the novel was meant to be "the most horrific tale," and so its organization and tonality had to contribute to the intended shock effect. Faulkner's technique is neither that of traditional detective fiction nor even that of the "hard-boiled school" of the thirties, and yet it produces its own kind of suspense and generates an intriguing opaqueness at times reminiscent of Dashiell Hammett's novels. Time, here, is *short*: but for the brief flashback-epilogue about Popeye's childhood (added in the final version), there is no plunge into the troubled waters of a remote past as in so many of Faulkner's other novels. In *Sanctuary* the past lacks depth and substance; there is only the past that accumulates as the narrative progresses. And, as noted earlier, the future is likewise a near, short-dated future. Even though the novel confines us within an endless circular nightmare, the narrative takes us speedily from a meager past to an empty future. Most often it bounces from one moment to the next, advances by fits and starts, and its broken, jerky progression resembles the time experienced by the characters themselves: the exploded time of terror.

The three sanctuaries

Space, in *Sanctuary*, offers no shelter. It is not meant to be inhabited; no one can feel at home in it. Like time, it is experienced as *expropriation*—alien, treacherous, whirling, and dizzying, a space with ever shifting boundaries, where one inevitably loses one's bearings, a space which appears either as a threatening outside or as a suffocating inside. There is no place here that does not eventually become a trap or a prison, a torture chamber or a stage for foul deeds; no sanctuary can be found that has not been or will not be desecrated.

The novel's title might be read as the generating metaphor of its text. It is at any rate one of its ironic keys, announcing as it does the principle of inversion and perversion which informs its whole structure and texture.

In contrast to other Faulkner novels, *Sanctuary* has no permanent locale. Its fictional space is divided into three arenas, corresponding broadly to its three major narrative sequences: the Old Frenchman place and its immediate surroundings, which provide the setting for the first third of the novel (chapters V-XIV), Memphis (chapters XVIII-XXV), Jefferson (chapters XXVI-XXIX). What connects these three arenas, apart from the comings and goings of the characters, is a set of common properties: those, precisely, which seem to relate them to a *sanctuary*, i. e., a closed space, a place forbidden to outsiders. Each of them constitutes a preserve, a territory claimed by a social class or group, a kind of micropolis ruled by laws of its own.[14]

A "gutted ruin rising gaunt and stark out of a grove of unpruned cedar trees" (8), the Old Frenchman place at once brings to mind the forbidding feudal manors and medieval monasteries of Gothic romance: it conveys the same sense of isolation and enclosure, decay and desolation, and much like the convents and castles of Mrs. Radcliffe or Walpole, the old ruined plantation house which has become a bootleggers' haunt stands for an extraordinary and autonomous world, remote from civilization, withdrawn from the jurisdiction of common law to be subjected to the will and whim of a master villain. It is therefore a set trap for the trespasser. Whoever blunders into it courts disaster. Horace Benbow, Gowan Stevens, and especially Temple will learn to their cost how perilous it is to cross the threshold of tabooed space.

Jefferson is to the Old Frenchman place as law to lawlessness, civilization to savagery. But only on the face of it. For the county seat of Yoknapatawpha, of whose civilizing function we are reminded by the courthouse and the jail, is just another space of exclusion. While offering protection to those who respect its institutions, adopt its values, and conform to its order—even hypocritically, like the judges and politicians of *Sanctuary*— it is intolerant of deviation and ruthlessly expels from its precincts all transgressors of its code, as evidenced by the harsh treatment given to Ruby, a former prostitute, and the savage lynching of Goodwin.

Memphis-Babylon, the underworld city of organized crime and prostitution, is a sort of middle ground or free zone, a place for more or less clandestine meetings and underhanded transactions between the "honest" citizens of Jefferson and the outlaws. Miss Reba is one of its most representative members, for she is above all a bawd, a *go-between*, and it is not fortuitous that the outrageous "affair" between Popeye and Temple Drake, who come from opposite extremes of the social spectrum, takes place in her brothel. Miss Reba provides the major part of the male population of Memphis with venal volupties, and she can pride herself on counting bankers, lawyers, doctors, even police officers among her patrons. Yet her house is indeed a *maison close*, another enclosed space, with a dubious marginal status, reserved for anonymous sex; a cozy ghetto of license and lust, conjoining in grotesque paradox the rules of the gangster milieu and the code of petty bourgeois respectability which the procuress does her comic best to enforce in her establishment.

The three main locales of the novel are sanctuaries through their enclosedness and their including/excluding function. But they lack one essential attribute of the traditional sanctuary: they are anything but *sacred* spaces. They may well serve as refuges for a while, but sooner or later the *right of sanctuary* will ineluctably be flouted.

With Faulkner, sanctuary functions in much the same way as virginity: the word as signifier is the tombstone of its referent. Or, as Claude-Edmonde Magny put it, Faulkner's sanctuaries "assume their sacred character only through the profanation which despoils them."[15] Popeye's spitting in the spring is the first of a long series of gestures of defilement. Moreover, the

Gothic description we are given of the Old Frenchman place marks it off at once as an evil place. Admittedly, before the intrusion of Popeye and Temple it may be seen as a kind of "savage Arcadia."[16] The presence of the feebleminded but rather harmless Tommy and that of the Goodwin family, whose survival is ensured, at least temporarily, by the motherly Ruby, can be viewed as a furtive, half-ironic reminder of a "natural" condition prior to good and evil, analogous in its primitiveness to the unpruned vigor of the surrounding "jungle." But no sooner have Popeye and Temple arrived than the place turns indeed into a haunt of evil. Suspicion takes over, aggressive gestures multiply around the desirable sexual object Temple has become to all the males present, and we then witness the irresistible rise of violence and terror up to the climax of Tommy's murder and Temple's rape.

Memphis is likewise the site of criminal acts and impious rites, and one can hardly fail to be struck by the similarity between the concluding events of the sequence at the Old Frenchman place and those of the Memphis episode. In both narrative movements the setting eventually becomes a stage for crimes: murder and rape in the first, murder in the second. The analogies between the two narrative closures are too many not to be deliberate: the two murders (neither of which is narrated) are interrelated through the match-and-fire motif associated with Popeye (see 102 and 254). It is remarkable, too, that both murders are followed by sinister mock rituals: the parodic nuptial rite enacted by Popeye's "seduction" of Temple after the killing of Tommy, a parodic funeral rite after that of Red.

The parallel is underscored by the symbolic equivalence of the two scenes' locales. The rape and the first murder are committed in a *barn*, a place metonymically associated with Temple, to whom it serves as shelter, but also a building used for storing grain, an emblem of natural fecundity, pointing here ironically to the sterile violence of the rape, just as its instrument, Popeye's corncob, does.[17] The rape thus proves a triple sacrilege, since it is simultaneously a violation of Temple's asylum, the profanation of a sanctuary of fecundity, and, as the heroine's first name suggests, the desecration of a "temple," a young woman's virginal body whose destination is also to be sown and harvested.[18]

As for the murder of Red and the funeral wake, their décor is a roadhouse and gambling joint named the Grotto. By its name if not by its function a potential asylum like the barn or the corncrib, it partakes of the same earth/womb symbolism, while the etymological affinities of *grotto* with *crypt* (a vault beneath a church used as a burial place) relate it even more directly to the novel's title. Evoking both sex and death, *grotto* admirably suits the site of Temple's and Red's last encounter, of Red's murder by Popeye, and of Red's funeral wake.[19] Linked to sexual depravation and murderous violence in much the same way as the crib or the barn, the Grotto appears as another inverted sanctuary for the celebration of unspeakable rites.

That the Old Frenchman place and the underworld of Memphis are only mock sanctuaries is hardly surprising. That the definition also applies to

Jefferson gives the novel's irony a further twist. In contrast to these haunts of lawless violence and sexual depravity, Jefferson might be expected to stand for the clear, clean, and orderly world of law and morals. Yet it soon becomes obvious that this opposition is a false one, for the presumed bulwark of justice turns out to harbor just as many turpitudes as a whorehouse or a criminals' den. The final proof of this is Goodwin's mock trial, the revelation in broad daylight of the corruption of the judges, the venality of the politicians, and the hypocrisy of Jefferson's "respectable" society. Imposture everywhere: the Jefferson courthouse is to justice what the Memphis brothel is to love.

The trial episode climaxes in a release of destructive violence, just as the two previous episodes did, and it ends likewise with the killing of an innocent. The only—but highly significant—difference is that this time the murder is collective: after the shooting of Tommy and Red, we now witness the lynching of Goodwin, burned alive in coal oil by a sadistic mob whose cruelty, whatever its pretexts may be, is just as horrendous as Popeye's.

While unfolding in three distinct areas, the novel's topography thus comes to inscribe itself under a single paradigm. The dense network of analogies through which these areas are interlinked constitutes what one might call a structural irony, an irony which gives the full measure of the novelist's demystifying intent. As in *The Beggar's Opera*, the underworld is used as a mirror image of the "upper" world. All classes come within the arc of Faulkner's satire; a whole society is brought to book.

In and out

Each of the three major locales of *Sanctuary* secures closure through a system of defenses and partitions which divide space into inside and outside. To pass from one area to another, to enter a "sanctuary" or leave it, implies the crossing of a threshold, and this crossing is never an indifferent matter, since to cross the boundary is to expose oneself to aggression or to escape from its threat, to lose the safety of a shelter or to find it again. Outside and inside are likewise menacing; all places are marked by the same ambiguity, the more so as no one ever knows for sure which side he is on nor what awaits him where he goes.

This uncertainty is easily perceptible in the *door* motif. Now allowing communication, now blocking it, the door entails a dialectic of enclosure and escape, security and insecurity. The locked door provokes anguish or provides reassurance, induces paralysis or invites breaking in. Depending on whether one is locked *in* or *out*, it means confinement or exclusion. The open door, on the other hand, points to the possibility of escape or retreat; ceasing to be a barrier or a protection, it becomes again a way out, the promise of an else-where—unless it turns out to be the lure of another trap.

At the Old Frenchman place, doors open and close over and over again. People come and go, rushing from one room to another, in pursuit or in flight. Yet motion is less chaotic than appears at first glance. An elementary etiquette regulates the comings and goings: to open a door, to enter a room is something that is not done in any way. Goodwin, for example, boorish though he is, signals his arrivals by the noise he makes: "[Ruby] heard the door open. The man came in, without trying to be silent" (84). Popeye, on the other hand, never announces himself unless he betrays himself by his smell: "Then, without having heard, felt, the door open, [Ruby] began to smell something: the brilliantine which Popeye used on his hair" (84). Later, Temple, in her room at Miss Reba's, finds "Popeye standing there, his hat slanted across his face" (166), without having seen or heard the door open.

Popeye is indeed throughout the one who has been, and whom nobody has known to be, *already there*, and whose presence therefore comes always as a total surprise. Never do we see him approach or go away. Everything happens as if he were given the preternatural privilege of turning invisible whenever and wherever he wants. Moving in a space without sound or distance, he appears and disappears *instantly*, like a demon or a phantom exempted from the laws of space and time.

The door thus comes to function as a touchstone, a test object, and the way of crossing its threshold as an index of character and behavior. While Goodwin's noisy entrances are pledges of relative candor and loyalty, Popeye's sudden intrusions are in his typical underhanded manner: his extreme discretion is in fact a maximum of indiscretion. Popeye moves about like a cat, like a thief, penetrating without warning wherever he pleases; or like a predatory animal lying in wait and ready to pounce upon its prey. And for him there are no game preserves (*sanctuary*, in the language of hunting, means "privilege of forest, close time"). Popeye abides by no rule, respects no limit, no distance; he stands outside all social and moral codes, which is to say that with him any possible transgression is to be expected.

Violating the private space of others, just as his voyeurism does, Popeye's stealthy entrances are the as yet benign symptoms of a compulsive need for intrusion, obtrusion, and aggression, of which the rape will be the grisly culmination. Temple's rape overshadows the whole novel, and though it is never told directly, but is only alluded to, the allusion reverberates everywhere.

Endlessly circling around that which it refuses to name, Faulkner's text shapes itself once again around a central gap. Hence, for example, the sexual overtones of the door, the more insistent as they are closely linked to two sharply contrasted female figures: Temple and Ruby.

Ruby takes no part in the general restlessness that has followed upon Temple's arrival at the Old Frenchman place. For quite a long time, she is referred to in the novel as "the woman"—a mother figure whose main function it is to prepare and distribute food. "A woman stood at the stove" (8) is the first sentence to mention her presence at Frenchman's Bend. Ruby spends most of her time in the kitchen, between the stove and the box where she keeps her baby. Everything designates her as a nursing mother and links her to the domestic values of fire and hearth. Ruby is in fact the only one to whom the dilapidated plantation house is *home*. Keeper of the house and guardian of its threshold (as Judith Sutpen, with much more of a tragic aura, will be in *Absalom! Absalom!*), she is most often seen "inside the door" (see 14, 15, 16, 17, 78, 84, 94, 99) immobile, on the lookout, determined, it seems, to bar the way to any intruder.

If Ruby is watching over her home and her child, Temple has only herself to defend, and she defends herself so weakly and with so little conviction that her behavior soon becomes suspect. The contrast between the two women is startling from the outset. Age, social background, morphology, clothes, gestures, attitudes, language, everything emphasizes their antagonism. While Ruby either does not move at all or moves within a very small field of action, Temple cannot keep still and runs from one place to another. Yet the door motif is associated with both, and whenever the narrative focuses upon Temple, references to doors, bolts, and locks begin to multiply. For Temple, however, the door is not a strategic position, a place to be occupied and, if need be, defended. If Ruby usually stands within the door, Temple stands before or behind it, uses it as a shield or confronts it as an obstacle. With her the door motif is drawn into another, far less stable pattern. As if contaminated by Temple's waking nightmare, the door thickens into a dreamlike object in a landscape of terror. Doors suddenly begin to resist:

> She had expected the door to be locked and for a time she could not pull it open, her numb hands scoring at the undressed planks until she could hear her fingernails. (91)

> Then she got to her feet and sprang at the door, hammering at it, watching the rat over her shoulder, her body arched against the door, rasping at the planks with her bare hands. (98)

> She leaned there, scrabbling her hands on the door, trying to pull it to . . . . (104)

> she clawed furiously at the door until she found the bolt, dropping the towel to drive it home. (155)

From a functional object the door has turned into something hard and heavy and opaque, whose secret malevolence seems to hold Temple back. Thus, after her first night at the crib, as she remembers the rat, she rushes to the door, claws at it, and eventually manages to open it. Yet no sooner has she sprung out than she springs back and bangs the door to, out of fear of the blind old man coming down the hill (91–92). The scene is an ironic epitome of Temple's desperate predicament: she springs out of the crib to escape from a first threat (the rat), yet outside she senses a second threat (the blind man), which compels her to seek shelter in the very place she had fled from a few seconds before.

Treacherous doors: they first harden into walls, block the exits, occasion delay, and once they have yielded, it is to open up a space just as menacing as the one just left. While preventing motion and communication, they also fail to shield, for whenever they ensure efficient enclosure, they become agencies of confinement. Let us reconsider the crucial scene in chapter XIII opposing Tommy and Temple to Popeye: at Temple's request, Tommy shuts the door of the corncrib, bolts it, then shakes it to test its solidity. "Hit's fastened," he says reassuringly. "Caint nobody git to you now" (105). After which Temple's faithful watchdog squats down before the door. As it turns out, however, Temple is less safe than ever. The fox is already with the goose, for here is Popeye coming down from a trap door in the loft overhead, outwitting Tommy and Temple, and taking the position in reverse. The reversal of the situation is nearly comic: Popeye, the still potential aggressor, and Temple, his intended victim, are confined within the same space, while Tommy continues mounting guard outside. It is a tragic reversal, too, for it plainly demonstrates the utter futility of protective measures in a world swayed by terror. When Popeye realizes that the door of the crib is bolted from without, he orders Tommy to reopen it, and in opening it to Popeye, Tommy signs his death warrant. A few moments later he will be shot down in cold blood by Popeye.

Popeye is the only character in *Sanctuary* whom doors obey. Discreet and diligent accomplices, they always make way for him and afford him the safety they deny to his victims:

> Temple neither saw nor heard her door when it opened. She just happened to look toward it after how long she did not know, and saw Popeye standing there, his hat slanted across his face. Still without making any sound he entered and shut the door and shot the bolt and came toward the bed. (166)

For Temple the bolted door is a reminder of her sequestration by Popeye; for the latter, however, it means permission to gratify his perverse fantasies with entire impunity.

Everything and everyone eventually yields to Popeye's mute violence. There is no need for him to break doors open; his acts of violence are the wanton discharges of unrestrained sadism. His casual murder of Tommy, recounted at the end of chapter XIII, is a case in point, the more significant as it is a prelude to and prefiguration of the rape, in which sex expresses itself in terms of death and death in terms of sex. Tommy's murder is the nuptial parade of the impotent gangster, the sinister travesty of a courtship scene: after shooting Tommy, Popeye turns at once and looks at Temple, waggling the pistol before putting it back in his coat (cf. 107). For him killing is the only way of proving his manhood to Temple, and the pistol exhibited in the scene as the instrument, if not the organ, of his "virility" is clearly a phallic prosthesis, like the dried-out corncob he is going to use for the rape. One might add that the sexual symbolism of the scene also surfaces in the reference to the yawning door (cf. 107). While the pistol is a penis surrogate, the door points to Temple's unconditional sexual surrender, as does her physical posture after the murder: "she sat there, the legs straight before her, her hands limp and palm-up on her lap" (107). Temple, at this point, has given up resistance and consented beforehand to the rape. The "temple" will not be defended.

Transgression

From inside to outside, outside to inside, the passage is effected according to various modalities, the most characteristic of which appears to be transgression, a term here to be taken both in its literal and etymological sense—*transgression*: a stepping across, a passing over, the crossing of a boundary in space—and in its figurative sense: a breach of contract, a violation of social, moral, or religious law. The act of transgressing is in this novel the act par excellence, and through its many occurrences it asserts itself as a kind of narrative paradigm. If *Sanctuary* had to be summed up in a single statement, "to transgress" would be its verb and "sanctuary" its metaphoric object. As to its subject, it would have to be a plural, for there is hardly a character in the book that, at one moment or another, does not become a transgressor.

In its most spatial and most obviously social form, transgression manifests itself as *intrusion*. The boundaries between the three major areas are of course no rigid barriers, and there are various transactional rules regulating the exchange of goods and services. Thus the male citizens of Jefferson know well where to buy the bootleg whiskey and where to gratify their sexual needs. Places like Goodwin's hideout and Miss Reba's brothel would simply not exist without their bourgeois customers, for their only *raison d'être* is to supply the latter with the pleasurable commodities of which official morality disapproves.

Economically, the three scenes of the novel's action complement one another. Socially, however, they remain antagonistic. There are no true laws of hospitality; the stranger may be a customer, but he never becomes a guest. To venture outside one's milieu is to lose the benefit of its protection. He who has crossed the border is no longer *at his place*, and being now in alien territory, under a jurisdiction which he does not know and is therefore most likely to transgress, he has become a virtual intruder.

Horace Benbow is an intruder *malgré lui*, and yet his stumbling into Old Frenchman place is enough to generate at once a state of suspicion and tension, as can be seen from his confrontation with Popeye at the spring as well as from Ruby's spontaneous animosity toward him: "That fool. . . . What does he want . . ." (14). Horace's fortuitous intrusion has a double effect: it exposes him to danger, yet he would not run any risk were he not himself perceived as a potential menace by those whose territorial limits he has unwittingly transgressed. The risks run by intruders are a function of the fears of the intruded. Horace is threatened to the extent that he is himself considered a threat.

The reception given to Temple is another, even more telling illustration of this axiom. Temple provokes from the start a far more inimical response. "What are you doing in my house?" Goodwin asks her (55). And Ruby reminds her over and over that she is *persona non grata*: "'Nobody asked you to come out here. I didn't ask you to stay. I told you to go while it was daylight'" (57). Ruby's only wish is to see Temple leave before it is too late, for she has sensed immediately the mortal danger her very presence represents for her and her family. What makes Temple so dangerous is above all her bland ignorance of the world she has entered. In her own milieu, her silly flirtatiousness would be of no consequence, while here it is misconstrued as an open sexual invitation. And since she is lusted after by several would-be rapists, she becomes at once an object of fierce sexual competition and eventually the cause of a brawl (see chapter VIII).

Temple's intrusion breeds extreme violence. Its significance is not only dramatic but social, and one might argue that the arrival of Horace, then of Temple and Gowan Stevens, at the Old Frenchman place is the intrusion of the Jeffersonian bourgeoisie into the *Lumpenproletariat* of bootleggers, gangsters, and whores. From the initial encounter of the two worlds, dramatized by the successive meetings of Popeye and Horace, Ruby and Temple, there develops a series of confrontations through which Faulkner's sardonic genius deploys the full range of its ironies and obliquities.

One of these ironies is that it is Temple, a Mississippi debutante, who precipitates the novel's disruptive action. It is through her agency and through Popeye's (it should not be forgotten that Popeye is also an intruder at the Old Frenchman place) that the process of evil is set off and the forces of destruction are unleashed. Before her arrival, as we have seen, the place was presided over by Ruby, and it is during the confrontation of the two women that Temple's intrusion takes on its full significance. Ruby's virulent diatribe against "honest women" in chapter VII leaves no doubt as to the irreducible antagonism between the coed and the former prostitute: "Oh, I know your sort. . . . Honest women. Too good to have anything to do with common people" (60). What feeds Ruby's anger is smouldering class hatred rather than sexual jealousy. Ruby speaks out on behalf of all those "that are not good enough to lace the judge's almighty shoes" (61). Temple she calls a "poor little gutless fool" (64), not even capable of true fear: "Afraid? You haven't the guts to be really afraid, anymore than you have to be in love" (65). Ruby's life has been sordid and miserable, but she has given, loved, suffered, and the implication is that among "white trash" there are probably more honesty, loyalty, generosity, and compassion than in Temple's shallow middle-class world.

Admittedly, there has been no shortage of prostitutes with golden hearts since Bret Harte, and in giving the finer role to the whore-madonna, Faulkner uses a fairly conventional trick. Ruby's inveighing, however, must be viewed functionally in the overall economy of the narrative: considered in retrospect, it appears prophetic, for the events to follow fully bear out Ruby's charges. Ironically, it is the treatment reserved to Ruby herself, when she in turn becomes an intruder in Jefferson, that confirms more than anything the appropriateness of the indictment. At Jefferson, her position is symmetrical to Temple's at the Old Frenchman place, but the effects of intrusion are by no means identical. While Temple, after sowing the seeds of violence and death about her, withdraws into the sanctuary of her family and her class, Ruby is expelled from any possible shelter by the righteous church ladies, and she loses even the man she loved.

If intrusion is one of the novel's constants, it is important, as well, to see how variable its consequences are. The intrusion motif is reused twice in a minor key, first in the scene with the town boys gathering outside the college to watch the dance (chapter IV), then in the Virgil and Fonzo episode (chapter XXI), where the motif is treated in the style of pure farce. This brief interlude is another tale of intrusion—the misadventures of two naive country boys in the world of urban prostitution—and thus provides a comic counterpoint to Horace's and Temple's "initiation into evil."

But does anything like true initiation occur? One may well wonder to what extent, if at all, Horace and Temple have been transformed by the *rite de passage* they have gone through. For both it simply ends in a discreet retreat to the sanctuaries they had provisionally left. While Horace has experienced the *Schaudern* of a brief season in hell, Temple has discovered the thrills of naked lust. Had there been a transgression according to the traditional patterns of passage rites, it would have resulted in a passage from innocence to experience and from ignorance to knowledge. In *Sanctuary*, however, transgression is merely a symptom of moral and social disorder, and all rites are rites in reverse. The logical correlate of intrusion is *expulsion*, but one of the grimmest paradoxes in the novel is that the main agents of intrusion are in no case those who bear its cost. Which shows once again how much the rules of the game have been perverted. The major intruders are Popeye and Temple, and the price exacted for their intrusion is high indeed, yet others must pay for them. After adjusting quickly and easily to Miss Reba's world, Temple returns to her own, seemingly little the worse for what has happened to her. As to Popeye, he is hanged—for a crime he has not committed. But the most revolting injustice of all is of course the atrocious lynching of Goodwin, who has committed no crime at all and is made to pay for Popeye's and Temple's crimes with his own life.

After all the intrusions and transgressions and the carnage they have provoked, we then witness the final expulsion rite through which the city of Jefferson frees itself symbolically from evil. But the ritual killing of Goodwin, the scapegoat, like the immolation of Christmas in *Light in August*, is at once a real murder and a mock exorcism, the climax of horror and the apotheosis of travesty. Ignominy has simply changed sides and been raised to a larger scale; one man's violence is succeeded by collective terror: the sadistic voyeurs who gleefully watch Goodwin burning alive are so many reembodied Popeyes. Far from being a cathartic counterviolence, the savagery of the lynch mob is the psychopathic killer's ultimate victory. And the transgression is this time the more outrageous as it has the tacit approval of the very people who should enforce respect of the law. At this point of extreme savagery we are even beyond "transgression," for transgression becomes impossible in a society that has regressed to the anarchy of the primal horde and where what seemed to be a monstrous exception to the rule is about to become a standard of endemic misrule.

XIII

THE MADNESS OF BODIES

> La biologie aurait raison, si elle savait que les
> corps en eux-mêmes sont déjà langage. Les
> linguistes auraient raison s'ils savaient que le
> langage est toujours celui des corps.
>
> Gilles Deleuze

Headless bodies

Unlike *The Sound and the Fury* and *As I Lay Dying*, the published version of
Sanctuary seldom delves into the inner recesses of individual minds and makes
no sustained attempt to conjure up the illusion of a "stream of consciousness."
There are Horace's reveries and hallucinations, to be sure, and we are even
allowed a few glimpses into Temple's thoughts, but the novel's main thrust is
away from inwardness. As in Dashiell Hammett's novels, albeit less systematically, we find in *Sanctuary* a fierce and scrupulous concentration on exter-
nals. The psychological veers toward the physical, the emotional toward the
sensory, and the focus is primarily on what happens to, in, and between
bodies. With reference to the first name of the female protagonist, *Temple*,[1] the
very title of the book is a carnal metaphor, and from the outset the protruding
and intruding eye, the *popeye* to which the voyeur-villain of the piece owes his
nickname, suggests the threat of encroachment and desecration. Moreover,
the novel's central scene is a rape, never actually recounted but whose outrage
reverberates throughout the text. *Sanctuary* is above all a chronicle of violation,
profanation, and destruction. What claims our immediate attention here is not
so much the characters' words, thoughts, or feelings as the silent language of
their bodies, the mute text written into the novel through their postures,
gestures, and motions.

Many of these signs and signals turn out to be perplexingly opaque or at the
very least deceptive. No fixed meanings are ascribed to them. Identical gestures and postures repeat themselves through different characters and situations, yet their significance and purpose can never be taken for granted and
their very legibility is often problematic. Under normal circumstances, body
signs and signals operate within established cultural codes and stable be-

havior patterns. They seldom do so in *Sanctuary* because more often than not encoder and decoder belong to different social groups with different codes.[2] Thus Temple's taunting and teasing at the Old Frenchman place are part of a ritualized erotic game—an act of flirting such as it was in the petting and necking twenties, what Ruby calls "playing at it" (64)—the rules of which are known and observed by the college boys she dates. But in the bootleggers' hideout those rules no longer apply. The underworld is another world with another code, portentously prefigured by the obscene scrawl with Temple's name on a lavatory wall referred to by Gowan in chapter IV (40). Frenchman's Bend is clearly not a place for ogling coquettes. As we have already seen, Temple's flirtatious provocation is perceived here as an open come-on, and it might be argued that all subsequent events—from murder through rape to murder—originate in the initial misunderstanding between the judge's daughter and the outlaws.

However, the failure of communication in *Sanctuary* is ultimately a matter of collapsing rather than conflicting codes. In point of fact, neither in the underworld nor in "normal" society does any code work properly as a control mechanism of social behavior, for everywhere the rituals of private and public life have been perverted or disrupted; nowhere does behavior conform to any fixed rule. Hence, nearly everyone involved in the novel's action lives in a state of constant suspicion and alarm. Ever on the brink of violence, each body lies closed upon itself, in wait for the redoubted aggressor or coveted victim, getting ready to fight or to flee. All contacts turn into confrontations. Aggression, violation, and destruction appear to be the only possible modes of relation in a world where the other is either prey or predator.

Sanctuary, at least the novel's first half, is perhaps best described as a pantomime or charade of terror, a nightmarish ballet in which mute tableaux of suspended gestures alternate with frantic movements of pursuit and flight. As in melodrama, the language of the bodies develops into a rhetoric of excess. One is left wondering, though, whether in their riotous expressivity the bodies point to anything beyond themselves. To *express* is to press out, to bring something inside to the outside, to make the invisible visible. In *Sanctuary*, however, there is no interior to be exteriorized, or (to change metaphors) there are no depths awaiting beneath the surfaces: body signs are at best indices of unease or symptoms of disease; they are no longer the tangible manifestations of an inner or transcendental world. The physical has ceased to gesture toward the meta-physical, just as it has ceased to reflect the psychological.

The Western tradition assumes subordination of the body to the mind or soul. In *Sanctuary* bodies avoid any lordship, escape all control. They are like chickens with their heads cut off or, to recall one of the most arresting scenes in the novel (so arresting that in the original text it appeared on the first page of the first chapter), like the black woman whose throat is slit with a razor and who, "her whole head tossing further and further backward from the bloody regurgitation of her bubbling throat," (118) runs out of her cabin and takes several steps before collapsing, finally dead.

Cut throat, gaping wound, spurting blood—this macabre vignette might be viewed as one of the many oblique reduplications (*mises en abyme*) of the novel's "primal" rape scene.[3] But the decapitation described here could also serve as a metaphor for less gruesome dis-locations: Temple, for instance, "losing her head" in the course of her frantic running before the rape, or later, in the Grotto, where she has her last rendezvous with Red:

> she found that her mouth was open and that she must have been making a noise of some sort with it. (250)

> She thought that perhaps she had passed out and that it had already happened. She could hear herself saying I hope it has. (250)

> She could hear herself shouting to the dice. (251)

Albeit induced by alcohol rather than by anguish there is again the same rift between body and mind, action and perception, and the same eerie sense of dissociation and doubling: one Temple speaks, another hears the words spoken as if they were uttered by the voice of a stranger.

Whether succumbing to drunkenness, nausea, or sheer terror, bodies drift away to act on their own. Individual will is lost; action no longer originates in the mind, it just registers in it. Consciousness is no more than a flare, a flicker, like the striking of a match in the dark: not only is it unable to cleave to the body; it is so volatile that its very existence is threatened at every moment with obliteration. Gowan Stevens, after getting drunk, retches in a lavatory and eventually passes out (see 35–37). Temple, in the Grotto scene, floats along in a "swoon of agonised sorrow and erotic longing, thinking of Red's body, watching her hand holding the empty bottle over the glass" (250). The mind is at best the impotent onlooker of the body's antics.[4]

Postures, motions

In *Sanctuary* everything conspires to make people give way to their bodies and the bodies surrender to their madness.

Body behavior becomes a function of terror: aggressive impulses or defense reflexes, almost mindless actions and reactions, an alternation of feverish tension and violent discharge form the elemental pattern of Faulkner's stark dramaturgy, a dramaturgy staged in a narrowing, constricting space and enacted in a time which has shriveled to a dazed sense of imminence.

One index of the mounting tension is *immobility*. Its significance, however, varies according to circumstance and character. With Ruby, standing in a doorway or leaning against a wall, it is primarily a posture of vigilance which she assumes to defend her territory against intruders. Popeye's stillness suggests a cat's guile, a snake's cunning, the suspended violence of a predator

about to spring. Temple's, on the other hand, either points to paralysis by fear
or hints at some private rite of magic self-protection:

> She moved the garments one by one under the quilt and lay down and drew the
> quilt to her chin. The voices had got quiet for a moment and in the silence Tommy
> could hear a faint, steady chatter of the shucks inside the mattress where Temple
> lay, her hands crossed on her breast and her legs straight and close and decorous,
> like an effigy on an ancient tomb. (75)

Temple plays dead to ward off sexual aggression. Her rigid posture is an
imaginary defense against the impending rape, as are the fantasized metamorphoses of her body which she later recalls in her confession to Horace Benbow.
But Temple never defends herself with anything but prophylactic fantasies
and magical gestures, and her immobility in this scene is highly ambiguous,
for her hieratic stiffness also evokes the passivity of the sacrificial victim.
Unlike Ruby, she is transfixed in mute fascination, stunned like a child in the
face of the inconceivable and at the same time secretly prepared to yield to it.
Surprised by Popeye in the crib, she sits "quite motionless, her mouth open a
little" (106). She is described in almost identical terms after the rape, on the
way to Memphis, as she sits in Popeye's car, "motionless, her mouth round
and open like a small empty cave" (144, see also 147), and again, at Goodwin's
trial, we find her "in her attitude of childish immobility, gazing like a drugged
person above the faces, toward the rear of the room" (304). In the courtroom
scene, Temple's stillness, her fixed gaze and blank face (see 299, 301, 302, 304)
betoken a state of total apathy, recalling the "drugged immobility" (120) of
Ruby's sickly child as well as anticipating the mood of psychic exhaustion
which takes over at the novel's close, and of which further evidence is
provided by Goodwin's impassiveness in jail and in court (see 283, 287, 288)
and Popeye's indifference on death row (see 329–30).

Immobility, then, is not necessarily an index of energy gathering to thrust
or parry; it may also connote a shrinking of vitality, the insidious contagion
of inertia if not a sheer surrender to death.

Another notable feature in *Sanctuary* is the frequency with which bodies are
shown to retract, contract, burrow, as if to reduce their exposure as much as
possible. Squatting—admittedly a common posture in the rural South—is
referred to too often in the early chapters not to be significant. In the opening
scene Popeye and Horace squat "facing one another across the spring, for two
hours" (5), and it is in the same attitude, "squatted on his heels in the chaff,
looking at the house" (105), that we see Tommy, Temple's ephemeral and
ineffectual bodyguard. Even more ominously, squatting becomes associated
with both voyeurism and defecation in the scene of chapter XI, where a
man—Popeye? Goodwin?—squatting "upon the glittering mass of leaves
along the crest of the ditch" (96), peers at Temple, huddled in the woods, trying
to relieve herself in privacy.

Equally striking are the many occurrences of "crouching," "cowering," and
"cringing." In the face of danger, man and animal alike recoil: "Under the bed

the dogs crouched against the wall in that rigid and furious terror" (162). By cowering, the body attempts to remove itself from sight and touch or at any rate to offer the smallest vulnerable surface. Temple's distraught behavior at the Old Frenchman place is not unlike that of Miss Reba's terrorized poodles: now she is in motion, running from one place to another, now she crouches against the porch door (69) or huddles up in a corner of the kitchen, first beside a shotgun and then beside the stove, drawing before her the box in which Ruby's baby sleeps. The phallic or maternal overtones of these talisman objects underscore the infantile pattern of her behavior. In search of a sheltering nook, Temple is unconsciously regressing to the womb, the earliest and safest of all "sanctuaries." Small wonder, then, that her cowering eventually becomes a curling up: after her first night in the barn, she "waked lying in a tight ball" (91), and later, in her room at Miss Reba's, with the door bolted and covers pulled over her head, she curls up again, "lying in a tight knot until the air [is] exhausted" (158).

Turbulences

All these repeated figures of suspension, withdrawal, and recoil attest to the paralyzing power of terror. Yet terror also generates turbulence—a turbulence ruled by the same principle of excess and exposing likewise the inescapable helplessness of the body. If immobilization petrifies the body in anguish or bemusement, motion sweeps it just as surely into a frenzied vertigo.

Turbulence sets in as soon as Temple arrives at the Old Frenchman place, and she is both its focus and its paradigm. Ruby quickly gauges the peril Temple represents, and she later tells Horace: "If she'd just stopped running around where they had to look at her. She wouldn't stay anywhere. She'd just dash out one door, and in a minute she'd come running in from the other direction" (169). Temple traverses the same space over and over again. Far from removing her from the threat, her brief, broken zigzag flights bring her back each time without fail to her point of departure:

> Still smiling her aching, rigid grimace Temple backed from the room. In the hall she whirled and ran. She ran right off the porch, into the weeds, and sped on. She ran to the road and down it for fifty yards in the darkness, then without a break she whirled and ran back to the house and sprang onto the porch and crouched against the door. (69)

> Tommy was standing in the hallway of the barn when Temple at last got the door of the crib open. When she recognised him she was half spun, leaping back, then she whirled and ran toward him and sprang down, clutching his arm. Then she saw Goodwin standing in the back door of the house and she whirled and leaped back into the crib. (104)

In her circular flights Temple turns upon herself like a living top. The ballet of terror which is the prelude to her rape presents us with the continuing spectacle of her pirouettes, and whether wheeling in space or pivoting upon herself, her body spins with dizzying speed. Yet once, at least, the rotation is performed in slowness. The effect is even more unsettling:

> Temple's head began to move. It turned slowly, as if she were following the passage of someone beyond the wall. It turned on to an excruciating degree, though no other muscle moved, like one of those papier-mâché Easter toys filled with candy, and became motionless in that reverted position. Then it turned back, slowly, as though pacing invisible feet beyond the wall, back to the chair against the door and became motionless there for a moment. (73)

Through contortions and distortions characters are dehumanized, their bodies disfigured into incongruous or hideous objects. Terror twists and tears the body's very fabric—skin, muscles, nerves, viscera. Yet even on the verge of disaster, the flesh continues to cringe and crawl into itself. Temple, as Popeye draws near, begins "to shrink into the bed, drawing the covers up to her chin," then writhes "slowly in a cringing movement, cringing upon herself in as complete an isolation as though she were bound to a church steeple" (166–67). Or consider her own account of Popeye's first touching her:

> Then it touched me, that nasty little cold hand, fiddling around inside the coat where I was naked. It was like alive ice and my skin started jumping away from it like those flying little fish in front of a boat. It was like my skin knew which way it was going to go before it started moving, and my skin would keep on jerking just ahead of it like there wouldn't be anything there when the hand got there. (229)

For a few more seconds the assailed body searches for its poor little tricks. But once these last defenses have failed, it erupts in an outburst of frenzy:

> Then [Temple] began to struggle.... She lay on the shuck mattress, turning and thrashing her body from side to side, rolling her head.... (85–86)
>
> she lay tossing and thrashing on the rough, sunny boards. (107)
>
> She caught his wrists and began to toss from side to side, opening her mouth to scream ... her body thrashing furiously from thigh to thigh.... (167)

Fearful cowering here gives way to hysterical gesticulation. At the Old Frenchman place before the rape as well as in the Memphis whorehouse after the rape, Temple tosses and thrashes on her bed, crazed with terror. Yet once she has herself become the sexual assailant, there is still the writhing of a tormented body: "She began to say Ah-ah-ah-ah in an expiring voice, her body arching slowly backward as though faced by an exquisite torture" (252). Pleasure or pain? The epithet "exquisite" could hardly be more appropriately ambiguous. Whether writhing with lust or cringing out of anguish, the body speaks almost the same language. The signs of agony and ecstasy are confusingly alike: the gasps and spasms of sex resemble the convulsions of terror, so that Faulkner's erotic scenes seem to take place in a torture chamber. In *Sanctuary*, as in most of his other novels, pleasure and pain are brought into uncomfortably close propinquity, and desire never ceases to be shadowed by suffering and death. Terror and nausea, violence and sex are braided in the same poisonous bouquet.

Behind the deceptive facade of melodrama, with its stark contrasts and brutal conflicts, one thus discovers a constant blurring of distinctions and blunting of differences. Even the opposition of motion and immobility tends to cancel itself in the shuffling back and forth between the extremes of frenzy and stupor. Movement consumes itself on the spot, its speed freezes, its energy expends itself in a vacuum, for nothing. The figure of the *vortex* is perhaps the one that best describes its self-contradictory, self-defeating character: motion turned upon itself, wasted in endless and pointless spinning.

Constrictions

This fascination with the paradox of "dynamic immobility" or "fury in itself quiet with stagnation"[5] could easily be traced in most of Faulkner's novels, but *Sanctuary* is probably the one in which it is most startlingly *embodied*, as if written into the very texture of the flesh, for here it is in their very substance that bodies partake of frozen turbulence.

In its emphasis on mechanic, metallic deadness and harsh angularity, Faulkner's delineation of Popeye is a case in point. Gnomelike stature, little doll hands, thin profile, stiff carriage, jerky motions, pallor and coldness—nearly everything about him intimates constriction and contraction, a chilly negation of the vital and the organic. His dress—a tight black suit and a "stiff hat all angles, like a modernistic lampstand" (6)—is in keeping, and so are all the similes applied to him: Popeye has the "vicious depthless quality of stamped tin" (4); his arm is "frail, no larger than a child's, dead and hard and light as a stick" (243), and his fingers are "like steel, yet cold and light as aluminium" (246). Popeye's body is a veritable collage, an implausible and uncanny conglomerate of heterogeneous materials and jarring qualities, in which the smoothness and softness of wax or rubber and the hardness of metal are paradoxically joined. Falling outside established categories and classifications, halfway between the organic and the inanimate, halfway between nature and artifact (or, to suggest a pictorial analogy, halfway between Francis Bacon's blotched creatures and Richard Lindner's steely thugs), Popeye is a hybrid, a freak, a monster both formidable and fragile, shaped in the likeness of the evil he blindly serves: a force of aggression born of infinite weakness, a lethal power risen from impotence.

Childlike thinness and fragility are among the many features that Popeye shares with Temple, his epicene victim/partner. Like his, her slim, barely nubile body appears to be fleshless and weightless, and it eventually undergoes the same process of reification. Consider, for example, how Temple is portrayed at the court trial:

> From beneath her black hat her hair escaped in tight red curls like clots of resin. The hat bore a rhinestone ornament. Upon her black satin lap lay a platinum bag. Her pale tan coat was open upon a shoulder knot of purple. Her hands lay motionless, palm-up on her lap. Her long blonde legs slanted, lax-angled, her two motionless slippers with their glittering buckles lay on their sides as though empty. Above the ranked intent faces white and pallid as the floating bellies of dead fish, she sat in an attitude at once detached and cringing, her gaze fixed on something at the back of the room. Her face was quite pale, the two spots of rouge like paper discs pasted on her cheek bones, her mouth painted into a savage and perfect bow, also like something both symbolical and cryptic cut carefully from purple paper and pasted there. (298–99)

Reduced to an inventory of clothing and a description of make-up, the portrait owes its only touch of vividness to sharply contrasted colors—the black of evil, the purple of lust, the pallor of death. Temple has been taken apart, her body disassembled, dissected, anatomized: her hair, her face, her hands, her legs have become *membra disjecta*, objects among objects, with no more life in them than the platinum bag or the glittering buckles of her slippers, their deadness matched by the white cadaverous faces in the courtroom.[6] Looming above the gaping crowd like a hieratic and derisive effigy of profaned virginity, Temple is no more than a grotesque carnival totem, a gaudy doll-idol in her ceremonial trappings of desire and death.

Constriction reveals itself in other ways as well: lack of air, shortness of breath, asphyxia. Many characters in *Sanctuary* have trouble breathing, suffocation is hinted at time and time again: "Gowan snored, each respiration choking to a huddle fall, as though he would never breathe again" (81). Temple, on the other hand, is often breathless: "Without stopping, she whirled and sat up, her mouth open upon a soundless wail behind her lost breath" (40–41). More disquietingly, there are the "short, whistling gasps" of Ruby's baby and Miss Reba's deep-throated wheezing, emphasized at her every appearance in the novel: "Her slightest movement appeared to be accomplished by an expenditure of breath out of all proportion to any pleasure the movement could afford her. Almost as soon as they entered the house she began to tell Temple about her asthma . . ." (150). Through the half-comic, half-pathetic figure of the old madam, the motif of suffocation resurges in all its physical urgency: "She drew her breath whistling, her mouth gaped, shaping the hidden agony of her thwarted lungs, her eyes pale and round with stricken bafflement, protuberant" (165). The horror of suffocation spreads throughout the novel. Miss Reba's two poodles are asthmatic like their mistress (see 161), and nature itself is repeatedly described as "choked" with weeds (see 20, 44, 49, 95, 102, 209).[7] Asphyxia thus becomes one of the novel's major metaphors: that of an exhausted, dying planet, a world at its last gasp. Not surprisingly, even apocalypse is envisioned as a process of slow suffocation: "The insects had fallen to a low monotonous pitch everywhere, nowhere, spent, as though the sound were the chemical of a world left stark and dying above the tide-edge of the fluid in which it lived and breathed" (233).

Mouths

Mouths agasp or agape. In *Sanctuary* they await us everywhere, and with the possible exception of eyes, the mouth is indeed the most frequently described part of the body. Miss Reba's "open mouth, studded with gold-fillings [gapes] upon the harsh labor of her breathing" (165); the mouths of her dogs gape 'pinkly upon needle-like teeth" (153); Popeye's "bluish lips [are] protruding as though he were blowing upon hot soup" (167); and Temple's and Little Belle's "painted" mouths are referred to over and over again.

The mouth is one of the body's gates. A place of input and output. Breath, food, speech—everything passes through it. Yet in *Sanctuary* its functions are often blocked. Terror stifles speech just as it stifles breath, and even screams are grimaces in a silent nightmare. In the seconds following the car crash, for example, we see Temple, "her mouth open upon a soundless wail," and Tommy, "his mouth open in innocent astonishment" (41). Similarly, in the scene before the rape, Temple screams, "voiding the words like hot silent bubbles into the bright silence about them" (107). And when she rides with Popeye to Memphis:

> Again, the bitten sandwich in her hand, she ceased chewing and opened her mouth in that round, hopeless expression of a child; again his hand left the wheel and gripped the back of her neck and she sat motionless gazing straight at him, her mouth open and the half chewed mass of bread and meat lying upon her tongue. (148)

In *Sanctuary* the mouth is more often the soundless O of dumbfounded amazement than the organ of articulate speech. Temple's round, open mouth suggests a child's bewilderment, as does Vardaman's in *As I Lay Dying*.[8] Yet it is also associated with food, another important motif in the novel, pointing even more directly to the close connection between sexuality and orality.

Ruby and Temple are in this respect polar extremes: the former in the role of nursing mother, the latter in that of voracious woman-child. Temple, in spite of everything that happens to her, almost never loses her appetite, and everyone hurries to feed her. Barely has she arrived at the Old Frenchman place when Tommy brings her something to eat. For lack of candy, Popeye buys her a sandwich during their ride to Memphis, and he sees to it that she is well-nourished at Reba's, where, after a moment's hesitation, she puts away her first boarder's meal (see 164).

Likewise related to food and feeding is the enigmatic figure of the blind old man whose baby diet is indicated by his name: "Pap."[9] The first time he appears, he is described as "an old man with a long white beard stained about the mouth," waiting for mealtime "with that tentative and abject eagerness of a man who has but one pleasure left and whom the world can reach only through one sense" (12–13). Oral gratification is the last pleasure of old age even as it is the first pleasure of infancy. Ruby feeds Pap in the same way that she feeds her baby, and his senility is indeed a second childhood, equally greedy, equally helpless:

> The others were already eating, silently and steadily, but the old man sat there, his head bent over his plate, his beard working faintly. He fumbled at the plate with a diffident, shaking hand and found a small piece of meat and began to suck at it until the woman returned and rapped his knuckles. He put the meat back on the plate then and Benbow watched her cut up the food on the plate, meat, bread and all, and then pour sorghum over it. (13)

Deprived of all but the pleasures of sucking and chewing, and wholly dependent on Ruby's mothering for the appeasement of his gluttony, Pap is the puzzling paradigm of oral regression.

The motif of *alcohol* belongs to the same pattern. Most of the novel's action in the first thirteen chapters unfolds at the site of a clandestine still, and it starts with Horace and Gowan stumbling across the bootleggers: the former is taken to their hideout by Popeye because he stopped at the nearby spring to drink *water*; the latter lands there because he wants to buy *liquor*. But for the lamentable defection of Temple's drunken escort, there would have been neither rape nor murder. The search for and consumption of liquor are in fact the immediate causes of the whole series of calamitous events.

With *Pylon, Sanctuary* probably holds the record for scenes of drunkenness in Faulkner's fiction. Horace, who merely intended to quench his thirst at the spring, leaves the Old Frenchman place inebriated—an ironic foreshadowing of the imminent arrival of Gowan, the "Virginia gentleman" who never sobers up between the moment he leaves the dance with Temple and the moment he shamefully abandons her. Miss Reba, who seldom appears without a tankard of beer, is in all likelihood a chronic alcoholic; Temple is utterly drunk at the Grotto nightclub; Red's wake ends in a drunken brawl, a scene comically paralleled by Uncle Bud's vomiting at Miss Reba's beer party. In most of these scenes alcohol begets mischief and violence, and it may be said to function at the very least as a catalyst of disorder.

Popeye, however, even though he is engaged in a lucrative liquor traffic, never drinks. He has good reason to abstain: "Alcohol would kill him like strychnine" (323). Popeye is so estranged from humanity that he is even barred from common vice. Yet his need for oral gratification is just as pressing: in his case it takes the surrogate form of compulsive smoking. "He wouldn't drink," Horace tells Miss Jenny after his return to Jefferson, "because he said it made him sick in his stomach like a dog; he wouldn't stay and talk with us; he wouldn't do anything; just lurking about, smoking his cigarettes, like a sullen and sick child" (113).

Avidity. Sick, sullen, greedy children. Devouring women. In Temple, the woman-child, the two voracities are one. Her mouth is by turns a child's mouth gaping with terror and the "bold painted" mouth of a seductress. From the first sketch of her to the last, the novel reverts many times to "her mouth painted into a savage cupid's bow" (224). While heightening its sexual appeal, the artifice of makeup also exposes the mouth as bait and threat. It is in Little Belle's rouged mouth that Horace detects what he takes to be woman's congenital duplicity: "In reaching for the [photograph], he knocked it flat; whereupon once more the face mused tenderly behind the rigid travesty of the painted mouth" (175). Woman's mouth provokes and pretends, and that which it both reveals and conceals is what it re-presents: the wounding wound of her sex. Intimated throughout the novel, the erotic significance of her mouth becomes obvious to the point of obscenity in the lurid "love-scene" between Temple and Red at the Grotto:

> When he touched her she sprang like a bow, hurling herself upon him, her mouth gaped and ugly like that of a dying fish as she writhed her loins against him. (252)

> With her hips grinding against him, her mouth gaping in straining protrusion, bloodless, she began to speak. (252)

> She strained her mouth toward him, dragging his head down, making a whimpering moan. (252)

Protruding, prehensile, predatory, Temple's mouth here testifies to her transformation from victim to aggressor. The teasing flapper has become a raving nymphomaniac, fastened like a leech to her paralyzed prey. The erotic quality of the scene borders on the ghoulish: when Temple finds her lover in the Grotto, the presentiment she has of his death is spice to her lust; the anticipation of pleasure is intensified by the anticipation of loss: "she was overcome by a sense of bereavement and of physical desire" (250).

Temple's mouth in this scene not only images uncontrollable and insatiable sexual craving; it also refers us back to the ever present menace of death by suffocation ("ugly like that of a dying fish"). Mouths are likewise omens of annihilation in the apocalyptic slaughter scene evoked for Horace by the seemingly trivial spectacle of dozing train passengers, "with bodies sprawled half into the aisle as though in the aftermath of a sudden and violent destruction, with dropped heads, open-mouthed, their throats turned profoundly upward as though waiting the stroke of knives" (176).[10]

Open mouths everywhere. The mouth, it would seem, is primarily a hole, something like a breach in the body's enclosure, or a tear in its fabric: the hole made flesh, flesh revealing itself as a gap. Hole imagery can be traced throughout the novel, yet its most significant uses occur with reference to Temple's body. Not only is her open mouth compared to "a small empty cave" (144), but through another rhetorical detour, another metonymical displacement, her eyes, both "empty" or "blank" (see 30, 74, 250) and "predatory" (30), are in turn likened to "two holes" (74) or again, in one of the many comparisons portending or echoing the unspeakable rape scene, to "holes burned with a cigar" (97).[11]

This, then, is what the mouth finally comes down to: a yawning gap, an unfillable hole, the orifice of nothingness. The organ of human need and greed turns into an instrument of destruction and death, and death, conversely, appears as a voracious, all-engulfing mouth.

It is worth noting, however, that in *Sanctuary* the mouth is almost as often associated with ejection and rejection as it is with absorption. Nausea is never far away, and several scenes actually end in *vomiting*. What occurs here is a violent inversion of the mouth's normal function: orality is, as it were, turned inside out, and paradoxically, it is perhaps the act of vomiting which in this world of helpless abandon comes closest to a gesture of refusal and protest. In the throes of nausea, the body repudiates itself as flesh, and it is quite revealing that in at least two scenes—the vomiting of the young coed in the dormitory after hearing of her girl friend's initiation into sex, and the vomiting of Horace after hearing Temple's confession—the experience of nausea coincides with the horrified discovery of sexuality.[12] Yet through a further paradox vomiting is also made to appear as a materialization of sex and death—of a death that expresses itself quite literally in the loathsome "black stuff" which oozes from Emma Bovary's mouth and stains her bridal veil shortly after her death (see 6) or again in the fluid substance, equally black, which Horace imagines rushing from a woman's body during his hallucination (see 234).

Discharges, distensions, diffusions

These nauseous disgorgings exemplify another mode of bodily disorder, apparently the reverse of constriction, but just as efficient in disrupting the body's integrity. Whereas constriction ends in blockage, paralysis, congealment, the centrifugal movement of discharge, distension, or diffusion pushes the body to loosen and open itself. In both cases, the body is reduced to a mere object and exposed as mere matter.

The constriction-relaxation polarity is already perceptible in the pairing and contrasting of the novel's characters. Morphologically, Popeye, Temple, and even Horace are alike in their thinness, while Miss Reba and Senator Snopes both partake of carnal plethora. In many scenes these contrasts are put to eloquent use: Temple's adolescent skinniness is opposed successively to Ruby's full-blown femininity and to Miss Reba's monstrous corpulence; Horace's thin nervousness, on the other hand, collides with Narcissa's bovine placidity and the disquieting bulk of the Senator. And even minor characters such as Miss Reba's two lady friends, Miss Myrtle and Miss Lorraine, are identified through most of the beer-party episode as "fat woman" and "thin woman" (see 263–67).[13]

Thinness indicates a drying up, a shriveling away. Fatness arouses the converse fear of unchecked, anarchic expansion. What is redoubted in the bloating of the flesh is no longer the withdrawal of life but its overflow, its absurd and sickening proliferation. In *Sanctuary* being fat is always a sign of excess and disease, pointing to a failure to maintain proper form and balance. Fatness is both unhealthy and unclean, as can be seen from the description of Gene, the bootlegger who provides free drinks at Red's funeral:

> Beside [the table] leaned a fat man in a shapeless greenish suit, from the sleeves of which dirty cuffs fell upon hands rimmed with black nails. The soiled collar was wilted about his neck in limp folds, knotted by a greasy black tie with an imitation ruby stud. (256)

The same imitation ruby stud and a similar (but less blatant, more hypocritical) combination of fat and filth are to be found in the portrayal of Clarence Snopes:

> In the bosom of his shirt, beneath his bow tie, he wore an imitation ruby stud which matched his ring. The tie was of blue polka-dots; the very white spots on it appeared dirty when seen close; the whole man with his shaved neck and pressed clothes and gleaming shoes emanated somehow the idea that he had been dry-cleaned rather than washed. (195)

In these merciless, harshly stylized portraits (one is reminded of the fierce cartoons of George Grosz and Otto Dix) we are offered the whole gamut of the nauseating: the shapeless, the misshapen, the greasy, the sleazy, the flabby, the filthy. Yet while with male characters such as Snopes and Eustace Graham, the clubfooted District Attorney, physical repulsiveness is paired with moral squalor, the amorphous and "mountainous" (153) figure of Miss Reba reactivates the ubiquitous obsession with female flesh. All breasts and buttocks— like some overripe matron out of a Fellini film—the Memphis madam is an outrageously parodic image of motherhood, even as the fleshless, almost sexless but tantalizingly sexy Temple becomes a savage travesty of the young virgin. Miss Reba's is rank and barren flesh—obesity heightened to obscenity. Reba *Rivers*: not living water, river of fecundity, but streaming decomposition, sagging and melting flesh borne in its debacle toward the indifference of the original flux.

The theme of liquefaction can also be traced through the *hemorrhage* motif. In *Sanctuary* blood has none of the symbolic (familial, genealogical, or racial) overtones it has in other Faulkner novels: it is nothing but *cruor*, real red blood flowing from wounded flesh. Gowan's shattered nose bleeds after the car crash; Van spits blood after the fight; blood spurts from the decapitated black woman, and Temple bleeds for hours after her violent defloration, "sitting with her legs close together, listening to the hot minute seeping of her blood, saying dully to herself, I'm still bleeding. I'm still bleeding" (143). Red blood, a traditional emblem of life, here becomes a warning of death and bleeding another reminder of the body's frailty: it takes little more than a cut or a tear for the flesh to empty itself of the precious liquid from which it draws its warmth and energy.

More discreetly yet just as disturbingly, the inevitability of effusion and diffusion is hinted at through the abundance and variety of bodily excreta. Spitting, for example, occurs several times, beginning when Popeye fouls the spring in the opening scene. References to the viscous flow of saliva abound: Gowan, drunk, leans against the wall above the urinal where he has just vomited, "swaying and drooling" (36). Temple lets her saliva ooze between Popeye's fingers whenever he clamps his hand over her mouth (see 144, 244). Moreover, excess saliva is often a sign of sexual excitement: Temple remembers Popeye, the impotent voyeur, "hanging over the bed, moaning and slobbering" (244), and she herself, at the Grotto, rubs her body against Red's, "dragging at his head, murmuring to him in parrotlike underworld epithet, the saliva running pale over her bloodless lips" (252–53).

Sometimes the body's fluids find their way to other orifices. In their vacant orbs, Pap's "cataracted eyes [look] like two clots of phlegm" (13). Or moisture seeps through the porous surface of the skin, as with the feverish perspiration of Ruby's baby, "its pinched face slick with faint moisture, its hair a damp whisper of shadow across its gaunt, veined skull" (120). In the diseased, ravaged body of the "crucified" child, death's work is nearly done. With its flesh drained and consumed, picked to the bone, Ruby's baby already seems to be sweating in the pangs of final agony.

The "black stuff"

"The obscene," writes Sartre, "appears when the body adopts postures which strip it of its acts and which reveal the inertia of its flesh."[14] In *Sanctuary* obscenity displays itself on almost every page: it is in the grotesquely frozen postures of fear, in the hysterical convulsions of anguish and lust, in the ignoble abandon of humiliated and defeated bodies, in the rigid immobility of corpses. Nausea in this novel results from the discovery of the body in its opaque inertia and the contingency of its being-in-the-world, from the recognition of a life which, barely begun, is already, inexorably, a hostage to time and death. Yet it is also, ironically, a blind, elemental gesture of protest, the organic expression of an inarticulate revolt against a condition which mocks our desire for autonomous and indestructible selfhood.

Bodies are not sanctuaries. No presence, no mystery dwells in them—unless it be that of their generation and death. What dignity could one find in these leaking sacks of skin? Bodies do not know how to contain and control themselves. Everything urges them to spill their slimy little secrets. Sweat, spittle, vomit, blood—through all these oozings and flowings and outpourings flesh bespeaks its incontinence and inconsistency, announces its carrion future. In the last resort, the language of the body comes down to this reiterated admission of its shame and misery—a nauseous epiphany, aptly epitomized by "that black stuff that ran out of Bovary's mouth" (6).

In Horace's hallucinatory vision, after he has listened to Temple's confession and contemplated the photograph of Little Belle, "something black and furious" (234) runs likewise out of the two girls' composite body, and it is very interesting to note that in the original text of the novel "the black stuff" was associated as well in Horace's memory with his own mother:

> After a while he could not tell whether he was awake or not. He could still sense a faint motion of curtains in the dark windows and the garden smells, but he was talking to his mother too, who had been dead thirty years. She had been an invalid, but now she was well; she seemed to emanate that abounding serenity as of earth which his sister had done since her marriage and the birth of her child, and she sat on the side of the bed, talking to him. With her hands, her touch, because he realised she had not opened her mouth. Then he saw that she wore a shapeless garment of faded calico, and that Belle's rich, full mouth burned sullenly out of the halflight, and he knew that she was about to open her and he tried to scream at her, to clap his hand to her mouth. But it was too late. He saw her mouth open; a thick black liquid welled in a bursting bubble that splayed out upon her fading chin and the sun was shining on his face and he was thinking He smells black. He smells like that black stuff that ran out of Bovary's mouth when they raised her head.[15]

In Horace's borderline reverie (he does not know whether he is awake or asleep), the staging of which recalls first the grape arbor scene in which he is watching Little Belle (the window, the garden),[16] the mother's lost body is miraculously retrieved, safe and sound.[17] Here she is, sitting on the side of his bed, if not his cradle, "talking to him." The dream begins blissfully with a regression to the time of infancy (= speechlessness) when her body and his communicated through touch, beyond—or rather beneath—the need for words, as they had done even more intimately before he was expelled from her womb. But the wish-fulfillment begins to turn into a nightmare as Horace comes to sense that far from being restored to its former integrity, the resuscitated maternal body is in fact an assemblage or palimpsest of the three women who count in his present life: Narcissa, the "serene" sister; Belle, the voluptuous wife; Ruby Lamar, the ex-prostitute (identified metonymically by the "shapeless garment of faded calico"). To the incest-haunted Horace, mother and sister, wife and whore blend into one synthetic figure of desire and dread. Yet the mother is also Popeye ("her fading chin"), and what she disgorges, what she delivers—her vomit, her son—is Popeye again.

At this juncture, readers of Freud might be reminded of the latter's contention that for the unconscious, feces, baby, and penis are the permutable representatives of "a 'little one' that can be separated from the body."[18] Indeed, it could be argued that this phantasmatic equation underlies the whole novel, for the "black stuff," the foul substance of nausea, at once relates back to the dual locus of childbirth and castration, the sex-mouth of woman, and points to Popeye, the "little black man" (113) with the bad smell, phallus-child and child-excrement, who is Horace's double.[19]

That this passage of the Ur-*Sanctuary* was expurgated by Faulkner when he revised the original text is probably not fortuitous; nor is it that the first reference to the "black stuff" in the novel is also a literary allusion, a fraternal salute from one writer to another, who was also an expert on nausea. One might then see it as well as a *mise en abyme*, a symbolic reduplication of the book within the book: black stuff, fallen on a white page; black bile, black humor, distilled into ink; terror and nausea exorcised in the very act of writing.

XIV

THE INFERNAL NURSERY

> Unschuldig ist . . . nur das Nichtun wie das
> Sein eines Steines, nicht einmal eines Kindes.
>
> Georg Wilhelm Friedrich Hegel

Childhood regained

If there is a single feature shared by the various behavioral patterns just evoked, it is surely their regressive, infantile character. A tale of terror and nausea, *Sanctuary* is also the *roman noir* of childhood regained.

Children and adolescents seldom appear in gangster novels. In *Sanctuary* they play a minor but highly significant role, especially in comic episodes such as the story of Virgil and Fonzo in chapter XXI and Miss Reba's beer party in chapter XXV. Childhood is traditionally equated with innocence; in Faulkner's novel, however, we watch children learning "this world's meanness" (265), that is, in the process of losing innocence and becoming involved in evil. But is there any innocence ever to be lost?

Whether Faulkner believed in original sin as a dogma of Christian faith need not concern us here, but to judge by his fiction, the least we can say is that he disbelieved in original innocence as a pristine, prelapsarian state of purity. This does not necessarily imply that he assumed man to be born into sin and guilt. The innocence of childhood, in his novels, is perhaps not "the seed of sin" it was for Calvin; it appears as evil's most fertile ground, however, the sine qua non of its growth and expansion. Or something like a primal blank or gap, the gap through which evil enters the world. Harmless only as long as it remains helpless.[1] Take for instance a character such as Tommy: he is a thirty-year-old child, a half-wit, an "innocent," but if he is no active agent of evil, he is no more "naturally" good than the idiot Benjy. Or take the symmetrical and contrasted figures of the *infant* and the *old man*: Ruby's sickly baby has no sooner started to live than it has begun to die—both a "crucified innocent"[2] and, inasmuch as its stunted childhood repeats Popeye's, an emblem of evil in gestation; Pap, the old man, blind, deaf, and gluttonous, has sunk into his second childhood on the threshold of death—a senile grimace of the same innocence. Between these extreme figures, in whom innocence coincides with a condition of utter weakness and so may be said to be at its zero degree, there extends the baleful rule of innocence *in action*. For as it turns out, innocence is redoubtable, not with the child, but with the adult in whom childhood lives on. The trouble with Popeye, Temple, *and* Horace (as, in different ways, with the Compson brothers in *The Sound and the Fury*, the Bundren brothers in *As I Lay Dying*, Christmas in *Light in August*, and Thomas Sutpen in *Absalom, Absalom!*) is their inability to outgrow childhood. It clings to them like a tenacious poison and in this indestructible childhood evil finds its most diligent accomplice. If there is a psychology of evil in Faulkner, this is the place to look for its roots; if there is a Faulknerian ethic, victory over childhood is one of its primary aims: to overcome evil, in Faulkner, is first of all to kill the despotic child that everyone carries within himself.[3] Only then does the *second innocence*, the only one worth achieving and possessing, become a serious possibility.

"My Lord, sometimes I believe that we are all children, except children themselves" (294), Horace cries out in one of his rare moments of lucidity, reminding us that the world of *Sanctuary* is upside down. No one in it, as we have seen, is at his place. Nor is anyone *at his age*. Children are not children—the two Snopes boys astray in the whorehouse and the bullet-headed little boy at the tea party are already participating in evil, and Ruby's baby is just a virtual Popeye—nor are grown-ups grown-ups. *Sanctuary* plunges us into an infernal nursery, a hothouse of regression and perversion, reaching back to the very brink of infancy. The "sense of the uncanny" that keeps haunting us as we read the novel certainly comes from the unfailing efficiency with which it stages our earliest miseries and earliest terrors, reactualizes our most archaic fantasies—those which Freud suspected in the "polymorphous pervert" and whose tremendous charge of anxiety was more fully revealed by Melanie Klein's investigations into the psyche of the little child.

Here is infancy in all its helplessness, anguish, and cruelty. From the novel's start we are given to understand that Popeye, the "tough guy," is a fearful kid scared by anything. After nightfall, when he leaves at last the spring in Horace's company, he chooses a longer route to avoid the darkness of the woods ("Through all them trees?"), and, as Horace notes, he "[looks] about with a sort of vicious cringing" (7). The flight of an owl suffices to make him panic:

> Then something, a shadow shaped with speed, stooped at them and on, leaving a rush of air upon their very faces, on a soundless feathering of taut wings, and Benbow felt Popeye's whole body spring against him and his hand clawing at his coat. "It's just an owl," Benbow said. "It's nothing but an owl." Then he said: "They call that Carolina wren a fishingbird. That's what it is. What I couldn't think of back there," with Popeye crouching against him, clawing at his pocket and hissing through his teeth like a cat. (7)

This scene has its faithful replica in chapter IX:

something rushed invisibly nearby in a scurrying scrabble, a dying whisper of fairy feet. Temple whirled, trading on something that rolled under her foot, and sprang toward the woman.

"It's just a rat," the woman said, but Temple hurled herself upon the other, flinging her arms about her, trying to snatch both feet from the floor. (87)

The rat is to Temple what the owl is to Popeye: the upsurge of "something," provoking intense fright, which Ruby and Horace attempt to dispel in identical words of reassurance: "It's just a. . . ." The same "grasping reflex" keeps recurring in different situations, particularly during Temple's moments of distraction: she clutches Gowan's arm and tells him she is scared when they first meet Popeye (51), even as she clutches Tommy's arm shortly before the rape (104). Later on, when left alone, for lack of a human presence she clutches objects (her coat, the covers of her bed) or her own body (see p. 78: "her arms crossed, her hands clutching her shoulders"). With Temple as with Popeye fright revives the terrors of childhood, and in the crib scene the infantile nature of the gesture is the more evident as it bespeaks the primitive urge to be carried, to find shelter in Ruby's maternal arms.[4] Mimicry, postures, language, everything with Temple is childish:

she peered around with the wide, abashed curiosity of a child. . . . (56)

she ceased chewing and opened her mouth in that round, hopeless expression of a child. (148)

she began to cry, hopelessly and passively, like a child in a dentist's waiting-room. (157)

she spoke like a child, with sober despair. (248–49)

She sat in her attitude of childish immobility. . . . (304)

Temple's body is likewise described as barely emerging from childhood: "Long legged, thin armed, with high small buttocks—a small childish figure no longer quite a child, not yet quite a woman" (94). Pubescent, both girl and woman, boy and girl, and neither. Incompletion, immaturity, indeterminacy. Temple's ambiguous attraction is that of a Lolitalike nymphet or baby doll.

Though devoid of all erotic appeal, a similar ambiguity as to age and gender attaches to Popeye, whose face is apt "to twitch and jerk like that of a child about to cry" (167). The stunted weakling, the wax-headed homunculus with doll hands is another prisoner of childhood, and in contrast to Temple—at least the later Temple of *Requiem for a Nun*—he will never break out of it, for, according to the doctor's diagnosis recorded in his biography, he was condemned from birth "never [to] be a man, properly speaking" (323). The key to Popeye's absurd and criminal fate is in his unerasable childhood, and

childhood lies at the core of all evil in *Sanctuary*. Not "Cherchez la femme!"
but rather "Cherchez l'enfant!" And look for the mute mother behind.

Couples, doubles, trouble

Popeye, the man-child, and Temple, the woman-child, constitute the central
"couple" in *Sanctuary*. There are many couples and doubles in the novel, and
coupling and doubling inform its whole structure, for the distribution of
characters as well as the management of the narrative are determined
throughout by a binary pattern. Dramatization is achieved through a series of
face-to-face encounters gradually yielding to more collective confrontations.
Prompted by chance meetings, pairs are formed, then break apart. Beginning
with Popeye and Horace at the spring, the pairs often consist of most unlikely
partners, warily watching each other, if not pitted against each other in open
conflict. Yet beyond the spectacular brutality of these confrontations, beyond
what is displayed on the stage, we must attend to the play of resemblances
and replications which secretly blunt the edge of antagonism and owing to
which the theater of *Sanctuary* opens onto another "scene" where all the
flaunted oppositions tend to annul themselves in the vertigo of *sameness*—the
very same which was believed to be other.

Horace, Popeye, and Temple are the novel's central triad. From their conjunctions arise the three major couples: Horace-Popeye, Horace-Temple,
Popeye-Temple.

To see more clearly what Horace and Popeye stand for, we shall have to
return once again to the opening spring scene. Faulkner has taken pains to
describe the two men from the outset as a sharply contrasted pair: Horace is
"a tall, thin man" (3), Popeye "a man of under size" (3); Horace is bareheaded,
Popeye wears a straw hat; Horace has a book in his pocket, Popeye carries a
pistol. Even before they have started to talk, there can be little doubt of their
opposing social identities: with his tweed coat and gray flannel trousers,
Horace is clearly a bourgeois, the pinched, black-suited Popeye just as obviously a seedy proletarian, if not a representative of what the nineteenth
century called the "dangerous classes." Further touches will be added to these
contrasted portraits in the course of the novel: physically, socially, and morally—insofar, at least, as morality is a matter of intentions—the Kinston lawyer
and the Memphis outlaw are perfectly antithetical figures. More than that: as
characters, they appear to belong to different registers, almost to different
genres. While Horace remains the most psychologized, most fully rounded of
the novel's protagonists, Popeye, for all his strange vividness or presentness,
is the most abstract, most emblematic, most phantasmal, and therefore most
opaque figure in the book. Horace would fit easily into a realistic psychological
novel; Popeye would not be out of place in a lurid Gothic romance.

But let us remind ourselves of the mirror-source, the geometric locus of the
inaugural scene:

> In the spring the drinking man leaned his face to the broken and myriad reflection of his own drinking. When he rose up he saw among them the shattered reflection of Popeye's straw hat, though he had heard no sound. (3)

The spring has turned into a liquid mirror for someone who at this point is still the anonymous "drinking man" but who, as we shall soon learn, is also a sad, aging Narcissus. It is in "the broken and myriad reflection" of his own face that Horace discovers Popeye. For Horace the first moment of his first encounter with Popeye, the very moment of surprise, is the flash of an *image*, that is, of a duplicate, and it is worth noting that through the superimposition of Horace's and Popeye's reflections, through their conjunction in the same mirroring, the image is itself redoubled.

Where Horace expected to find a *self-image*, he discovers, mingled with his, the unexpected *image of another*. Determined by their positions on both sides of the reflecting spring water, the relation between him and Popeye is presented from the start as a specular relation of mutual opposition and of symmetry, and what the novel's opening scene recounts is in fact the birth of a *double*.

First a hidden gaze, then a dislocated reflection, Popeye eludes from the beginning any direct visual apprehension, and his status as character in a presumedly "realistic" novel is indeed extremely problematic. For Horace at least, Popeye acquires visibility only through the relay of a replication, the mediacy of an image. And this image is not simply Popeye's, that of a stranger, a mysterious other; it is also—most familiar—his own: a blurred and broken double image, a liquid fusion of reflected faces, a symbolic mingling of identities, portending confusions and conflations to come.

Much as they differ from each other, Horace and Popeye are indeed twin figures, and that their initial conjunction is effected through the lure of an image, of the imaginary, is of course not quite fortuitous.[5] Granted, Popeye is not quite Dr. Benbow's Mr. Hyde; nor is he a patent double like William Wilson's *doppelgänger* in Poe's tale or Hermann's in Nabokov's *Despair*. It is remarkable, though, that three at least of his attributes link him to the doubles found in folklore or fantastic fiction. There is first of all his disconcerting dreamlike quality: Popeye, as Michel Gresset notes, "is to the 'man' as the nightmare monster is to the dreamer."[6] Then there is his ghostliness: as we saw earlier, throughout the novel he appears and vanishes like a phantom—a figure the more unsettling for seeming weightless and empty. Moreover, his metallic, robotlike rigidity and all the similes underscoring his artificiality relate Popeye to the waxwork figures, mechanical dolls, and automata whom Freud, in his essay on the *Unheimliche*, the "uncanny," explicitly identified as recurrent embodiments of the double.[7]

The singular nature of the relationship established between the two men clearly deserves close scrutiny. What induces it is the shock of surprise; what sustains it is fascination. *Fascinum* and *fascinatio* are the Latin words for the "evil eye" of popular superstition,[8] and eyes and gazes are precisely what is throughout at issue in *Sanctuary*. The fascinating power of Popeye's evil eye is in fact nothing but the power bestowed upon it by the transfixed eye of the beholder, its only measure the fascinated impotence of Horace.

Even as all human identity, arising as it necessarily does out of difference, is determined and affected from the very moment of its constitution by otherness (to be identical to oneself, one has to be other than the other), all otherness results from a process of *alter*ation or *alien*ation, a re-presentation of the self-same on the scene of the *Unheimliche*. In Popeye Horace encounters the other, *his* other. "I be dog if he aint skeered of his own shadow," says Tommy of Popeye. To which Horace replies, "I'd be scared of it too. . . . If his shadow were mine" (21–22).[9] But Popeye's shadow, just like his reflection in the spring water, *is* Horace's. The same-as-other, difference-in-sameness is of course something he is reluctant to acknowledge, and the sense of uncanniness he experiences derives precisely from the unexpected resurgence of the obscurely known, the familiar, the intimate (*heimlich*), and from its instantaneous cancellation by denial or repression (*un-*). Horace is fascinated, but his fascination blinds him prophylactically to its cause: instead of recognizing Popeye as his dark, demonic double, his secret sharer, he hastens to expel and repel him as the radically Other and hypostatizes him into absolute Evil.

Conflating as he does in a single figure, hyperbolically, the fearsome innocence of omnipotent/powerless desire and the fierce aggressiveness born of frustration, Popeye is in a sense to Horace what Benjy and Jason, taken together, are to Quentin in *The Sound and the Fury*. Indeed, in all of Faulkner's fiction, Popeye is surely the most "condensed" representative of Eros subjected to Thanatos and the most compelling "materialization" of lubricious and murderous impotence. Horace fits into the same fantasy cluster save that he is rather on the side of neurosis, while Popeye's extreme criminal behavior points definitely to perversion or psychosis.

Both sons of invalid mothers, Horace and Popeye stand for the neurotic and psychotic, passive and active, masochistic and sadistic poles of the same incapacity to live according to what Lacanians would call the law of desire. With both, the regressive urge is revealingly underscored by the incest motif. Horace's equivocal feelings for his sister and stepdaughter are archly echoed by Popeye's dutiful love for his mother: "He goes all the way to Pensacola every summer," says Miss Myrtle, and Faulkner, tongue in cheek, has her comment: "A man that'll do that cant be all bad" (269). In the novel's first version a succulent touch of fetishism had been added to Popeye's mother fixation: in "the turnip-shaped silver-watch . . . which he had inherited from his grandfather" Popeye piously preserved "a lock of his mother's hair in the back of the case."[10]

Voyeurism is another, even more blatant sign of immaturity and perversion. It is crudely clinical with Popeye watching Temple and Red fornicate in the whorehouse room. As Miss Reba reports, "Minnie said the two of them would be nekkid as two snakes, and Popeye hanging over the foot of the bed without even his hat took off, making a kind of whinnying sound" (273). All of the impotent gangster's sexuality is concentrated in his "pop-eyes," his gun serving as its occasional executive organ. Voyeurism and violence are his surrogates for the sexual act he is unable to perform. Barred from reciprocity, his maimed and morbid sexuality can be gratified only at a distance, by proxy, through the private peepshows he manages to stage in a brothel, and the closest he ever comes to orgasm is either passively, by way of painful exacerbation of its impossibility, or actively, through sadistic infliction of pain on others.

Voyeurism, however, is not always just a compensation for impotence. In *Sanctuary* nearly all males, whatever their age or social condition, are voyeurs, and Horace is no exception.[11] Not that he watches through windows like Tommy or peeps through keyholes like Senator Snopes. But Popeye's watching Temple and Red in the bordello is just a cruder version of Horace's watching Little Belle and her college boys in the grape arbor. It is noteworthy, too, that Horace's sexual musings are all prompted by visual stimuli. From first to last he is trapped in the fascination of optical images. What stirs him erotically is not so much Little Belle herself as her reflections and effigies. The immediate cause of his twisted reveries, halfway between desire and terror, is nearly always something seen and watched. Most revealing in this respect is the double mirror scene which Horace himself describes to Ruby:

> then I saw her face. There was a mirror behind her and another behind me, and she was watching herself in the one behind me, forgetting about the other one in which I could see her face, see her watching the back of my head with pure dissimulation. (16)

As mirrors turn into peepholes, watching becomes mutual, a dizzying blend of voyeurism and narcissism: Horace spies on Little Belle, who spies on Horace, spying on her spying on him. Once more the positions of the watchers are perfectly symmetrical, and in forgetting (overlooking) that Little Belle's "dissimulation" is the exact counterpart of his own, Horace fails once more to acknowledge the symmetry. But how could he acknowledge it? Blind bondage to the imaginary is the essence of his being and behavior.

With Little Belle's photographic picture, Horace has apparently no such symmetry or mutuality to fear. Pictures reduce motion to stillness, body to image. Small, flat, inanimate, easy to manipulate, a "dead cardboard" (174) at the discretion of the beholder, the glossy photograph has all the virtues of a fetish-image, and yet each time Horace contemplates it—first in a hotel room in town, after his interview with Ruby about Temple (174–75), later in his own house, after listening to Temple's confession (234)—the absence that it frames comes strangely and hauntingly alive, "like something familiar seen beneath disturbed though clear water" (175). As in Poe's tale "The Oval Portrait," it is almost as if life had been drained out of the real Little Belle and into the photograph, and as if, through some kind of eidetic reduction, the photographic reproduction of her Mona Lisalike "sweet, inscrutable face"

(174) had captured the generic essence of her being. In revealing "a face older in sin than he would ever be" (175),[12] the inert copy turns out to be more compelling than its living original, and fills Horace with "a kind of quiet horror and despair" (175); its dark magic has such power over him that it takes him twice to the brink of hallucination, and the second time, as Little Belle's eroticized picture blends with the "slow, smoke-like tongues of invisible honeysuckle" (234) and the searing memory of Temple's words, he barely reaches the bathroom to vomit.

Furthermore, intimately associated with the enchantments of the image, there is what represents to Horace the very *scene* of desire, the grape arbor:

> From my window I could see the grape arbor, and in the winter I could see the hammock too. But in the winter it was just the hammock. That's why we know nature is a she; because of that conspiracy between female flesh and female season. So each spring I could watch the reaffirmation of the old ferment hiding the hammock; the green-snared promise of unease. What blossoms grape have, that is. It's not much: a wild and wax-like bleeding less of bloom than leaf, hiding and hiding the hammock, until along in late May, in the twilight, her—Little Belle's voice would be like the murmur of the wild grape itself. (14)

A scene watched "from my window," that is, a scene stamped by the imprint of desire: there is no fantasy scenario that has not its frame. The grape arbor is to Horace what the cedars were to Quentin Compson: a green curtain half hiding the theater of sex, i.e., the hammock on which Little Belle, much like Caddy in *The Sound and the Fury*, abandons her body to the caresses of her lovers. The same troubling site recurs in all its components: vernal and crepuscular, fraught with heady fragrances and full of secret whispers. Carnal effervescence merges with the "old ferment" of the "female season." Nature "is a she," female, fluid, fecund, and women partake of her elemental force and cunning. For the Faulknerian idealist as for Baudelaire, "La femme est *naturelle,* c'est-à-dire abominable."[13] But the abominable is also the desirable, and once again the relation of the male gaze to the female object of desire is taken in the whirligig of attraction and recoil.

Horace's eyes are irresistibly drawn to the "green-snared promise" of the desired-abominated spectacle. But what does Horace actually see? As a rule, the longer he looks at what fascinates him, the less he actually sees. Typically, the first time he examines the photograph of his stepdaughter, he begins by shifting it "until the face [comes] clear" (174), but before long the picture shifts "as of its own accord" (175), the image "[blurs] into the highlight" (175), and only once it has lost its distinctness does it come eerily alive. In much the same way, the grape arbor discloses what it conceals, conceals what it discloses. Both an incentive and an impediment to vision, it is the eye's target, tease, and trap, that by which it is both fixated and frustrated. A *screen*, in both senses of the word: a device meant to remove from view, a tantalizing wall of foliage and bloom, and a blank surface inviting projection, on which the actually seen as well as the suspected unseen are soon to dissolve into the sensed, the imagined, the imaginary. The grape arbor stands here for the enclosed, bounded space of fantasy—another, inner "sanctuary," referring back to the "primal scene" in which all fascination originates, and of which a child-voyeur was once the bemused and mesmerized witness.

The position of the excluded third party is even more inescapably Popeye's. The difference separating him from Horace—admittedly a decisive one—is the distance between fantasizing and acting out. With both, frustration begets envy and resentment: Horace envies Little Belle's flirts, just as Popeye envies Red. Yet through rape, abduction, and sequestration, Horace's inadmissible wish comes true. It would seem that Popeye succeeds where Horace fails: he appropriates, confines, and isolates the object of his desire for his exclusive benefit. Can there be desire without envy? Could jealousy be the key to it all? At any rate *Sanctuary* provides an amazing illustration of "the logic of jealousy" which Gilles Deleuze detected in *A la Recherche du temps perdu*: "There is an astonishing relation between the sequestration born of jealousy, the passion to see, and the action of profaning: sequestration, voyeurism, and profanation—the Proustian trinity."[14]

Popeye thus becomes the *avenger* not only of Horace but of all the fretting and thwarted lovers in Faulkner's early fiction, from George Farr and Byron Snopes to Quentin Compson. It is of course a derisory revenge. Popeye may sequester Temple in a brothel room (a parodic version of the Presbyterian Hell where Quentin wanted to isolate himself and his sister out of the "loud world"), yet in eliminating his rival he deprives himself of the indispensable accessory to his voyeuristic *grand guignol*. As an inordinately aggrandized negative of the neurotic attitudes dramatized in the earlier novels, Popeye's psychotic acting out supplies the proof *per absurdum* of the beastly madness at the core of "romantic" desire.

If there is any validity to my contention that Faulkner's fiction, especially in its first major phase, is in many ways a spectral analysis of narcissism, Horace and Popeye appear as its extreme complementary impersonations. Horace represents it ironically in its most anemic, most Prufrockian aspects, Popeye in its most monstrous form. If taken as fictional elaborations of the writer as desiring subject, Horace might be seen as a new avatar of the artist as Narcissus Bound, Popeye as his portrait as Narcissus Unbound. With both one can hardly fail to be struck by the extreme savagery of Faulkner's portrayal. Never before had he been so ferocious with his characters, never had he handled them so roughly. In these unsparing caricatures one can measure the distance traveled since *The Sound and the Fury*. Horace is an aging, balding Quentin miserably surviving himself, a Quentin whose fresh despair would have turned into the sour compromises of middle age, just as Little Belle, the object of his half-incestuous reveries, is a devalued Caddy, much closer to Caddy's daughter or to Temple Drake than to the poignant naiad of *The Sound and the Fury*.

While Horace-and-Little Belle may be seen as a *debased* version of Quentin-and-Caddy, they are also, within the novel, a *softer* replica of Popeye-and-

Temple. The two couples are indeed in many ways similar, and their homology is highlighted in the narrative sequence leading from Temple's confession to Horace at Miss Reba's to Horace's hallucination at the close of chapter XXIII. On his way from the brothel to the station, Horace suddenly glimpses a couple: "In the alley-mouth two figures stood, face to face, not touching; the man speaking in a low tone unprintable epithet after epithet in a caressing whisper, the woman motionless before him as though in a musing swoon of voluptuous ecstasy" (232). Just before, Horace was thinking of "the only solution" (232), the annihilation of all the people involved in the lurid story, including himself. With the appearance of the couple (a prostitute and her pimp?), the outer world breaks into his somber thoughts, and Eros into Thanatos: the nameless woman's "voluptuous ecstasy" announces the "voluptuous languor" (234) of Little Belle's face on the photograph as well as Temple's "floating swoon of agonised sorrow and erotic longing" (250) in the later Grotto scene. Immediately after, Horace recalls the blank eyes of a "dead child" (232): there is clearly also a dead child in him, the living adult, whose repressed concupiscence makes itself heard in "unprintable epithets" and makes itself visible through this obscene couple, and he must wish his eyes too were "empty globes" (232), for if they were, he would be blind to lust. We are thus prepared for the concluding hallucination scene, after Horace has reached home and contemplated the photograph of Little Belle. The interplay of identifications and projections now climaxes in the "streaming blackness" (234) sweeping along a young naked woman who might be either Temple or Little Belle, and is in fact a composite of both. Through Temple's shocking confession Horace has been brutally confronted with what beckoned to him from behind the grape arbor and from the photographs of his stepdaughter: the triple horror of sex, woman, and evil. And yet this could also be a moment of self-revelation: the naked crucified body surging up in his hallucination—another dreamlike condensation—is not only a conflation of Temple and Little Belle, it is also his own, both male and female, violating and violated, and the "something black and furious [roaring] out of her pale body" (234) is his own vomit.

The hallucination is one of the novel's pivotal scenes: a moment of shattering truth, symptomatically spoken by fantasy, even though acknowledged only through violent repudiation. This is the instant when Popeye's and Temple's "real story" and Horace's fantasy life join and overlap, and as Horace hallucinates the violation Popeye has perpetrated "in the flesh," the horrified spectator of evil is at last unmasked as vicarious *participant*.

The revelation has been built up to by Horace's own drunken confession to Ruby in chapter II and by the earlier spell of hallucination described in chapter XIX. Let us equally note that Horace is attracted to Temple both through Popeye, the double of the desiring subject, and through Little Belle, the double of the desired object. Without their mediacy there would be no Horace-Temple "couple."

This "couple" has been called the "Faulknerian couple *par excellence*."[15] Considering that Horace and Temple are both generic figures, it is Faulknerian indeed: Horace is another figuration of the desiring male subject in the by now familiar guise of the *defeated idealist*, whereas Temple turns out to be a new avatar of the *foolish virgin*, and their pairing, albeit of secondary importance in terms of plot, looms large as a summation of the fierce and irreducible sexual antagonism that haunts nearly all of Faulkner's fiction. Quite remarkable too is again the symmetrical nature of the relation. Horace, the sad old young man "with something of the air of a guilty small boy" (110), whom Goodwin asks, "What sort of men have you lived with all your life? In a nursery?" (293), is hardly more of an adult than young Temple. True, he is much older and assuredly more reflective, more sensitive, with at least an embryo of moral imagination, but although his personality offers far more facets than hers, the basic components of his psychic makeup are about the same: incestuous fixation and its usual correlative, narcissism. With both we find again the hard kernel of "innocence."

What needs to be emphasized, however, is less the couple's typicality than the startling way in which it is aggrandized or, to borrow a metaphor from photography, "blown up." Horace is the Faulknerian idealist at his most impotent, Temple the Faulknerian virgin at her deadliest. Of all of Faulkner's couples, this one is the most violently *distorted*—like a savage caricature, but also like a dream image. Furthermore, in one sense Horace and Temple are both *remainders*. Horace is the last in a long series of troubled aesthetes and, as we have already noted, his role in the book is his very last. Temple likewise closes the procession of narcissistic virgins whom Faulkner had borrowed from the Decadents to make them the epicene heroines of *The Marionettes* and his early novels.

Sanctuary is a kind of close-out sale: Faulkner discards the characters who had so far held the leading roles in his obsessional theater. While staging the final show in melodramatic manner, he also pushes it toward burlesque. The actors have become grotesquely gesticulating puppets whose strings he pulls with furious contempt before rejecting them to their nothingness.

Of these puppets Popeye and Temple are the most terrifying; they form the most outrageous couple ever invented by Faulkner. At first glance, but only at first glance, the scandal lies in the forced union of opposites. Popeye and Temple seem to constitute a living antithesis, and their incompatibility can be verified at every level: actantial (active/passive; aggressor/victim), sexual (male/female), social (lower class/upper class). To these oppositions might be added those which have been suggested by allegorical readings such as George M. O'Donnell's: North versus South, modernism versus tradition.[16] Through their accumulation the antithesis is tightened to a maximum. Yet while flaunting disparities, the novel's text surreptitiously hints at secret affinities and complicities. We have already noted Temple's and Popeye's common marks of deficiency and lack as they appear through their morphologic (thinness, lightness, fragility) and psychic (infantility) similarities. Furthermore, Temple the flapper and Popeye the gangster both appear as sociomythic figures of the twenties and are as such more typed and more dated than the other characters in the book. Lastly, sexual difference itself tends to get blurred: Popeye's pseudo-virility is matched by Temple's equivocal femininity.[17] Symbolically both are under the sign of castration: Popeye is an impotent phallambulus; Temple is in turns woman-child and phallic woman, persecuted maiden and devouring vamp. Castrated and castrating, both.

The scandal embodied by the coupling of Popeye and Temple is therefore double. It is produced first of all by the cancellation of the bar separating two antithetical terms, the unnatural conjunction of what was meant to remain disjoined, the paroxysm of transgression represented by the rape. But the first scandal reverses itself into a second, even more intolerable: the fact that the rape has only been a simulacrum, that no transgression has actually occurred, that the differences were all undermined from the start, and that they eventually collapse into one another. The scandal of scandals is that in the last resort Popeye is not the cause and agent of evil he was assumed to be but only the catalyst of its enactment and exposure.

The Popeye-Temple couple is the more monstrous as it results as much from the near incestuous union of two figures twinned in evil as from the forced marriage of contraries. A marriage fertile in harvests of death: their coupling functions like a formidably efficient killing machine. In the manuscript of *Sanctuary* one can read the following reflection about Popeye: "To think of the thug in the same instant with any woman, to imagine him with a sweetheart was as monstrous as to imagine the mating of two automatic pistols."[18]

The eclipse of the Law

In *Sanctuary* the monstrous is by no means the exceptional: the abnormal is the norm, misrule the rule. Taken together, Popeye and Temple are the emblem of a whole society, the magnifying but hardly distorting mirror reflecting rampant perversion and corruption.

If the novel owes much of its disturbing power to the duplication and overlapping through which victims and victimizers, "honest people" and criminals are conflated, it also owes it to the procedures of multiplication by which the *dramatis personae* are made exemplary. Most revealing in this regard are the crowd scenes, such as those focalized through Horace in chapter XIX:

> The waiting crowd was composed half of young men in collegiate clothes with small cryptic badges on their shirts and vests, and two girls with painted small faces and scant bright dresses like identical artificial flowers surrounded each by bright and restless bees. When the train came they pushed gaily forward, talking and laughing, shouldering aside older people with gay rudeness, clashing and slamming seats back and settling themselves, turning their faces up out of laughter, their cold faces toothed with it, as three middle-aged women moved down the car, looking tentatively left and right at the filled seats. (177)

The procession became three streams, thinning rapidly upon the dawdling couples swinging hands, strolling in erratic surges, lurching into one another with puppyish squeals, with the random purposelessness of children. (179–80)

[Horace] stood there while on both sides of him they passed in a steady stream of little colored dresses, bare-armed, with close bright heads, with that identical cool, innocent, unabashed expression which he knew well in their eyes, above the savage identical paint upon their mouths; like music moving, like honey poured in sunlight, pagan and evanescent and serene, thinly evocative of all lost days and outpaced delights, in the sun. (180)

The nostalgic lyrical note introduced in the last passage reminds one of Horace's Proustian penchant for *jeunes filles en fleurs* as well as the lush mannerisms of Faulkner's early poetry; it barely mitigates, however, the cruelty of the description we are given of the student population of Oxford, Mississippi. As Wyndham Lewis noted in his (otherwise unfair) essay on *Sanctuary:* "No one is likely to accuse Faulkner, after reading it, of a weakness, I think, for these herds of nasty children."[19] These young people are noisy and exuberant as all young people are assumed to be, but their carelessness is portrayed without sympathy, and of the train scenes watched by Horace—the two cheating students (177–78), their dirty jokes (178–79), their rudeness vis-à-vis adults (179)—there is none that does not reveal the callousness and sheer stupidity of these squealing "puppies."

These acidulous vignettes, which are without direct connection with the plot but have been significantly placed in the middle of the novel, provide further evidence of the omnipresent theme of "innocence": these vulgar and vociferous young men are indeed nothing but spoiled brats. Their female companions are not any better, and their "identical" short bright dresses, "identical" violently painted mouths, and "cool, innocent, unabashed" eyes remind one irresistibly of Temple and Little Belle.

What Horace sees is a crowd of Temples and Little Belles. Much in the same way, he will discover later on, before the lynching of Goodwin, an assembly of budding Popeyes. "I saw her," says one of the "drummers" he overhears. "She was some baby. Jeez. I wouldn't have used no cob" (309). And after the lynching, the mob, its appetite whetted, threatens to lynch Horace himself: "Do to the lawyer what we did to him. What he did to her. Only we never used a cob. We made him wish we had used a cob" (311). It is only a short step from the obscene jokes of the students to the salacious and sadistic comments of the drummers and from the "artificial flowers" to Temple, the flower of evil and death. Whether the crowd consists of teenagers or adults, whether it is an everyday crowd or an angry mob, it is always the same primitive horde, the same pack of wolves or herd of sheep, ignoble, more or less, according to the occasion.

Not only rubies are spurious in *Sanctuary*. Temple's rape? A mock mating between a half-virgin and a manikin, occasioned by the desertion of a false gentleman. Red's funeral? Sheer travesty. Goodwin's trial? A charade from first to last, with false judges, a false witness, a false innocent, and a false culprit. Horace's efforts on behalf of justice? The velleities and blunders of a would-be knight.

Imposture carries the day. The law is mocked throughout or rather, the way it is enforced in Jefferson, the law mocks the law. Lee Goodwin's and Popeye's trials are outrageous parodies, and the clinching irony is that the true culprit in the first trial is sentenced in the second for a crime he did not commit. To save appearances, to perpetuate the myth of its respectability, is all that the local bourgeoisie cares about. Temple, the daughter of a judge, sends Goodwin off to death by her perjury, and when the trial is over, her father hurries to make her leave the courthouse so she can say no more. Narcissa tells her brother cynically: "I dont see that it makes any difference who did it. The question is, are you going to stay mixed up with it?" (193). Justice is the last consideration of its official custodians. Eustace Graham, the clubfooted district attorney, violates the secret of his office to obtain from Narcissa the information that will allow him to win the case; Clarence Snopes, a Mississippi senator, spends most of his time prowling brothels and sells information to the highest bidder.

In *Sanctuary* all law-defending agencies are missing or failing. A lawless society: a fatherless society, in which the tyranny of the king-child does not permit the paternal function to manifest itself otherwise than in a perversely parodical way. In the Old Frenchman place this function falls ironically to Pap, a blind, deaf, and mute old man, who spends his days sitting "in a splint-bottom chair," his head turned toward the sun he cannot see, his hands crossed over a knotty stick (45, 96, 107). Earless and eyeless, a senile Tiresias whose blindness is compensated by no gift of clairvoyance, he is the novel's most arresting symbol of humiliated and degraded fatherhood. Temple implores him in vain before her rape, even as in her moments of extreme anguish and dread she vainly repeats the propitiatory magic formula "My father's a judge" (55). She invokes her father as if he were God, but in her hour of need the real father fails to answer her prayers just as the heavenly Father does. At the novel's close, we shall see Mr. Drake with his daughter in the Luxembourg Gardens, sitting like Pap, "his hands crossed on the head of his stick" (333). A father both too distant and too close, excessive and failing: Temple's attachment to him, we should not forget, is also placed under the sign of incest.[20]

There are other hints of perverted father-daughter relationships. Thus Temple's father fixation is paralleled by Horace's attraction to his stepdaughter, and another instance of twisted fatherhood is provided by Ruby's account of the killing of her first lover by her father (see 61). The scene not only points ahead to the assassination of Red by Popeye; it also foreshadows Popeye's own fatherly role, which Cleanth Brooks was the first to detect: "If [Temple] hates Popeye—or perhaps because she hates him for his power and authority—she finds in him something of the father."[21] *Daddy* was slang of the twenties for "lover," but that Temple uses the word whenever she wants to placate Popeye gives it particular relevance, and it is also interesting to note that once Temple has been sequestered, Popeye turns into a sugar daddy, showering her with expensive gifts and spending long quiet moments by her bed. In Popeye the primal tyrant-father represents himself in the guise of king-child and imposes himself as the ludicrous and terrible ruler of *Sanctuary*'s nursery world.

Popeye stands for brute force without law, the unmitigated violence of evil, Horace for law without authority, the empty abstraction of the good. "You've got the law, justice, civilization," Horace tells Goodwin in jail (137). What follows cruelly belies his naive humanistic creed. But Faulkner's irony has many twists, and it is remarkable that the law is also invoked by its most zealous violators. "There should be a law": this reflection runs like a refrain through the novel. Thus Clarence Snopes in his anti-Semitic tirade: "the lowest, cheapest thing on this earth aint a nigger: it's a jew. We need law against them" (280). Popeye, the outlaw, expresses the same wish at the sight of the disorder provoked by alcohol: "I told him about letting them sit around all night, swilling that goddam stuff. There ought to be a law" (101). At the close of the novel Horace echoes them ironically in complaining to Little Belle about the summer nights: "Night is hard on old people. . . . Summer nights are hard on them. Something should be done about it. A law" (314). That Horace wishes to outlaw the disturbing summer nights comes as no surprise, and we can see here how little he has learned from his confrontation with evil: the law he dreams of is an antinature, antisex, and antiwoman law, a law that would spare him all the embarrassments and vexations of reality. It is likewise amusing to hear Snopes and even Popeye call for laws. The laws they are considering are of course those that would protect their own interests. But the irony cuts deeper than appears at first glance. Everyone also seems to deplore the lack of an order that would, if need be, shield them against themselves or at least provide their actions with the sanction of legality. One easily imagines Popeye and Snopes in a police state: they would have been happy there, one as torturer, the other as informer.

If a more ideological reading of the novel were attempted, one should refrain from construing it simply as a plea for law and order. The stakes of Faulkner's critique are more complex, even if one concedes that its most obvious targets are the disorder and corruption of the American society of the "roaring twenties." A satire on modernism? While acknowledging the necessity of change and adjustment to change, Faulkner, like many of his contemporaries, was viscerally hostile to the new urban and industrial society, and like them, he was upset by the social and cultural transformations that took place in America in the wake of World War I. No doubt *Sanctuary*, like *The Sun Also Rises* and other works of the twenties, belongs to a period of extreme misogyny (noticeable on both sides of the Atlantic in literature as well as in painting) that started in the late nineteenth century and was reinforced by the panic that struck Western males in the face of the first "sexual revolution" and the concomitant emergence of the "new woman." Yet it would be another mistake to reduce the novel to a sexist tract. That there is an undercurrent of misogyny can hardly be denied, but after all, men, in *Sanctuary*, fare hardly better than women, and it is worth noting that Ruby Lamar and Miss Jenny are among the rare characters who are spared the novelist's strictures. No more than he sets tradition against the turpitudes of modernity does Faulkner burden women with all sins. The evil at issue in *Sanctuary* is the monopoly neither of a time nor of a gender.

Far from exhausting the novel's thematics, social critique and satire are only one of its aspects. In his introduction to *The Portable Faulkner* Malcolm Cowley views the novel as "an example of the Freudian method turned backward, being full of sexual nightmares that are in reality social symbols."[22] What Cowley means by "Freudian method" is far from clear, and the little he says about it rests on the dubious assumption that the meanings of a literary text are under the writer's full control, so that it will suffice to find the key to their code—the author's intentions—to decipher its message in its entirety. To equate the relation of the sexual to the social with that of signifier to signified is a gross oversimplification. The novel's satiric thrust is certainly not to be ignored, but the "sexual nightmares" of *Sanctuary* are not metaphors conceived in the cool transparency of pure intention. They are the book's very substance, what it puts into words, what it sets on stage.

Terror and nausea are, as we have seen, its major modes: terror born of the ever present imminence of annihilation, nausea provoked by the glutinous tyranny of flesh and sex. In *Sanctuary* sexuality inevitably assumes a destructive character; conversely, death is always the ultimate aim and fulfillment of desire. The failure of the law not only entails chaos and corruption; it inaugurates the rule of death: anarchy is one with thanatocracy. Death is in power, the "little black man" is its most spectacular representative, and after having been its zealous servant, he will be in turn its prey. A consenting prey: Popeye is as indifferent to his own death as he was to that of others, and his hanging will be in fact a manner of suicide. Yet Horace also calls for death after listening to Temple's confession:

> Better for her if she were dead tonight, Horace thought, walking on. For me, too. He thought of her, Popeye, the woman, the child, Goodwin, all put into a single chamber, bare, lethal, immediate and profound: a single blotting instant between the indignation and the surprise. And I too; thinking how that were the only solution. Removed, cauterised out of the old and tragic flank of the world. (232)

For Horace the death wish is associated with the horrified discovery of "the logical pattern to evil":

> Perhaps it is upon the instant that we realise, admit, that there is a logical pattern to evil, that we die, he thought, thinking of the expression he had once seen in the eyes of a dead child, and of other dead: the cooling indignation, the shocked despair fading, leaving two empty globes in which the motionless world lurked profoundly in miniature. (232)

Before long Horace's nightmare fills the whole world:

> The insects had fallen to a low monotonous pitch, everywhere, nowhere, spent, as though the sound were the chemical agony of a world left stark and dying above the tide-edge of the fluid in which it lived and breathed. The moon stood overhead, but without light; the earth lay beneath, without darkness. He opened the door and felt his way into the room and to the light. The voice of the night--insects, whatever it was—had followed him into the house; he knew suddenly that it was the friction of the earth on its axis, approaching that moment when it must decide to turn on or to remain forever still: a motionless ball in cooling space, across which a thick smell of honeysuckle writhed like cold smoke. (233–34)

The dead child's "two empty globes" reflect an earth "ball" which is itself at its last agony; the nightmare has taken on cosmic proportions. It should be remembered, though, that the apocalyptic vision follows the shock undergone by Horace during Temple's confession and "illustrates," so to speak, the rise of nausea culminating, at the chapter's close, in Horace's vomiting. The apocalyptic vision, then, turns out to be another projection of his private obsessions. The "point of view" is unmistakably his, and so we should beware of ascribing to the narrator or author what belongs to a character in the book.

Yet it is worth recalling that the end-of-the-world motif and the honeysuckle motif also occur in other Faulkner novels, and that in *Sanctuary* itself, Horace's vision is foreshadowed as early as chapter XVIII:

> [Temple] watched the final light condense into the clock face, and the dial change from a round orifice in the darkness to a disc suspended in nothingness, the original chaos, and change in turn to a crystal ball holding in its still and cryptic depths the ordered chaos of the intricate and shadowy world upon whose scarred flanks the old wounds whirl onward at a dizzy speed into darkness lurking with new disasters. (158)

In both passages there is spheric and circular imagery: the "disc suspended in nothingness" is homologous to the "motionless ball in cooling space" as well as to the dead child's "empty globes." It is the same vision of darkness, disaster, and death, the same terror in the face of an inscrutable, drifting universe, which for man is at best an "ordered chaos" (or Joyce's "chaosmos"). Yet if the first passages quoted obviously refer to Horace's anguished musings, the last cannot be reasonably attributed to the futile Temple. The narrative, at this point, is no doubt focalized through her, since it is she who watches the dial "change from a round orifice in the darkness to a disc suspended in nothingness," but her shallow mind can hardly be credited with the stark vision growing out of her visual perception. As it happens, Temple is at this moment thinking of something else: "She was thinking about half-past-ten-oclock The hour for dressing for a dance, if you were popular enough not to have to be on time" (158).

So we have to bow to the textual evidence: Horace is not alone in picturing the world in apocalyptic terms. It is as if his diseased, dirt-and-death-haunted imagination has contaminated the whole book. Nausea seeps from every thing and every place; the heaven tree described at the beginning of chapter XVII brings to mind the famous chestnut tree in Sartre's *Nausea*: "The last trumpet-shaped bloom had fallen from the heaven tree at the corner of the jail yard. They lay thick, viscid underfoot, sweet and oversweet in the nostrils with a sweetness surfeitive and moribund" (131). Or consider the funeral languor of the final scene:

> she seemed to follow with her eyes the waves of music, to dissolve into the dying brasses, across the pool and the opposite semi-circle of trees where at sombre intervals the dead tranquil queens in stained marble mused, and on into the sky lying prone and vanquished in the embrace of the season of rain and death. (333)

This is how *Sanctuary* ends: death has literally the last word. What we have been listening to was "a voice of fury like in a dream, roaring silently out of a peaceful void" (311). Now it roars just as silently back. Faulkner's sonorous finale evokes a "dying fall,"[23] a slow, soft sliding back into inertia. And all convulsions gone, all violence provisionally spent, life, paradoxically, is about to resume its customary course, just as it does at the end of *The Sound and the Fury*, *As I Lay Dying*, and *Light in August*. Again one wonders: what kind of "life"? In the ironic guise of a reversion to normalcy, it would seem that the novel's triple denouement marks the ultimate surrender to nothingness: here is Popeye on death row in Alabama, calmly counting the days left before his hanging; here is Horace back in Kinston, defeated and resigned to defeat, locking the back door of his domestic sanctuary upon Belle's injunction; here are Temple and her father in Paris, dead souls among the "dead tranquil queens" (333) of a crepuscular garden. "It had been a gray day, a gray summer, a gray year" (332): after the red of terror and the black of nausea, here is the grisaille of absolute nondifferentiation.

True, narcissism is apparently the last thing to die. As he stands on the scaffold with a rope around his neck waiting to be hanged, Popeye asks the sheriff to "fix" his hair, and Temple, sitting in the Luxembourg Gardens, takes out her compact to look at her sad and sullen face. But at this point nothing anymore "makes a difference." Everyone is sinking into apathy, overcome by sheer lassitude, and Popeye's brutal execution is neither more nor less preposterous than death on the installment plan, the slow, quiet dying in the dreary round of dwindling days—life measured out, Eliotically, in coffee spoons or in "a fading series of small stinking spots on a Mississippi sidewalk" (19).[24]

After a frenzy of looking and watching and spying, all we are left with is the blank stare of a dead child: cold inanimate globes, emptied of the outrage and despair that gave them life; unsouled mirrors reflecting a moribund earth. Is this to say that *Sanctuary* is a nihilistic novel, a kind of prototype of the "absurd" fiction that was to sprout in Europe, then in America, in the wake of postwar existentialism? To say so would be to argue the identity of Horace's and Faulkner's visions, and it is precisely in the gap between their perspectives that the book's ambiguity appears—an ambiguity never to be reduced, for Horace *is* and *is not* the focus of perception and evaluation; the viewpoints of author and character are at once distinct and undissociable.[25] Horace, as we have seen, is a character under constant suspicion, and through him the ravages of self-deluded idealism are once again unsparingly exposed. Yet the distance taken from Horace does not prevent his aversion for reality from infecting the whole book.

The fascination of evil and the fascination of nothingness: surely Faulkner himself also felt their power and the temptation to yield to them. Contrary to his sad hero, however, he was able to break the insidious enchantment by the countermagic of his writing. "The tragic poet," as Malraux has pointed out, "expresses what fascinates him, not to rid himself of fascination (its object will reappear in his next work), but to alter its nature: for, by expressing it with other elements, he incorporates it within the relative world of things conceived and mastered. He does not defend himself against anguish by expressing it, but by expressing something else with it, by bringing it back into the universe. The deepest fascination, that of the artist, derives its strength from being both horror and the possibility of conceiving horror."[26]

Sanctuary is this fascination held and withheld in words. Of all Faulkner's novels it is beyond contest the darkest, written like none of the others in the ink of melancholy.[27]

Four
Versions of the Sun

XV

IN PRAISE OF HELEN

Timeless mother,
How is it that your aspic nipples
For once vent honey?

Wallace Stevens, "In the Carolinas"

Venus Genitrix

[*Light in August*] began with Lena Grove, the idea of a young girl with nothing, determined to find her sweetheart. It was . . . out of my admiration for women, for the courage and endurance of women. As I told the story I had to get more and more into it, but that was mainly the story of Lena Grove.[1]

Most readers would probably dispute that *Light in August* is "mainly the story of Lena Grove," and there is good reason to question the accuracy of Faulkner's account of its genesis.[2] If not literally true, however, the statement has its own truth, the truth of its maker, the poet's truth, and it is indeed in Lena, a young pregnant woman on a dusty summer road, that the novel has its beginning and its ending. More than that: Lena holds the novel together, enfolds it in her monumental serenity, makes it what it is: a story full of sound and fury set against a background of pastoral stillness, a tale of darkness fringed with light.

And in a tenderly humorous way *Light in August* is indeed an homage (from the French *homme*, man, male) to Woman, an invocation to Venus Genitrix in the tradition of Homer and Lucretius,[3] a graceful tribute to feminine fertility, feminine endurance, and feminine triumph. Lena is the radiant figure at the novel's gates, and from one gate to the other her trajectory draws a straight line, as economical as light itself—a straight line which would be at the same time the most accomplished circle.

Lena comes to us, comes back to us from the plumbless depths of a time before time, prior to the nightmare of history, a time slow and simple, ruled by the regular rhythms of mere alternation: "backrolling now behind her a long monotonous succession of peaceful and undeviating changes from day to dark to day again, through which she advanced in identical and anonymous and deliberate wagons as though through a succession of creakwheeled and limpeared avatars, like something moving forever and without progress across an urn" (7). Lena moves in the timeless time of eternal recurrence, along a soft curve retracing and rejoining itself in a circle ever rebegun. As to her own time (if we can credit her with a time of her own), it is like a smaller circle within the large one, closed in upon itself, throbbing with the pulse of living matter, and so quite naturally attuned to the unchanging cycle of days, months, and years. For Lena and in Lena time flows smoothly, following its predetermined course, "with the untroubled unhaste of a change of season" (57). She lives each moment as it comes, here and now, and accepts whatever it brings. In sharp contrast to Dewey Dell, her rebellious and tormented sister in *As I Lay Dying*, she "is waging a *mild* battle with the providential caution of the old earth of and with and by which she lives" (29, italics added). Of and with and by: Lena is but another name for *natura naturans*.

Her swollen body shows nature at work in the fecund field of female flesh, and Lena hears and feels "the implacable and immemorial earth, but without fear or alarm" (31). Nothing can hurt her. No need even for her to fight to achieve her ends. Her ends are in her beginnings, the harvest is in the seed, it is all a matter of growing and ripening. Lena has just to wait, and her patience is inexhaustible. Unlike Joe Christmas's journey, her own is not a restless, aimless wandering, nor is it a true quest. Her destiny bears her along, and she bears it within herself, like the child soon to be born.

Everything for her comes at its appointed hour, in the appointed place. Lena has no permanent dwelling, but why should she care? She is at home wherever she goes. Her naive wonder and puzzled pleasure in measuring the distance she has already traveled—"My, my. A body does get around" (32)—clearly indicate that to her space is not at all the ever-receding, inaccessible horizon which it will be to Christmas. Hers is the realm of *immanence*: she is as safely inside space as she is inside time, cradled in its folds like the fetus in her womb. Conversely, space appears to be the cosmic double of her own body: both welcoming, hospitable, and closed, concentric—space as it was described by Plato in the *Timaeus*, that is, a receptacle, a vessel, a matrix, as though it were the mother or nurse of all becoming. Significantly, all its predicates—luminosity, stillness, warmth, and a unique combination of torpor and alertness—also apply to Lena herself. Woman's body and the world's body call for each other and respond to each other in preestablished concord, joined by a happy complicity which nothing, apparently, will ever be able to break.

Lena therefore never stands out *against* the landscape. The natural world at peace with itself—the pastoral world—is her true milieu, gathering around her as if to shelter her in its seamless and boundless mantle. And if her habitat seems to be a solid earth, it is infused by light, a light which lightens matter, slows down motion, and in which time itself almost comes to a standstill: "The wagon moves slowly, steadily, as if here within the sunny loneliness of the enormous land it were outside of, beyond all time and all haste" (30).

The first chapter of *Light in August* celebrates the victory of light and space over the darkness of time and the triumph of the mythic over the actual. "Mythological Antiquity," writes Catherine Clément, "is precisely that: the privilege of space over time. . . . Mythology cancels time, and opening up space, renders human achievements indefinite. Immortality finds there its foundation." And she adds that with the advent of Christianity space lost this privilege and ceased to be the locus of life: "Time and its tragic consequences—sin, guilt—then became the straight gate to immortality."[4]

Lena belongs to this pure mythic space prior to the fall into time, and as has often been pointed out, she turns out to be herself a mythic figure, a new avatar, in Faulkner's fiction, of the primal mother or earth goddess. Admittedly, she is a very earthy earth goddess, a deity mildly astonished at finding herself in the plump young body of a very ordinary mortal woman, yet in her absolute serenity she is assuredly Olympian.

Faulkner called her after Helen, the Spartan princess assumed to have caused the Trojan war, the daughter of Zeus whose bewitching beauty matched that of the fairest goddesses. He thereby associated Lena even more closely with the symbolism of the novel's title, since etymology links *Helen* to Greek words denoting the brightness of light.[5] *Grove*, her patronym, is likewise loaded with mythic suggestions, bringing to mind the Ephesian Diana (or Diana Aricina), the Roman goddess described by Frazer in the first pages of *The Golden Bough*, whose cult used to be celebrated in a sacred grove of the Alban hills. Yet Lena evokes not only pagan goddesses. The "faded blue" of her sunbonnet and her dress, along with her "palm leaf fan" (6), may remind one of Mary, the Virgin Mother, as she might have been portrayed in her ample gown by Piero della Francesca or Giovanni Bellini, and once Lena has found her meek Joseph in Byron Bunch, there will be another Holy Family on the road.

Helen and Diana were originally goddesses of vegetation and fecundity, and if the Virgin Mary has not been divinized, she came close to holding in the symbolic economy of the Christian West the place which the Great Mother of earlier cultures had left vacant. The mythological configuration in which Lena is embedded is then clearly that of the archaic *Magna Mater*. It will not do, however, to catalogue her as another earth mother and let it go at that. As a character in a novel, Lena is both more and less than a replica of her mythic models. Myth and fiction belong to different cultural registers, and whenever a novelist uses mythic figures and mythic patterns, it is to transform them for his own purposes. It is therefore important to see how myth is deflected and altered in the writing process.

To begin with, one should perhaps take a closer look at the mythic material itself. In their search for large and simple truths, Jungian critics would have us believe that all mythic figures can ultimately be reduced to stable, monolithic archetypes.[6] In fact, nearly all gods and goddesses, especially when they involve themselves in human affairs, turn out to be ambiguous and contradictory figures. This duality or duplicity holds true for Helen and Diana as well as for the Virgin Mary. Helen was believed to be the daughter of Zeus, but there was no consensus on the identity of her mother, who may have been either Leda, a daughter of Oceanus, or Nemesis, the goddess of retribution, who was herself the daughter of Nyx (Night). Helen, in her unsurpassed beauty, is the "bright," the "shining" one, and yet her half-divine, half-human origins are wrapped in mystery and darkness, even as there is darkness in her fate and in the fatality she became to thousands of Greeks and Trojans in provoking, albeit involuntarily, a murderous war. And, as Aeschylus suggests in *Agamemnon*, there is also darkness in "that name for the bride of spears and blood, Helen, which is death . . . death of ships (*helenas*), death of men (*helandros*) and cities (*heleptolis*)."[7] Diana is no doubt a different figure, but she too has a double face: at one and the same time a woman and a robust huntress, a fierce virgin and the patron goddess of brides, wives, mothers, and children. And the Virgin Mary stands for a similar duality in the Christian tradition: a woman born of woman and yet conceived (and conceiving) without sin; a second Eve exempted from the first Eve's evil inheritance; both mother of Jesus and immaculate virgin.

Lena obviously also partakes of the paradoxical myth of the virgin mother, in which the role of sexuality and the procreative function of the male are blandly ignored. Of course, hers is not an immaculate conception, untainted by carnality; the reader soon learns under what circumstances she was seduced. Everything seems to suggest, however, that the identity of the father does not really matter and that there is no need to find him promptly. If it is not Burch, it will be Bunch. In the novel's comic epilogue, the family triad is at last completed, order is restored, but even then Byron Bunch, the future husband and father, is still like an intruder, an alien to the primordial and autarkic couple formed by mother and child.[8]

Lena is unique because she is one, and she is one because she is two, two in one, one in two—thanks to the child-supplement, the child-phallus, which makes her whole. She is the one who lacks nothing. Fulfilled *and* intact: mother *and* virgin.

"An older light than ours"

Lena's exceptional status is confirmed by her privileged relationship to *light*, the import of which in the novel, especially in connection with Lena, Faulkner himself pointed to in an interview:

> in August in Mississippi there's a few days somewhere about the middle of the month when suddenly there's a foretaste of fall, it's cool, there's a lambence, a luminous quality to the light, as though it came not from just today but from back in the old classic times. It might have fauns and satyrs and the gods and—from Greece, from Olympus in it somewhere. It just lasts for a day or two, then it's gone, but every year in August that occurs in my country, and that's all that title meant, it was just to me a pleasant evocative title because it reminded me of that time, of a luminosity older than our Christian civilization. Maybe the

connection was with Lena Grove, who had something of that pagan quality, of being able to assume everything, that's—the desire for that child, she was never ashamed of that child, whether it had any father or not, she was simply going to follow the conventional laws of the time in which she was and find its father. But as far as she was concerned, she didn't especially need any father for it, any more than the women that—on whom Jupiter begot children were anxious for a home and a father. It was enough to have had the child. And that was all that meant, just that luminous lambent quality of an older light than ours.[9]

Here we are back at the place and time of beginnings: in Greece, under its sky and sun, in its warmth and light. Faulkner's Greece is not quite his own invention; he inherited it from a dream which has been with us for centuries. From the Renaissance through Romanticism to the Symbolists Greece haunted the Western imagination like the nostalgic memory of a lost world of innocence and wholeness, and it is indeed as a lost "home" that the young Faulkner, the enthusiastic reader of Keats, Swinburne, and Mallarmé, redreams it in his early poems. The first chapter of *Light in August* thus echoes the texts of Faulkner's literary apprenticeship, but it is also easy to see how much he has moved away from them. The Greece of his poems was a highly formalized and rather conventional Greece. In the novel, Arcadia has become a part of Yoknapatawpha County. The light of August in Mississippi, as Faulkner himself notes, *"might have* fauns and satyrs and the gods" of Greece in it, but the landscape and the figures in the landscape are now recognizably southern. The imaginary, this time, resurges within the reality of an intensely felt and densely textured fiction.

What it refers back to is a golden age, the time "of a luminosity older than our Christian civilization," and, we might add, poles apart from Christianity and its somber world of sin and retribution. Lena-Helen partakes of that "luminosity" and has something of "that pagan quality of being able to assume everything," which sets her apart from all the other characters in the novel, especially from her negative double, Joanna, sadly weighed down by her "burden" of inherited guilt. Lena draws all her strength from her spontaneous and total acquiescence in the cosmic order. Hers is not an abject submission like that demanded by the harsh puritanical God of Jefferson, but a serene and joyful acceptance of her destiny as a woman and a mother: *amor fati.*[10] Since her innermost will coincides with the world's will, how could she ever enter into conflict with the Law? Lena is Helen, and her world is Hellas, a world where the gods are still close, a true cosmos where the severance of the human and the divine has not yet been consummated.[11] So she can paradoxically be a docile handmaiden of the species as well as a living example of *autarkia*, the virtue of self-sufficiency which Greek wisdom valued over all others. Lena travels by herself, but hers is "the sunny loneliness of the enormous land," under the benevolent gaze of the gods of Olympus, and not at all the barren solitude in which Christmas, Joanna, and Hightower live out their desperate lives.

The first chapter of *Light in August* offers us another version of Faulkner's pastoral. The model is still Greek. However, if the tamely erotic texts of Faulkner's youth were full of lusting fauns and tantalizing nymphs, Lena is anything but a maenad. The Greece she comes from is certainly not that of the drunken cohorts of the goat-god, the nocturnal and riotous Greece of the bacchanalia. Serene and simple Lena walks in the light of day, the "lambent" light of a late summer day, clear, soft, and warm. There is not the faintest touch of the Dionysian in the evocation of her world. This Arcadia is utterly chaste, and if a tutelary god were needed, it could only be Apollo, the "bright one," the god of measure and wisdom and master, according to Nietzsche, of "the beauteous appearance of the dream-worlds."[12]

Space around Lena floats indeed in dreamlike suspension: "Fields and woods seem to hang in some inescapable middle distance, at once static and fluid, quick, like mirages" (30). And amid this dreamscape in broad daylight Lena herself appears as a mirage, a "fair appearance," a dream woman, too fair to be true.

Lena was no doubt meant to represent Nature in her generous fertility; yet, as in all pastorals, the "good" nature which she is assumed to embody is no longer there, has in point of fact never been there except as a soothing illusion conjured up by the wistful staging of a myth. Besides, when the procession of identical wagons in which Lena is traveling is likened to "something moving forever and without progress across an urn" (7), Faulkner's pastoral calls attention to itself as a work of art. And, revealingly, the reference here is to a plastic medium, to the arts of space, whose privileges Faulkner must have sometimes envied and with which he seems to have competed more vigorously in *Light in August* than in any of his other novels. We know, however, that the image of the urn, used by Faulkner in other texts and other contexts, is also a *literary* allusion, an intertextual effect, the first emergence in *Light in August*, that is, of Keats's "Ode on a Grecian Urn," a poem in many ways reread and rewritten in and by the novel.

At this point it may be worth recalling that, even though the poet speaks to the urn and allows it to speak in the last two lines, Keats's poem is an ode *on*, not *to*, a Grecian urn. Like Homer's famous description of the shield of Achilles, it is an *ekphrasis*, a verbal transposition of a plastic work of art, a word-shaper's tribute to a sculptor of marble in the *ut pictura poesis* tradition. And, beyond its descriptive purpose, it is also a reflexive and interrogative text in which the function of art and its relation to life and truth are crucial issues. The answer is given laconically at the close of the poem: beauty is truth, truth is beauty. This aphorism has given rise to much speculation among critics, but in essence it is an idealistic equation in the Platonic spirit of Greek philosophy and in the Apollonian spirit of Greek art. Keats seems to endorse it, and yet Dionysus is not missing from the ode:

What men or gods are these? What maidens loth?
What mad pursuit? What struggle to escape?
What pipes and timbrels? What wild ecstasy?

These eager staccato questions, the first prompted by the contemplation of the urn (the poem will leave them unanswered), all evoke the dark god of music, dance, and madness, and it is remarkable that most of the semantic oppositions patterning the ode could be subsumed under the antithesis Dionysus/Apollo: the disorder of the "mad pursuit" is contrasted with the fixed order of the represented scene, the turbulence of the unleashed passions with the "silent form" of the Attic vase, the transient ardor of life with the permanence of the "Cold Pastoral." Apollo cannot do without Dionysus, for from the Dionysian depths comes the dark, as yet unshaped and uncontrolled primal *matter* from which all Apollonian works of art, be they urns, odes, or novels, ultimately proceed. A reversal takes place, however: the "wild ecstasy" gives way to aesthetic stasis, its savagery caught in the eternity of the fair *form*. The first tableau engraved on the urn is clear evidence of this reversal and offers an eloquent example of the Apollonian representation of the Dionysian: an amorous pursuit, yet petrified; the arrested motions and suspended gestures of a human passion forever unfulfilled; a stilled scene set against the green foliage of perennial spring. Immune to the ravages of time and change, sheltered from aging and death, but also barred from all earthly bliss, the lovers on the urn are the mute, transfixed impersonators of desire, or rather of the *idea* of desire, a pure idea dwelling in marble, the truth of which is made visible through the beauty of a semblance. "Beauty is truth, truth beauty," but for the equation to become effective the mediacy of the ideal is indispensable. Reality must be cleansed and refined into the incorruptible ideality of art—whence these silent forms, these "unheard" melodies, not meant for the "sensual ear" but for the eye or the soul. Keats's urn exemplifies the victory of the sculptor-god over the god who dances. Or, again, the triumph of light over darkness.

If we now turn back to the first chapter of *Light in August* and reread it through the "Ode on a Grecian Urn," it will appear that both are steeped in the same light and that in both the light source is the sun of a twice mythic Greece. True, the opening scene is to some extent an obverse reflection of the poem's scene of desire: the partners have exhanged roles; from pursued the maiden has become pursuer, and for the time being there is no "bold lover" in sight. Yet again day prevails over night. What night? The primal night associated by all mythologies with the uncanny and terrifying "realm of the Mothers," the dark chaos from which all life springs and to which all life returns. As a pregnant woman, Lena might be expected to have her share in the darkness. Faulkner's *mise en scène*, however, is handled in such a way that darkness almost never reaches her, and she nearly always appears to be flooded with light, from both without and within.[13]

Lena is light, as "Helen was light,"[14] and she is also, according to one of the oldest metaphors of womanhood, an urn, a body-vessel destined to receive man's seed. It is interesting to note that it is precisely in such terms that Hightower, in chapter XX, evokes "*The* woman . . . the Passive and Anonymous whom God had created to be not only the recipient and receptacle of the seed of his body but of his spirit too, which is truth or as near truth as he dare approach" (514–15). Again Keats's ode is close to the textual surface, with its beautiful truth and its truthful beauty. Lena is the emblem or allegory of their union. It is highly significant, though, that for Hightower—and perhaps for Faulkner too—truth comes *to* woman but does not come *from* her: she may represent it to man, embody it as a symbolic figure; she is neither its seeker nor its finder. Only man, as Hightower suggests, carries the spiritual seed capable of transmuting matter and of generating the sublime clarity of beauty and truth.

To the binary oppositions we have detected so far (darkness/light, matter/form, nature/art), we must therefore add that of feminine and masculine, probably the most decisive of all insofar as it points to the deeper meaning of the others and subsumes them in the process of idealization, the wily trick of white magic through which both pastoral landscape and the figure of Lena are produced in the text.

Lena is the woman who casts no shadow, the woman subjected to the law of light, to its measure and order—the Apollonian order of visible forms. Being a maternal figure, she is of necessity related to the earth, yet what determines her import more than anything else is her relationship to light. Lena is the Mother wed to the Sun—*la Mère allée avec le Soleil*, to misquote Rimbaud—and what the mythic wedding amounts to is a tacit reaffirmation of the phallocentric principle of feminine dependence and subordination, a surreptitious way of putting woman back into her place, under the unchallenged sovereignty of the sun-father.

The mother supplies matter; the father inseminates and informs it, gives it a shape and a name, promotes it to a higher order. The idea or, rather, the fantasy is by no means new, and can be found in philosophers such as Plato and Aristotle as well as with the Aranda tribe or the Trobriand Islanders studied by Malinowski.[15] It probably also permeates most male fictions about woman, and *Light in August* is no exception: female characters have to be imaginatively reappropriated and reshaped according to the demands of male desire. A woman cannot be apprehended in her unique, irreducible individuality; she must be made to stand for something else, something larger, so as to be more effectively diminished. Lena is both a real woman (or, to be more specific, a woman plausibly rendered according to the realistic code) and a metaphorical woman, an unmarried pregnant country girl and "the still unravish'd bride of quietness," even as the urn is at once an image of fertility, a symbol of the work of life, and, through Keats's intercession, a paradigm of the work of art. Denied as desiring body and dissociated from the "act of darkness," which would jeopardize her mythic purity, she is, at least in the first pages, a mother *not yet* a mother, still at one with her child: the ideal mother, the mother ideal, the-mother-to-be, suspended out of time, prior to birth and death, a pure mirage of "inwardlighted" stillness and togetherness.

Moments of euphoria are rare in Faulkner. The opening scene of *Light in August* is one of them. From the outset it holds us spellbound, and its spell is the exact reverse of what we experience in reading the first pages of *Sanctuary*: not a dark spell, not the sinister power of an evil eye, but a slow vertigo, a happy languor, in which perhaps something repeats itself of the little child's fascination with its mother, and something, too, of the later fascination of adults with childhood. As Maurice Blanchot argues:

> If our childhood fascinates us, it is because childhood is the age of enchant-ment—an enchanted age—and this golden age seems to be suffused in a wonderful, invisible light. But in fact this light is foreign to visibility, has nothing to make it visible, is no more than a reflection. Doubtless the mother-figure's importance derives from this enchantment. It could even be said that if this figure is so fascinating it is because it first appears while the child still inhabits the reflected light of enchantment and the mother is the essence of such enchant-ment.[16]

Interestingly, Blanchot's evocation of the enchanting mother of childhood calls in turn for the light metaphor, and it is noteworthy that the quoted passage is part of an essay on the specific spell of writing. Could it be that the enchantments of literature all originate in the bright or dark enchantments of childhood and that writing is always an attempt to retrieve the plenitude of the origins by re-membering the resplendent body of the lost, forgotten, and unforgettable mother? "To write," Blanchot contends, "is to accept that solitude where fascination lurks."[17] This is indeed what writing was for Faulkner at his most daring: a solitary venture into the twilight territories of the unknown, a singlehanded confrontation with the alluring and fearful powers arising out of an ever-present and ever-pressing past—a fascination both surrendered to and heroically resisted. For us, his readers, however, there can only be the radiance of words, the spell of a text, the incantations of a book called *Light in August.*

From light to fire

Perhaps one should also note that in the novel itself the enchantment of luminous motherhood is short-lived, that it is only one moment in its unfold-ing, and that even in the first chapter it works only intermittently. The pastoral note is not sustained; as early as the second page the description of an abandoned sawmill and the devastated land around—"a stumppocked scene of profound and peaceful desolation, unplowed, untilled, gutting slowly into red and choked ravines beneath the long quiet rains of autumn and the galloping fury of vernal equinoxes" (4–5)—compromises the harmony of the well-tended garden. Moreover, at the close of the chapter, when Lena's wagon crests the last hill before Jefferson, she sees two columns of smoke on the horizon, one of which arises out of "a clump of trees some distance beyond the town" (32). A house is burning. Light has already turned into devouring fire.

And even Lena will be deprived of her magic aura, briefly but significantly, when she is about to give birth to her child. As Byron runs to the cabin where Lena lies in labor, he still believes that he will be "met by her at the door, placid, unchanged, timeless" (440). But

> Then he passed Mrs Hines in the door and he saw her lying on the cot. He had never seen her in bed before and he believed that when or if he ever did, she would be tense, alert, maybe smiling a little, and completely aware of him. But when he entered she did not even look at him. She did not even seem to be aware that the door had opened, that there was anyone or anything in the room save herself and whatever it was that she had spoken to with that wailing cry in a tongue unknown to man. She was covered to the chin, yet her upper body was raised upon her arms and her head was bent. Her hair was loose and her eyes looked like two holes and her mouth was as bloodless now as the pillow behind her. (441)

The bright screen image has momentarily dissolved. Paradoxically, at the instant when Lena is about to give life, life has deserted her, and it looks as if she has withdrawn into another alien and barely human world, speaking now in "a tongue unknown to man" not unlike that of "the bodiless fecundmellow voices of negro women" (126) in Freedman Town, from which Joe Christmas flees in revulsion and terror. Indeed, with her loose hair, her empty eyes, and her bloodless mouth, Lena has become in turn a disquieting figure of almost monstrous strangeness.[18] One might argue that she only appears as such to Byron Bunch and that for him this is a decisively sobering moment, forcing him at last to acknowledge the harsh laws of reality. Yet, whether he will ever conquer the blindness of his romantic love and recognize Lena as a woman with a mind, a body, and a life of her own remains extremely doubtful.

Faulkner's portrayal of women is a complex issue. His detractors have charged him with blatant misogyny; his defenders transfer the accusation to his male characters, and at first sight it seems indeed fair and reasonable to exempt Faulkner from the prejudices voiced by his sexist heroes. Yet the fact that Lena and nearly all of Faulkner's women are held throughout in a male's gaze and a male's discourse raises serious questions about the "realism" of the portraits. We can of course try to dissociate fact from fantasy, investigate all the social and psychological determinants of Faulkner's women, and in most cases it will appear that they have been less sinning than sinned against. The trouble is, though, that to reach this conclusion we must stand back and betray our first reading experience. For it is precisely to the extent that they are fantasized or mythified that most of his women become compelling characters. And, as we shall see in the next chapter, the sexist stereotypes of his men are often powerfully reinforced by the insidious rhetoric of the narrator.

With Faulkner, more often than not woman turns out to be merely a male self's other, the phantasmal projection of his repressed desires and unacknowledged fears. Only on rare occasions—in Faulkner's rendering of Addie Bundren, for instance—is her otherness acknowledged as the otherness of another's self. Whether praised or disparaged, idolized or demonized, she hardly ever comes into her own, and, arising as they do of the same phantasmagoria, Faulkner's consoling, motherly Eve figures are in the end just as equivocal as his lurid Lilith figures. The celebration of Lena in the role of earth goddess is in fact little more than a precarious rite of exorcism, and the scene of her delivery gives it away. Take off the fair mask of light, and all that is left is the stark enigma of spawning flesh.

XVI

THE CRACKED URNS

> La plume aura toujours déjà trempé dans le
> meurtre de la mère, de la femme, pour écrire
> en noir, au sang noir (comme de l')encre, la
> coagulation de ses droits et plaisirs.
>
> Luce Irigaray

The other women

There are other women in *Light in August*—women of a different otherness,
dark women in dark houses in dark groves, whom the rays of the sunfather
have not yet reached, whom his sovereign light has not yet sublimated.
Women in the shadows, women of and from the night.

Other urns, flawed and foul. On the night when young Christmas learns
that Bobbie Allen, his first mistress, is menstruating, he flees into the phallic
woods:

> He reached the woods and entered, among the hard trunks, the
> branchshadowed quiet, hardfeeling, hardsmelling, invisible. In the notseeing
> and the hardknowing as though in a cave he seemed to see a diminishing row
> of suavely shaped urns in moonlight, blanched. And not one was perfect. Each
> one was cracked and from each crack there issued something liquid, death-
> colored, and foul. He touched a tree, leaning his propped arms against it, seeing
> the ranked and moonlit urns. He vomited. (208–9)

The urn here is still a metaphor of the feminine, but the Greek vase has become
the "unclean vessel" of the Bible. It no longer stands for permanence, wholeness, and integrity; its "suave shape" no longer fulfills its luring purpose; its
imperfection has become visible. The row of urns which Christmas "seems to
see" in the woods is the negative of the Keatsian vase associated with Lena in
the novel's first chapter, even as the place, time, and circumstances of the
spectacle reverse those of the initial scene: daylight, the condition of seeing,
yields to the "notseeing" of night; the fatherly sun gives way to the motherly
moon, the free, open space of the road to the smothering enclosure of the

"cave." As to the urns themselves, the dark secret withheld in their flanks and now leaking from their cracks is no other than the foulness of death.

Learning from a friend about menstruation—"the temporary and abject helplessness of that which tantalised and frustrated desire; the smooth and superior shape in which volition dwelled doomed to be at stated and inescapable intervals victims of periodical filth" (204)—young Christmas was so horrified that he shot a sheep and then "knelt, his hands in the yet warm blood of the dying beast, trembling, drymouthed, backglaring" (204). This time there is no homeopathic cancellation through the ritual slaughter of an animal. Instead of another blood sacrifice, we witness Christmas's nightmarish vision of the cracked urns, which, like Horace's hallucination in *Sanctuary*, objectifies his revulsion from blood, sex, and woman, and ends likewise in vomiting. Menstrual bleeding, to him, can only be a reminder of woman's unhealable "wound," an anguishing confirmation of the deadly menace of female "castration."[1]

What was denied in the fetishized mother of the first chapter returns with a vengeance. Apart from Lena, the one without lack, the solar urn with its smooth fecund flanks, all urns are flawed; apart from her, all women, as Christmas and most of the novel's other males perceive them, appear as wounded and wounding, castrated and castrating, frail and lethal. As if their very femininity were a contagious disease.

This *evil femininity*—what Doc Hines, in his biblical invectives, calls "the divine abomination of womanflesh"—is orchestrated in *Light in August* with unprecedented starkness and stridency, except where Lena stands in her inviolate and inviolable innocence: at the beginning and the ending, on the white margins of the book, at the edges of the black "pit" yawning in its middle.

As Lena, the alibi-woman, the screen-mother, recedes, here comes the other woman, the woman-as-other. Her faces are many, and she appears in various guises in Faulkner's gyneceum: married or single, submissive or rebellious, placid or hysterical, desexed or sex-hungry, they form a disparate gathering in which the downtrodden or neglected wife (Mrs. McEachern, Mrs. Hines, Mrs. Hightower) keeps company with the soured spinster (Joanna Burden) and the vulgar prostitute (Bobbie Allen). But they very much resemble one another in their miseries, are alike in their batteredness. If viewed together and from afar, what strikes one first is their subordinate status in a cultural organization devised by and for men, condemning them to either submit to masculine tyranny or resort to ruse and dissimulation, the traditional weapons of the weak. Indeed, what we are told in the narrative about woman's place and role within the couple, the family, the patriarchal order of southern society, reads like a sad chronicle of humiliation and oppression.[2] To acknowledge this, however, is not to exempt Faulkner from all misogyny, for the representation of women in *Light in August* cannot be reduced to a series of narrative and descriptive statements to be read with cool detachment. To see how it actually works, in the text and on the reader, we must attend to all its rhetorical modalities and try to measure the persuasive power of the resulting effects.

Beneath the fairly realistic description of the plight of women in the novel's "world," we have to trace the inscription of the feminine in its text. Breaking across the boundaries of "character," a signified, both massive and mobile, evanescent and irrepressible, keeps insisting in the text, the signifiers of which are disseminated over the textual surface and combine with others to generate figures and configurations which are so many tropes of femininity. Interweaving the threads of private fantasy and common prejudice, a discourse on femininity unfolds its lexicon and displays its rhetoric, a discourse speaking the feminine in order the better to silence it. Aggressive and regressive, reductive and redundant, it equates, over and over again, woman with female, mother with matrix: *tota mulier in utero* is the axiom by which it is sustained throughout.

Nocturnes

Let us follow Christmas in his descent to Freedman Town, the black district of Jefferson: "On all sides, even within him, the bodiless fecundmellow voices of negro women murmured. It was as though he and all other manshaped life about him had been returned to the lightless hot wet primogenitive Female" (126). The last five words—a capitalized noun and four epithets—are not only an apt epitome of the archaic masculine representation of womanhood underlying the novel; they could almost be viewed as a pool of tropes, or even as the "matrix" of the metaphorical or metonymical operations by which this representation inscribes and reinscribes itself in its text. For references to darkness, heat, wetness—the three physical predicates of the "primogenitive Female"—will recur many times, less as direct qualifiers of women as characters than as rhetorical intensifiers of the feminine.

Luminous Lena is the exception that confirms the rule: femininity, in *Light in August*, is first of all that which partakes of the engulfing darkness of the night, of its risks of confusion and savagery. Not surprisingly, most of the scenes in which Christmas encounters women take place in the dark. As a child of five, at the orphanage, it is behind a curtain, squatting in "the rife, pinkwomansmelling obscurity" (134) of the dietitian's closet, that he gorges himself on her toothpaste and overhears her lovemaking. As an adolescent, it is at dusk, in the darkness of a deserted sawmill shed, that he meets the young black prostitute. Nocturnal, all his dates with Bobbie Allen and the "urn scene" in the woods; nocturnal, his first encounter with Joanna Burden and the sexual frenzy which marks the "second phase" of their affair: "The sewer only ran by night . . . he knew that she was in the house and that the coming of dark within the old walls was breaking down something and leaving it corrupt with waiting" (281–82). Night is the time of disorder, dissolution, defilement, debauchery. With its coming, boundaries blur, prohibitions and inhibitions collapse, releasing wild desires and energies, and Christmas is soon to witness the grotesque and frightening spectacle of Joanna's nymphomania. The nights of the "second phase" give birth to another Joanna locked in fierce combat with the one he knew:

> two creatures that struggled in the one body like two moongleamed shapes struggling drowning in alternate throes upon the surface of a black thick pool beneath the last moon. Now it would be that still, cold, contained figure of the first phase who, even though lost and damned, remained somehow impervious and impregnable; then it would be the other, the second one, who in furious denial of that impregnability strove to drown in the black abyss of its own creating that physical purity which had been preserved too long now even to be lost. Now and then they would come to the black surface, locked like sisters; the black waters would drain away. (286)

Two Joannas, then: one lunar, lunatic, the daughter of darkness, a prey to the furious madness of her sex; the other rigid, cold, contained, the spectral double and foil of her demented "night sister" (288), the Joanna of daylight. But note that the diurnal Joanna is also the masculine Joanna: "And *by day* he would see the calm, coldfaced, almost *manlike*, almost middleaged woman who had lived for twenty years alone, *without any feminine fears at all,* in a lonely house" (283; italics mine). Once again the light/dark and male/female oppositions come to overlap. The day woman, the text suggests, is less of a woman than her night double: it is only in the secret of darkness that Joanna, as she acts out her repressed desires, reveals the true "nature" of her sex.

"Something more than water"

Equally remarkable, in the narrative of the "second phase," is the extensive reuse of the other major attributes of the "primogenitive Female": heat and wetness. Joanna's sexual frenzy is remembered by Christmas as the torrid darkness of Hell itself: "he was at the bottom of a pit in the hot wild darkness" (296). But the darkness is liquid as well: "he began to see himself as from a distance, like a man sucked down into a bottomless morass" (285). Again, as in *The Sound and the Fury* and *As I Lay Dying*, not to mention *Mayday* and "Nympholepsy," water is associated with woman, sex, and death, and perhaps nowhere else in Faulkner does this metaphorical cluster impose itself on the reader as forcefully as in the twelfth chapter of *Light in August*. From the outset, the "second phase" is placed under the sign of the *sewer:* "It was as though he had fallen into a sewer" (281). As for Quentin in *The Sound and the Fury* or Horace in *Sanctuary,* the nightmare of sex materializes as a liquid nausea: the putrid water of the sewer, the stagnant water of the morass, the thick black water of the pool, already prefigured (or echoed in anticipation, if we follow chronology) in the narrative of the twenty-four hours preceding

Joanna's murder: "In the less than halflight he appeared to be watching his body, seeming to watch it turning slow and lascivious in a whispering of gutter filth like a drowned corpse in a thick still black pool of more than water" (117). It is in the same "thick black pool" that Christmas sees Joanna's double body drown. "More than water," less than water: thickened, darkened, viscous, polluted and polluting, a medium and agent of corruption and decomposition, dead and deadly, and at the same time erotic water, in which corpses turn, "slow and lascivious."

The revulsion from thick liquidity is first and foremost a revulsion from the female body, which is phantasmically conceived as soft, fluid, formless matter threatening engulfment and as "matter out of place," as *dirt*. Dirt is earth; earth, fecund and foul, is woman. Dirt is filth, and all filth comes down to "womanfilth," as Doc Hines puts it, the "periodical filth" of menstrual blood, which for Christmas as for other Faulkner males is the visible trace of woman's "curse," the unmistakable sign of her fallen and soiled condition. The "thick still black pool" is indeed "more than water": a metaphor of female blood, a metonymy of female flesh. The circuits of the imaginary have led us once more from the material to the bodily and from the physical to the physiological. In Faulkner's *rhétorique profonde* (to borrow Baudelaire's phrase) there is scarcely a figure that does not turn out to be a figure of the body.

Food

These figures are now drawn in black, in the sticky ink of nausea, now in pink, the suave color of desirable flesh, as they are in the pivotal (and almost too overtly "Freudian") toothpaste scene of the sixth chapter, in which the smooth pink toothpaste gulped down by little Joe is equated with the pink and tender body of the chubby dietitian. But on the chromatic scale of Faulkner's imagination black and pink are hardly antithetical; they complement each other like outside and inside, appearance and truth: while pink is the alluring color of the promised flesh, the deceptive veneer of seduction, black is the color of the female body in its rank secret.

And what applies to colors also applies to substances. To the little orphan the toothpaste is at first something sweet, unctuous, delectable, a surrogate of the maternal milk from which he has been severed since birth and which he absorbs greedily in the "rife, pinkwomansmelling obscurity" (134) of the dietitian's womblike closet. Toothpaste, however, is no nourishment nor even a natural substance. As "the cool invisible worm" (133) coils out of the tube, and as Christmas smears it into his mouth, we almost grow sick with him, the more so because the toothpaste is invested with those tactile qualities of softness and sliminess which in Faulkner, as in Sartre and Céline, invariably suggest feelings of nausea. As object of desire/revulsion and as correlate of the feeding woman (explicitly designated as such in the text), it belongs to the same register of the imaginary as the much more sinister metaphors previously mentioned: the "deathcolored" liquid, seeping from the cracked urns, or the black water of sewers and pools. The sweet, sticky, sickening toothpaste initiates Christmas's first experience of nausea, just as the starkly dreamlike childhood scene, of which it is the derisory emblem, constitutes the originary traumatic event on which his adolescent and adult sexual experiences are patterned.

That the first scene to emerge distinctly in Christmas's memory—memory which "believes before knowing remembers"—is this early scene of his orphaned childhood is of course not fortuitous. While the child, crouching "among the soft womansmelling garments and the shoes" (132), gulped down toothpaste ad nauseam, the dietitian, on the other side of the curtain, was making love with a young intern. Hence the little thief was also, without seeing or understanding, a little voyeur,[3] an involuntary witness to the clandestine copulation of his nurturing mother with an unknown male. And it is by the end of this "primal scene"[4] that his nightmare begins. First reversal, first disaster: the object of desire is no longer desirable, "no longer sweet" (134). As "hands [drag] him violently out of his vomit," he looks "into a face no longer smooth pink-and-white, surrounded now by wild and dishevelled hair whose smooth bands once made him think of candy" (135). The heretofore maternal figure has been metamorphosed into a terrifying Medusa, and at the same instant her accusing, hysterical voice has changed him into a "little nigger bastard" (135). A fatal slippage has occurred: from desire to nausea (from pink to black); from innocence to guilt-ridden anguish (from white to black).

A slippage, a fall, a monstrous second birth: "'Well, here I am'" (134), Christmas says to himself when "it happens." Here he is, the instant and immediately rejected child of a hysterical woman and a faceless father. From that moment on, nothing will be the same again. For the first time Christmas's sense of blackness has been enmeshed with the temptations and terrors of sex. For the first time and forever. Christmas, at this point, has irreversibly entered the memory of his future. The traumatic scene will never stop festering in his mind. Henceforth womanhood, food, and sexuality will be joined with his racial obsession in a single knot of fear, shame, guilt, and resentment. "There was something in him trying to get out, like when he had used to think of toothpaste" (172), we are told as, nine years later, Christmas, now an adolescent, enters the dark shed where he is about to have his first (failed) sexual experience. Indeed, the die is cast, a pattern has been set for his whole sexual career: of his subsequent encounters with women, from his early meeting with a young black prostitute through his affair with Bobbie and his many anonymous promiscuities to his involvement with Joanna, there is scarcely one that does not end in similar fashion with extreme bewilderment and violent repudiation. In one way or another, all of them appear as compulsive reenactments of the primal scene at the orphanage.

During the scene, eating/vomiting and lovemaking take place at the same time in the same setting, separated only by a thin curtain (an accessory of

Faulkner's sex theater already used in *Sanctuary* and also found in his next novel, *Pylon*). Spatial contiguity and temporal coincidence are bound to suggest analogies between the two activities: the double *mise en scène* sets up, symbolically, an equivalence between eating and copulation, mouth and sexual organ or, to put it less anatomically, the oral and the genital.[5]

In *Light in August* the sexual, the feminine, and the alimentary partake throughout of the same ambivalence and are therefore, to a greater degree even than in *Sanctuary*, permutable. Hence the pattern of absorption and rejection, eating and vomiting. Christmas never stops seeking and fleeing the woman-mother who would finally appease that hunger beyond hunger which he has felt since childhood and which keeps harassing him throughout his life until the final moment of peace, just before his surrender, when he "feels dry and light" and realizes with relief that he does not "have to bother about having to eat anymore" (372).

To eat, for Christmas, is to submit to the needs of the body and to acknowledge dependency on woman, and indeed, almost all the women encountered by him are food providers, beginning with the dietitian at the orphanage, the prototype of all the others, whose very designation in the text (Atkins, her family name, is only mentioned twice) bespeaks her nurturing function, and whom the child identifies entirely with the idea and the pleasure of eating:

> The dietitian was nothing to him yet, save a mechanical adjunct to eating, food, the diningroom, the ceremony of eating at the wooden forms, coming now and then into his vision without impacting at all except as something of pleasing association and pleasing in herself to look at—young, a little fullbodied, smooth, pink-and-white, making his mind think of the diningroom, making his mouth think of something sweet and sticky to eat, and also pinkcolored and surreptitious. (132)

As for the next woman to play a major role in Christmas's early years, Mrs. McEachern, the foster-mother, his relationship to her is most memorably illustrated in the scene where she secretly brings him a tray of food after he has been whipped and sent to bed supperless by McEachern. He dumps the food onto the floor in a violent gesture of refusal, but an hour later, he rises from the bed and "above the outraged food kneeling, with his hands [eats], like a savage, like a dog" (171).

Later, at seventeen, he meets Bobbie Allen, his first and perhaps only love, in a dingy backstreet restaurant. Like the dietitian, Bobbie is related to food by her job, and moreover she is also related professionally to sex, since she is not only a waitress but a prostitute. Their relationship—a sad parody of romantic first love—starts with the ordering of a pie and a cup of coffee, and while wooing her, Christmas brings her, one night, "a stale and flyspecked box of candy" (210). Like the toothpaste in the early orphanage scene, candy is "something sweet and sticky to eat," and like the latter, it is metonymically associated with sex: "He watched her come to the bureau and set the box of candy upon it. While he watched, she began to take her clothes off, ripping them off and flinging them down" (215). That night, in exchange for his gift, he enjoys for the first time Bobby's naked body, and during the same night he learns that she is a prostitute. Spoiled sweets, soiled love.

Finally, Christmas's fateful encounter with Joanna results from a quest for food, and his clandestine entry into her house is, significantly, by way of the kitchen: "Then he climbed into the window; he seemed to flow into the dark kitchen: a shadow returning without a sound and without locomotion to the allmother of obscurity and darkness . . . he also seemed to see in the darkness as he moved as unerringly toward the food which he wanted as if he knew where it would be; that, or were being manipulated by an agent which did know. He ate something from an invisible dish, with invisible fingers: invisible food" (252–53). Invisible food is "dark" food, and so twice suspect. The account includes here its own commentary: this is another scene of repetition and return in which Christmas's sure, unerring, and necessary gestures succeed one another as if in a dream. And for once, it would seem, the dream is not a bad one: the darkness is, this time, the darkness of the maternal womb regained. "If it is just food you want," says Joanna, "you'll find that" (254).

Take or be taken

But it is not "just food" that Christmas wants, and this scene is only the first link in a whole chain of events, the beginning of a tragic sequence which will lead him to murder and to his own destruction. In retrospect, the "invisible food" waiting for Christmas in his future lover's kitchen could be seen as a bait, the taking of which will lead to his being taken—in another kitchen, Hightower's, where Percy Grimm later robs him of his genitalia.

Take or be taken: that's the question. When Christmas enters Joanna's house, he is already in the role of thief, and the theft is a prelude to the rape. Now, if Christmas robs or rapes, if he always *takes*, it is for fear that something might be freely *given*. When stealing money from Mrs. McEachern's hoard, he tells her: "I didn't ask you for it. . . . Remember that. I didn't ask, because I was afraid you would give it to me. I just took it. Don't forget that" (230). When Byron Bunch kindly offers to share his meal with him, Christmas, denying his own hunger, answers contemptuously: "I ain't hungry. Keep your muck" (37). Even as he vomits the dietitian's toothpaste and dumps his foster-mother's food, he hurls Joanna's dishes against the wall and curses them as "Woman's muck" (262). Muck is mud or manure; muck stinks. For Christmas, food is excrement, and woman is both. Of course, he is not able to do without food, nor, for that matter, without women. But it is necessary for him to feel that he is taking something by stealth or by force. Christmas can only be a brutal intruder or a thankless parasite. His hosts are his enemies, but the hostility is his. Just try for a second to imagine him sitting at a table breaking bread with others in the sharing of a communal meal, and you will realize that conviviality is not for him.[6]

Christmas would rather fast than feast. Here again everything is already determined in childhood, during the toothpaste scene. And let us recall its singular denouement: after discovering the child hidden behind the curtain, the dietitian, instead of punishing him, tries to buy his silence by offering him a silver dollar. Christmas expected to be whipped, not to be bribed. Her incongruous offer, which he cannot begin to comprehend, leaves him "still with astonishment, shock, outrage" (138), and as he looks at the dollar, he seems "to see ranked tubes of toothpaste like corded wood, endless and terrifying; his whole being coiled in a rich and passionate revulsion. 'I dont want no more,' he said. 'I dont never want no more,' he thought" (138). So here, on the heels of the first, comes a second shock, a second revulsion. The dollar scene repeats and intensifies the trauma of the toothpaste scene. The dollar solidifies, as it were, the toothpaste, and the row of tubes prefigures the row of cracked urns: a multiple nightmare projected on the "endless" succession of days.[7] A new element is added to the network of imaginary equivalences formed by women, food, and dirt: "filthy" money. But if Christmas is once again on the verge of nausea, his reaction this time is less passive, less purely physiological: it shows *astonishment*, which, as we have already seen in *As I Lay Dying*, is in Faulkner the signal of consciousness awakening to the existence of scandal and to the scandal of existence. It also marks the beginning of a deep sense of *outrage*, which rapidly turns into angry revolt. In the first scene, Christmas's nausea was the uncontrolled outcome of a hardly conscious psychosomatic process; in the second, he also responds with his mind and expresses his refusal through words. Without knowing it, Christmas seems to have derived a lesson from the first experience: he has learned to be wary, he is becoming inured. From this point on, he will categorically reject any attempt at seduction by a woman. Rather than accepting what is offered, he will forcibly take what has been refused him, so as not to be taken himself and maintain his aloofness.

Dark houses

Mistrust henceforth rules his conduct with all women and above all with those such as Mrs. McEachern and later the Joanna of the "third phase," who "mean well." Their tortuous benevolence, their insidious softness, their proneness to secrecy and conspiracy seem more threatening to Christmas than the overt and predictable brutality of men:

> It was not the hard work which he hated, nor the punishment and injustice.
> He was used to that before he ever saw either of them. He expected no less, and
> so he was neither outraged nor surprised. It was the woman: that soft kindness
> which he believed himself doomed to be forever victim of and which he hated
> worse than he did the hard and ruthless justice of men. (185)

Christmas thus joins the ranks of Faulkner's fierce misogynists, for whom woman is a permanent threat. Woman means confinement and constriction, mothering means smothering, a condition most eloquently symbolized by the *dark house:* as we know from manuscript evidence, "Dark House" was the title originally chosen for this novel, yet even in its absence it is silently at work in the text.[8] Most houses mentioned in the book appear at night; all the houses known to Christmas, from the orphanage to Joanna's house, are associated with a female presence, and in each instance he ends up by fleeing them—except the last one, Hightower's house, where he finds his ultimate refuge, in death. And without exception, they are all nocturnal: "The house squatted in the moonlight, dark, profound, a little treacherous. It was as though in the moonlight the house had acquired personality: threatful, deceptive" (188). The passage describes the McEacherns' house at the moment when Christmas escapes to meet Bobbie. The house bespeaks threats and treachery—but whose? A little further on, we find out: "Up the dark lane, in the now invisible house, the woman [his foster-mother] now lay asleep, since she had done all she could to make him late" (189).

House, darkness, woman, sleep. The same configuration already appears in chapter V:

> Ahead, rising from out a close mass of trees, he could see one chimney and one gable of the house. The house itself was invisible and dark. No light shown and no sound came from it when he approached and stood beneath the window of the room where she slept. . . . (116)

Dark and disquieting, in the middle of trees (the term used most frequently is *grove*, which is also Lena's last name), Joanna's house, more than any of the others, appears under the ambiguous sign of enticing/threatening femininity. Here is the description of Christmas's long wait in front of it, just before he enters it for the first time:

> The house was now dark; he quit watching it then. He lay in the copse, on his belly on the dark earth. In the copse the darkness was impenetrable; through his shirt and trousers it felt a little chill, close, faintly dank, as if the sun never reached the atmosphere which the copse held. He could feel the neversunned earth strike, slow and receptive, against him through his clothes: groin, hip, belly, breast, forearms. His arms were crossed, his forehead rested upon them, in his nostrils the damp rich odor of the dark and fecund earth. (251)

Darkness, dampness, penetrating odors, the slow palpitation of the "dark and fecund" earth—the text once again calls up the signs of the great terrestrial motherhood. For Christmas, the outcast, this is one of the few moments in his life when he experiences and accepts the immediacy of physical contact with nature, and when his body communes peacefully with the obscure workings of the earth. As the whole scene confirms, this is a short-lived return to maternal darkness, but the mother-house itself remains forbidden, and penetration always implies a breaking-in, a violation, a rape:

> One day he realized that [Joanna] had never invited him inside the house proper. . . . And when he entered the house at night it was as he had entered it that first night; he felt like a thief, a robber, even while he mounted to the bedroom where she waited. Even after a year it was as though he entered by stealth to despoil her virginity each time anew. (257)

If he is no longer lost in the inhospitable immensity of the outside, Christmas does not find in Joanna's house the warmth and safety of the secretly desired shelter. Her house is no doubt an inside, yet it is anything but a home. As long as Joanna is alive, however, Christmas lacks the energy to flee. For although her house never welcomed him, it holds on to him with a magnetic force:

> he was ready to travel one mile or a thousand, wherever the street of the imperceptible corners should choose to run again. Yet when he moved, it was toward the house. It was as though, as soon as he found that his feet intended to go there, that he let go, seemed to float, surrendered, thinking *All right All right* floating, riding across the dust, up to the house. . . . (260)

Joanna's house is the fatal house, the trap set by fate. Christmas can only defend himself against his preordained destiny by seeing it through and accomplishing a double gesture of destruction: killing Joanna and setting fire to her house.

This house symbolism is related to another recurrent metaphor of lethal femininity: the *pit*.[9] Drawing Christmas to it like a beckoning chasm, Joanna's house eventually comes to stand for the vertigo of the yawning void, the irresistible fascination with the all-absorbing abyss, the very matrix of abjection. As an adolescent, when, in the darkness of the shed, he approached the young black prostitute, he already "seemed to look down into a black well and at the bottom saw two glints like reflections of dead stars" (172). Sex and terror, abyss and vertigo. Christmas will be seized by the same horror and terror during his liaison with Joanna on those bacchanalian nights when the foul "sewer" waters flow. At these moments, he senses the formidable attraction of the abyss and feels sucked down into a bottomless morass. This nightmare of engulfment haunts Christmas up to the eve of his crime and, in the text, it reappears revealingly in the account of his descent into the black section of Jefferson:

> As from the bottom of a black pit he saw himself enclosed by cabin shapes . . . as if the black life, the black breathing had compounded the substance of breath so that not only voices but moving bodies and light itself must become fluid and accrete slowly from particle to particle, of and with the now ponderable night inseparable and one. (125–26)

To Christmas the experience is that of a *regressus ad uterum*, a return to the womb-tomb of "the lightless hot wet primogenitive Female" (128), twice symbolic in that the "black pit" is the place where sexual phobias and racial terrors come together.

The scene in Freedman Town ends with Christmas running up the hill, "out of the black hollow" to "the cold hard air of white people" (126). But he does not escape the abyss. Several days before his death, when the manhunt begins, it seems to Christmas that he can "see himself being hunted by white men at last into the black abyss which had been waiting, trying, for thirty years to drown him and into which now and at last he [has] actually entered, bearing now upon his ankles the definite and ineradicable gauge of its upward moving" (364). Christmas anticipates his own death as a drowning in deep darkness. But the *black* abyss now stands out in sharp contrast to *white* men, as a metaphor of race. However, in the previous occurrences of the trope, the racial was already discernible beneath the sexual, and, as we have just seen, in the Freedman Town scene, the two meanings impose themselves with equal force. The metaphor, at this point, is the more compelling for coming to the reader—at least to the attentive reader—already charged with the memory of its prior contexts and hence invested with the meanings that these contexts have imprinted on it. So we read it quite "naturally" as a double metaphor: of sex and of race. And also, at the end of the novel, as a figure of *destiny*, the metaphor of an inescapable circular journey: from a cursed birth to a cruel death—from one abyss to the other.

From woman to woman: in *Light in August*, as in most of Faulkner's other novels, woman speaks the origin and the end. She remains close to doorways, watches over thresholds, at entrances as well as exits. Is this not precisely Lena's place and role in the novel?

Three figures, two faces

Christmas's flights ironically cancel themselves by circling back to where they began. He begins by fleeing the world of women for the world of men; after a "brief respite," he must escape "back into it to remain until the hour of his death" (133). A return of and to the same? Not quite. For as the end approaches, the feminine is divested of all that made it so disturbingly ambiguous, and the only fascination that remains is the pure fascination with death.

Genitrix, mate, destroyer: it is in these three roles that Freud evoked woman in "The Theme of the Three Caskets."[10] It is also in this triple function that she appears in *Light in August*. When Christmas goes looking for food in Joanna's house, he is in search of the nursing Mother. He first finds a mate, a mistress, if not a wife, and later a smothering mother; it is in her house that his destiny is sealed, that death awaits him at the bottom of the "black pit." Even though she is herself a victim, Joanna is another of Faulkner's *femmes fatales*: because of her, Christmas must die.

Lena, too, is fatal, though not at all lethal: fatal to Byron Bunch, who, falling madly in love with her the first time he sees her, is drawn out of the dullness of his bachelor's routines, and fatal, as if by ricochet, to Hightower, whose friend's transformation transforms him in his turn. Thus, both Joanna and Lena act as Destiny's messengers. But whereas Joanna brings suffering and death, Lena gives life or occasions rebirth. If the former is Atropos, the inexorable, the third of the Parcae, the latter plays only the first and second of the roles that fall to women; she is first of all the *mother*, which, as we have seen, is her great mythical function, and at the end of the novel she becomes the *mate* when, as she resumes her journey, she is joined by Byron Bunch. But perhaps this is saying too much, for if these are indeed Lena's roles, she does not entirely fill them. Everything occurs as if she were always one part behind: in the first chapter, where the signs of her pregnancy multiply, she is *not yet* literally a mother, and in the epilogue, when we see her resisting Byron's timid advances, she is *not yet* a man's companion. In one sense, she remains to the end the "still unravish'd bride of quietness," and if she represents a fertile Eros, most of the time she does so in such an ideal way that—as on Keats's urn—the settling of payments to real life always seems to get deferred.

In the symbolic pairing of Lena and Joanna, one recognizes once again two halves of the same old myth. Their antithetical and complementary relation-hip in the novel's pattern refers us once again back to the gesture of division, which, since Faulkner's beginnings as a novelist, has been the hallmark of his representation of the feminine. Lena and Joanna are opposites like day and night, sun and moon: one is wise, the other mad; one is fertile, the other barren. Womb and tomb, refuge and abyss, Eve and Lilith, once again. While Lena is a gratifying image of the good mother, Joanna is a terrifying image of the bad one. Both have their iconographic referents: for Lena, it is the Virgin and Child, the reassuring *Madonna col bambino*, as Western painting and sculpture have celebrated her since the thirteenth century; for Joanna, the devouring and castrating woman, it is the head of Medusa—"She would be wild then, in the close, breathing halfdark without walls, with her wild hair, each strand of which would seem to come alive like octopus tentacles" (285)—an emblem the more appropriate as it refers to a woman punished with monstrousness for a forbidden sexual encounter.

The Virgin Mother, classical icon of fetishized or sublimated maternity, and Medusa, standard symbol of castration:[11] it is nearly always between these imaginary poles that the magnetic field of Faulknerian femininity unfolds.

We must refrain, however, from attempting to void the novel of its uncer-tainties and ambiguities. If it is true that the image of woman is split and mythicized along the lines of readily recognizable and long-established dichotomies, on closer inspection the contrasts turn out to be less clear-cut than they appeared to be, and the play of signifiers in the text—to what extent intended, in what measure unconscious?—gives rise to suggestions or rather countersuggestions calling the whole pattern into question. Let me signal one minor but particularly revealing example. The rhetoric woven around Lena tends to present her as a wholly positive figure: pregnancy notwithstanding, her relationship to sex is presented as distant, and to death she seems to have none at all. It is perhaps not entirely irrelevant, however, to point out that the word *grove* occurs many times in the novel in contexts invariably involving sex or death,[12] nor is it indifferent that it is in the vicinity of the oak grove surrounding Joanna Burden's house that Joanna is slain and Lena gives birth to her child. Lena's last name is thus charged, laterally, with connotations which might seem inappropriate to the character as such. Are we to infer that even Lena does not escape the mark of sex and death? Must every woman's name have its share of shadows? *Lena Grave?*

XVII

THE PERILS OF PURITY

> Who can say, I have made my heart clean,
> I am pure from my sin?
>
> Proverbs

> Gardez-vous de la pureté: c'est le vitriol de
> l'âme.
>
> Michel Tournier

From feminine to masculine

What the discourse on the feminine conveys is the *negative*, that which the positive affirmation of the masculine subject rises from and rises against. The feminine code is but the masculine code turned inside out, or rather outside in—its secret, shameful *other*.

In the scene of the failed sexual initiation recounted in chapter VII, Christmas, after furiously kicking at the black prostitute, fights with the other boys: "There was no She at all now. They just fought; it was as if a wind had blown among them, hard and clean" (173). What the "hard and clean" wind blows away is the *odore di femmina* and the smell of the "nigger," the nauseating emanations of the "womanshenegro." Elsewhere, in chapter XII, it is the memory and promise of "the street lonely, savage, and cool" (285) that counterbalances Christmas's terror of the female abyss. It is as if by removing just one element from the feminine "set" and replacing it by its masculine counterpart, one could successfully neutralize its charge of negativity. Consider the description of the night scene with Christmas standing before Joanna's house in chapter V:

> The dark air breathed upon him, breathed smoothly as the garment slipped down his legs, the cool mouth of darkness, the soft cool tongue. Moving again, he could feel the dark air like water; he could feel the dew under his feet as he had never felt dew before. (118)

It is dark, the air is liquid—and thus a feminine milieu—but the dewy grass is *cool*, and it would seem that this is enough to exorcise the darkness and restore water to its cleansing function. Purification is precisely at issue here: this is the last night before the murder; Christmas has just been cursing Joanna "with slow and calculated obscenity" (117) and he now cuts off with his pocket knife the last button that she had sewn on his undergarment, stripping off his clothes to expose his naked body to the cool night. These ritual gestures reveal, as Maurice Edgar Coindreau has noted, "a desire for purification. . . through a most intimate contact with the redeeming nature,"[1] but it is important to note that the preliminaries to the purification rite are the rejection of a woman and the denial of any debt to her. By cutting off his buttons (round objects like the silver dollar which he refused to accept from the dietitian), Christmas erases the marks of his dependency on Joanna (or, to put it another way, cuts the umbilical cord chaining him to another surrogate Mother), and if one considers the crime soon to follow, his gesture is also a rehearsal of the murder. The button is cut off with a *knife* as Joanna's throat will be slit with a *razor* (and as, later, Christmas will be castrated with a knife): the symbolic violence of the private ritual foreshadows the actual violence of the murder. What follows is the rare moment of peace when Christmas can "feel the dew under his feet as he [has] never felt the dew before." As in the earlier scene where he is lying in the grass in front of Joanna's house and feels the earth striking through his clothes, there is here again something like intimacy between his body and nature, a nature which is itself evoked sensuously, almost sensually, like a living organic body, but a body deprived of its animal heat, with a "cool mouth" and a "soft cool tongue." As so often with Faulkner (and with many other American writers), the repudiation of woman entails an almost instantaneous assent to a resexualized nature. It is precisely after Christmas has broken off all his relations with women that he has the feeling of being close to the earth, as if the removal of the "bad object" immediately allowed him a guilt-free relation to the retrieved "good object." Christmas at this point deludes himself into thinking that in stripping everything that attaches him to their world he has rid himself at last of women. He would like to be as naked and innocent as on the day he was born, but his desire has in effect only changed its object; unbeknown to him, it has shifted to the third and last "figure," death, and Christmas's devious path from the extinction of impure desire to the desire for death within purity at last regained is not unlike the route followed by Quentin in *The Sound and the Fury*.

The pure and the impure

Purity as such escapes precise definition but we can trace it through a number of "objective correlatives." Its texture: a rocklike hardness. Its weather: cool and dry. Its favorite elements: air and fire. Its color: a virginal white. Its space: a closed-in, clean, well-lighted place. No women and no blacks allowed.

Whether they are suicidal young men (Bayard Sartoris, Quentin Compson, David Levine), passive dreamers (Horace Benbow, Hightower, Harry Wilbourne), nostalgic primitivists (Isaac McCaslin), or raging rebels (Joe Christmas), most of Faulkner's male characters demonstrate the same yearning for purity. Indeed, purity is one of the essential values of masculinity in the novelist's puritan world.[2] Many men die for it; none can live by it. For purity is a property always already lost and never retrieved. As Vladimir Jankélévitch has pointed out, "No one can assert about himself, at this very minute: 'I am pure,' *purus sum.*"[3] Purity cannot exist in the first person and the present tense, within and for consciousness, nor is it to be found at any time in the teeming outer world. Like virginity in Mr. Compson's definition, it is "a negative state," an abstract ideal condition retrospectively inferred from the tangible process of its corruption.

The affirmation of purity is nothing but the denial of the impure. What comes first is an obsession with dirt, a phobia of defilement, and in Faulkner the climactic moment in the search for purity is never its attainment but the shattering revelation of its failure through nausea, the revulsion produced by utter disgust. For that which is denied is of course not thereby removed and is the less removable as it turns out to be coextensive with the entire world of experience. Life's kitchen is messy and smelly; it is anything but a clean, well-lighted place. Nothing is therefore more disturbing to Faulkner's squeamish idealists than the gross organs and gross appetites of living flesh, and the supreme threats to purity are the carnal presence of woman with her enveloping sexuality and that of the black male in what is assumed to be his rank animality.

The desire for purity is a desire for pure desire, or, as Hightower puts it, for "virginal" desire, the ideal object of which would be a fleshless and sexless body, a glassy essence out of time, a transparent form gleaming in the cold abstract perfection of the as yet uncreated. It is an impossible desire for an impossible object, and its inflexible logic leads it to *demand* the impossible, to want reality closed out and unreality made real. We have seen this logic at work in the suicidal courses of Bayard Sartoris and Quentin Compson. The motivating force behind it is soured nostalgia and vindictive resentment, and where it takes over, violence is never far away. For purity can be restored only through purgation, and purgation can be achieved only by way of subtraction and destruction. Violence is its sole weapon, death its last recourse. Since he cannot have what he wants, the fanatical purist always ends by destroying either himself or those he holds in his power, taking revenge on life by calling for the *tabula rasa* of death: the incorruptible purity of nonlife, the aseptic void of nonbeing.

Indeed, beginning with Sir Galwyn of *Mayday*, nearly all of Faulkner's idealists (before the "positive" heroes of his late fiction) turn into knights of nothingness. Christmas is one of them, although his marginal status does not allow him to cultivate his idealism as romantically as the young patricians Quentin Compson and Bayard Sartoris and the ex-minister Hightower do. Purity is already what he attempts to restore after his first outraged discovery of the uncleanliness of the other sex, when he tries to wash away the stain of menstrual blood with the blood of a slaughtered sheep. The day before the murder, the same desire leads him to strip off his clothes in the cool of the night, to go to the deserted stables to breathe in the smell of the horses ("It's because they are not women. Even a mare horse is a kind of man," 119) and to shave himself near a spring (which recalls Quentin's careful toilette before his suicide). Characteristically, the ritual cleansing is related in both cases to women and to death. However, whereas in the slaughtering of the sheep purification and sacrifice were one, the second purification rite is a prelude to the sacrifice, the intended murder of Joanna, which, as Christmas well knows, will have to be paid for by his own death. It is with these two impending deaths in mind that he purifies himself. Because of the shadow cast on his present by his inescapable future, he is being granted a few moments of peace such as he has never known before. Reflecting upon his miserable life, he comes to realize that it was peace which he had been seeking all along: "*All I wanted was peace*" (123), he thinks despairingly before he kills Joanna. This reflection will be echoed in his thoughts when, after the ordeal of the descent into Freedman Town, he finds himself again among whites: "'That's all I wanted,' he thought. 'That dont seem like a whole lot to ask'" (127). And several days after the murder, having tried to evade his pursuers for an entire week, exhausted by lack of food and sleep, he thinks again about all that he has been missing:

> It is just dawn, daylight: that gray and lonely suspension filled with the peaceful and tentative waking of birds. The air, inbreathed, is like spring water. He breathes deep and slow, feeling with each breath himself diffuse in the neutral grayness, becoming one with loneliness and quiet that has never known fury and despair. 'That was all I wanted,' he thinks, in a quiet and slow amazement. 'That was all, for thirty years. That didn't seem to be a whole lot to ask in thirty years.' (364)

This scene is almost a replica of the scene in chapter V when Christmas exposed himself to the darkness: it is dawn again, the air cool and limpid like spring water, and once again Christmas acquiesces in the nature from which he has held himself, almost all his life, so rigidly apart and becomes for a brief moment one with its deep calm. Paradoxically, it is during his last week, when he comes to the point at which he no longer needs to eat and sleep and even loses his awareness of time, and when he realizes the futility of flight and the ineluctability of death, that he finds at long last "peace and unhaste and quiet" (372).

Peace, for Faulkner's males, is never a natural condition, as it is for Lena Grove; nor is it ever achieved through the deliberate pursuit of inner balance. More often than not it is a welcome yet unexpected release from tension and turbulence, a euphoric sense of exhaustion that comes when all violence has been spent, and the deepest peace always comes on the threshold of death. To young Christmas it would come after he had suffered physical violence, in the aftermath of McEachern's whippings or the beating taken from Bobbie's friends; later, he experiences it in anticipation of violence to come, as when he is about to kill Joanna or after the murder, during the few days before his arrest, but he is never as serene as in his last moments, as he lies bleeding and dying on Hightower's kitchen floor. His is of course an extreme case, but it is noteworthy that Byron likewise feels peaceful after having been beaten by Burch (485). Violence is in Faulkner's world a shortcut to peace, and peace, a return to quiescence, is what nearly all the male heroes of his early and middle period—from Donald Mahon to Bayard Sartoris to Horace Benbow to Quentin Compson to Darl Bundren to Christmas to Harry Wilbourne to Isaac Mc-Caslin—are desperately seeking.

"I just wanted peace" (341), Hightower says, as Horace said before him in *Sanctuary*, and he thinks that his "martyrdom" has bought him immunity. While Christmas only finds true peace at the end of his life journey, as a brief respite on his way to death, Hightower chose immobility over movement, contemplation over commitment, death over life, and did so from the very start. He did not join the seminary and become a minister out of devotion to the Church; his "vocation" was to find a sanctuary for his life-denying, safety-seeking self:

> He believed with a calm joy that if ever there was shelter, it would be the Church; that if ever truth could walk naked and without shame or fear, it would be in the seminary. When he believed that he had heard the call it seemed to him that he could see his future, his life, intact on all sides complete and inviolable, like a classic and serene vase, where the spirit could be born anew sheltered from the harsh gale of living and die so, peacefully, with only the far sound of the circumvented wind, with scarce even a handful of rotting dust to be disposed of. That was what the word seminary meant: quiet and safe walls within which the hampered and garmentworried spirit could learn anew serenity to con-template without horror or alarm its own nakedness. (527–28)

Following the urn evoked in chapter I and the cracked urns "seen" by Christmas in chapter VIII, here the urn serves as a metaphor for the ideal future dreamed by young Hightower. Like the former, it is associated with peace and serenity; like the latter, it is conceived of as a receptacle. This time, however, the receptacle, instead of being flawed, is a perfect tabernacle, a holy temple of the spirit that is to become the place of a second birth, immaterial and immaculate, owing no debt to woman: a rebirth of the *spirit* or *truth* (for Hightower the two are indistinguishable), restored to the disembodied purity of its origins and therefore capable of gazing upon its "nakedness" without shame or fear.

While Hightower's reverie of disincarnation might be related to the Platonist or Gnostic tradition, it obviously owes next to nothing to Christianity, and with the "classic and serene vase"—a triple metaphor for the Church, the seminary, and "sheltered" life—we have come back to Keats's ode. But in Hightower's anemic version, Keatsian idealism has been reduced to futile aestheticism and is at best the noble alibi of a gaudy dream.

Like Bayard Sartoris, Hightower is haunted by a legendary past of heroic follies and fascinated by a monumentalized kinsman, but he has condensed them into one dazzling vision of daredevilry and death—a vision rerun every night, like a cherished movie, the images following one another in the same predictable order—and is content with waiting, at sundown, for his grandfather's galloping cavalry to thunder past. As a character, Hightower stands exactly at the intersection of Faulkner's two youthful temptations: the heroic and the aesthetic. His relationship to the idealized dead double is no longer, as it still was with Bayard Sartoris, a process of active identification and appropriation: there is no challenge left to take up, no manhood to be tested, no actual death to reenact. The repetition compulsion has been internalized to such a point that it can only occur in the hallucinatory mode, through the recurrence of a phantasmal vision that is apparently gratifying— did not Hightower sacrifice everything for it?—and becomes its own end and excuse.

Here the conjuring away of the real to the benefit of the imaginary reaches its extreme limit: everything takes place on a mental screen of daydream and pseudo memory. And the contrast between the dreamer and his dreamed double is indeed startling: what better foil could we find for the gallant horseman, the splendid centaur amid "the wild bugles and the clashing sabres and the dying thunder of hooves" (544), than Hightower, the fat, flabby, unwashed recluse, sitting at his window and waiting every night for the resurrection of a dead epic romance? There is a secret tie, though, between the hero and his worshiper: their shared scorn for ordinary life if not for life as such. What the first one sought through defiant arrogance in the face of death, the second seeks in the closed private space of his phantom theater: an "apotheosis," the magical ascension to a timeless realm of "truth" and "beauty" where the spirit would be free of the flesh. If heroic action and aesthetic contemplation are two different modes of existence, their ultimate purposes are not far apart. Moreover, as Faulkner began to discover in writing *Flags in the Dust*, there is already an unmistakable touch of aestheticism in heroism itself and one of exhibitionism in the desire to end with a flourish or, as the French say, *en beauté*. With Hightower, however, the heroic impulse turns totally inward. Although he still subscribes to the manly ideal of the heroic deed, he no longer adopts it as a model of behavior. Haunted by nostalgia for the perfect *act* but unable to venture into the world and translate his desire into action, Hightower withdraws into the idealness of the ideal and transmutes his dream into a visionary object for rapt contemplation until it becomes "that fine shape of eternal youth and virginal desire which makes heroes" (533).

Idealism in Faulkner appears in various guises, not all of which are so disastrous in their effects. Byron, for instance, might be considered a "good" idealist, yet what makes him a positive figure is precisely his capacity to outgrow the naive romantic assumptions with which he started. In essence idealism is hostile to life, and each time it stakes its exorbitant claims to rule over life, it can only bring destruction and death. And while the more reckless court and often receive a violent death, the Hightowers follow the slower route of death-in-life and suffer their voluptuous martyrdom in the limbo of fantasy and memory. Having grown up among three "phantoms" (his invalid mother, his remote father, and the old black woman who told him stories) and a "ghost" (the dead grandfather), Hightower, like Quentin in *The Sound and the Fury*, has in turn become "a shadowy figure among shadows, paradoxical " (537). Born at the wrong time, "about thirty years after the only day he seemed to have ever lived in—that day when his grandfather was shot from the galloping horse" (66), he "had already died one night twenty years before [he] saw light" (527). Hightower has turned away from the world and sacrificed his own life so that his grandfather may live and die again. As a result, his present as well as his future can be conjugated only in the passive voice and in the past tense. Outside the past there is nothing for him but empty time, dead time, in which nothing ever happens, "as though the seed which his grandfather had transmitted to him had been on the horse too that night and had been killed too and time had stopped there and then for the seed and nothing had happened in time since, not even him" (69).

Blindings

Hightower, the stillborn, who has lost his place in the chain of the generations, is the victim of his own idealism. He is not, however, its only casualty. Its second victim is his wife, and she dies of it in the most sordid of circumstances. As in Faulkner's other novels, from *The Sound and the Fury* to *Go Down, Moses*, the idealist's relation to woman in *Light in August* is a stumbling block and touchstone; it is that which puts idealism to the test. It is true that in the novel's narrative present Hightower does not deal with women except in the end when he delivers Lena's baby, but his general comments on the other sex are among the most damning to be found in the book: "There have been good women who were martyrs to brutes, in their cups and such. But what woman, good or bad, has ever suffered from any brute as men have suffered from good women?" (347). Hightower repeatedly maligns women in order to dissuade Byron from fulfilling his amorous plans, and in his own life he has been too self-absorbed ever to pay heed to a woman's needs. As he himself comes to recognize in chapter XX, his wife rapidly became a stranger to him; he told her about "the depth of [his] hunger" but let her know at the same time that "never and never would she have any part in the assuaging of it" (538).

Only through misunderstanding could a woman intrude into Hightower's sheltered life. To protect himself from the hazards of love, young Hightower armed himself in advance with a lofty love "ideal," which, like Don Quixote and Emma Bovary, he had found in a book, and at his first meeting with his future wife, he "believed at once that she was beautiful, because he had heard of her before he ever saw her and when he did see her he did not see her at all because of the face which he had already created in his mind" (528–29). In the same way, when he came to Jefferson, it was "to forward [his] own desire" (538), and his congregation was as invisible to him as his bride had been: "I came here where faces full of bafflement and hunger and eagerness waited for me, waiting to believe; I did not see them. Where hands were raised for what they believed that I could bring them; I did not see them" (538). Here one catches idealism at its persistent work of obfuscation: Hightower fails his congregation as he fails his wife because he is not even able to acknowledge their existence. For idealists like him, it is never a question of coping with real people in a real world but of either subjecting them to prewritten scripts or ignoring them altogether. Idealism is a *blinding* force, in both senses of the word: blinding the beholder and blinding at the same time the object of the gaze as one would blind a window. In his stubborn refusal to see others as other and to accept them as such, the idealist drains relationships of all mutuality. The other can only be the mirror of his dreams, the instrument of his will, or the target of his hatred. What we are told about the first encounter of Hightower and his wife-to-be could be easily extended to other encounters. Hines, McEachern, Joanna, Grimm, and Christmas are indeed afflicted with the same disease: "because of the face which they have already created in their minds," they are unable to see the face in front of them. Their eyes, often described as both empty and staring, are organs not of perception but of projection. Solipsistic self-blinding is of course not an accidental weakness of the Faulknerian idealist: denial, as we have seen, is his first impulse, the founding moment of idealism, just as it is the founding moment of fetishism.

Hightower is therefore able to believe in love as long as it continues to be a seductive fiction, a beautiful empty form. Marriage, on the other hand, less amenable to idealization, does not seem to him at any time to be desirable: "to him it was not men and women in sanctified and living physical intimacy, but a dead state carried over into and existing still among the living like two shadows chained together with the shadow of a chain" (529). As it gives shape and substance to the imaginary, Hightower's idealism hollows out and devalues the real. Marriage, to him, can be a nothing but a perfunctory pairing of dead shadows. To his wife, however, its shadowiness became devastatingly real as it took her from despair to abjection, from abjection to a sordid death. Later, but too late, when the hour of truth has come, Hightower will plead guilty, recognizing at last that his monstruous indifference had led his wife to disgrace and suicide: "at that moment I became her seducer and her murderer, author and instrument of her shame and death" (462).

From angel to beast

In *Light in August* three women die victims of men's blind and blinding madness: Hightower's wife rejected, debased, and sacrificed on the altar of a dream; Milly, the unmarried mother, literally bled to death by Hines's fanaticism; and finally Joanna, whose throat has been slit by Christmas in expiation for a guilty passion. All three deaths can be laid at the feet of male idealism and its ravaging misogyny. Joanna's case, however, deserves closer attention insofar as she herself endorses masculine standards, thus contributing to her own ruin as well as Christmas's. When Christmas first meets her, she is a mannish spinster, a virago with angular features, tough and inflexible, with a man's muscles and voice as well as a man's mental habits; she is masculine even in the struggle of the rape scene: "There was no feminine vacillation, no coyness of obvious desire and intention to succumb at last. It was as if he struggled physically with another man for an object of no actual value to either, and for which they struggled on principle alone" (258). At this point Joanna's behavior seems so unwomanly that the following day Christmas has the feeling that "what memory of less than twelve hours knew to be true could never have happened" (258), and he wonders who raped whom: "'My God,' he thought, 'it was like I was the woman and she was the man'" (258).

Christmas is dumbfounded by Joanna's harsh determination. As she has fought loyally and accepted her defeat in accordance with men's rules of battle, there has been no real rape—just violence but no real violation. Even in the face of renewed assaults the fortress remains impregnable :

> Even after a year it was as though he entered by stealth to despoil her virginity each time anew. It was as though each turn of dark saw him faced again with the necessity to despoil again that which he had already despoiled—or never had and never would. (257)

Joanna cannot be conquered and possessed. She is so fiercely entrenched in the sanctuary of her virginity that defloration does not seem to make any difference. From the first night on, making love to her becomes a kind of Poesque necrophilia: "beneath his hands the body might have been the body of a dead woman not yet stiffened" (259). Before the "second phase" sets in, Joanna lets herself be taken without letting herself go, inviolable beyond violation. Ironically, in her own way, very different from Lena's, she is also a "still unravish'd bride." But even more significant is her adamant refusal to learn from and to be altered by what happens to her; like all of Faulkner's idealists, she is, or thinks she is, "impervious" to experience. In this respect she belongs undeniably with the more rigid of Faulkner's males: her mental inadaptability and moral inviolability are close to what is called elsewhere (in *Absalom, Absalom!*, for instance, apropos of Thomas Sutpen) "innocence," a preeminently masculine attribute, and the exact opposite of that innate knowledge of and spontaneous complicity with life, that rich store of experience always already available and prior to any real experience, which, in Faulkner's fiction, is the presumed prerogative of woman.

This innocence may be fractured, but it can never be completely destroyed. The masculine Joanna of the first period survives in the second and clearly has the upper hand in the third. In her own way, Joanna follows one of the idealist's classical paths: she does not pass from innocence to experience but from prim purity to abject corruption, and within her corruption purity persists like a hard pebble buried in slime:

> Now it would be that still, cold, contained figure of the first phase who, even though lost and damned, remained somehow impervious and impregnable; then it would be the other, the second one, who in furious denial of that impregnability strove to drown in the black abyss of its own creating that physical purity which had been preserved too long now even to be lost. (286)

For the intransigent idealist, confrontation with reality either ends in horrified withdrawal into some "sanctuary" or becomes a hellish journey into abjection, madness, or death. With Joanna the fascination for the pure reverses itself characteristically into an intoxication with the corrupt. Everything that has been denied and repressed then irresistibly returns and submerges her like a mud slide, as she passes from harsh abstinence to the most unrestrained lust:

> Now and then she appointed trysts beneath certain shrubs above the grounds, where he would find her naked, or with her clothing half torn to ribbons upon her, in the wild throes of nymphomania, her body gleaming in the slow shifting from one to another of such formally erotic attitudes and gestures as a Beardsley of the time of Petronius might have drawn. (285)

On the face of it, Joanna's frantic behavior is nothing but the late eruption of a libido too long repressed by the stiff corset of puritanism. Once within puritanism's grasp, however, one does not leave:

> At first it shocked him: the abject fury of the New England glacier exposed suddenly to the fire of the New England biblical hell. Perhaps he was aware of the abnegation in it: the imperious and fierce urgency that concealed an actual despair at frustrate and irrevocable years, which she appeared to compensate each night as if she believed that it would be the last night on earth by damning herself forever to the hell of her forefathers, by living not alone in sin but in filth. She had an avidity for the forbidden wordsymbols; an insatiable appetite for the sound of them on his tongue and on her own. She revealed the terrible and impersonal curiosity of a child about forbidden subjects and objects; that rapt and tireless and detached interest of a surgeon in the physical body and its possibilities. (283)

The strong emphasis on the *forbidden* clearly indicates that prohibition has become so erotically charged for Joanna that its transgression can no longer be resisted. Yet once broken, the taboo keeps haunting her guilt-ridden consciousness and she plunges body and soul into sexual frenzy, with a keen and almost exultant awareness of her sin and the absolute certainty of her damnation. Moreover, her "avidity for the forbidden wordsymbols" and her "formally erotic attitudes and gestures" are telling evidence of Joanna's need to *speak* and *stage* her sin (a need not unlike Addie's during her adulterous affair in *As I Lay Dying*), as if speech and theatrics were required to make it real and significant. Filth is filth only if it is named; sin is a role to be played. Hence the necessity of turning fornication into a series of "faultlessly played scenes" (289). "The obscene," as Gilles Deleuze has pointed out, "is not the intrusion of the body into language but their common reflection."[4] The spectacle of the obscene is intended for Christmas, the "nigger" whom Joanna chose for a partner and whose outraged eyes reflect and confirm her own abasement; but it is first and foremost for herself: as she is watching herself being watched, she is both actress and witness, exhibitionist and voyeuse (why do we hesitate to make this word feminine?), torturess and martyr—a perverse, sadomasochistic couple bound together in a single body. Her sexual vertigo by no means cancels self-division. Joanna does not give herself, nor does she thirst for orgiastic *jouissance*. Her body is no more *her own* in debauchery than it was in chastity, and that she explores its "possibilities" with "the terrible and impersonal curiosity of a *child*" suggests the replay of a "primal scene" in which she at once acts as excited impersonator and watches as bewildered witness.

What this doubling or splitting once again brings to light is both Joanna's psychic immaturity and her—acquired, not innate—bisexuality. Her flesh is adult female flesh, but the eye she casts over the show is both a child's and a man's eye: to Joanna as to Christmas the discovery of the "black abyss" is the supreme horror.

Qui fait l'ange, fait la bête. The angel plays, in the end, the beast, but it is a beast only *in the eye* of the beholding angel. And we all know this angel's gender.

The exterminating angel

Joanna for a time plays the beast. But the angel wins out over the beast, and during the final phase of their relationship, Christmas discovers her other face, "a face cold, remote, and fanatic" (294). Joanna has regained her self-control, and when Christmas "in a kind of baffled desperation" wants to touch her (gently, it seems: even Christmas has his almost affectionate moments[5]), she repels his hand "with the calm firmness of a man" (294). She has by then rejoined the men's camp, and her new face, the cold mask of fanaticism, could be that of McEachern, of Doc Hines, or of Percy Grimm. Having renounced all sexuality, denied all femininity, she becomes once again her Fathers' docile daughter, the inheritor of their order and values, and the unquestioning executor of their last wills, and so turns again into a prim do-gooder. Enjoining Christmas in turn to make a show of submission, she asks him to *kneel down,* to pray at her side, and to accept publicly his black identity—a demand the more unacceptable to Christmas as it is an almost verbatim repetition of McEachern's injunctions when he was a boy. For Joanna, it is a question of expiation as well as submission, and death now appears to her as the inescapable conclusion to their guilty affair: "Maybe it would be better if we both were dead" (305), she says to Christmas after one of their last violent confrontations. And later, after having unsuccessfully implored him to join her in prayer, she comes to acknowledge the fact that death is by now for both the only possible way out:

> "Then there's just one other thing to do."
> "There's just one other thing to do," he said.
> 'So now it's all done, all finished,' he thought quietly, sitting in the dense shadow of the shrubbery, hearing the last stroke of the far clock cease and die away. (308)

The time has come indeed to settle the scores. Time to kill and time to die. Joanna dies by the hand of Christmas, who slits her throat,[6] Christmas by the hand of Percy Grimm, who castrates him. Double murder, double suicide: Joanna longed for death and Christmas knows her death will have to be paid for by his own. And from decapitation to castration the gesture that cuts is repeated over and over. Death works with a sharp blade, a razor or a knife, fast, efficient, flawless, cutting off as neatly and precisely as a surgeon's scalpel would a gangrenous limb. The point, in effect, is to cleanse, to eradicate evil, to restore purity and reestablish law and order, and the fact that the two victims of these sacrificial murders are a white woman and a putatively black man is of course no coincidence.

Joanna's murder is something of a matricide but also something of a parricide insofar as she has become the reincarnation of repressive paternal authority. However, what is regarded as the supreme, inexpiable violation of the southern law serves the social system and will reinforce its racist order. Christmas killed Joanna because she wanted him to become a reformable "nigger." But killing her is a public admission that he is an unreformable one. To kill a white woman, for Christmas, is to acknowledge his "black blood." Hence it is also to appoint himself unwittingly to fulfill the ritual function of scapegoat. From this point onward, all the conditions are met for the ceremony of his execution, "the symbolic murder of darkness by light."[7] A new victory, then, of the "light in August," but no longer the light that shone in chapter I, Lena's "lambent" light; the soft radiance of motherhood has turned into the savage glare of the avenging sun in which Christmas's handcuffs glint in the last minutes before his death. As for Grimm, Christmas's pursuer, killer, and castrater, his face then reveals "that serene, unearthly luminousness of angels in church windows" (510).

Christmas is now the beast to be slaughtered, and Grimm appears on the scene as the exterminating angel, the angel of light with a butcher knife, sent out by the invisible "Player" to punish the murderer and avenge his victim.

Through Christmas's scapegoating racial purity is restored, white supremacy reaffirmed; through his emasculation the danger that hung over southern ladyhood is warded off. At least until the next time.

It has been argued that "Grimm's action does not commit the community,"[8] and his social representativeness can of course be questioned. Faulkner himself saw in him a proto-Nazi, a prefiguration of Hitler's storm troopers, but he added that this type of man was not very common in the South nor anywhere else.[9] Yet if the novel underscores Grimm's alienation from the community, his initiatives after Christmas's arrest, though opposed by the sheriff, are not rejected by his fellow citizens: "without knowing that they were thinking it," the narrator tells us, "the town had suddenly accepted Grimm with respect and perhaps a little awe and a deal of actual faith and confidence, as though somehow his vision and patriotism and pride in the town, the occasion, had been quicker and truer than theirs" (504). Joanna's murder and the need to punish the murderer in an exemplary way provide Grimm with the long-awaited opportunity to emerge from anonymity and to gain at last public recognition—not by defying the law but by becoming its living embodiment, and it is worth noting that in the beginning he only wants to ensure that Christmas is properly tried and hanged: "We must let the law take its course. The law, the nation. It is the right of no civilian to sentence a man to death. And we, the soldiers in Jefferson, are the ones to see to that" (498). Grimm, then, sees himself, not as an adept of random violence but as a vigilant patriot and staunch defender of his community's values, armed with "a sublime and implicit faith in physical courage and blind obedience, and a belief that the white race is superior to any and all other races and that the American is superior to all other white races and that the American uniform is superior to all men, and that all that would ever be required of him in payment for this belief, this privilege, would be his own life" (498). Yet once Christmas has broken away and tries to escape, Grimm feels that order can no longer be restored in the orderly way and that he must therefore take the law into his hands. Ironically, his very love of obedience leads him to indiscipline, his very respect for the law compels him to hunt down Christmas like an animal.

Like McLendon, the leader of the lynching party in "Dry September,"[10] Grimm is a dutiful criminal, a pure-hearted killer, the more ruthless as he possesses the absolute certainty that he represents Good in its never-ending crusade against Evil. His heroic task may be dirty work, but he performs it without flinching, with the jubilant dedication of a "young priest" (512). The killing has nothing to do with a settling of scores; Grimm's abstract idols leave no room for private conscience and individual emotion, so that there is "nothing vengeful about him either, no fury, no outrage" (509). A mindless and cold-blooded little monster, one of those angelical robots from whom totalitarian ideologies have always recruited their heroes and their martyrs, Grimm is Faulkner's portrait of the idealist as a "Fascist galahad."[11]

In his fanatic racism Grimm is of course very much like Hines (one stands for racism in its patriotic and paramilitary version, the other for its religious, fundamentalist variant), and yet far deeper affinities unite him to the meek Hightower. One is a brooding quietist, the other a self-righteous activist, but the army is to Grimm what the Church was to the young Hightower: a sanctuary, a refuge of purity, an antilife institution. And World War I is for the former what the Civil War was for the latter. Both are latecomers, feeling like History's orphans and dreaming of an heroic era gone by. More intriguingly, Grimm's short biography in chapter XIX brings to mind the sense of belatedness and frustration associated with Faulkner's own youth, for Faulkner too was "too young to have been in the European War," and he too was thought to be "just lazy and in a fair way to become perfectly worthless, when in reality [he] was suffering the terrible tragedy of having been born not alone too late but not late enough to have escaped first hand knowledge of the lost time when he should have been a man instead of a child" (496–97).[12] After Julian Lowe, the young "cadet" in *Soldiers' Pay*, Grimm, the young frustrated warrior and would-be hero, is clearly another retrospective self-portrait in miniature, yet its much harsher irony shows how far Faulkner has come from the glorious dreams of his youth. Indeed, all that is left of them in *Light in August* is Hightower's derisory celebration of a henhouse raider and the gruesome exploit of Grimm, a knight in uniform whose horse is a bicycle and whose sword is a butcher knife. In their utter estrangement from reality and their grotesque dedication to abstractions, these quixotic figures could almost be comical. Yet we are not allowed to forget that a woman pays for Hightower's fantasies with her life and that a man dies a dreadful death at the hands of Percival the Sinister, the ignoble knight of white supremacy. The logic of idealism is always the same, and the purer the idealism, the more devastation it leaves in its wake.

XVIII

THE FATHERS

> ... alle Religionen sind auf dem untersten
> Grunde Systeme von Grausamkeiten.
>
> Friedrich Nietzsche

Strangers in Jefferson

As has often been pointed out, none of the main characters of *Light in August* belongs to Jefferson.[1] Hightower and Joanna have both been relegated to the margins of the city. Around the apostate minister, the community has drawn the successive circles of scandal, reproval, and rejection, and a similar ostracism has struck the negrophile daughter of carpetbaggers. As to Christmas and Lena, no matter how much they differ from each other, they are likewise strangers, and both are essentially nomads, people on the move: for Lena, Jefferson is just a brief stopover; for Christmas a long halt after many years of wandering. Even minor characters such as Lucas Burch, Doc Hines, and Percy Grimm are figures on the fringe, and Byron Bunch himself is considered by his fellow citizens to be a harmless eccentric.[2]

Outsiders, outcasts, Ishmaels. Christmas has been called "the most solitary character in American fiction,"[3] and he is perhaps also the most American of solitary heroes in Western fiction. "The essential American soul," wrote D. H. Lawrence, "is hard, isolate, stoic, and a killer."[4] The definition holds for Christmas, who claims his solitude with a savage pride, and we need only compare him to Büchner's Woyzeck, his European brother in humiliation, to realize how much defiance there is in his isolation. Lena, although her solitude is anything but loneliness, is, like Christmas, an orphan; and even if she is destined to have eventually a family of her own, in the novel she is only a pregnant girl in search of a father for her child. The lack of familial ties can also be observed in the other characters: Hightower is a childless widower, Joanna a spinster, Byron a bachelor, and Lucas Burch and Percy Grimm likewise single. Not that the family is entirely missing from the novel: in his flashbacks, the narrator provides a good deal of information on Hightower's and Joanna's parents and ancestors; the point, however, is that the family is kept in the backgound and seldom intervenes directly in the present action. In *Light in August* the familial institution does not act as a mediating agency between the characters and their social environment as it does in most of Faulkner's earlier and later books. It is as if Faulkner had seen to it that in this novel individuals are directly confronted with society at large.

The title of Cleanth Brooks's classic study of *Light in August* aptly summarizes its central division: "The Community and the Pariah."[5] And Brooks is equally right to call attention to the specific nature of the milieu in which the destinies of its characters are acted out: not a modern urban setting but a traditional rural society, such as could still be found in the Deep South of the twenties and thirties—a society or, to use Brooks's term, a "community," a tightly knit social organization, with something like an "organic" character, whose stability is guaranteed by unanimous acceptance of inherited values and unquestioning compliance with established cultural codes. Brooks, however, is not content with underscoring the community's pull and power; he celebrates it as a "positive norm,"[6] the ideal standard by which all individual actions ought to be judged. The causes for Christmas's or Joanna's sufferings are then not far to seek: if both lead miserable lives and die violent deaths, it is essentially because, in departing from the social roles prescribed to them, they have forfeited their right to membership in the community. Conversely, if both Hightower and Byron Bunch are eventually "redeemed," it is because they have found their way back into the communal fold. In his reading of the novel Brooks refers several times to the characters' state of "alienation," but he never seriously considers the possibility that alienation might originate, at least partially, in some flaw of the social fabric itself. To him the outsiders and outcasts of *Light in August* are primarily deviants, and his assumptions about deviance are those which have been held by conservative social thinkers from Plato to Parsons: deviance proceeds from anomie, i.e., lawlessness, a lack of temperance and restraint, a collapse of personal morality.[7] Which is to say that, whatever the circumstances may be, conformity is right, rebellion wrong: in the last resort the wretched of the earth have only themselves to blame for their wretchedness.

There is little in Faulkner's novel, however, to warrant such a reading. Admittedly, a good man is not too hard to find, and not all outsiders are brutally rejected by the community. Thus, although Lena has transgressed its sexual code, everybody, even the outraged Mrs. Armstid, takes her in and treats her with charity. But the benevolence accorded to the unmarried pregnant girl should not make one forget Hightower's beating up by the Ku Klux Klan or Christmas's murder and mutilation by Percy Grimm. Extremist groups such as the KKK and fanatic individuals such as Grimm may not be typical; still, they do the community's dirty work and act as the unofficial agents of collective violence. Technically, the assassination of Christmas is perhaps no "lynching,"[8] but it is condoned beforehand by the mob hysteria which sets in as soon as it is rumored that a white woman has been murdered by a "nigger":

So the hatless men, who had deserted counters and desks, swung down, even including the one who ground the siren. They came too and were shown several different places where the sheet had lain, and some of them with pistols already in their pockets began to canvass about for someone to crucify. (316)

The community, then, to put it mildly, cannot be exonerated of all guilt. Even if it seems to disavow its self-appointed defenders and avengers, it supports their misdeeds by its cowardice and sanctions them by its consenting silence.

In *Light in August,* as in most of Faulkner's novels, the individual and the collective are inextricably entangled. No one, not even the outsider, is outside society; and not only are we all within society, but no sooner are we born and given a name than society is *within us* and starts to shape our minds and lives.

Blood(s) and shadows

Hence any conflict with society is bound to become a war on two fronts: the enemy is both without and within. Christmas's destiny is a case in point. The conflict he is engaged in is at once an open contest with the community and a psychomachia, a long fierce struggle of self against self, and it is one of the novel's supreme ironies that the origin of this dual conflict lies not at all in actual racial difference but in fantasies—both public and private—about race. Christmas is not a black man pitted against the white community; he probably is not even a mulatto. There is no factual evidence for his mixed blood: his being partly black is sheer conjecture, and it should be remembered that the first person to conceive the hypothesis and to convert it into a certainty is Doc Hines, the rabid racist who happens to be Christmas's grandfather.[9] Christmas's cruel secret is the unresolved riddle of his birth. His is, according to Faulkner himself, "the most tragic condition a man could find himself in—not to know what he is and to know that he will never know."[10] He does not know, but he often thinks he knows; he believes because he has been made to believe.[11] As a child, at the Memphis orphanage, he became aware of himself as an object of contempt and hatred through the other children's taunting voices, the dietitian's invectives, and above all Hines's watchful gaze.[12] Under more favorable circumstances, discovering himself different might have been a normal stage in the individuation process, perhaps even a positive step toward autonomy; for Christmas, though, it marked the beginning of his schizoid sense of himself as self-estranged and foreboded a future of isolation, alienation, and fragmentation. And once the judgment passed upon him by hostile others had been internalized, he would never stop loathing himself, consumed both by the white racist's hatred of the "nigger" and the black man's hatred of his white oppressor.

To have an identity: to be one; to have two identities: to be no one. Christmas is a walking oxymoron and its negation: both white and black, and *neither.* He might choose, he could "pass," yet he chooses not to choose, refuses to settle for either of the ready-made identity patterns urged upon him by southern society. Were he able to merge or transcend them, he could achieve a self beyond race truly his own, but the feat cannot be accomplished and the dice are loaded anyway. So all he can do is cling to his refusal, persevere in his no-saying, affirm what is left of his humanity and freedom through repudiation and revolt.[13]

In delving into the depths of Christmas's memory, Faulkner enables the reader to trace his tragedy back to its origin in childhood and youth. *Light in August*, however, though largely focused on the ravages of racism in an individual psyche, does not leave its public dimension out of account. Christmas's journey into darkness starts in an orphanage under the petrifying stare of a paranoid grandfather, and when it reaches its final stage, there is once again an evil eye, but this time it is the collective eye of the lynch mob gathered around Joanna's burning house: "It was as if all their individual five senses had become *one organ of looking*, like an apotheosis" (319; italics mine). Between the "ordinary" racism of the white community, most often latent but easily reactivated in times of tension, and the virulent, never-abating racism of fanatics like Hines or Grimm, the difference is at best one of degree, and little is needed to cancel the difference. Racism in Jefferson is a chronic and endemic disease, to the contagion of which no one, whether white or black, is totally immune.

Yet just as Christmas's split self has been generated by an old man's manic suspicion, racism rests on nothing but preconceptions and misconceptions and draws its power from a shared fiction. In the course of his erratic career Christmas is victimized by various people, but all of his victimizers pay allegiance to the same myths, and Christmas, the victim, is himself trapped within them. It could hardly be otherwise: he has been educated entirely by white people; the only standards which have ever been available to him are white standards. Race hatred was instilled into him by his grandfather; McEachern, his foster-father, taught him the harsh virtues of white Protestant manhood and a solid contempt for women. Their teaching has made him what he is: a racist, a sexist, and a puritan. Mentally and emotionally, he is indeed a white southern male—or would be, did he not believe himself to be tainted with blackness.

What makes Christmas's position untenable is that he feels simultaneously imprisoned in and excluded from his white fathers' value system. However stubborn his desire to refuse, however heroic his will to resist, his entire being is caught in the social machinery, and at the end, inexorably, as in Kafka's *Penal Colony*, the death sentence will be inscribed on the prisoner's flesh. As Christmas himself comes to realize toward the close of his desperate search/flight, he has never been able to break out of the "circle" of his predetermined fate, and even his death is a false exit, since his crime—the slaying of a white woman—and its punishment—his being killed and castrated—provide the long-awaited opportunity to coerce him into a recognizable identity and make him play a repertoried role: in death, as scapegoat,

Christmas has at last become of service to the community. And through the sacrificial magic of atonement, he has at last become *one*.

It is through the very paradox of his predicament that Christmas develops in the novel into a highly emblematic figure. Not that he typifies in any way the South in social or ethnic terms. But his eccentricity takes us to the very core of the southern experience. Christmas is anything but representative of the South, yet in his single and singular fate he embodies its ambiguities and contradictions, acts out its conflicts, exemplifies in almost allegorical fashion the principle of division which holds it together and threatens to tear it apart.

In much the same way Joanna Burden, for all her New England antecedents, is more southern than Yankee—not because she is a typical southern woman but because she allows Faulkner to highlight some of the recesses of the southern mind.[14] Besides, Joe and Joanna, already twinned by their first names, are very much alike. Whereas Joe has known neither of his parents, Joanna bows under the "burden" of a family tradition, but they share an abiding obsession with race, transmitted to them at a very early age and closely associated with the indelible memory of a father, a grandfather, or both. These figures are in turn surprisingly similar. Though alleged to be from New England, Joanna's grandfather Calvin is in his theological fanaticism a worthy match for Doc Hines: both regard the black man as the accursed of God and the emblem of white man's guilt; the abolitionist's militant negrophilia and the white supremacist's demented negrophobia are antithetical rationalizations of the same racist delirium. Furthermore, if Joe's father, according to rumor, might have been a Mexican, Joanna has been named after Juana, her father's first Mexican wife, who looked exactly like Evangeline, her father's French Huguenot mother. In the chronicle of the Burdens, as recounted by Joanna to Joe in the middle of chapter XI, these women and their progeny are evoked as if they belonged to another race, and the physical contrast between Calvin and his son Nathaniel is heavily emphasized: "the tall, gaunt, Nordic man, and the small, dark, vivid child who had inherited his mother's build and coloring, like people of two different races" (266). Even more revealing are Calvin's outraged remarks when he sees Juana's son for the first time: "'Another damn black Burden,' he said. 'Folks will think I bred to a damn slave and now she's got to breed to one too'. . . . 'Damn, low built black folks: low built because of the weight of the wrath of God, black because of the size of human bondage staining their blood and flesh'" (272). Prurient puritans, the male Burdens were obviously attracted to "dark" ladies and beset with the exotic sin of miscegenation. No wonder then that Joanna, their female descendant, should repeat the pattern in reverse in becoming the mistress of a man whom she believes to be a mulatto and who may remind her—incestuously?—of her half-Mexican half-brother, shot at age twenty "by an ex-slaveholder and Confederate soldier named Sartoris, over a question of negro voting" (273).

Like Joe's, Joanna's initiation into evil took place in early childhood. According to her own testimony, she was (re)born into guilt on the day her father took her to the grave of her grandfather and her half-brother to invest her with the curse of the white race:

> Remember this. Your grandfather and brother are lying there, murdered not by one white man but by the curse which God put on a whole race before your grandfather or your brother or me or you were even thought of. A race doomed and cursed to be forever and ever a part of the white race's doom and curse for its sins. Remember that. His doom and his curse. Forever and ever. Mine. Your mother's. Yours, even though you are a child. The curse of every white child that ever was born and that ever will be born. None can escape it. (278)

Speeches are acts; words inflict wounds. At once testament, verdict, and prophecy, the paternal pronouncement is irrevocable; it marks Joanna forever. There could hardly be a better illustration of the performative power of language: the father's words have conjured up a solid world of division and guilt, and for Joanna their magic is to last to the very end, their evil enchantment will never be dispelled:

> I had seen and known negroes since I could remember. I just looked at them as I did at rain, or furniture, or food or sleep. But after that I seemed to see them for the first time not as people, but as a thing, the shadow in which I lived, we lived, all white people, all other people. I thought of all the children coming forever and ever into the world, white, with the black shadow already falling upon them before they drew breath. And I seemed to see the black shadow in the shape of a cross. And it seemed like the white babies were struggling, even before they drew breath, to escape from the shadow that was not only upon them but beneath them too, flung out, as if they were nailed to the cross. I saw all the little babies that would ever be in the world, the ones not yet even born—a long line of them with their arms spread, on the black crosses. (278)

The father's *speech* is followed immediately by the daughter's bleak *vision* of universal and endless agony. But ironically, the crucified child is first of all Joanna herself, nailed by her own father to the cross of a triple identity, a triple filiation. Through the baptismal rite on the ancestral grave she has forever lost her innocence and entered at once the family line, the white southern community, and the communion of the damned, her fate sealed once and for all by the unappealable decree of three blended voices: the actual, living voice of her father, the posthumous voice of her grandfather and, lending absolute authority to both, the remote overvoice of the heavenly Father.

The Father—especially the Dead Father—is always the one who names, separates, places, marks, and casts the spell, whether through his voice or his eyes.[15] Like so many of Faulkner's doomed characters, both Joanna and Joe testify in their ultimate helplessness to the Father's irresistible power, and the identity impressed upon the former is hardly more viable than the latter's nonidentity: fractured and fraught with guilt from the start, marked out for

suffering and disaster. Joanna will never escape from the "black shadow," nor
will Joe ever cease to perceive himself through the hate-filled eyes of a white.
There is nothing metaphysical or theological about Faulknerian predestina-
tion: it is all a matter of evil utterances and evil eyes, of human, all too human
predictions and previsions.

Sex and race

Joe's and Joanna's encounter is the fortuitous but fatal collision of two lives
under the same curse, the same paternal *malediction,* and their affair the
inevitable working out of two complementary self-destructive designs. By the
end of their stormy relationship Joe has become for Joanna the "shadow" and
the "cross"; for Joe, Joanna ends up as an ominous reincarnation of his first
persecutor, "cold, dead, white, fanatical, mad" (304). The time is ripe then for
their final confrontation; the process of mutual annihilation is now to come to
its predictable end. When Joanna, recalling her father's speech and identifying
with her fathers' will, starts to "pray over" Joe and insists on confining him
within his mythic "Negro" identity, Joe has no other course left to him than
to kill her. Even in the earlier "sewer" phase, however, when she was in "the
wild throes of nymphomania," Joanna would call him "Negro! Negro!
Negro!" (285). Race and sex are at stake in their liaison from first to last, as
they have been in Joe's life since his traumatic toothpaste experience. As an
adult, he cannot make love to a white woman without telling her about his
black blood, and after his disastrous experience with Bobbie the idea of a white
woman consenting to sleep with a black man is as unbearable to him as to any
white racist. It takes two policemen to prevent him from killing a white
prostitute for her indifference to his blackness, and her attitude upsets him so
deeply that after the incident he stays "sick for two years" (248). Conversely,
having chosen to live "as man and wife with a woman who resembled an
ebony carving," he is unable to share her bed without "his whole being
[writhing] and [straining] with physical outrage and spiritual denial" (248).
At each encounter, sexual difference is exacerbated by (presumed) racial
difference. Always the antagonist, Joe feels black with a white woman and
white with a black one. Sexual intercourse is to him twice cursed and twice
tabooed, and so experienced each time as a monstrous mating, a kind of
reciprocal rape bound to end in either nausea or murderous fury.

In Yoknapatawpha County sexism and racism go hand in hand. Luminous
Lena notwithstanding, Woman and "Negro" alike appear throughout most of
Light in August as carriers of strangeness and disorder, as uncanny, menacing
figures of radical otherness. They appear as such to the white-male characters
in the novel, and unless in our reading we choose to resist the images conjured
up in our minds, this is also how they are likely to affect us. *Light in August* is
indeed a tale of "darkness."[16] Its haunting rhetoric of corruption, with its

Hawthornian light-dark imagery and its rich array of liquid metaphors (pools, pits, sewers, swamps, morasses), invariably refers back to the *other race* or the *other sex* or both and suggests over and over again the disquieting closeness of an abysmal blackness in which both are secret sharers. The supreme horror, the ultimate abomination is therefore the "womanshenegro" (172): blackness at its thickest and foulest, blackness with a vengeance.

Nowhere in the novel is this phantasmal equivalence of femininity and negritude as flagrant as in the scene at Freedmen Town recounted at the end of chapter V, just before the long retrospective sequence opening the next one. Christmas's nocturnal visit to the Negro section of Jefferson is his descent into Hell, an apposite recapitulative *mise en abyme* of his whole life as well as a prefiguration of his imminent death. Darkness here has conquered everything and everybody. Even light has been absorbed into the opaque and fluid substance of the night, and for Christmas the night, filled with "the bodiless fecundmellow voices of negro women" (126), turns into a nightmare, the nightmare of "the lightless hot primogenitive Female" (126), which threatens to engulf his precarious manhood.

Yet the dark pit, from which he soon flees in revulsion and terror, is described as a place of teeming fertility, and the voices he hears there are the mellow murmuring voices of primal motherhood. But to Christmas the (m)other's tongue is an alien idiom, "a language not his" (125), which he cannot and will not understand and listen to, because it speaks the unspeakable, the "other" without a name. Like all male characters in the novel, Christmas fears and hates the raw powers of life embodied by the "primogenitive Female": life is only bearable to the extent that it is "manshaped" (126).

Life at its enigmatic source is disorderly, random, unpredictable. Hence the male strategies of containment, division, and control and the establishment of a repressive, male-made, and male-centered social order founded on the subjection of women to men and blacks to whites. Hence also the need for an ideology—or a mythology—capable of investing this social order with a measure of legitimacy. In *Light in August* the most vociferous spokesman of racist and sexist ideology is Doc Hines, yet nearly everybody subscribes to its basic tenets: only the white man can claim the dignity and privileges of sovereign humanity; he alone is entitled to lay down the law. Women and blacks, the dangerous representatives of that which exceeds and negates all representation, are assigned to an inferior essence, quite "naturally" destined to occupy subordinate positions in the social structure.

Such is the dominant discourse, and Faulkner allows us to measure its effects, to see how it works, how it warps, and how it kills. Count the corpses: Milly Hines bled to death by her own father, Hightower's wife driven to suicide, Joanna slain and beheaded, Christmas shot and emasculated—three women and one "nigger." Their tragic deaths are eloquent testimony to the murderous violence of southern ideology; yet, as we have already seen, its everyday ravages, though less visible and more insidious, are no less appalling: crippled minds, split selves, destruction from within. Christmas is no doubt the most exemplary case of self-division and self-laceration, but just as he wavers between his racial identities, so Joanna switches back and forth between her sexual identities. At the beginning of their affair, Christmas is impressed by, perhaps even secretly attracted to, her "mantrained muscles" (258), her "mantrained habit of thinking" (258), and deeply perplexed by the "almost manlike yielding of [her] surrender" (257). Even more stubbornly than she resists her outside aggressor, Joanna resists her own femininity, denying her flesh and sex in the very act of surrender, inviolate in violation. As we have seen, even in her second "phase," when yielding to the filth and fury of seemingly naked lust, her mind keeps hovering above the obscene spectacle of the sinning flesh like a horrified voyeur.[17] Her "dual personality" (258) persists, and what she is then seeking is not erotic gratification so much as forbidden knowledge about evil and the unpardonable transgression of the paternal law. In wallowing in sex with a "nigger," she attempts to revenge herself upon her father and grandfather, and her revenge would be complete if Christmas made her pregnant: "A full measure. Even to a negro bastard child. I would like to see father's and Calvin's faces" (291–93).

Joanna is at war with her womanhood, and her womanhood is at war with her Fathers. Christmas loathes his "blackness," and his "blackness" resents his "whiteness." For neither can there be acceptance of otherness within self. Subjection or abjection is the only alternative.

Masculine standards, white standards: tracing identical boundaries, serving identical purposes, they are the pillars of the power system, known as the Law, which governs the community, and to which every one of its members is summoned to submit. And woe to the offenders: sooner or later they will be dismembered—not only ostracized but broken apart, body and soul.

Puritan asceticism

For once the hackneyed phrase "dominant ideology" seems perfectly appropriate. Southern ideology, however, has yet another, more official component: puritanism,[18] ideological discourse at its most articulate and most intimidating, the common idiom by means of which the community defines and vindicates its priorities and whose authority is the more undisputed as it is assumed to be derived from divine transcendence itself. Indeed, whenever racist or sexist prejudice is spelled out, as it is by Hines, McEachern, and Joanna's father and grandfather, the rhetoric assumes at once the harshly prophetic accents of Old Testament eloquence, and the final justification for any belief or behavior is nearly always theological. The rantings of backwoods fanatics like Hines can of course be readily dismissed as crude travesties of true Christianity and even as debased versions of its Calvinistic variant. The point, however, is that apart from Gavin Stevens, the lawyer with degrees from Harvard and Heidelberg, Hightower, the renegade Presbyterian minister, and Byron Bunch, Faulkner's triumphant comic rebel (he is the only male in the novel not irremediably locked into his cultural conditioning), no one in Jefferson seems able to express ideas on moral, social, or racial matters outside the framework of ingrained religious concepts. Puritanism imposes itself as an all but exclusive way of thinking and speaking, and insofar as it filters people's thoughts and words, it controls their very lives, netting them in its rigid code of prescriptions and prohibitions, requiring strict observance of its norms, and calling for ruthless punishment whenever the norms are violated. A collective neurosis like all cultures, the puritan culture dramatized in Faulkner's novel originates in and rests upon repression. What sets it apart is that the amount of repression exacted is exceptionally high, the neurosis exceptionally severe. Based on the presumption of man's innate depravity, puritan morality stresses the need to discipline the body and mortify the flesh to ward off temptation. Flesh is filth, sex is sin or, as Hines puts it, "bitchery and abomination" (398). Life, for the puritan, can only be life in death and for death, and to Joanna, the martyr of Calvinism, and Christmas, the puritan *malgré lui*, it is indeed nothing else.

With the exposure and denunciation of puritanism as life-negating, we are of course on fairly familiar ground. *Light in August*, however, goes well beyond the by now commonplace equation of puritanism with sexual repression. For if it leaves us in no doubt about the debilitating effects of the puritan ethos on individuals, it allows us as well to detect the economic uses of repression: it is not simply a matter of subduing and disciplining bodies in order to save souls; the sexual energies deflected from their natural goals are destined to become socially productive through work.

Simon McEachern, Christmas's Presbyterian foster-father, is in this respect the key figure: work is one of the articles of his faith; his is the Protestant "work ethic" in all its rigor but also with its typical sense of ownership. In fact, his relations to other persons are all patterned on those of owner to owned. On arriving at the orphanage, he looks at the five-year-old Joe with "the same stare with which he might have examined a horse or a second hand plow" (156–57) and takes delivery of him as though he were a mere commodity. Once he has adopted him, he treats him like an object to be fashioned at will by its possessor. True, McEachern is also a man of duty, ready to assume responsibility for his possessions, and so pledges himself to take care of the child as he has done so far of his wife, his cattle, and his fields. The adoption, for him, is ruled by a businesslike mutual agreement, and he informs Joe without delay of what he takes to be its terms:

> "You will find food and shelter and the care of Christian people. . . . And the work within your strength that will keep you out of mischief. For I will have you learn soon that the two abominations are sloth and idle thinking, the two virtues are work and the fear of God." (159)

In teaching Joe the Presbyterian catechism, McEachern will do his best—and worst—to beat these virtues into his recalcitrant mind. However, if the boy must be taught the prophylactic virtue of toil, it is equally important for his foster-father that he should be given proper training for his future tasks. Joe is his putative son, after all, who someday will inherit his property. Hence the gift of the heifer, a highly pedagogic gesture intended to teach the boy "the responsibility of possessing, owning, ownership" as well as "foresight and aggrandisement" (179). Yet once again McEachern's pedagogy fails: Joe sells the cow to buy himself a new suit. Had he sold it for a purely financial profit, McEachern claims, he would have forgiven him; what he cannot condone is that Joe has sold it *for his pleasure* or, more precisely, for "whoring" (181). The sin is the more unpardonable in that it combines waste with lechery. Sexual morality and economic morality are the two sides of the same coin: to McEachern as to all puritans, gratuitous expenditure and instant sensuous gratification are anathema; work, thrift, the pursuit of profit, and the accumulation of wealth are approved of as intrinsically virtuous. Renounce the pleasures of the flesh, work hard, and get rich *ad majorem Dei gloriam:* such are the major commandments of McEachern's religion, which owes at least as much to Benjamin Franklin as to Calvin.

Sober manners, stern self-control, coldness in interpersonal relations, devotion to work, thrift, and gain—all these features remind one of the "worldly asceticism" which Max Weber regarded as essential to the rise of capitalism.[19] And in this connection one might also note the many hints in the novel at what Weber called the "religious foundations"[20] of Protestant asceticism. In *Light in August* religious imagery is pervasive but never so abundant as in the chilling scenes of Joe's indoctrination by McEachern:

> [The boy] was looking straight ahead, with a rapt, calm expression like a monk in a picture. (164)

> Save for the surplice he might have been a Catholic choir boy, with for nave the looming and shadowy crib. . . . (165)

> Then he returned to the bed, carrying the empty tray as though it were a monstrance and he the bearer, his surplice the cutdown undergarment which had been bought for a man to wear. (170)

> The boy's body might have been wood or stone; a post or a tower upon which the sentient part of him mused like a hermit, contemplative and remote with ecstasy and selfcrucifixion. (175–76)

Hieratic postures, sacerdotal garments: it is as if the stark simplicity of the Presbyterian catechesis were given the lie by the ceremonious formality of Catholic liturgy. The immediate purpose of this imagery is no doubt to underscore the disturbing ritualistic quality of McEachern's and Joe's sadomasochistic relationship, yet there are other characters in the novel who are likened to monks and hermits and thus bring to mind the monastic practices of another age. Once again, Faulkner plays on contrasts and continuities, suggests the permanence, across centuries, of cultural traditions, and points to the recurrence of identical types of behavior. Whatever the differences beween the mystical asceticism of early Christianity and the secular asceticism of puritan America, they both bespeak the same compulsive urge to raise mind above matter and soul above flesh, the same inordinate pride in the guise of humility. Puritan asceticism turns out to be yet another detour and disease of desire. What is repressed returns and takes revenge. Pain changes places with pleasure, and it is in violence, spontaneous or ritualized, individual or collective, that the puritan seeks the "ecstasy" he is forbidden to experience otherwise:

> Pleasure, ecstasy, they cannot seem to bear; their escape from it is in violence, in drinking and fighting and praying; catastrophe too, the violence identical and apparently inescapable. *And so why should not their religion drive them to crucifixion of themselves and one another?* (405)

In Hightower's thoughts—which one would be tempted to suspect if they did not seem to have the narrator's approval[21]—puritanism is explicity accused of being the main cause of violence and suffering. Christ's sacrifice on the cross is no longer associated with the glad tidings of redemption: "crucifixion" has become an ironic paradigm of the torments men inflict upon themselves and on others.

On Sunday evening, at twilight, sitting once again at his window, Hightower is listening to the music that comes to him from the church where he used to preach:

> The organ strains come rich and resonant through the summer night, blended, sonorous, with that quality of abjectness and sublimation, as if the freed voices themselves were assessing the shapes and attitudes of crucifixion, ecstatic, solemn, and profound in gathering volume. Yet even then the music has still a quality stern and implacable, deliberate and without passion so much as immolation, pleading, asking, for not love, not life, forbidding it to others, demanding in sonorous tones death as though death were the boon, like all Protestant music. (404–5)

This is the music we listen to in *Light in August:* a sinister celebration of death inspired by a religion of death. Whether in writing the novel Faulkner intended to indict Christianity or at any rate Protestantism remains debatable. For all we know, he was by no means hostile to the Christian religion, and a judicious appraisal of his fictional treatment of religious matters would obviously require a good deal of circumspection and tact. One can hardly fail to be struck, however, by the fierceness of the attack in the two passages just quoted. Nietzsche at once comes to mind, and the impassioned critique of "ascetic ideals" in his *Genealogy of Morals.*[22] Faulkner a Nietzschean? Certainly not, and yet when writing *Light in August* he was perhaps not far from sharing Nietzsche's assumption that all religions were "at the deepest level systems of cruelties."[23]

Disjunctions, exclusions, closures

Puritanism, sexism, racism. What joins them is obviously more than a vague ideological kinship: a structural homology, an identical functioning.[24]

Each of them generates an order by way of distinctions and disjunctions. Thus puritanism, in accordance with the converging traditions of Christianity and Platonic idealism, reasserts the old dualistic patterns of Western thinking—reality and ideality, matter and spirit, body and soul—and radicalizes them in terms of the Calvinistic division of mankind into the elect and the reprobate. Sexism likewise takes advantage of sexual difference to disjoin masculine from feminine, and racism takes advantage of a difference in skin color to separate white from black. The disjoining is of course anything but neutral. It is a matter of sorting out, of identifying, categorizing, and classifying. Its purpose is the production of a workable taxonomy, which in turn will lead to a mandatory hierarchy of values.

One divides to oppose: ideal versus real, male versus female, white versus black. One term in the binary opposition is always valued over the other. Whereas ideality, masculinity, and whiteness are exalted, their opposites are abased. To divide is to pass judgment, to name the categories of good and evil, to assign them to fixed locations, and to draw between them boundaries not to be crossed. On the good side, *inside,* the clear, clean, orderly space of all that is valuable; on the other, *outside,* the alien, enemy territories of darkness and disorder, the abject kingdom of evil.

To enforce these divisions in society and ensure their maintenance, it is important that they should be guaranteed by solid barriers blocking off all circulation, all communication between what has been ordered to be kept apart. A society founded on rigid divisions and arbitrary exclusions can only be a *closed* society,[25] regulated by immutable taboos and demanding from its members total subjection to its law. Personal identity is anyway never a mere matter of individual preference, but in a closed society there is no choice at all. Identities are defined and distributed according to the prevalent codes: everyone must be tied to a class, a race, a gender. To have a clear-cut identity is a social imperative. *Either/or,* male or female, white or black, elect or nonelect. Above or below.

Small wonder, then, that any sign of ambiguity, any swerve from the straight path of conformity should be interpreted as a potential threat to the established order. Nothing is more detestable or more alarming to such a society than the in-between, the intermingled, the impure—that which blurs its neat fictions and undermines its dogmatic certainties. Characteristically, in the community of Jefferson, all illicit contacts are perceived as contagions, all breaches of rule as defilements, all punishments as purgations, and the threat posed to the community by such figures as Hightower, Joanna, and Christmas is indeed that of their ambiguity. Joanna, the "nigger lover," is not quite a woman, at any rate not a white southern woman (though she becomes a martyr of southern womanhood in the public legend after her death); Hightower, the unfrocked minister suspected both of being a homosexual and of having slept with a black woman, is not quite a man. It is Christmas, however, who provokes the greatest outrage:

> He never acted like either a nigger or a white man. That was it. That was what made the folks so mad. For him to be a murderer and all dressed up and walking the town like he dared them to touch him, when he ought to have been skulking and hiding in the woods, muddy and dirty and running. It was like he never even knew he was a murderer, let alone a nigger too. (386)

These are the comments of the "town" on Christmas's behavior at Mottstown, shortly before his capture. They express amazement, indignation, and a deep sense of malaise. The mere existence of Christmas has suddenly become an unbearable scandal. But what renders it so scandalous is not that he is assumed to be the black rapist and murderer of a white woman; it is rather that everything in him denies that assumption. What makes "the folks so mad" is not the presumed miscegenation, the guilty mixture of black and white blood, but the lack in Christmas of any trace of miscegenation, the visible invisibility of his blackness. This "nigger" is white; the blackness in his whiteness cannot be ascertained. Neither his physical aspect nor his style of behavior conforms to racist stereotypes. Now if a black man can look and act exactly like a white man, if appearances fail to match and confirm essences, whiteness and blackness alike become shady notions, and once the opposition white/black has broken down, the whole social structure threatens to crumble. Christmas is thus a living challenge to the community's elemental norms and categories. Whether on purpose or not, whether knowingly or not, he subverts its either/or logic, calls attention to the fragility of the law, and points to the unacknowledged origin of racism by showing it up as a *cosa mentale*, a mere thing of the mind. This is clearly more truth than a closed society can bear, and to persevere in its closedness, to maintain the distinction between a pure inside and a corrupt outside, it must kill Christmas without further delay.

In *Tristes Tropiques* Claude Lévi-Strauss distinguishes two opposing types of society: *anthropoemic* (from the Greek *emein*, to vomit) and *anthropophagic* (from the Greek *phagein*, to digest).[26] Whereas anthropoemic societies expel their deviants by "vomiting" them into prisons and asylums or putting them to death, anthropophagic societies absorb and "digest" them by assigning a specific function to them within the community. The society portrayed by Faulkner in *Light in August* obviously belongs to the first category, and given the importance of nausea in his fiction, the vomiting metaphor seems particularly relevant. Like Faulkner's many self-tormented idealists, from Horace Benbow to David Levine, this society becomes sick whenever it is confronted with its "others," and it ends up vomiting what it cannot digest. *Intolerance,* in every possible sense, including the medical one.

The meaning of sacrifice

If the gesture of exclusion repeats itself throughout Faulkner's work, however, the account of Christmas's death at the hands of Percy Grimm, the tribal god's avenging angel, suggests more than rejection and retaliation. Indeed, *Light in August* is the first of Faulkner's novels to evoke the execution of an outcast as a sacrificial act. As in all scapegoat ceremonies, a reversal seems to have taken place: from *agos*, a figure of defilement, Christmas has turned into *pharmakos*, a collector of communal guilt and agent of purification, and at the point of death he is transfigured and reborn into myth. The ritual meaning of the murder, then, exceeds that of ostracism; its stakes are higher and far more complex: in killing the sacrificial victim, it is a question not only of driving out a present evil but also of making amends for a past one, of paying off an arrearage. The propitiatory, commemorative, and reparative function of sacrifice is always in reference to a collective guilt felt in relation to the *divinity*. In other words, with the sacrificial rite, we enter into a sacred economy of credit and debt.

In this regard, one will note that in the rhetorical orchestration of the scene in chapter XIX in which Percy Grimm pursues Christmas, the references to the divine "Player," the emphasis on the sun's savage glare, Grimm's assimilation to angel or priest—everything contributes to giving the manhunt the solemn aura of a sacred ceremony. Remarkable too (and already often remarked upon), at the end of the chapter is the singular reversal suggested by the highly rhetorical description of the dying Christmas:

> But the man on the floor had not moved. He just lay there, with his eyes open and empty of everything save consciousness, and with something, a shadow, about his mouth. For a long moment he looked up at them with peaceful and unfathomable and unbearable eyes. Then his face, body, all, seemed to collapse, to fall in upon itself, and from out the slashed garments about his hips and loins the pent black blood seemed to rush like the rush of sparks from a rising rocket; upon that black blast the man seemed to rise soaring into their memories forever and ever. They are not to lose it, in whatever peaceful valleys, beside whatever placid and reassuring streams of old age, in the mirroring faces of whatever children they will contemplate old disasters and newer hopes. It will be there, musing, quiet, steadfast, not fading and not particularly threatful, but of itself alone serene, of itself alone triumphant. Again from the town, deadened a little by the walls, the scream of the siren mounted toward its unbelievable crescendo, passing out of the realm of hearing. (513)

The description is not without its ambiguities, but its most striking feature is the radical reversal it evokes.[27] Prior to this moment, blood was mostly a metaphor of defilement and malediction, but now, all of a sudden, it turns into a radiant sign of glory. Losing its density and opacity, it takes on the lightness of breath and the brilliance of fire and gushes from the mutilated body as if from a fountainhead. A stream of blood, an insolent spurt of life, Christmas's dying evokes paradoxically an ultimate defiance of death, and his annihilation becomes a triumphant ascension. But is this not the central paradox of all sacrifice? As Georges Bataille has noted: "It is the common business of sacrifice to bring life and death into harmony, to give death the upsurge of life, life the momentousness and the vertigo of death opening on to the unknown. Here life is mingled with death, but simultaneously death is a sign of life, a way into the infinite."[28]

Whoever speaks of sacrifice speaks also of the sacred. And the sacred is both the holy and the unholy, the pure and the impure.[29] In ancient Rome, *sacer* was the name given to the criminal expelled from the community. The sacred, then, is not only in the ritual act of sacrifice; the victim, too, is endowed with sacred qualities.[30] Christmas, as Faulkner describes him in his last agony, clearly partakes of this sacredness. At the very moment when he dies to life, he is reborn in death. The same individual who was, during his lifetime, less than a man in the community's eyes, becomes, through his sacrificial death, a superhuman figure. Projected into the heavens of myth and forever fixed in men's memories, the lowest of the low accedes posthumously to the immortality of heroes or saints, if not of gods. At the same time he accedes to the immortality of art: "not fading," Christmas has become in his own turn a figure on the urn, where his triumphant serenity joins that of Lena Grove.

Death and resurrection: convinced that Faulkner drew his inspiration from Frazer's *Golden Bough*, a number of critics have taken pains to establish Christmas's mythical identity. Adonis? Mithra? Osiris? Dionysus? Jesus Christ? One can always ferret out analogies, and Christmas could easily be assimilated to some dying god. But there is little point in making an inventory of parallels if it is only to dissolve everything into the tepid universality of all too predictable archetypes. Whatever Faulkner's indebtedness to Frazer's anthropological bric-a-brac, the only mythology truly relevant to critical inquiry in *Light in August*—as in *The Sound and the Fury*, *Go Down, Moses*, and *A Fable*—is clearly the Christian one. Biblical allusions, notably references to the life and death of Christ, are indeed too numerous, too pronounced, and above all too interrelated to be dismissed as merely ornamental.[31] More than *The Sound and the Fury*, this book can be read, on one level, as a transcription of the Scriptures. But here again one must avoid the easy route of a reductive decoding. As Michel Serres has pointed out, "the elaborate projection of *Light in August* is not simple, cylindrical or conical, as one would say in geometry"; "neither is it a simple inversion."[32] Too many critics believe that their work is done once they have spoken of irony. But if there is irony in the repetition and reversal of a familiar mythic pattern, the irony itself is more complex than has been generally assumed.

As a Christ figure, Christmas appears at once as the inversion of his model and the inversion of this inversion. Blasphemous, ungodly, violent, criminal, he is the Antichrist, whose gospel is one of revolt and hatred, and who sows the seeds of evil and destruction.[33] Nevertheless, in his role as victim, bearing the invisible "cross" of his invisible "black blood," he is also Christ humiliated, persecuted, tortured, and crucified afresh. A double and contradictory figure, therefore: in the same way that he is white *and* black, Christmas is both Christ *and* Antichrist. This does not imply, however, that we should read his ambiguities and contradictions from within a traditional religious framework. Although Faulkner shows great insight into religion as an anthropological donnée, one is struck once again by his strictly secular use of Christian references. Like his later, apparently much less negative Christ figures, Isaac McCaslin in *Go Down, Moses* and the corporal in *A Fable,* Christmas lacks a transcendental dimension. And because nothing is more alien to Faulkner's thought than Christian eschatology, Christmas is at the same time deprived of any transhistorical significance. All Christmas has in common with Christ are the trials of his martyrdom and the ignominy of his death.[34] In this regard, Faulkner's work continues an American tradition that goes back to Trancendentalism: that of a thoroughly humanized Christ, son and brother of man rather than Son of God, exemplary in his stoic suffering and selfless sacrifice but whose Passion is considered as the mythic prototype of an endlessly reenacted human drama, not as the supreme and unique redemptive moment of divine incarnation. It is this image of Christ that casts its shadow on *Light in August*: neither the Messiah nor Christ the King, but the "man of sorrows," the universal paradigm of all human agonies. Christmas's story, however, is not just an allegory of *innocence* crucified, as, for instance, Billy Budd's appears to be (at least on the face of it) in Melville's tale. Though their deaths and their posthumous destinies as legendary figures are evoked in similar terms, Christmas lacks the Adamlike purity of Melville's hero. Christmas is guilty *and* innocent—guilty for what he does, innocent for what he endures. Faulkner's Christ, at least in this novel, is a *tragic* one.

The debt to the Father

It remains to be seen how this version of the Christian myth relates to the novel's sexual and racial theme. Unlike Christ's, Christmas's death is a payment for a double debt: his own guilt, which he contracted with his crime, and the community's, which, as sacrificial victim, he must take upon himself vicariously. Let us remember that in the community's eyes Christmas is guilty as much for the rape of a white woman as for her murder, and in reprisal for these two crimes he is not only killed but also castrated by Percy Grimm. Race and sex are clearly the major stakes of sacrificial violence here, and it can be safely assumed that the unadmitted collective guilt which is projected and seeks to exorcise itself is of the same order as the victim's.

What does Christmas represent as black *pharmakos?* On what stage is the theater of sacrifice played out?

Joel Kovel, in his Freudian reading of racism, argues that the order established by white racists, particularly in the South, rests on a sort of collective resolution—or, as I would rather suggest, a collective representation—of the Oedipus complex, with the white woman in the position of forbidden mother and the black man projected in the double role of incestuous son and rival father: "the Southern white male simultaneously resolves both sides of the conflict by keeping the black man submissive, and by castrating him when submission fails. In both these situations—in the one symbolically, in the other directly—he is castrating the father, as he once wished to do, and also identifying with the father by castrating the son, as he once feared for himself."[35]

Double identification, double projection, generated by transgressive desire and fear of retaliation: these are precisely the mechanisms at work in Christmas's death. Remember that his birth cost the life of his father and mother, that his first crime was the attempted murder of McEachern, his foster-father, and the second was the rape and murder of a white woman. It is also noteworthy that Christmas's destiny evokes in several ways the Oedipus legend.[36] Everything, therefore, prompts us to see Christmas as another *son* figure. But to the extent that all sacrifice is the repetition and re-presentation of the murder of the father, the collective crime in which, according to Freud, all societies originate, the killing of the son is necessarily both a substitutive murder and a retributive one. Christmas therefore also functions as a father surrogate; his killing is also a displaced and disguised parricide: castration and murder are simultaneously the acting out of an oedipal desire and its punishment. As for Grimm, the sacrificer, his relation to the sacrificed victim might be defined as a chiasma: father to son, son to father, he occupies the same position as his victim—on the other, the safe side of the mirror, where the desire to murder takes on the austere aspect of civic duty.

Ambi-violence, which brings us back to the play of doubling. It is everywhere, inscribing itself even in the name casually given to the foundling one Christmas evening. Joseph, his "Christian name," comes from Doc Hines, the delegate of God the Father; his "sacrilegious" name is given by women, "the Jezebel of the doctor" who was his first nursing mother, and the other "young sluts" in the orphanage: "It is so in the Book: Christmas, the son of Joe. Joe, the son of Joe. Joe Christmas" (424). This mock baptism, where alcohol takes the place of the baptismal water, marks nevertheless the meeting of a body and a name, and Christmas will make this fortuitous name his own, claiming his right to it in the face of those who would try to impose another.[37]

Joe Christmas, a double name, ironic and prophetic: Joseph, the name of a *father* given by a (grand)father; Christ(mas), the name of a *son*, given by women. Son and father, Christmas is both, through his name as well as through his sacrificial role, as was Jesus Christ himself, inasmuch as the mystery of his incarnation and his resurrection partakes of the omnipotence of God the Father. We have seen, however, that the Christ suggested by Christmas was a suffering son rather than a sovereign father. Moreover, "Joseph," the character's first name, does not refer to Christ's "real" father but to Mary's discreet human companion, the nominal father. In the father-son duality, the emphasis falls clearly on the second term: Christmas is Christ only in his passive sonship, in his Passion, his suffering and death, and his resurrection in the memory of myth is merely the commemoration of a crucifixion that begins over and over again.

In the name of what God? A God neither merciful nor just. If one insists on his relationship to the Judeo-Christian tradition, one would have to say that he much more closely resembles the Yahweh of the Old Testament than the Man-God of the New. And one could of course also evoke the implacable God of the Calvinists. But Faulkner's God—or, not to take risks, the God of and in his fiction—is not even a jealous one. The metaphors referring to him in *Light in August* as in the other novels leave no doubt whatever about his evil nature. Unlike Einstein's God, Faulkner's is here, as in *Flags in the Dust*, the supreme "Player," willingly playing dice or chess with his Creation. And for mankind he is the inescapable and ruthless "Opponent," a power omniscient and omnipotent, more infernal than celestial, manipulating men as if they were pawns or puppets and leading them with sadistic glee to their destruction.

William Ellery Channing once observed that "the God of Calvinism, if made a model of human conduct, would turn men into monsters."[38] This is precisely what happens in *Light in August* to all the father figures who take themselves for the duly mandated representatives of the "wrathful and retributive Throne" (225). Just consider McEachern and Doc Hines: both are in their Lord's confidence and are certain that, whatever they do, they do his bidding. And not only do they see themselves as the instruments of divine power; occasionally they even identify with it: "Dont lie to me, to the Lord God" (145), Hines tells the dietitian. Monsters indeed, but monsters unaware of their monstrosity, with the best of alibis. How could anyone find fault with the docile servants of God's will?

Whether divine or human, fatherhood ensures authority and immunity. While the sons inherit all the liabilities, the fathers enjoy the exercise of undisputed power. Within the family, they arrogate the prerogatives of the *pater familias*. The wives are reduced to servility; the children are compelled to blind obedience. The father commands, controls, punishes, and he possesses the power of life and death over his progeny. Hines allows his daughter to die in childbirth and does not rest until her son also dies; McEachern believes himself to be likewise invested with a divine mission and lays claim to the same discretionary powers; and Grimm, the frustrated son, will be transformed in his turn into a sadistic and homicidal father.

Only in fatherhood, the focus and model of all male power, does masculinity fulfill itself in mastery, and fatherhood, the apotheosis of masculinity, unquestionably also informs the organization, ethos, and religion of southern society as depicted in the novel. The god which it has invented for itself is clearly an idealized Father, patterned on its own white ruling fathers. "God aint no nigger" (423), one of the blacks working at the orphanage tells Christmas, and Joanna talks "to God as if He were a man in the room with two other men" (308).

In this patriarchal order everything comes back to the Father. Christmas's tragedy is the most extreme and most poignant exemplification of this inexorable law, but, in another fashion, the stories of Joanna and Hightower are just as telling. The analogies between these two characters have often been commented upon, but their most profound resemblance lies in their imprisonment in the past, in their bondage to the Fathers. It is the voice of the Fathers that communicated to the young Joanna those terrible words which seal her destiny, and she will die for having, at once, obeyed and disobeyed their injunction. Similarly Hightower, unable to free himself from his grandfather's ghost, is himself doomed to chronic ghosthood.

Though the destinies of these three characters are quite different, they are all marked by *filiation*. But at one generation removed: the decisive relationship is not between child and father but between grandchild and grandfather. Before his adoption by McEachern, Christmas is taken in by Doc Hines, whose heinous stare fixes his destiny as cursed pariah. Christmas's case involves a living grandfather and dead parents; for Hightower and Joanna, it is a question of living parents and a dead grandfather. As to the mothers, one can hardly fail to note once again how closely they are associated with absence or death. Christmas's mother dies in childbirth, and Joanna tells nothing about her own except that she was the second wife of Nathaniel Burden who ordered her like an item out of a mail order catalogue from his cousin in New Hampshire (cf. 274). In Hightower's memory, on the other hand, the mother does loom very large, but she is remembered most vividly as the thin-faced, almost skeletonlike, dying mother, with "the two eyes which seemed daily to grow bigger and bigger, as though about to embrace all seeing, all life, with one last terrible glare of frustration and suffering and foreknowledge" (524). Remarkable, too, as far as Hightower and Joanna are concerned, is the remoteness of the real father, the begetter, who cuts a wretched figure in relation to his own father. Whisky drinkers, cigar smokers, crude, brazen, and pugnacious (each of them committed murder, and each dies a violent death), the first Calvin Burden and the first Gail Hightower were by no means dun and dour puritans, and their uninhibited, exuberant vitality stands in sharp contrast to the cramped austerity of their sons. Half-barbarians of the sturdy race of pioneers and warriors, they belong to a heroic bygone time. Not so Hines, Christmas's grandfather: "the dirty old man," with his almost lecherous hatred for women and blacks, is but an obscene caricature of their conquering virility. In relation to his grandson, however, his is indeed the lethal power of the indestructible survivor.

Here, then, reemerges the towering primal figure of the magnified Ancestor, the Sovereign Ghost, already invoked in *Flags in the Dust* and, more obliquely, in *The Sound and the Fury*, and to be found again in *Absalom, Absalom* and *Go Down, Moses*. In its mythical function, this figure evokes the formidable Father of prehistoric times, the *Urvater* postulated by Freud in "Totem and Taboo," who wielded absolute power, in the pure arbitrariness of force. Hence once again the deadlock of the father-son relationship, destined either to bog down in alienating identification or to culminate in a fight to the death in which the son is inevitably destroyed.

It has been said that Christianity is a religion of the Son. In *Light in August* the only god is the Father, the Tyrant-Ancestor, and religion, in Yoknapataw-pha, is a closed economy of endless revenge and endlessly accumulating guilt, in which violence can only breed further violence. Christmas's death may well have been enshrined in the collective memory of Jefferson, but it serves no cathartic purpose. Christmas no doubt dies for his sins, but in dying he pays off neither his debt nor that of the community. His is a *passion inutile*, a useless sacrifice, a Passion without redemption—just one more grisly tale in the disconsolate chronicle of the South. And there will have to be other expulsions and other "crucifixions." How could the infinite debt to the Fathers ever be extinguished?

XIX

CIRCLES

> The way up and the way down are one and
> the same.
>
> Heraclitus of Ephesus

Straight and curved

Christmas dies, Christ is recrucified. Once again but not for the last time. At dawn, the same day, in the murdered son's cabin, a child is born. The indefatigable Player is already rearranging his pawns on the chessboard, ready for a game: the same one.

At first sight, whether tragic or not, fate, in *Light in August*, seems to follow a single rectilinear line. Thus Lena is following her straight way, the *road* straight ahead of her, with inexhaustible patience and unerring resolve. From Alabama to Mississippi, from Mississippi to Tennessee, her progress continues without a hitch or a detour, depending on hospitable wagons and hospitable people in a steady rhythm that is barely slowed down by a few days' stop in Jefferson, long enough for her to deliver her child. Faces and places turn round Lena as she moves along: after "the sunny loneliness of the enormous land" (30) comes Jefferson with its crowded streets and the bustle of collective life. Lena, however, is only in transit there; she will always be a stranger to its noise and disorder, skirting its turmoils and tragedies without ever being directly involved in them, serene like a peaceful river flowing through a burning city. As she moves through the novel she moves across the land, "just travelling" (558), intact, intangible, identical at the end to what she was at the beginning, except that she will have moved, time will have passed, and a child will have been born.

Another straight line, the *street* is to Christmas what the road is to Lena. Both are places of passage, distances to be covered, but while the dusty road follows the lay of the land, is open to every horizon, and communicates with the whole of the surrounding space, the street is part of the stony geometry of cities. It is no doubt still a traveled path, offering the perspective of an over-there; yet, more rigidly than the road, it constrains movement to a predetermined direction. Patterned by its inflexible linearity and the double verticality of its walls, half open, half closed-in, it constitutes the space of a false freedom—a prison all the more oppressive for being half open.

> The street, a quiet one at all times, was deserted at this hour. . . . He went on, passing still between the homes of white people, from street lamp to street lamp, the heavy shadows of oak and maple leaves sliding like scraps of black velvet across his white shirt. Nothing can look quite as lonely as a big man going along an empty street. Yet though he was not large, not tall, he contrived somehow to look more lonely than a lone telephone pole in the middle of a desert. In the wide, empty, shadow-brooded street he looked like a phantom, a spirit, strayed out of its own world, and lost. (125)

Such is Christmas's street, the desolate nonhome of the rootless. As in Hopper's bleak, anonymous cityscapes, the street appears here as a place of chilling emptiness and loneliness. Christmas's street is invariably deserted. No companionship, no encounter ever fills the void, and drained of the little reality he still has, Christmas himself becomes a forlorn phantom in a dead city.

"Knowing not grieving remembers a thousand savage and lonely streets" (242). Thus opens chapter X, which tells of Christmas's fifteen years of wandering. The street is its emblem; it defines its space, measures its duration from that night when he was beaten by Bobbie's friends: "From that night the thousand streets ran as one street, with imperceptible corners and changes of scene" (246). A thousand streets, one street, *the* street:

> The street ran into Oklahoma and Missouri and as far south as Mexico and then back north to Chicago and Detroit and then back south again and at last to Mississippi. It was fifteen years long: it ran between the savage and spurious board fronts of oil towns. . . . It ran through yellow wheat fields. . . . And always, sooner or later, the street ran through cities, through an identical and wellnigh interchangeable section of cities without remembered names. (246–47)

Christmas has roamed a continentwide territory, but there is no "open road" in his America. The street remains identical to itself wherever he goes, straight throughout its detours.[1] Like Bigger Thomas, the protagonist of Wright's *Native Son*, Christmas has fled from place to place, but "one place was the same as another to him" (248), for he has never found a place to flee *to*. His flights have all been from one exile to another. Nameless and empty, the street gives Christmas no respite: "in none of them could he be quiet. But the street ran on in its moods and phases, always empty: he might have seen himself as in numberless avatars, in silence, doomed with motion, driven by the courage of flagged and spurred despair" (248).

Christmas's street was already heralded in chapter VI by the orphanage's "quiet and empty corridor" in which his frail child's figure appeared "sober and quiet as a shadow" (131). Besides, there is hardly a character in the novel who does not at some point visualize his or her life as a corridor. To the dietitian at the orphanage it looks "straight and simple as a corridor with [the janitor] sitting at the end of it" (139); Joanna sees "her whole past life, the starved years, like a gray tunnel" (290). Percy Grimm sees "his life opening before him, uncomplex and inescapable as a barren corridor" (497). And even Lena's recent past "is a peaceful corridor paved with unflagging and tranquil faith and peopled with kind and nameless faces and voices" (7). The corridor can be empty or full of people, agonizing or peaceful, but each time the image of a predetermined path imposes itself. Whether looking back at the way they have come or looking ahead to scrutinize their future, Faulkner's characters perceive themselves as moving points on a straight line, heading in a direction that they have not chosen and that—for better or worse—they will have to follow to the end.

Parallel or intersecting roads, streets and corridors draw destiny's implacable geometry. And while they are places within the represented space, they also function as recurrent, permutable signs within the textual space, their reiteration gradually transforming them into fixed essences eluding time. The streets, monotonously following one another during Christmas's long wandering, overlap to reveal in transparency the image-idea of *the* street, just as in chapter I the roads followed by Lena eventually merge into *the* road.

Yet Faulkner's lines are never simply linear; sooner or later, his roads and streets always get bent or twisted. The unfolding line curves round, turns back on itself, draws a circle. In the first chapter, the wagon in which Lena rides through the silent August afternoon is "like a shabby bead upon the mild red string of road," and the road in turn is likened to "already measured thread being rewound onto a spool" (8). Christmas's progress comes likewise to evoke a circular journey, and Christmas himself views it as such on the eve of his capture: after trying to evade his pursuers for seven days, he has "lost account of time and distance," yet as he reenters "the street which ran for thirty years," he suddenly realizes that it "had made a circle and he is still inside of it," and that he has "never broken out of the ring of what [he has] already done and cannot ever undo" (373–74). And yet one page before, we are told that "Again his direction is straight as a surveyor's line, disregarding hill and valley and bog" (372). Like Lena's road, then, Christmas's street evokes circular closure. But instead of representing self-sufficient plenitude or, in Paul Claudel's phrase, "the inexhaustible in the closure,"[2] as it does for Lena, the circle here becomes the symbol of inescapable guilt and doom. Christmas's circle is a trap, a cage within which he is endlessly turning round and which will hold him captive until he faces death.

The paradoxical conjunction of the straight line (variants: road, street, corridor, tunnel) and the circle (variants: wheel, sun, spool, button, bead, urn, silver dollar) provides the design of the entire novel. For while the stories of the central characters unfold in time from a beginning to an end, the telling keeps doubling back on itself, and the rich, complex patterning of the novel is dominated throughout by circularity.

Rotations

Sitting beside the road, watching the wagon mount the hill toward her, Lena thinks, 'I have come from Alabama: a fur piece. All the way from Alabama a-walking. A fur piece.' Thinking *although I have not been quite a month on the road I am already in Mississippi, further from home than I have ever been before. I am now further from Doane's Mill than I have been since I was twelve years old.* (1)

"'My, my. A body does get around. Here we aint been coming from Alabama but two months, and now it's already Tennessee.'" (559)

The last paragraph of the last chapter echoes the first paragraph of the first chapter. The novel ends as it begins, with Lena on the road, and her comments express identical wonderment about the distance she has covered. The last scene is a nearly perfect replica of the first: the same character appears in the same setting, thinking nearly the same words. Nothing, however, is exactly the same. Lena has traveled from Alabama to Mississippi and is now moving into Tennessee (it is indeed her moving that is the subject of her comment), time has passed ("*a month* "/"two months"), and though she is still on the road, she is no longer alone (a change signaled by the pronominal shift from "I" to "we"). In the fictional world, there is thus no return to the starting point, but repetition with a difference, and in its spiral-like movement through space and time Lena's curve remains open, since her journey, begun before the novel begins, will continue on beyond the novel's ending.

Lena's circle—the circle with the purest curve and the longest radius—is the novel's most visible contour, its outer rim as well as the paradigm of its inner structure. For other curves, other circles will unfold tangentially to or concentrically within Lena's. Thus the first chapter begins and ends on the road as the novel does, closing with Lena's words: "My, my, . . . here I aint been on the road but four weeks, and now I am in Jefferson already. My, my. A body does get around" (32)—the first repetition of the novel's incipit as well as the second, this time almost literal anticipation of its ending.

The narrative opens in the present tense and tilts almost immediately into the past (with a flashback on Lena starting in the second paragraph, ending on page 4), then shifts back from the past to the present up to the end.[3] The same narrative scheme is found in the next three chapters: they all start in the present tense and revert to it after a detour through a distant (chapters II and III) or recent past (chapter IV). Each of the first four chapters is built on the same circular model, but these circles, in turn, are enclosed in a new circle signaled by Lena's return at the end of chapter IV and the second repetition of her refrain (this time quoted by Byron): "'My, my. Here I have come clean from Alabama, and now I am in Jefferson at last, sure enough'" (111).

These four chapters, the first three of which are expository while the fourth already foreshadows the ending, form the first narrative movement of *Light in August*.[4] Past and present alternate in all of them, but the present is the axis of reference. With chapter V, the narrative circles back to the Friday of Lena's arrival in Jefferson but focuses for the first time on Christmas. It takes us from midnight to midnight—another circle, recounting his last twenty-four hours before the murder. All of the chapter is in the past, and so prepares us for the much longer flashback movement into Christmas's earlier life which constitutes the middle portion of the novel, from chapter VI through XII. The narrative then comes back to the other characters, the threads of the narrative are retied where they were cut, and in the second section of chapter XIII the present becomes again the major tense. As tense of motion and action as well as of the eternal now, the fullness of time, it is par excellence the tense of the circle, and is therefore also the predominant tense in all the scenes irradiated by Lena's presence. And after the narrative of Christmas's and Hightower's stories has been completed (chapters XIX and XX), the novel comes full circle when Lena, like a bright star having followed its prescribed orbit, reappears, as serene and steadfast as ever. "A body does get around."

Lena-Christmas-Lena. Present-past-present. At the threshold of the novel, chapter I—which, surprisingly enough, was not included in the first draft of the narrative[5]—stands like a convex mirror, reflecting in proleptic miniature the overall pattern of the narrative to come: four introductory chapters in the present (I-IV), eight chapters in the past (V-XII), and the nine climactic and conclusive chapters in the present again (XIII-XXI). Granted, this is a very broad outline, and in fact time divisions are not quite so clear-cut. The novel's narrative economy no doubt calls for much closer attention to its multiple articulations and to the shifting relations between structure, mood, and voice. The little we have said should suffice, however, to show that this novel—as a whole but also in nearly every one of its parts—is dominated by the figure and ruled by the law of the circle and finds within it its form and its formula.[6]

Repetitions and differences

The circle, then, is to be understood dynamically, as an active *circling* or *circulation*. To identify it as the unifying principle of the novel's narrative design is clearly not enough; it is also worth inquiring how it affects its textual economy. In *Light in August*, circulation operates on all levels: it takes place between words or sentences as well as between scenes or sites or characters, generating various intersecting patterns of eddying repetition. Hence an eerie sense of *déjà-vu*, the already seen, the already read, the familiar made strange through its very repetition.

The refrainlike recurrence of Lena's musing in chapters I, IV, and XXI clearly functions as a structural rhyme, but one could easily find other textual repetitions. Hardly less conspicuously than in *As I Lay Dying*, words, phrases, and sentences recur within a chapter (the three occurrences of *"Something is going to happen to me"* in chapter V) or rebound across chapters (the incipits of chapters VI and VII), often connecting fairly distant moments in the text, such as McEachern's "Kneel down" (167) echoed by Joanna's "Kneel with me" (310), Mrs. Armstid's "you men" (18) much later repeated by Mrs. Beard (462), or again Hines (145) and McEachern (224) confronting women with "Jezebel." Words and word clusters, identical or more or less synonymous, punctuate the text with their emphatic repetition—the vocabulary of serenity, for example, in chapter I, light and darkness imagery in chapter V, street and pit imagery in chapter X and XII or, even more subtly, the diction of the "Ode on a Grecian Urn" saturating the text in chapter XX.

Repetition weaves its way through signifiers as well as signifieds. Faulkner's narrative itself moves in circles, forward and backward, multiplying calls and recalls, anticipations and retrogressions through the recurrence of similar situations and similar actions, so that most incidents in the novel can be placed in one or several series. One such series—the most prominent in *Light in August* and one that runs through the whole of Faulkner's fiction— consists of flight and pursuit scenes. Hines pursues his daughter Milly and the circus man with whom she is running away and later persecutes the surviving grandson. McEachern pursues young Christmas to the schoolhouse where he dances with Bobbie. The sheriff, his men, and his bloodhounds, and then Percy Grimm and his acolytes hunt him down after the murder. And in nearly all these pursuits the pursuer knows exactly where to track down the pursued and acts with the same "blind and untroubled faith in the rightness and infallibility of his actions" (507). On the other hand, counterpointed against the manhunts, a comic inversion of pursuers and pursued marks the Lena Grove story: Lena first pursues her seducer Lucas Burch and then is in turn pursued by Byron.

Many scenes are thus replayed several times, either with the same actors or a different cast, as if they were successive versions of, or variations on, the same dramatic scheme.[7] To give one specific example: in chapter VII we are told that after several whippings by McEachern, little Christmas "fell at full length to the floor and did not move," and that a few hours later "he came to" in his attic room and "lay for some time, looking peacefully up at the slanted ceiling" (167). The scene is echoed at the close of chapter IX, when Christmas, then a young man, is beaten nearly senseless by a stranger: "his eyes were still open, looking quietly up at them. There was nothing in his eyes at all, no pain, no surprise. But apparently he could not move; he just lay there with a profoundly contemplative expression" (240). This description in turn foreshadows Christmas's dying in chapter XIX: "But the man on the floor had not moved. He just lay there, with his eyes open and empty of everything save consciousness" (513). Yet we might also relate it to the description of Byron Bunch after his fight with Joe Brown: "He feels no particular pain now, but better than that, he feels no haste, no urgency, to do anything or go anywhere. He just lies bleeding and quiet" (485). Or even to Lena, shortly after giving birth: "She just lay there, propped on the pillow, watching him with her sober eyes in which there was nothing at all" (473).

There is hardly a gesture, an attitude, or an action in the novel that does not occur at least two or three times. Lena looks out over Jefferson from the crest of a hill; so does Christmas. Christmas interrupts worship in country churches; so did Hines and Hightower's grandfather. Lena and Burch escape through windows; so does Christmas. Moreover, the same fixed postures and the same blank faces follow the reader from one scene to another, generating the double motif of the statuelike body and the masklike face. Characters are repeatedly compared with hard matter, wood, stone, or rock, as if they were no longer living bodies freely moving in space but inert effigies or figures on a frieze. Christmas is compared to "a large toy" (138), "a tomb effigy" (169), and, in the flagellation scene in chapter VII, "a post or a tower" (175), McEachern to a rock in chapters VI and VII, Hightower to an "eastern idol" (98, 346), Hines's wife to "something made of stone and painted" (407), the cashier of the bar to a "carved lioness guarding a portal" (192), and at one point Hightower, Byron, and Mrs. Hines appear "like three rocks above a beach, above ebbtide" (421). Faces lose their expressiveness and congeal into hard blank stone masks. Mrs. Armstid's face "might have been carved in sandstone" (19), McEachern's profile juts "granitelike" (168), and during the final chase, Christmas and Percy Grimm look and move about like masked hieratic actors from some ancient ritual drama reenacted for the thousandth time.

The time always comes for Faulkner's characters, however, when the masks fall, when the statues spring to life, when confrontation can no longer be avoided. This critical, often climactic moment is nearly always preceded either by a long period of expectation or by the short tension of a *face to face*, a typical situation in *Light in August* as in all Faulkner novels. Such is the case with Lena and Mrs. Armstid's confrontation at the beginning of the novel, Byron and Hightower's in chapters IV and XIII, the dietitian and Hines's in chapter VI, Christmas and McEachern's in chapter VII, Christmas and Bobbie's in chapter VII, Christmas and Joanna's in chapter XII, Byron and Burch's in chapter XVIII, and finally Christmas and Percy Grimm's during the final chase in chapter XIX. True, there are also friendly meetings such as the weekly conversations between Hightower and Byron. More often, however, these encounters end in silent hostility and mounting tension. Then only the eyes talk: guarded, watchful stares, locked in mutual fascination, sometimes yielding to unbidden and unspoken intimacies, as when Lena and Mrs. Armstid "look at one another, suddenly naked, watching one another" (19) or when Burch, looking at Lena before his final flight, is "stripped naked for the instant of verbiage and deceit" (477). Consider also the following confrontation between Christmas and Joanna: "Their faces were not a foot apart: the one cold, dead white, fanatical, mad; the other parchmentcolored, the lip lifted into the shape of a soundless and rigid snarl" (304). Shortly after, Joanna slaps her lover, and he, in his turn, hits her in the face.

The passage from face to face to hand to hand confrontation is almost inevitable. Violence also repeats itself in series and cycles, with a dull, implacable regularity. Not only Christmas's final moments but his whole life has been a calvary. As a child, he is whipped by his foster-father. As a young man, he is slapped in the face by Bobbie and then beaten up by her friends at Max's restaurant, and finally, when he is captured, his face is bloody for having been beaten by Halliday and Hines. Unlike Christ, however, Christmas fights back and gives as many blows as he receives. From the young black girl in the shed to the white prostitute, from Bobbie to Joanna, there is not one woman in his life whom he does not end up hitting. Similarly, from the playmates of his childhood to Brown, his associate, there are few men with whom he does not fight: "Sometimes he would remember how he had once tricked or teased white men into calling him a negro in order to fight them, to beat them or be beaten; now he fought the negro who called him white" (248). His career in violence started with (what might have already been) a murder and culminates in (what may well be) another, and even after killing Joanna, he will continue to strike out, attacking black people in a church during his final flight and knocking down Hightower before being shot down by Grimm.

Christmas's story is another "story full of sound and fury," but in this novel it is caught up in a general economy of violence, marked throughout by either sexual conflict—"that spontaneous compulsion of the male to fight with or because of or over the partner with which he has recently or is about to copulate" (173)—or racial tension. On the other hand, although the action of *Light in August* takes place in the twentieth century, the tumultuous chronicles of the Burdens and the Hightowers remind us that violence is an integral part of the legacy of the South, and it is probably not accidental that, before she dies, Joanna, the inhabitant of an old colonial mansion, threatens Christmas with an old pistol dating from the Civil War.

Violence repeats itself in space and time, and, as if to emphasize the serial character of its returns, the novel evokes it through a succession of identical gestures. Thus, in most of the violent scenes, the blows are struck to the face and all the main characters—with the predictable exception of Lena—are, at one point, wounded in the head: McEachern bleeds from the head when he is floored by Christmas in the ball scene, as do Byron after his savage fight with his recalcitrant rival and Hightower when he is knocked out by Christmas— not to mention Joanna's nearly severed head.[8] Masklike faces, bruised and bloody, merge in the reader's mind as they come to merge on the "wheel" of Hightower's final vision in chapter XX.

Repetition informs Faulkner's characterization as well as his dramaturgy. Not that his characters lack individualization, but it would seem that individualization operates from a common root or common fund. In *Light in August* as in Faulkner's other novels, the invariant shows through the variable, similar patterns arise from the play of doubling and difference, connecting characters and at the same time hollowing them out by reducing their uniqueness. Generated in a kaleidoscopic manner through ever-new combinations of the same set of features, the characters thus come to look like differential forms, all born of some division within the same. Probably no novelist escapes the constraints of such *combinatoires*. Faulkner, however, far from concealing them, displays them, as constraints both of his writing and of his "world." The characters remain particularized figures, but they are stamped with a common pattern; their identities repeat one another, so as to merge, at least asymptotically, in a common identity, improper and recurrent.

As a result, each individual, however isolated he may be in his sense of himself from the outer world, is a kind of monad reflecting all the others. If, for example, we consider Christmas and Lena as the novel's two polar figures, we can see that their opposition is built on a series of clear-cut contrasts but that at the same time they are united by a series of hardly less obvious similarities: both are orphans, both have deprived childhoods, both escape through windows to meet their first lovers and are betrayed by them; both become wandering "strangers." The distribution of roles is patterned by contrast and symmetry in Faulkner's entire work, but in *Light in August* couples and doubles are multiplied even more conspicuously than in the previous novels. First of all, there is a series of couples, in the common acceptation of the term, among which the most significant are two heterosexual couples, one "positive" (Byron-Lena), the other "negative" (Christmas-Joanna), and two equally contrasted male couples (Byron-Hightower, Christmas-Brown). Moreover, characters are paired either through parallelism (Hightower-Joanna, McEachern-Hines) or through antithesis (Lena/Joanna), and with self-divided figures such as Christmas and Joanna this binary division finds its internal duplication in the characters themselves.

Beyond these paired oppositions, larger groupings occur according to the functions assigned to each character in the novel's narrative economy. If Christmas is considered as protagonist, it becomes obvious that his *opponents* (from Doc Hines to Percy Grimm) largely outweigh his mostly potential *helpers* (little Alice at the orphanage, Mrs. McEachern, Byron, Mrs. Hines, and Hightower). We have already seen that Christmas's antagonists can be divided into two complementary sets, one aggressively male (Doc Hines, McEachern, Joanna, Percy Grimm as representatives of the repressive Father), the other insidiously female (all the women who, from the dietitian to Joanna, assume the ambiguous role of nourishing/devouring Mother). The same symbolic figure, the same actantial function, then, can be actualized in several different characters. Conversely, a single character can come to embody several figures or play several roles: in relation to Christmas, Joanna combines both parental figures under the sign of castration, and Grimm, in a similar manner, appears as another frustrated son while occupying the position of the punishing father with respect to Christmas. Such iteration of figures and functions is bound to derealize characters, depriving them of their uniqueness and denying them a fixed identity.

Faulkner's games with names have likewise disruptive effects. The name is the character's major and permanent signifier; it is also a standard characterization device which Faulkner sometimes seems to use as Fielding, Dickens, and Thackeray did. The way he uses it, however, is anything but naive, for at the same time he alerts us to the tenuous, arbitrary relation of names to the named. In *Light in August* Byron, the most name-conscious character in the novel, at one point addresses himself questioningly: *"you just say that you are Byron Bunch . . . you are just the one that calls yourself Byron Bunch today; now, this minute"* (468), and yet he is also the one who reflects that "a man's name, which is supposed to be just the sound for who he is, can be somehow an augur of what he will do, if other men can only read the meaning in time" (35). Names are used for purposes of designation and recognition; they individualize and socialize, but it would seem that they also announce character and destiny. *Nomen est omen*, and "he that has an ill name is half hanged." Indeed, Christmas is a dead man once it is known that he is a "nigger,"[9] and moreover his suffering and sacrifice were inscribed beforehand in his last name and his initials. "Do you think it was just chanceso [sic] that Madam should have been away that night and give them young sluts the chance and call to name him Christmas in sacrilege of My son?" (422) Hines asks. And Christmas's name seals indeed his fate: "Halliday saw him and ran up and grabbed him and said 'Aint your name Christmas?' and the nigger said it was" (386). While Christmas refuses to deny his name, other characters in the novel either want to or do change theirs. Thus Hightower's adulterous wife registers in a Memphis hotel under a false name, but after she has committed suicide, the police find "her rightful name where she had written it herself on a piece of paper and then torn it up and thrown it into the waste basket" (72): the torn-up name—the husband's name—identifies the mangled body and points accusingly at the "murderer."

Names are given and lost, even as their bearers are born and die. To read a destiny is to decipher a name, and in one sense the whole text of *Light in August* is nothing less and nothing more than a hazardous unriddling of names. And as if to underscore its hazards, Faulkner plays once again, as he did in *Flags in the Dust* and *The Sound and the Fury*, on homonymies (there are two "Gail Hightowers" and two "Calvin Burdens") and homophonies (Grove/grove, Gail/gale, Burch/birch, Grimm/grim), and he even sees to it that "Christmas" reappears in "fading letters" on Hightower's sign (62). One character, Joe Christmas, has his "heathenish" name changed when he is adopted by the McEacherns; another, Lucas Burch, hides behind the pseudonym "Joe Brown," and, ironically enough, Lena and Byron's first encounter occurs only because of a paronymy: "Burch," the name of the fugitive seducer, and "Bunch," that of the future husband (see 54), are two signifiers differentiated by a mere letter. For the characters in the novel the confusion of names can be fraught with untoward consequences, though its outcome is likely to be a happy one for Lena and Byron. As for the reader, he no doubt hardly risks mistaking one character for another, yet what these games with names suggest is that one name can be used for another, is of equal value with another, and that a name is actually only a haphazard sign with no real privilege in the larger circuit of signs forming the text. The characters' names are no doubt metaphors and oracles, but their status turns out to be as uncertain as the identities to which they are supposed to refer. "What's in a name?" *Light in*

August leaves us at a loss, for through their interplay and interferences, their resemblances and repetitions, it is just as if names had been voided of the precious substance attributed to them and turned into empty shells.

The "wheel of thinking"

Signs and meanings recur and revolve, as scenes and characters do, within the revolutions of a text. The circle spins, slows, stops, starts again, in the same direction or in the opposite direction, in the "right" direction or the "wrong" direction. Even the sun might take a bad turn. For Christmas, for example, toward the end of his flight, time, the succession of days and nights, is disrupted: a night of sleep is followed by another night "without interval of day"; a day is followed by another day "without any night between or any interval for rest, *as if the sun had not set but instead had turned in the sky before reaching the horizon and retraced its way*" (367; italics mine).

To each character his or her circle, to each circle its turns and returns. Lena's is the first and last circle, the fertile open circle of inexhaustible reproduction, the agrarian cycle of springs and summers, sowing and harvest, the luminous cycle of the Virgin-Mother under the kindly protection of the Sun-Father. But push the wheel in the opposite direction or a bit further in the same direction and you come upon Joanna's late summer and autumn cycle, the ebbing tide of decline and decay, the dark cycle of the Foolish Virgin under the curse of the Dead Fathers.

Christmas's destiny is likewise locked in a circle of suffering and death. From empty street to empty street, from "dark house" to "dark house," he wanders through his life like a furious sleepwalker, and during his final flight he himself comes to recognize the circle of his fate as "the ring of what [he has] already done and cannot ever undo" (374). And Christmas's circle inexorably coils inward toward the sacrificial scene of his murder. The *pharmakos* is immolated afresh; once again the son is crucified for his guilt and his innocence.

But there is yet another circle in which the others will all come together: the great revolving *wheel* of thought, which dominates Hightower's final meditation in chapter XX.

Set between a tragic narrative (Christmas's death) and a comic one (the latest of Lena's departures), between a closed cycle and an open curve, this transition chapter is itself a loop. "Now the final copper light of afternoon fades" (514) is its opening statement, and it ends with "the dying thunder of hooves" (544). Dying is present at the beginning and at the end, and the whole chapter could be read as the evocation of one of those extremely fast panoramic visions which, it is said, sometimes occur during mortal agonies, even though Hightower's death—unlike Christmas's in the preceding chapter—is but a symbolic one.[10] The public theater of sacrificial violence has narrowed to a private drama, a mental scene of representation, memory, and fantasy. Its time is twilight, a time of suspension, between light and dark, life and death, as well as a time of revelation, a time for epiphanies. Its space is "the street . . . prepared and empty, framed by the study window like a stage" (514). Representation is here what is "offered to the view" (*theatron*), but also what re-presents itself anew. The overall movement of the text is indeed one of *return:* the long-delayed return of the thunderous vision of the grandfather's final charge (foretold at the beginning and described in the end), the long return toward childhood, the family past, with its three "ghosts" and its "phantom," and lastly the self-probing and self-accusatory return that induces the movement of the "wheel." In these returns, however, all is not sheer repetition. Hightower's habitual fantasy script is for once disrupted by precisely that which the text indicates through the figure of the "wheel." For the latter is not a delusion machine; it is, in the narrator's own words, the "wheel of thinking" (541), turning on its own course, and compelling Hightower to think what he does not want to think. Turning slowly at first, like a wheel in heavy sand, as Hightower still resists the knowledge awaiting him, it will drive him, in spite of himself, to acknowledge truth, and first and foremost truth about himself, the unpalatable truth of his selfish and misspent life: "Out of the instant the sandclutched wheel of thinking turns on with the slow implacability of a medieval torture instrument, beneath the wrenched and broken sockets of his spirit, his life" (541).

But as it whirls faster and grows lighter, "freed now of burden, of vehicle, axle, all," the wheel "seems to engender and surround itself with a faint glow like a halo" (542). The faces which Hightower had seen at first expressing astonishment, outrage, and fear, and in which he had watched himself as in mirrors, are now "not shaped with suffering, not shaped with anything: not horror, pain, not even reproach. They are peaceful, as though they had escaped into an apotheosis; his own is among them. In fact, they all look a little alike, composite of all the faces which he has ever seen" (542).

As in the final description of the dying Christmas in the previous chapter, a serene "apotheosis" has been achieved. The differences between the faces are now blurred, and yet Hightower can still distinguish them one from another:

> his wife's; townspeople, members of that congregation which denied him, which had met him at the station that day with eagerness and hunger; Byron Bunch's; the woman with the child; and that of the man called Christmas. This face alone is not clear. It is confused more than any other, as though in the now peaceful throes of a more recent, a more inextricable, compositeness. Then he can see that it is two faces which seem to strive (but not of themselves striving or desiring it: he knows that, but because of the motion and desire of the wheel itself) in turn to free themselves one from the other, then fade and blend again. (542–43)

The entire cast of the novel comes back for a final pageant. Their faces are still distinguishable but they are carried along by the same round, swept along by the same leveling movement. Individual features fade away, differences dissolve. Just as the same position indicates midday and midnight on the clock's face, the same position is assigned on the circle of light to the once hostile faces of Percy Grimm and Christmas, the faces of the killer and the slain, the last to appear in Hightower's reverie. The strife and the coincidence of opposites are already inscribed in the wheel's whirling movement and have been inscribed there since the beginning of time, in keeping with "the desire of the wheel" and not with a will that could be ascribed to any of their ephemeral impersonators.

What knowledge, what wisdom, what forgiveness is "the wheel" assumed to offer? Hightower's final vision can be read as his late and painful initiation to the community of man, or even, in Christian terms, as his entry into the communion of sinners. Driven out of his "high tower" by Byron and forced to confess his guilt, Hightower comes to identify with Christmas, his brother in crime. He now is guilty among the guilty, murderer among murderers, man among men, finally returned from the world of ghosts. Sparked by the death of Christmas and the birth of Lena's child, Hightower's moment of awareness appears symbolically as another death followed by another birth. His spiritual rebirth, though, cannot be taken for granted, and little is gained by making Hightower a disciple of Buddha, assumed to find enlightenment through acceptance of the "pari-nirvana."[11] A revelation no doubt occurs, and the deep shock it provokes in him is such that he thinks indeed that he is dying from it. He survives, though, and does not even "die" to the world. If the experience of the "wheel" leaves him in an unusual state of lightness and vacuity, it does not lead at all to the extinction of the desiring self. Far from it. In the end, Hightower falls back into his fantasy, and the phantom horsemen return, "as though they had merely waited until he could find something to pant with, to be reaffirmed in triumph and desire with, with this last left of honor and pride and life" (543–44). Hightower has not broken out of his enchanted circle, the hour of "liberation" or redemption has not yet come.[12]

As in other novels by Faulkner, in *Light in August* a moment of visionary insight is bestowed upon one of the characters. The meaning of this vision, however, is to be sought neither in the character's psychology nor in some religious or metaphysical system outside the text. If the whole text is patterned according to the principle of circularity, the vision described in chapter XX must be understood as still another circle within the circle, another internal reduplication of the novel, one of those places where what we might call, for want of a better term, the "thought" of the text, is re-unfolded and re-inscribed. Not Hightower's thought nor even Faulkner's, but a thought turning in its closure, a knowledge always already there and always to come, always to be written and read, a questioning never to be completed.

The locus of the questioning is the circle, the sign raised to the highest power, reduplicated by Hightower's "wheel." So far each destiny seemed to draw its own circle in utter isolation. All of them, now, are carried along in a general circulation, a gyratory movement in which they appear as if chained one to the other. Hightower's vision brings us closer to this central, fixed, and exalted point of view which would be that of an all-seeing God, "the final and supreme Face Itself, cold, terrible because of Its omniscient detachment" (539) and from which everything would be perceived to be at equal distance, in equal light, equalized, like a vast, horrendous human Comedy.

From this timeless perspective, the trajectories of Christmas and Lena would have to be represented by curves joined end to end rather than by disjointed circles. And indeed, the end of one life-cycle coincides with the beginning of another. A child is born the day Christmas dies, in the Negro cabin where Christmas lived, not far from the house in which Joanna has just been murdered. A birth at dawn, a death in the afternoon. Life dies away to soar again out of its ashes. Old Mrs. Hines, mistaking the newly born and still unnamed child of Lena for her own lost grandson, stubbornly insists on calling him "Joey," and Lena herself becomes so confused that she briefly imagines Christmas as her child's father:

> "She keeps on talking about him like his pa was that . . . the one in jail, that Mr Christmas. She keeps on, and then I get mixed up and it's like sometimes I cant—like I am mixed up too and I think that pa is that Mr—Mr Christmas too." (452)

Christmas is symbolically reborn both as Lena's son and Lena's husband, a child and the child's father.[13] Indifferent to time and its "avatars," life begets itself ever again at the crossroads of death. The waste earth becomes fertile again. "Poor woman," Hightower thinks, remembering Joanna. "Poor, barren woman. To have not lived only a week longer, until luck returned to this place. Until luck and life returned to these barren and ruined acres" (449). It then seems to Hightower that he can see all about him "the ghosts of rich fields, and of the rich fecund black life of the quarters, the mellow shouts, the presence of fecund women, the prolific naked children in the dust before the doors; and the big house again, noisy, loud with the treble shouts of the generations" (449). To Christmas, during his visit to Freedman Town, the same scene of teeming fertility had been a suffocating nightmare. The same scene and not the same. The wheel has turned.

Through its turns and returns, its coincidences and confusions, *Light in August* thus urges the reader to discover and decipher this game of repetition and difference, of chance and necessity in much the same fashion as Hightower does through his rapt contemplation of the turning "wheel." The latter's experience of epiphany has been aptly defined by one critic as "a serene moment of Apollonian vision" in "the Dionysian dance of life."[14] But it is also an Apollonian vision *of* the dance, and Hightower's vision condenses and reduplicates what the reader himself has already "seen." Interestingly, in chapter XX the urn, still another image of roundness, reemerges in Hightower's reveries as the "classic and serene vase" (528) of Keats's ode, as if to recall that works of art, after all, are not quite resourceless: if they pretend to truth, they will acknowledge the world's turmoil, but they will also draw it into the Apollonian play of forms and signs. In representing the tragic and framing it in a tale, the novel imposes the rules of its own game and affirms its precarious mastery over the world. Tragedy both captures the tragic and loosens its hold on us by putting it into words and having it performed on a stage. Whatever terror or pity we are made to feel, we are not in danger of being engulfed by them. Stories, no matter how sad or gruesome, gratify our desire to live and die vicariously and assuage our deep need to see and to know. Watching spectacles and listening to narratives are always pleasures. This is how a "dark house" can become "light in August."

Narratives are transactions within the economy of desire, and it is interesting to note that the epilogue of *Light in August* almost seems to have been intended as a lighthearted reminder of their contractual nature. The novel's conclusion offers a double shift: while moving away from the tragic-naturalistic atmosphere of the previous chapters and bringing us back to the comic-pastoral mood of the beginning,[15] it accomplishes an ultimate narrative shift by introducing a new intra-diegetic narrator. Three weeks after Christmas's death and the birth of Lena's baby, a furniture dealer, back home after a trip to Tennessee, tells a story to his wife. The locus of the narration is the conjugal bed, in which they have just made love, and its object is "an experience which he had had on the road, which interested him at the time and which he considered amusing enough to repeat" (545). Why amusing? "Perhaps the reason why he found it interesting . . . is that he and his wife are not old either, besides his having been away from home . . . for more than a week" (545). What makes the story interesting to him has obviously something to do with the happy reunion of the young couple, and the more so as its subject is another young couple, Lena and Byron, the comic story of an amorous pursuit, a love yet to be consummated. The dealer who, like V. K. Ratliff, belongs to the family of Faulkner's vernacular raconteurs, tells the story with good-natured humor. But what gives his tale its full meaning is the occasion of the narrative utterance and the identity of the narratee, the woman listening in the dark. The story is meant for her, told to her as a kind of post-coital gift, and the gift is perhaps not without ulterior motive, for it would seem that the narrator expects something in return for what he supplies; his telling, fraught with erotic hints and double entendre, is a mischievous invitation to rebegin. The stake of the narrative exchange, then, is overtly sexual: in gratifying his wife's desire for a story, the furniture dealer attempts to rekindle her desire for him, and to all appearances the attempt is successful. As the narrator, gently laughing at his wife's impatience, well knows, a tale is to be exchanged for a body, and for once the postponement inherent in all narrating will be short; for once the waiting will be rewarded with true release.

As in *The Sound and the Fury, As I Lay Dying,* and *Sanctuary,* the ending here returns us to the triviality of the everyday. It would seem, however, that it does so much more smoothly and lightheartedly than in the previous novels. With its last story—our last glimpse, through the furniture dealer's eyes, of Lena and Byron on the road—*Light in August* at once closes on a note of muted affirmation and breaks out of its closure, to reenter the free circulation of stories told and listened to. This peaceful, almost cheerful ending, though, cannot obliterate what has gone on before; nor was it meant to. It may even serve as a humorous reminder of that which *Light in August* has been about all along and for which, as an object of exchange, it must ultimately stand for writer and reader alike: the body of desire. The writer never tires of playing with this body, endlessly recapturing it to lose it again.[16]

In *Light in August* Faulkner set out once again to fill an empty space, but all he could do was to pursue his work of mourning and rearticulate absence. Its sound and fury spent, what his novel leaves us with in the end is an odd sense of stillness: the haunting stillness of the circle—a "silent form," like Keats's urn, "[teasing] us out of thought." As we have seen, the circle is here much more than one trope (one "turn") among others; it is the master trope presiding over the novel's structure, generating its iterative movement, and even ruling the play of its meaning. It is not only the *fixed*, enclosing, and organizing figure from which the book takes its form but the *moving* figure, like a wheel turning indefinitely on its axle, which drives it along. All the signs inscribed on its circumference reappear with each new rotation; all meanings produced in the text are both activated by its spin and contained by its rim. The circle controls the text's turbulences, binds its fragments, erases its differences, and rounds off its contradictions. Its closure, however, offers nothing but the blank space of indeterminacy, for whatever the circle is made to mean is at once canceled out by its opposite. If it emblematizes time as the continuous and invariable succession of identical instants, it also stands for the round of eternal becoming and eternal return which disorients time and deprives it of all destination. Indeed, more than any of Faulkner's previous novels and almost as insistently as the later *A Fable*, *Light in August* points to the ancient and universal concept of cyclic time, a concept very close to the timelessness underlying mythic vision and therefore poles apart from time and history as we have understood them in the West since the advent of Christianity.

Here is a world in which events, whether fortunate or disastrous, repeat themselves over and over again, and their repetition does not occur *in* time, in relation to a beginning, an origin, and a goal, a *telos;* repetition is time's absolute essence, the essence of a nonoriginal and nonoriginating *now* containing and dissolving all pasts and all futures. *Sub specie aeternitatis:* one sole and selfsame cycle always beginning anew. And if time is destinationless, if nothing ever happens that has not happened before and will not happen again, the very notion of unique events befalling unique individuals and determining unique destinies becomes inconceivable. With the novel's ending in mind, it may be tempting to think that the powers of life will eventually prevail over the forces of darkness and death. But what the "wheel of thinking" suggests is a world beyond hope and despair. Nothing is ever gained or lost, for there are neither final victories nor irreparable disasters. And if the actors change, the repertoire is always the same. There will always be outcasts to serve as scapegoats, Percy Grimms to kill them, and Lenas to repeople "the good earth," just as there will always be corporals to rebel and generals to have them shot. Only the overall play of the world is real, the ceaseless processsion of passing generations, of which the master, if there were one, could only be an indifferent or else cruel God, one like the ruthless "Player" watching over Christmas's murder.

Instead of bringing us closer to a full understanding, the circle absorbs everything it touches into its enigmatic, apparently meaningful, yet ultimately purposeless patterns of repetition and deferment and threatens us with the empty perfection of the cipher. These patterns can be acknowledged; they cannot be known. Neither outside nor inside the circle can the reader find a fixed point from which to read the whole as a whole, and this holds true of the circle of Faulkner's text as much as of the circle of his fictive world. Like Hightower and the other characters in the book, we are inescapably caught in the turning of the "wheel." But this is after all the fate of all reading, once it has suspended its own linearity to attempt interpretation. So we keep on trying to make sense, circling and recircling around the missing center—unless we content ourselves with just enjoying the show, like gods or children, as Lena does at the novel's end, looking out from a truck and "watching the telephone poles and fences passing like it was a circus parade" (559).

EPILOGUE

UNDER THE SIGN OF SATURN

> Hypocondrie mélancolique: C'est un terrible
> mal, elle fait voir les choses telles
> qu'elles sont.
>
> Gérard de Nerval

From the outset Faulkner had a feeling *for* words, but not until he wrote *The Sound and the Fury* had he acquired the full capacity to feel *through* words, and to feel through them for more than a complacent mirror. Sinking its roots in the desires and terrors of childhood and adolescence, this novel was in one sense more deeply autobiographical than all of his earlier work, but its "depth" was such as to allow it to leap beyond the confessional mode and to develop into something other and better than fictionalized autobiography. To Faulkner it was surely also an act of exorcism, a catharsis, a disengagement from the tangles of youthful self-involvement through the vicarious death of a sacrificial double. Not that the writer's self was suddenly healed of its wounds; writing is not therapy. The work of desire, grief, and memory, the long and difficult process of mourning, remembering, and forgetting, was in fact barely begun. But Faulkner was at last a writer on his own, and his writing was henceforth free to clear other paths, to open up other spaces, well beyond the shivering theater of Narcissus.

From his early *fin-de-siècle* masquerades to his full engagement in the work and play of fiction, Faulkner's growth as writer had been a fairly long one. But once established, mastery was preserved for at least ten years. After *The Sound and the Fury,* his fiction kept changing and expanding; it would be wrong, however, to assume that his work went on following a steadily rising curve. True, *Absalom, Absalom!* is an even greater accomplishment and probably Faulkner's most daring and most original contribution to the novel as a genre. But whatever individual preferences may be, the four novels I have examined all belong to the same plateau of excellence. One critic has argued that "without Faulkner's work of the next ten years *The Sound and the Fury* would itself seem a literary curiosity, an eccentric masterpiece of experimental methods and 'modernist' ideas."[1] It seems to me that had Faulkner written no other book *The Sound and the Fury* would nonetheless belong with the handful of novels that altered the art of fiction during the early decades of the twentieth century. In the books Faulkner wrote after it, he no doubt widened the range of his fictional investigations and approached the complexities and ambiguities of southern experience from other angles; but to hold that *Light in August* and *Absalom, Absalom!* are better novels because they deal more frontally and more fully with the racial problem is to measure artistic excellence by extremely dubious standards. All too often critics with sociohistorical interests tend to confuse the merits of a literary work with the tangible magnitude of its themes and what they take to be the political correctness of their treatment. They would do well to ponder Proust's warning: "Fools believe that the big dimensions of social phenomena provide an excellent opportunity for penetrating the human soul; they should realize that in sounding the depths of an individuality they would have a better chance to understand these phenomena."[2]

It would be as serious a mistake, however, to sever Faulkner's *oeuvre* from its cultural moment and to leave his lifelong obsession with the South out of account. No matter how admirable his verbal performances, our first response to them is not tranquil aesthetic contemplation. What we discover in first reading Faulkner is not only the pulse and power of his language but a fierce urgency to tell which goes well beyond the will to style he shared with other modernist writers. As we read on, we no doubt also come to note how often his narratives call attention to the snarls and stumbles on their paths and how often his fiction gestures toward its own artifice. Faulkner's work is not realistic in any traditional sense; it hardly pretends to offer faithful offprints of reality. If to be a modern artist is to insist on one's medium and to claim that meaning can only be found in *process*, Faulkner is certainly as modern as any of his contemporaries. Yet we would diminish his novels greatly if we read them merely as tales about their own telling. Writing, to him, was not an intransitive verb (as dogmatic deconstructionists would have us believe); it was still a telling, a way of speaking of the world, in the world, to the world.

"The people to me come first, the symbolism comes second," said Faulkner, when asked about *Light in August*,[3] and on many other occasions he made similar statements about his priorities as a fiction-writer. While to those who would like to think of him as a traditional novelist his emphasis on "people" is a welcome confirmation of the notion that he was primarily a creator of "lifelike" characters, it is more likely to embarrass those who see him essentially as a modernist. Did Faulkner really mean what he said or was he just taking the humanistic stance he was expected to take after winning the Nobel Prize? However, Kafka, a very different sort of writer, even less associated with standard realism, apparently had the same priorities: "What matters are people, only them, people."[4] So we should perhaps ask ourselves what this trivial term could possibly mean to them. What they had in mind was certainly not the abstract universal "man" of the philosophers, nor man as the quantifi-able object of scientific discourse. Could it be, then, that in defining "people" as their central concern they simply redefined with deliberate flatness what has always been the novel's proper province: ordinary human beings in the various vicissitudes of their ordinary lives?

Such a broad definition, however, hardly increases our understanding of what Kafka and Faulkner were up to as modern novelists. Writing novels has always been reflecting on what it means to be human, and well before the advent of modernism, the concept of "man" had already become fairly problematic. People were not for Flaubert what they had been for Balzac, nor were they for Conrad or James what they had been for Dickens. By the end of the nineteenth century, it was no longer possible for a serious novelist to portray them as the typical representatives of an immutable "human nature." The time was irrevocably past when fiction provided intelligible and legitimizing pictures of the way we live; novels were becoming more and more reports on the strangeness of being human in a world itself stripped of its reassuring familiarity.

Faulkner's novels are just such reports, the more disturbing as they come from a slightly archaic rural world which we would like to meet our conven-tional pastoral expectations. For central to nearly all of them is a keen sense of estrangement, born of the outraged discovery that no one ever masters the conditions of his life, let alone its meaning. And whether in terror or wonder, his "people" all make the same discovery at their own expense over and over again. The ultimate fascination of Faulkner's novels lies neither in the stories they tell nor in the characters they present but in the rendering of the enig-matic, ever-baffling conjunction of minds and bodies with events which we call "experience." Many of Faulkner's characters are of course extremely vivid figures, but what captivates us in his fiction is not so much what people are or think they are as *what happens to them* and how they remember or refuse or repress what has happened to them—what becomes of them when their lives, snatched up by forces beyond their control and understanding and most often even beyond their awareness, have been sealed into irreversible destinies. One may choose to call this a tragic vision, but the nature of the vision depends on the beholder, and in Faulkner's gaze the show is always just as likely to turn into grim comedy. "There's not too fine a distinction between humor and tragedy," he once observed, for "even tragedy is in a way walking a tightrope between the ridiculous—between the bizarre and the terrible."[5]

What needs to be stressed, however, is that, no matter how massive and inscrutable, the forces we watch at work on his people are always forces of this world. Whatever his debt to Christianity and his private beliefs, no twentieth-century novelist is in the last analysis less other-worldly than Faulkner; his language presses at the edge of the knowable but never hints at any metaphysical *Hinterwelt* beyond the private fantasies or common myths of his characters. We need only think of his fellow southerner Flannery O'Connor to realize at once how thoroughly secular a writer Faulkner was.

Heroism and art were the only possibilities of transcendence he cared about as a novelist, and in his greatest books the stress falls invariably on the limitations and failures of the human mind, not on its powers and achievements. Indeed, nearly all of his work could be read as an illustration of Marx's statement that "it is not the consciousness of men that determines their existence, but on the contrary their social existence that determines their consciousness."[6] Not that Faulkner can be easily fitted into the realist-naturalist tradition and its mechanistic explanation patterns. His involvement with his creatures was far too intense, his feelings about the South, past and present, too much of a passionate love-hate relationship to permit the detached, objective stance of an outside observer, and his "private cosmos" is too fiercely idiosyncratic ever to be reduced to a sociological document. Writing the South was Faulkner's way of reading the South, but like the telling of the Sutpen story by Quentin and Shreve in *Absalom, Absalom!* it was always also a vehement imaginative (re)enactment.

Novels first appeal to our feelings and fantasies. Psychoanalytic criticism tends to treat them as mere exfoliations of the imaginary; the cruder Marxists dismiss them as deceitful ideological constructs. That fiction grows out of the unconscious and around private and collective fantasies is obvious enough, and Faulkner's work is a case in point. Yet, much as it arouses emotions, novelistic imagination at its most demanding is surely also one of the higher forms of intelligence, and the final object of its pursuit is neither wish fulfillment nor indoctrination but knowledge. Milan Kundera goes perhaps too far in contending that "knowledge is the novel's only morality,"[7] but he is certainly right in claiming that novels are ways of knowing the world as it cannot otherwise be known.

Among other things, great novels are also works and worlds of thought. In discussing twentieth-century fiction, critics take this for granted in highly intellectualized novels such as those of Joyce, Proust, Musil, or Broch. They are generally less willing to do so in dealing with Faulkner. Much has been written, of course, about Faulkner's "ideas," and there has been no lack of speculation about what is presumed to be his "vision of life." But surprisingly little has been said so far about his thought as it actually moves in his fiction.

What this thought is about is not far to seek. What is there for a novelist to think and write about but the unavoidable commonplaces of misery, injustice, madness, and crime? And what can he do apart from constructing fictitious models of singular cases? In Faulkner's fiction, however, it would seem that the models always need revision, that the construction is forever provisional; there is always a sense of energies as yet in motion, of turbulences not yet stilled. Thinking, in Faulkner at his best, is never allowed to cool into thought. For when he is at his best, his thinking is at one with his telling and writing: not the articulation of prior thought but the fever of thinking itself, still hot on the page.

Hence the compelling experiential quality of his language and what has so often been deplored as its obscurity. Like all thinking, Faulkner's is a sorting out, a patterning, a way of trying to make sense of the world. But rather than reaching out for the clarity of neatly conceptualized certitudes so as to bring consciousness to rest, it keeps deferring the moment of closure, turning backward and inward, brooding over the confusions of experience and memory, lingering in uncertainty, and staying as close as possible to the astonishment and sense of outrage of which it was born.

Instead of assuming the world of human affairs to be available to lucid description and reasonable interpretation, Faulkner's thinking starts from the premise—shared by many modern writers—that it is opaque. To begin to know the world, then, is to acknowledge that the meanings we bring to it are little more than the precarious fictions of our desires and the erratic impositions of our wills. Faulkner's novels, at least those he wrote from the late twenties to the early forties, are precisely designed to promote such an acknowledgment by pointing to a reality beyond themselves which language fails to encompass and articulate. At the same time, however, they suggest that language is not altogether resourceless and that there are other ways of thinking and speaking the world than those which govern common discourse. Ordinary reasoning is ruled by an "either/or" logic which, because of its insistence on irrefrangible identities and clear, clean spaces between them, is totally unable to account for the many complexities and indeterminacies of human behavior, and as we have seen, the same rigid binary logic informs the ideology of the segregationist and sexist society which Faulkner depicts in his novels. In his own thinking, however, as we can trace its search through the unfoldings and refoldings of his fiction, nothing is ever simply this or that. Identities are not perceived as separate entities but as precarious nodes in a tangled world of ceaseless interaction and change.

It is true that Faulkner's patterns of perception and his rhetorical penchants reflect a powerfully "polar imagination," tending to emphasize extreme tensions and irreducible oppositions.[8] Oxymoron, the pairing of contraries, is, as we know, one of Faulkner's favorite figures of speech, and paradox and irony are his favorite modes of thought. Indeed, no fictional language has ever made fuller allowance for conflict and contradiction, and the familiar concepts of "paradox," "ambiguity," and "tension" may therefore seem to apply almost ideally to Faulkner's work. The point is, however, that, contrary to New Critical assumptions, there is no unifying principle under which they can be subsumed. Paradoxes, with Faulkner, insist on remaining paradoxes; they refuse to be eventually dissolved in the plenitude of the completed text. The self-sustaining wholeness of the "well-wrought urn" may well have been his aesthetic ideal, but it is persistently belied by his novelistic practice. No matter how carefully designed, his novels cannot but display their unresolvedness, an unresolvedness which they manage to contain but are unable to transcend. Discordances do not fade into harmony; fractures are not healed, fragments not gathered into meaningful wholes.

This does not imply, though, that Faulkner was engaged in a quixotic quest for failure. What the tense polarities and radical discontinuities of his work bespeak is less a helpless or complacent dwelling in ambiguity than a stubborn, all but heroic resistance to easy resolutions. In Faulkner writing is motion, action, process—sometimes playful performance, more often feverish struggle. Its most fascinating moments are not those of sovereign mastery; they occur when *force*—the onrush of affects, the energies of thought at work, the raw powers of language—exceeds and defies *form*. Faulkner's thinking, at such moments, is thinking out of need and under pressure, impatient to do its business. And yet there is no hurrying toward judgments, no rush to conclusions, but always an infinitely careful and honest weighing of all the available evidence. Not the brutal alternatives of "either/or" but the acknowledged perplexities of "neither/nor" or the scrupulous gatherings of "and . . . and."

Faulkner's thought moves by collections and recollections, connections and disconnections, endlessly reshaping and reinterpreting, seeking to encompass its chaotic material in ever-widening circles of conjecture and speculation. Its movement is one of indefinite centrifugal expansion; its divisions are never exclusions. None of his major novels can be reduced to a simple "message." Instead of a single general truth, they all offer heaps of singular local truths, bodied forth in a multiplicity of imaginary selves and patiently traced through the intricate webs of their interrelationships. Faulkner's wisdom is what has always been the novel's wisdom: the brave and humble wisdom of uncertainty.

The wisdom of uncertainty is an uncertain wisdom, likely to frustrate those who expect writers not only to raise questions but to answer them. The ordinary reader wants reassurance that evil is plain evil and that innocence is above suspicion; he would like to find in fiction a world where everything stays "in its ordered place" or which can be changed for the better. Hence, among early reviewers, the regret that Faulkner did not put his remarkable talent to more positive use[9] and the general sense of relief that came in the fifties when Faulkner officially rallied to the camp of the humanists. The essence of his wisdom, however, is found in his darker novels. Faulkner was born into literature under the sign of Saturn, the remote, slow planet of detours and delays, the black sun of melancholy; his was the saturnine temperament of the solitary writer, and saturnine too are the torpid landscapes of his fiction: "Like our rivers, our land, opaque, slow, violent, shaping and creating life in its implacable and brooding image."[10]

From the fifteenth to the seventeenth century, the drawings and engravings of many European artists illustrated the fate of Saturn's children; most of them represent either hermits and prisoners in their cells, weighed down by desolate reveries, or lost pilgrims, wretched beggars, and exhausted vagrants who have still a long way to go.[11] Faulkner's doomed characters are likewise condemned to brooding seclusion or aimless wandering. Haunted by loss, suffering, and death, his great novels all reflect awareness of the futility of human endeavor and the immutability of misfortune in the flow of time; each of the four works I have discussed here turns out to be a literary *vanitas*.

With Faulkner the writer, though, the sense of futility never became an alibi for escape or retreat; nor did his own brooding ever cease to be the restless passion of an energetic mind in search of truth. Hence his darkest novels are also those where we find the sharpest insights into southern culture. Faulkner's wisdom is neither haughty withdrawal from nor cynical acceptance of the world as it is. One thing at least he knew for certain: that evil was rampant in the society in which he lived. As he himself noted, for a southern writer of his generation, the alternative was either "to draw a savage indictment of the contemporary scene or to escape from it into a makebelieve region of swords and magnolias and mockingbirds which perhaps never existed anywhere."[12] Faulkner soon chose the former course; *Sanctuary* was indeed a "savage indictment," and from *Flags in the Dust* to *Go Down, Moses* all his Yoknapatawpha novels were to be highly critical treatments of the South.

Yet at the same time Faulkner could also legitimately claim that "it is himself that the Southerner is writing about, not about his environment."[13] For environment, to him, was not a reality outside his self; the legacies and liabilities of his milieu were something so deeply internalized and so bitterly resented that he "unconsciously [wrote] into every line and phrase his violent despairs and rages and frustrations and his violent prophesies of still more violent hopes."[14]

Violence is often Faulkner's fare. His comments on the predicament of the southern writer confirm the suspicion that its dramatization on the fictional scene is most often the writing out of an inner violence, that the conflicts staged in his novels are in one sense all intensely personal affairs. Perhaps because Faulkner came from a culture in which, not so long ago, there were no clearly marked boundaries between the public and the private,[15] his work, while exemplifying the "inward turn" characteristic of the modern novel, is probably more intimately in touch with social forces than that of any other major American novelist of our century.

"I am telling the same story over and over, which is myself and the world," Faulkner once wrote to Malcolm Cowley.[16] Yet the more he told the story, the more his self receded and the more generously he responded to otherness. From *The Sound and the Fury* to *Light in August*, we can measure the road traveled: while Quentin, the young self-lacerating patrician, is still to some extent a projection of the writer's *self*, Christmas, the rootless proletarian, the desperate pariah of uncertain identity, is definitely *another*. As Gilles Deleuze has suggested, to write, at its most adventurous, is perhaps always "to become something else."[17] For Faulkner, in *The Sound and the Fury*, it was to become by turns a speechless idiot, a neurotic young man, a spiteful petit bourgeois. In *As I Lay Dying* it was to become an addled old woman, a bemused pregnant girl, a confused child, a forlorn son drifting toward madness. In *Light in August* it was to become a "white nigger." This empathetic self-obliteration clearly had its limits and Faulkner was well aware of them: it is not a matter of chance that in *The Sound and the Fury* the fourth section *is not* Dilsey's interior monologue and that all the blacks are seen from without. But to invent the troubled psyche of a character apparently as remote from the writer's own experience and environment as Christmas, more than the talents of an illusionist were required.

Faulkner possessed what is probably the novelist's rarest gift: the faculty of decentering and displacement, the aptitude to cross boundaries and inhabit other landscapes of the mind, the capacity to allow oneself to be traversed by unknown currents and tap their intensities. And the deeper he plunged into the riddles of his *oeuvre*, the more that *oeuvre* effaced him. In his later years, when his best work was behind him, Faulkner, who had so desperately wanted literature to bring him fame and glory, came to desire that effacement to the point of wishing "to be, as a private individual, abolished and voided from history, leaving it markless, no refuse save the printed books,"[18] and even regretted having signed his books.

His signature can of course no longer be erased; there is just no way to prevent the work he has left us from being the sovereign unfolding of a name, from being the place where this name assumes a body. Faulkner has disappeared *into* his work (like the painter in the Chinese legend who disappears into one of his canvases), not *from* his work. And one might even say that he has painted himself into it, that the sum of his writings forms the incessantly rebegun rough draft of an immense self-portrait. Except that once finished, this portrait would no longer be in any way the portrait of a self fascinated by its own reflection. Faulkner represents himself, not full face, arrested in rapt attention, as does Velasquez in *Las Meninas*, but with his back turned to the viewer, as does Vermeer in his *Art of Painting*. Were it not for the brush and the hand holding it, this could be a portrait of anyone. Let us not, therefore, look for the unique face of a singular man. The portrait of the artist by himself, if it aspires to some sort of truth, can only be the portrait of a man unknown.

NOTES

Introduction: Masks and Mirrors

1. "L'Apres-Midi d'un Faune" (with no accent on the "e") appeared in *The New Republic* on August 6, 1919. Reprinted in *EPP*, pp. 39–40. For a close reading, see Lothar Hönnighausen, "Faulkner's First Published Poem: 'L'Apres-Midi d'un Faune,'" *William Faulkner: Materials, Studies, and Criticism* (Tokyo), 6 (May 1984), 1–19.

2. *SP*, p. 7.

3. On Faulkner's role-playing, see Joseph L. Blotner, *Faulkner: A Biography* (New York: Random House, 1974), vol. 1, pp. 232–33, 255, 324–25, 351, 369.

4. For photographs from this period, see Blotner, *Faulkner*, pp. 200, 225, and Jack Cofield, *William Faulkner: The Cofield Collection* (Oxford, Miss.: Yoknapatawpha Press, 1978), pp. 53, 55, 56.

5. *American Heritage Dictionary of the English Language* (1978).

6. See Faulkner's Foreword to *The Faulkner Reader* (New York: Random House, 1954), pp. ix–x: "This was 1915 and '16; I had seen an aeroplane and my mind was filled with names: Ball, and Immelman and Boelcke, and Guynemer and Bishop, and I was waiting, biding, until I would be old enough or free enough or anyway could get to France and become glorious and beribboned too." Also in *ESPL*, p. 180.

7. *The Letters of John Keats*, ed. M. B. Forman (London: Oxford University Press, 1935), p. 228.

8. Ibid., p. 72.

9. Marcel Proust, *Contre Sainte-Beuve*, ed. Pierre Clarac (Paris: Gallimard, Bibliothèque de la Pléiade, 1971), pp. 221–22. My translation.

10. *MOS*, p. 251.

11. "The Lilacs" is as yet unpublished, but its title poem was to appear in a somewhat different version in *A Green Bough*. The other completed poem sequences are "Vision in Spring" (summer 1921), "Orpheus, and Other Poems" (1923), "The Marble Faun" (probably begun in 1918 and published after revison in 1924), and the sonnet sequence "Helen: A Courtship" (summer 1926).

12. *MF*, p. 6.

13. On Faulkner's poetry, see Harry Runyan, "Faulkner's Poetry," *Faulkner Studies*, 3 (Summer–Autumn 1954), 23–29; George P. Garrett, "An Examination of the Poetry of William Faulkner," *Princeton University Library Chronicle*, 18 (Spring 1957), 124–35; Cleanth Brooks, "Faulkner as Poet," *Southern Literary Journal*, 1 (December 1968), 5–19; H. Edward Richardson, *William Faulkner: The Journey to Self-Discovery* (Columbia: University of Missouri Press, 1969), pp. 47–60, 104–15; Martin Kreiswirth, "Poetry and Imitation," in *William Faulkner: The Making of a Novelist* (Athens: University of Georgia Press, 1983), pp. 2–17. The latest, best informed, and most comprehensive studies of Faulkner's literary beginnings are Judith L. Sensibar, *The Origins of Faulkner's Art* (Austin: University of Texas Press, 1984), and Lothar Hönnighausen, *William Faulkner: The Art of Stylization in His Early Graphic and Literary Work* (Cambridge: Cambridge University Press, 1987).

14. See *EPP*, pp. 57–59, 61.

15. On *Vision in Spring* as a poetic sequence, see Sensibar, *The Origins of Faulkner's Art*, pp. 104–205.

16. Garrett, "An Examination of the Poetry of William Faulkner," 125.

17. On the Pan motif in English literature from 1890 to 1930, see Patricia Merivale,

Pan the Goat-God: His Myth in Modern Times (Cambridge, Mass.: Harvard University Press, 1969).

18. *MF*, p. 12.

19. Richard P. Adams, *Faulkner: Myth and Motion* (Princeton, N.J.: Princeton University Press, 1968), p. 77.

20. Phrase from Melvin Backman, in "Faulkner's Sick Heroes: Bayard Sartoris and Quentin Compson," *Modern Fiction Studies*, 2 (Autumn 1956), 95–108.

21. See "The World and Pierrot. A Nocturne" and "The Dancer," in *VS*, pp.10–29, 67–75. On Faulkner's Pierrot, see Sensibar, *The Origins of Faulkner's Art;* Hönnighausen, *William Faulkner: The Art of Stylization*, pp.128–35; and Michael Kreyling, "Faulkner's Pierrotic Hero," *Figures of the Hero in Southern Narrative* (Baton Rouge: Louisiana University Press, 1987), pp. 125–53.

22. Two of the four known copies were published in limited facsimile editions in 1975: one by the Bibliographical Society of the University of Virginia and the University Press of Virginia, the other at Oxford, Miss., by the Yoknapatawpha Press. A third facsimile edition was published in 1977 by the University Press of Virginia and the Bibliographical Society of the University of Virginia, with a textual apparatus and an excellent introduction by Noel Polk.

23. *MAR*, pp.1–2.

24. *MAR*, pp. 2–3.

25. Pierrot's vogue began in 1825 with Jean-Gaspard Debureau's pantomimes at the Funambules. A group of writers, including Flaubert (*Pierrot au sérail*, 1840) and Théophile Gautier (*Pierrot posthume*, 1847), wrote scripts for him. Baudelaire, Champfleury, Gautier, Banville, Verlaine, Rimbaud, Mallarmé, Huysmans, and Rostand all wrote about Pierrot, and Jules Laforgue often wrote *as* Pierrot. In England the harvest was no doubt less abundant than in France, but even before the publication in 1899 of *The Symbolist Movement in Literature*, Arthur Symons's extremely influential book, Pierrot had made his entry into English literature. *Pierrot of the Minute*, a play by Ernest Dowson illustrated by Beardsley, appeared in 1897, and in its wake many poets were to write Pierrot poems, among them such major figures of modern poetry as T. S. Eliot, Wallace Stevens, and Conrad Aiken. See Robert F. Storey, *Pierrot: A Critical History of a Mask* (Princeton, N.J.: Princeton University Press, 1978), and Martin Green and John Swan, *The Triumph of Pierrot: The Commedia dell'Arte and the Modern Imagination* (New York: Macmillan, 1986). On the clown figure in romantic and modern art and literature, see also Jean Starobinski's fine essay *Portrait de l'artiste en saltimbanque* (Genève: Albert Skira, Les sentiers de la création, 1970).

26. Introduction to *MAR*, p. xvii.

27. Faulkner owned a copy of Wilde's play in the American 1912 edition, which included Beardsley's illustrations. See J. Blotner, *William Faulkner's Library: A Catalogue* (Charlottesville: University Press of Virginia, 1964), p. 77.

28. *MAR*, pp. 43–48.

29. For a fuller discussion of Marietta's metamorphosis into a work of art and a more detailed examination of Faulkner's various borrowings, see "The Iconography of Faulkner's *Marionettes*," in Hönnighausen, *William Faulkner: The Art of Stylization*, pp. 128–53.

30. *MAR*, p. 55.

31. *MOS*, p. 250.

32. William B. Yeats, *Uncollected Prose*, ed. John P. Frayne, vol. 1 (London: Macmillan, 1970), p. 103.

33. "Verse Old and Nascent: A Pilgrimage," *Double Dealer*, 7 (April 1925), 129; *EPP*, p. 115.

34. *EPP*, p. 72.

35. *EPP*, p. 71.

36. "American Drama: Inhibitions," *Mississippian* (March 17, 1922), 5; *EPP*, p. 93.

37. "Books and Things: Joseph Hergesheimer," *Mississippian* (December 15, 1922), 5; *EPP*, p. 101.

38. *EPP*, pp. 101–2.

39. *LG*, p. 253.

40. "American Drama: Eugene O'Neill," *Mississippian* (February 3, 1922), 5; *EPP*, p. 86.

41. *EPP*, p. 87.

42. *EPP*, p. 94.

43. *EPP*, p. 86.

44. *EPP*, p. 94.

45. See Carvel Collins, Introduction, *MAY*, pp. 8–10.

46. *EPP*, pp. 42–50.

47. *EPP*, pp. 90-92.

48. See *William Faulkner: Proses, poésies et essais critiques de jeunesse*, trans. Henri Thomas (Paris: Gallimard, 1966), p. 8.

49. *EPP*, p. 91.

50. Michel Gresset, "Faulkner's 'The Hill,'" *Southern Literary Journal*, 6 (Summer 1974), 12.

51. *EPP*, p. 91.

52. *EPP*, pp. 91–92.

53. *EPP*, p. 92.

54. Jorge Luis Borges, *Labyrinths: Selected Stories and Other Writings*, trans. and ed. Donald A. Yates and James E. Irby (New York: New Directions, 1962), p. 182.

55. Gresset, "Faulkner's 'The Hill,'" 14.

56. *US*, pp. 331–37; originally published in *Mississippi Quarterly*, 26 (Summer 1973), 403–9.

57. *US*, p. 332.

58. *US*, p. 334.

59. Swinburne was probably the first writer to turn Pan into a god of terror. "A Nympholept," one of his great "panic" poems, may have inspired Faulkner's title.

60. *US*, p. 334.

61. *US*, p. 335.

62. Quentin's death by water in *The Sound and the Fury* is foreshadowed by that of Sir Galwyn of Arthgyl, the knight-errant in *Mayday*, the pseudo-medieval tale which Faulkner wrote in late 1925 or early 1926. Before embracing "Little sister Death," Galwyn sees in the river "one all young and white, and with long shining hair like a column of fair sunny water." Similarly, in "The Lilacs," the opening poem of *A Green Bough*, an aviator pursues "a white woman," whom he stalks "through the shimmering reaches of the sky"; at the moment when he feels her arms and her "cool breath," a bullet strikes him "in the left breast." See *MAY*, p. 87, and *GB*, p. 8. The drowning metaphor reemerges in many of Faulkner's novels. See *FD*, p. 243: "And then Belle again, enveloping him like a rich and fatal drug, like a motionless and cloying sea in which he watched himself drown"; *WP*, pp. 44–45: "[Harry Wilbourne] seemed to be drowning, volition and all, in the yellow stare"; *T*, p. 95: "[Eula Varner was] still not moving: just standing there facing me so that what I smelled was not even just woman but that terrible, that drowning envelopment."

63. *Metamorphoses*, III, 192–93.

64. The sketches have all been collected in *NOS*.

65. Reported by Faulkner in "A Note on Sherwood Anderson" (1953), *ESPL*, p. 7.

66. "Dying Gladiator," *Double Dealer*, 7 (January–February 1925), 85; "The Faun," *Double Dealer*, 7 (April 1925), 148; "The Lilacs," *Double Dealer*, 7 (June 1925), 185–87. The first two were reprinted in *EPP*, pp. 113, 119; the third, after revision, became the first poem of *A Green Bough*.

67. "On Criticism," *Double Dealer*, 7 (January–February 1925), 83-84; "Verse Old

and Nascent: A Pilgrimage," *Double Dealer*, 7 (April 1925), 129–31; "Sherwood Anderson," *Dallas Morning News*, 3 (April 26, 1925), 7. See *EPP*, pp. 109–12, and *NOS*, pp. 132–39.

68. Review of *Ducdame*, a novel by John Cowper Powys; first published on March 22, 1925, in the literary supplement of the *Times-Picayune*; reprinted in *Mississippi Quarterly*, 28 (Summer 1975), 343–46, with an introduction by Carvel Collins.

69. Among them many poems, a number of which are mentioned and quoted in Blotner, *Faulkner* (390–91, 392, 397, 398–99); "Literature and War," a short essay probably written in 1925, edited by Michael Millgate in *Mississippi Quarterly*, 26 (Summer 1973), 387–93; and two sketches, "The Priest" and "Don Giovanni," collected in *US*, pp. 348–51, 480–88.

70. In *Soldiers' Pay* as well as in *Mosquitoes* Faulkner quotes poems he will later include in *A Green Bough*.

71. Michael Millgate, "Starting Out in the Twenties: Reflections on *Soldiers' Pay*," *Mosaic*, 7 (Fall 1973), 9.

72. See *GB*, pp. 7–11.

73. *SP*, pp. 82–83.

74. *SP*, p. 295.

75. *SP*, p. 224.

76. *SP*, p. 225.

77. On motivation in *Soldiers' Pay*, see Cleanth Brooks, *William Faulkner: Toward Yoknapatawpha and Beyond* (New Haven, Conn.: Yale University Press, 1978), pp. 82–92.

78. See Blotner, *Faulkner*, pp. 192–97.

79. See Barbara Hand, "Faulkner's Widow Recounts Memories of College Weekends in Charlottesville," *Cavalier Daily*, 21 (April 1972), 4: "Mrs. Faulkner said that her husband used her as a model for one of his characters in his first novel, and that it 'hurt my feelings terribly.'"

80. *FU*, p. 257.

81. For fuller treatments of structure and technique, see Ilse Dusoir Lind, "Faulkner's *Mosquitoes*: A New Reading," *William Faulkner: Materials, Studies, and Criticism*, 4 (July 1982), 1–18, and Kreiswirth, *William Faulkner: The Making of a Novelist*, pp. 84–99.

82. See Frederick L. Gwynn, "Faulkner's Prufrock—and Other Observations," *Journal of English and Germanic Philology*, 52 (January 1953), 63–70.

83. For Faulkner's models, see Blotner, *Faulkner*, pp. 514–22.

84. Hemingway parodied Anderson's style in *The Torrents of Spring* (1926). Faulkner did so in his introduction to *Sherwood Anderson and Other Famous Creoles*, a collection of caricatures by William Spratling, published in December 1926. The publication of the book was resented by Anderson and was probably the immediate cause of his break with Faulkner.

85. Concern with the breakdown and inversion of traditional sex roles appears in such romantic and late romantic texts as Gautier's *Mademoiselle de Maupin*, Swinburne's "Hermaphoditus," and Pater's "Diaphaneity" and in French nineteenth-century novels commonly associated with realism. Balzac, Stendhal, Flaubert, and Zola all portrayed effeminate males and viriloid females, if not androgynes and castrati. Little attention has been accorded to the significant place occupied by homosexuality and hermaphroditism in Faulkner's early fiction. Sexual ambiguities appear not only in *Mosquitoes* but also in *Soldiers' Pay* and "Elmer," the uncompleted novel of 1925. Faulkner's interest in them is less prominent in his later work but never totally vanishes, as can be seen in *Sanctuary, Light in August, Absalom, Absalom!, The Unvanquished*, and *The Wild Palms*.

86. See Fairchild's reflections in *Mosquitoes*, p. 231.

87. *MOS*, p. 75.

88. *MOS*, p. 186.

89. *MOS*, p. 210.

90. *MOS*, p. 210.

91. See Joyce W. Warren, "Faulkner's Portrait of the Artist," *Mississippi Quarterly*, 19 (Summer 1966), 121–31.

92. *MOS*, p. 339.

93. *MOS*, p. 154.

94. James Joyce, *A Portrait of the Artist as a Young Man*, ed. Chester G. Anderson (New York: Viking Press, 1968), p. 217.

95. Ibid., p. 172.

96. *MOS*, p. 339.

97. *A Portrait of the Artist as a Young Man*, p. 170.

98. *MOS*, p. 11.

99. On this point, see Kenneth William Hepburn, "Faulkner's *Mosquitoes*: A Poetic Turning Point," *Twentieth Century Literature*, 17 (January 1971), 19–27.

100. *MOS*, p. 329.

101. *MOS*, p. 11.

102. In his essay on fetishism Freud refers to "the Chinese custom of mutilating the female foot and then revering it like a fetish after it has been mutilated. It seems as though the Chinese male wants to thank the woman for having submitted to being castrated." Gordon's first sculpture is a fetish in much the same way: through mutilation woman's unbearable "wound" is both acknowledged and denied. See "Fetishism" (1927) in the *Standard Edition of the Complete Psychological Works of Sigmund Freud*, ed. and trans. James Strachey (London: Hogarth Press, 1964), vol. 21, p. 157. All further references to Freud will be to this edition, which will be cited hereafter as *SE*.

103. *MOS*, p. 322.

104. *MOS*, p. 339.

105. James Joyce, *Stephen Hero*, ed. Theodore Spencer (London: Jonathan Cape, 1956), p. 83.

106. Ibid.

107. Edited by Dianne L. Cox, the text of the unfinished typescript of the novel, now at the University of Virginia, was published in the Summer 1983 issue of *Mississippi Quarterly* with a foreword by James B. Meriwether. The beginnings of other versions subsist under various titles: "Growing Pains," "Elmer and Myrtle," "Elmer," "Portrait of Elmer Hodge." A completed short story entitled "A Portrait of Elmer," probably written in the thirties, was included in *US*, pp. 610–41. See Thomas L. McHaney, "The Elmer Papers: Faulkner's Comic Portraits of the Artist," *Mississippi Quarterly*, 26 (Summer 1973), 281–311.

108. Jenny Steinbauer describes "Faulkner" first as "a funny man," then as "a little kind of black man," and reports his self-definition as "a liar by profession" (*MOS*, pp. 144–45). In *Sanctuary* Popeye is described in almost identical terms by Horace Benbow: "that little black man" (*SAN*, 113). On Faulkner's three "signed" self-representations, see Michel Gresset, "Faulkner's Self-Portraits," *Faulkner Journal*, 2 (Fall 1986), 2–13.

109. Cf. *MOS*, pp. 246–47, 249, 252, and *GB*, pp. 21, 49, 61.

110. Review in *New York Herald Tribune Books*, June 19, 1927, 9; reprinted in *William Faulkner: The Critical Heritage*, ed. John Bassett (London: Routledge and Kegan Paul, 1975), pp. 66–67.

111. "William Faulkner, Who Wrote 'Soldiers' Pay,' Again Manifests Brilliancy, Promise and Foibles," *New York Evening Post*, June 11, 1927, section 3, 7; reprinted in *A Reviewer's ABC* (New York: Meridian Books, 1958), pp. 197–200, and *The Critical Heritage*, pp. 63–65 .

112. *Flags in the Dust* was edited by Douglas Day and published in 1973 by Random House. The text is based on a composite typescript that Faulkner retained with an earlier handwritten copy.

113. *LG*, p. 255.

114. See *Father Abraham*, edited, with an introduction and textual note, by James B. Meriwether (New York: Random House, 1983).

115. Reported by Faulkner in "A Note on Sherwood Anderson," *ESPL*, p. 8.

116. Joseph Conrad, "Books," *Notes on Life and Letters* (London: Dent, 1949), p. 6. The essay was first published in 1905.

117. *FU*, p. 285.

118. Introduction, *FD*, p. x.

119. *SL*, p. 211.

120. On Faulkner's models for *Flags in the Dust*, see Michael Millgate, *The Achievement of William Faulkner* (New York: Random House, 1966), p. 25; Blotner, *Faulkner*, pp. 532-38, 545–46.

121. Quoted in Blotner, *Faulkner*, pp. 531–32, from the manuscript deposited at the Yale University Library.

122. *FD*, p. 46.

123. *FU*, p. 23. See also p. 48 and "Ad Astra," *CS*, pp. 407–29.

124. See Cleanth Brooks *William Faulkner: The Yoknapatawpha Country* (New Haven, Conn.: Yale University Press, 1963), p. 103. Hereafter referred to as Brooks, *The Yoknapatawpha Country*.

125. For Bayard's literary sources, see Dieter Meindl, *Bewusstsein als Schicksal: Zu Struktur und Entwicklung von William Faulkners Generationsromanen* (Stuttgart: Metzler, 1974), pp. 90-106.

126. *FD*, p.170.

127. *SAR*, p. 203.

128. *FD*, p.187.

129. Horace resembles Faulkner in many ways: he is of small stature; he is a tennis player and a pipe smoker, a friend of children and a devotee of Shakespeare and Keats, and like the author he marries a divorcée. Moreover, the early versions of the novel contain samples of Horace's Decadent poetry very similar to Faulkner's own early verse.

130. *FD*, p. 8.

131. Judith Wittenberg, "Vision and Re-Vision: Bayard Sartoris," in *Critical Essays on William Faulkner: The Sartoris Family*, ed. Arthur F. Kinney (Boston: G. K. Hall, 1985), p. 326. On Byron Snopes, see also John T. Matthews, *The Play of Faulkner's Language* (Ithaca, N.Y.: Cornell University Press, 1982), pp. 53–56, and James G. Watson, *William Faulkner: Letters and Fictions* (Austin: University of Texas Press, 1987), pp. 64–66, 69–75.

132. On this point, see William Empson's chapter on "double plots" in *Some Versions of Pastoral* (Middlesex: Penguin Books, 1966). On their use in other Faulkner novels—especially in *The Wild Palms*—and their ideological implications, see Michael Grimwood, *Heart in Conflict: Faulkner's Struggles with Vocation* (Athens: University of Georgia Press, 1987).

133. *FD*, p. 432.

134. *FD*, p. 5

135. *FD*, p. 14.

136. *FD*, p. 427.

137. *FD*, p.120.

138. *FD*, p. 433.

139. *FD*, p. 94.

140. *FD*, p. 426.

141. See letter to Horace Liveright, October 16, 1927, in *SL*, p. 38.

142. *AA*, p.143.

One. The Struggle with the Angel

I. The Quest for Eurydice

1. Faulkner's introduction survives in several partial and complete manuscript and typescript drafts. Two of them have been published: "William Faulkner: An Introduction for *The Sound and the Fury*," *Southern Review*, N.S., 8 (October 1972), 705–10; "An Introduction to *The Sound and the Fury*," *Mississippi Quarterly*, 26 (Summer 1973), 410–15. Both versions were edited by James B. Meriwether.

2. "An Introduction for *The Sound and the Fury*," 708.

3. Ibid., 710.

4. Ibid.

5. Ibid. No one, to my knowledge, has noticed how much the anecdote about the old Roman recalls the story of Pygmalion in Ovid's *Metamorphoses*: Pygmalion falls in love with a beautiful ivory statue he has created, bedecks it with jewels, fondles its curves, and takes it to bed, praying to Venus that his wife be (or be like) his "ivory girl." The "Pygmalion complex" is of course common among artists, and the transformation of the manufactured woman into a living female body is probably every male novelist's dream.

6. See André Green, *Un Oeil en trop : Le Complexe d'Oedipe dans la tragédie* (Paris: Editions de Minuit, 1969), pp. 35–40.

7. Estelle Oldham, one of the models for Caddy, is compared to "a lovely vase" in one of Faulkner's letters. See Blotner, *Faulkner*, p. 563. On the symbolism of the urn/vase image, see David Minter, *William Faulkner: His Life and Work* (Baltimore: Johns Hopkins University Press, 1980), p. 102.

8. "An Introduction for *The Sound and the Fury*," *Southern Review*, 710.

9. Ibid., 709.

10. Ibid.

11. Ibid.

12. Ibid., 710.

13. Ibid., 709.

14. Ibid., 710.

15. *FU*, p. 61. See also *LG*, p. 146.

16. Quoted in James B. Meriwether, "Notes on the Textual History of *The Sound and the Fury*," *Papers of the Bibliographical Society of America*, 56 (Third Quarter, 1962), 289.

17. See *FU*, pp. 61, 77; *LG*, pp. 92, 146, 180.

18. *FU*, p. 61.

19. Samuel Beckett, *Proust and Three Dialogues with Georges Duthuit* (London: John Calder, 1965), p. 125.

20. *LG*, pp. 146–47. See also p. 222.

21. The working title of the short story was "Twilight." See Blotner, *Faulkner*, p. 566. Faulkner had already written two stories about the Compson children: "That Evening Sun Go Down" (published in March 1931; included in *T13* and *CS*) and "A Justice" (included in *T13* and *CS*).

22. *LG*, p. 238.

23. *LG*, pp. 220–21.

24. *LG*, p. 180. Significant too is Faulkner's offer to provide an appendix to the novel for the Viking *Portable Faulkner*, which Malcolm Cowley was editing in 1945. The many additions he made there to the original account of the Compson family (a number of which, incidentally, are inconsistent with the novel) are tangible testimony to his feeling that the story was "still not finished." First published in the *Portable Faulkner* in 1946, the "Appendix: Compson 1699–1945" was republished in a slightly different version in the Modern Library double volume of *The Sound and the Fury* and *As I Lay Dying* (1946) and the Random House edition of 1966. Hereafter referred to as "Appendix."

25. *LG*, p. 238.

26. On the processlike quality of the novel, see Donald M. Kartiganer, *The Fragile Thread: The Meaning of Form in Faulkner's Novels* (Amherst: University of Massachusetts Press, 1979), pp. 3–22.

27. Robert Musil, *Der Mann Ohne Eigenschaften* (Hamburg: Rowohlt, 1952), p. 1640. My translation.

28. "A Primitive Like an Orb," *Collected Poems* (New York: Alfred A. Knopf, 1951), p. 443.

29. "Le Double et l'absent," *Critique*, 29 (May 1973), 403–4.

30. Reported by M. E. Coindreau in "Preface to *The Sound and the Fury*," *The Time of William Faulkner* (Columbia: University of South Carolina Press, 1971), p. 41. The autobiographical source of the Damuddy episode is presumably the funeral of Faulkner's grandmother Lelia Swift Butler in 1907. Faulkner was then ten years old—approximately the same age as Quentin at the time of Damuddy's death in the novel.

31. Coindreau, *The Time of William Faulkner*, p. 49.

32. "An Introduction for *The Sound and the Fury*," 710.

33. Note also the phonic kinship of *muddy* and *Damuddy*.

34. Freud, "Fetishism," *SE*, vol. 21, p. 154.

35. Ibid., p. 155.

36. Revealingly, in one of his later interviews Faulkner confused Caddy's pear tree with an apple tree (see *FU*, p. 31). With regard to the Edenic connotations of the scene, note that before Caddy climbs the tree "a snake [crawls] out from under the house" (*SF*, 42), and a few moments later Dilsey says to her, "You Satan. . . . Come down from there" (51).

37. *LG*, p. 244.

38. *FU*, p. 6.

39. Consider also what Faulkner told M. E. Coindreau: "the same thing happened to me that happens to many writers—I fell in love with one of my characters, Caddy. I loved her so much I couldn't decide to give her life just for the duration of a short story. She deserved more than that" (*The Time of William Faulkner*, p. 41). Among the figures anticipating Caddy one might mention Juliet Bunden in "Adolescence," a story written in 1922; Frankie, in an untitled story seemingly written in 1924; Jo-Addie in "Elmer," the uncompleted novel begun in 1925; the nameless girl who turns out to be "Little sister Death" in "The Kid Learns" (1925); and Dulcie, the little heroine of *The Wishing Tree* (1927). Most of the young female characters in Faulkner's first three novels are also related to Caddy in some way or other, Patricia Robyn (*Mosquitoes*) being the one who bears the closest resemblance to her. The heroine of *The Sound and the Fury* is of course much more complex than any of these figures, and Faulkner's involvement with her has deep autobiographical sources. In creating her, he drew more than ever before on memories of his own childhood and adolescence. It seems safe to assume that Estelle Oldham, whom he had come to know as a little boy and with whom he fell in love as a teenager, served as a model for Caddy. But so did Sallie Murry, the tomboyish cousin to whom, as Blotner points out, Faulkner "had been almost as close as a sister" (*Faulkner*, p. 568). And one might do well to remember that Estelle also served as a model for the devastating portrait of Cecily Saunders in *Soldiers' Pay*. Which is to say that Caddy, even though she rose out of the depths of Faulkner's private experience, is above all a literary creation.

40. Further name confusions are induced by the presence of two Quentins (uncle and niece) and two Jasons (father and son) and by the change of the idiot's name from Maury to Benjamin. While pointing to inbreeding and degeneracy in the Compson family, these confusions refer more generally to the precarious status of the self. Name confusion leads to identity confusion. Although Faulkner's characters preserve recog-

nizable features, the device tends to blur the boundaries between them. What is at stake here is the very concept of *character* and its function in the novel.

41. The importance of this image and of the scene it heralds is confirmed by the manuscript. Originally section 2 started thus: "One minute she was standing there. The next Benjy was yelling and pulling at her. They went down the hall to the bathroom and stopped there, Caddy backed against the door. . . ." This page of the manuscript is reproduced in James B. Meriwether, *The Literary Career of William Faulkner: A Bibliographical Study* (Princeton, N.J.: Princeton University Library, 1961), illustration II.

42. The reversible girl = tree metaphor can be traced back to Faulkner's earliest work: in *The Marble Faun* poplars are compared to "slender girls"; girls are likened to trees in *The Marionettes* as well as in *Soldiers' Pay* and *Mosquitoes*.

43. Jean-Paul Sartre, *Baudelaire* (Paris: Gallimard, 1947), p. 201. My translation.

44. The phrase is from Harry M. Campbell and Ruel E. Foster, *William Faulkner: A Critical Appraisal* (Norman: University of Oklahoma Press, 1951), p. 54.

45. Paul Claudel, *La Ville*, 2d ed. (Paris: Mercure de France, 1920), p. 307.

46. For a discussion of Caddy in psychological and moral terms, see Catherine B. Baum, "'The Beautiful One': Caddy Compson as Heroine of *The Sound and the Fury*," *Modern Fiction Studies*, 13 (Spring 1967), 33–44; Eileen Gregory, "Caddy Compson's World," *Merrill Studies in The Sound and the Fury*, compiled by James B. Meriwether (Columbus, Ohio: Charles E. Merrill, 1970), pp. 89–101.

47. Henry James, *Notes and Reviews* (Cambridge, Mass.: Dunster House, 1921), p. 226.

II. The Agony of Dispossession

1. "The title, of course, came from the first section, which was Benjy. I thought the story was told in Benjy's section, and the title came there. So it—in that sense it does apply to Benjy rather than to anybody else, though the more I had to work on the book, the more elastic the title became, until it covered the whole family" (*FU*, p. 87).

2. Clément Rosset, *Le Réel: Traité de l'idiotie* (Paris: Editions de Minuit, 1977), p. 42.

3. See Irena Kaluza's helpful linguistic-stylistic study, *The Functioning of Sentence Structure in the Stream-of-Consciousness Technique of William Faulkner's "The Sound and the Fury"* (Krakow: Nakdalem Uniwersytetu Jagiellonskiego, 1967), reprinted by Folcroft Press in 1970. According to Kaluza, reported dialogue represents 56 percent of the Benjy section, indirect quotations introduced by "he said" and the like 21 percent, and "stream of consciousness" proper 23 percent.

4. According to L. Moffitt Cecil, Faulkner allows Benjy a working vocabulary of some 500 words, including slightly over 200 nouns, 175 verbs or verbals, 61 adjectives, 37 adverbs, 25 prepositions, and 13 conjunctions; see "A Rhetoric for Benjy," *Southern Literary Journal*, 3 (Fall 1970), 32–46, esp. 38–42. See also Seiji Sasamoto, "The First Section of *The Sound and the Fury*: Benjy and His Expressions," *William Faulkner: Materials, Studies, and Criticism* (Tokyo), 4 (July 1982), 19–36.

5. Kaluza's study establishes that 686 (84 percent) of the 814 sentences of Benjy's idiolect are generated by basic syntactic patterns and 462 (67 percent) are one-unit simple sentences.

6. Noam Chomsky, *Syntactic Structures* (The Hague: Mouton, 1957), p. 107.

7. On "the mirror stage," see Jacques Lacan, "Le stade du miroir comme formateur de la fonction du Je," in *Ecrits* (Paris: Editions du Seuil, 1966), pp. 93–100.

8. Freud, "Beyond the Pleasure Principle" (1920), *SE*, vol.18, p. 15.

9. Ibid.

10. *FU*, p. 64.

11. The theme of the brother-sister relationship is already outlined in Faulkner's early story "Adolescence" and in his uncompleted novel "Elmer"; it recurs in

Mosquitoes and, with markedly incestuous undertones, in *Flags in the Dust*. It also figures prominently in *As I Lay Dying, Absalom, Absalom!,* and *The Hamlet.*

12. *LG,* p. 146.

13. See Faulkner's statements on this point in *LG,* pp. 245–46.

14. Benjamin, the new name given to the idiot, means in Hebrew "child of the right hand," i.e., favorite child. According to Faulkner's testimony, however, it was not chosen with ironic intent. Confused with Joseph, the son sold into Egypt, it was meant to suggest abandonment and exile, as can be seen from Quentin's reflections in section 2 (195). See also *FU,* p. 18.

15. "An Introduction to *The Sound and the Fury,*" 414.

16. *LG,* pp. 147–48.

17. *FAB,* p. 296. See also "Appendix," pp. 423–24, and *LG,* p. 246.

18. Besides being an identification motif, Luster's search for the lost quarter in the first section provides an ironical parallel to Benjy's quest and foreshadows Jason's chase after Miss Quentin (who has run off with his money) in section 4.

19. *FU,* p. 64.

20. See Carvel Collins, "The Interior Monologues of *The Sound and the Fury,*" in *Merrill Studies in The Sound and the Fury,* pp. 59–79. The original version of this essay appeared in *English Institute Essays, 1952,* pp. 29–56.

21. See "Appendix," p. 423.

22. The phrase drew comment in one of the first essays to be written on the novel: James Burnham's "Trying to Say," *Symposium,* 2 (January 1931), 51–59.

23. See *FU,* pp. 4–5.

24. See "Appendix," p. 422, and the letter about *The Sound and the Fury* that Faulkner wrote to Ben Wasson in 1929, in which he stated that Benjy "tries to rape a young girl and is castrated" (*SL,* p. 44).

25. These image associations are echoed in the second monologue: Quentin links death and sleep (see 133, 199), and several times invokes hell-fire. Moreover, his suicide at the end of section 2 is symmetrical with Benjy's going to sleep at the close of section 1.

26. Seventeen narrative units are devoted to the day of Damuddy's death. See 19–21, 22–23, 23, 25–32, 37, 38 (two units), 40–42, 42–43, 43, 44, 51–52, 70, 71, 83, 83–84, 84–85.

27. See Edmond Volpe, *A Reader's Guide to William Faulkner* (New York: Farrar, Straus, 1964), pp. 103–4.

28. See ibid. For a fuller discussion, see Charles D. Peavy, "Faulkner's Use of Folklore in *The Sound and the Fury,*" *Journal of American Folklore,* 79 (July–September 1966), 437–38.

29. *LG,* p. 245.

30. *FU,* p. 95.

31. On Faulkner's use of italics for indicating time-shifts, see James B. Meriwether, "The Textual History of *The Sound and the Fury,*" in *Merrill Studies in The Sound and the Fury,* pp. 9–11. Faulkner rejected Wasson's suggestion to replace italicization by wider spaces between lines, reminding his editor that he "purposely used italics for both actual scenes and remembered scenes for the reason, not to indicate the different dates of happenings, but merely to permit the reader to anticipate a thought-transference, letting the recollection postulate its own date" (*SL,* p. 45). Faulkner's own preference was for printing the Benjy section in inks of different colors.

32. I am referring here to Roman Jakobson's definition of the two axes of language: the syntagmatic axis, based on the principle of contiguity, and the paradigmatic one, based on analogy. See "Two Aspects of Language and Two Types of Aphasic Disturbances," in *Fundamentals of Language,* ed. Jakobson and Morris Halle (The Hague: Mouton, 1956).

33. Benjy is "a mirror of moral conscience, in which the various members of the family can see their own actions reflected and implicitly evaluated." Lawrence

Thompson, *William Faulkner: An Introduction and Interpretation* (New York: Barnes and Noble, 1963), p. 36. See also James M. Mellard, "Caliban as Prospero: Benjy and *The Sound and the Fury*," *Novel*, 3 (Spring 1970), 233–48.
    34. *LG*, p. 246.

III. The Young Man, Desire, and Death

    1. See Kaluza, *The Functioning of Sentence Structure*, p. 73.

    2. For a fine discussion of Quentin's "voice," see Stephen M. Ross, "The 'Loud World' of Quentin Compson," *Studies in the Novel*, 7 (Summer 1975), 247–57.

    3. *The Sound and the Fury* is polyphonic not only in its manifest structure but also in the very texture of each of its four parts. In all sections there is an interweaving of many voices. If Faulkner may be considered Dostoevski's American heir, it is because of the polyphonism—or, to use another term from Mikhail Bakhtin, the *dialogism*—of his novels rather than because of a common thematics.

    4. On this point, see Jane Millgate's perceptive essay "Quentin Compson as Poor Player: Verbal and Social Clichés in *The Sound and the Fury*," *Revue des Langues Vivantes* (Bruxelles), 34 (1968), 40–49.

    5. Shreve alludes ironically to Lochinvar, the hero of a ballad included in the fifth canto of Scott's *Marmion* (106), and makes an oblique reference to the sixth canto of Byron's *Don Juan* (107); Spoade calls Quentin "the champion of dames" (191), and to Herbert Head he is a "half-baked Galahad" (126). The very name Quentin suggests gallantry and romance (*Quentin Durward*), and the irony is the more pointed here as the same name was borne by the first of the Compsons.

    6. Jean-Paul Sartre, "Time in Faulkner: *The Sound and the Fury*," trans. Martine Darmon, in *William Faulkner: Three Decades of Criticism*, ed. Frederick J. Hoffman and Olga W. Vickery (East Lansing: Michigan State University Press, 1960), p. 230.

    7. Read in Freudian terms, the equation sex = dirt might be considered an index of regression to the anal-sadistic stage of psychosexual development. The Natalie scene would then represent an abortive attempt to accede to genitality and the hog wallow scene a return to pregenital sexuality. The traits associated with anal fixation are extremely numerous in the Quentin section: obsession with the pure/impure, sadistic impulses, compulsive orderliness and cleanliness, ablution rites, phobia of stains and soiled objects. In this respect as in others Quentin closely resembles his brother Jason: both are related to what Freud calls the "anal character" through their emphasis on orderliness, their extreme obstinacy, and their strong sense of ownership (plain avarice with Jason, emotional possessiveness with Quentin). See Freud, "Character and Anal Erotism" (1908), *SE*, vol. 9, pp. 167–75.

    8. The hog wallow scene points forward to Quentin's allusion to Euboelus (170), the swineherd who plunged with his herd into the chasm formed in the earth when Hades emerged to rape Persephone. The sexual implications of the mythic reference are reinforced by the Rabelaisian and Shakespearean image of "the beast with two backs." Fusing these two references with a third one (the Gadarene swine described by Mark and Luke in the New Testament), Quentin resumes the image at the end of his monologue in the startling evocation of "swine untethered in pairs rushing coupled into the sea" (202)—a vision of apocalyptic sexuality as well as a prevision of Quentin's death by water.

    9. *LA*, p. 204.

    10. On homeopathic, or imitative, magic, see James Frazer, *The Golden Bough*, abridged ed. (London: Macmillan, 1963), pp. 16–49. The first critic to use the phrase with reference to Faulkner's fiction was Jean-Jacques Mayoux, in *Vivants Piliers: Le roman anglo-saxon et les symboles* (Paris: Juilliard, 1960), p. 265.

    11. Here again one is reminded of the anal phase, during which the concepts of dirt and property polarize infantile behavior. Since this is also the time of separation from the mother, dirt, excrement—what is expelled from the body—becomes linked with

the ambivalent feelings generated by the child's (re)expulsion from the mother's body. Caddy has become a "dirty girl" to Quentin insofar as she is no longer an extension of himself, i.e , his property. The dirt motif is thus directly related to the central experience of loss.

12. Tertullian's metaphor finds an almost literal illustration in the blue-eyed girl with "long golden curls swinging downward above the ordure" whom Fairchild, as a twelve-year-old, saw through the seat of an outhouse. See *MOS*, p. 234.

13. Faulkner himself pointed to the symbolism of the muddy drawers. See *LG*, p. 245.

14. Rats often appear in scenes with sexual overtones. In the barn scene Quentin and Natalie hear a rat in the crib. The image of the rat is also associated with Caddy: after she has lost her virginity, her eyes are compared to "cornered rats" (171). In Faulkner's unfinished novel "Elmer" the same image occurs; it also figures in the closing section of *Mosquitoes* and in the rape scene in *Sanctuary*.

15. References to stained objects abound in section 2. Apart from those already mentioned, consider "a red smear on the dial" (91), "a man in his stained hat" (101), and "a soiled pink garter" (107), where the connection between Quentin's phobia and his sexual obsessions is particularly evident. Dirt and stain imagery is a recurrent feature in Faulkner's novels, most conspicuous in the sexual nightmare of *Sanctuary*.

16. Suspecting Quentin's taste of the clean and pure, Herbert Head thinks he can buy his friendship with a brand-new fifty-dollar bill: "look at it it's just out of convent look not a blemish not even been creased yet see here" (125). One notes the image of the convent, linking physical cleanliness with chastity.

17. "One cannot 'plan' to kill oneself. One can make preparations for it and act in anticipation of the final gesture which still belongs to the normal category of things to be done, but this gesture is not made with a view to death, it does not envision death, it does not hold it in its grasp. Hence the love of minute detail, the patient and manic attention to trifling matters often evinced by someone about to die. Other people are surprised and say: 'When you want to die, you don't think of so many things.' But in fact one doesn't *want* to die, death cannot be an object of volition, it is impossible to want to die, and so the will, stopped short on the uncertain threshold of what it cannot accomplish, resorts with its calculating wisdom to grappling with everything it can still seize hold of in the neighborhood of its limits." Maurice Blanchot, *L'Espace littéraire* (Paris: Gallimard, 1955), p. 105. My translation.

18. Later Caddy gives her brother's name to her own daughter: symbolically, Quentin II is both the fruit of the imaginary incest and Quentin's homologue as Caddy's child.

19. Several critics assume that there is a "suicide pact" between Quentin and his sister. The assumption has been questioned by Charles D. Peavy in "A Note on the 'Suicide Pact' in *The Sound and the Fury*," *English Language Notes*, 5 (March 1968), 207–9. There is no final proof in these matters, but Quentin is obviously not meant to be taken as a reliable narrator of his past.

20. "Appendix," p. 411.

21. On Quentin and Hamlet, see Cleanth Brooks, "Primitivism in *The Sound and the Fury*," *English Institute Essays, 1952*, pp. 13–14, and William R. Taylor, *Cavalier and Yankee* (New York: Anchor Books, 1963), pp. 137–40.

22. Bland's symbolic function is further emphasized by imagery assimilating him to a royal personage (104, 121, 138), and his mother is likewise compared to a queen. No doubt irony plays its part in these similes, but to Quentin this regal couple is also a mythicized image of the parental couple. Moreover, through the superimposition of the husband-wife relationship on the son-mother relationship, one can see the incest motif emerge once again. The ambiguous intimacy between Mrs. Bland and her son, her wide-eyed admiration for his amorous exploits, her ecstatic marveling at his handsomeness (121), are in themselves suggestive of near-incestuous relations.

23. In the confrontations between Quentin and his sister's lovers the contrast between his impotence and their manliness is underscored by the ironic use of phallic symbols: Ames's revolver, Head's cigar. One recalls that Ames offers to lend Quentin his revolver and Head offers him a cigar, both of which are refused. His attitude confirms the denial of sexuality in which his impotence originates. It seems safe to assume that this symbolism was intentional: similar phallic imagery is found in Faulkner's uncompleted early novel "Elmer," whose immature hero to some extent prefigures Quentin. The contrast between Quentin and his rivals is further suggested through their respective relations to the elements of water and fire. For Quentin water means both death and desire, and one of the last memories in his monologue is significantly a remote childhood memory about the nights when he would get up to go to the bathroom, "seeking water" (199). Ames and Bland, his surrogates, on the other hand, have both gained mastery over the female element: Bland is an accomplished oarsman, and Caddy tells Quentin that Ames has "crossed all the oceans all around the world" (172). At the same time these two figures are related to fire (a traditional symbol of male potency): Bland through his association with the sun, Ames through his remarkable marksmanship and his association with bronze and asbestos.

24. Mr. Compson's reflections upon time in the opening of the second section (86) as well as his speculations about virginity (132–33) are missing from the manuscript. It is most significant, too, that while many of the references to "Father said" were added upon revision, Faulkner removed "said" from Quentin's final (imagined) conversation with Mr. Compson (202–5). In the manuscript, Faulkner followed the normal pattern of reported speech ("He said. . . and I said. . . ."); in the published version, the only clues to change of speaker are the pronouns that are run into the prose without any punctuation mark. Moreover, to suggest the shrinking of Quentin's self, Faulkner substituted "i" for "I." On this point, see Faulkner's comments in *FU*, p. 18.

25. It is important to bear in mind, though, that the conversations reported by Quentin are to some degree imaginary. When Faulkner was asked if Quentin had talked of incest to his father, he answered that he never did. See *FU*, pp. 262–63.

26. *FU*, p. 3.

27. Ibid.

28. See also "Appendix," pp. 404–5.

29. One might even argue that there is an ironic permutation of roles: the weak but affectionate Mr. Compson becomes a parodic mother figure; Mrs. Compson acts at times as a father substitute, especially in her harshly repressive attitude toward Benjy and Caddy. A similar inversion can be seen in Quentin and Caddy: Quentin is the weakling; Caddy has inherited the reckless courage of the original Compsons. In their childhood games, Quentin remembers, "she never was a queen or a fairy she was always a king or a giant or a general" (198).

30. On Lacan's concept of the Name-of-the-Father, see *Ecrits*, pp. 812–13 and passim. Whereas Freud's oedipal father might be taken for the real father, Lacan's Name-of-the-Father is both condition and effect of the symbolic law and operates exlusively in the field of language.

31. I am referring again to two of Lacan's concepts. The imaginary, the symbolic, the real are to Lacan the three essential registers of the psychoanalytic field. The first is marked by the prevalence of a narcissistic relation to the image of a similar being, as evidenced by the "mirror stage" in the early development of the child. The second refers to the symbolic systems structuring interhuman relationships, especially language.

32. The phrase is from Guy Rosolato, "Du Père," *Essais sur le symbolique* (Paris: Gallimard, 1969), p. 49. My translation.

33. Ibid., p. 48. My translation.

34. Quentin's desire to avoid oedipal involvement is also attested by the fantasy of being his father's father, i.e., unfathered: "*Say it to Father will you I will am my fathers Progenitive I invented him created I him Say it to him it will not be for he will say I was not*

and then you and I since philoprogenitive" (140). In Faulkner's fiction being fatherless is considered alternately as a positive privilege and a fatal flaw. It means total self-possession for Lucas Beauchamp, "who fathered himself, intact and complete" (*GDM*, p. 118); for Joe Christmas, in *Light in August*, it is a source of anguish and alienation. The fantasy of self-generation is of course also that of the writer—both son and father to his work.

35. "Appendix," p. 411. Italics added.

36. See Freud "Mourning and Melancholia" (1917), *SE*, vol. 14, pp. 243–58.

37. References, literal or oblique, to mourning abound. The most ironic, perhaps, is in section 3, when Jason recalls his mother going "around the house in a black dress and a veil. . . crying and saying her little daughter was dead" (264), after she has seen one of the boys from town kissing Caddy. Equally remarkable is the mythic reversal of the motif in the Easter celebration of the final section, where the sorrow and despair over death eventually yield to the joyful certitude of resurrection.

38. Identification with the lost sister would account in some measure for Quentin's feminine features and for the latent homosexuality which seems to characterize his relationship to Shreve ("Calling Shreve my husband," 88).

39. Quentin's wish to erase Ames out of existence, significantly linked with his revulsion from sex and his horror of procreation, reveals itself most startlingly in this fantasized *coitus interruptus*: "If I could have been his mother lying with open body, lifted laughing, holding his father with my hand refraining, seeing, watching him die before he lived" (91). There are strong suggestions here of the primal scene, and it is most remarkable that Quentin identifies with the mother figure and her desire—a negative desire, refusing maternity, refusing the child's birth before its conception: it is Quentin's own relation to his mother, or rather her relation to him, that is projected onto the fantasy scene.

40. Freud notes that in the condition of melancholia the superego is transformed into "a pure culture of the death instinct." See "The Dependent Relationships of the Ego" (1923), *SE*, vol. 19, p. 53.

41. The equivalence death = wedding also appears in the assimilation of the marriage announcement to a bier ("*It lay on the table a candle burning at each corner upon the envelope tied in a soiled pink garter two artificial flowers,*" 107) and in Quentin's reflections about the trunks assembled for Caddy's trip to French Lick, the Indiana resort town where she was to look for a husband ("*Bringing empty trunks down the attic stairs they sounded like coffins French Lick. Found not death at the salt lick,*" 108–9).

42. The fusion of Eros and Death is strongly suggested in the evocation of Quentin's suicidal drive in the "Appendix": "who loved death above all, who loved only death, loved and lived in a deliberate and almost perverted anticipation of death as a lover loves and deliberately refrains from the waiting willing friendly tender incredible body of his beloved, until he can no longer bear not the refraining but the restraint and so flings, hurls himself, relinquishing, drowning" (411).

IV. Of Time and the Unreal

1. The word *shadow* occurs repeatedly in the first section. In the second it becomes one of the key words, the most frequently used (53 occurrences) after *water* (61 occurrences).

2. In Quentin's monologue shadow and darkness are associated on several occasions with woman and sex. See, for example: "walking along in the shadows and whispering with their soft girlvoices lingering in the shadowy places" (169). See also the description of Caddy's encounter with Dalton Ames, in which the fusion of shadows suggests sexual union of the bodies: "their shadows one shadow her head rose it was above his on the sky higher their two heads" (177); "her shadow high against

his shadow one shadow" (177); "leaning down her shadow the blur of her face leaning down from his high shadow" (178).

3. When questioned on the significance of the shadow motif in Quentin's section, Faulkner answered: "That wasn't a deliberate symbolism. I would say that that shadow that stayed on his mind so much was foreknowledge of his own death. . . ." (*FU*, p. 2). In this respect one should note Faulkner's implicit reference to the fears about shadows in popular beliefs. To lose one's shadow or to walk on it has been considered an evil omen in many cultures, and Quentin recalls the superstition of blacks about "a drowned man's shadow" (102) as he stands on the bridge and looks at his shadow in the water below him.

4. The jeweler is himself a rather intriguing figure. There is something faintly demonic about him, and the brief sketch we are given of him has many symbolic connotations. Functionally, insofar as he is expected to answer Quentin's questions, he reminds one of Mr. Compson, the *father*. Metonymically, through his profession and environment, and above all through his "rushing" eye (95), he is turned into a symbol of *time*, and "the metal tube screwed into his face" (95) relates him more specifically to mechanical time. Quentin's description of him is focused exclusively on his *eye*, as though he were a Cyclops in his infernal smithy. In myths and folklore, the unique eye has often been associated with either subhuman or superhuman vision, divine or demonic knowledge. It is precisely because of his presumed knowledge of time that Quentin pays a visit to the jeweler. Yet the latter's eye is also "blurred" (95): Father Time will not reveal his secret.

5. Sartre, "Time in Faulkner," p. 228.

6. In his interview with Loïc Bouvard, a French graduate student, in 1952, Faulkner said that he was influenced "by Bergson, obviously" (*LG*, p. 72). There is no evidence, however, that he read him as seriously as Proust or Eliot did. The relationship between Faulkner and Bergson should be assessed in terms of confluence rather than influence.

7. On Sartre's misquotations and misinterpretations, see Henry J. Underwood, "Sartre on *The Sound and the Fury:* Some Errors," *Modern Fiction Studies*, 12 (Winter 1966–67), 477–79.

8. See Sartre, "Time in Faulkner," pp. 226–27.

9. I prefer this more literal but also more suggestive translation of *enfoncement* to *suspension*, the term by which it has been rendered in *Three Decades of Criticism*.

10. The first to call attention to this motif was Melvin Backman, in *Faulkner: The Major Years* (Bloomington: Indiana University Press, 1966), pp. 24–26. As Backman points out, the same triad appears in the opening pages of *Sanctuary*.

11. *A la recherche du temps perdu*, III (Paris: Gallimard, Bibliothèque de la Pléiade, 1954), p. 872. My translation.

12. See Lawrence Thompson, "Mirror Analogues in *The Sound and the Fury*," *English Institute Essays*, 1952, pp. 83–106.

13. Here again there is a significant parallel between sections 1 and 2. At the close of section 1, after being undressed by Luster, Benjy looks at himself and begins to cry (84); at the close of section 2, Quentin looks at himself in the mirror, noticing his black eye and the bloodstain on his vest. In both scenes there are references to physical injury, and both scenes point ironically back to Caddy. In Benjy's case, the implied reference to his castration sends us back to its cause: the attempted rape of the Burgess girl, whom Benjy mistook for his sister; Quentin's black eye and bloodied vest recall his fight with Bland, whom he mistook for his sister's first lover.

14. Paul Valéry, "Mélange" (1939), *Oeuvres*, I (Paris: Gallimard, Bibliothèque de la Pléiade, 1957), p. 332. My translation.

15. The first page of the manuscript of *The Sound and the Fury* bears the title *Twilight*. However, it is impossible to determine whether this title was intended for the short

story that Faulkner originally planned to write or for the first section or for the complete novel. The twilight symbolism fits Benjy's monologue as well as it does Quentin's, and insofar as it evokes decline it equally well epitomizes the story of the Compson family. The twilight motif appears very early in Faulkner's work, notably in "The Hill," and is also found in the later novels *As I Lay Dying, Light in August,* and *Absalom, Absalom!*

16. Faulkner himself suggests that "when he wants the old fish to live, it may represent his unconscious desire for endurance, both for himself and for his people" (*FU*, p. 18).

17. See *SP*, p. 57: "If a man could be freed for a moment from the forces of gravity [he] would be a god, the lord of life, causing the high gods to tremble on their thrones: he would thunder at the very gates of infinity like a mailed knight." The flight motif can be traced back to Faulkner's early prose and poetry; it reappears in a number of his stories and novels from *Soldiers' Pay* through *Pylon* to *A Fable*. Flying often stands for the heroic quest for "glory" through a meteoric death.

18. Bland's rowing is significantly associated with his mother's presence. Quentin describes them "moving side by side across Massachusetts on parallel courses like a couple of planets" (103), and refers to "the wet oars winking him along in bright winks and female palms" (127). Bland's godlike ascent is conditioned by his ideal relationship to his mother.

19. A similar dissociation occurs in "Carcassonne," a short story presumably written in 1926 and originally published in *T13*, pp. 352–58. It also presents the monologue of a dying or dead young man. His body lies "on the rippled floor, tumbling peacefully to the weavering echoes of the tides," while he rides a horse *"with eyes like blue electricity and a mane like tangled fire, galloping up the hill and right off into the high heaven of the world"* (p. 358).

20. On Quentin as a poet, see François Pitavy, "Through the Poet's Eye: A View of Quentin Compson," in *William Faulkner's "The Sound and the Fury" : A Critical Casebook,* ed. André Bleikasten (New York: Garland, 1982), pp. 79–99.

21. Quoted in Blotner, *Faulkner*, p. 1522.

22. "Appendix," p. 412.

23. The strongest case for Quentin as a "moral agent" is made by Mark Spilka in "Quentin Compson's Universal Grief," *Contemporary Literature*, 11 (Autumn 1970), pp. 451–69.

24. "Appendix," p. 412.

V. The Poison of Resentment

1. See James M. Mellard, "Faulkner's Jason and the Tradition of Oral Narrative," *Journal of Popular Culture*, 2 (Fall 1968), pp. 195–210.

2. Significantly, *you* occurs in the second sentence of Jason's speech. Most often his *you* is all-inclusive, referring at once to Jason himself as receiver of his own message, to an implied audience of people sharing his cultural values, and—outside the time-space of the novel—to the reader. While in the first two sections most of the components of the speech event are problematic, they are all strongly marked in the third—evidence that we are moving closer to normal communication patterns.

3. While in the first two sections time-shifts are very frequent, there is only one major flashback in the third: Jason's reminiscence of his father's funeral and of the yet earlier scene when Mr. Compson brought home Caddy's infant child.

4. George Washington Harris's Sut Lovingood was one of Faulkner's favorite characters in fiction: "I like Sut Lovingood from a book written by George Harris about 1840 or '50 in the Tennessee mountains. He had no illusions about himself, did the best he could; at certain times he was a coward and knew it and wasn't ashamed; he never blamed his misfortunes on anyone and never cursed God for them" (*LG*, p. 251). The traits which Faulkner admired in Harris's character are precisely those opposing him to the self-deluded and self-pitying Jason: Sut Lovingood knows he is a rogue and

judges himself as harshly as the sordid world in which he moves. See Stephen M. Ross, "Jason Compson and Sut Lovingood: Southwestern Humor as Stream of Consciousness," *Studies in the Novel*, 8 (Fall 1976), 278–90.

5. See Robert C. Elliot, "The Satirist Satirized: Studies of the Great Misanthropes," *The Power of Satire: Magic, Ritual, Art* (Princeton, N.J.: Princeton University Press, 1960), pp. 130–222.

6. See James M. Mellard, "Type and Archetype: Jason Compson as 'Satirist,'" *Genre*, 6 (June 1971), 173–88.

7. See Elliot, "The Satirist Satirized."

8. "Interviews in Japan, 1955," in *LG*, p. 149.

9. John Longley, *The Tragic Mask: A Study of Faulkner's Heroes* (Chapel Hill: University of North Carolina Press, 1963), p. 144.

10. Wayne C. Booth, *The Rhetoric of Fiction* (Chicago: University of Chicago Press, 1961), p. 307.

11. For fine treatments of Jason's humor, see James M. Cox, "Humor as Vision in Faulkner," and William N. Claxon, Jr., "Jason Compson: A Demoralized Wit," in Doreen Fowler and Ann J. Abadie, eds., *Faulkner and Humor* (Jackson: University Press of Mississippi, 1986), pp. 1–20, 21–33.

12. James Dahl, "A Faulkner Reminiscence: Conversations with Mrs. Maud Faulkner," *Journal of Modern Literature*, 3 (April 1974), 1028.

13. As Gary Lee Stonum argues, "Jason's scorn, like Quentin's horror over Caddy's loss of honor, is rooted in a feeling that an ideal has failed him. The almost hysterical concern for his own current position as a quasi-father in the household and the half-admitted sorrow he expresses at Mr. Compson's funeral suggest that behind this scorn is a disappointed image of the father as an anchor of meaningfulness in a healthy family." *Faulkner's Career: An Internal Literary History* (Ithaca, N.Y.: Cornell University Press, 1979), p. 86.

14. On Jason's indebtedness to his father's philosophy, see Duncan Aswell's insightful essay "The Recollection and the Blood: Jason's Role in *The Sound and the Fury*," *Mississippi Quarterly*, 21 (Summer 1968), 211–18; reprinted in *William Faulkner's "The Sound and the Fury:" A Critical Casebook*, pp. 115–22. It is noteworthy too that Mr. Compson (as quoted by Quentin) occasionally makes reflections which would not be out of place in Jason's speech: "watching pennies has healed more scars than jesus" (204).

15. See Brooks, *The Yoknapatawpha Country*, p. 339.

16. This incident relates Jason's childhood to Popeye's in *Sanctuary*: Popeye cuts up two live lovebirds and a kitten. Jason's action is of course less gruesome: he is a Popeye with inhibitions.

17. The first two sections provide many indications about Jason that presage what he will become as an adult. He is a fat and greedy child; he is a loner and never misses a chance to tattle on his siblings; he is always seen with his hands in his pockets and chooses to play treasurer when his playmates launch into kite-making.

18. See Faulkner's comment: "to him all the rest of the town and the world and the human race too except himself were Compsons, inexplicable yet quite predictable in that they were in no sense whatever to be trusted" ("Appendix," p. 421).

19. For further comments on this subject, see Charles D. Peavy, "Jason Compson's Paranoid Pseudocommunity," *Hartford Studies in Literature*, 2 (1970), 151–56.

20. "We must remember that a man is not necessarily humble or even modest because he has consented to mediocrity. On the contrary, there is a passionate pride among the mediocre, and anti-Semitism is an attempt to give value to mediocrity as such, to create an elite of the ordinary." Jean-Paul Sartre, *Anti-Semite and Jew*, trans. George J. Becker (New York: Schocken Books, 1948), p. 23.

21. Longley, *The Tragic Mask*, p. 147.

22. "Appendix," p. 420.

23. For Jason's indebtedness to the formulaic manner, see Mellard, "Faulkner's Jason and the Tradition of Oral Narrative."

24. Aswell, "The Recollection and the Blood: Jason's Role in *The Sound and the Fury*," 216.

25. See Vickery, *The Novels of William Faulkner*, pp. 30–31; Millgate, *The Achievement*, p. 99; Brooks, *The Yoknapatawpha Country*, pp. 325–26.

26. See, for example, George O'Donnell, "Faulkner's Mythology," *Kenyon Review*, 1 (Summer 1939), 285–99; reprinted in *Three Decades of Criticism*, pp. 82–93.

27. See "Appendix," p. 420, and Faulkner's letter to Malcolm Cowley in *SL*, p.197.

28. See *M*, pp. 322–27, 330, 332, 334.

29. Irving Howe notes that "like those quasi-intellectuals who abandon old allegiances to become the spokesmen of a rising new class, Jason formulates the values of Snopesism with a cleverness and vengeance which no Snopes could express." William Faulkner: A Critical Study, 2d ed. (New York: Vintage Books, 1962), p. 50.

30. See Richard Hofstadter, "The Pseudo-Conservative Revolt—1954," *The Paranoid Style in American Politics and Other Essays* (New York: Vintage Books, 1967), pp. 41–65. Hofstadter borrowed the phrase from *The Authoritarian Personality*, published in 1950 by Theodore W. Adorno and associates.

31. *FU*, p. 17.

VI. An Easter without Resurrection?

1. *LG*, p. 147. See also p. 245 and *FU*, p. 32.

2. See Margaret Blanchard, "The Rhetoric of Communion: Voice in *The Sound and the Fury*," *American Literature*, 41 (January 1970), 555–65.

3. That Faulkner knew about the meaning of jaybirds in folklore is attested a few pages later, when Luster throws a rock at the birds, shouting "Git on back to hell, whar you belong at" (311). See Charles D. Peavy, "Faulkner's Use of Folklore in *The Sound and the Fury*," 442–43.

4. "Appendix," p. 421. In *The Mansion* we are told that a few years later Benjy set fire to the house and burned to death in it. These facts are not consistent with the information provided in the "Appendix." Benjy's death and the destruction of the house by fire are obviously afterthoughts, probably suggested to Faulkner by the similarities between the Compson story and that of the Sutpens.

5. John V. Hagopian, "Nihilism in Faulkner's *The Sound and the Fury*," *Modern Fiction Studies*, 13 (Spring 1967), 46.

6. On leaving Jefferson, Jason thinks that "every damn one of them will be at church" (353); Dilsey, back in the house, "[enters] a pervading reek of camphor" in Mrs. Compson's room (345), while Jason misses the camphor that would relieve his headache (363). Lastly, at one o'clock, Dilsey tells Luster and Benjy that Jason will not be home for dinner (348); the latter, at the same moment, is leaving Mottson, where people are "turning peacefully into houses and Sunday dinners" (363).

7. According to Faulkner, "The narcissus was given to Benjy to distract his attention. It was simply a flower which happened to be handy that 5th of April. It was not deliberate" (*LG*, p. 246). Whether deliberate or not, this flower is an apt emblem for the self-centered Compsons. Lawrence E. Bowling, on the other hand, reminds us that beyond its roots in Greek mythology "the narcissus has also a Christian tradition, for it is the flower which in the Bible is called 'the rose' and is identified with Jesus (Isaiah 35:1, Song of Songs 2:1). Thus the narcissus, like Benjy himself, symbolizes not only the world's selfishness but also its need for love. The association of Benjy's narcissus with the Savior is made more specific and significant by the fact that the flower has been broken twice, the two breaks symbolizing the two crucifixions: the first by the ancient world and the second by the modern world." "Faulkner and the Theme of Innocence," *Kenyon Review*, 20 (Summer 1958), 485–86.

Given the novel's thematics, it seems equally relevant to call attention to the etymological link between *narcissus* and *narcotic*. The ancients knew about the soporific or deathlike effect of the flower and used it for the adornment of tombs. The association of the narcissus with death is also evident in the story of Demeter and Persephone. The Homeric Hymn to Demeter establishes a close connection between the narcissus and the rape of Persephone by having Hades use the beauty and fragrance of the flower to lure her into the underworld. In Quentin's allusion to Euboelus (170), there was already an implicit reference to the rape of Persephone, the mythical equivalent of the abduction of Caddy by Dalton Ames.

Lastly, the flowers associated with Benjy could be read as images of his mutilated manhood. Like jimson weed, the narcissus may be another inverted phallic symbol, the more plausibly so as it belongs in the category of *broken* things, references to which are particularly numerous in sections 1 and 2, that is, where castration is at stake. It appears, moreover, that all of Benjy's objects and playthings represent and compensate losses, whether they are phallic substitutes like the flowers or, in D. W. Winnicot's phrase, "transitional objects" (i.e., substitutes for the mother's breast) like the cushion. The most obviously symbolic of these objects is the soiled satin slipper, a reminder of Caddy and her wedding but also a classic sexual fetish—which sends us back again to the pervasive issue of castration.

8. As Beverly Gross notes, "the ending of *The Sound and the Fury* is a significant and suggestive reflection on the novel as a whole. It concludes not an action, but the enactment of a process; the novel ends not with an ending, but with an unforgettable epitome of itself." See "Form and Fulfillment in *The Sound and the Fury*," *Modern Language Quarterly*, 29 (December 1968), 449.

9. Hagopian, "Nihilism in *The Sound and the Fury*," 47.

10. Purple and maroon are royal colors, but in the Christian tradition purple is also a liturgic color (associated with Advent, Lent, and Good Friday) and the color of martyrdom. The terrestrial symbolism of purple, with its suggestions of sacrificial suffering, mourning, and penitence, is contrasted with the celestial symbolism of blue. When Dilsey later reemerges from her cabin, she is dressed in blue gingham. In medieval color codification blue was the color of chastity and therefore of the Virgin; in the novel, it also stands for Benjy's innocence. In the episode of the Easter service the symbolic equation of Dilsey with the Virgin and of Benjy with Christ is repeatedly suggested (342–44).

11. In this the portrait of Dilsey announces the tribute that Faulkner was later to pay to her and to her kin: "They endured" ("Appendix," p. 427).

12. See letter to Malcolm Cowley, *SL*, p. 202.

13. *LG*, pp. 244–45. An early casting of Dilsey is to be found in "The Devil Beats His Wife," a story Faulkner began after his return from Europe in December 1925 but never completed. A number of critics assume that Dilsey was modeled on Caroline Barr, the "mammy" of the Faulkner family to whose memory *Go Down, Moses* was dedicated thirteen years later. The resemblances, however, are rather tenuous. Molly, Lucas Beauchamp's wife in *Go Down, Moses*, comes much closer to being a portrait of Caroline Barr.

14. Brooks, *The Yoknapatawpha Country*, p. 343.

15. See George E. Kent's sharply critical assessment of Faulkner's "mammies" in "The Black Woman in Faulkner's Works, with the Exclusion of Dilsey," part II, *Phylon*, 36 (March 1975), 55–67.

16. This is not to say that there is no significant contrast between whites and blacks. Some of Quentin's observations aptly summarize the function of blacks in the novel: "a nigger is not a person so much as a form of behaviour; a sort of obverse reflection of the white people he lives among" (98); "They come into white people's lives like that in sudden sharp black trickles that isolate white facts for an instant in unarguable truth like under a microscope" (195). Dilsey and, to a lesser degree, her husband, her

children, and grandchildren testify to the virtues which Ike McCaslin attributes to blacks in *Go Down, Moses:* endurance, pity, tolerance, fidelity, love of children (see *GDM*, p. 295). In the younger generation of the Gibsons, however, these virtues seem to be less developed than among their elders, as can be seen, for example, from Luster's occasional cruelty toward Benjy. And there is nothing to suggest that the Negroes are morally superior to the whites because they belong to a different race. Dilsey, with her customary clear-sightedness, tells her grandson Luster that he is just as fallible as his white masters: "Lemme tell you somethin, nigger boy, you got jes es much Compson devilment in you es any of em" (319). Faulkner's treatment of blacks in *The Sound and the Fury*, albeit not free of stereotypes, is never tritely sentimental, testifying to a tact and intelligence seldom found among white southern novelists. But, though the contrast between the white family and the black community provides an oblique comment upon the downfall of the Compsons, racial relationships are not central in *The Sound and the Fury* as they are in *Light in August, Absalom, Absalom!, Go Down, Moses*, and *Intruder in the Dust*.

17. In his interviews Faulkner stressed the principle of cohesion represented by Dilsey in the Compson household. See *FU*, p. 5, and *LG*, p. 126.

18. Dilsey's solicitude for Benjy is already emphasized in the first section. She is the only one to remember his thirty-third birthday and to celebrate it with a cake she buys with her own money. The manuscript of the novel includes no reference to Benjy's birthday—an indication that in revising the section Faulkner felt the need to provide further illustration of Dilsey's kindness and so to prepare the reader for the full revelation of her personality in section 4. See Emily K. Izsak, "The Manuscript of *The Sound and the Fury*: The Revisions in the First Section," *Studies in Bibliography*, Bibliographical Society, University of Virginia, 20 (1967), 189–202.

19. T. S. Eliot, *Collected Poems, 1909–1962* (New York: Harcourt, 1963), p. 178.

20. See Victor Strandberg, "Faulkner's Poor Parson and the Technique of Inversion," *Sewanee Review*, 73 (Spring 1965), 181–90.

21. On Faulkner's indebtedness to the tradition of the oral sermon, see Bruce A. Rosenberg, "The Oral Quality of Reverend Shegog's Sermon in William Faulkner's *The Sound and the Fury*," *Literatur in Wissenschaft und Unterricht*, 2 (1969), 73–88.

22. Claude Lévi-Strauss, *The Raw and the Cooked*, trans. John and Doreen Weightman (New York: Harper and Row, 1969), pp. 15–16.

23. See Rosenberg, "The Oral Quality of Reverend Shegog's Sermon."

24. References to empty eyes or troubled vision abound: the "blurred" eye of the jeweler (95), Caddy's eyes "like the eyes in the statues blank and unseeing and serene" (187), Benjy's vacant gaze (369, 370), not to mention the empty eyes of the Confederate soldier (370). The picture of the eye on page 360 also points to the importance of the motif of seeing/not seeing.

25. Gabriel Vahanian, *Wait without Idols* (New York: George Braziller, 1964), p. 111. See also Amos N. Wilder, "Faulkner and Vestigial Moralities," *Theology and Modern Literature* (Cambridge, Mass.: Harvard University Press, 1958), pp. 113–31.

26. See *FU*, pp. 86, 117 ; *LG*, pp. 246–47.

27. Roland Barthes, "Criticism as Language," *Times Literary Supplement* (September 27, 1963), 739–40; translated from "Qu'est-ce que la critique?" *Essais critiques* (Paris: Editions du Seuil, 1964), pp. 256–57.

28. Brooks, *The Yoknapatawpha Country*, p. 348.

29. Paul Eluard, *Poésie Ininterrompue* (Paris: Gallimard, 1946), p. 32.

Two. Requiem for a Mother

VII. A "Tour de Force"

1. In 1946 Random House published the two novels together as one Modern Library volume, but Faulkner was by no means enthusiastic about reprinting them

together. Several of his letters to Robert Linscott testify to his strong objections to their pairing. On one hand, he told Linscott that he "had never thought of TSAF and AS I LAY DYING in the same breath" (*SL*, 221); on the other, he found them too similar in style and technique: "It's as though we were saying 'This is a versatile guy; he can write in the same stream of consciousness style about princes and then peasants,' or 'This is a universal writer; he has written about all the kinds of people in Miss. in the same style'" (*SL*, p. 118).

2. Calvin Bedient, "Pride and Nakedness: *As I Lay Dying*," *Modern Language Quarterly*, 29 (March 1968), 65.

3. *FU*, p. 207.

4. Faulkner, "An Introduction for *The Sound and the Fury*," *Southern Review*, 8 (October 1972), 709.

5. Ibid.

6. See *FU*, pp. 87,113, 115, 207; *LG*, pp. 180, 222, 244.

7. "I sent it to Smith and wrote him that by it I would stand or fall." Introduction to the Modern Library issue of *Sanctuary*, p. vii; reprinted in *S*, p. 339.

8. Ibid.

9. See R. W. Franklin, "Narrative Management in *As I Lay Dying*," *Modern Fiction Studies*, 13 (Spring 1967), 57–65. Franklin takes Faulkner to task for the apparent inconsistencies of the novel's temporal structure. Franklin's argument has been scrupulously and brilliantly rebutted by Stephen M. Ross in "Shapes of Time and Consciousness in *As I Lay Dying*," *Texas Studies in Literature and Language*, 16 (Winter 1975), 723–37.

10. *LG*, p. 244

11. See A. J. Greimas, *Sémantique structurale* (Paris: Larousse, 1966), pp. 172–91.

12. See Gérard Genette, *Narrative Discourse* (Ithaca, N.Y.: Cornell University Press, 1980), pp. 164–85.

13. Several attempts have been made to identify a central narrative consciousness. See, for example, M. E. Bradford, "Addie Bundren and the Design of *As I Lay Dying*," *Southern Review*, 6 (Fall 1970), 1093–99; David M. Monaghan, "The Single Narrator of *As I Lay Dying*," *Modern Fiction Studies*, 18 (Summer 1972), 213–20; Daniel Ferrer, "In Omnis Jam Vocabuli Mortem," *Poétique*, no. 44 (November 1980), 490–503. Bradford sees Addie's ghost as the single "auditor" of the other character's reveries; Monaghan contends that the only way to account for the novel's inconsistencies is to posit her as its single narrator. According to Ferrer's much more sophisticated argument, the whole text is hallucinated by Darl. These more or less ingenious explanations testify to the critics' need to unify and rationalize, but there is no conclusive evidence for the existence of an overall narrative agency.

14. Stephen M. Ross, "'Voice' in Narrative Texts: The Example of *As I Lay Dying*," *PMLA*, 94 (March 1979), 302.

15. Many critics have commented in particular on Vardaman's extremely "literary" description of a horse in the concluding paragraph of his first monologue (52).

16. Quoted by Terry Eagleton in *Walter Benjamin* (London: Verso, 1981), p. 128. The review appeared in the *Athenaeum* on December 5, 1874.

17. On questions of voice and enunciation, see the closely argued article by Ross mentioned in note 14 above and Ann Lecercle-Sweet's shrewd comments in "The Chip and the Chink: The Dying of the 'I' in *As I Lay Dying*," *Faulkner Journal*, 2 (Fall 1986), 46–61. My own comments are indebted to both studies.

18. See Richard Bridgman, *The Colloquial Style in America* (New York: Oxford University Press, 1966).

19. See Stonum, *Faulkner's Career*, pp. 101–2: "Each character draws on the same category of imagery, and these categories thus serve as a sort of authorized lexicon for the fictional world." Frederick N. Smith likewise points out that "the style of the book—at least in chapters narrated by one of the Bundrens—is characterized by an

oddly restricted vocabulary." See "Telepathic Diction: Verbal Repetition in *As I Lay Dying,*" *Style*, 19 (Spring 1985), 67. Smith's article offers an extremely perceptive discussion of Faulkner's use of repetition in the novel, even though some of its conclusions seem questionable.

20. Smith, "Telepathic Diction," 70.

21. On "holes," see Lecercle-Sweet, "The Chip and the Chink," 46–49.

22. On Faulkner's use of secrets in *As I Lay Dying*, see Robert Dale Parker's fine discussion in *Faulkner and the Novelistic Imagination* (Urbana: University of Illinois Press, 1985), pp. 23–58.

23. *SL*, p. 75.

24. See Larbaud's preface to *Tandis que j'agonise*, trans. Maurice Edgar Coindreau (Paris: Gallimard, 1934), pp. ii–iii.

25. *FU*, p. 87.

26. See Barrault's *Réflexions sur le théâtre* (Paris: Jacques Vautrain, 1949), p. 49, and Antonin Artaud, "Un spectacle magique," *Nouvelle Revue Française*, 45 (July 1935), 136–38.

27. For relevant discussions of *As I Lay Dying* as comedy, see Fred Miller Robinson, *The Comedy of Language: Studies in Modern Comic Literature* (Amherst: University of Massachusetts Press, 1980), pp. 51–88, and Patricia R. Schroeder, "The Comic World of *As I Lay Dying,*" in Doreen Fowler and Ann J. Abadie, eds., *Faulkner and Humor* (Jackson: University Press of Mississippi, 1986), pp. 34–46.

28. Irving Howe, *William Faulkner*, 2d ed. rev. (New York: Vintage Books, 1962), p. 189.

29. Backman, *The Major Years*, p. 51.

30. Walter Brylowski, *Faulkner's Olympian Laugh* (Detroit: Wayne State University Press, 1968), p. 86.

31. Karl E. Zink, "Flux and the Frozen Moment: The Imagery of Stasis in Faulkner's Prose," *PMLA*, 71 (June 1956), 285–86.

32. Edmond L. Volpe, *A Reader's Guide to William Faulkner* (New York: Noonday Press, 1964), p. 126.

33. Elizabeth M. Kerr, "*As I Lay Dying* as Ironic Quest," *Wisconsin Studies in Contemporary Literature*, 3 (Winter 1962), 13.

34. See, for instance, Michael Holquist, ed., *The Dialogic Imagination: Four Essays by M. M. Bakhtin* (Austin: University of Texas Press, 1981).

VIII. A Dying Life, a Living Death

1. See Blotner, *Faulkner*, pp. 634–35. There are several similarities between the Oresteia and the Bundren story: Clytemnestra and Addie are both unfaithful wives, Agamemnon and Anse deceived husbands; Whitfield has the same role as Aegisthus; while Darl, the dispossessed son, is another Orestes.

2. See "Spotted Horses" (1931) in *US*, pp. 165–83, and Blotner's note in *Faulkner*, pp. 689–90. One early short story version was published in 1986 with a useful introduction by James B. Meriwether; see "As I Lay Dying," *Mississippi Quarterly*, 39 (Summer 1986), 369–85.

3. E. Pauline Degenfelder reminds us that *licgan*, from which *to lie* is derived, originally meant "to lie down" in the marriage bed. See "Yoknapatawphan Baroque: A Stylistic Analysis of *As I Lay Dying,*" *Style*, 7 (Spring 1973), 148. Addie's own repeated use of "lie" and "lay" in relation to Anse—"I lay with him in the dark" (158), "I would lie by him in the dark" (159), "Then I would lay with Anse again" (161)—suggests a sexual meaning for the title.

4. Jean Rousset, *La littérature de l'âge baroque en France: Circé et le paon* (Paris: José Corti, 1954), p. 116. My translation.

5. Edgar Morin, *L'Homme et la mort* (Paris: Editions du Seuil, 1970), p. 123. My translation.

6. Maurice Blanchot, *L'Espace littéraire* (Paris: Gallimard, "Idées," 1968), p. 351: "le cadavre est sa propre image."

7. On the motif of the unburiable cadaver, see John K. Simon, "The Scene and the Imagery of Metamorphosis in *As I Lay Dying*," *Criticism*, 7 (Winter 1965), 1–22; J. Russel Reaver, "'This Vessel of Clay': A Thematic Comparison of Faulkner's *As I Lay Dying* and Latorre's *The Old Woman of Peralillo*," *Florida State University Studies*, no. 14 (1954), 131–40.

8. *WP*, 138.

9. With regard to the fairly obvious sexual symbolism of "Dewey Dell," it is interesting to note that from the sixteenth to the eighteenth century "dell" was a slang word first for a virgin, then for a prostitute.

10. The manuscript reads: "Dewey Dell's wet dress shapes for the blind eyes of 3 dead men those mammalian ludicrosities" (MS, p. 67). In the story context, the three men must be Cash, Anse, and Darl. The permutation of "blind" and "dead" indicates the symbolic equivalence of the two words: not to see is to be dead. But there is also the suggestion that in relation to the inexhaustible fertility of the "feminine principle," the male is always already dead.

11. Rabi, "Faulkner and the Exiled Generation," in *Faulkner: Two Decades of Criticism*, p. 129; translated from "Faulkner et la génération de l'exil," *Esprit*, 19 (January 1951), 56.

12. This is Gaston Bachelard's term. See *L'Eau et les Rêves* (Paris: José Corti, 1942), p. 111: "les quatre patries de la mort."

13. See, for instance, Carvel Collins, "The Pairing of *The Sound and the Fury* and *As I Lay Dying*," *Princeton University Chronicle*, 18 (Spring 1957), 114–23.

14. Charles Baudelaire, "Madame Bovary," *Oeuvres complètes*, ed. Y. G. Le Dantec (Paris: Gallimard, Bibliothèque de la Pléiade, 1954), pp. 1008–9. My translation.

15. This is not to say that Anse is only a figure of impotence. Before as well as after Addie's death, he is the one who gives orders (see 16, 27, 47, 89), and he takes advantage of his father status to steal Cash's and Dewey Dell's savings and trade off Jewel's horse for a new span of mules. Anse exploits his children materially, just as Addie manipulates them psychologically.

16. The term *omnipotent* appears in the manuscript in relation to Addie, and it is not surprising that it should occur in one of Darl's monologues. See MS, p. 19.

17. See Eugénie Lemoine-Luccioni, "La grossesse comme crise narcissique," *Partage des femmes* (Paris: Editions du Seuil, 1976), pp. 31–41.

18. See Robert J. Kloss, "Faulkner's *As I Lay Dying*," *American Imago*, 38 (Winter 1981), 429. Faulkner's depiction of the mother-son relationship may somehow reflect his own sense of bondage. Phil Stone thought that "all the Falkner boys were tied to their mother and resented it" and that this was "probably partly responsible . . . for an animosity toward women that he saw in Bill." Blotner, *Faulkner*, p. 631.

19. See Parker, *The Novelistic Imagination*, p. 25–26.

20. For this Hegelian digression I am indebted to Daniel Ferrer's brilliant essay "In Omnis Jam Vocabuli Mortem," *Poétique*, no. 44 (November 1980), 490–503.

21. Georg Wilhelm Friedrich Hegel, *The Phenomenology of Mind*, trans. J. B. Baillie, 2d ed. (London: George Allen and Unwin, 1949), p. 472. I have changed the translation of "bewusstloser Begierde" from "the desires of unconscious organic agencies" to "unconscious cravings."

22. Ibid., p. 471.

23. Ibid., p. 469.

24. On the funeral service, see Warwick Wadlington's perceptive comments in *Reading Faulknerian Tragedy* (Ithaca, N.Y.: Cornell University Press, 1987), pp. 103 and 111.

25. Hegel, *The Phenomenoloy of Mind*, p. 475.

26. In Anse's second speech the participle *laughing* is placed twice in such an

ambiguous way as to refer both to Darl and Addie: "Setting back there on the plank seat with Cash, with his dead ma laying in her coffin at his feet, laughing" (93); "And Darl setting on the plank seat right above her where she was laying, laughing" (94).

27. Eric J. Sundquist, *Faulkner: The House Divided* (Baltimore: Johns Hopkins University Press, 1983), p. 33. Once the temporal distance between events and their telling has been properly acknowledged, the narrative discontinuities cease to be inconsistencies. Cash would not refer to "Mrs Bundren's house" (218) before the family's arrival in Jefferson if he did not speak from a time well after Anse's remarriage.

28. Freud, "Totem and Taboo" (1913), *SE*, vol. 13, p. 65.

29. Daniel Lagache, "Le travail du deuil," *Oeuvres I* (Paris: Presses Universitaires de France, 1977), p. 245.

30. See Hyatt H. Waggoner, *William Faulkner: From Jefferson to the World* (Lexington: University of Kentucky Press, 1959), pp. 78–79, and Parker, *Faulkner and the Novelistic Imagination*, pp. 27–31. Waggoner and Parker draw attention to the scene at Addie's deathbed in which Anse tries awkwardly to express his affection, but both overlook the fact that after unsuccessfully mimicking his daughter's gestures, "his hand [falls] to his side and [strokes] itself again, palm and back, on his thigh" (48).

31. Freud, "Mourning and Melancholia," *SE*, vol. 14, p. 255.

32. Addie is often associated with wood imagery, and the loading of lumber into the wagon coincides with her death. Living trees, on the other hand, are linked to sexuality: Addie's and Whitfield's secret trysts, like Dewey Dell's and Lafe's, take place in the "secret shade" of the woods.

33. "In mania, the ego must have got over the loss of the object (or its mourning over the loss, or perhaps the object itself), and thereupon the whole quota of anticathexis which the painful suffering of melancholia had drawn to itself from the ego and 'bound' will have become available. Moreover, the manic subject plainly demonstrates his liberation from the object which was the cause of his suffering, by seeking like a ravenously hungry man for new object-cathexes." Freud, "Mourning and Melancholia," p. 255.

34. When Jewel calls his horse a "pussel-gutted bastard" and a "sweet son of a bitch" (13), he is unwittingly referring to himself. Jewel's horse, associated in turn with fire, sun, birds, and snakes, has some of the characteristics of the Mother and the Father. To see the horse as a symbol of virility only is to ignore its multiple valorizations in Faulkner's bestiary.

35. On Dewey Dell and Addie, see Kathleen Komar, "A Structural Study of *As I Lay Dying*," in *Faulkner Studies 1* (University of Miami, 1980), 53. According to Komar, Dewey Dell "undergoes an uncanny transformation, a kind of possession by Addie's ghost," as can be seen from her adoption of Addie's tragic vision in her third section (106–8). It is true that when she refers to "the womb of time: the agony and the despair of spreading bones, the hard girdle in which lie the outraged entrails of events" (106), she sounds very much like Addie in her monologue. But Darl or even Vardaman often does too, and as we have seen, in their use of heightened diction Addie and her children occasionally sound like Faulkner himself at his most rhetorical. Moreover, as far as the relationship of the Bundrens to their mother is concerned, I would argue that they are all "possessed."

36. In a number of pre-Columbian and African cultures (for example, the Dogon), the fish is closely associated with rites of fertility, birth, and rebirth. The fish is also an emblem of Christ, which is of interest considering that the fish caught by Vardaman will be the object of totemic consumption. Needless to say that for psychoanalysts the fish is likewise an overdetermined symbol, standing both for sexual intercourse and the position of the fetus in the womb. See in particular Sandor Ferenczi, *Thalassa: A Theory of Genitality* (New York: Psychoanalytic Quarterly, 1938).

37. See Melanie Klein, *The Psycho-Analysis of Children*, trans. Alix Strachey (London: Hogarth Press, 1932).

38. Michel Gresset, *Fascination: Faulkner's Fiction, 1919–1936*, adapted from the French by Thomas West (Durham, N.C.: Duke University Press, 1989), p. 225.

39. See Gresset's comments on the sexual symbolism of the river scene in Diction-naire des oeuvres contemporaines (Paris: Laffont-Pompiani, 1968), pp. 693–94. Refer-ring to Sandor Ferenczi's essay "The Symbolism of the Bridge" (Further Contributions to the Theory and Technique of Psycho-Analysis, New York: Basic Books, 1952, pp. 352–56), Gresset points out that while the mother is represented both by the river to be crossed and by the landscape to be reached, the bridge may be equated with the father's penis. The whole river scene could thus be read as a symbolic representation of the fertilization of the womb. This interpretation is all the more plausible as the farmers say the bridge was first crossed by Doctor Peabody on his way to the house of a woman in labor (cf. 78). We must not forget, however, that the bridge was washed away by the rising floodwaters—another reminder of male impotency in the novel.

40. "In dreams as in mythology, the delivery of the child *from* the uterine waters is commonly presented by distortion as the entry of the child *into* water; among many others, the births of Adonis, Osiris, Moses, and Bacchus are well-known illustrations of this." Freud, *The Interpretation of Dreams, SE*, vol. 5, p. 401.

41. In his interview with Jean Stein vanden Heuvel, Faulkner focuses on the outcome of the funeral journey and ranks the Bundrens with those of his characters who, like Lena Grove, manage to come to terms with reality: "The Bundren family in *As I Lay Dying* pretty well coped with [their fate]. The Father having lost his wife would naturally need another one, so he got one. At one blow he not only replaced the family cook, he acquired a gramophone to give them all pleasure while they were resting. The pregnant daughter failed this time to undo her condition, but she was not discouraged. She intended to try again and even if they all failed right up to the last, it wasn't anything but just another baby" (*LG*, p. 254).

IX. Turns of Madness

1. Gaston Bachelard's phrase. See *L'Eau et les Rêves*, 123: "cosmos de la mort."

2. *GDM*, pp. 130–31.

3. The most powerfully dramatized case of nonrecognition in Faulkner's fiction is of course Thomas Sutpen's refusal to acknowledge Charles Bon as his son in *Absalom, Absalom!*

4. Manuscript and typescript evidence shows that in the opening Darl section Faulkner substituted "Addie Bundren" for "Maw."

5. Anse describes Darl in almost identical terms: "he's got his eyes full of the land all the time" (32).

6. *FU*, p. 110.

7. As we have seen, there is clearly a contradiction on this point between Vernon Tull's testimony, as reported in his first speech (25–30) and echoed by Cora (19), and Darl's account in the fifth section (15–18).

8. For a close reading of this passage, see Robert Hemenway, "Enigmas of Being in *As I Lay Dying*," *Modern Fiction Studies*, 16 (Summer 1970), 133–46.

9. See *FU*, p. 110.

10. On this point, see R. D. Laing, *The Divided Self: An Existential Study in Sanity and Madness* (London: Tavistock, 1959). The case studies of schizoid and schizophrenic patients presented by Laing offer many close similarities with Darl's madness. There could scarcely be better proof of the depth and accuracy of Faulkner's imaginative insight. On Darl's madness, see Leon F. Seltzer, "Narrative Function vs. Psychopathol-ogy: The Problem of Darl in *As I Lay Dying*," *Literature and Psychology*, 25, no. 2 (1975), 49–64: David Kleinbard, "*As I Lay Dying*: Literary Imagination, the Child's Mind, and Mental Illness," *Southern Review*, 22 (January 1986), 51–68.

11. *FU*, p. 113.

12. *FU*, p. 111.

13. According to the *American Heritage Dictionary*, to mismatch is "to match un-suitably or inaccurately, especially in marriage."

14. The allusion to the Rabelaisian and Shakespearean "beast with two backs" occurs in connection with incest in Quentin's monologue in *The Sound and the Fury*.

15. Charles Baudelaire, "De l'essence du rire," *Oeuvres complètes*, p. 717.

16. It is this "exterminating laughter" that Clément Rosset analyzes in the closing pages of his *Logique du pire* (Paris: Presses Universitaires de France, 1971).

17. Michel Foucault, *Madness and Civilization: A History of Insanity in the Age of Reason*, trans. R. Howard (New York: Pantheon, 1965), p. 16; translated from *Histoire de la folie* (Paris: Plon, 1961), p. 19.

18. See, for instance, M. E. Coindreau, "Le Puritanisme de William Faulkner," *Cahiers du Sud*, 22 (April 1935), 266–67.

19. Foucault, *Madness and Civilization*, p. 16.

20. Sören Kierkegaard, *Concluding Unscientific Postscript*, trans. David F. Swenson and Walter Lowrie (Princeton, N.J.: Princeton University Press, 1941), p. 175.

21. See *FU*, p. 112.

X. The Real and Its Representations

1. *MOS*, p. 130.

2. Ibid.

3. Walter Benjamin, "The Storyteller: Reflections on the Works of Nicolai Leskov," *Illuminations*, trans. Harry Zohn (New York: Schocken Books, 1969), p. 94

4. Joseph Conrad, *Lord Jim* (1900) (London: Penguin Books, 1957), pp. 171–72.

5. On this point, see Paul R. Lilly, Jr., "Caddie and Addie: Speakers of Faulkner's Impeccable Language," *Journal of Narrative Technique*, 3 (September 1973), 170–82. Lilly views the Addie section as "a special dramatization" of Faulkner's "theory about the nature of language" (171). For a judicious critique of Lilly's argument, see John T. Matthews, *The Play of Faulkner's Language*, pp. 40–42.

6. Jean-Paul Sartre, *L'Idiot de la famille*, vol. 1 (Paris: Gallimard, 1971), p. 41. My translation.

7. "I find it impossible to communicate with the outside world," Faulkner told Loïc Bouvard in 1952. "Maybe I will end up in some kind of self-communion—a silence—faced with the certainty that I can no longer be understood. The artist must create his own language. This is not only his right but his duty. Sometimes I think of doing what Rimbaud did—yet, I will certainly keep on writing as long as I live" (*LG*, p 71).

8. Rosset, *Le Réel: Traité de l'idiotie*, p. 82. My translation.

9. *AA*, p. 251.

10. Foucault, *Madness and Civilization*, pp. 288–89.

Three. The Blackness of Darkness

XI. "The Most Horrific Tale"

1. Introduction, *Sanctuary* (New York: Modern Library, 1932), p. v. Faulkner's Introduction is included in the Editor's Note of *SAN*, p. 337. All further page references are to *SAN*.

2. On the revisions, see Linton Massey, "Notes on the Unrevised Galleys of Faulkner's *Sanctuary*," *Studies in Bibliography*, 8 (1956), 195–208; James B. Meriwether, "Some Notes on the Text of Faulkner's *Sanctuary*," *Papers of the Bibliographical Society of America*, 55 (1961), 192–206; Millgate, *The Achievement of William Faulkner*, pp. 113–23; Gerald Langford, *Faulkner's Revision of "Sanctuary,"* (Austin: University of Texas Press, 1972), pp. 3–33; Warren Beck, "The Transformation of *Sanctuary*," *Faulkner* (Madison: University of Wisconsin Press,1976), pp.191–260; Noel Polk, "Afterword," in *SO*, pp. 293–306.

3. *LG*, pp.123–24.

4. See *FU*, p.90, *LG*, p.122.

5. See *LG*, p. 255.

6. Blotner, *Faulkner*, p. 179.

7. The available versions of the text of *Sanctuary* are the holograph manuscript, the carbon typescript, the unrevised galleys (now all at the University of Virginia), the revised galleys (now at the University of Texas), the text of the original edition, and the text based on Faulkner's typescript established by Noel Polk.

8. *LG*, p. 123.

9. To write this scene Faulkner drew on memories of his visit to Paris in August and September 1925. In the letters he then wrote to his mother and to his aunt Alabama McLean, there are frequent references to the Luxembourg Gardens (see *SL*, pp. 11–22). In one of them, dated September 6, he wrote: "I have just written such a beautiful thing that I am about to bust—2000 words about the Luxembourg gardens and death. It has a thin thread of plot, about a young woman, and it is poetry though written in prose form" (*SL*, 17). These "2000 words," of which no material evidence is left, were probably the first draft of the final scene of *Sanctuary*.

10. His role, however, will be resumed in some of the later novels by Gavin Stevens, another idealistic but far more resilient lawyer.

11. On *Sanctuary* as Horace's dream, see Noel Polk, "'The Dungeon Was Mother Herself': William Faulkner: 1927–1931," in Doreen Fowler and Ann J. Abadie, eds., *New Directions in Faulkner Studies* (Jackson: University Press of Mississippi, 1984), pp. 61–93.

12. Title given by Cleanth Brooks to his chapter on *Sanctuary* in *The Yoknapatawpha Country*, p. 116.

13. On *Sanctuary* and the Gothic novel, see David L. Frazier, "Gothicism in *Sanctuary*: The Black Pall and the Crap Table," *Modern Fiction Studies*, 2 (Autumn 1956), 114–24; reprinted in *Twentieth Century Interpretations of "Sanctuary,"* ed. J. Douglas Canfield (Englewood Cliffs, N.J.: Prentice Hall, 1982), 49–58.

14. This repsychologization is particularly evident in a number of recent attempts to "explain" Temple, generally with the purpose of finding extenuating circumstances for her behavior. True, Temple should not be dismissed as a little bitch who gets what she deserves. However, what these well-meaning defenses of her fail to acknowledge is the shrill rhetoric of Faulkner's characterization, which, even in the early chapters focusing on her horrendous ordeal at Old Frenchman place, precludes true sympathy and eventually turns her into a despicable figure, whatever the "facts" may be. The description of Temple in the Grotto, "hurling herself upon" Red, "her hips grinding against him, her mouth gaping in straining protrusion, bloodless" (252), is part of our reading experience; her being a confused teenager with an emotionally deprived childhood is not. See in particular Joseph R. Urgo, "Temple Drake's Truthful Perjury: Rethinking Faulkner's *Sanctuary*," *American Literature*, 55 (October 1983), 435–44, and Elisabeth Muhlenfeld's eloquent essay "Bewildered Witness: Temple Drake in *Sanctuary*," *Faulkner Journal*, 1 (Spring 1986), 43–55.

15. See Sundquist, "*Sanctuary*: An American Gothic," *Faulkner: The House Divided*, pp. 44–60.

XII. Terror and Transgression

1. This scene has drawn many comments, especially by French critics. The most penetrating are by Jean-Jacques Mayoux, "The Creation of the Real in Faulkner," in Hoffman and Vickery, eds., *William Faulkner: Three Decades of Criticism*, pp. 156–59, and Gresset, *Fascination*, pp. 193–98. See also Arthur F. Kinney, *Faulkner's Narrative Poetics* (Amherst: University of Massachusetts Press, 1978), pp. 177–78, and George Toles, "The Space Between: A Study of Faulkner's *Sanctuary*," *Texas Studies in Literature and Language*, 22 (Spring 1980), 28–30.

2. Mayoux, "The Creation of the Real in Faulkner," p. 158.

3. "He was merely symbolical of evil. I just gave him two eyes, a nose, a mouth

and a black suit. It was all allegory" (*LG*, p. 53). In a later interview, however, Faulkner called Popeye "another lost human being" (*FU*, 74).

4. Gresset, *Fascination*, p. 196.

5. *SO*, p. 23.

6. Gresset's phrase in *Fascination*, p. 155.

7. See William Rossky, "The Pattern of Nightmare in *Sanctuary*, or, Miss Reba's Dogs," *Modern Fiction Studies*, 15 (Winter 1969–70), 503–15; reprinted in *Twentieth Century Interpretations of "Sanctuary,"* ed. Canfield, pp. 70–78.

8. Imperviousness to evil is one of Horace's major complaints about women. As he puts it in a letter to Narcissa omitted from the published version, "That's what hurts. Not that there is evil in the world. . . . It's that they can be so impervious to the mire which they reveal and teach us to abhor; can swallow without tarnishment in the very stuff in the comparison with which their bright, tragic, fleeting magic lies" (*SO*, p. 282). Horace's letter is echoed by the letter Faulkner wrote to Ben Wasson, his first literary agent, while working at the novel. What he was really interested in, he told his correspondent, was "how all this evil flowed off of [Temple] like water off a duck's back." There can be no doubt, then, that whatever she may be for the reader, Temple was perceived by her creator as a totally amoral creature. In the same letter Faulkner observed that "women are completely impervious to evil," which suggests that some at least of the sexist commonplaces voiced by his male characters received his full approval. See Blotner, *Faulkner*, p. 613.

9. The same sentence occurs in *Light in August* (p. 130), *Pylon* (p. 300), *Miss Zilphia Gant* (the novella first published in 1932; *US*, p. 380), and, in a slightly different tense, *The Wild Palms* (p. 204).

10. André Malraux, Préface, *Sanctuaire*, trans. R. N. Raimbault and H. Delgove (Paris: Gallimard, 1933), pp. i–iv. For a not quite satisfactory translation, see "A Preface for Faulkner's *Sanctuary*," *Yale French Studies*, no. 10 (Fall 1952), 92–94.

11. Sartre, "Time in Faulkner: *The Sound and the Fury*," in *Three Decades of Criticism*, p. 226.

12. Jean Paul Sartre, *Saint Genet* (Paris: Gallimard, 1952), p. 9. My translation.

13. The scene of Red's murder originally included the following statement: "Popeye shot him in the back of the head." See manuscript, p. 67.

14. On "sanctuary" as a central metaphor in Faulkner's novels, see Philip M. Weinstein's fine essay "Precarious Sanctuaries: Protection and Exposure in Faulkner's Fiction," *Studies in American Fiction*, 5 (Autumn 1978), 173–91.

15. Claude-Edmonde Magny, "Faulkner or Theological Inversion," in Robert Penn Warren, ed., *Faulkner: A Collection of Critical Essays* (Englewood Cliffs, N. J.: Prentice Hall, 1966), p.71

16. Cleanth Brooks's phrase for Frenchman's Bend in his study of *The Hamlet* in *The Yoknapatawpha Country*, p. 167.

17. According to the *Oxford English Dictionary*, *barn* may designate a place of worship. *Crib*, another recurrent word in the novel, suggests the cave-manger setting of the birth of Christ—another index of the ironic inversions at work in the text.

18. As Michel Serres notes in *Feux et signaux de brume*, "All sailors will tell you that the Ear of grain is the Alpha of the Virgin. Or Faulkner in *Sanctuary*" (Paris: Grasset, 1975, p. 111). Spica (from the Latin *spica*, "point," ear of grain) is indeed the brightest star in the constellation Virgo, and in Babylonian astrology the Virgin's name was *Ki*, an abbreviation of *Ki-hal*: that which pierces the earth. In Greece, Demeter, the goddess of harvests, was celebrated on the day when the star called Ear of grain rose at dawn. There is no proof that Faulkner was aware of these astronomical and astrological associations, but as his fiction offers at least another coincidence of this kind, it may seem reasonable to allow him benefit of doubt. Readers of *Go Down, Moses* might be intrigued to learn that in astrological texts the *Lion* is termed "the Noble Dog" or "the Great Dog."

19. On the symbolism of the grotto in Western art and literature, especially in the Decadent 1880s, see Ewa Kuryluk, *Salome and Judas in the Cave of Sex* (Evanston, Ill.: Northwestern University Press, 1987). On the wake for Red, see William B. Stein, "The Wake in Faulkner's *Sanctuary*," *Modern Language Notes*, 75 (1960), 28–29. Stein aptly calls the wake a "profane Mass for the Dead."

XIII. The Madness of Bodies

1. For a reader with a Christian background, the girl's first name brings to mind the Pauline metaphor of the body as "temple of God" or "temple of the Holy Ghost." The metaphor was in current use in Victorian manuals of sexual education for girls: "Your body is a beautiful house in which you dwell, and not only that but it is a sacred temple in which God dwells with you. . . . A temple, you know, is a place of worship, and it is the same as if He called the body a church. We feel that we must behave very properly when in church" (Mary Wood-Allen and Sylvanus Stall, *What a Young Girl Ought to Know*, Philadelphia, 1899, pp. 105–6; quoted in Stephen Kern, *Anatomy and Destiny: A Cultural History of the Human Body*, New York: Bobbs-Merrill, 1975, p. 159).

As Leslie A. Fiedler has noted, Temple is also the name of one of the prototypical heroines of American fiction. Suzannah Rowson's *Charlotte, A Tale of Truth*, a sentimental novel à la Richardson published in 1791 and one of the first American bestsellers, was a seduction story, and its pathetic heroine was named Charlotte Temple. See Fiedler, "From Clarissa to Temple Drake: Women in Love in the Classic American Novel," *Encounter*, 8 (March 1957), 14–20, and *Love and Death in the American Novel* (New York: Criterion Books, 1960), pp. 311–12.

2. Even in verbal exchange, communication often falters, as can be seen from Horace's attempts at conversation with Popeye, Ruby, and Lee.

3. See also "Upon the table lay a damp, bloodstained cloth and a burning cigarette" (82) and "One finger, ringed with a thick ring, held her lips apart, his finger-tips digging into her cheek" (244). In displaced form, the repressed scene keeps returning again and again.

4. Similar dissociations occur in other Faulkner novels. In *The Sound and the Fury*, Benjy's mind is likewise alienated from his body's motions, and in *Light in August*, when Joe Christmas is crouching in the dietitian's closet, he seems "to be turned in upon himself, watching himself sweating, watching himself smear another worm of paste into his mouth which his stomach did not want" (*LA*, 134; see also 261).

5. The two phrases are borrowed from *As I Lay Dying*, pp. 68 and 150.

6. Farther on, her face is in turn anatomized and reified: "From a short distance her eyes, the two spots of rouge and her mouth, were like five meaningless objects in a small heart-shaped dish" (301).

7. Cesare Pavese observes that "we continually feel that anguish, that *nearly physical constriction* which we feel watching a film in slow motion. The entire adventure of Temple in the plantation house—the first half of the book—is the most notable example of this *asthmatic* style." "Faulkner, a Bad Pupil of Anderson," in *Cesare Pavese, American Literature: Essays and Opinions*, trans. Edwin Fussell (Berkeley: University of California Press, 1970), p. 145 (italics mine). Pavese's essay was published orginally in *La Cultura* (April 1934) under the title "Faulkner, cattivo allievo di Anderson."

8. See *AILD*, p. 43.

9. "Pap" also points to the impotent father figure. To these two meanings the dictionary adds a third: nipple, teat. Papa, mamma, pabulum: all infantile sexuality concentrated in a single word.

10. The reference to throats to be cut is also significant in this scene. As Aubrey Williams has pointed out, in *Sanctuary* "man's neck is repeatedly seen as stretched, or prepared, or shaven for the noose, the knife or the guillotine." See "William Faulkner's 'Temple' of Innocence," *Rice Institute Pamphlets*, 47 (October 1960), 65–66; reprinted in *Twentieth Century Interpretations of "Sanctuary*," p. 68.

11. On the symbolism of the hole, see Sartre's brilliant analyses in the fourth part of *Being and Nothingness*, trans. Hazel E. Barnes (New York: Philosophical Library, 1954), pp. 612–14. Sartre comments upon the obscenity of everything which "gapes open" but sees the hole in existential terms as "an appeal to being." In *Sanctuary* it appears as a call to nothingness.

12. The discovery of sex is likewise associated with nausea in the toothpaste episode in *Light in August*.

13. Other minor characters are likewise identified by their fatness or thinness. See pp. 148, 156, 221, 308, 312.

14. Sartre, *Being and Nothingness*, p. 401.

15. *SO*, p. 60.

16. Faulkner's windows and curtains often open onto the "other scene" of the unconscious and serve to frame his characters' fantasies. As Catherine Backès-Clément has noted, "For Freud, the primal scene, even if it is the transposition of a noise heard through a partition, is the first spectacle and the model of all others. It is through a window that the first spectacle is watched, and the significance of the window is to be sought, not in the spectacle seen, but in the gaze itself." See "De la méconnaissance: fantasme, texte, scène," *Langages*, 8 (September 1973), 41. My translation.

17. In the fiction Faulkner wrote in the late twenties and early thirties, mothers are seldom in good health. Like Horace in *Sanctuary*, Quentin Compson has an ailing (or hypochondriac) mother in *The Sound and the Fury*. Young Hightower's in *Light in August* is an invalid, and Addie, the mother of the Bundren children in *As I Lay Dying*, is at the point of death. Maternal deficiency is inscribed in the very body.

18. Freud, "From the History of an Infantile Neurosis," in *SE*, vol. 17, p. 84.

19. In an early review of the novel, Lawrence S. Kubie had already emphasized the phallic qualities of the character. See "William Faulkner's *Sanctuary*: An Analysis," *Saturday Review of Literature*, 11 (October 20, 1934), 226; reprinted in *Twentieth Century Interpretations of "Sanctuary*," p. 31. In his fantasizing Horace tries to "clap his hand" to his mother's mouth—a gesture repeated by Popeye with Temple: "his hand came over her mouth, hard, his nails going into her flesh" (244). On Popeye and Horace as doubles, see T. H. Adamowski, "Faulkner's Popeye: the 'Other' as Self," *Canadian Review of American Studies*, 8 (Spring 1977), 16–51; reprinted in *Twentieth Century Interpretations of "Sanctuary*," pp. 32–48.

XIV. The Infernal Nursery

1. "There is no crime which a boy of eleven had not envisaged long ago. His only innocence is, he may not be old enough to desire the fruits of it, which is not innocence but appetite; his ignorance is, he does not know how to commit it, which is not ignorance but size" (*R*, p. 46). For comments on childhood, see also *AA*, p. 246.

2. At the close of chapter XVII, the child's posture is compared to "the attitude of one crucified" (141). There is another reference to crucifixion in Horace's hallucination in chapter XXIII (see 234).

3. On the necessity of "killing the child" within us, see Serge Leclaire, *On tue un enfant* (Paris: Editions du Seuil, 1975).

4. According to psychoanalysts Imre Herman and Geza Roheim, the "grasping reflex" is a primordial gesture, both libidinal and aggressive, in which all human behavior originates. See Imre Herman, "Sich Anklammern, auf Suche gehen," *Internationale Zeitschrift für Psychoanalyse*, 22 (1936).

5. The phonic kinship between their names is also noteworthy: the soft double *b* of "Benbow" echoes the more explosive double *p* of "Popeye."

6. Michel Gresset, "Le regard et le désir chez Faulkner," *Sud*, no. 14/15 (1975), 59, note 60. My translation.

7. See Freud, "The Uncanny" (*Das Unheimliche*) (1919), *SE*, vol. 17, pp. 219–52.

8. According to the *Oxford Latin Dictionary*, *fascinum* is (1) an evil spell, bewitch-

ment; (2) a. the penis, b. a phallic emblem (worn round the neck as a charm); c. a kind of sea-shell. As the last three meanings suggest, *fascinum* connotes sexual ambiguity.

9. Further evidence of the secret Horace-Popeye connection appears in the novel's original text. For instance, at Old Frenchman place, while explaining his desertion of Belle, Horace watches Popeye "as though he were the one he must establish himself with. . . ." (*SO*, 50). Shortly afterward, fearing Popeye will kill him, he tells himself, "You'd think there'd have to be a kinship between two who looked on death at the same time, even though it was from opposite sides" (*SO*, 52).

10. See *SO*, p. 50.

11. See pp. 30, 43, 73–74, 146, 220. Voyeurism, in *Sanctuary*, is not only sexual; there is also the voyeurism of death: "All day long a knot of them stood about the door to the undertaker's parlor, and boys and youths with and without schoolbooks leaned with flattened noses against the glass, and the bolder ones and the younger men of the town entered in twos and threes to look at the man called Tommy" (116–17). The association of death and childhood in this scene reminds one of the Compson children's curiosity about their dead grandmother in *The Sound and the Fury* and the confrontation of the Bundren children with their mother's corpse in *As I Lay Dying*.

12. Cf. Walter Pater's famous eulogy of Leonardo's *La Gioconda*, one of the first literary portraits of the late nineteenth-century *femme fatale*: "She is older than the rocks among which she sits; like the vampire she has been dead many times, and learned all the secrets of the grave." *The Renaissance* (London: Macmillan, 2d ed. revised, 1877), p. 135. Faulkner refers explicitly to Mona Lisa's smile in "Episode," one of his 1925 New Orleans Sketches. See *NOS*, p. 107.

13. Baudelaire, "Mon coeur mis à nu," *Oeuvres complètes* (Paris: Gallimard, Bibliothèque de la Pléiade, 1954), p. 1207. Italics in the text.

14. Gilles Deleuze, *Proust and Signs*, trans. Richard Howard (New York: George Braziller, 1972), p 125; translated from *Proust et les signes* (Paris: Presses Universitaires de France, 1964; 4th. ed. rev., 1976).

15. Gresset, *Faulkner ou la fascination: Poétique du regard* (Paris: Klincksieck, 1982), p. 245. This statement was not translated in *Fascination*, the English version of Gresset's study.

16. George M. O'Donnell, "Faulkner's Mythology," *Kenyon Review*, 1 (Summer 1939), 285–99.

17. Temple's androgynous nature is inscribed in her first as well as in her last name. A drake is a male duck, and the word's etymology refers back to *dragon*. When Temple tells Miss Reba her first name, the latter shows surprise: "'You got a boy's name, aint you?—'" (153).

18. Manuscript, p. 17.

19. Wyndham Lewis, "The Moralist with the Corn-Cob," in Seamus Cooney, ed., *Men without Art* (Santa Rosa: Black Sparrow Press, 1987), p. 52. Originally published by Cassell in London in 1935.

20. The incestuous nature of their relationship is hinted at several times. The description of the Judge escorting his daughter to the courthouse suggests a wedding ceremony (304–5), and at the novel's close, their trip to Paris resembles a honeymoon.

21. Brooks, *The Yoknapatawpha Country*, p. 135.

22. Malcolm Cowley, Introduction, *Portable Faulkner*, p. 15.

23. On "the dying fall," see Michel Gresset, "Of Sailboats and Kites: The 'Dying Fall' in Faulkner's *Sanctuary* and Beckett's *Murphy*," in Michel Gresset and Noel Polk, eds., *Intertextuality in Faulkner* (Jackson: University Press of Mississippi, 1985), pp. 57–72.

24. On the setting of the Luxembourg Gardens scene and its symbolic meaning, see Giliane Morell, "The Last Scene of *Sanctuary*," *Mississippi Quarterly*, 25 (Summer 1972), 351–55. According to Morell, "the ultimate irony of the scene, and of the book, is that [Temple] should be sitting there in front of the Senate, in front of the Temple of the Law" (354). On the novel's ending, see also George Garrett, "'Fix my hair, Jack': The

Dark Side of Faulkner's Jokes," in Doreen Fowler and Ann J. Abadie, eds., *Faulkner and Humor* (Jackson: University Press of Mississippi, 1986), pp. 216–31.

25. Comparison of the manuscript and the published text is instructive in this respect. Thus the evocation of the grape arbor, as it appeared originally in the second chapter, was not explicitly associated with Horace. In the final version it is integrated into Horace's speech at the Old Frenchman place, and so can no longer be ascribed to the narrator.

26. Malraux, Préface, *Sanctuaire*, p.iv. My translation.

27. Since *Sanctuary* is to Faulkner as *La Nausée* is to Sartre, let me recall that the latter's first title for his novel was "Melancholia," after the Dürer engraving.

Four. Versions of the Sun

XV. In Praise of Helen

1. *FU*, p. 74.

2. Textual evidence reveals not only that the initial pages are among the most heavily revised but also that during composition Faulkner shifted various blocks of material into the beginning position. At different times the novel seems to have begun with each of the other narrative strands: with Hightower's biography (now chapter III) and with Christmas's capture (now chapter XV). See Carl Ficken, "The Opening Scene of William Faulkner's *Light in August*," *Proof*, 2 (December 1972), 175–84; Regina K. Fadiman, *Faulkner's "Light in August": A Description and Interpretation of the Revisions* (Charlottesville: University Press of Virginia, 1975), pp. 31–32.

3. See, for instance, the superb invocation to Venus in the opening lines of *De Rerum Natura*: "Aeneadum Genitrix, hominum divomque voluptas, / alma Venus, caeli subter labenta signa." Lucretius's lines are echoed by Spenser in *The Faerie Queene*, book IV, canto 10, stanzas 44–46.

4. Catherine Clément, *Miroirs du sujet* (Paris: 10/18, 1975), pp. 174–75.

5. On the etymology of the name, see Ch. Daremberg and E. Salia, *Dictionnaire des Antiquités grecques et romaines*, III, p. 56. There are allusions to Helen in Faulkner's work from his early writings to *The Town* and *The Mansion*, and in a conversation in the latter novel Ratliff and Stevens explicitly identify Helen with light. It is also worth recalling that among the women Faulkner loved there was Helen Baird.

6. For a Jungian reading of *Light in August*, see, for example, David Williams, *Women: The Myth and the Muse* (Montreal: McGill-Queen's University Press, 1977).

7. From Aeschylus to Ronsard, poets have derived *Helen* from *helein* (to take away, to steal, to ravish). The poets' etymology is not the philologists'.

8. In point of fact, as we find him depicted in the furniture dealer's humorous account of the final scene, Byron is not even a serious intruder but rather a troublesome child. To the dealer, he looks like a little boy "with his face all shined up like a kid trying to do something for you before you change your mind about something you promised to do for him" (549). Lena likewise treats him like a small child: "*What do you reckon happened, with a big gal like that, without any warning that it was just him, and a durn little cuss that already looked like he had reached the point where he could bust out crying like another baby? . . . I be dog if I dont believe she picked him up and set him back outside on the ground like she would that baby if it had been about six years old*" (555).

9. *FU*, p. 199.

10. See Faulkner's comments in his interview with Jean Stein: "I would say that Lena Grove in *Light in August* coped pretty well with [her fate]. . . . She was the captain of her soul" (*LG*, p. 253).

11. See Faulkner's reflections after his visit to Greece in *FU*, pp. 129–30.

12. Friedrich Nietzsche, *The Birth of Tragedy*, trans. W. A. Haussmann (New York: Macmillan, 1924), p. 23.

13. On page 20 Faulkner calls her "inwardlighted."

14. *M*, p. 133.

15. See Jean-Joseph Goux, "Matière, différence des sexes," *Matière et pulsions de mort* (Paris: 10/18, 1975), pp. 123–67.

16. "The Essential Solitude," in *The Sirens' Song: Selected Essays by Maurice Blanchot*, ed. and intro. Gabriel Josipovici, trans. Sacha Rabinovitch (Brighton: Harvester Press, 1982), pp. 107–8.

17. Ibid., p. 108.

18. Her loose hair reminds one of the dishevelment of the Medusalike Joanna. The comparison of her eyes to "two holes" is also used in *Sanctuary* to describe Temple Drake.

XVI. The Cracked Urns

1. Fear of menstrual blood, however, can be found in a number of cultures. Mary Douglas describes a tribe in New Guinea holding the belief that contact with menstrual blood or a menstruating woman will, in the absence of appropriate countermagic, sicken a man, cause persistent vomiting, "kill" his blood, and eventually lead to his decline and death. See *Purity and Danger: An Analysis of the Concepts of Pollution and Taboo* (London: Ark Paperbacks, 1984), p. 147.

2. See Judith Bryant Wittenberg, "The Women of *Light in August*," in Michael Millgate, ed., *New Essays on Light in August* (Cambridge: Cambridge University Press, 1987), pp. 103–22. On the perception of women by male characters, see Gail L. Mortimer's comments in *Faulkner's Rhetoric of Loss* (Austin: University of Texas Press, 1983), pp. 17–26.

3. Since Christmas overhears the scene, *écouteur* would be a more appropriate term, but unfortunately it does not belong to the jargon of perversion.

4. Even though the two partners in the scene are lovers, the dietitian is extremely reluctant to make love: "No! No! Not here. Not now. They'll catch us. Somebody will—No, Charley! Please!" (133). What Christmas witnesses is not quite a rape, but there is violence, which is also in keeping with the standard script of the "primal scene," generally interpreted as an act of violence inflicted by the father upon the mother. No wonder that once he has become an adult, Christmas is unable to envision sex without brutality.

5. As so often with Faulkner, the metaphor here derives metonymically from the diegesis, i.e., from the spatiotemporal context of the narrative. In Faulkner as in Joyce and Proust, metonymy is a pervasive mode of metaphorization, probably inherited from Flaubert.

6. In sharp contrast to Christmas, Lena exhibits a healthy appetite and thoroughly enjoys her food: "She eats slowly, steadily, sucking the rich sardine oil from her fingers with slow and complete relish" (31).

7. One thinks of the row of canned food which in *The Wild Palms* becomes for Harry Wilbourne the symbol of the passage of time.

8. The original title appears on the title page of the final manuscript, now at the University of Virginia. It is crossed out, and "Light in August" is written above in Faulkner's hand (see Meriwether, *Career*, pp. 66–67, and Blotner, *Faulkner*, p. 701). According to Blotner, the title refers primarily to the cloistral dimness of Hightower's house, but in fact most of the houses described in the novel, from the home of Lena's parents to the house of the furniture dealer, are described as "dark." "A Dark House" was also considered as a possible title for *Absalom, Absalom!* (see Blotner, *Faulkner*, pp. 828–30).

9. As with all the previously discussed metaphors, *pit* is the devalorized term of a binary opposition. The descending verticality of the pit is opposed both to horizontality (Lena's peaceful progress along the road) and to ascending movement (the index of spiritual "aspirations").

10. Freud, *SE*, vol. 12, pp. 291–301.

11. See Freud, "Medusa's Head" (1922), *SE*, vol. 18, pp. 272–74. Note that the dietitian is also described as a disheveled Fury. See 135.

12. The first occurrence of *grove* is on page 4, in reference to Lena's father: "They buried father in a grove." The association between grove and father is even more pronounced in Joanna's autobiographical account in chapter XI: "I think it was something about father, something that came from the cedar grove to me, through him. A something that I felt that he had put on the cedar grove, and that when I went into it, the grove would put on me so th.t I would never be able to forget it" (277). On the other hand, the notion of a grove is linked to two other places which connote sexuality: the schoolhouse where Christmas dances with Bobbie and attacks his foster-father (cf. 223), and above all, Joanna's house, "hidden in its shaggy grove" (130; see also 249).

XVII. The Perils of Purity

1. Preface to *Light in August*, p. xi.

2. See Michel Gresset, "Les deux pôles de l'idéalisme faulknerien," in *William Faulkner: Ontologie du discours*, *Delta* (Montpellier), no. 25 (October 1987), 17–86.

3. Vladimir Jankélévitch, *Le Pur et l'impur* (Paris: Flammarion, 1960), p. 5.

4. Gilles Deleuze, *Logique du Sens* (Paris: Editions de Minuit, 1969), p. 326.

5. The first of these moments occurs in the much earlier scene when Bobbie and Christmas lie in bed together and talk, Christmas telling her about his failed experience with the black girl "quietly and peacefully, lying beside her, touching her" (216). In Faulkner's world, peaceful communication can be established through talk or touch, never through sight. As Rosa Coldfield argues in *Absalom, Absalom!*, "*there is something in the touch of flesh with flesh which abrogates, cuts sharp and straight across the devious intricate channels of decorous ordering*" (*AA*, 139).

6. Most readings of the novel assume that Christmas is the murderer, even though the murder scene is not reported in the text. Questioning that assumption, Stephen E. Meats argues the possibility that Christmas did not murder Joanna but simply left her unconscious after hitting her with the pistol, and that the actual slaying was done the next morning by Brown. It is quite true that if there are heavy presumptions, no conclusive evidence is offered within the book that Christmas committed the murder. On the map he drew for *Absalom, Absalom!*, however, Faulkner refers to "Miss Joanna Burden's, where Christmas killed Miss Burden," which proves at least that Christmas is the murderer in his creator's eyes. But if he did kill Joanna, we cannot be sure whether *murder* is the proper word, for, as John N. Duvall rightly points out, there is much to suggest that Christmas killed in self-defense. See Meats, "Who Killed Joanna Burden?" *Mississippi Quarterly*, 24 (Summer 1971), 271–77; Duvall, "Murder and the Communities: Ideology in and around *Light in August*," *Novel*, 20 (Winter 1987), 101–22.

7. Gresset, *Fascination*, p. 209.

8. See Brooks, *The Yoknapatawpha Country*, p. 52.

9. "I wrote that book in 1932 before I'd ever heard of Hitler's Storm Troopers, what he was a Nazi Storm Trooper, but then I'd never heard of one then, and he's not prevalent, but he's everywhere. . . . I think you will find him . . . in all countries, in all people." *FU*, p. 41.

10. *CS*, pp. 169–83. First published in *Scribner's* (January 1931).

11. *SL*, p. 202.

12. Percy Grimm and Faulkner also have similar fathers. Grimm's is a "hardware merchant" (496); Faulkner's had bought a hardware store at the beginning of 1912. See Blotner, *Faulkner*, p.150.

XVIII. The Fathers

1. The absence of family ties was noted as early as 1949 by Phyllis Hirshleifer in "As Whirlwinds in the South: An Analysis of *Light in August*," *Perspective*, 2 (Summer 1949), 225–38.

2. Chapter II introduces Christmas as "the stranger" (33), and the same word

designates him five times in the following two pages. Lena is likewise called a "stranger" (9), and so are Joanna (50) and Brown (296). Hightower is described as "the fifty-year-old outcast who has been denied by his church" (52).

3. Alfred Kazin, "The Stillness of *Light in August*," *Three Decades of Criticism*, p. 253. The essay appeared originally in *Partisan Review*, 24 (Autumn 1957), 519–38.

4. D. H. Lawrence, *Studies in Classic American Literature* (New York: Viking Press, 1964), p. 62. Lawrence's essays were first published in 1923.

5. See Brooks, *The Yoknapatawpha Country*, p. 47.

6. Ibid., p. 69.

7. On the concept of anomie in social theory and its ideological implications, see Alvin W. Gouldner, *The Coming Crisis of Western Sociology* (New York: Avon Books, 1970).

8. See Brooks's observations on this point (of honor?) in *The Yoknapatawpha Country*, pp. 51–52.

9. It is remarkable that the manuscript version of chapter V includes references to Christmas's "black blood" and "Negro smell," which Faulkner only removed when he wrote the final text. On this point, see Fadiman, *Faulkner's "Light in August*," pp. 42–43.

10. *FU*, p. 72.

11. When asked by Joanna how he knows that one of his parents was "part nigger," Joe admits that he does not know and adds with sardonic bitterness: "If I'm not [a nigger], damned if I haven't wasted a lot of time" (280).

12. This, according to the narrator, is what he then "might have thought" had he been older: *"That is why I am different from the others: because he is watching me all the time"* (152). The scenes at the orphanage remind one of the transformation of an innocent child into an abject monster which Sartre describes in *Saint Genet*. Sartre remarks that "the gaze of adults is a *constitutive power* which has changed [Genet] into a *constituted nature*" (p. 55). Between Genet's childhood and Christmas's there are several intriguing analogies: the former, at seven, was committed to the charge of Morvan peasants; the latter, at five, is adopted by a couple of Mississippi farmers.

13. Malcolm Cowley defines Christmas as "an abstraction seeking to become a human being" ("The Stillness of *Light in August*," 524). It is rather the other way around: Christmas is a human being seeking not to become an abstraction. Faulkner criticism treats him all too often as if he were a human cipher or an archvillain, or regards him as a character totally bent on self-destruction. Thadious M. Davis is closer to the truth when she notes that "Joe's refusal, though effectively defeated, is a positive, progressive impulse, but one doomed to failure because it cuts so sharply against the grain of traditional Southern life and thought." *Faulkner's "Negro": Art and the Southern Context* (Baton Rouge: Louisiana State University Press, 1983), p. 133.

14. For perceptive discussions of Joanna, see R. G. Collins, *"Light in August:* Faulkner's Stained Glass Triptych," *Mosaic*, 7 (Fall 1973), 122–30; Susan Hayes Tully, "Joanna Burden: 'It's the dead folks that do him the damage,'" *Mississippi Quarterly*, 40 (Fall 1987), 355–71.

15. On the role of paternity in Faulkner's fiction, see my essay "Fathers in Faulkner," in *The Fictional Father: Lacanian Readings of the Text*, ed. Robert Con Davis (Amherst: University of Massachusetts Press, 1981), pp. 115–46.

16. According to *Light in August: A Concordance to the Novel*, ed. Jack L. Capps (Faulkner Concordance Advisory Board, 1979), *dark* occurs 134 times, *darkness* 35 times.

17. Here puritan and libertine are very much alike, as in the case of Laclos's Madame de Merteuil: "je ne désirais de jouir, je voulais savoir [I was not seeking sensual pleasure but knowledge]." *Les Liaisons Dangereuses* (Paris: Gallimard, Bibliothèque de la Pléiade, 1951), p.177.

18. This aspect of the novel has drawn much critical comment. The most useful study is Ilse Dusoir Lind, "The Calvinistic Burden of *Light in August*," *New England Quarterly*, 30 (September 1957), 307–29.

19. See Max Weber, *The Protestant Ethic and the Spirit of Capitalism*, trans. Talcott Parsons (New York: Scribner's, 1930). Weber's influential essay first appeared in 1904–5.

20. See ibid., p.95.

21. In this passage it is impossible to distinguish the narrator's from Hightower's point of view. The perspective here is dual or mixed, as it often is in this novel.

22. Consider the following reflections: "an ascetic life is a self-contradiction: here rules *ressentiment* without equal, that of an insatiable instinct and power-will that wants to become master not over something in life but over life itself, over its most profound, powerful, and basic conditions; here an attempt is made to employ force to block up the wells of force; here physiological well-being itself is viewed askance, and especially the outward expression of this well-being, beauty and joy; while pleasure is felt and sought in ill-constitutedness, decay, pain, mischance, ugliness, voluntary deprivation, self-mortification, self-flagellation, self-sacrifice." Friedrich Nietzsche, *On the Genealogy of Morals*, trans. Walter Kaufmann (New York: Vintage Books, 1969), pp. 117–18. There is scarcely a sentence in this passage that could not be applied to Faulkner's novel.

23. Ibid., p. 61.

24. See John Tucker, "William Faulkner's *Light in August:* Toward a Structuralist Reading," *Modern Language Quarterly*, 43 (June 1982), 138–55.

25. The distinction between "open society" and "closed society" was first made by Henri Bergson in *Les Deux Sources de la morale et de la religion* (1932). The terms were reused in a secular and rationalistic sense by Karl R. Popper: "the closed society is characterized by the belief in magical taboos, while the open society is one in which men have learned to be to some extent critical of taboos, and to base decisions on the authority of their own intelligence"; *The Open Society and Its Enemies*, vol. I, 5th ed. (Princeton, N.J.: Princeton University Press, 1966), p. 202. My own use of the phrase refers back to Popper. Popper's definition of the closed society, in its emphasis on the latter's "semi-organic" character (cf. ibid., p. 173), is a liberal's unsympathetic redefinition of Brooks's "community."

26. See Claude Lévi-Strauss, *Tristes Tropiques*, trans. John Russell (New York: Atheneum, 1968), p. 386.

27. On the semantic and syntactic ambiguities of the scene, see James A. Snead's comments in *Figures of Division* (New York: Methuen, 1986) pp. 97–98. As Snead rightly points out, the reader can determine neither whether "the pent black blood" is to be taken literally or figuratively, nor who is meant by the remembering "they."

28. Georges Bataille, *Erotism: Death and Sensuality*, trans. Mary Dalwood (San Francisco: City Lights Books, 1986), p. 91.

29. On the ambiguity of the sacred, see Roger Caillois, *L'Homme et le sacré* (Paris: Gallimard, Les Essais, 1950), pp. 37–72. See also René Girard, *La Violence et le sacré* (Paris: Grasset, 1972).

30. On the sacredness of the emissary victim, see Henri Hubert and Marcel Mauss, "Essai sur la nature et la fonction du sacrifice," in Marcel Mauss, *Oeuvres I* (Paris: Editions de Minuit, 1968), pp. 193–352, and René Girard, *Le Bouc émissaire* (Paris: Grasset, 1982).

31. When asked about Christmas, Faulkner stated that he had not intended him as a Christ figure (see *FU*, p. 119). Parallels notwithstanding, Christmas's career is not systematically patterned on the life of Christ, and some of the correspondences "discovered" by ingenious critics are demonstrably false. Thus Christmas is thirty-six or thirty-seven, not thirty-three, when he dies.

32. Michel Serres, *Hermès III: La traduction* (Paris: Editions de Minuit, 1974), p. 265.

33. Christmas is likened to Satan (225, 354), but so are Hightower (74) and Doc Hines (410–11).

34. When asked whether he intended any "Christ symbolism" in Christmas, Faulkner replied: "No, that's a matter of reaching into the lumber room to get out

something which seems to the writer the most effective way to tell what he is trying to tell. . . . Everyone that has had the story of Christ and the Passion as a part of his Christian background will in time draw from that. There was no deliberate attempt to repeat it. That the people to me come first. The symbolism comes second" (*FU*, p. 117).

35. Joel Kovel, *White Racism: A Psychohistory* (New York: Vintage Books, 1971), pp. 71–72.

36. On Christmas and Oedipus, see Longley, *The Tragic Mask*, pp. 193–95.

37. Christmas rejects the name which his foster-father wants to impose on him: "*My name aint McEachern. My name is Christmas*" (160). Later, when the restaurant owner asks for his name: "It's not McEachern," he said. "It's Christmas" (203). For the child, to claim his first name is to claim his difference in the face of his new father, and to be true to his origin. And since for McEachern "Christmas" is a heathenish name, it is also a way of claiming his pariahhood. On this point, see T. H. Adamowski, "Joe Christmas: The Tyranny of Childhood," *Novel*, 4 (Spring 1971), 240–51.

38. William Ellery Channing, *Works* (Boston: George G. Channing, 1849), vol. 1, p. 238.

XIX. Circles

1. For a brilliant exploration of the flight motif in the American novel, see Pierre-Yves Petillon, *La grand-route* (Paris: Editions du Seuil, 1979).

2. Paul Claudel and André Gide, *Correspondance* (Paris: Gallimard, 1955) p. 91: "l'inépuisable dans la fermeture."

3. On Faulkner's hesitations over tenses in the manuscript, see François Pitavy, *Faulkner's "Light in August"* (Bloomington: Indiana University Press, 1973), pp. 47–49.

4. For a chapter-by-chapter analysis of the entire novel, see ibid., pp. 13–35.

5. See Fadiman, *Faulkner's "Light in August,"* p. 195.

6. As Richard Chase astutely noted in his discussion of the novel, "The symbolism that seems most profoundly organic with the action and meaning of the book is that of the circle, and I would judge that, like any interesting symbol, this was half consciously intended by the author but has implications within the book of which he was probably not entirely conscious when he wrote it." *The American Novel and Its Tradition* (Garden City, N.Y.: Anchor Books, 1957), p. 217.

7. On recurring scenes, see Pitavy, *Faulkner's "Light in August,"* pp. 38–40.

8. Phyllis Hirshleifer was the first to point to the motif. See "As Whirlwinds in the South," 227–28.

9. To call someone "nigger" is of course not to name a person but to deny his individuality and humanity. A "nigger" is not even a separate entity; he is simply an emanation of "niggerhood." The white people who gather around Joanna's corpse all believe that "it [is] an anonymous negro crime committed not by a negro but by Negro" (315). On this point, see Richard Godden, "Call Me Nigger: Race and Speech in Faulkner's *Light in August*," *American Studies*, 14, 2 (1980), 235–48.

10. Many critics assume Hightower dies at the end of chapter XX. According to Faulkner, however, "He didn't die. He had wrecked his life. He had failed his wife. He had failed himself, but there was one thing that he still had—which was the brave grandfather that galloped into the town to burn the Yankee stores, and at least he had that. . . . He had to endure, to live, but that was one thing that was pure and fine that he had—was the memory of his grandfather, who had been brave" (*FU*, p. 75).

11. See Beach Langston, "The Meaning of Lena Grove and Gail Hightower in *Light in August*," *Boston University Studies in English*, V (Spring 1961), 46–61.

12. The question of "redemption" is mentioned in nearly all studies of Hightower. See, for example, John S. Williams, "The Final Copper Light of Afternoon: Hightower's Redemption," *Twentieth Century Literature*, 13 (January 1968), 205–15.

13. On this scene, see Arnold Weinstein's stimulating essay, "Fusion and Confusion in *Light in August*," *Faulkner Journal*, 1 (Spring 1986), 2–16. A similar confusion occurs

at the end of *Flags in the Dust* when Miss Jenny talks about Narcissa's child as if he were Johnny Bayard. See *FD*, p. 409.

14. Darrell Abel, "Frozen Movement in *Light In August*," *Boston University Studies in English*, 3 (Spring 1957), 43.

15. On the novel's ending, see H. C. Nash, "Faulkner's 'Furniture Repairer and Dealer': Knitting up *Light in August*," *Modern Fiction Studies*, 16 (Winter 1970–1971), 529–31; Marianne Torgovnich, "Storytelling as Affirmation at the End of *Light in August*," *Closure in the Novel* (Princeton, N.J.: Princeton University Press, 1981), pp.157–75; Ronald Wesley Hoag, "Ends and Loose Ends: The Triptych Conclusion of *Light in August*," *Modern Fiction Studies*, 31 (Winter 1985), 675–90.

16. "L'écrivain est quelqu'un qui joue avec le corps de sa mère . . . pour le glorifier, l'embellir, ou pour le dépecer, le porter à la limite de ce qui du corps, peut être reconnu." Roland Barthes, *Le Plaisir du texte* (Paris: Editions du Seuil, 1973), p. 60.

Epilogue: Under the Sign of Saturn

1. Sundquist, *Faulkner: The House Divided*, p. 3.

2. Marcel Proust, *Du Côté de Guermantes*, II, p. 22. My translation.

3. *FU*, p. 117.

4. Quoted by Marthe Robert, in "Kafka sans idées," *Art Press International*, no. 16 (March 1978), 14. My translation.

5. *FU*, p. 39.

6. Karl Marx and Friedrich Engels, *Basic Writings on Politics and Philosophy*, ed. L. S. Feuer (New York, 1959), p. 43.

7. Milan Kundera, "The Novel and Europe," *New York Review of Books* (July 19, 1984), 15.

8. See Walter J. Slatoff, *Quest for Failure: A Study of William Faulkner* (Ithaca, N.Y.: Cornell University Press, 1960).

9. See, for example, Lillian Smith's assessment of Faulkner in Helen White and Redding Sugg, Jr., comps., *From the Mountain* (Memphis, Tenn.: Memphis State University Press, 1972), pp.153, 208–10.

10. *AILD*, p. 41.

11. See Raymond Klibansky, Erwin Panofsky, and Fritz Saxl, *Saturn and Melancholy* (London: Thomas Nelson and Sons, 1964), pp.204-7, and Jean Starobinski, "L'Encre de la mélancolie," *Nouvelle Revue Française*, 11 (March 1963), 410–23. I am indebted to Starobinski for my book's title.

12. "An Introduction to *The Sound and the Fury*," *Mississippi Quarterly*, 26 (Summer 1973), 412.

13. Ibid.

14. Ibid.

15. As Walker Percy once remarked in commenting on Mississippi, which is also his native state, there was an "absence of a truly public zone" separate from the interior life of the family, so that the latter came to coincide with the actual public space it inhabited." "Mississippi: The Fallen Paradise," *Harper's*, 230 (April 1965), 170. On the relations between public and private realms in the Old South, see also Bertram Wyatt Brown, *Southern Honor* (Oxford: Oxford University Press, 1982).

16. Letter dated early November 1944, in *SL*, p. 185.

17. See Gilles Deleuze and Claire Parent, *Dialogues* (Paris: Flammarion, 1977), p. 54.

18. Letter to Malcolm Cowley, 11 February 1949, in *SL*, p. 285.

INDEX

CPSIA information can be obtained
at www.ICGtesting.com
Printed in the USA
FSOW02n0601011116
26805FS